THE MOUNTAIN EMPIRE LEAGUE

a NOVEL by
Marshall Adesman

The Mountain Empire League

Marshall Adesman

Published by

ARKETT PUBLISHING
division of Arkettype
PO Box 36, Gaylordsville, CT 06755
806-350-4007 • Fax 860-355-3970
www.local-author.com

Copyright © 2023 Marshall Adesman

All rights reserved under International and Pan-American Copyright Conventions.
No part of this book may be reproduced or transmitted by any means
without permission in writing from the author.

ISBN 979-8-8689-0725-8

Printed in USA.

Cover design by Tim Smith

Acknowledgements

No book is written by just one person, and *The Mountain Empire League* is no exception. There are many people who need to be singled out, and we would like to take a moment to do that here.

My two fabulous editors, miss tree turtle and Francinia Williams, guided this work for a couple of years. With her vast experience in the field, miss tree turtle convinced me to be more direct and more concise (though this final version is still longer than she would have preferred!). Francinia Williams' sharp eye, understated manner and knowledge of baseball were exactly what I needed at exactly the right time. I will always be extremely grateful to both of them for their sagacity.

I was blessed to have some excellent beta-readers. A couple of friends from SABR (Society for American Baseball Research), Bryan Steverson and Steve Weingarden, weighed in with excellent comments on portions of the manuscript, as did old friend and colleague Dave Denny and another old friend and one-time co-author Chris Holaday. Two noted authors—Julie Huffman-Klinkowitz and Jerome Klinkowitz—rode herd on me from the beginning, making sure that the writing was crisp; Jerry, especially, constantly cautioned me to remember that I was not writing an essay that would be published in some journal.

My sister, Sharon Furlong, was also an important beta-reader, as was my wife, Susan. They were both important because they came to this project without a real baseball background, and were thus able to examine the manuscript from both a literary and historical perspective. Their insights were outstanding and generally spot-on.

A variety of people chipped in with numerous important services. Tim Smith was able to design our unique and intriguing cover after just two or three conversations, while Joel Levitt directed me to the path that brought me to Tim, and Doug Maurer of the Asheville Tourists sent along some photos that helped to inspire the cover. Billie Wheeler took a set of wonderful photos, one of which we have used here, with others found on my website; that would not have become a reality without fabulous assistance from Chuck Reisinger, Maria Bajgain, Katherine Kantner, and Ed DiGangi.

Lou Orkell, from Arkettype, was my final shepherd, agreeing to publish my manuscript and do the important formatting, with an occasional editorial correction tossed in for good measure. When you hold this book in your hand, please pay particular attention to how good it feels; no electronic device can ever replace the thrill of holding a writer's words and thoughts, and Arkettype, in my biased opinion, makes you feel like you are settling down with an old friend.

I regret that it took me so long to complete this manuscript, because my dear friend and baseball mentor, John Dittrich, did not live to see it completed. So much of what I learned about running a minor league team came from his tutelage, and his untimely death is felt every single day by so many.

Finally, this book is dedicated to my wife, Susan, my partner for better than forty years, the *yin* to my *yang* (or maybe it's the other way around?). Your help, with this book and in this life, is immeasurable, and can never be repaid. If there is such a thing as reincarnation, I hope I get to live with you again, especially if we are a pair of pampered house cats!

Marshall Adesman

The Mountain Empire League—The Basics

It is common knowledge that Jackie Robinson became the first African-American to play major league baseball in the 20th century. His groundbreaking feat has been the subject of numerous books and articles, as well as two motion pictures.

Robinson's success on the field was all the more impressive when one realizes how much vitriol he faced every day. He was the Rookie of the Year in 1947 and led his Brooklyn Dodgers to the World Series, despite the hatred expressed by other players and managers around the league, to say nothing of the epithets that rained down on him from the stands in ballparks around the league. The hardships he had to endure paved the way for athletes of color in all sports.

What is often overlooked are those other athletes, the ones who attempted to follow in his massive footsteps. This was most notable in baseball's minor leagues, because so many of them were located in southern states, whose naturally-warmer climates were especially conducive to playing baseball for five or six months. Unfortunately, this time period also coincided with the waning days of the Jim Crow era, in which African-Americans found themselves relegated to second-class (or lower!) status. Meaningful efforts to change this abomination in the United Sates did not gather real momentum until the Civil Rights movement of the 1950s, which led directly to the Civil Rights Act of 1964 and the Voting Rights Act of 1965.

But what of the black ballplayers of the 1950s? If a young man, inspired by Jackie Robinson, attempted to climb the ladder to the major leagues, what kind of reception did he receive in the minor leagues? And how did it affect him? Several people have written about their experiences, or talked for publication, outlining the discrimination and hatred they faced simply trying to succeed in a sport that is difficult enough as is.

My book is a work of fiction, based on facts. The Mountain Empire League never existed, none of the cities in the league have ever existed, except for Edens Ridge, which was a small Northeast Tennessee town in the 19th century that was eventually absorbed into Kingsport. And all of the main characters are fictional.

Much of what takes place in the book is, however, factual, with the information coming from numerous accounts in previously-published works. So when our hero, Oddibe Daniels, is thrown at by both pitchers and infielders, that is accurate. When he has to run away from a potential beating after a game, that is accurate. In addition, I spent about a dozen years working on the business side of minor league baseball, from the late 1970s through 1990, and incorporated quite a few incidents that I experienced myself, either directly or indirectly, into this book. Many of the secondary and tertiary characters found here are based on people I knew, or interacted with, during my years in the game. And several actual people make brief appearances, such as Satchel Paige, Pete Suder and George Trautman.

And the issue of language needs to be mentioned. There is a lot of cussing in this book, and it is included simply because those words are common among ballplayers, in the clubhouse, in the dugout, in their everyday life. I am sorry if anyone disapproves. Now, the use of the more despicable words, the racial epithets, you **should** find offensive. They are used because they were all-too-common at that time, and you need to find them horrific. Historically accurate, yes, but nevertheless vile and contemptible, more so because they still get used today.

My purpose in writing *The Mountain Empire League* was to explain how the world still had a long way to go in the immediate aftermath of Jackie Robinson. To the best of my knowledge, no work of fiction has ever focused on the hardships faced by young African-American men who were hoping to make a career for themselves in professional baseball. The story of the sport's integration, most especially in the minor leagues, needs to be told, because it is filled with a great many unsung heroes. Through the use of a fictional league and characters, I have attempted to tell that tale, and salute them as the pioneers they were.

I do not believe this is strictly a "baseball novel." Baseball is most assuredly the backdrop, but it is a book about America, the nation we were and the nation we were trying to become. Set primarily in 1951 and 1952, we are exposed to a country that was beginning to see and hear the rumblings of social change, sights and sounds that, sadly, have not abated with time.

ONE

⚾ ⚾ ⚾

It had been the very best summer of his life, and it was about to get better.

For 22-year-old Jack Simpson, being a professional baseball player was all he had ever wanted, and in 1937, his fifth year in the minors and second in the New York Yankee system, he was truly living the dream. Hadn't started out all that well—despite his good spring, he'd been sent back to Joplin when a couple of other players became the talk of St. Pete and got that plum assignment to Norfolk. His manager, former major league catcher Benny Bengough, saw his slumped shoulders and quickly set him straight.

"Quitcherbitchin, kid," said Benny, "you still got plenty to learn. Besides, this gives you a chance to show them you know how to make a silk purse outta a sow's ear, know what I mean? Make the best of it, go out and have a great year and you'll be in Norfolk soon enough. For now, you get to play baseball AND look at my pretty mug every day, what could be better?"

Benny was right. Several players had been released that spring, and had it been him, what would he have done? Things seemed to be getting a little better throughout the country, to be sure, but times were still plenty hard and jobs were still tough to come by, and look at him. *You're getting a steady paycheck for playing a game, quitcherbitchin.* And Benny always made it fun, made you want to come to the ballpark. So he worked hard, didn't over-swing, just went with the pitches and was batting a robust .337 in late June.

One of those boys who'd made it to Norfolk broke his ankle trying to turn a double into a triple earlier that month. The Tars shuffled their outfield a bit, elevating one of their erstwhile reserves, but he had trouble handling the curve, a very common occurrence in the bushes. The Yankees put in a call to Joplin.

"Show 'em what you got, kid," Benny had said when he called Mrs. Davis' boarding house to give Jack the news. And when the young outfielder said "I'll miss you, Benny," the old catcher had quickly replied "Fuck me, kid, you concentrate on you."

Norfolk was in the midst of a tight race with the Asheville Tourists for the Piedmont League championship, and they really needed an outfielder who could play day after day. "The pitchers are tougher here in Class B," said Johnny Neun, the former Tiger and Brave first baseman who was managing the Tars. Jack followed Bennie's advice and bore down every day, every at-bat, which resulted in a fine .284 mark over those final two-plus months. He also played well in the outfield, as he usually did, impressing his new skipper, who knew a thing or two about defense himself, having completed an unassisted triple play for Detroit ten years earlier.

There was some real talent on that team, guys who would eventually make it all the way to the majors. Like the whole infield—Ed Levy at first, Pete Suder at third, and Mickey Witek and Gar Del Savio up the middle, plus catcher Red Hayworth. Terrific pitching—Hi Bithorn rolled to ten quick wins before being promoted to

Binghamton, on his way to becoming the first Puerto Rican native to play in the majors. Norm Branch won fourteen and three others won in double figures. And of course there was Tommy, Tommy Holmes, playing just his first year after being signed out of Brooklyn Tech and the Bushwicks semi-pro team. He had so much potential he didn't need to start at the lowest rung of the minor league ladder—Class D—and he proved it by batting .320, with 25 homers and 111 runs batted in. Everyone knew he would become a star, and he did, with a lifetime big-league batting average of .302, plus a couple of All-Star Game appearances. The Tars only lost one playoff game and claimed their second straight Piedmont League title.

Perhaps even more memorable than winning the title, though, was when his folks came to see him play in early August. That hadn't happened since high school, just four years earlier but seemingly a lifetime ago. Sarge really hated taking vacation, he secretly thought the twice-weekly newspaper he edited and published, the *Fulton County Chronicle,* couldn't manage without him, but Pamela had put her foot down.

"Virginia isn't all that far from Pennsylvania, you know, wouldn't take us all that long to drive down there. I hear it's pretty country, I've never been, neither have the girls, it oughta be fun!" When her husband didn't respond, her demeanor turned more serious.

"Ben, we haven't had a vacation in I don't know how long, and this seems to me to be the perfect opportunity. We get to see our boy play ball, against other professionals, some of the best players in the country. And Norfolk, Norfolk's near Richmond, isn't it? You've always said you wanted to visit the Confederate capital. Bet we could probably go through Appomattox, too, either on our way down or coming back…"

"The girls would be bored," said Sarge, trying to mask his growing enthusiasm. "They don't share my love for Civil War history, and you don't either, for that matter."

"But Norfolk is on the water, I'll bet the girls would love to get in some beach time, and I…frankly, I wouldn't mind it either." She then gave him a sly smile and a quick wink. "Been a long time since I've seen you in a bathing suit, Ben Simpson, you never know what that might…stir up."

Just having them in the stands was a thrill, but the seventh inning proved to be the real highlight. That's when he lined a bases-clearing triple against the league's best pitcher, Portsmouth's tough lefty Harry "The Cat" Brecheen, who would later be the star of the 1946 World Series. While Cubs' manager Elmer Yoter was making his pitching change, Jack was able to look into the stands, and it was easy to locate his family. They were the ones still out of their seats, his mother clapping, his sisters jumping, and his father just standing there, beaming, almost glowing. Nothing, no nothing, not on a ballfield, anyway, would ever feel that good again.

Right after his family headed back home, Pete Suder asked him if he wanted to make a little extra money once their season ended.

"Guy I know puts together a barnstorming tour every year in September and October. We travel around western Pennsylvania, West Virginia, sometimes into Maryland, playin' every day, or close to it, sometimes two towns a day, ya know? We play a lotta town teams, easy pickins, but sometimes we go against some other minor leaguers, sometimes against good Negro League guys, those games are a lot more fun 'cause they're more challenging. And we can each make some decent dough and still be home 'fore Thanksgiving. Waddya say?"

Jack's mind quickly flashed back eleven years, to 1926, when his father took him over to Chambersburg. The Phillies' second baseman, Max Bishop, had put together a barnstorming team, and both Simpsons were thrilled to see major and minor leaguers live and up close. Jack remembered how it made him feel, and the chance to bring that excitement to other boys almost gave him goosebumps.

"Count me in, Pete."

Growing up in Clay County, there were a couple of things Walter Daniels knew. For sure he wanted to get out of Clay County. Out of Georgia altogether, if he could. Just because his daddy was a farmer and his granddaddy had been a farmer didn't mean he had to work the land, too. He did like using his hands, making things, building things, fixing things, but feeding chickens and slopping hogs just wasn't the life he saw for himself. But that was Clay County—if you lived there, you tilled the soil. That was true of the Creek and Seminole tribes who had been inhabiting the land for centuries. That was true of the Africans forcibly brought in to pick cotton.

And it was compounded by Jim Crow. The Confederates may have lost that war, but it sure didn't seem like it in Clay County. Walter and his family always had to watch what they said and how they acted around white folk. Don't look 'em in the eye, always say "yassir" and "no ma'am," and you still couldn't be sure what might happen to you. Fellow had been lynched in Clay County before Walter was born, but plenty of people remembered it, brought it up now and again, just in whispers. It was always there, in the back of their minds, with the knowledge that it could certainly happen again.

Must be a better way, Walter thought, *a better place. Maybe Chicago, or Boston, or New York, some place like that.* His daddy just snorted.

"What, you gonna go to Chicago or Noooo Yawk? Whatchoo gonna do up dare, Mista High-n-Mighty, be one of dem stock traders? Mebbe go huntin' wit' young Mista Roo-zee-velt? I gits it, why don't you jes' go up to Washington, DC and hep Mista Hardin' run da country? Da's it, you go run da country, you kin do it, yassir. Betta start walkin' now 'fore the cold weatha come. You gonna need to getchoo some betta shoes 'cause it snows up dare in Washington, DC. You do dat, boy, you go run da country. Ha!"

Unfortunately, President Harding died before Walter could offer his services.

Working on a farm, of course, meant more than dealing with animals; there was always wood to be split and fences to be mended and things to be fixed. Wielding an axe or a hammer had helped Walter develop that barrel chest, those strong arms and wrists, the broad shoulders, all of which gave him another skill—he could swing a baseball bat.

Lots of boys played ball all over Georgia, and Clay County was no exception. Walter and a few of his friends from neighboring farms started their own little team, the Hayseeds they called themselves. Pretty soon they were playing other informal squads around the county, just a fun thing to do on a Sunday afternoon. Walter wasn't fast but he could hit the ball hard, really drive it into the gaps, so he generally batted fourth or fifth in the lineup. And he had those good, strong hands, making him a natural for third base.

A lot of times local people would come watch the boys play, bringing plenty of food with them so that after the game both teams could chow down, and you'd better believe those youngsters were grateful. And sometimes a stranger or two would be out there, watching, maybe making notes, and the boys speculated that they were scouts.

"They gotta be scouts, why else they be writin' stuff down? They is lookin' at us!"

"Well no chance they lookin' at you, you done struck out twice today."

"Ain't no scouts cummin' roun' here to Clay County, you crazy?"

"Man, they might be Homestead Grays! Or Chicago American Giants."

"Chicago American Giants, shit, might as well be da New York Giants. Mebbe that was John McGraw hisself, eh? Shit."

"John McGraw ain't no colored man, dat man was as black as you."

"You ain't never seed John McGraw, you don' know what he look like."

"Wait, I know, I know. Weren't John McGraw, was ol' Joe Jackson. He cain't play no more but he scoutin' players for da White Sox. Dat's who it was, Mista Shoeless Joe hisself!"

And the boys all laughed, part of the fun of playing baseball.

Summer of 1927, a challenge came from the boys in Early County, and so the Clay County kids put together an all-star team of sorts and met their southern counterparts at a neutral site. Folks came from both counties, and the boys heard there was money being wagered, not just on the outcome of the game but sometimes on particular at-bats:

"Four bits sez he strike him out right here."

"Yeah? You on!"

Walter hit three doubles, including a shot down the left-field line that started the scoring, and bullets to right-center that drove in runs both times, the last one knocking in the go-ahead tally in the tenth. Those three two-baggers earned him several handshakes after the game that surprisingly included a few dollar bills.

As they were getting into the wagons that would take them back home, a man approached and called Walter by name. A tall, slender Negro, he seemed to walk with a confidence not generally seen on the farms of Clay County. Everyone stopped, it was one of those men who had been seen taking notes at some of their games! Wasn't John McGraw or Joe Jackson, though.

"Mista Daniels, may I speak with you for a minute? Won' take long, I know you boys wanna git-on home."

Walter didn't respond because he simply didn't know what to say.

"My name is Tom Butler, and I work for the Asheville Royal Giants baseball club. I bin watchin' you for a while now, and I like the way you play the game. Mebbe I kin cum see you one night, you an' your pappy, talk a little baseball?"

Walter still wasn't sure what to say, and he was very much aware that all the other boys were staring at him. Finally he mumbled "yeah, sure, whateva you want, we home ever night."

Mr. Butler smiled. "I be over one day this week, then." He turned and smiled at the wagons. "Great game, boys, y'all played real well. Have a nice trip back home." And with that he walked away. All eyes were on him for a moment before they turned, almost as one, to stare at Walter, who felt very self-conscious as he climbed into the wagon.

No one said anything for a moment or two as they clucked at the horses, then finally "Boney" Burnett whistled and said "Damn, Walter, you gonna be a BALLplayer!"

The Royal Giants were not in an "organized" league, they were barn-stormers, a traveling team that moved around, playing similar squads throughout the Southeast. But their schedule proved to be quite irregular. Sometimes they were in and around Asheville for days on end, other times they were elsewhere in North Carolina, or in Tennessee or Virginia or South Carolina. And sometimes they'd go for a few days, or longer, without playing. No games meant no money coming in, and finding any kind of day labor was plenty difficult in Depression-ravaged America.

But going back to Clay County was not an option for Walter, and not just because of all the things his Daddy would have said to him. He had met someone, a local young lady named Lilliana Lewis, and in short order they had married and produced a daughter, Annie. Now in late August of 1929, with another baby on the way, he took a job as a janitor and general handyman at Stephens-Lee High School, and signed to play weekends and summers with the Asheville Black Tourists, who offered a much more structured schedule.

After the stock market crashed two months later, the opening act for what would become known as the Great Depression, getting a full-time job made Walter Daniels appear to be prescient.

Oddibe was born in February, which meant the extra $75 a week or so that Walter brought home every summer by playing ball for the Black Tourists came in very handy. (Berenice was born in 1934, while Willie, "the accident," arrived in 1941.) And Walter liked this arrangement—he had a steady, comfortable, paying job for most of the year, and in the summer, he could still play a little ball and get paid for his efforts.

Snow was falling in late January of 1934. He was leaving Stephens-Lee for the day when he saw an old familiar face leaning against an automobile.

"Tom Butler! Landsakes, I haven't seen you in ages! How are you, sir?"

"Fine, Walter, just fine. And you, and Lilly? How many young'uns you got now? Here, wait, let's get into my Chevy Stovebolt, it's cold out here today!"

They spent a few minutes catching up, then the old Royal Giants scout got to the point.

"I'm workin' on puttin' together my own barnstormin' team, Walter, and makin' it bigger and better than the Black Tourists. We'll play some real good teams, filled with minor leaguers, Negro Leaguers, maybe even get a few big-league boys to join us. White and Black, we'll play 'em all for sure, don't matter to me."

He took a breath, and when Walter said nothing, Tom Butler continued his sales pitch.

"Right now, what I'm doin' is workin' to put this all together, and tryin' to figger out who might could be with me. I got a firm commitment from Big House Kirkland, you know him, the catcher, right? Thought so. And Willson Carmichael, he'll anchor our outfield. Burger Boyd said he'd pitch and maybe play a little first, and you know people will come out just to watch him strut around out there." The both laughed, thinking of some of the legendary stories about the veteran southpaw, some of which might actually be true; the Burger Man was never afraid to toot his own horn.

Still smiling, Tom Butler zeroed in.

"Walter, I'd like to put you down for third base. I'll pay $85 a week, guaranteed, and I'm lookin' to line up eleven weeks of play. No need to try and do the math, I can tell you that's almost a thousand dollars for the summer, old friend."

Walter whistled. "That's a lotta money, Mr. Butler, you sure you gonna be able to come up with that and have enough left for yourself? I mean, I 'spect you ain't doin' this outta the goodness of your heart…sir."

Butler smiled. "Good question. I already got one sponsor, Sunbeam Chevrolet, they gonna supply all our cars, just like mine, here, no charge. When I told 'em we'd be playin' up in Tennessee and Virginia, that really got 'em excited, I believe they're thinkin' 'bout goin' into them markets themselves. And…"

"Mr. Butler, sorry to interrupt, but how you gonna have a cullud team playin' any white teams in the South? That ain't done, leastways not down here. Maybe up north…"

"I know people, Walter, people I met all those years I was scoutin' for the Royal Giants. They wanna make this happen as much as me. I don't have to tell you that we're still in this Depression, people all over still hard up for money. Black team playing White team, people will pay to see that, even in the South. Pay good money, Walter."

In the end, they made a verbal agreement. By late April, the Tom Butler All-Stars would either be a reality or a pipe dream, but one way or another he'd let Walter Daniels know. "This way, if I've struck out, you still got plenty-a time to sign up with the Black Tourists again. Deal?"

They shook on it.

In a way, the West Virginia coal mines were good to Jack Warhop. He made a little money and also got to pitch for local teams sponsored by his employer, the Chesapeake and Ohio Railroad. This won him some recognition and, soon enough, a professional baseball contract, which allowed him to leave the mines at the age of 21, his lungs pretty much intact.

Just average height and weight, he fooled hitters with a "submarine" delivery. Essentially throwing underhanded, its' unorthodoxy makes it a difficult adjustment for most professional hitters. Highly successful in the minors, Warhop was signed by the Detroit Tigers, who then sold him to the New York Highlanders.

When Byron Bancroft (Ban) Johnson formed the American League, he knew his fledgling major league needed a strong anchor in New York. After two years, the Baltimore Orioles were sold to three businessmen and moved to New York, where a ballpark was very hastily constructed in upper Manhattan's Washington Heights neighborhood. How hasty? When the park opened, part of right field had to be roped off to prevent outfielders from being swallowed up by a swamp. (Eventually a fence was erected, making it a choice target for hitters, even in that dead-ball era.)

The team was called the Highlanders and had middling success over the years, never winning a pennant though they did contend a couple of times. After the 1912 season, the team left swampy Hilltop Park for the new, fifth edition of the Polo Grounds, where they became tenants of the Giants, long-time "lords" of New York baseball. And they changed their name to the Yankees.

Jack Warhop probably cared little about this history when he joined the team late in the 1908 season (except for keeping an eye on that short porch in right field). Starting in 1909, he became a regular member of the Highlanders/Yankees pitching rotation, throwing better than 200 innings five times, and fashioning an excellent career Earned Run Average of 3.12, a much better arbiter of his abilities than his overall losing record of 68–92. Beginning in 1916, he became a baseball gypsy, pitching in minor leagues all around the country, occasionally adding the title of "manager" to his resume. He was, in fact, still taking an occasional turn on the mound in 1934, when he was 50 years old.

And he also kept his hand in the game by organizing barnstorming trips during the autumn. Though now a resident of Illinois, he always returned to West Virginia, and its environs, for a few weeks, so his fellow Mountain State boys (and a few of their neighbors) might have a chance to pick up some extra cash.

Somewhere along the line he and Tom Butler had become acquainted and found they could work together. The nation's racial mores be damned.

"I just wanted to let you know I got a few studs this year, Tom," Warhop told Butler in a long-distance phone call. "Suder's back, he's prob'ly our best player, plus a righty from Ohio named Wahonick, John Wahonick, he's, uh, conveniently wild..."

"You usually do, Crab," replied Butler, using the nickname the old hurler had answered to for years. "I ain't worried, I got me some good fellas, too. We got guys what can hit, that's for sure. Little light on the mound, but we make up for it with our bats."

Warhop laughed. "Ain't gonna be playin' many 2–1 games, eh?"

"Not much past the first inning or two." They both found that amusing.

"OK, Tom, see ya in the mountains in October."

"Lookin' forward to it, as usual."

The Tom Butler All-Stars played their way north from Asheville. They had a couple of games in Tennessee, though one got cancelled when the county sheriff got word to Butler that "trouble may be a-brewin', a smart fella would think hard 'bout stayin' away this year." They added a game in Prestonburg, Kentucky, though, and also played a couple of contests in Virginia before getting to the Mountain State. Their opponents were generally local teams that featured guys who had not played seriously since high school, and for good reason. Sometimes, though, they ran across a good player or two. If Tom thought they had even the smallest chance of making it in the minors, he would get their contact information and pass it along to any number of white scouts he knew, including Jack Warhop. While the black team was normally superior, they made sure never to blow out the opposition. It was simply good business—they wanted to be invited back next year, and were also mindful of angering some fans in the grandstands who were just looking for a reason to stir up trouble. A close game generally kept the hotheads at bay.

The Warhop Warriors played a little in southeastern Ohio and a lot in western Pennsylvania before reaching West Virginia a few days ahead of their Negro counterparts. While there was no real "home-team advantage" for touring teams, playing a couple of games in and around Morgantown would at least get the fans familiar with the players Jack Warhop was trotting out onto the field.

The travel book that Butler always utilized to find housing and eateries for his barnstorming players had turned up several available homes and boarding houses for them to utilize while they were in the Morgantown area. Once he had made sure everyone was settled in at their respective locales, he went to his lodging and was surprised to find a message waiting for him.

> Tom, there's huge interest in our game, so I've turned it into a day-night doubleheader. Hope you don't mind, but that'll be two separate admissions and more money for all of us. See you at the field.
>
> Jack W.

Saturday, October 16, was clear and cool. "Be a good day for a baseball game," Tom said, as the players assembled at the ballfield located in the southeastern portion of the municipal park. "Be a little chilly tonight," said Burger Boyd. "Lemme pitch the second game, Tom. I won't screw around, just work on getting' outs so we don't freeze our asses off after the sun goes down."

"Oh, it won't be that cold," said Butler. But he did agree to pitch Boyd in the newly-scheduled nightcap.

The grandstands were packed and still the people were coming, so the outfield was roped off for standing room only. "That's good," said Big House. "Make it easier to hit the ball out in the crowd." His teammates just snickered. "Only a ground-rule double if'n you hit it out there," said Walter, to which Kirkland just responded with a drawn-out "Shit."

To a man, the Negroes' built-in radar homed in on one of Warhop's reserve players, a lanky young man with sandy brown hair. No one remembered ever seeing him before, but they sure recognized the type—he kept looking over to their bench and chuckling, with a periodic discharge of tobacco juice, followed by another look and a grin. Yeah, gotta watch out for him. Walter volunteered to find out who he was, so he went over to the first Warhop player he saw.

"Afternoon," said Walter to the white player, a young man, well built, with a pleasant face and, when he took off his cap to wipe his brow, a prematurely-receding hairline.

"Afternoon," he replied. "Jack Simpson."

"Walter Daniels," he said with a nod. "Good trip so far?"

"Yeah, been fine. Games have been…hell, no use sugar-coatin' it, they been pretty easy, for the most part. We're lookin' forward to playin' you here today, we're expectin' some good competition."

"And you'll get it," said Walter, with a quick smile. "Was wonderin'…we was all wonderin' if you could tell us who that guy is, your teammate." And he shot the lanky dude a fast glance.

"Yeah, his name is Chum Benton," said Simpson. "Back-up outfielder. Not much talent, if you ask me. He's here, I guess, 'cause he'a a friend of Belcher, one-a our lefties. From somewhere 'round here, I think. A real…" Simpson looked down at the ground, which he seemed to be massaging with his foot. Finally he looked back at Daniels.

"Not my favorite fella," he said. "Smart to keep an eye on him."

They nodded at each other and headed back to their respective benches.

Butler's players were hardly surprised that the fans considered them to be the "villains," and Chum Benton helped it along with a steady chatter from the bench, using language that encouraged the fans to follow suit.

"Looky here, we got us a team full-a n—s. No n—s ever gonna be able to beat no white men." *("Go back to Africa, n—s, this here's a white man's game.")*

"Call the zoo, bunch-a their monkeys done escaped!" *(A few people in the crowd made monkey noises.)*

"Glad you're here, rastus, I need me some fresh gator bait." *("Rastus, rastus.")*

When the leadoff man for the Butler All-Stars grounded out to short, Benton was emboldened.

"All right, all right. Fuckin' coon, you don't belong here, why don't you go home and pick some cotton?"

Someone in the crowd started singing "Old Man River." On the bench, Walter snorted. "If you gonna sing that song, 'speshully that song, would sure he'p if you could actually carry a tune." His teammates laughed, but that only infuriated Benton.

"What y'all laughin' at, n—s? Why you nappy-headed sons-a bitches, come on over here and shine our shoes."

Jack Warhop finally—finally!—got to his feet and ambled over to Chum Benton.

"That's enough outta you, meat. Zip your lip, and keep it zipped."

"But coach…"

"This is just a game, not a Klan rally. If you can't keep yer yap shut, I'll…"

Benton stood up; he was several inches taller that his manager, and a good thirty years younger.

"You'll what? Whatcha gonna do, old man?"

Warhop moved within inches of his player's face. Having held his own against the likes of Ty Cobb, Frank Baker, Nap Lajoie and others during his major league career, he was not going to be intimidated by this bumpkin.

"I will pick you up by the nuts and deposit you right in the middle of that other bench. Bet them fellas would love to get to know you better."

A few of the white players worked hard to suppress their laughter. Benton looked around for some support and, finding none, simply sat down. But the fuse had been lit.

Willson Carmichael led off the third inning. The pitcher, Wahonick, got the first pitch over for a strike, but the second one was wild and hit the centerfielder, just above the elbow. Carmichael grimaced but, as is customary, didn't give the opposition the satisfaction of rubbing the spot.

This brought up Big House Kirkland. The powerful catcher wanted nothing more than to hit a towering home run well beyond the roped-off section of fans, but instead he hit a hard line drive right up the middle, directly at the pitcher. Wahonick instinctively threw up his glove, which no doubt protected him from serious injury. The ball, however, did ricochet off the glove, hit his head, and then bounce slowly behind the mound. Despite his lack of speed, Big House easily made it safely to first.

The crowd was now stirred up. "Hey ump, that jig just tried to kill our pitcher, you gotta do somethin'." (Warhop had recruited three local fellows to serve as umpires. They were happy to handle ball-and-strikes, and plays at the bases, but were not inclined to get in the middle of a racial conflict.)

This brought up Walter Daniels with runners on first and second and no outs. Like Big House, he wanted to hit the ball hard; unlike his teammate, he did not, sending a routine ground ball to short, a sure double play.

The shortstop flipped the ball to his second baseman, who stepped on the bag, retiring Big House, and a follow-up throw to first would undoubtedly get Walter for the double play. But the infielder held the ball for an extra second, looking at the sliding Big House the whole time. And the veteran catcher recognized that look, the look of pure hatred, and he knew what was coming.

The throw to first was low, much lower than normal, low enough to possibly hit the incoming runner right between the eyes. Big House threw up his hands in self-defense and deflected the ball, prompting the umpire to immediately thrust his right fist in the air and yell "Interference! Runner interfered with the throw, it's a double play."

Truthfully, it was the right call, but that didn't prevent Tom Butler from tearing over from the coaches' box, screaming something about "intent"—"that throw was meant to injure my baserunner!" Both benches emptied, fans started screaming again, and suddenly Big House and the much-smaller second baseman began pushing, then pushing back, and quickly punches were being thrown, and players on both sides began squaring off.

Not everyone, however—some All-Stars and some Warriors immediately began trying to calm their teammates. It was rather difficult, but Walter was finally able to pull Big House off the physically-overmatched infielder. "Get your hands offa me," the catcher kept yelling, but Walter just pulled him away and over towards their bench.

"Cool off, man, cool off. Remember where you are. Wanna spend the night in a West Virginia jail?" That arrow struck home. Big House sat down, and Walter ran back to the infield.

He found Jack Simpson serving as one of the peacemakers, having run in from left field. "We're OK here, Daniels, it's over, it's over. Right, fellas?" He stared at his teammates, who grumbled an assent and began ambling back to their bench.

"Thanks, man," said Walter, and Simpson nodded.

"Appreciate your help out here," he responded. The two men nodded again, and within moments the game resumed. Though tensions remained high, there were no further incidents or fisticuffs. And for the record, both teams recorded wins that day. The Warhop Warriors took the day game, 6–5, while Burger Boyd, taking advantage of Jack Warhop's mediocre portable lighting system, was virtually unhittable in the nightcap, giving up just two singles in a 4–0 win. And everyone left Morgantown with a fresh infusion of cash.

A sunny, warm afternoon sure brought the fans out, so Jack and Nashota had to park a little further out than they had expected.

"Quite a crowd for a semi-pro industrial league game," he said.

"Looks like more people than we sometimes get in April and early May," she said, wryly. He just frowned, knowing she was (unfortunately) correct.

Jack and Nashota Simpson operated the Edens Ridge Wolves of the Mountain Empire League, an independent Class D ballclub in baseball's coast-to-coast minor league system. Even though their playing season was officially over, they were in picturesque Asheville, North Carolina on this Saturday in late September 1951, scouting possible talent for next year's team. Specifically, one player in particular.

They had parked on the first-base side of the small ballpark, and as they walked towards the main gate, they passed a much smaller entrance marked "Coloreds Only." "I'll never get used to that," said Nashota, shaking her head. "You know, when I lived here in the 'Paris of the South,' I'd often sit out here. Occasionally someone would come over to me and whisper 'Ma'am, this here area is just for coloreds,' and I'd tell 'em..."

"Yes, yes, I know, you'd point out that you were Cherokee and thus not white and you felt more comfortable out here anyway, loved having the sun on your face..."

Nashota grinned. "Guess you've heard it before, *U-ya-hia*." To which he replied "I would hope that husbands and wives wouldn't keep secrets from one another." That made her laugh out loud, that pervasive noise that always made people instinctively turn to see what was causing such a howl. Of course, people always looked at Nashota—she was always the most beautiful woman in the room, easily the most beautiful woman Jack Simpson had ever known, far more attractive than so many Hollywood stars. She was also bright and athletic and full of ambition. It was her eyes, however, that most people saw first and remembered long afterward. They were large and dark and piercing and commanded attention. When she was happy her eyes sparkled like stars in the night sky, but when she was angry or upset, oh my! Those eyes would narrow into slits, and could penetrate anyone within her sights, reducing them to little more than a melted puddle of *a-ma* (the Cherokee word for water).

Officially, she was the Business Manager of the Wolves, nestled in the small Northeast Tennessee town of Edens Ridge, but in actuality, she ran the operation from top to bottom, allowing him to concentrate on signing the players and then managing them on the field.

She had to compose herself before continuing her thought. "So wait, you're saying that if I start having an affair with someone back home, I need to let you know because we don't keep secrets? That's really…"

"'Scuse me, 'scuse me." Her fantasy was interrupted by a voice coming from over his right shoulder. He looked in that general direction and saw a burly Negro man, with a small boy, hustling his way.

"Friend of yours?" asked Nashota. Jack looked once, then a second time. "I'm not…might could…"

"Jack Simpson? Is that you, Jack Simpson? From The Warhop Warriors back in…"

"1937! It is, it's me! And you're Walter Daniels, right? Well I'll be. Walter Daniels, good to see you after all this time" Jack instinctively thrust out his right hand, but Daniels' face clouded and he lowered his voice.

"Cain't do that, Mr. Simpson, not out here. Please."

"I HATE IT! I hate it. This…country." And Nashota proceeded to walk in a small circle, speaking entirely in her native tongue. After a moment she calmed down, allowing Jack to speak.

"My wife, Mr. Daniels, Nashota Cozens Simpson. She's a full-blood Cherokee, and she often reverts to the mother tongue when she's upset." And Walter smiled, bowed his head a bit and said "Ma'am." Then he looked at Jack and said "What brings y'all out here today?"

"We're looking at a…ohmygoodness. Nashota, what's the name of the young man we're scouting?"

"Oddibe Daniels…wait, sir, did Jack say your name was…"

"Walter Daniels, yes, ma'am. Oddibe is my oldest son, second born-a four. This here's my youngest, Willie," giving him a quick hug.

Since the game would be starting soon, Jack gave Walter the basics about their affiliation with a minor league team and their search for talented players. Daniels could barely believe his ears; all he could say was "A professional team? My Oddibe? Be a pro ballplayer, like Jackie? Good Lord!" They agreed to meet at that exact spot after the game, though Jack warned "Fifty-fifty chance it'll be a no, Walter. I might tell you that your son is a good semi-pro player, but that's it. I hope you understand." Then they headed to their separate entrances, which elicited a new stream of invectives from Nashota.

Several days later, the Simpsons drove back to Asheville for dinner at the Daniels home. Nashota logically volunteered to drive, since she had lived there for several years, long before she and Jack had met. But she also didn't want him behind the wheel when his mind was so distracted, 'cause ever since they had seen him play, all Jack Simpson could talk about was Oddibe Daniels.

"He was just phenomenal, 'Sho, incredible. That play he made in center was…was…what was your word? Extraordinary! I tell ya, this young man, he could be a force, I can see it, he could dominate games from centerfield. Like Reiser when he was healthy, or DiMaggio, either one. Or Mays, or this Minoso kid on the White Sox. I really believe that."

"What about his hitting?" she asked.

"Needs work, that's for sure, his offense is not as advanced as his defense. But I'm sure I can help him, work with him. Maybe we'll tinker a bit with his swing, or where he sets up in the batter's box, we'll see, we'll see how he does and how he adjusts when the pitchers start figurin' him out. No need for him to hit with power, we just gotta get him on and his speed will do the rest." He chuckled. "Our league won't know what hit them."

It was the perfect lead-in for Nashota's next thought.

"They'll know, Jack, and they will need to know about him in advance, doncha think? Do you really think Wells will just approve this contract without asking questions. The other league directors…"

"They'll be fine, 'Sho. 'Cept for Truck, the rest will…"

"And BJ, he won't be in favor. And I don't know about a couple of the others, either. I mean, this is a big deal, Jack. The league has never had a Negro player, I'm sure the other directors will want to have a say…"

They turned onto the Daniels' street, so the matter was left hanging.

Needless to say, the excitement level was through the roof in the Daniels household. A professional contract would be wonderful for Oddibe, of course, that was the most important thing. But they also realized this would be good for the Negro community of Asheville, maybe even the whole State of North Carolina. They would be proud to have their son add his name to a growing list that was headed up by none other than Jackie Robinson! Why, even if he never played an inning in the big leagues, he would always be known in a similar way—the first Negro in this Mountain Empire League, and the first Negro from Asheville to play professional baseball. Didn't matter how much he'd get paid, almost didn't matter how he'd fare on the field. Just having him be the first, being a pioneer like Jackie, was about enough for Walter and Lilly.

So they welcomed Jack and Nashota Simpson into their modest home on a Tuesday evening, apologizing for the mess. *(What mess?* thought Nashota. The place was spotless. Lilly had stayed up late three nights in a row making sure her home was as immaculate as the Biltmore House.) They served a meal of chicken and potatoes and greens and cornbread, with a healthy side of baseball talk.

"Weren't that somethin', Mista Simpson, the Giants comin' back like that and ol' Thomson hittin' that home run like he did. I been watchin' this game f'mos-a my life, saw Cobb play a exhibition game once, saw Satchel pitch a-coupla times. Saw Josh, too, saw him hit one ovah a bank-a trees in dead center, that ball might still be travelin' somewhere out in space!"

Everyone laughed, and Walter continued. "Thomson's home run weren't hit nearly as far. Really just a pop-up next to what Josh did. Oh, and Cool Papa, saw him, too, no man could run like him."

Jack nodded. "Saw Josh once in Philly but he didn't hit one out that day. Never did see Cool Papa, sure wish I had. You know what they said 'bout him: 'if the ball takes two bounces, put it in your pocket.'"

Walter laughed. "Tha's right, tha's right, an' it was true. But I tell-ya, Mista Simpson, with all this, I ain't never seen nothin' like what happened with the Dodgers and Giants, ever, have you?"

"No, not really, leastways not in a game that meant so much. That was quite the game," said Jack.

"I was wonderin' why Mr. Dressen pulled Newcombe out. I thinks I woulda lef' him in, I even tol' that to m'boy right then an' there," said Walter.

"And I said no, takin' him out was the right thing to do, he was getting' tired. Don't you think, Mr. Simpson?" asked Oddibe, turning to Jack, who smiled; there was nothing he liked better than talking baseball.

"Yes," said Jack, "Newcombe seemed to be out of gas, I think I'd have done the same thing." And Oddibe turned back to his father and smiled, pleased to have found a new ally.

"What about this World Series, then?" asked Walter. "I thinks winnin' this game will give them Giants all the confidence they need 'genst th'Yankees, doncha think? They now have, uh, they have…aw shoot, they's a word fer it an' I just cain't…"

"Momentum, is that what you're lookin' for, Pop?" asked Oddibe, and Walter jumped on it.

"Momentum, tha's it, tha's th' word, the Giants got it an' they kin use it to beat th' Yankees, I think." And immediately Oddibe said "I think so, too!"

"I hate to disagree," Jack said, "but Casey has a fresh pitching staff, and his team isn't so emotionally exhausted. And they've won the last two years, they know what it takes. I think the title stays in the Bronx." This led the three men to compare the two teams, position by position, and eventually they agreed that time would tell.

Nashota insisted on helping with the kitchen clean-up, even though Lilly said that Berenice regularly took care of it. Moments after they had finally decided to split up tasks, Jack poked his head in the doorway.

"'Sho, we've agreed to terms, we need your paperwork."

"Really?" asked a surprised Nashota. "So quickly?" Her husband smiled. "Yes," he replied. "Just like that. He really wants to play."

The Simpsons decided to stay the night in a little motel in the northern part of Asheville. Neither one was anxious to try and drive over the mountain in the dark, and besides, Nashota could see the look in her husband's eyes and knew how excited he was right now. She'd seen it when he had asked her to marry him, and again when they had their wedding ceremony on the reservation. The last thing she wanted to do was spoil the mood, but she felt she had to ask the question again.

"Jack, sweetie, are you sure the league will approve this contract?"

He had used a couple of pillows to prop himself up in the bed. He looked at her, said "That again," and swung his legs around so they touched the floor and he could look her in the eye.

"OK, I've been thinking about this. Yes, there are gonna be people that…have somethin' to say, like Truck and BJ, maybe Don Harrell. But in the end, it's just the league president's call, he's the only one that gets to approve or disapprove contracts."

"Yes, but you know Wells. You know him fairly well, actually, better than me, longer than me, that's for sure. And this will make him…nervous, to say the least. Very nervous."

"Now, you're short-changing yourself, hon. You know as well as I that the one thing Wells wants more-n anything is this world is for all-a us Mountain Empire League teams to line up major league affiliations. If he can arrange that, it'll be the crowning achievement of his career, no doubt." He paused, figuring this logical explanation would suffice, but she said nothing, so he continued.

"We all see what's happening in the baseball world. The Dodgers and Giants and Indians, they're winning ballgames and pennants with their Negro players. The floodgates have opened up and is in the process of drowning the old system." He smiled, pleased with his inspired analogy. "It won't be long 'fore all the big boys have signed Negro players, and they gotta put 'em someplace. More leagues in the South than in the North, certainly on the B, C and D levels. Day is comin', sooner rather-n later, that a big league team won't affiliate with any minor league that won't accept their Negro players."

The Mountain Empire League directors were an eclectic group. Lanny Maxwell of the Mettin Foxes was known to all as "Truck." He claimed to own the biggest independent trucking company in all of Virginia, but his nickname more likely derived from the way he dealt with people—steamrolling them as if he was a runaway eighteen-wheeler. He was also rumored to be high up in Virginia's Klan hierarchy. The same was said of Bobby Joe "BJ" Lewis in Shirley, Kentucky. He was the garrulous, loud owner of the local Chevy dealership, and the Cardinals baseball team. And no one could ever really get a fix on Donald Harrell, the quiet CPA who managed the Kruse Ducks, just a few miles east of the Simpsons' Edens Ridge Wolves. Might be Klan, might be shady, there have always been rumors, but nothing more.

In Jack's opinion, the other directors were a lot more stable and reliable. Charles Underwood was a quiet, thoughtful banker who had been the prime mover in bringing a team to Blackmer, Kentucky. Though it was the second-smallest town in the league, the Blackbirds nearly filled their little ballpark every night and showed a tidy profit year after year. Jeriome Hoffman owned the largest beer distributorship in Southwest Virginia and was probably the wealthiest man associated with the league, but he was really pretty down-to-earth. Despite a very occasional bout of bluster, the Beck Bears' owner was well-liked and respected by his fellow directors. Soft-spoken Jules Gray, a vice president with the munitions company based in Weare, ran his Mustangs with reserve and an impressive efficiency. This was in contrast with the other director from North Carolina, John Robertson. A career baseball executive with a gift for gab, he was a salesman extraordinaire who specialized in bringing people into his ballpark. Unfortunately, his spending habits meant that he annually had to scratch and claw in order for his Buchanan Bees to turn a profit.

"I can see Wells passing the buck, 'Sho. I know that's what you're thinkin', and you may be right. But aside from Truck and BJ and maybe Harrell, the other directors will side with us. They're good men, honest men, reasonable men. And look—Truck and BJ, all-a us, we're just hopin' to make a little money every year, you know that. The Dodgers and Giants and Indians, they're drawing more people to their ballparks than ever." He gave a short laugh. "If there's one language every baseball executive in every league in this country understands, it's the language of money. Push comes to shove, the only color they'll see will be green."

Jack swung his legs back onto the bed. "Oddibe's contract will be approved. We may have to argue our case, but it'll happen."

Nashota took off her blouse and skirt and hung them up. Then she slipped into the bed next to him and nuzzled against his shoulder.

"I sure hope you're right," she said quietly. And after she had fallen asleep, he softly said "Me, too."

TWO

Because of his name, Herbert George Wells Boggs had taken control of himself at a very early age. His mother started off calling him Herbert, which his father hated, so they began using George, which the young man hated, especially once he began going to school. Since H.G. was obviously taken, he switched to Wells and was satisfied for the rest of his life.

His mother was the former Mary Taylor, privileged child of one of the Pennsylvania Railroad's top executives. At Cornell University, however, her world was turned upside down by Eli Boggs, a dynamic firebrand enamored of Socialism and the New York Giants baseball team. Despite her proper upbringing, Mary had great difficulty resisting him (she told herself) and, after twice fearing she had become pregnant, the two eloped after their junior year, much to the chagrin of their respective families. (They did redeem themselves a bit by returning to Ithaca to get their degrees, thus fulfilling promises made to both sets of parents.)

The newlyweds knocked around for a time before landing in Knoxville, Tennessee shortly after Mary had given birth to Wells in the spring of 1903. The Southern climate suited them, and conservative East Tennessee proved to be the perfect foil for Eli's Socialist views, because he loved nothing more than stirring up the pot. "I'm like a teacher," he would frequently tell his son, "I'm helping people to think straight." For those who "chose to learn," he started a newspaper that, surprisingly, became modestly successful despite its unabashedly anti-Klan editorials. In fact, the paper made Eli Boggs something of a celebrity in Knoxville, so much so that he was asked to run for Mayor, which he did with relish. He said whatever he liked and for the rest of his life wore his decisive defeat as a badge of iconoclastic honor.

Young Wells at first thought he wanted to be a lawyer and enrolled at the University of Tennessee, but stayed for only one year. "It's not challenging," he told his parents. "I think I can learn just as much by working, and I'd be getting paid at the same time." (Besides, he really didn't look very good in orange.) But he did have a plan, and in June of 1922 he took the train to New York City to spend time with Grandma and Grandpa Taylor, who were delighted to have him. His grandfather immediately got him a job selling train tickets in Grand Central Station. Wells liked interacting with people and found himself intrigued by business, not just the dollars-and-cents but the whys-and-wherefores. He frequently came home at night with questions for his Grandpa Taylor, who was more than happy to teach the young man about the finer points of capitalism, something that obviously had not been learned from that Socialist father of his.

"Son, your daddy thinks that capitalism is evil, but let me tell you—that is simply not true, it's actually the very rock upon which this country is based. What's evil is that sometimes a handful of businessmen abuse it and they're the ones who give capitalism a bad name! Allows people like your father and that Debs fellow to point their fingers and rail against crooks like Doheny and Sinclair, against the whole system! But those bums, they're just bad seeds, a tiny minority. Most of us are upright, honest entrepreneurs who follow the rules of law and the rules of business."

"There are rules to business?" Wells' curiosity was peaked. "I didn't know that, what are they?"

"Glad you asked, Wells, glad you asked. They aren't rules that are written down, but every good businessman knows them, knows he has to follow them if he wants to be successful. Not everyone does, of course, but let me put it this way—those rules form the road to success, and if you stay on that road you'll have a good and prosperous life."

Mr. Taylor was a little late coming home the next night, and after supper he brought Wells into the den and handed him a piece of paper.

RULES OF BUSINESS

Work hard, but work smart. Just because you put in a lot of hours doesn't mean you're being productive.

Make a budget and stick with it. And develop a good working relationship with a bank.

Hire the best and smartest people and then listen to them. When they come up with good ideas, utilize those ideas and reward the ones who thought them up.

Make the best possible product. And if your first attempt is not exactly what you want, be persistent and keep working at it.

Charge a fair price.

Treat your employees, your customers and your vendors exactly the way you want to be treated.

Always, ALWAYS, be honest, with both your customers and your employees.

"Been thinking about this much of the day and spent some time here and there, when I could, of course, jotting down some notes. Waited while Eunice typed them up for you, that's why I was late tonight, but I wanted…"

Mr. Taylor indicated the paper Wells was holding. "We were talking yesterday about the rules of business, remember, and I thought you might want to know exactly what they are. If you study these and memorize them and—really, this is the most important—live by them when you go out into the business world, you'll do just fine."

Wells looked at them quickly, then up at his grandfather. Mr. Taylor smiled broadly, something he didn't do all that often, then stood up.

"You have any questions, just come to me and ask. Otherwise, that's all for tonight." And with that the tall Defender of Capitalism left the room.

It was clear to Wells that he was holding his lesson for the evening, so he wandered into the kitchen, brewed himself a cup of tea, then went back to the den and read what his Grandpa had prepared for him.

⚾ ⚾ ⚾

Wells continued to work every day at Grand Central and take "master classes" at night with Grandpa Taylor, all of which led to a major announcement, when the whole family was together at Thanksgiving.

"I've decided to go back to school," he said, and before he could continue his parents said "Wonderful!" simultaneously.

"But not UT, I could never go back there. Sorry, Mom, sorry, Dad. No, I've decided I want to study business, and I'm going to apply to the University of Pennsylvania's Wharton School. Hopefully, I will be accepted and can start next fall."

Grandpa Taylor immediately said he was as proud as he could be and "I will happily pay for tuition, room and board." Eli Boggs, however, was having none of it.

"You've been poisoning his mind, that's what's been going on while he's been living here with you!" He leaned on the table and pointed his finger in about as menacing a gesture as Wells had ever seen from his father. "You've turned him away from everything Mary and I have taught him, all we hold close to our hearts."

"Boy's old enough to make his own decisions, Eli," Mr. Taylor said quietly, with a trace of a smirk. "I have not…"

Wells' father quickly interrupted. "And let me tell you, the Boggs family does not take charity, no sir! I have a good job and make a decent living and provide for my family, and no one has to pay my bills. If my boy wants to go to Wharton, fine, but we'll be footing the bill, Mary and me, thank you very much."

"It's hardly charity, Eli. We're not talking about some street urchin, he's my grandson." Mr. Taylor shifted in his chair. "You may not realize how expensive Wharton is and, uh, well, I know you have a good job but so do I and I think, uh, not trying to…well, look, Eli, I just think we're in a little better position…"

"There you go again!" Eli rose from his chair as his decibel level increased. "You are always in some way criticizing my work, and my beliefs. You have never…"

"Father! Eli! No good will come of shouts and accusations." Mary realized she needed to get in the middle of this before things got completely out of hand. "Let's all sit down and talk about this calmly and rationally. Rationally."

For a moment the only sound in the room was Wells' sister, Janine, chewing on a turkey leg.

"Eli," said Mary, slowly. "If Father is right about this school, he may have a point, it may be more than we…um, would have budgeted for Wells' college, especially since Janine is also planning on going for her teaching degree next year."

"UT is just fine with me," said Janine, looking right at her brother, who just rolled his eyes.

"I think we can, um, we, uh, ought to be able to devise a plan to share the expense of Wells' schooling," said Mary.

There was silence. It was Janine who, inadvertently, broke the tension and the logjam. "I think Wells ought to pay something, too."

Everyone looked at her. She felt conspicuous, suddenly becoming the center of attention while gnawing on that turkey leg. But Janine realized they were expecting her to make her case.

"Well, why shouldn't he have to pay, it's his education, isn't it? He's been working for the past few months, and living here rent free, he ought to have at least a little bit stashed away, right?" Ha, this was perfect, she could finally get back at him for that time he caught her with Johnny Trainor and threatened to tell Mom and Dad.

"Janine, I must say, that is not a bad idea, not bad at all," said Mr. Taylor. He then turned to his son-in-law. "Perhaps, Eli, you can agree to pay forty percent, and I will pay forty percent, then Wells can pay the remaining twenty percent. Perhaps that way you and I will be happy and Wells will learn some valuable lessons, both in and out of the classroom."

And with that, détente was achieved and the Great Thanksgiving Day battle came to an end.

In the fall of 1923, Wells Boggs took the train to Philadelphia to begin his studies at Wharton. And the University of Pennsylvania wound up fitting Wells like a glove (plus he looked much better in red and blue!). The business classes he took were challenging and exciting, and he liked keeping company with his upper-crust classmates. He also liked that, on occasion, he could take the trolley to either the Baker Bowl or Shibe Park to see the Phillies or Athletics play. Wells couldn't hit a baseball if he was swinging a tree trunk, but all aspects of the game fascinated him, and he frequently questioned strategic moves and, occasionally, business practices he observed. In September of 1925, as he was beginning his senior year at Penn, he attended a game against the Cubs and then wrote a letter to William Baker, the Phillies' owner, criticizing the operation of the concession stands, which Wells found to be "sloppy and inefficient." To his surprise he received a response, signed by Mr. Baker himself:

> Dear Mr. Boggs:
>
> Thank you so much for your thoughtful letter. I often receive mail from fans, but they are generally filled with suggestions about moves they think we ought to be making on the field, like trading our entire outfield for Babe Ruth. So I was pleased to read something that was thoughtful, intelligent, well-written and not at all a waste of my time. I can see that your Wharton education is paying off!
>
> I would like to invite you to come into my office some time so we may discuss some of these thoughts and ideas you have been good enough to share. Please call the number listed at the top of this letterhead and ask for Miss Owens; I will alert her to be expecting to hear from you.

Thank you again for your interest in the Philadelphia Phillies, and I look forward to meeting you in person in due course.

Respectfully,

William F. Baker
President, Philadelphia Phillies

    An appointment was quickly made. Mr. Baker was polite and cordial, listened to Wells, answered his questions and actually seemed to be taking notes. He asked Wells what he planned to do when he graduated from Penn, and when Wells said he thought he would try for a master's degree at Wharton, Baker snorted. "You can learn a helluva lot more working in the real world than by reading about it in books. What they write in those textbooks ain't always the way it really is, son. If I was you I'd get me a job, start earning my way, that's the best education you will ever get."

    After Wells left his office, Baker buzzed his secretary. "See if you can find Harry Land, down in Bradenton, Florida, will you? Thanks." Baker was planning to move the Phils' spring training base there in 1926, and knew that the (Class D) Florida State League was planning to add teams, including one in Bradenton. This bright young man ought to be putting that Wharton degree to work in professional baseball, he thought.

    Wells had also, unknowingly, made an impression on Baker's secretary. Not for herself, mind you, she was a couple of years older than he and already planning her December wedding. But Miss Owens had a younger sister, Georgia, who really needed some direction in her life, and a good, smart, solid young college man might be just the thing. She guessed that her boss had also been impressed with the lad and that she'd eventually be asked to bring him in again. If that were the case, she would make sure her sister just happened to be in the office at that time.

    Grandpa Taylor had been more than a bit disappointed when the boy told him he was going to work in baseball. He had a Wharton degree, after all, surely it was worth something more significant than a game. And if it had to be baseball, then why not with a major league team? Mr. Taylor knew Charles Stoneham a little and would have been happy to use that connection to get the boy a job up at that funny-shaped Polo Grounds park but no, headstrong and confident, young Wells wanted to make his own way, on his own terms.

    So he went to Bradenton, Florida, as the new Business Manager for the Growers of the Florida State League. Wells loved the job but hated the hot, sticky weather, and distrusted his boss, Mike McDonnigle. A sharp dresser with a winning smile, even the inexperienced Wells Boggs soon realized that the team's president regularly violated all of the Rules of Business his grandfather had ingrained into him. His suspicions were verified when, once the team hit the road following their final homestand of the season, McDonnigle took off with the concession and gate receipts from the previous three games. (Never caught by U.S. officials, he likely ran afoul of some *crimináles*—his body was found on a Cuban beach about three years later.)

Mr. Asher, the league president, quickly determined that Wells had not been complicit in any way with McDonnigle's fiscal shenanigans. He and the Florida State League's Board of Directors also decided they were more comfortable operating as a six-team league, which led to them dropping Bradenton, Ft. Myers and Lakeland and adding the Miami Hustlers, with Wells Boggs appointed as the Business Manager.

He did not make the trip to South Florida alone. He had been introduced to the petite Georgia Owens the second time he had met with Phillies' owner William Baker. They had two dates before he left for Miami, with their courtship continuing through the US mails, except for the one time she had taken the trains down to Bradenton to be with him and seal the deal. A few weeks after the McDonnigle disaster had been put to rest, newspapers in both Philadelphia and Knoxville carried a small notice of the nuptials between Miss Georgia Owens and Mr. Herbert George Wells Boggs. "A brief honeymoon in Atlantic City will be followed by the young couple relocating to Miami, Florida, where Mr. Boggs will be operating a minor league baseball team."

But The Magic City proved to be even less hospitable than Bradenton. It seemed to be hotter and more humid for longer periods of time, making it hard to move, hard to breathe, hard to work in the ballpark, hard for people to come out to the ballpark. Plus, the economy fell into the toilet after the real estate boom came to a crashing halt and, if that wasn't enough, monster storms seemed to blast the area every year. When the Okeechobee Hurricane hit in September of 1928, they took it as a sign from God.

Once again, Mr. Asher had a solution. He had many friends in baseball and he put Wells in touch with one of the most significant, Mr. William G. Bramham, who ran four leagues from his law office in Durham, North Carolina. Wells sent him a letter, outlining his background and experiences and explaining his desire to work in a good "baseball town," and one September evening Mr. Bramham unexpectedly called him long-distance. The two chatted for nearly an hour, and then a week or so later Mr. Bramham called again, this time with an offer to come up to Durham and run the local club, the Bulls, members of the (Class C) Piedmont League. The young couple were both so anxious to leave Miami that Wells said yes before he even knew what salary was being offered.

It proved to be a good move for everyone. Wells and Georgia liked the tobacco town, and both sets of parents found it easy to get to Durham to visit, especially once grandchildren began to arrive. And after a few years, a once-in-a-lifetime opportunity arose—Business Manager of the Knoxville Smokies. Members of the Class A Southern Association, the Smokies were just two rungs below the majors, and of course the hometown team he had been rooting for since childhood. Wells jumped at the chance.

Hollywood might have seen this as a match made in heaven and written a feel-good ending. Truth, however, can be much harsher. Knoxville was unquestionably the Southern Association's weakest franchise. The city had lost and regained franchises over the years, and this incarnation, shifted from Mobile, Alabama in July of 1931, had consistently struggled, both on the field and at the box office. Wells' primary

The Mountain Empire League

goal was to improve things, but it was difficult when the product on the field was so disappointing—the team rarely won more games than they lost. Didn't matter if they affiliated with the Brooklyn Dodgers or Pittsburgh Pirates or New York Giants, or were completely independent, they still lost, and attendance—and revenue—suffered.

It all came to a head in 1944. With the club continuing to lose and playing to sparse crowds, the team's owners came to Wells (ironically!) just a couple of weeks after the euphoria of D-Day.

OWNERS: "Wells, there is a matter of some urgency that we need to discuss. And please understand, this is in no way a criticism of you, far from it. You are one of the hardest-working people we know, and if anyone could have turned this franchise around, it is you. The fact is…um, the way we see it, Knoxville is not a good baseball town, not for minor league ball, anyway. UT just has too much of a hold in these parts. And we've lost a lot of money, you know that as well as we do. Mr. Evans, our league president, has been advising us and, um, we, uh, we've decided to move the franchise."

WELLS: "Move the franchise? Where? When?"

OWNERS: "Mobile, Alabama. They want us, we just…"

WELLS: "Mobile? Really? This franchise came here from Mobile, they had trouble supporting baseball down there…"

OWNERS: "We know, we know. But we're desperate, and they assure us things are different now than they were, what, back in 1931? Look, we know how bad things are in the minors, we know it might not be any different down there, but we just can't afford to lose any more money here. We think we might have a fighting chance in Mobile."

WELLS: "When are you thinking…?"

OWNERS: "In a week or two. Now Wells, you need to understand, this does not affect your job at all, we want you to move with us, move with the franchise, continue as the General Manager. Just in a new town."

WELLS: "A week or two, my God! I can't believe it."

OWNERS: "We just need to iron out a couple of little details. Once we do that, we'll sign the contract, pack up and move south, probably around July 1 or thereabouts. Hopefully you'll be leading the way."

This certainly put Wells in a quandary. He and Georgia and the kids had a home they loved, just some 25 minutes away from where his parents lived, how could he ask them to uproot themselves on such short notice, especially with school set to begin again in just a few weeks? On the other hand, he didn't relish the idea of quitting and trying to find a job somewhere while the war raged on. Georgia objected, of course, but they worked out a deal, whereby he went with the team to Mobile while she and the kids stayed in Knoxville and he sent her money every week. He decided that, if he really liked it in Alabama, he would somehow talk his wife and children into joining him full-time, which would of course mean selling their home and relocating for the first time in almost a decade. And if he didn't like it, he'd resign when the season ended and, in early December, journey up to Buffalo, New York, where the minor leagues would be holding their annual winter meetings, and see if he could find a new job in baseball.

Mobile proved to be OK, with enthusiastic fans, but Wells never really warmed to the town. Maybe it was because the humidity brought back not-so-fond memories of Miami. Maybe it was because he found the Gulf of Mexico to be pretty enough but not nearly as lovely as the Great Smoky Mountains. Maybe it was just because he missed his family, in addition to having to pay for separate residences. Whatever the reason, Wells completed the season, tendered his resignation, and went back to Tennessee.

He did not, however, go to Buffalo. Never one to keep her opinions to herself, Georgia fired away as if she had been on the front lines at Aachen:

- "I am not interested in moving anywhere and our children are not interested in moving anywhere!!
- "What kind of a marriage would that be, hmmm, what kind of family life would we have if we were here all year long and you weren't? Our children need their father here for them, don't you see that? What's wrong with you?"
- "I have never taken you for THAT kind of man, the kind who leaves his family at a time like this. In case you hadn't noticed, we're still at war!"
- "Besides, how many baseball jobs are out there right now, anyway? Can't be that many, you've told me a million times how much this war has hurt the sport, how many teams and leagues have gone belly-up." (She had a point: only 70 U.S.-based minor league teams were able to make it through the 1944 season.)
- "Know what I think? I think you could easily find yourself a job somewhere in or around Knoxville, you've made lots of contacts over the years, you know lots of people, I'm sure someone would be happy to have a man with your talents working for them."
- "And don't forget, your parents have been here forever and your father knows just about everyone in town, even people who hate his guts! If none of your contacts can help you out, I'll bet he can come up with someone who could offer you a job that would pay the bills and keep you here at home, where you belong."
- "And that, Wells Boggs, is that!"

It was couple of weeks before Halloween, right around the time that Allied troops were liberating the Greek capital of Athens, that Wells went to work for WNOX radio, 990 on your AM dial, selling advertising time to local businesses. The work wasn't difficult, it was really kind of similar to what he had been doing before, talking to people and convincing them to spend their money with him. But it wasn't quite the same. There was something about shooting the breeze with a man about the game, about the good moments from last season (and there were always at least a few), and about the high expectations for the coming year. Since Pearl Harbor, baseball's importance was in bringing a couple of hours of joy to kids whose fathers were on some battlefield in Europe or some destroyer in the Pacific, to say nothing of their mothers whose blood froze every time there was a knock on the door. More than most businesses, baseball was special, it made the daily war news just a little more tolerable, and it was why he had always looked forward to coming to work every day. The bottom line is important, sure, and Lord knows he tried everything he could think of to make the team more profitable, but DAMN, baseball is not just another business, it's more than dollars and cents, lots more. For Wells, it meant adding a new line to his grandfather's Rules of Business: **Make it so that people love your business as much as you do.** Working at WNOX was fine but it was just a job. It didn't take long before Wells was trying to figure out how he could get back into baseball. And he had him an idea.

The Nazis surrendered in May of 1945, three weeks after the baseball season had begun, too late for him to put his plan into action, but plenty of time to try to make it a reality for 1946. He talked to quite a few people, including his old friend and mentor William Bramham, who had become president of all the minor leagues back in 1932. Bramham encouraged Wells, and when Japan capitulated in August, Wells decided to act. First, of course, he had to go through Georgia.

"You want to say that again, Wells honey, and go real slow this time?" When Georgia called him "Wells honey," he knew he was in trouble. But he was determined.

"I'm puttin' together a four-team league, the Mountain Empire League. Be Class D, the lowest rung on the ladder, but we'll be part of the National Association, the minor leagues, and we'll be bringin' baseball to towns that haven't had baseball before but who really want it."

"And how do you know that, Mr. Baseball, hmmmmm?" *Oh boy, she was heating up.*

"'Cause I been talkin' to a lot of people, Georgia. Look, you remember William Bramham, from Durham? You know he's been runnin' the minors for years, and he agrees with me that everything's gonna start gettin' back to normal and now's the perfect time to make a move. He's behind me one hundred percent, already approved a playin' schedule of 132 games, startin' early May and runnin' to the middle of September. And I've got firm commitments from four cities—up at Edens Ridge and Kruse here in Tennessee, Northeast Tennessee, and in Buchanan and Weare over in North Carolina. We're gonna be ready to go come spring!"

"And what do you get out of this? No, more important, are you gonna get paid at all for…whatever…whatever it is you'll be doing? Will you be able to feed your family?"

This part brought a smile to Wells' face. "Honey, I'm the guy in charge, I'm the league president! The four teams I mentioned, they all have to pay league dues, which goes towards my salary and umpires' salaries and league expenses. That's all set. And the best part is I don't have to go anywhere, I can run things from right here in Knoxville." He touched her arm. "I never forget my family, Georgia, I could never do that. You and the kids, you're the most important people in the world."

She didn't look at him for a moment while she mulled things over. Finally she looked up.

"This is just crazy, Wells Boggs. Who in their right mind goes off and starts a…a league, a whole baseball league, especially now when the world is just trying to get back to normal after this horrible war? You have a job, a good job, we're able to keep our heads above water, at this time that's about all we can ask, and you want to go off and do something foolish like this? Makes no sense to me, no sense at all. What about WNOX? Are you just gonna walk out on them, is that part of your plan, too?"

"I'm no fool, Georgia, Mr. Aubrey knows all about this and he's been encouragin' me. I'll be keepin' my job, at least part-time, he's given me his word so, see? We'll have money comin' in from two sources, which means in no time we'll be doin' twice as good as we are now."

Georgia was not amused. "I don't understand your thinking. You've got this good job, you make decent money, we're doing OK, why you have to go off…half-cocked like this? You've told me a million times about how leagues fold all the time, and here you are trying to start one from scratch, with absolutely no guarantee that it can succeed. Why would you even think of something like this, Wells? What's wrong with doing what you've been doing?"

"Because it's not baseball!" For the first time in a long time, Wells raised his voice to his wife. "I loved workin' in baseball, I just loved it, and I miss it, I miss it like crazy. The radio station is fine but I can't do it for the rest of my life, Georgia, I just can't. This is a real chance for me to be doin' somethin' I love, and be doin' it right here, at home. A while back you said you didn't want to move, so look, we don't have to move, everythin' stays the same 'cept for the fact that I'll back doin' what I really love. You gotta see that, Georgia."

"I see my children not having enough to eat, or having holes in their shoes or their shirts. I see us having trouble paying the mortgage, maybe having to borrow money from your family or my family. I see us…" She started to cry. He immediately put his arms around her, and she looked up at him.

"I'm scared, Wells, this scares me. We're fine as we are, things are just fine, there ain't no need to…to…to muck it up." He wiped her eyes. "Maybe you could wait 'til 1947, or 1948, see how things go, see what happens in the country, in the world, see if we do get back to normal, then jump in and start your league. You could do that, right, you could wait a year at least, couldn't you? Those cities…"

"Those cities want their baseball and they want it now. I have promised them that we will be startin' in the spring, in the spring of 1946, I have promised Mr. Bramham, and I can't go back on my word, not to him, not to all these people. That's not who I am, you know that prob'ly better'n anyone."

She threatened to take the kids to Philadelphia. She pouted for two full days, barely speaking to him, "displacing" him to the couch.

The cloud unexpectedly lifted as they were washing the dinner dishes.

"Promise me," she said in a small, quiet voice, "that we'll always have food on the table and a roof over our heads."

And with that, the Battle for Georgia came to an end.

The telephone rang in the Simpson house.

"Wells, how are you? How's the family?" Jack was surprised to hear from his league president.

"We all fine down here, Jack, just fine. How's that pretty li'l wife of yours, hmmm? You gonna be able to bring her to Columbus for the Winta Meetins this year? I know you'll be comin', they's gonna be some important discussions takin' place, on television and bonuses and open leagues like ours. Lots to talk about, like always."

"I'll be there, Wells, but Nashota might…"

"Jack, sorry to cut you off but this is long distance and I gotta question, hope you don' mind my askin'. It's about this contract that came in the mail yesterday, no, day before, this boy you just signed name of Oddibe…" He fumbled for the papers, then read the name. "Oddibe Daniels."

"Yeah, Oddibe. Great looking kid, real fast, natural in center and leading off, what about him?"

"Well, I never heard a name like that, Oddibe, it's diff'rent, and I've lived in the South my whole life and heard me some, heh, unusual names. My mechanic's name is Tilden, for instance, and Georgia has her a very good friend named Lulia, and two-a our very best friends are Boyce and RaeNelle Johnson. I was just wondering if, uh, if maybe he was, uh, if, uh…Jack, where'd you find him?"

No, Wells, don't be doing this. We shouldn't be having this discussion, I thought you were better than this.

"Industrial league down in Asheville. Actually, you'll especially appreciate this—Nashota spotted him first and told me about him. I watched him play twice and I gotta tell you, Wells, I been real impressed, I think this kid could go places, I can see big-league teams getting interested in him. He can really run, catch everything out in the outfield, like Mays but not as big…" *Ouch, I may have opened the door.*

And sure enough Wells jumped on that Mays reference. "Are you tryin' to tell me he's a Nigra? Jack, come on, ya gotta come clean here."

Jack hesitated, cleared his throat. No use lyin', they'd find out sooner or later. "Yes, Wells, he's a Negro. But look, teams are signing them every day, we can't be left in the dust. If we don't act quickly, we'll…" He had to word this carefully. "…we'll get ourselves a reputation that we don't really want, one that won't help us in the long run. Major league teams are falling over themselves signing up Negro League players and…and even semi-pro kids like Oddibe, and they won't look kindly on clubs and leagues that remain all white. Won't look good to potential parent organizations, now would it?" *The hammer, use the hammer!* Jack knew it was Wells' fondest dream for all eight teams in the Mountain Empire to land secure partnerships with big league teams, so he was happy to make sure this seed got planted early. "Besides, I had to move quick, there were other teams watching him, I didn't want to lose out." Maybe that was true, maybe not. He certainly had seen at least two other fellows at Oddibe's ballgames who may have been scouts or managers or in some way employed by other minor league teams, they had that look. If they were smart they'd have been looking at Oddibe.

There was a long silence, followed by a sigh, followed by Wells audibly scratching his face, followed by "Jack, I don't care what color the boy is, y'all know that, but I think that the other teams in our league need to know what you're proposin' to do and, maybe, well, maybe they, uh, they may, um, want to, uh, weigh in, you know, give their 'pinyuns, know what I mean?"

"Wells, this don't affect them none. I never have a say in who Weare signs or who Mettin signs or who Blackmer signs, we don't share roster information 'til just a few days before we open, this oughta be the same thing. He's just a kid I'm bringing in because I think he'll make my team better, that's all."

"Jack, this is different and you know it and you know why. I'm with you, ought not to make no difference, for sure, but…"

"Then if you're with me, Wells, nothin' else oughta matter. Look, I'm sure you remember that all the other major league owners voted against the Dodgers' bringing up Jackie Robinson. Even the American League guys, and they don't ever play Brooklyn. Vote was 15–1 against, but Commissioner Chandler stood behind the signing and allowed it to go through. That's where you are now, Wells, you gotta stand behind me and let it go through."

A barely-audible "hmmmf" escaped from Wells' throat before he responded.

"We live in hard times, Jack, I don't need to tell you, and I think we at least oughta bring this up to all our directors. Hmmm, what you say, Jack, is that all right with you?"

No it is not, Jack thought, but he also knew it didn't matter what he said, Wells had made up his mind to take it to the full league. Imagine, a league president having his directors rule on a contract signing. The fall league meeting, generally short and dull but genial, had suddenly gotten interesting, and complicated, real fast.

"Bob, it's amazing how your instincts never seem to fail you."

The speaker was George Trautman, President of the National Association of Professional Baseball Leagues. That was the formal name of what most people simply called the minors, a conglomeration of 51 leagues and more than 400 teams located in all 48 states, as well as selected cities in Mexico and Canada. Headquartered in Columbus, Ohio, Trautman had quickly felt overwhelmed when, after his election as president in 1947, he tried to understand and deal with the disparate situations of all those teams. How could he best help his constituents?

The idea came to him in the shower—Field Representative. He would figuratively divide the country into four quadrants, with the Mississippi River and the Mason-Dixon Line roughly being the lines of demarcation. He would hire four people, all veteran baseball men, to "patrol" their respective sectors, loosely configured to be the Northeast, Southeast, Northwest and Southwest. Each field rep would visit all of the teams in their sector at least once per season and try to help the club operators with any difficulties they may be having, or offer proposals on better ways to function. The field reps would also keep Trautman informed of all their findings, consulting by phone so that quick suggestions could immediately be offered in potential trouble spots.

Trautman interviewed a number of veteran minor league executives, former managers, major league scouts, even a couple of college coaches, and eventually selected his quartet, who began their tenures on January 1, 1949. One of the men he hired was Bob Rhodes, who was now reporting back on the results of the contentious Mountain Empire League meeting.

Rhodes was an Idaho farm boy whose first love had been the discus throw, and who had been good enough to be a member of the U.S. Olympic Team in 1912. He did not win a medal in Stockholm, but he did become good friends with a member of the Sac and Fox nation from Oklahoma named Jim Thorpe. Maybe it was because they were both "westerners," or because they both loved baseball as well as track and field, but the two hit it off. Thorpe, of course, proved to be the star of the Games, winning the gold medal in both the pentathlon and decathlon, and when King Gustav V of Sweden handed Thorpe his medals, he said "Sir, you are the greatest athlete in the world."

Rhodes returned to Idaho to complete his studies at Lewis-Clark State College, and after graduating the following spring, he decided to try his hand at professional baseball. Old pal Thorpe, playing for the New York Giants, offered to help and arranged to have Rhodes meet the team in St. Louis and try out for manager John McGraw. To his dying day Bob Rhodes believed he had performed well, but McGraw simply shook his hand, told him he was a good player, said "thanks for coming," and that was all; no contract was offered.

The Cardinals, however, were interested. Their playing manager, Miller Huggins, always got to the ballpark long before his players, so he sat in the dugout that morning and watched Bob Rhodes get put through his paces. When he learned the youngster had not been signed by the Giants, Huggins got permission from his front office to make the kid a Card.

But Rhodes never made the majors, never even got close. He did, however, become a minor league general manager, successfully utilizing that business degree he got from Lewis-Clark, until George Trautman hired him to become one of the new Field Representatives. He was assigned to cover the Southeast, which included, of course, the Mountain Empire League, where he had an open invitation to attend any of their quarterly meetings. "Be happy to," he had told Wells Boggs. "Your meetings can be really lively and entertaining."

Quite true. One meeting was always held in conjunction with baseball's annual convention, the Winter Meetings, and another was a short, half-day get-together held at the site of the league's mid-summer all-star game. Those meetings were all right, but the most interesting ones were hosted by Wells in Knoxville in February and October. Scheduled over a weekend, he and the directors were not only able to complete their league business, but they invariably had a good time doing it. The meeting would begin informally on Friday night with a social that featured a buffet and drinks, and sooner rather than later Boggs would always stand up and announce "Conviviality, my friends. We have plenty to discuss this weekend, but tonight there will be none-a that, tonight is just for conviviality and good fellaship." Almost everyone knew the words by heart and mouthed them along with their president, which didn't bother Wells at all, he just loved those weekend meetings, especially the Friday night socializing.

Which is exactly what Nashota disliked the most. The sessions held on Saturday morning and afternoon, followed by the closing gathering on Sunday morning, were good. Important league matters were discussed, and she could often pick up several useful business or promotional pointers that she might try to put into practice in Edens Ridge. But Friday night could be interminable for her, since she was generally the only female present. Even though she always deliberately dressed very plainly that evening, all too often she found herself the recipient of unwanted stares as more and more alcohol was consumed. Once someone had even grabbed her ass. She was sure it was one of the Maxwells, probably the father, Lanny, but she couldn't be sure so she didn't say anything to Jack, no need to stir up something needlessly. But any time she saw either of the Maxwells looking at her she gave them as cold an eye as was humanly possible and they would quickly look away, probably fearful she was trying to put some Cherokee hex on them. If Nashota could have turned them into stone or something, she would have considered it to be her positive contribution to the human race.

On this October night in 1951, the eight league directors were all there, as was their president, Wells Boggs. There were also four other invited guests—Nashota, since she was the Wolves' Vice President and Business Manager; Beau Maxwell, Lanny's son and the field manager of the Mettin Foxes; Lionel Ticknor, both the field manager and Vice President of Operations for the Buchanan Bees; and Bob Rhodes. When Jack mentally took attendance and came up with a head-count of thirteen, he frowned, being a baseball guy and therefore superstitious by nature.

Circulating around the room and continually answering the question every baseball executive gets asked every off-season—"had a good year?"—Simpson was finally able to corral his wife, Ticknor and Rhodes in a corner.

"I want to give you both an alert about something that's going to be on the agenda, either tomorrow or Sunday. I've signed a young man to a contract but Wells is hesitant to approve it until he runs it by the league's directors."

"Since when do other teams get to approve someone else's players?" asked Ticknor. "I'll be damned if I'd let that happen to me. I think the world of you, Jack, but you have no right to tell me who I can have on my team."

"I agree, Lionel, I agree, I don't think…"

"What did you do, Jack?" asked Rhodes, looking at him warily. "Who have you signed?"

"North Carolina kid named Daniels, young, just 21, no professional experience but a great talent…"

"He can really play, Bob," said Nashota, quickly. "I saw him a few times in Asheville and told Jack I thought he could help us…"

"He can make us, not just help us, he could make us the best team in the league. He can run, really run, fast as anyone I've ever seen, fast as…" *Be careful here.* "…fast as Ashburn or Pee Wee or that TCU kid, Busby. I wanna have him lead off and make things happen, and put him in center and take charge of the outfield." Ticknor and

Rhodes just looked at him. "It's a standard contract, no reason, really, for Wells to bring it up this weekend, but he says he's going to."

"Makes me wonder why," said Rhodes. "What aren't you telling us, Jack?"

Husband looked at wife, wife looked back, then she flashed that camera-ready smile and said cheerily "He's a Negro. We haven't had any Negro players in the league and Wells doesn't...well, he probably wants everyone to share in the decision to admit one."

Silence, cold silence. *Is this what they call a pregnant pause?* Jack wondered. Then Bob spoke.

"Geez, Jack, that's a pretty bold step, don't you think? What are the other clubs saying?"

"I haven't talked to anyone but the two of you," Jack replied, gesturing to both Ticknor and Rhodes. "Not politicking here, I just thought I'd give you a sneak preview, like at the movies."

"Well, Jack, I don't have a vote, least not officially, but I can pretty well predict that John will vote with you," said Lionel. "And lemme tell you—if he hesitates for even a second I may just twist his nuts right there at the table, that oughta help him think straight." Nashota couldn't help but laugh, which turned a few heads. "'Bout time this league joined the rest of baseball," he concluded, as he polished off his drink. *Good old Lionel,* thought Jack, *he's nothing if not a straight shooter.*

Bob Rhodes spoke quietly.

"Jack, the National Association is absolutely positively firmly behind the integration of the game. We've had, um, a couple of problems in other leagues, but on paper, our office will be completely behind you."

"On paper? What does that mean, on paper?" Nashota wanted to know. "We don't play the games on paper, Bob, we want to play this young man in our ballpark, and in the league's seven other ballparks..."

"And that's where the problem may be, Nashota. There are a few Negroes in other leagues, but they've all been in the North. A coupla Southern leagues integrated this past season, Carolina, West Texas-New Mexico, but in both cases it was only for a few weeks, not even a month..."

"Carolina League, that's right, fella played in Danville, didn't he?" Jack asked excitedly. "That means he played in Virginia, the capital of the Confederacy, and the heavens didn't explode, we didn't have a flood for forty days and forty nights, there wasn't even any trouble, was there? Did he play in North Carolina, too, they have teams in North Carolina, did he play there?"

"Yes, he did, at least, I know he played in Raleigh and Winston..."

"If they didn't kill him in those places, Jack's kid will be just fine in Buchanan and Weare, I can tell you that for a fact," Ticknor said quickly. "Can't be sure 'bout our Virginia towns, but I doubt Mr. Underwood and Windy would let anything happen in Blackmer, I'm betting they vote with you. Obviously you're voting yes, Jack, so that's four, you just need one more, you can probably persuade Harrell..." And a thought made him grin mischievously. "...Just tell him how many people will show up and how much money he'll make every time you bring your Wolves into Kruse, he'll be in your hip pocket!" And Lionel Ticknor let out such a loud laugh that everyone else in the room, without exception, turned their heads and wondered what in heaven's name was so funny over there.

Nashota and Jack both felt better about things, but Bob Rhodes still looked uneasy. "Like I said, Jack, the National Association will stand behind you. If you want, I can even call Mr. Trautman at home tonight and tell him what you're planning, but you have to be certain you think this all the way through. If you get the OK, the two of you…" and he indicated Nashota, as well "…need to make sure this kid is protected at all times, in every ballpark, on the bus, in whatever house or apartment he rents. He'll need a place to sleep in all the other cities…"

Jack jumped in quickly. "Not Kruse," he said. "We commute back and forth."

"Right, right," said Rhodes. "But you'll need to find a place for him in the other six cities, you know the hotels won't take him. He won't be allowed to eat with the team, either, you'll need to find places for him to take his meals. And he'll need to be accepted by his own teammates, don't forget that, Jack. There were some players on the Dodgers who got up a petition against Jackie, and Lippy moved to squash it right away, remember?" Simpson nodded. "A couple of those players eventually got shipped out of Brooklyn, you might have to deal with something like that, too, so be prepared."

Saturday morning's meeting began with old business, which was dispatched quickly, and then each club gave a summary of their season. They would start with financials, shift over to any negatives, like rainouts, and follow up with the positives, which often were successful promotional ideas that brought people into the ballpark. One of Blackmer's biggest nights of the year, for instance, was Advertisers' Night, in which all of the team's sponsors were given free tickets to pass out to their customers, which brought the fans out in droves. Don Harrell didn't see how this could be a positive. "Your gate receipts were next to nothing, how could that be a good night?" he asked. In his calm and quiet way, Charles Underwood responded by reading off the night's numbers at the concession and souvenir stands, concluding with "We only had two nights all year in which we sold more food, and our souvenir sales for that game were in the Blackbirds' top five for the year. We definitely plan to hold an Advertisers' Night every year from now on." Nashota also spoke and told about how they had brought in the acrobatic Jackie Price. "Sure we had to pay him $125," she said, in response to a question. "But we had a full house that night and they were all paying customers, so we easily covered his fee right at the box office. And of course we sold a ton of food and drink and the like. I've already contacted him about coming back sometime next summer."

Next up was a discussion of the schedule for 1952, which brought the annual request from BJ Lewis—"Last year's schedule worked so well, why don't we just do it all over again?" Since Jeriome Hoffman's Beck Bears had won their first league championship with this schedule, he joined Lewis in arguing for the exact same slate of games. In the end, however, it was decided, as usual, to set up a committee to gather special requests from all members. Edens Ridge, for example, always wanted to be home during the last part of the town's annual Mountain Magic Festival, a week-long celebration of music and food and culture and life in general in the beautiful Blue Ridge Mountains. Jack always made sure that the Festival dedicated one night to the team, which went all out to make it one of the year's most memorable events. General admission seats were free to all comers, and there were tons of prizes, all donated by sponsors. Hamburgers, hot dogs, soft drinks and popcorn were basically sold at just above cost, and the grandstands were filled with strolling musicians, clowns and any other form of entertainment he and Nashota could rustle up for two or three hours. Requests like these were forwarded to the committee, which eventually drafted a new schedule and presented it to the directors at their next gathering, held during baseball's annual Winter Meetings. (In 1951, it was scheduled for early December in Columbus, Ohio.) Jack always volunteered for that committee.

They took a short break at that point and, as Jack was getting another cup of coffee for Nashota (he had never developed the habit himself), Wells strolled by, quietly said "You up next, Jack," and kept on walking.

"Now we have a con-track-shoo-al matter to discuss," said Wells, slowly dragging out the key word when they all got back to their seats. "Jack Simpson has signed him a new player, boy named Oh-to-bee Daniels…" Jack was reminded of his days in Mrs. Morritt's class in elementary school, when she painstakingly taught them to sound out words. "…and I have asked him to tell y'all 'bout him. Jack?"

Nashota quickly squeezed his hand as he stood up. "OK, thanks, Wells. This YOUNG MAN…" He made sure to emphasize those words, Nashota had cautioned him last night to do everything he could to stay away from the word *boy*. "…has been playing in Asheville, little weekend industrial league. I…we, actually…" he looked at his wife and smiled…"we've been real impressed with him. Terrific outfielder, very fast, gets a great jump, I figure…"

"OK, you signed a new kid, fine, happy for you," said John Robertson. "I've signed two fellas myself and expect to reel in two or three more in the next week or so." He knew what was going on, Lionel had filled him in, and this was his way to try and help the situation. "Now Wells," he continued, looking right at his league president. "This is nothing that we need to be discussing, is it? We are allowed to sign anyone who does not already have a valid contract with another team, why is this on our agenda? No disrespect to you, Jack," he said, looking over to Simpson. "But I suggest we just move on, shall we?"

"Jack," said Wells slowly. "You wanna, um, give us, um, all the facts here, please?"

That got everyone's attention. What wasn't Jack saying? A couple of directors leaned forward a bit in their chairs, while Bob Rhodes muttered "oh brother" quietly to himself.

Jack looked at Nashota again and she said, "Just say it, Jack." He cleared his throat, hesitated, then finally said "My new centerfielder, Oddibe Daniels, is a Negro."

He could feel the air being sucked out of the room as everyone seemed to quit breathing at once.

Not for long, of course. "A Nigra? You want to play a Nigra on your team? Are you crazy?" It would be fair to say no one was surprised that Truck Maxwell was the first person to speak up. Or that BJ Lewis quickly followed.

"We don't have no Nigras in our league, Jack, you know that. Ain't had none up til now, don't see no need to change."

"Why not? Why shouldn't we change?" John Robertson had leaped to his feet. "Look what's happening in baseball, look at that playoff series they just played, Dodgers and Giants, how many Negroes were on the field? Dodgers had…"

"Tha's diff'rent, tha's may-jah leegs, tha's up in Noo Yawk and places like that," said BJ. "They ain't a-playin' where we play, in Virginny and Nawth Caroline and Kaintuck and Ten-Uh-See. They gots lotsa Nigras up there to come on out and cheer for their boys, we don't got that here." Jack was surprised that Lewis sounded more disappointed than angry.

"That's not true, BJ," said Robertson, "We have plenty of Negroes in all our towns, why else would we have separate entrances and bathrooms and concession stands?"

"BJ is right," yelled Truck. "They kin do what they like in Noo Yawk, they can play all the Nigras they want, turn baseball from the good ol' American game it is to nigraball, tha's their bizness. Down here we gots our own ways of doin' things, and that don't include playin' Nigras in this here league." He looked at Jack." "That boy-a yers can play in his industrial league ever' day of the year, don't matter to me, but he ain't gonna play in my league, in our league, not if I got somethin' to say 'bout it."

Robertson jumped on this. "And we really don't have anything to say about it, now do we? It's like I said earlier, all contracts go to the league president, we have no say in who signs who."

Now everyone seemed to be talking at once, and Wells, for the first time all day, had to use his gavel. "Quiet, quiet, let us have some order here." He banged the gavel again, just for good measure, which prompted Lionel to ask "Wells, you thinking of running for judge?" which thankfully brought out a couple of snickers.

"John is right, I gets to approve all contracts, but in this case I wanted to find out what y'all think. I don't have nothin' 'gainst no Nigras, never did, but bein' as this would be a first for our league, I think we all need to say our piece, then I can decide what oughta be done."

"Tell you what," said Truck, "I'll make this real easy—I VOTE NO!!" And he pounded the table in front of him for extra emphasis. Not quite as loudly but just as convincingly, BJ Lewis said "I'm with Truck."

"Gentlemen, there is no motion on the floor, we can't vote on something that has not yet been proposed," said Don Harrell.

Truck didn't hesitate. "Fine, then I move…" But before he could go further Jules Gray spoke up.

"Just a moment, Truck, may I say something here, please?" Truck shot him a look. "Sorry to interrupt, Truck, but I'd like to say something if I may. Mr. President?" He looked at Wells, who wished he was somewhere else right now, maybe fishing on Douglas Lake.

"All right, Jules, go ahead. Truck, we'll get back to you in just a minute, OK?"

"Thank you, Wells. Gentlemen," said Gray, looking around the room, "this is an important decision we need to make. I think Wells was right to bring it to us first, sorry Jack, but I believe we need to…to think about this very carefully. Yes, there are Negroes playing in other minor leagues, mostly in the North right now, but I think it's only a matter of time before they are playing everywhere. We need to think about that, think about whether the time is right for us, for our league, for all of our towns and all of our fans. I don't believe we ought to make a hasty decision. I believe we should think about it overnight, sleep on it, and then decide tomorrow."

"I have a question, Mr. President, may I?" It was Charles Underwood.

"Oh for heaven's sake!" exclaimed Truck Maxwell, but Wells said "go 'head, Charles."

"Thank you. Jack, how old is this boy, um, young man, you've signed?"

Nashota stood up. "I can answer that, Charles. He is 21, in fact he'll be 22 before we even get to spring training."

"So this is a legitimate contract, then, he is of legal age. Gentlemen," continued Underwood, "this is something we also need to consider. If we reject this agreement, young Mr. Daniels and his family could sue us for breach of contract, and if they won, I doubt we could afford to pay up. We'd be out of business, plus we'd owe a small fortune to our lawyers and to this young man. We must keep this in mind."

"No Nigra gonna sue no white man, no court gonna 'low that, not here in the South," said an exasperated Truck Maxwell. "What kind of talk is that, Charles, you just talkin' crazy."

Underwood had a quick response. "We are a league that plays in four states, Truck. We are therefore interstate commerce, just like your trucking business. You know what that means, maybe better than anyone here—we could be sued in Federal court. Different ballgame there."

The room was quiet—this was a lot to think about and mull over. Truck Maxwell, speaking slowly and deliberately, broke through the quiet.

"Mista Prez-ee-dent, may I PLEASE make my motion now?" Wells nodded, Truck continued. "I would like to move that this league, the Mountain Empire League, formally an' 'fishly REJECT…" and this he said loudly, with emphasis, "…this proposed contract between the Edens Ridge team and this, this, ni…" Beau nudged him forcibly, "young man, this Daniels fella. I so move," he said and looked around the room, feeling satisfied while also searching faces.

Wells said nothing for a few seconds, allowing Truck's words to hang in the air. Then he said, "We have a motion on the floor, do we have a second?"

The silence was deafening.

Truck, still standing, looked around the room again, this time with a look that said *well, who's with me here?* Nothing. Now he looked hard at BJ Lewis, because he knew, he just knew, that the Shirley car dealer was on his side. He had known BJ for years, knew what kind of man he was, knew how he thought, what he believed, so why in hell was he staring at his shoes and not speaking up? Maxwell panned the room again, hoping that someone would say something…

It was Wells who broke the silence. "There's a motion on the floor, do we have a second?" This time he waited just a handful of seconds before he continued. "With no second, this motion cannot be discussed and is dropped."

Truck was about to explode when Jules Gray jumped to his feet. "Mr. President, I would like to make a motion, if I may." Wells nodded. "Mr. President, I would like to move that we table the discussion of the Daniels contract until tomorrow morning. This will give us all…" He looked around the room and made sure his gaze fell on each of his fellow directors, one by one, before continuing. "…ALL…a chance to think about it. Really think about all the things that have been brought up here today, perhaps had a chance to talk about it amongst ourselves, or with others. Then we can bring it up again and, I think, make an informed decision."

"What a crock-a shit, they's only one kind of informed dee-si-shun to make here," snarled Maxwell. "And who you gonna talk to, Jules? Gonna call Harry Truman or Hubert Humphrey? Sheeeeet." Nashota had to drop her head so the others wouldn't see her giggle at the thought of Truck having a conversation with the fiery young senator from Minnesota.

"Actually, I think I need to consult with my manager, Gene Conn. His input will be important."

Other directors murmured an assent, they had probably been thinking the same thing.

Wells quickly jumped in. "We have a motion on the floor, do we have a second?" "I second," said Charles Underwood. "Any further discussion?" asked Wells.

"Mr. President," said Bob Rhodes, "I know I am not officially a member of this league, but I wonder if I could make a comment; actually, pass along some information, to all of you?"

"I have no objection, what about y'all?" Maxwell snorted but said nothing, a couple of people said, "go ahead," so Wells nodded to Rhodes.

"Gentlemen, I need to tell you that this issue is coming up more and more in the minors. More and more Negroes have been playing in more and more leagues, and yes, they have been primarily in the North, like Jules said earlier, but that's not gonna last for long. Mr. Trautman has been told, in no uncertain terms, that the big-league clubs are all committed—well, most-a them, anyway—to signing good Negro talent, as many kids as they can. And once they do, they'll be placing them with their farm clubs, no matter where those teams are located. I know this league does not have any major league affiliations right now but that could change, they're always looking and I know Wells wants to make it happen. You need to…you REALLY need to think about this. If you want to buddy up with the majors, you'll have to play by their rules, and they are gonna want to send some of these boys to you." There was a low undercurrent of voices in the room. Rhodes paused for a second, then continued. "And here's something else to keep in mind. It is the official policy of the minors—Mr. Trautman and the entire National Association—to NOT stand in the way of anyone who wants to play professional baseball. In other words…" and here he looked right at Truck Maxwell. "…a legitimate contract is a legitimate contract and must be honored."

Maxwell looked away in disgust. Rhodes turned to Nashota.

"Did he sign a standard, official, National Association contract?"
Nashota smiled and said, "Yes he did."
"And he has already had his 21st birthday?"
"Yes he has," said Nashota.

Bob Rhodes looked around at the group. He paused to let this sink in, then said "Gentlemen, a contract is a contract. That's all I have to say, Mr. President, thank you."

"Thank you, Bob," said Wells. "Anyone else got anythin?" No one spoke. "Good. Well then, we have a motion on the floor to table this contract matter until first thing tomorra mornin'. All those in favor?" Six hands went up. "Opposed?" Maxwell raised both of his arms. "Only one vote, Truck, sorry. I counted seven, does that mean someone abstains?" Quiet for a few seconds, then BJ Lewis said "yes, I abstain." "Six votes in favor, one opposed, one abstains, the motion carries," said Wells, banging his gavel. Happy to have bought another day, he glanced at his watch. "Gentlemen, I see where it is already almost half-past noon. I suggest we adjourn for lunch and come back here at, say, two o'clock. Any objections? No? Then we are adjourned until two."

That evening, even though he knew Georgia would be angry, Wells went to the hotel lobby because he felt he needed to be available to his directors if they wanted to talk. But there was no one there. He waited for about half an hour and then went home, where he worked with Eli on memorizing the Gettysburg Address and commented on the girls' homecoming gowns when they asked his opinion, and slept much better than he thought he would.

His directors, however, were absolutely discussing the same topic, just in separate places, away from the lobby. Charles Underwood, Jules Gray, Jeriome Hoffman, Don Harrell and B.J. Lewis all went to their respective rooms and called their respective managers. The Simpsons dined with Bob Rhodes, Lionel Ticknor and John Robertson at a barbecue place Bob knew, and talked about the state of baseball.

"Jackie and Campy and Monte Irvin and this Mays kid, they're changing the game, right before our eyes," said Nashota.

"That Mays, he had twenty homers in less than a full season, jeez," remarked Lionel.

"And the Mountain Empire League," said Bob, as he polished off another hush puppy, "sure needs to get with it or else they're gonna be steamrolled right out of existence."

Only the Maxwells, father and son, ignored the issue at hand by enjoying the entertainment at The Golden Dolphin, an establishment filled with young ladies who spent as much time dancing and socializing with the predominantly-male clientele as they did serving food and drinks.

Truck Maxwell was the only one nursing a hangover the next morning; the other dozen quietly filed into the conference room. There was no chit-chat, there was no light-hearted banter, everyone simply sat down and waited.

Wells took his seat at the front of the room. He had no idea how today would play out and he didn't like that, didn't like not even having an inkling. The only thing he was sure of was that today would be a day he'd always remember, like where he had been when he heard about Pearl Harbor, or when he'd asked Georgia to marry him. It would be a major one in the history of the Mountain Empire League.

He quickly called the roll, then said "We have an item of business left over from yesterday, the contract of one Oh-to-bee Daniels, submitted to the league for approval by the Edens Ridge Wolves. Y'all were supposed to be sleepin' on it, does anyone have any thoughts or questions 'bout this?"

Everyone seemed to shift in their seats at the same time, then Charles Underwood stood, looked at the group and said, "Mr. President, I would like to make a motion at this time that the Mountain Empire League formally approve Mr. Oddibe Daniels' contract to play with Edens Ridge for the 1952 season." He sat back down.

"I second that motion," said Jules Gray.

"Motion has been made and seconded," said Wells. "Is there any discussion?"

"Y'all know what I think," said Truck, not standing up. "I may be the onlyest one here talkin' the plain, God's-honest truth. Jack," he said, turning to look Simpson right in the eye, "did you really think 'bout us, think 'bout how somethin' like this would affect all-a us in the other towns in this league, hmmm?" He now looked at everyone else, one by one. "Did y'all think 'bout this last night, 'bout findin' a place for this boy to sleep and eat and even just get himself to your ballparks? Ya gotta think 'bout this, fellas, ya just gotta. We ain't ready for this yet, I really don't think we are." He looked down at his hands, looked up again, but said nothing more.

"Anyone else?" asked Wells.

"I called Karl Hines last night," said BJ, "and I'm bettin' a bunch-a y'all called your managers, too. Mine said sure, go 'head, we need to have cullud fellas in this-here league, it's the wave of the future, that's just how Karl put it, the wave of the future. I don't believe he's right, I think we ought not to let this young man play for us, but if I vote no..." He let out a very audible sigh. "If I vote no, my manager will be mad at me and he might quit. Or things'll get strained 'tween us an' then we'll start to fightin'..." He sighed again and shook his head. "And y'all know me, I'll get mad and fire him an' hafta go find someone else and, boys, I don't wanna do that. I like ol' Karl, he's a good man and a real good manager, no need to tell you. So I...I don't want him mad at me, I wanna live with him all year." He looked right at Maxwell. "I just wanted you to know, Truck, know why I can't vote witcha this time."

"Shit," said Truck Maxwell, quietly.

No one else spoke until Don Harrell quietly said, "let's vote."

"It has been moved and seconded to accept the contract of Mister Oh-to-bee Daniels for the 1952 season," said Wells. "All those in favor?" Six hands went up. "Opposed?" That was Harrell somewhat surprisingly joining Maxwell. "The ayes have it," said Wells, "the contract is approved." He banged his gavel, rather quietly this time, then said "let's take a short break."

Harrell practically ran over to Jack. "I called Vic last night, Jack," he said, referring to his manager, Vic Rutherford. "And I was real surprised, he said we didn't need that kind of problem in the league and asked me to vote no. I was all set to vote yes, I could see how your boy would bring more people into my ballpark, but I was like BJ, I couldn't go against my manager." Jack had never seen Harrell like this before. The CPA was always rather crisp and business-like in his dealings with others, but this was a different side to him, a human side, a caring, passionate, emotional side that Jack, for one, had never experienced. "It's OK, Don," he said, "I understand."

Bob Rhodes came over. "This might work out better than we think, Jack. Look, I spoke with Mr. Trautman and we will help you all we can over the next few months, getting prepared-n-shit." Wells came over at this point, and Bob immediately included him in the conversation. "I'm just telling Jack that the National Association is behind this. I'll get ahold of some of the other leagues that have gone through it, get their input, their advice, find out what the league needs to do and what the teams all need to do. Truck was right about one thing, everyone needs to think about hotels and restaurants and whatnot, I'll get as much information as I can and then maybe we all oughta get together somewhere and set out a plan of action, what do you think?"

"You don't mean a special league meetin', do ya, Bob?"

"No, just the four of us, then once we know what we want to do and what we have to do, you can send out a memo to the rest of the directors. Maybe we'll even put it on National Association stationery, make sure everyone knows it's coming right from the top."

"I would be very glad for your help, Bob, for all the help we can get. Maybe we can meet in Columbus in December, during the Winter Meetings"?

"That gives me 'bout six weeks, I think I can get all my information by then. Might even be able to get Mr. Trautman to sit in with us for a little while. Let's do that, let's shoot for Columbus."

THREE

On a recruiting trip back in January, Jack had hit a patch of ice in western North Carolina that required a night in the local hospital, more of an annoyance than anything else. But the other party in the accident had not been nearly as lucky, which meant saying goodbye to one of his oldest companions, his 1942 Studebaker Commander, and replacing it with a new-to-them 1949 Dodge Meadowbrook. Shortly afterwards he left for spring training, followed immediately by the 1951 season, so the Meadowbrook, really, hadn't been used for much more than in-town driving. It needed a road trip, as did the Simpsons, so they motored up the road to Pennsylvania and spent Thanksgiving with Jack's family. "First time in a while," proved to be a common refrain from old Sarge, as well as Jen and Jo, especially when Jack was obviously surprised that Jen's boy was going to be five in February. ("You really don't know? You really thought he was still a toddler?" Jen really was miffed.) Only his mother never said anything about how long it had been since they had made the trek to Fulton County.

From there the Meadowbrook headed west, to the Deshler-Wallick Hotel in Columbus, Ohio, site of the 1951 baseball Winter Meetings. Nashota, for one, had always found these national meetings to be fascinating, a mixture of business and bluster and thoroughly doused with a healthy supply of liquor. There was a great deal of back-slapping as long-time friends and acquaintances reunited for the first time since the previous year, discussing how their seasons had gone and recounting amusing incidents. They talked about successful promotions ("I tell ya, that Max Patkin is so funny, you can't help but laugh. The crowd was in stitches, I'll definitely be bringing him back."). They laughed about ideas that bombed ("Whoever thought Lefthanders Night was a good idea? Oh yeah, that was me!"). And people drank to excess, making it baseball's version of the office Christmas party.

Because she was one of the very few female executives in the game, Nashota was treated differently in deference to her sex, meaning no one clapped her on the back or called her by some bizarre and vaguely-obscene nickname. While she appreciated that, she was not nearly as fond of the condescending way many people spoke to her, assuming that, despite her title, she was "just a girl" who knew very little about the game or its inner business workings. Her Mountain Empire colleagues knew differently, of course, and could have warned team presidents or general managers not to tangle with her, but they didn't. There were now more than forty leagues operating under the National Association umbrella, which meant over three hundred people were often milling about and, as Charles Underwood had once put it, "the statistical probability of Nashota going one-on-one with some unsuspecting asshole is pretty high." None of her MEL colleagues wanted to miss out on that show. Like the afternoon she ripped a diminutive member of the California League, in front of a gathering crowd, for calling her "little lady," pointing out that while she certainly

The Mountain Empire League

WAS a lady, HE was the one looking up at HER. The poor bastard, not recognizing it was time to retreat, made a snide remark, which brought out the other gun. "I would like to point out something to everyone present," she announced, as many of her league associates bit their lips in anticipation. "I can tell you, for an actual fact, that every hair on my head is just as real and as natural as the day I was born, unlike someone standing in front of me right now." Or when she wanted to attend a business seminar and was told it was only open to GM's or business managers. Oooh, did that set off a minor shitstorm! Before the smoke had cleared, she had quoted the Wolves' income and expense figures for the year from memory, then launched into a brief lecture on how two different promotional nights had each put almost $5,000 into the team's coffers. The upshot was that she was almost immediately asked to serve on a minor league financial advisory committee, reporting directly to President Trautman himself! Don Harrell, who had also attended that meeting, later reported to his fellow Mountain Empire directors that it had been worth every penny he had spent driving from Kruse just to witness her in action.

("And did you accept the committee appointment?" asked an incredulous Jack when, later, she told him everything that had happened. "You bet your *ti*," she said triumphantly.)

But for Jack and Nashota, these 1951 Winter Meetings were primarily about a man who wasn't there—Oddibe Daniels. So on Sunday morning, she and Jack and Bob Rhodes went up to Wells Boggs' suite. A couple of years before, Wells had complained to his directors that other leagues sprung for a suite for their presidents and he didn't see why the Mountain Empire couldn't do the same. "I never ask you for any kind-a egg-strava-gances, now do I? Do I? No, I do not. And this one, this will be just once a year, that's all." The directors had agreed (a little reluctantly, reflected by the 5–3 vote), and now he had a nice breakfast buffet sent up so that the four of them could get down to business without any interruptions.

As promised, Bob had sketched out a list of things that needed to happen, and after he passed out copies they went over them, point by point:

PREPARING FOR ODDIBE DANIELS

I. EDENS RIDGE
 a. Advertisers, publicity, and other businesses
 b. Local clergy
 c. He'll need a place to live/eat/shower
 d. Friendly faces

II. SPRING TRAINING
 a. Hotels, restaurants, travel
 b. Teammates

III. M.E.L. SEASON
 a. Hotels and restaurants in all league cities
 b. Bus and driver
 c. Teammates

"You've got to think about this chronologically, and that means right from the beginning," said Bob, immediately taking charge of the proceedings. "Jack, Nashota, the first section is completely directed at the both-a you, while the next two sections are for everyone, the whole league, OK?" They all nodded, and he continued.

"Before anything is done you're going to have to go to all of your advertisers, Jack, Nashota, and tell them what you're doing. You're going to have to point out how important this is for the town, the league, the whole region. We are recommending that you be very positive, very excited." He put on his "salesman's face." *"This is such a wonderful honor for our town, being the first to break the color line. We might get great publicity in the state, maybe nationwide, and everyone who is supporting us, all our good partners like you..."* He paused for emphasis. *"...will be along for the ride. It proves you're progressive, eager to forge ahead, break free from the past, be a part of the new America, the nation that fought hate and repression in Europe and Asia."* He hesitated, obviously thinking, then said "Really emphasize that last point, about why we fought the war, been over six years and some people may already be forgetting."

Nashota took notes furiously on a pad she had brought, Jack just listened.

"This may sound cold," Bob said, "but you've got to have your business owners behind you. If even a couple of them come out and make a statement supporting you, it should make this go a lot more smoothly. People will say, 'well, if the XYZ Company is for this, if the newspaper is for this, then I guess I'm for it, too.' Go after your biggest businesses, and your local paper and the most-listened-to radio stations. And you'll need your clergy, a few of the more influential ones, and city leaders, the mayor and city council, and the Chamber, too, they need to be behind you."

"And what if they aren't?" asked Jack. "What if I can't get all this support? Our Mayor and Board of Alderman are all a bunch of good old boys, nice fellows for the most part but not exactly the kind you'd expect to rock the boat. Our biggest business is Eastman, based in New York State so that may be good. But I'm sure our local people will have to go right to the top before they'd be allowed to say anything, and they may just choose to keep their mouths shut. And what if we get opposition right away? What if our businesses and city officials and the newspaper aren't in our corner, or suggest that we ought not do this? Does that doom the whole idea, are we out before we've even left the batter's box?" The question hung like a heavy cloud that was just itching to let go of a couple of inches of rain. "I don't want people who know next-to-nothing about us, who have just the tiniest vested interest in us, exercising any control whatsoever. I don't want this to be like the UN, that Security Council, is it? Just one damned 'no' vote can kill an entire resolution, even if everyone else votes 'yes.'"

"You need these people, Jack, you can't just force the issue, this has gotta be a group effort, otherwise it'll be like running in shit."

"Bob, look at the third line, (c), place to live and eat and shower." Nashota spoke quietly, without expression, but her face spoke volumes. She looked at her husband. "Where is he going to shower, Jack?"

"We have showers at the ballpark, I don't underst...oh." The lightbulb suddenly came on.

The room fell silent for a few seconds before Rhodes stated the obvious. "He's gonna need a place to change before the game, and clean up afterwards."

There were several more silent seconds before Nashota said "I'd have no problem bringing him over to our house, let him shower, and then take him home once he's all done."

"We don't know where he'll be living, 'Sho," said Jack. Might be a way's away from our house, or from the yard, or both. We don't know that yet."

"Besides, I know you have plenty to do after a game, you want him to just sit and wait for you 'til you're finished? Doesn't really seem very practical." One of Bob Rhodes best features was his ability to hit the nail on the head, quickly and succinctly, and this was no exception.

There was more silence until Jack spoke.

"Between our locker room and the concession stand, we have that storage space. It's pretty large, we could cut it in half, put a wall in there, plus a shower and sink and toilet, hook it to the water line in the concession stand, that would work."

"Won't be a lot of room in there, Jack," Nashota said.

"Would the City be willing to do the work for you?" asked Rhodes.

"Probably. Maybe. Hell, I dunno. I know plenty-a people at City Hall, I think I…I might could sell them on the idea…"

"When you get them behind you, Jack, when you show them how important this is gonna be, and all they have to do, really, is make a small modification to the ballpark, as well as publicly support you, tell the world…"

"One thing at a time, Bob. Let's see if we can just get a shower in there, OK?"

"What if they won't do it, Jack?" Leave it to Wells to splash some cold water. "I mean, they own the park…"

"Then I'll do it myself, dammit. Me-n Bob Dean, maybe a coupla other guys. Bob knows everybody down at the railroad, I'm sure he can get some guys, work a weekend or two and have it all done." He looked at Nashota. "It won't be a huge space, but enough for a small shower. Toilet don't take up much room. Maybe not a sink, but a spigot so he can wash his hands. We'll get it done."

"He may also be able to clean up wherever he's living. We can keep that in mind when we're looking for a place for him."

"Sure, 'Sho, that could be another option," Jack said. "But I think Bob's right, if I pitch it properly to the City, they'll do the work, or at least let Bob and I handle it." Nashota replied with a simple nod and small smile.

Jack looked down at the page Bob Rhodes had given them, then up at his old friend.

"I think…my thinking is, we line up first getting him a room in someone's house, make sure he can go get groceries, make sure he can get to the ballpark every day…Hmmm, you didn't put that down on this sheet, oughta be there. But if we can get these taken care of first, that's when we go to the City and the Chamber and the businesses. That's when we tell them we've got this all arranged, it's gonna happen and it's gonna be such a great thing for Edens Ridge and we'd sure like their support. I think that may be the way to go. City will see it's all set, they'll get behind us, maybe even build that shower." Jack looked at Nashota. "What do you think, *tsu-na-da-da-tlu-gi?*"

"What does that mean?" asked Wells with a smile.

"'Sweetheart', he calls me that a lot," she said.

"And what do you call him?" Wells wanted to know, still smiling.

That made Nashota laugh. "Depends on what he's done!" which brought guffaws from both Bob and Wells but just a wan smile from Jack, who knew how true that was.

Rhodes was scribbling on his copy. "So we're flip-flopping lines, (a) becomes (b), (c) becomes (a), (b) drops down to (c)." Which brought a question from Nashota.

"Is that all right, Bob? Is it OK to do that, or would that cause a problem? Should this…" and she rattled that paper "…should this be a directive or a guideline?"

"No, it's not a guideline, the National Association isn't telling you what to do here," said Rhodes. "We are making suggestions, though, things we think ought to be done, and I guess…" He paused as he thought this through for a few seconds. "If you want to move things around a bit, I guess that would be OK. I can see the logic in it, in doing it in any order that you think will work in your town. But I have to tell you both, you can't ignore those businesses, you've got to get them, and your city leaders, behind you."

He paused, then looked right at Jack. "To answer your question, Jack, if you don't get at least some of the big poobahs in Edens Ridge—your newspaper, your major radio stations, your city…what'd you call them, aldermen? If you don't get some of these cats, this is not going to go well, for you and the team and the league and especially that young man. That's why we're having this meeting, Jack, to get you, and Wells, too, to get you all prepared. Mr. Trautman wants this to succeed, I want this to succeed, and we think…"

"OK, Bob, I got it." He looked at Nashota. "We can probably do (b) and (c), the new (b) and (c), at the same time, hmmm? We can make a list of people we need to talk to and split it up…"

"Some of those men won't talk to me, Jack, you know that. We'll have to come up with a list and then I can go to the ones I know. But I think I can get Oddibe a place to stay, I know a couple of ladies who have rooms they might want to rent, I can talk to them."

"Negro ladies?" asked Bob. "It would probably be best if he stayed with Negro families. Do you have a Negro section in Edens Ridge?"

Nashota gave him a quizzical look. "Yes, we have Negro families. They are primarily on the east side of town, right near the ballpark, in fact, I'm surprised you haven't noticed that before, Bob." And now she gave him a smile that wasn't designed to be welcoming, causing Jack to send out a telepathic message: *danger, danger, back away slowly and carefully!*

"I've got a large territory to cover, so I'm in and out of a town in a day or so, you've seen how I work. I generally just go to the ballpark and the hotel, maybe a diner after a game, then in the morning I'm back on the road, no time to really see the area. I go into Atlanta at least once a year, but about the only place I ever get to see is Ponce de Leon Park!" Bob was satisfied with this explanation—*message received, over and out.*

"OK, Bob, Nashota and I will start working on (a), (b) and (c) as soon as we get back to town, and especially once the holidays are over. But what is (d), what do you mean by "friendly faces"? And Wells nodded here and said, "I was wonderin' that myself."

"Good question, Jack, let me ask you one," said Bob. "What's the first town you ever played in?"

"Eau Claire, 1933. Only played there a couple of months that year 'cause I signed out of high school, then went back the next year…"

"Ever been to Eau Claire before 1933?"

"No, of course not," said Jack. "I'd never been west of Chambersburg, Pennsylvania up to that time. I'd never heard of Eau Claire, couldn't even spell it 'til I saw it on my bus ticket."

"So you didn't know anybody in town, or on the team, before you arrived?" asked Bob.

"No, not a soul."

Bob smiled. "I'm betting, then, that the first thing you did was meet the guys, your new teammates, and started making friends. And maybe…" He looked at Nashota but decided to go ahead, this would have been long before she met him. "…then maybe after a while you made a few friends in town, people who weren't in the clubhouse."

"Yeah, I made a couple of friends, not in town, though, I wasn't there long enough. Different the next year, I was there all season…" BOOM!! Just like thunder inevitably follows just seconds after a flash of lightening, Bob's point hit Jack as he was about to recount, in detail, his success at Eau Claire in 1934. "Oh, I get it, he's gonna need to have at least a couple of buddies on the team. Well, you know, we can't guarantee anything for sure, but we'll work on it, Bob. I'll talk to everyone I plan to bring back from last year and everyone I invite to a tryout, make certain no one objects to playing with a Negro. We don't need no Dixie Walkers here, now do we? Maybe I can spot a guy or two or three who'll be likely to step up and make the kid feel welcome, comfortable…"

"Your own Pee Wee Reese!" Wells chimed in.

The three men chuckled; Nashota knew that both Walker and Reese were Dodgers and she made a quick notation on her pad to ask Jack why those specific names had been brought up.

"If you look at the outline I passed out," Bob continued, "you'll see that I have a line for "Teammates" under both SPRING TRAINING and M.E.L. SEASON. That's exactly what I was talking about; Jack, you've got it figured out but Wells, it also applies to you, or at least to the other teams in the league. We don't need any troublemakers, or as few as is absolutely possible. It will be up to you, as league president, to work with the other seven teams to make sure we don't have very many Slaughters or Chapmans."

(Slaughter and Chapman, Nashota wrote in her pad, with a question mark.)

"Very many?" asked Jack. "Does that mean the National Association will tolerate some abuse?"

"It means," said Bob with a sigh, "that the National Association expects there will be a few bad apples. We're not likely to catch them all in advance, but Wells, you have to work hard with your teams, right now before the season even starts, to keep the number of incidents to a minimum. The last thing we want is for this young man to be run out of the league."

"Bob, I can't ask my teams to give their players a civics test," said Wells. "Each manager is lookin' for players who knows how to play, and who plays to win. Don't matter who they vote for, or what they think 'bout segregation or the NAACP or what happened there in Cicero. Only matters if they can throw strikes or hit the curve or field the routine grounder. I don' see how I can ask my managers to look beyond that. What if the next Ty Cobb comes to a tryout camp, are we s'posed to turn him away 'cause he don' like culluds?"

There was silence in the room; Wells had, perhaps innocently, asked the question that struck right at the heart of the matter. Everyone looked at Bob, who was looking only at Wells.

"Yes," said Bob Rhodes, quietly but firmly.

"Yes?" asked Wells. "Yes what? What do you mean, Bob?"

"You asked me a question. What if someone finds the next Ty Cobb, but he's gonna cause trouble over our bringing in a Negro. You asked if a team is supposed to turn him away if they see that's the case, and the answer is yes. It is their job to find out this kind of thing in advance and it is your job, Wells, as the head of this league..." And here Rhodes shook his finger at Boggs, something the league president did not appreciate. "As the head of this league, it is your job to tell your managers and team presidents to weed out any troublemakers in advance. If they fuss or raise any sort of ruckus, you tell them this is an order that's coming directly from the top, right from Mr. Trautman, himself. And if they want to complain, you get in touch with me and I will come speak to them in person. And that's exactly what I want you to do, Wells—if anyone gives you shit, either before the season begins or once play has started, you call me and I'll get involved immediately. My home number is at the bottom of the paper I gave you, but of course during the season I'm traveling most of the time, so just call Marge in the Columbus office. I've written her number down too, she'll always know where to reach me, and I'll get back to you just as soon as I can. The National Association will back you up one hundred percent, and if necessary we'll take all the flak. Understood?"

Rhodes let out a deep breath and looked at Wells, who looked at his shoes, then at Jack and Nashota and finally back to Bob. "Understood, Bob. I understand perfectly."

Bob was ready to move on. "Jack, you also need to remember about spring training. The odds are, whatever hotel you'll be using won't accept the boy, you'll have to..."

Nashota jumped in. "Daniels," she said sharply, "His name is Oddibe Daniels." Bob just looked at her. "Not 'the boy' or 'the kid,' he has a name, Oddibe Daniels. Please use it."

Bob paused, nodded, continued. "You will undoubtedly have to find a place for Mr. Daniels to stay while you're all at spring training, plus bus travel or cabs, some way for him to get back and forth to the ballpark. For that matter, you probably should also be in touch with whoever owns the yard, might be the city or county, they may have laws against integration, a lot of towns do, you know."

That rang a bell in Wells' head. "I think that might could actually be the case in our league. What are we s'posed to do if, say, they's a law in, oh, Blackmer, 'genst whites and culluds bein' together in a public park?"

"Are Negroes prohibited from attending games in any of your cities?" Bob asked, already knowing the answer. "Well, no," said Wells, slowly, which allowed Bob to jump back in quickly. "Then you're fine in that regard. I doubt any of your club operators, even Truck Maxwell, will ask the city fathers to pass a law that takes money out of their pockets."

"We all train near each other, in Okaloosa County, in the Florida panhandle. Eglin Air Force Base is right there, a lot of flyboys come out to see the games," said Jack.

Bob smiled and looked at Nashota. "Okaloosa, is that one of your words?"

She shook her head. "Choctaw, not Cherokee. Means 'black water.'" And when he looked at her quizzically, she said simply "I asked a coupla years back."

Bob nodded. "Know anybody over at Eglin? Having the Feds there will help a great deal with any problems that arise or roadblocks that 'suddenly' crop up."

Jack and Nashota both snickered a bit, Wells smiled, and again Bob looked perplexed. "My oldest brother, Dyami, has been in the Air Force since before the war, since it was the Army Air Corps and then the Army Air Forces," said Nashota. "He was the one who actually put us in touch with the right people in Okaloosa two-three years ago, I'm sure he'd be happy to help us again." Still chuckling, Jack chimed in. "Yes, and the town fathers in Okaloosa will most certainly listen to the MAJOR. He is very well respected down there." He turned to his wife. "We'll just work through him, 'Sho, he can get a lot more accomplished than we can," and Nashota nodded.

"If he can help you with lodging for Daniels, maybe also give you names of a few places he can eat, that would be terrific." Nashota kept writing as Bob started up again. "And this will be the best time for you to be working with your players, one on one. They'll be seeing Daniels every day, on the field, in the dugout, in the clubhouse. It has to be no big deal for them. If they accept him, no questions asked, then 'most everyone else around the league will accept him, too." He looked at Wells. "You mentioned PeeWee earlier, Wells, and that is exactly right. PeeWee let it be known that Jackie was a Dodger, he was their teammate and the normal rules applied—mess with him and 23 other guys will be gunning for you. OK, any questions so far?"

Bob paused. No one said anything, so he picked it back up.

"Last section, and Wells, this goes back to what we were talking about a little while ago. You need to make sure that all the other teams in the league are prepared for Mr. Daniels. It would be nice if the hotels all gave him a room but I know that won't be happening, so you'll need to be sure he has a place to sleep, a DECENT place to sleep, not some flophouse. He'll also need to know where he can get him some food in every town."

He shuffled his papers, then looked at Jack. "Do you own your bus and pay your driver, or do you work through a local company?" Nashota was quick to respond. "We co-own a bus with Kruse, we decided to split the cost with Don a couple of years ago. That's why we try to arrange the schedule so we're never on the road at the same time. Doesn't always work out, maybe once or twice a year we have an overlap and then someone has to go to Dick Rockingham, he owns a bus company that services all of Northeast Tennessee. I don't think he'll be a problem, but I'll talk to him myself." And of course she wrote herself a note.

"When you talk to him, Nashota, tell him there just can't be any issues with any of their drivers At the very least, he'll need to know who he can assign to you and who he can't." She nodded and wrote some more.

"Beck and Mettin each have their own buses," said Wells. "Blackmer does, too, and they lease it out to Shirley when it don't conflict. Weare and Buchanan, I'm pretty sure they both lease, or did Weare go and buy one?" He looked at Nashota. "I kinda remember they was talkin' 'bout buyin' but I can't recall right offhand what they went and did."

"They talked about it," said Nashota. "They did speak with me and I gave them some numbers which showed 'em how much we'd saved, but I don't think they've done it yet." She shrugged. "I guess we can't force them be practical."

"Will it really matter?" Jack asked, and Bob quickly responded. "It might," he said, "if the drivers say they're not going to take "their boys" to play against a team that has a Negro. Even if the driver is a player or coach or trainer, like you've got, Jack." He thought for a couple of seconds. "I don't know if it's a very strong possibility but it could come up, Wells, so you'll need to address it with your teams in advance." Boggs nodded, Nashota scribbled.

Bob looked at his papers again, remained silent, then looked up. "I think that's all I've got on my list." "That's plenty," mumbled Wells, quietly, almost like he was thinking out loud. Bob ignored him. "Anyone have any other questions?" They all looked at one another, then at Rhodes. "Guess not, Bob," said Jack. "You've given us plenty to think about, and to do."

"Just one more thing," said Bob. "I've said it already but I want to say it again—the National Association is completely and totally behind this. We want this integration to be a success, and we will do whatever it takes to make it happen. Hopefully all of you, and the rest of the league, are ready to make the same commitment." "You know you can count on us," Jack said emphatically; Nashota nodded and Wells, after a brief hesitation, followed suit. But every time he thought about Truck Maxwell he felt a pain in his gut.

The holidays always come hard on the heels of the Winter Meetings. For the Daniels family, Christmas in 1951 was especially joyous. While they had promised not to say a word to anyone about Oddibe's professional contract, it would not prevent them from going to church on Christmas Eve. Led by Lilliana, they lingered as the rest of the worshipers filed out when the service was over. "Momma?" asked Berenice, but Lilly simply said, "One minute, baby." Then she grasped her daughter's right hand with her left, and her husband's left hand with her right, and bowed her head. Walter followed his wife's lead and the three children, not really sure what was happening, did the same. And Lilly quietly, privately, whispered a personal prayer of thanks, and asked that Oddibe be granted extra strength for the road he was about to take.

In general, for about three weeks after the Winter Meetings, baseball people (for the most part) put the game on the back burner and get busy with other things. There are gifts and trees to buy. Better hurry up and start addressing those Christmas cards, assuming they've even been purchased! String the lights, set out holiday decorations—all the year-end Christmas-y things that makes December both memorable and stressful.

January is different. January begins the real meat of the selling season, the time of year that often determines whether or not a team will show a profit for the year. But for team presidents and field managers in the Mountain Empire League, the registered letter that arrived from President Wells Boggs on the 11th really jump-started their 1952 baseball season. He had asked Nashota to write the first draft and then he fine-tuned it to contain a little more of his voice before shipping it out. Wells assumed it would be the source of surprise and discussion among his league's senior people, and he was right. And he would hardly have been shocked that the loudest uproar came out of Mettin, Virginia.

Beau Maxwell was in a really good mood and eager to share some major news with his Dad—he had just landed a new sponsor, that breakfast-and-lunch place that had opened up on Broad Street back in September. They had agreed to an ad on the program's score pages, running along the bottom. It was a very prominent spot and, Beau thought, made for a significant new addition to the Foxes' family. He was whistling as he approached his father's office, but was stopped in his tracks as Truck Maxwell's profanities rang through the empty ballpark.

"Goddam, sumbitch," he screamed. "God-DAM! Motherpussbucket, lily-livered, Lincoln Loyalist piece-a shit. Goddam you to hell, Wells Boggs."

He was holding some papers and waving them about while he turned the air blue. He didn't even seem to notice that Beau had run in and, carefully taking the papers from his father's hand, thoroughly read their contents.

"Dad. Dad. DAD!" Beau needed to shout if he wanted to get a word in. "This ain't no surprise, we voted last month and approved the boy's contract, this is just ol' Wells followin' up. No need to put yourself out all over again. Now lemme tell ya…"

"Don't you be tellin' me any goddam thing, goddammit! Bad enough they is tryin' to make us play with…with…THEM…" Beau was surprised, and grateful, his father didn't go to his standard and favorite bastardization of the word "Negro." Truck pointed to the letter in Beau's hands. "Votin's one thing, but now our 'steemed league president is tellin' me how to run my club, tellin' me how to do my job in my town! Shit, he thinks he knows Mettin 'cause he comes here two-three times a year for a whole day or two each time. That makes him a expert, huh? Now he knows what we want, who we is, how we s'posed to behave, how we s'posed…"

"Dad," said Beau, looking it over once more, "this letter ain't sayin' anythin' of the sort. He's just tellin' us what our responsibilities are as members of the league, that's how I see it. It's really just a reminder…"

"Reminder my ass!" exploded Truck, and he grabbed his keys and threw them across the room in exasperation. "I think I need to remind that prick-faced dandy who really runs this-here league, it's us team presidents, we hired his chubby little ass and we can fire it right quick." A new thought passed through his brain. "No, firin' is too good, way too good. I gotta mind to get me a coupla the boys and go on down there to Knoxville one evenin' and put the fear-a God into him and his family, show him what we think 'round here 'bout…'bout…" He was sputtering a bit, maybe finally running out of steam. "…'bout this kind-a shit. This ain't Brooklyn, this ain't Cleveland, this ain't even St. Louis, goddam Veeck. This is the South, this is the Confederacy, this is STILL the Confederacy, doncha know? These damn Yankees think they can come in here and tell us what to do in our league, it's OUR league, dammit, who they think they are?" And he sat down in his chair, having worn himself out. Beau had been noticing that his father seemed to tire a little more easily these days.

While the father sat and caught his breath, the son read that letter one more time.

MOUNTAIN EMPIRE LEAGUE

| Blackmer, Kentucky | Buchanan, NC | Edens Ridge, TN | Beck, Virginia |
| Shirley, Kentucky | Weare, NC | Kruse, TN | Mettin, Virginia |

Dear Truck:

First of all, let me express my wish that you and your family had a healthy and happy Christmas and New Year's. I'm sure you join me in hoping that 1952 will be a truly great year for all of us in the Mountain Empire League.

You will no doubt recall the important exchange we had at our December meeting in Columbus, Ohio, regarding the contract offered to outfielder Oddibe Daniels by Edens Ridge, and the vote that came out of that discussion. While we still have some three months before our new season begins, I feel—as does National Association president George Trautman—that we must begin working now to prepare each of our towns for this significant, ground-breaking event. I think if we do this conscientiously but quietly, we will minimize any problems that could arise. Mr. Trautman and I both agree wholeheartedly that the Mountain Empire League, through its Trustees and Field Managers, has the capability to make this transition take place just as seamlessly as possible. I have stated that to Mr. Trautman, and I sincerely believe that we will prove to be a model for having white and Negro ballplayers play together on the same field.

To make this a reality, there are a number of steps that we feel need to be taken this off-season:

TRUSTEES

- Please speak with your major business, civic and religious leaders and tell them what the League has decided to do. Please make it clear that this action has been approved by the very highest levels of professional baseball, and that all of us are hoping they will continue to support you and your team. If they could speak positively about you and help spread the word throughout town, so much the better.

- When Edens Ridge comes to your town, it would be nice if all the players, including Oddibe Daniels, could be housed in the same motel. We realize, however, that may not be possible. We ask you, then, to please make arrangements for him to stay with a high-quality local person or family, perhaps a minister in a Negro church, or a boarding house that comes highly recommended. (This section does not apply to Kruse, since the Wolves and Ducks are within NAPBL-recognized commuting distance.)

- In speaking to businesses, please be sure to include restaurants, and determine which ones will be happy to accept Mr. Daniels' money. It would be ideal if the entire team could eat together, either before or after a game, but we recognize that this is very unlikely.

- If you own your own bus, please be sure your driver or drivers are well aware of the situation and will not object to carrying the team into Edens Ridge. If you lease a bus, please talk to the head of the company as soon as you can. Make him aware of the upcoming change in the League, and make sure he and his drivers have no objections to carrying the team into Edens Ridge. If there is a problem, please notify me immediately and Bob Rhodes and I will work with you and do everything we can to smooth things over.

FIELD MANAGERS

- Field managers, it is most important that you are completely in agreement with having Oddibe Daniels playing against your club this season. We ask that you emphasize to your athletes that he is just another player and should not be treated any differently than anyone else wearing a uniform from another club. This means that the National Association of Professional Baseball Leagues, and the Mountain Empire League, do not and *will not* condone any unsportsmanlike conduct directed specifically at Mr. Daniels. That includes pitches aimed at his head, his hands, his elbows or his knees, though pitching inside is certainly permitted. It also includes aiming throws at his head while he is running the bases, spiking him, or making unreasonably hard tags on him when he slides into any base. And this especially means making sure that there are no rabble-rousers on the team; we do not want any Dixie Walkers, or Ben Chapmans, for that matter.

- And this last paragraph is directed at both the Trustees and Field Managers. As you assemble your team in the spring, and as you make changes periodically during the season, you must be sure that any players you are considering for your roster are made fully aware of the special circumstances in the League this year, and have no objections. Mr. Trautman and I want to emphasize this point very strongly—**we will not tolerate the kind of ugly behavior that has shown up elsewhere, most notably with the Philadelphia Phillies in 1947.** We want to demonstrate to the rest of America that we are better than that! I have therefore been given the power by Mr. Trautman to crack down hard on any players, managers, coaches or others who might give the League a black eye, and please know that I WILL EXERCISE THAT POWER. Please be sure, then, that you talk to all players as they try out for your team. If you suspect that any of them may prove to be the source of difficulties, especially when playing against Edens Ridge, **DO NOT SIGN THEM**, no matter how talented they may appear to be. That decree comes directly from Mr. Trautman.

You may find that you have questions about some of the points raised here. If so, I would encourage you to call me, and I will be happy to try to provide an answer, even discuss the entire matter with you. This is, as you might expect, undoubtedly the most significant thing that any of us will be involved in this year, even overshadowing the pennant race! I firmly believe that we have a chance to do something here that will be remembered long after each of us is gone. I look forward to working with you to make this season a success, both on and off the field. Please remember that we are in this together, and I am constantly here for you.

With all good wishes I am, as always,

Wells
Herbert George Wells Boggs
President

"Black eye," said Truck, with a little laugh. "I thought that part was pretty funny." Beau just sighed.

For Jack and Nashota Simpson, the real work was about to begin, and they knew it. On the drive back from Columbus, they crafted a "plan of action." (Jack had initially called it a "plan of attack," but Nashota nixed that right away, simply saying "The war has been over for six years, Sergeant.") They would divide up the businesses and clergy, she would search for a place for Oddibe to live, and he would deal with Win Appleton over at the *Edens Ridge Gazette*. He would also talk to a few members of the Board of Mayor and Aldermen, but she volunteered to speak to the Mayor, Dick Curtis.

"I thought you hated him," said Jack.

"I do," she replied, then quickly caught herself. "Oh, hate is such a strong word, I'm sorry, I take it back. But I do dislike him, he is such a…a…*a-s-gi-na*."

"I assume that's not good," he said with a smile, and when she replied "devil," he snorted and laughed at the same time.

"But he seems to like me," she said. "He's always pleasant, though solicitous. And since he also owns The Curtis Motor Lodge, maybe I can renew his contract at the same time."

Jack had no objection, simply replying "Be my guest."

Because of the Daniels signing, Mr. and Mrs. Simpson had both found the Winter Meetings to be uncharacteristically stressful, which seemed to tie in with them not getting as much sleep as they would have liked. And there certainly wasn't any playtime, they were too wound up for that. There hadn't been any in Pennsylvania, either. "Ew, your parents are just next door!" Nashota had whispered one night when Jack started getting amorous, and that was that. And shortly after returning from Ohio, they drove over to Cherokee for Christmas, as they usually did. That tradition also included the "no frolicking" rule in the Cozens house. ("Ew, my parents are just next door!") So not very long after the Meadowbrook safely made the journey back to Edens Ridge from Columbus, Jack and Nashota found themselves rolling around in their bed, taking care of some very necessary business. They had concentrated so intently on enjoying themselves, and each other, that it was not until later when they realized they had simply forgotten to use any protection this time.

"The best laid schemes o' Mice an' Men gang aft agley," wrote Robert Burns, the national poet of Scotland. Translated into baseball-English, it meant that, if the Wolves fielded a good team in 1952 and made the playoffs, their manager would likely have more on his mind than his starting rotation.

FOUR

Baseball is a game of failure. The very best batters do not get a hit seventy percent of the time. The very best fielders are always candidates to make an error, sometimes at the most inopportune times. The very best pitchers have nights when they look like rag-arm bums.

Minor league club operators are also very aware of failure. A team's overall financial success is frequently predicated on how well you do during "the selling season." What happens in the winter can literally make or break you, fiscally, before the very first pitch of the year is thrown.

Jack and Nashota, along with every other minor league operator on the planet, spent the fall and winter knocking on doors, asking for support for their team. Doesn't matter if the ballpark is covered with snow for days at a time, the preparation for the new season never lets up. They offered a variety of advertising opportunities, from signs on the outfield fence ("the largest and most distinctive way to be seen at Bill Washington Park") to ads in the program and on the roster insert, to sponsoring specific nights at the ballpark. Businesses could opt for a package deal that might include any combination of a fence sign, a program ad, season tickets and a promotional night. The price for these combos—all-too-obviously nicknamed "Double Play," "Triple Play" and "Grand Slam"—was discounted off the "rack rate" to try and stimulate sales. And making sales is vitally important for the team, especially in the off-season, because it is their only source of revenue during the fall and winter months. If the Simpsons wanted paychecks to be able to buy groceries and pay their standard monthly bills, they needed to make sales. "They don't sell themselves," Jack would frequently say. "For us, baseball is never over."

During the "selling season," it was normal to lose an advertiser or two or three, with economics generally being the reason. And typically those losses would be offset by adding a new customer or two or three, making it a great day when either Jack or Nashota would bring in a signed contract from a new business. But this year they had an added worry, the concern that some of their good commercial patrons would refuse to re-up simply because the team was planning to integrate. So every renewal was a cause for minor celebration in the Simpson household.

As they had discussed in Columbus, they divvied up responsibilities. "I have a feeling, 'Sho, that a lot of men in town would have more trouble saying 'no' to you than to me." He smiled. "I know you won't want to hear it, but a pretty face can often accomplish more than one with a stubble." And she had agreed, though she couldn't help asking, with a wry grin, "Then how come neither political party will be running a woman for President this year?" Knowing the question was rhetorical, he chose to ignore it.

And they had their successes. Lee Meadows had renewed his real estate company's clever fence sign ("WE COVER MORE REAL ESTATE THAN ALL THREE DiMAGGIOs COMBINED!"), and had expressed no reservations over Oddibe joining the team. Herb Barber agreed to renew, though he "truthfully ain't that crazy about havin' a cullud boy on the team." It didn't really affect his business at all, though—his people cleaned up the ballpark after games—and he knew that if he didn't renew his sign, the Wolves wouldn't do business with him and he'd lose that nice, steady source of summertime income. "Y'all might as well go ahead and do whatcha gonna do and don't mind me."

Renewing LaDonna Holmes was a no-brainer. Probably Nashota's closest friend in town, she ran The Back Porch, "THE Place To Be for Breakfast and Lunch in Edens Ridge." She had started off doing the cooking while her husband, Steve, greeted every customer and took care of the finances. When he decided to join the Marines in 1942, he gave her a few quick business lessons, kissed her goodbye and told her he'd be back "once we take care of these Japs." He almost made it all the way through before he and his Second Battalion landed on a rock named Iwo Jima. Joe Rosenthal's Pulitzer Prize-winning AP photo may have celebrated a hard-fought victory, but more than 20,000 men, American and Japanese, did not make it off that island. LaDonna kept the place shuttered for three days and then went back to work because that seemed to be the only thing to do. She tried to be the smiling hostess, but she didn't have Steve's talent for it, plus she missed making flapjacks. She quickly pivoted, leaving the bills and the books for after hours, while she hired someone to manage the dining area, allowing her to happily go back to the kitchen. She was very careful with her money, but when then-bachelor Jack Simpson became a breakfast regular, she agreed to purchase a small ad, mainly just to help him out. Her eventual friendship with Nashota led her to cautiously try a larger ad, which included a discount coupon. That summer, when she found it necessary to hire an extra person because so many additional customers were coming through the door with that coupon, she became a die-hard member of the "Wolves Pack," which was the name adopted by the booster club.

"About time you added a colored boy," she said when Nashota came in one afternoon and explained what she and Jack were planning. "You tell him he can come in here to eat, though I prob'ly have to put him at a back table, sure he'll understand. But I'll feed him good and give him the same break I give all our boys!" And the two friends clinked their coffee cups, which LaDonna had freshened up with something a bit stronger than Maxwell House.

Not everyone, however, proved to be quite so agreeable.
- Jim Morris from JDM Printing. He had been printing the team's souvenir program since the very first season. He still wanted to have the print job but was not willing to buy his ad and fence sign any more.
- Nick Mancuso from Nick's Barber Shop. Jack always got his hair cut there and had been sending the players to him as well. No more. "I don't like coons," Nick said when Jack told him about the plan. "I can't put my name in a program of a team that has…has…one-a them on the field."

- Bob Biggerstaff from Biggerstaff Distributing. The largest Budweiser wholesaler in Northeast Tennessee, he spent lots of money with the ballclub, buying a fence sign, program ad (on the highly-visible score page) and four season tickets, plus he sponsored a major promotional night every year. In exchange, he was the beneficiary of the team's most exclusive perk—Budweiser was the only beer sold at the ballpark. But when it came to race, money was apparently secondary to Bob Biggerstaff. "If I stay with you," he said to Jack, "I'd be giving my blessing to your…experiment, or whatever you want to call it. Not interested. I ain't in favor of what you're doing." When Jack pointed out that the team was expecting to draw more fans, Negro fans, Biggerstaff snorted. "They don't drink my beer," he said. "Malt liquor, ain't that what they like? Now if you'll excuse me…"
- Cloyd Christian from Christian Portraits. Jack was quite surprised that the local photographer was so opposed, but when he left he noticed, for the first time, that despite the walls being dotted with numerous photos of "satisfied customers," none of them were Negro faces. "Some Christian," Jack mumbled to himself.
- Buddy Martin from Martin and Sons. They supplied the team with candy, bags of unpopped popcorn kernels, salted-in-the-shell peanuts, things like that. "Buddy, there are Negro people who come out to our ballpark and buy your products from us," said Jack. "Why didn't you ever object to that? Didn't stop you from taking our money, did it?" "That's different," said Martin, but when Jack asked how, his former supplier just said "you oughta leave now, Jack." "I'm going," said Jack, "and I guarantee I won't be back."
- Tom Edwards from Edwards Insurance. This was a major shock. "Tom, I can't believe this, I would never have expected this of you and Sarah Lou," said Nashota. "The two of you have been to our house…" "The one has nothin' to do with t'other," Edwards said in his slow drawl. "We just don't never do business with culluds, never have, never will. And if you do, if you put one on your payroll, then we can't support you, Nashota, sorry. Now please, my next appointment is waiting for me." She turned to go, stopped, turned back. "Tom, would you sell a policy to an Indian?" "No, 'course not," he said without looking up. "But you have, you know. For the past few years. What do you think of that? And I can tell you that this full-blooded Cherokee and her white husband won't be renewing their policies." She left without waiting for his reaction.
- Gray Gamadge from Kettle Creek. The Wolves had always run several promotions that involved plants or flowers, and Gray had always either donated them or sold them to the team at a deep discount. "Sorry, Nashota, but I can't keep doin' business with you if you have a Nigra on your team, that's jus' the way I feel." "Even if we said we'd pay full price for the flowers?" she asked. He was silent for a moment and then, looking down at the flowers on the table in front of him, said "Even then. Sorry."
- Rich Lamson from Rich's Restaurant. This one wasn't as much of a surprise as some of the others. A dapper dresser who generally affected a pleasant and affable demeanor, Jack always found Lamson to be rather phony and a bit "oily." Told about Oddibe, he immediately took umbrage, saying "Jack, no, what are you doing? Have

you lost your mind? You can't do this, you can't mix the races out on the ballfield." What was happening in the major leagues meant nothing to him. "Look, I've got nothing against the coloreds, the few that I've met have all seemed to be quite nice, but…but…centerfield? Jack, anyone playing center needs to have some brains, he needs to know what he's doing out there and sort of be in charge of the whole outfield. A colored boy just doesn't have that…that…that capacity, Jack, I know you know that."

- Cole Katt from Katt and Son Auto Repair. With two 1940s vehicles that got a lot of use around town, both Simpsons had come to know Cole and his son, Cal, pretty well, and had been able to sell them a sign and a half-page ad. Jack had never dreamed they wouldn't renew, but was wrong. "Sorry, Jack, I just can't go along with you on this," said Cole. "Ain't nothin' personal in't, is purely business. I got some customers that don't like coloreds, I know it, they've told me so lotsa times. I keep supportin' you, I'll lose business, can't 'ford that. Sorry, Jack, really, I am. Tell 'Shota we said hi." Katt turned away but, sensing a possible opening, Simpson said "I will, but I may have to sic her on you." The car guy stopped for a moment and, without turning to face Jack, quietly said "Please don't do that," before continuing into his shop.

But the worst, by far, had been Dick Curtis. Nashota didn't often find herself speechless, but her conversation with Dick Curtis proved to be one of those occasions.

There was only one hotel in Edens Ridge and it was owned by Curtis. Actually it wasn't a hotel at all, it was The Curtis Motor Lodge, but because it was local it had been where all the visiting teams had stayed from the very beginning. Truth be told, though, it was not the most popular destination among the league's players. While Curtis did make sure the rooms were always clean, he offered no perks whatsoever, and his "restaurant" was nothing more than a snack counter. Curtis was also something of an ass, a blowhard with a Clark Gable moustache whose opinion of himself was much higher than anyone else's. But he was a staunch supporter of the team, having served as president of the "Wolves Pack" for a time, and was now the Mayor of Edens Ridge.

So signing him up for his fence sign and box seats seemed to be a mere formality. It became anything but.

"By the way, Dick," said Nashota, as she pulled a blank contract out for him to sign, "I need to tell you that this year we are going to have a young Negro man playing in our out…"

"A what? You're going to have what? A Negro? There is going to be a Negro playing for the Wolves? My Wolves? Are you crazy, girl? Have you and your husband lost your ever-lovin' minds?" She thought he was being sarcastic, no one said "ever-lovin'" any more, but he continued.

"The big leagues is ruinin' the game, just ruinin' it, I say, with all these cullud fellas out there. That Branch Rickey, he started it all by bringin' in Jackie Robinson, they should both rot in hell, and now all these others. That Mays booner kid who played in the Series, and Campy-somethin' and…and even ol' Satch Paige is out there. What next? You gonna put uniforms on monkeys and teach 'em to hit and run and throw? This just ain't right, it ain't right."

Nashota sat there, hoping there was a punch line, a grin, a laugh, something to say, "just fooling, good for you, now lemme sign that contract so we can both get on with our day." But there was nothing except this odd twitch—his moustache, which was starting to display a little more grey, seemed to be moving involuntarily.

"Dick," she said slowly, "I hope you don't mean all that."

"Look, Nashota, I like you," he said, leaning forward. "You're a good girl, always treated me fair, you-n your husband both. Lotsa Injuns ain't like you, can't be trusted, I'm sure you know that yourself, right? But, shoot, them culluds…" He looked away, shook his head, looked back at her. "Them culluds, ain't a-one-a them worth a damn, I don't care 'bout that Bunche fella or none-a them, they ain't no good. Some of 'em can sing and dance, I guess, like the Nicholas Brothers, and ol' Satchmo, he can sure blow the horn, but most of 'em are just good for shinin' shoes or cleanin' houses. They don't belong on a ballfield, not with good white boys, anyways."

"We have made a commitment, Dick, we are bringing in a young man named Oddibe Daniels…"

"Oddibe? What kind-a fool name…who gives their child such a name, huh? Only a cullud…"

She raised her voice a bit even though she knew she shouldn't. "He will be playing center field for us this summer. I'm sorry if you don't like it, but we are going to be doing it. Now, truthfully, it won't really affect you at all, none of the other teams have signed any Negroes, at least not right now, so they wouldn't be staying with you…"

"And I wouldn't let 'em if they tried. I can't have no culluds stayin' at my hotel, I have a reputation to think of!"

Nashota stood up, trembling. It was all she could do to keep from screaming in his face. She was actually surprised to realize that her right hand was knotted in a fist, and she quickly relaxed it, and then internally worked on the rest of her, but remained standing.

"Dick, Jack and I made a decision that we would tell all our sponsors what we are doing this year, bringing in Oddibe, and if anyone objected we would not re-sign them. That includes you. Now, if you…"

"I'm the only hotel in town, there ain't no place else for you to go, missy. Y'all need to think about that."

"And you," she exploded *(sorry, Jack, I just can't help myself)*, "You need to think about this—six teams come in here every year and stay at your…your hotel. How many rooms do they take? At least ten, right? Maybe one or two more. Ten nights for each. That's not counting moms and dads who come to town to watch their boys play, or scouts who come in, or when Wells Boggs or Bob Rhodes comes to town. You get all that business all summer long." She paused to let that sink in, then continued. "Unless you apologize for all you just said, unless you take it all back, I'm prepared to walk out of here and find a new place for the league to stay, and you'll have to fill those rooms some other way."

He stood up, put his hands on his desk, and glared at her. "No one tells me what to do, hear? No one, 'specially no Injun! I give the orders, and I'm orderin' you to git! Go on, get outta here, you…you…squaw."

She peeled out of the motor lodge, sped around the corner and parked, trying to collect herself. *I won't give him that satisfaction of crying,* she thought, but it took every bit of willpower she had.

Once she calmed down she started thinking about what was next. Curtis was right about one thing, he had the only motor lodge in town *(hotel, my ass!),* and except for Kruse, which just commuted back and forth, the rest of the teams had to stay somewhere. *Great,* she thought, *I don't have a place for Oddibe to sleep yet, and now I don't have a place for six teams, either.*

They needed to talk, so on Friday evening they had a little supper, washed and dried the dishes, and grabbed a couple of beers.

"I can't believe Tom and Sarah Lou," said Nashota. "I mean, we've socialized, we've had them over, I consider them to be friends…"

"Doesn't matter," said Jack, sipping his beer. "I'll bet the subject of Negroes and whites was never brought up when we were together."

"Don't you think, Jack, that if a person hates Negroes he would also hate Indians? Tom admitted he wouldn't sell to an Indian, but he insures the team even though I'm the Business Manager, and I'm married to you, and we have our life insurance with him…"

"And that'll change," said Jack emphatically. "We'll shop around for a new insurance agent, and I'll find someone else to cut my hair, and…" he lifted up the bottle, "no more Buds in this house, OK? Plenty of other brews to choose."

"Fine with me," she said. "But Jack, Biggerstaff buys a lot from us, and…"

"And we buy a lot from him. Long term, he'll probably feel it more than we will."

"Really? How? You think that dropping him…Explain to me how this will benefit us?"

He took another swig. "It makes us expand our horizons. It gets us out meeting more people, making new friends." He smiled. "It gives more businesses the chance to work with us. We don't have to just sell Budweiser any more, we can approach other distributors, which means we can sell more ads, more tickets, more nights. We just need to tell them about…about Oddibe right away, in case we run into more people like Tom Edwards and Bob Biggerstaff."

Nashota wrote down the names of the businesses they'd lost, and then shifted the discussion to coming up with replacements.

"For Kettle Creek, the flower people, I have an idea about that. Same with the photo guy, Cloyd Christian. I think I know how to replace both of them." Jack just nodded, so she continued.

"Royal Privette has a nice little flower shop. He won't be able to buy a half-page ad like Gray Gamadge, but I'll bet he can afford a quarter-page, or maybe something on the roster insert. And I was thinking we could design a little promotion around his name. We wander around the ballpark every night, see, and we choose a family, mom and dad and kids, or at least one child, and we move them down to a box seat for that game. Mom gets a small bouquet of flowers, Dad gets, I dunno, something, I have to think on that a bit, kids get maybe an ice cream or popcorn from the concession stand. And we call them the evening's Royal Family, sponsored by Royal Privette Florists. Get it, playing off his name?" Her husband just looked at her. "Jack? You heard me, right? What do you think? Jack?"

He cleared his throat. "I think, I think…goddam, woman, that's fucking brilliant! Sorry, I didn't mean to cuss, sorry, but damn, that's fu…that's a terrific idea, just…just…first-rate. Do you think you can sell it to him?"

There were a handful of curse words that Nashota really hated, and the f-word was one of them. Not that she wasn't averse to letting loose now and then, though she generally did it under her breath, or in Cherokee. This simply meant that people either didn't hear her or, more likely, didn't understand her, and both were all right with her. But on this occasion, well, on this occasion, she would forgive Jack Simpson his trespass.

"Yes, I think he'll go for it, as long as I don't make him buy a big ad. And if I promise that I'll be the one picking out a worthy family every night, I think that may seal the deal with him."

"What about July and August, especially August, when you'll be very pregnant? Aren't you gonna want to be taking it easy by then?"

Very few people knew about the pregnancy. Nashota had told her sister, Tehya, and then the two of them had gone over to Cherokee to give their parents the good news. And Dr. Tracy, of course, who had examined Nashota, told her she was healthy and fit and things looked good in these early stages. The baby was due, she thought, in late September.

"I think I'll be fine," she said, quietly pleased that Jack was concerned. "If I need help towards the end, I'm sure someone will step up." She smiled. "You know Dorothy's gonna be acting like my mom the whole time, and LouEtta, um, I'll bet…I'll bet LouEtta will be hovering around all the time, too. Don't worry, we'll cover it."

"OK," he said, "I'll let you handle…" Considering that he had not minded being an active participant in the baby's conception, she found his hesitancy to discuss any aspect of her pregnancy amusing, and she giggled. He ignored that, continuing to concentrate on sales and promotions. "We're gonna need a car guy, maybe I can sell a garage on the idea of giving away a free oil change or a tune-up as the gift for Dad, something like that. Along with their ad." Jack was newly energized. "Good, good, what else were you thinking?"

"Well, you remember Tehya's friend, Cattrenia Barraclough? She used to work…"

"Yeah, she worked at the munitions plant with your sister, but she quit and moved…up this way, wasn't it? Isn't she somewhere around here? And wait, wait, didn't she get in some trouble a while back? Why would you bring her name up?"

"She did get into a bit of trouble, but it wasn't her fault. She married a guy who was no good, a crook, was always being arrested for petty theft and things, and he was a real jerk with her, used to slap her around. One night they got into a fight and he came at her with a knife and she defended herself, hit him with the toaster, imagine that?" She chuckled at the thought. "Busted his wrist, I think, and put a dent in his head, too. Prob'ly killed the toaster." He snorted. "They were both arrested but she only got 30 days for disorderly conduct, then she divorced him and moved up to Kingsport and got on at Eastman. Still works there, but she's been trying to start her own photography business. I've seen a little of her work, and she's good, Jack. I was thinking she could be the one to replace Christian Portraits. Maybe give away a free photo session or, um, perhaps, come in for family pictures and get a free one for every one you buy, something like that."

This time Jack was a little skeptical. "I dunno, 'Sho, people might be leery of dealing with someone like that, lady with a record and all..."

"If a white woman had defended herself against a man with a knife, no one would say anything, they'd call her 'courageous' or 'hero' or something. Ah, but let it be an Indian woman and people don't want to have anything to do with her, now how fair is that? Aren't we trying to fight that kind of thinking by bringing Oddibe in here? Hmmmmm?"

Jack drank the last of his beer and sighed. "Honestly, I just want someone who can play center and bat leadoff, tell you the truth." He could see her nostrils were starting to flair again. "But if you vouch for her, that's enough for me. See if you can sell her. Any other ideas?"

"No, not right now, anyway," she said sharply.

"OK, so you're going to work on replacing Kettle Creek and Christian Portraits, I'll see about replacing Biggerstaff Distributing and Edwards Insurance and Cole's. There are other restaurants we can get to replace that snake Rich Lamson, same with a barber shop. But we have to find a new printer, that's essential, someone has to print our program and roster insert and special tickets and be willing to buy a fence sign and program ad. And we have to find a place for the players and umpires and guests to stay."

"We'll have to go into Kingsport for a hotel. As for printers, I know there's a couple of printers now in Edens Ridge..."

"They're small, though, don't know if they can handle as much business as we generate..."

"We won't know unless we talk to them," she said. "There was that fella who came in to see us last spring, I think I saved his card. I'd be happy to go in and talk to him, if you'd like."

"I dunno, hon..."

"Jack," she said, very firmly, "you just said it, a printer is essential. Let me go in and see samples of his work. If we think this man will be able to do a good job for us, and he doesn't object to Oddibe, I'll make a deal with him. We have..."

"He has to buy a fence sign, at the very least. No negotiations on that—no fence sign, no business from us, yes?" Nashota smiled and nodded, then asked "OK, now what about Buddy Martin? Losing him is bad, Jack, most of our concessions came from him, how..."

"I know what he's meant to us, you don't have to remind me. But Don Harrell swears by his guy, Tony Shale, and he's only maybe fifteen minutes away, I'll bet he won't mind burning a little gas in exchange for all of our business. I plan on calling him first thing Monday morning and making an appointment. Now, if we don't line him up, then I'll get worried, but right now I'm more concerned with finding a printer and a hotel."

"I'll get us a printer, Jack, leave that to me. And I can call hotels, make appointments…"

"We can both do that," he said, and she nodded as she stood up and asked "Want another beer?"

"Do we have anything other than Bud?" When she shook her head, he did the same. "Not 'til we have us up a new beer guy."

"I think we have a cold bottle or two left, and we paid for 'em…"

"You're right," he said, standing up. "Hate to waste money. What say we finish them off and then smash them, symbolizing…" He said that last word very slowly. "…symbolizing the end of our relationship with Bob Biggerstaff!"

She laughed. "As long as we do it outside, I don't want to be sweeping glass off our floor for days and weeks."

Before getting back to dealing with local businesses, Jack turned his attention to Win Appleton.

The two had first met in 1946, when Jack had been hired to be Lionel Ticknor's coach. Winston Stanley Appleton, born and raised in nearby Hawkins County, was the sports editor and chief baseball writer for the *Edens Ridge Gazette*. As that initial Mountain Empire League season progressed, Jack and Win began learning about each other through numerous pre- and post-game conversations. They were both fans of the Philadelphia teams, for instance, though Jack came by his interest naturally, as a native Pennsylvanian. Win, on the other hand, had started pulling for them earlier, in 1913, primarily because of Frank Baker of the Athletics, better known as "Home Run" Baker because, in that "dead ball" era, he was the game's premier slugger with his twelve home runs. (In contrast, Ralph Kiner had hit 42 round-trippers in 1951, which led the majors. The ball hadn't been "dead" for many years.) Win admired him so much he decided he would become a major league third baseman, but that is where the Simpson and Appleton career paths diverged. While Jack Simpson was able to develop his skills and play ball professionally, Win Appleton found that any physical activity like baseball caused him to cough and wheeze, which led to a diagnosis of asthma and the realization that his ball-playing days were over—a has-been at the age of eight! But he learned he had a talent for writing when his father returned from the Great War and Win wrote an essay for school that he called "Why I Am So Proud Of My Father." His teacher, Mr. Spooner, was impressed enough to submit it to the local newspaper, *The Rogersville Review*, and they not only printed it, they gave Win 50 cents for his efforts, and told him to "feel free to submit anything else you write, young man." Just a few weeks shy of officially becoming a teenager, Win Appleton realized what he'd be doing for the rest of his life.

After Nashota agreed to marry Jack, the Simpsons and Appletons frequently got together, primarily in the fall or winter, when Jack wasn't in uniform. Nashota had even given cooking lessons to the oldest girl, Eugenia, when her mother, Talitha, had needed some minor surgery in 1949. (Eugenia had proved to be such an apt pupil that she remained the family's primary chef, and was hoping to make this her career.) A dinner in a private, quiet setting struck Jack as the best place to let Win in on their major news.

Talk was small throughout dinner. Eugenia had been dating someone for a brief while but that now seemed to have run its course, "kind of like a virus," she said, with a little chuckle. She really did not seem all that upset, and Nashota assured her that the right person was out there, somewhere, and she'll meet him sooner or later. The twins soon got bored and asked to be excused so they could listen to *Louisiana Hayride,* and though Win frowned, Talitha gave them permission "as long as you don't make the radio too loud."

Jack decided the time was right.

"Say, Win, 'Sho and I are going to be doing something, with the ballclub I mean, and we were wondering…um, we were hoping that, uh, maybe you, uh, maybe you could help us a bit."

"Sure, Jack, I'm always happy to assist the Wolves whatever way I can. Need me to pitch?" Win laughed. "I'm well rested, haven't thrown a ball since the twins were five or six, maybe seven, so I'm VERY well rested. And just 'cause I'll be 46 in March doesn't mean anything, Satchel Paige is still chuckin' for the Brownies, and he's only a few months younger-n me. At least, that's what he admits to!" And he laughed again.

"You know, a team can never have enough pitching," Jack said with a smile. "If I think we're a little thin when we come back from Florida, we'll give you a uni.," to which Appleton quickly replied "It'll have to be a pretty big one to cover this body!" Everyone found that to be hilarious.

Jack, still with a smile on his face, leaned forward in his chair. "No, this is something else. We have…" he looked at Nashota for encouragement and she gave him a little smile and a nod. "We have signed a young man to play center for us this year, and I think he's gonna be terrific. Over time, you understand. He's kinda raw, been playing in an industrial league for a coupla years, ever since he got outta high school down in North Carolina." Jack could certainly ramble on if he was nervous. "But he's real fast, can steal bases and he'll play centerfield like crazy, we haven't ever seen anyone this good defensively in this town." Jack stopped to take a breath. Win was looking at him, not sure where this was going, so Jack plunged ahead.

"Thing is, Win, he's got all this ability, and he's a nice kid…"

"Real nice kid," said Nashota.

"But there are…." He hesitated, looking for the right words. "…some people who…er, some people will object, um, may object, may object, to our playing a…a…a colored boy in our outfield. Or…um…or maybe…um…anywhere on the field."

"A colored boy? You signed…to play…he's gonna play here in Edens Ridge?" Win practically catapulted himself out of his chair.

"Negro," said Nashota and Eugenia, almost in unison, with the eldest Appleton child continuing the thought. "Colored is so demeaning, Dad, almost like they're still slaves, and they're not, you know, it's been almost ninety years…"

"I don't need a history lesson from you, young lady," said Win. "We've always said 'colored,' there's never been a problem with that term…"

"It's not very popular these days, Win," said Nashota, quietly. "They much prefer 'Negro.'"

There was a brief but heavy silence, and finally Win said, "All right, Negro. The fact is that this league has never had any players who weren't white…"

"Windy Haines had that big outfielder, Villareal, two years ago, no, been three years now, he could hit the pi…'scuse me, ladies, I mean to say, he could really hit the baseball." Eugenia giggled, Talitha smiled weakly while Nashota just rolled her eyes at her husband. "And Jerry Hoffman signed that shortstop, Garcia, year before last, real slick fielder…"

"Over the hill, both-a them, not major league prospects, and besides, they weren't Negroes." Win said the word slowly and with special emphasis. "They were all from Cuba, big difference."

"All right, please explain that to me," said Nashota. "I remember those young men and I remember them being just as dark, as…as…as black as our Oddibe, yet there was hardly any fuss raised at all. I remember some catcalls from the stands, but nothing serious, nothing like what Jackie Robinson went through."

"Who's Oddibe?" asked Win, and Nashota quickly replied. "Oh, sorry, we haven't told you his name. Oddibe Daniels, that's the young man we've signed. First name is spelled O-D-D-I-B-E. Daniels is just like you'd expect."

"I'm pretty sure there were some objections," said Win, who really wasn't sure at all. "But look, they were from another country, that's what made it different, see? They weren't Americans…"

"So, wait, wait, this game, this AMERICAN game, this game that's been known for years as AMERICA'S NATIONAL PASTIME, isn't that right, Jack?" Ewald John Simpson simply nodded and kept his mouth shut, he knew better than to get in the way when the Nashota Express was building up a full head of steam. "This…America's National Pastime doesn't object, much, when some darker-skinned ballplayers come over here from Cuba, but if a young man from North Carolina wants to try and make his living playing baseball, people raise a holy stink? That makes no sense!" Nashota stood up and began pacing around the room. "Why in…of course, I shouldn't be surprised, if anyone should know better it's me, right? I'm the one whose ancestors got force-marched halfway across the country, white men, white EUROPEAN men, oppressing the true Americans, people born here, right here. Lived on this land for centuries, CENTURIES, long before the Europeans came over and began calling it America…"

"OK, let's calm down, 'Sho, we're veering off our path here." Jack felt it was time to step in before she said something she could not take back. "We're just talking about baseball, just a little game of baseball."

"She makes a good point," said Eugenia, who had never heard this kind of conversation before and was totally fascinated by it. But before she could say anything else, her mother jumped in.

"Win, Jack, perhaps the two of you should discuss this in private, in the den, while we…"

"I'd like to stay and listen, Mom, I think this is so interesting, and important."

No one moved, no one said a word. Nashota was trying to compose herself but was still breathing a little heavily.

"She can stay, Tal," said Win, softly, but Talitha, her cheeks flushed, stood up.

"If it's all the same to you, I think I'd rather be in the kitchen. Would anyone like anything?" she asked, her voice cracking. Without waiting for a response, she simply walked out of the room.

Jack tried to get back on point. "Win, let me tell you why we're bringing this up," but Win Appleton's mind was now elsewhere.

"Jack, let me see to my wife. You know how…how delicate she can be, especially when it comes to current events, she has trouble sometimes…" There was a catch to his voice as he trailed off. Looking at the floor, he quietly said "Maybe we should finish this another time. How 'bout I meet you at the ballpark on Monday, late in the day?"

It actually wound up being Tuesday. Nashota, returning to the ballpark with a signed contract and some encouraging words to relay to Jack, immediately recognized Win Appleton's car in the parking lot. They were not in the office so she wandered about looking for them, and found them sitting in the grandstand, drinking from a bottle Win had brought to help insulate against the cold. And it was cold, barely above freezing, typical for late January in the mountains. She shook her head and muttered to herself *"Nu-da Yu-ne-gas,"* and she went back to the office, took care of her paperwork and left them alone.

A short while later the door opened and they came in, both a bit unsteady. Win touched the brim of his hat and simply said "Nashota," and just as simply she said "Win," trying to suppress a smile. Jack wrote something on a piece of paper and gave it to Win, who nodded, smiled at her and left. Her husband sat down, looked at the floor, then at her and said, "Win's on board."

"That's good. I have some good news, too, some great news, in fact…"

He cut her off. "I wanna hear it," he said, and she could now hear that his tongue was a little thick. "I wanna hear it, I really do, but I think I need some coffee first." He stood up, then sat down again. "I also think it might be best if we went home now. You drive. Prob'ly safe to leave the Meadowbrook here overnight, doncha think?"

She chuckled. "Yes, it'll be fine. Let's go on home." She shook her head and laughed more robustly and said to herself, *"Nu-da Yu-ne-ga."*

A minor league baseball team can have a brief but significant impact on a town's economy. "Brief" because their season is short, from April into September. "Significant" because they are essentially throwing a party every time they open their door, with anywhere from several hundred to a few thousand guests attending. That means an awful lot of food and drink must be on hand, as well as enticing souvenirs. During the spring and summer, a minor league team is, perhaps, a town's most active merchant, purchasing supplies and employing a small army of local people who perform a wide variety of tasks.

Which is why, given the opportunity, many Edens Ridge businesses jumped at the chance to affiliate with the Wolves. Where Gray Gamadge, Buddy Martin and the like only saw black and white, Royal Privette, Tony Shale and others saw green.

Nashota had absolutely no trouble selling the "Royal Family" idea to Privette, who opted for an ad on the roster insert and made her a promise. "If this promotion brings in a significant amount of new business, I'll give strong consideration to buyin' one-a those fence signs for 1953." And Cattrenia Barraclough was so thrilled to be listed as the "Official Photographer of the Wolves" that she actually shed a couple of tears when she signed her contract for a quarter-page ad (to be paid out over four months). Oh, and neither had any problem with the addition of Oddibe Daniels to the roster.

It took some rummaging around, but Nashota found the business card the new printer had given them some months before, so she went to see him. Good idea, bad result—the business was already shuttered, with a large FOR SALE OR LEASE sign in the window. That certainly put a damper on the day, but then she had an idea when she walked into The Back Porch for lunch.

"LaDonna, your menus look great, who prints them for you?"

"You like them, 'Sho? I helped to design them myself, I like a lot of color, you know that, and they did a good job, I think, making them colorful but tasteful." That made LaDonna Holmes laugh, and since she was a big girl with a big laugh, it always made everyone around her smile, at the very least, when she let go with one of her frequent belly-laughs. "Tasteful, maybe I could make 'em tasty, too, huh? That would be somethin', edible menus, what a scream!"

Nashota was used to her friend's fits of silliness, so she waited a moment 'til she calmed down, then said "You'd probably go broke replacing all those half-eaten menus, LD. But I'm interested in the printer, who do you go to?"

"Oh, yeah, sorry, I got sidetracked. Ron Bruce is his name, he's just around the corner on Second Street, you go in there and tell him I sent you. In fact, tell him I said that if he wants to keep…" She stopped here for a moment, giving some thought to the rest of her sentence. "…THINGS as they are, he'll work with you and join the Pack." And she smiled and then giggled and had to work hard to stifle another gut-busting laugh.

Nashota didn't need to resort to veiled blackmail, just mentioning that she and LaDonna were friends and that The Back Porch was a major team sponsor was enough for Ron Bruce. That and the economics, of course.

"How many people come on out to the ballpark every year?" he wanted to know.

"Last year we drew 88,000, best in the league. Our goal is to hit 100,000 someday…"

"And how many programs did you sell?"

"I'm glad you asked that, because every year that's a pet project of mine," she said proudly. "We sold about 7,300 programs, which breaks down to one for every twelve people who walk into the ballpark…"

"That's not all that much, I would think you could do better," he said.

"Don't forget, Mr. Bruce, we sell quite a few season tickets, plus our book tickets, which lets people come to ten games. If they buy a program the first time they come to see us, they don't really need another one unless they want a roster insert."

"Exactly," said Ron Bruce. "You need an incentive to get them to buy more often, and I've got just the thing. 'Scuse me, Mrs. Simpson, for just a minute." He dashed off to the back of his shop and returned a moment later with what looked like a newspaper.

"Do you print the *Gazette* here," Nashota asked.

'Naw, they do that themselves. But one day I got to wonderin', so I asked around and found that printin' a newspaper is a whole lot cheaper than printin' the kind-a program you been usin'. Look, with a newspaper format, you can change it 'bout as often as you like. Every month, every week, every day, no matter, and it ain't gonna cost you as much as puttin' out somethin' in book form, like you got here. Now, addin' color will make the price go up a fair amount so you may want to just go with black-and-white, or maybe only put color on the front page, like the *Gazette* does on the Fourth of July. Still, it'll cost you a whole lot less, and I guarantee you'll sell a bunch more than 7,300. I'm willing to bet you double your sales."

Of course, Nashota said she'd have to talk it over with Jack, but she also said she, personally, was excited to give this a try. For his part, Ron Bruce said that if they allowed him to print their program, as well as the roster insert, he'd be happy to buy a fence sign, a half-page program ad, an ad on the insert sheet, and probably three or four of those books of tickets.

Jack was more than a little skeptical, but Nashota was prepared for that. She and Mr. Bruce had done some figuring before she left, and she showed Jack how much cheaper it would be, on a per-unit basis, to print their program in newspaper format.

"The really nice thing, Jack, the best part, is not having such a heavy expense up front. We print just so-many programs for the opening homestand and pay for them, and then we can do the same for the next homestand, and the next, see? And we can make changes, write new articles, put in new photos. The program will be fresh all the time, people will want to buy it…"

"Yeah, but it's a newspaper, 'Sho, will people want to be reading a newspaper at the ballpark? And will they be able to keep score in a newspaper?"

"Of course, silly," she said. "You always see people sitting in Rorke Park, next to the library, on a nice day reading the paper, it'll be the same thing at our ballpark. And if people can do the crossword puzzle in the *Gazette,* they can keep score, too." In the end that argument seemed to work, so Jack agreed to give it a try, at least for the 1952 season, which automatically increased their pre-season sales, since Jim Morris had never bought any tickets.

Jack, meanwhile, had found Tony Shale more than eager to stock the Wolves' concession stand. "Don Harrell has always told me you're a right-good fella," Shale said when they met. "And I believe ol' Don, I been knowin' him for years, we went to school together. I'd be proud to work with you, Mr. Simpson, and I'll do ya a right-good job, too."

"It won't be a problem, hauling things to us from here in Kruse?" Jack asked.

Shale laughed. "Bought me a coupla new trucks last year, top-a the line, they get 'leven or so miles to the gallon. Don't know if it's even two gallons from me to you and back, ain't nothin' 'tall. And if ya need somethin' in a hurry, we can be to ya in a half-hour, don't you worry none."

And when Jack brought up about Oddibe, he was surprised by Tony Shale's response.

"This ain't somethin' I tell many people since, ya know, lotsa folk here are…oh, funny 'bout some things, so please keep it under yer hat, OK? I thought my oldest boy would go into the business with me but he weren't much interested, he likes to sing and dance, so he went on up to Noo Yawk afta he grad-ee-ated high school. Gotta admit, he makes a good living, he's in this new version of "Pal Joey" right now, me and the missus went up there month or so ago to see it and she wants to go again. Anyway, he married this gal coupla years back, she also sings and dances, and she's, um, pretty dark, if you know what I mean." Shale smiled. "Tell ya the truth, she's a real nice girl, Evangeline's her name, Vangy he calls her, he thinks she walks on water. Livin' in Noo Yawk, they're OK, still got some problems once-n-awhile, he says, but nuthin' like if they lived down here. They nervous 'bout visitin', and we wonder what'll happen when they have kids, we'd hafta go up there…" He stopped, lost in thought somewhere, then came back to Jack. "Maybe your boy, your Negro player, maybe he'll get people to, uh, help 'em see things a little different, and they won't mind so much if Vangy come to see her in-laws."

"Mr. Shale…"

"Tony, Jack, you call me Tony, we partners now."

"Tony, you may be asking a lot of us, we're just a Class D minor league team."

Shale laughed. "I know. Man can dream, eh? Now lookit, let's talk turkey." And he signed on for a Grand Slam—fence sign, half-page ad, tickets and a promotional night, the popular Christmas in July ("I'll supply the candy and some other treats, you supply the Santa and the snow!" Shale said with a big, hearty laugh).

Harry Brown was quite surprised when Jack told him the team was shopping for a new insurance agent. "You been with Tom Edwards from the beginning, ain't he kin to Bill Washington?"

"He is," said Jack, "a cousin to Rhetta, if I remember right. But they're both gone now, so I don't feel that I have to stay with him. Truth is, Harry, I've had no quarrel with Tom or our policies or our rates, but the reason I'm looking to leave is…"

"This boy you're bringin' on the team, right?" Jack nodded. "Heard 'bout it a few days ago. Word's gettin' out, Jack, people are talkin', they was lotsa chattin' goin' on 'fore the Chamber breakfast on Tuesday."

Jack was surprised, and also curious. "Well, what were people saying?"

"Different things. Everybody got their own 'pinion, you know, some for it, some agin it, some just don't know. That's me, I ain't real sure how I think 'bout it, if I'm bein' honest with you. I kinda think you may be doin' the right thing, but I wonder if this is the right time, if we maybe oughta be waitin' a bit. I also wonder if this is the right place, the right town I mean, maybe Beck would be a better place for the league's first Negro, or one of them towns in Caroline. Ha, 'speshully Buchanan, I know ol'

Lionel is always itchin' to thumb his nose at people, tell 'em to go, well, you know, you worked close with him so I don't have to tell you."

Jack cleared his throat. "Harry, I have to have insurance on the ballpark, and get that separate dram policy to sell beer. Tom's told me he won't do business with me, so I'm coming to you, you're my first choice. Will you work with me, or do I have to look elsewhere?"

Harry Brown didn't answer right away. He shifted in his seat, then picked up a paper clip and began playing with it. Finally he spoke.

"I'd sure like the business. What's it gonna cost me?"

Jack wasn't sure if his question was more rhetorical than practical, but he opted to stay on the business road. "Tom Edwards used to buy a fence sign, but he dropped that two or three years ago in favor of an ad and a couple of seats. I'll be happy if you wanted to do the same thing."

Brown continued to bounce the paper clip against his desk. "I wouldn't mind one of them signs, but I ain't sure I can afford it. Can you give me any kinda deal?"

Now it was Jack's turn to ruminate. He knew that Harry liked to come to ballgames, maybe he could do something there. "We make it a policy to not discount our fence signs, that's the best advertising we offer, but..." The wheels were turning hard and fast. "Tell you what, Harry, if you buy a sign and one box seat, I'll give you a second seat, no extra charge. What do you think? And Nashota and I are planning to move all our personal insurance, too, car, house, life, it ain't much, I know, but we'll give you that business as well."

The paper clip stopped bouncing against the desk. "Be happy to have you and your lovely wife as our customers, Jack. Proud and happy. What if I bought the sign and two seats, could you give me two more?"

Jack was always willing to make some sort of arrangements involving seats, figuring that whoever occupied them would wind up buying food and drink. He smiled, said "deal," and stuck out his hand, and when Harry Brown grasped it, Jack got a little lump in his throat while mentally crossing another business off his list.

The fact that Edens Ridge had a team at all was because of Bill Washington. There had never been anything more than high school baseball in town, but Washington, who managed one of Eastman's facilities, had a vision, which became a dynamic presentation, which swayed Wells Boggs. Washington then lobbied hard with the town's leadership until they appropriated enough money to get the dilapidated old high school field to meet basic minor league specifications. Finally, Washington got the Board of Mayor and Aldermen to allow the Wolves to sell beer at the newly-renamed Bill Washington Park, though some people had expressed opposition.

"If you're opposed to beer," Washington found himself saying over and over, "then don't buy a beer. Just enjoy the game. Have fun watching the kids in the stands enjoying the game. Having fun is what it's all about, not beer." To Board members, Washington stressed the dollars. "We have estimated how much money will come into our town if we have minor league baseball. Hotels, restaurants, people will be coming into town and spending money. We can't afford to give that up. But if we can't sell beer, we won't succeed, and we'll lose our franchise. Hell, I'm not sure I'd even stick with this project if you turn down my beer request. Got someone else ready to run this thing?" By a strong 4–1 margin, the BMA gave the Wolves permission to sell beer, and Bill Washington soon signed an exclusive contract with Biggerstaff Distributing. But now that was up for grabs, and two men were reaching out.

Paul Martino was a big, burly guy whose booming voice and New Jersey accent stood out like a sore thumb in Northeast Tennessee. Wounded severely enough at the Bulge to warrant a discharge, he was able to come home and get an early start on a job search, and landed with Miller Beer. After completing his apprenticeship, he was assigned to first one, then another cold and snowy town, so when he was given the chance to breathe life into a stagnant distributorship in Appalachia, he grabbed it with both hands, as much for the weather as for the business opportunity. In his first year in Edens Ridge he would sometimes privately make fun of the "yahoos" and their "funny accents," unaware of how he sounded to them. In his second year he met Ella Hord and the teasing stopped, and by 1950, when their first child was born, he was finally able to convince his mother to leave Long Branch and learn to love barbecue. (Added bonus—Lisa DeMaestri had moved down from South Philly the year before and made a cannoli that Ma Martino herself labeled as *"molto buono."*)

Now Jeff Toussaint, he came from a totally different part of the country — Lafayette, Louisiana, where his family had been selling alcohol for years, even during Prohibition. "It's easier now that it's legal," his father had once told the young Jeffery, "but before the repeal it was probably more fun because it was so much more of a challenge!"

When a massive heart attack took his father unexpectedly at age 59, the business went to Jeff's older brother, Malcolm, and the two discovered they had different ideas about how things should be run. Jeff found himself complaining to his mother, who finally decided she'd had enough.

"Jeffery," she said, "I love you very much, but I love your brother, too. He is now in charge, and you need to accept that. If you cannot, then it might be best if you found a new place to live."

"Are you saying you want me to leave Lafayette, *maman?*" he asked incredulously.

"I don't want you to leave, *mon coeur,* but it might be the best way to keep you and your brother from trying to kill each other."

The war in Europe took care of the problem. Like Jack Simpson, Jeff thought that this was no time for neutrality, that right-thinking people needed to get involved in this obvious battle of Good versus Evil. So Toussaint headed north, to Canada, to become a gun jumper, doing what some 9,000 other Americans (including Jack Simpson) did prior to Pearl Harbor. In Europe he met a fellow named Royal Privette from some place in Tennessee he had never heard of, though Royal made it sound like a small slice of heaven.

"No, we won't be accepted there, Jeff, are you nuts? Lotta people in town still fuss 'bout the Confederates losing the War of Northern Aggression."

"Then we need to go to some place like New York, or California, or maybe Toronto, I liked Toronto when I was there, didn't you? A big city where people won't look down on us, beat us, call us…that…those horrible words."

After a quiet moment, Royal said "I'm a small-town guy, Jeff, I don't think I can live in one-a those places. I'd just as soon go home, and if you don't want to join me, I understand."

"Well, we gotta come outta this alive first," said Toussaint, and they both smiled and nodded.

Royal was seriously wounded at Juno Beach on D-Day, and a doctor told Jeff that his friend's chances were "Touch and go, soldier, touch and go." He then left to look after other wounded dog faces, and when he was out of earshot, Jeff grabbed Royal's hand and whispered "Tell you what, *mon cher*, I'll make you a deal, we like to make deals down in Louisiana, you know. You pull through and I'll come live in that little town-a yours, all right? Do we have an agreement?" Royal was no doubt in some other dimension and didn't say a thing, but he survived the night, and the next, and many more, and was eventually shipped home. The next year, true to his word, Jeff Toussaint found his way to Northeast Tennessee.

Edens Ridge, of course, proved to be nothing like Lafayette, or any place he had ever been, since none were quite this small. At least he and Royal were together, almost literally. They had discussed sharing a place and decided that would arouse too much suspicion, so they hatched a plan and had the patience to make it work. Jeff bought a small house in an older neighborhood and then, when the house next door became available some months later, Royal snapped it up, so they could go back and forth relatively easily. And when one of the town's small beer distributorships went bankrupt trying to compete with Biggerstaff, Jeff bought it and brought in Pabst Blue Ribbon, then Falstaff Beer, and finally Hamm's and made a go of it.

Both Martino and Toussaint were thrilled when Jack came to see them; they had both been wanting to have their product in Bill Washington Park but had been blocked by Biggerstaff's exclusive deal. Now they both went after it with gusto, offering to buy grand slam packages and, in the case of Jeff Toussaint, even more. "I'll take two fence signs, Jack," he said, without blinking an eye. "Promote PBR on one and Falstaff on the other, and make my program ad be for Hamm's, or maybe switch Hamm's and PBR, I dunno, I'll have to think 'bout it. But that's the kind-a thing I'm willin' to do if you make me your exclusive beer vendor, my friend."

No deal. Jack had decided he wanted to do business with both men, and was willing to take less from each in order to offer more variety to his fans. There was, of course, the possibility of a deal breaker, and Jack made sure to bring it up early in his conversations.

"Before you get too excited, let me tell you about one of our new players. He's gonna be our new centerfielder, and…"

"Jack, I don't give a good goddam about who's out there on the field for you, those kids won't be drinking my beer." Subtle was not Paul Martino's middle name.

"You need to know about this player, Paul. His name is Oddibe Daniels and he's a Negro. We plan on making him the first Negro in the Mountain Empire League."

Jack paused to get a reaction. Martino didn't say anything for a few seconds, then "So?"

"Well, Paul, some people are telling me they object, and there might be some trouble..."

"Fuck 'em," Martino said emphatically. "I'm tired of this racial shit." He stood up and started walking around his office. "Don't get me wrong, I love living down here, happy to raise my kids here rather than Jersey, but sometimes this black-and-white crap drives me nuts. I'm Catholic, you know, I go to church on Sundays, I read the same Bible as everyone else. I sure don't remember Jesus sayin' anything about putting your knee on someone's neck. But some people, some of 'em my neighbors, they seem to go outta their way..."

"Paul, let's not get worked up, OK?" Martino was a big fellow and Jack was afraid he might have a heart attack, or some sort of fit at the rate he was going. "We're talking beer here, not politics or religion, and you've answered my question, it don't matter to you..."

"Hell no!" Martino's voice was generally the loudest in the room, but this phrase may have broken decibel records. "And listen, when I'm out at the ballpark this summer, if someone starts spoutin' that kind-a shit near me, I'll deal with him personally, Jersey style!"

Jeff Toussaint was much more soft-spoken but no less emphatic. "Good for you, Jack Simpson, good for you. Too many people get discriminated against, believe me, I've seen it first-hand..." He paused, then continued. "I oppose it completely and totally, and applaud you for taking a stand. I am with you one hundred percent. Now where do I sign?"

In the end Jack convinced both men that they could do well even if the other was also selling his product to Wolves fans. Toussaint only took one sign, as well as a program ad and a promotional night, while Martino opted for a sign and four box seats and a night. And Jack was pleased to know that these two combat vets would be in the foxhole with him.

The day Jack had been turned down by Cole Katt had been a rough one, so he popped over to see Elnora Vines, who always made him smile. At one time she had been the Wolves' office manager/secretary, but the position was really part-time, from late March through September. She would then have to find a new job, generally at Adams, the grocery store, which she really disliked. After the 1950 baseball season, she sat Jack down and said "Someone done gave me this ideal," using the Northeast Tennesssee colloquialism for the word "idea." "They said there was lotsa people like you, didn't need a secretary full-time, but could use someone to simply answer the phones and take messages. That got me to thinkin' and wonderin', so since July I been talkin' to folks, seein' if I could maybe line up enough people, clients..." Being able to use that word made her beam. "Get me enough clients to make a go of it, you know? And I think I'm off to a good start, Jack. I got six for sure, got a seventh who I think will throw in with me, and a coupla others are thinkin' it over." She paused, which allowed Simpson to ask a question.

"So are you thinking of this just for the fall and winter, or all year long?"

She gave him a wistful smile. "Full time, Jack, twelve months a year. Can't hardly expect someone to give me a commitment if I don't give it right back to 'em, know what I mean? I think…I'm gonna be 57 in December, Jack. Been workin' for someone, somewhere, my whole life. Doin' this, I'd kinda be my own boss, and I'll be doin' somethin' I know how to do. I figure if I'm gonna step out on my own, now's a pretty good time, doncha think?" He didn't say anything, so she continued.

"Got my eye on a little place downtown, right in the middle of everythin', near the bank and Harry Brown's and Phil Ross, the jeweler, pretty good location. Southern Bell will rent me as many lines as I need, put a different number on each so I know how to answer, you know, make it sound all professional-like. Only other thing I need is plenty-a paper and pencils." She looked down at the floor, then back up to Jack. "Guess what I'm saying is that my next paycheck from you will be my last. I know you won't be needin' me 'til spring but, with any luck, this new business will have taken off by then and, uh, you'll, uh, need to find a new in-season secretary."

She stopped and waited for him to say something. And waited. To Elnora, it seemed like forever before he broke the silence.

"I know something else you need," he finally said, and when she asked "What?" he smiled for the first time and said "Another client. This sounds perfect for us, for the Wolves, for the off-season, sign us up."

So on this afternoon, he sat for a while with Elnora at her 15-month-old business, pouring out his tale of the day's woes, occasionally interrupted as she answered different calls. She wasn't impressed.

"I remember you've had other days like this in other years, and things always got better, didn't they? Bad days seem to lead to better days. Maybe this'll help," she said, handing him a slip of paper. "This gal called earlier and left a message, sounds like it could have some potential. You can use the call room."

One thing Elnora had learned when she had started the business was that most of her clients wanted to return those calls pretty quickly. Even though it was not in her original budget, she decided to spend a little more money and put in a new wall, creating a new room. She then put in three small desks, each with a phone, a pen and a pad of paper. A client was free to use one of the phones, which is exactly what Jack did.

"Holston Hotel, how may I help you?" The female voice sounded bright, cheerful and young.

"I'm looking for…" he glanced at the paper Elnora had given to him. "Miss Phoebe Moon. This is Jack Simpson of the Edens Ridge Wolves baseball team, returning her call."

"This is Phoebe Moon!" she said. "Thank you so much, Mr. Simpson, for getting back to me. I'm the assistant manager of the Holston Hotel here in Kingsport, and I was wondering if there was some way we could work with you this season. To be honest, sir, a little birdie told me that visiting teams won't be staying at The Curtis Motor Lodge any more, and I wanted to invite you to come over here and look at our place. We have done some major remodeling that we're real proud of, and think we would be a very good locale for the Mountain Empire League."

Jack always tried to be prompt, so shortly before 10 am the next day, he was staring into the large, expressive eyes of Miss Phoebe Moon. She was tall and very attractive, with a shock of curly black hair, and an engaging smile. Jack's first thought was *shit, all my players are going to be chasing after her.* They shook hands and she said "Welcome to the new and improved Holston Hotel. Can I get you anything?" with a big smile.

Get your mind out of the gutter, mullion, he thought, *you may not be old enough to be her father but it'd be close, and you've got a baby on the way...*

"No thanks, I'm fine."

"Well, if you need anything, you just ask, OK?" *Oh, brother!* "Let me show you around."

This lobby, she told him, had just undergone a renovation, its first new look since before the war. She then took him into the dining room, which was clean and neat and being readied by the staff for the expected lunch crowd. "We know that ballplayers keep, um, somewhat unusual hours. We're prepared to work with them, make sure they're fed, even if they want breakfast at, oh, 10:30 in the morning, or lunch at, maybe four o'clock."

"That breakfast time may be about right, but an afternoon meal is more likely to be somewhere between two and three or so. How late does the kitchen stay open?"

"At night, you mean? Generally we're all finished around nine, which I know is not good for the players. We wanted to ask you about that, actually—how important is it for us to be able to provide them a meal after a game?" she asked.

Jack scratched his head. "I can tell you that no hotel in the league does that. When we go on the road, we generally play the game, find some greasy spoon for hamburgers, then head back to the hotel. If you were to stay open you'd automatically become the players' favorite place in the league, but I'm not sure if it would be very profitable for you, know what I mean? Plus, you'd have to make sure each player paid, the ballclubs don't pick up those tabs. Could prove to be more trouble than it is worth.

Her brain was hard at work. "Perhaps...oh, we could, maybe, put out some cold cuts and bread and mustard and chips," she said brightly. "Everyone could just get off the bus, come in and make a sandwich or two, and sit and eat in the dining room or take it up to their rooms, whatever they'd like. We could staff it with one person who'd be there to help out, answer questions, and collect money, maybe a dollar per sandwich? How does that sound, Mr. Simpson?" And Jack had to admit it seemed like an idea that might work.

The sleeping rooms were like the dining area, clean and neat. Not that the players would care, but the walls were all painted a muted blue, which contrasted with the brown dressers. The rooms with two beds were plenty large enough for two athletes, while the single rooms seemed to Jack to be exceptionally spacious.

"Am I right, Mr. Simpson, to think that each team will be needing about a dozen rooms?"

"Yeah, give or take. We can carry up to nineteen players, though occasionally we might have less, plus there's the manager and the bus driver, who's also the coach. And nowadays some teams have a radio guy. The players all double up, so that's nine rooms, one player shares with either the bussie or the blabbermouth, the odd man out gets his own room, as does the manager, so yeah, that's twelve."

"We're prepared," said Miss Moon, looking very serious, "to comp the manager's room."

"That's good, teams will certainly appreciate it. They started doing that in both Buchanan and Weare last year and the rest of us said we'd see what we could do in our towns. Of course, I knew Dick Curtis would never go along, that man can squeeze a nickel..."

Phoebe giggled. "My father doesn't have a lot of nice things to say about Mr. Curtis, either." She noticed she was receiving a blank look from Jack. "My family owns the Holston Hotel. Technically my father is the manager and I'm the assistant manager, but I pretty much handle day-to-day operations." She gave him a thin smile. "Of course, if you'd feel more comfortable talking to Dad, I can..."

"No, no, not at all," Jack said quickly. "I'm happy working with you, you're doing a fine job."

She smiled, obviously pleased with the compliment. Jack thought it would be a perfect time to discuss business.

"Dick Curtis has been purchasing a fence sign and four box seats from us. If we move the other teams in the league over to you, we would need at least that much, perhaps a bit more..."

She smiled again. "Mr. Simpson, I'm happy to work out terms with you, but remember, we're having this conversation because that little birdie..."

"Little birdie's got a big mouth," said Jack, which made her laugh out loud.

"Now Mr. Simpson, you wouldn't be trying to take advantage of me just because I'm a girl, would you? I'm sure you're better than that." If they had been playing chess, she would have been able to say "check" at this point, so he just kept his mouth shut.

"We'll take the sign and the seats and we might like to do something to promote our restaurant, maybe run an ad on the score page, what do you think? We'll also offer the comp room and the late-night cold cuts, and give the teams a competitive rate. Do you need anything else?"

There she goes again, he thought. *I wonder if she does this deliberately, or if it's all very genuine, or maybe she's just a little naïve?*

This was a good time to bring up Oddibe. "Yes, ma'am. Before we go any further, there's something you need to know." He explained everything to her, including the fact that none of the other teams in the league—the ones who would be staying at the Holston—would be bringing in any Negro players. He also felt it necessary to say that "Odds are, Oddibe wouldn't ever have any reason to come over here..."

"Mr. Simpson!" Her smile was gone. "The last thing that my family and I care about, the VERY LAST THING, is the color of anyone's skin." She paused for a breath before continuing.

"I realize you don't know me, so I guess I can forgive you this time." She gave him another smile, but much weaker. "My father is part Cherokee, my mother is a mix of several cultures, including Cuban. I consider myself a real Heinz 57." She giggled, then continued. "If the Harlem Globetrotters came to this area, we'd be proud to have them all stay with us." She looked down, and then said, quietly, "Truthfully, I can't believe that your league has never had a Negro player before. Not ever?" Jack shook his head, and so did she. Then Phoebe Moon smiled, a little more broadly. "The Holston Hotel will be proud to work with you, sir, very proud. Now, Mr. Simpson, is there anything else?"

Jack let out an audible sigh, then smiled. "Let's go to your office," he said, "and I can draw up one of our contracts, and I imagine you'll have something for me to sign." And now she gave him one of those huge smiles. She nodded, and even held the door for him as they headed back towards the lobby.

That evening Jack and Nashota Simpson made love like they were newlyweds.

FIVE

Vernell Gibson was always happy when Nashota dropped in and she, in turn, enjoyed spending time with him, though he did like to talk, about anything and everything. He owned The Specialty Shop, and he boasted that he could get all sorts of novelty items for your business, no matter what your business was, and he could get it "at a price that will make you smile." The Wolves would convince a local entrepreneur to sponsor a promotional night out at the ballpark and give away pens or keychains or kazoos, and they would buy these items from Gibby, who would make sure the sponsor's name was very prominently displayed. In return the big man—he was about six feet tall but had to weigh at least 350 pounds ("I haven't been able to look down and see my feet in years" was one of his favorite lines)—proved to be a great friend of the ballclub. He bought a quarter-page ad and eight box seats, which he often gave away to good clients. Boy Scouts, people from his church, anyone he knew that was going through a rough patch, he would give them some tickets. "Have a good time," he would say. "You deserve the kind of enjoyment that only a night at the ballpark can provide." And of course, he was also a loyal member of the Wolves Pack; in fact, he sat on their Executive Board.

"Have you talked to any of the church leaders?" he asked Nashota in his booming voice. And when she said "no, not yet," he said "Let me take you in to see Father Feeney. Do you know him?" She shook her head. "Thought not, I'll introduce you, been a member of his parish for years, longer than I can count. Let me call him right now, when would you like to go see him?" Before she could respond, he grabbed his phone and dialed the priest's number from memory.

"Connor? Vernell. How are ya, you old mackerel snapper? You gonna put us to sleep again on Sunday?" Nashota was rather taken aback by his tone; he was, after all, talking to a priest! (And mackerel snapper, that was a new one for her.) Gibby saw the look on her face and just grinned, then he laughed at something Father Feeney was saying.

"Yeah, well you certainly have no room to talk. You keep hittin' the suds, you'll be matching me pound for pound in no time." He paused while Feeney had another comeback, then let out a huge laugh that almost shook the room.

"That was a good one, Connor, I'll have to remember that for Friday's Kiwanis meeting. But listen, I had a real reason for calling, besides just shootin' the shit with the likes-a you. Do you know Nashota Simpson, wife of the Wolves' boss?" A pause, then "The Wolves, Edens Ridge Wolves, the baseball team. You dumb mick, we been out there a hundred times over the past few years, were you blasted or hung over every time?" Another pause, then another laugh. "All right, all right. Anyway, Nashota handles the team's business affairs, and she has something she wants to talk to you about. I thought I'd bring her over and introduce you, when are you free?" He gave her a smile while he listened, then got all serious again. "Now did I say today? I asked when you're free...yes, we can make an appointment, whatever will work for you, am I right about that?" This last was directed right to Nashota, who nodded. "She said yes. Tomorrow at 10? Let me check." He looked at her and she smiled and nodded again. "Yes, that will be fine, I'll bring her over." Pause. "Yes, I have to be there, I'm making the introduction, remember? Besides, if you're drunk, I'll need to pour coffee down your throat so you'll be able to carry on a reasonable conversation with this woman. Got that?" And after another brief pause he roared once more, almost rattling the walls. "All right, save it for another day. We'll see you tomorrow morning. Try not to get in any trouble before then, OK? Bye, Connor." And with that he hung up, looked at Nashota and said, "You be here tomorrow by 9:30, I'll drive us over."

Father Connor Feeney had been very pleasant when Gibby had introduced him to Nashota, and he listened to everything that was said, quietly nodding and saying "Uh huh" several times. But he never came out and said he was in full support of what the team was planning to do. In fact, he was pretty noncommittal.

"Our Church, of course, always welcomes any and all who come and worship," he said. She noticed that his hands never remained quiet. "We are all God's children." He stopped and seemed to be trying to find more to say, then just looked at them rather blankly. Gibby jumped all over him.

"Is that all you've got? Bunch of platitudes? Hell, I can get that much wisdom reading the *Edens Ridge Gazette,* and that rag ain't worth a…"

The cleric quickly jumped in. "What you must understand, my dear," he said, "is that we have to be very careful. The Klan…they're not a huge presence in our area, thank the Lord, but they are here and sometimes they, uh, they make themselves heard, very, um, um, emphatically. And they hate Catholics every bit as much as they hate Negroes and Jews, so I…" He hesitated again, looked down, then back at Nashota. "I am very hesitant to do something, or say something, that would cause them to direct any violence our way. We are a small congregation…" He stopped again, obviously in thought, before coming back to his original point.

"We are a small congregation and I would hate for anything to happen to any of my parishioners, or to the building itself, because we took a particular stand."

One of Nashota's great skills was her ability to think on her feet. "Father, please forgive me if I've not made myself clear," she said. "We are not asking you to say anything publicly." Technically that was true, but privately, she was hoping that area ministers would begin preaching sermons about racial equality once they had all been made aware of the Wolves' impending integration. "We just wanted you to know what's going to be happening in our town, so you would not be…um…blindsided when we bring Oddibe with us out of spring training."

"Now, I do have a thought, Mrs. Simpson," said the Father. "We are a small congregation, as I mentioned, but we are part of a larger group." *The human race,* thought Nashota, but she kept that to herself. "A few years ago, several churches in the area got together to form a consortium, the Northeast Tennessee Interfaith Council, which we call NETIC. We meet monthly to discuss issues of common interest, and also ways that we can work together to promote peace and harmony. All religions believe in this, and we thought…that is, a few of us thought, that we ought to work together to try and remind our people, all of our people, that this is really basic to everyone in our community, everyone."

Gibby beamed at this statement, and Nashota jumped on it.

"How can I meet these people? Would it be possible for me to address this Council sometime soon? It would be a great opportunity for them to hear what I've just told you, and talk about it. Frankly, Father," and here she leaned forward in her chair, "I think if the Council would publicly support us, it would mean so much, and would be…" Now it was her turn to search for the right words.

"Very significant." Gibby hit it right on the head.

"My thought exactly!" said the cleric. "Our little church doesn't amount to a hill of beans…"

"Oh, please, Connor, 'Casablanca,' really?" said Gibby. Father Feeney ignored him, again.

"…but if you get all the churches, representing all denominations in your corner, you'll…you'll really have something there. Let me make a call."

Father Feeney was as good as his word, getting them a spot on February's agenda. Jack and Nashota worked hard on their presentation, even thoroughly rehearsing it until they were satisfied that it struck the right tone. They wrote it so that they both would participate, first one then the other, back and forth, talking about how Oddibe was a good ballplayer and an even finer young man, a good church-going, God-fearing young man.

"From a baseball standpoint," said Jack, "the team needs someone with his skills. Night after night, he will give us a better chance to win."

"But winning on the field is not nearly as important as winning off the field," Nashota said, with emphasis. "This is absolutely the right thing to do at this time in our nation's history."

"We fought a war for freedom," said Jack. "I was in that war, some of you may have been as well, in one way or another, but really, we were all involved, every one of us, day after day, whether overseas or right here at home."

"And we are fighting yet another war so that people living in the small country of South Korea can be free," said Nashota. "Our democracy shines such a brilliant light around the world. So many people want to be like us, it is time that we followed our own ideals in our own country."

"Oddibe Daniels is an American citizen, same as you and me," Jack continued. "In fact, it's very possible that his family has been in this country longer than any of ours. All he wants is a chance to play professional baseball, to match his skills against other young men. All we ask is your support, in any way, shape or form."

Nashota looked around the room, said "Thank you for your time," and they sat down.

The applause from the assembled religious leaders was rather tepid.

Reverend Hagan Cornell, the president of NETIC, returned to the microphone. "I'm sure we are all very happy that Mr. and Mrs. Simpson came over to Kingsport to talk to us this morning. Thank you," he said, turning around to smile at them as they sat behind him. "I know you have..." and here he turned back to the larger group in front of him. "You have given us things to think about." He glanced at his notes and then continued. "I have been asked by Father Feeney to let y'all know that Mr. and Mrs. Simpson will be stickin' around for a while, with him..." and he nodded in the priest's direction..." in case anyone would like to speak with them." This was their cue to quietly move back to their seats.

When the meeting was over, most of the men smiled at them but continued to the door. "No one is coming by!" whispered Nashota to her husband. "Can you believe this, not a single person?"

Father Feeney heard her even as he was looking out towards his colleagues. "Have faith," he said quietly. There was something he was expecting and he smiled as he saw it developing. He looked at his guests. "I think," he said, "you are about to have some visitors."

Two young men walked briskly their way, one easily a head taller than the other. They eased themselves into the row right in front of them, and extended their hands.

"Thank you so much for coming today. I am Rabbi Halevi of Congregation Veyidgu Larov, the area's Jewish community," said the shorter one as Jack and Nashota stood to shake hands.

"And I am Reverend Robert Thomas from The Good Shepherd Episcopal Church," said the other. He had curly, reddish-brown hair that Nashota thought was very appealing. He also had a pleasant face that seemed to have a touch of sadness in it. "There should be..." he looked around and said "we were expecting a couple of others to join us..." He kept looking and finally spotted someone and waved his arm. "Ah, there's one now."

They saw an older gentleman hustling up the aisle. He was tall and slender and his face was deeply lined; he was certainly much older than either of their two new acquaintances, and he was most likely a good five or ten years older than Father Feeney. "Sorry I'm late, I got caught in a conversation with a couple of our colleagues..." he looked back behind him..."which seems to still be going on! Get a bunch of ministers together and the talk can go on for hours!" Everyone chuckled and the rabbi said, "You were probably the one doing the most talking."

The four religious leaders laughed at that one, and then the older man turned to Jack and Nashota. "Sorry, I haven't introduced myself yet, I'm Reverend Maurice Stapleton from the Brookdale Baptist Church."

There was a moment or two of general pleasantries, then Rev. Stapleton said "I think it might be a good ideal if we found a...a quiet, neutral location for us'n to talk, what y'all think?"

"Getting close to lunch time," said Father Feeney, "maybe we could..."

"We're supposed to...I was hoping we'd have one more person join us...oh, there he is."

A tall, somewhat angular man made his way towards them, flashing a sheepish, lopsided grin as he got closer.

"Sorry I's late, I was headed this way and got waylaid by Hagan. He was, uh, doin', oh, whatcha might call politickin'. Hagan's got a problem…"

"I'm sure we'll be getting into all that later," said Reverend Thomas, sounding a bit annoyed.

The newcomer frowned at him, then looked at Jack and Nashota and gave them that uneven smile of his.

"Anyway, please forgive me for bein' tardy," he said slowly, naturally drawing out every syllable of every word. *His sermons must last forever*, was Jack's immediate thought. "I am the Reverend Roy Ammons of the Calvin Street Methodist Church. I was so pleased that you came to us this mornin', and I am excited for what you are proposin' to do in our little community."

Nashota responded with her multi-megawatt smile. "You're not late at all, Reverend. We were just chit-chatting…"

"And deciding about lunch." Father Feeney was obviously a man on a mission.

Nashota quickly picked up on the thread. "If you don't mind coming over to Edens Ridge, we have a wonderful little place, The Back Porch, the owner is a friend of mine…"

"As well as a supporter of our team," Jack added.

"Yes," said Nashota, "And I know she'd be happy to host us. More importantly, I think it'll be a good, out-of-the-way place where we can talk." They all agreed and quickly arranged for a carpool over to Edens Ridge, where LaDonna seated them towards the back of the restaurant.

"If you ask me," said Rabbi Halevi, jumping right into it, "you should not have bothered coming to talk to us, you should have just gone ahead with your plans. Now you've given some pastors a window and they'll use it to deliver sermons about 'our way of life' and all that, get their parishes stirred up against you."

"No one will do that," said Rev. Stapleton as he took a bite of LaDonna's home-made cornbread, but Reverend Thomas immediately disagreed.

"Cornell will, I could hear the wheels in his head spinning when he said, 'you've given us things to think about.' He probably went right back to his church and immediately started working on this Sunday's sermon."

"Hagan's not so bad," said Rev. Stapleton. "I admit he can be a bit over-bearing at times…"

"A bit? He's like a tank," said Rabbi Halevi, then he turned to Jack. "I applaud you for fighting in the war. I wanted to go but my father's deceased, I'm an only child, so they said I had to stay home and care for my mother. I worked days and went to college at night."

"You must be younger than I thought," said Jack, and the rabbi grinned. "I'm 27, be 28 shortly after your season begins. This is my first congregation."

"He's a baby," said Reverend Thomas. "Until he got here, I was the youngest member of NETIC. I don't feel like such a kid anymore. And I have to tell you, this is really great chicken."

"Tell the owner, I'm sure she would love to hear it," said Reverend Stapleton. "And you're both a coupla young'uns. I'm 67 and been at Brookdale now for 21 years. Tell you what, long as my heart holds out, I'd like to stay on for 'nother 21. This ain't my first parish but it's my best, my wife and I, we just love it here in Tennessee."

"Where you from, Reverend?" asked Jack.

"Over yonder," he replied with a grin while he took a drink of his sweet tea. "In Virginia, Duffield to be exact. Went to school there, through high school. Went to Duke, though, for my divinity degree. Few years 'fore Robert here," he said, nodding towards Reverend Thomas.

"Few decades might be more accurate," replied his colleague, wryly, as he finished his second piece of chicken.

"Now is that any way to speak to your elders, Robert?" asked Rev. Stapleton. He then looked at Jack and Nashota and winked. "He's always got it in for me. We have some great debates, though I always come out on top. Maybe he's a little, oh, resentful, is that it, Robert?"

"You only think you win, truth is…" and now he looked at the whole table, "truth is, we do have some great debates, they're pretty stimulating, but no one ever wins or changes the other person's mind." Reverend Thomas smiled, then immediately got serious again. "But this time we can't be debating, we all have to be together. What Jack and…" He paused, then looked a little sheepishly at Nashota. "I'm sorry, I've forgotten your name, please forgive me."

"Nashota," she said. "It's Cherokee. Nothing to forgive, it's not a name you hear every day."

"Still, I apologize. Anyway, what Jack and Nashota were talking to us about is so important, and they're right, now is the time."

"Ah-men," said the rabbi. "I am behind you one hundred percent, and I'll bet I'm speaking for 'most everyone in my congregation, too. Jews have always been on the front lines of the battle for individual freedom, most Jews, anyway, just forget about Judah Benjamin, OK? We're with you," he said with emphasis, looking right at Jack and Nashota, who were both wondering who this Benjamin fellow was. "You can count on me and Veyidgu Larov. We may be small, unlike Brookdale, but we'll be with you."

"I'm with you, too." said Reverend Thomas. "Good Shepherd isn't large either, let's face it, if you're not a Southern Baptist in Northeast Tennessee you're not going to be very large. But we've got 92, little less than Connor has, and I know my flock will be behind you. Tell you what, I'll pledge right now that I'll organize a group from my church to come out one night and cheer hard for that young man."

"Good," said Jack, "I'll hold you to that."

"My congregation," said Reverend Ammons, "is actually a decent size. We got two Methodist churches in Kingsport, mine and First United, we both gen-uh-ruh-lee fill our pews on Sunday, or come real close. There's also one over to Kruse, and that new one on Center Street in Kingsport. Small place, used to be a store-a some sort. I think they opened up around Thanksgiving, serving the people who live closer to downtown."

Reverend Stapleton laughed. "That prob'ly fried Cog's bacon," which the other ministers also found amusing. "He thinks downtown is his terry-tory, bet he's none too pleased. He just barely reck-a-nizes me-n my flock." And he laughed again.

"Pardon me," said Jack, but Cog is…"

"Reverend Stephen Coggins of the First United Methodist Church of Kingsport. Weren't here today, no surprise, he hardly ever comes to one-a our meetins. He's a very busy man, very busy, just ask him, he'll be real happy to tell you."

The Reverend Ammons was eating a club sandwich. "Lotta food here, might just have to see 'bout takin' some-a this home for later." He did swallow some more coleslaw, then leaned back in his chair."

"Mistah and Missus Simpson, if I could…" He paused while Jack said "please, go right ahead."

"Can't speak for anyone else, 'course, but I do know somethin' 'bout the Methodists in this area. Now, not so much 'bout the AME church, you'll need to talk to Ish Clark, he knows his people way better-n me. But as to the others, I can tell you that my con-gre-gay-shun is much more likely to support you than Cog-n his folks. Got more, um, high rollers over there at First, people who got it real good, for the most part. Not very eager to rock the boat, if'n you know what I mean. That ain't who you'll find at Calvin Street. Oh, we got us a few old boys with money, but most-a my people are just good solid folk, hard-workin', hopin' to make a better life for theirselves and they kids. I know, sometimes people like that are Klan, I know. Cain't say that none-a my people ain't Klan. But I will say that 'most everyone is just not that way, and you can count on the Calvin Street Methodist Church bein' behind you, yes-siree. And if we support you, ha!" He let out a short laugh. "You just watch. If-n I bring some-a my con-gre-gay-shun out to your games, I know Cog will feel ob-lee-gay-ted to do it, too, am I right?" He looked at his fellow ministers.

"He'll take it as a challenge," said Reverend Stapleton. "He'll wanna have a bigger group than you, that's for darn sure. He hates finishin' second in anything." And the assembled clergymen all laughed out loud.

"Thanks so much to all of you, thank you. Let me ask you something, though" said Nashota, who then continued with a new thought. "There are Negro churches in the area, I know there are, I think we have at least two in Edens Ridge," she said. "Aren't any of them members of NETIC?" Everyone I saw this morning was white, why is that?"

No one spoke. There was more chewing, more drinking, and considerable shifting in chairs.

"You're not going to tell me that a group of religious leaders discriminates against fellow religious leaders, are you? I can't believe that!"

"No, no, that's not it at all, no, no, no." They all spoke at once, even the quiet Father Feeney. "Then what?" asked Nashota. More silence.

"Gentlemen," said Jack with great authority, "if I may, I would like to offer you some friendly advice. I know this woman, and I can tell you that she will not let you leave here until someone has answered her question, and answered it truthfully. So if you value…," and here he paused to carefully choose his words. "If you value any and all body parts, I suggest that someone speak up." She kicked him, he flinched a bit but continued. "And if you're not telling the truth, she'll know it. I don't know how, but she'll know it, must be a Cherokee thing." She kicked him again and this time he instinctively yelped, which brought laughs from the rest of the table.

Father Feeney surprisingly broke the silence. "It's Hagan," he said. "He's not very, uh, what's the word, welcoming, that's a good one, he's not very welcoming to Negro ministers."

"We used to have several come to our meetings, one was real active, Reverend Clark, Roy mentioned him a moment ago. He's right there in Edens Ridge, maybe you know him? No? Well, you ought to," said Reverend Stapleton as Nashota made a mental note to seek him out.

"One by one they all stopped coming after Cornell was elected," said Reverend Thomas, staring at his iced tea. "I was told he would say…say…things to them, let them know he really didn't want them around, all with a smile on his face. He never asked them to serve on any committees, never asked for their involvement or participation on anything, never did a single thing, really, to make them feel like they were real members of NETIC." He took a drink from his cup. "Connor's right, he never made them feel welcome, so sooner or later they all left. Sumbitch." This last was mumbled, followed by a thin little smile and a shrug.

"I can relate," said Rabbi Halevi. "I'm not his favorite person. If I never came to another meeting, it wouldn't upset him in the least."

"How did he ever get elected?" Jack asked.

"No one else wanted the job," said Reverend Stapleton, and Father Feeney's vigorous nods backed him up. "After Reverend Bennett passed away—he was the head of NETIC 'fore Hagan—coupla people asked me 'bout doin' it but I told 'em I'm too old, already past sixty. And Wilma's health ain't the best, mine ain't either, sometimes, so I just said no, ain't for me, find someone else. And they asked Hagan."

"He campaigned for the job," said Father Feeney. "He was willing to back off if you wanted it because you have seniority, but he let it be known he'd take it if you didn't. And you didn't."

There was silence for a moment before Rabbi Halevi spoke up.

"Y'all know I'm behind you, I've already said so. Whatever you might need," he stated, looking right at Jack and Nashota, "whatever it may be, I'll do everything I can to help you get it, you understand? You have my complete and total support. Now," he turned to his fellow clergymen, "what about the rest of you? These people need our backing, they need us to talk to our congregations, they need us to talk to our colleagues, what about it?"

"We're happy to have your help with your parishes, and, frankly, with other clergy," said Jack. "We need your help, the response this morning wasn't, um, quite as, oh, enthusiastic as we would have liked."

"I'm with you, Jack, Na…Nashota," said Reverend Thomas, pleased that he was able to remember her name. "You can count on me."

Their waitress came by to see if anyone needed anything else, with Reverend Thomas asking for "a bit more tea, please, sweet." Meanwhile, the older clerics looked at each other, no one seemingly anxious to speak first. When the waitress left, Rabbi Halevi said, simply, "well?"

"My congregation will be split," said Father Feeney. "If I take an active role, one way or another, I risk alienating half my people, and we're small, we don't even have a hundred members. I think if anyone asks me, and I'm sure some will, I'll tell them that a good Christian wouldn't care who's out there on that field, and besides, it is just a game, after all. That's what I'll say if they ask. But I'm not going to preach about it, though I'm sure Gibby will be on me every week to do it." He looked directly at Nashota because he felt she would be the more sympathetic. "That's just how I feel, I hope you can understand that."

She didn't blink. "I understand, Father. Catholics are a minority in this community, but this means you know what it feels like to be a minority. As a Cherokee I certainly do! And our Oddibe will be a minority, the only Negro on the playing field, night after night after night…"

"I'm not against you, Nashota, not by any means," Father Feeney interrupted. "I think what you're doing is good, and it's right, and it's long overdue here. I just have to think of my church, our membership numbers are down, I can't afford to lose more."

There was silence for a moment, and then Nashota sighed and, with clear resignation in her voice, said "I must say I'm a bit disappointed that you won't play an active role. But as long as you won't work against us, and if people ask, you tell them how you feel, personally."

"Oh yes, oh yes, I'll definitely do that, yes," said Father Feeney, and with that she just nodded and looked down at her hands, which were clasped on the table.

"Already tol-ja, you can count on me and my flock," said Reverend Ammons.

Which left Reverend Stapleton, who licked his lips. "I have to be honest," he said finally. "If I were a bettin' man, and of course I'm not, we don't believe in it. But if I was, I'd bet that most of my people will not be real happy to see a cullud boy out on the playing field this spring and summer. Me, I don't care, don't bother me 'tall, but I'm sure some-a my folks might get themselves all riled up. But I think Connor has the right ideal, so if anyone asks me, I'll be happy to tell 'em it ought not to matter who-all is out there a-playin' ball 'slong as he's on one-a our uniforms. Gotta root for the home team, right? Boy out there trying to win just like ever'one else on our team. And we might could remember that he's a Christian, a good Christian boy, didn't you say that this morning? We always gotta get behind anyone that's a Christian. That's what I'll tell anyone who asks, but I ain't gonna preach 'bout it, don't think my folk would want me to do that. Guess that's my position."

That seemed to bring the luncheon to a close. They all exchanged business cards and headed for the door. Reverend Thomas made it a point to tell LaDonna how much he liked her chicken and said he'd be back. "Now that they've finally got the road done between Kingsport and Edens Ridge, won't take me any time at all to ride over here."

Outside, Rabbi Halevi shook hands with both Jack and Nashota and said, "I meant what I said, I want to help, I really want to get involved." "Why, Rabbi?" asked Nashota, and he smiled. "In our *shul*—Yiddish for synagogue —we have a group of young people, Young Judea, they call themselves. They have a room that they use for meetings, and it has photos on the wall. David Ben Gurion, the Israeli Prime Minister; Chaim Weizmann, President of Israel; you'd expect them. But they also put up Emma Lazarus, the poet." Nashota must have had a blank look on her face because he said, "give me your tired, your poor, your huddled masses yearning to breathe free," and she made the connection.

"There are also three Negro men on the wall," the Rabbi continued. "Dr. Ralph Bunche, the diplomat and winner of the 1950 Nobel Peace Prize. A. Philip Randolph, the labor leader and founder of the Brotherhood of Sleeping Car Porters. And Jackie Robinson. These people are all up there because our youngsters admire them all very much. Equal rights for all is an important issue for our Young Judea group, and I'm sure you know why. They all came through a war, had fathers or older brothers off fighting, and maybe…" His face quickly became serious. "Maybe some of them had relatives over there, in the 'Old Country' who, um, may have…may not have…had it so easy." He paused and quietly said *"Alehém Hashalóm,* may they rest in peace." He shook his head and coughed. "Anyway, it's easily the most important thing that's happened in their lifetime so far, fighting a war to beat a system that wanted to exterminate some people and enslave the rest of the world."

He coughed, then concluded. "If I don't get involved, if I don't back you with every bit of my being, I would be failing these kids, I could never walk into that room again, I really would have no right to even keep my job. That's why I'm with you, and I'm betting that many of my parishioners, and all of Young Judea, will be with you, too. If there's anything we can do to help, you just give me a call."

Jack told Nashota that he wanted to speak with Reverend Clark.

"I can, um, approach him a little differently than you would, more from a historical point of view." She looked at him blankly. "I know a little about what happened when Jackie Robinson was brought up to Brooklyn five years ago. I think if he and I talk in those terms, it will have a little more impact, understand?"

She didn't, not completely, but she was comfortable letting him handle items that were specifically about baseball, so she nodded.

First on Jack's agenda for the day was making another trip to see Jehosie Jackson. While unable to afford nearly as much as the Katts, Mr. Jackson did sign a contract for a quarter-page ad, which made Jack happy. This not only gave the team a new auto repair shop, it became the first Negro-owned business to throw their support behind the Wolves. And now, since he was literally in the neighborhood, Jack decided to go around the corner and visit the Jericho Chapel AME Church.

The Reverend Ishmael Clark was not a large man, but he had a firm handshake and warm smile that immediately put a person at ease. Plus he served a mean cup of coffee.

"Well, first of all, I want to tell you I'm not here to try and sell you anything…" Jack began, but he was quickly interrupted.

"That's good, Mr. Simpson, 'cause we don't have anything to spare, 'cept words!" He laughed heartily, while Jack just smiled.

"I did want to tell you about something that we are gonna be doing out at the ballpark this coming season. I, um, I'm telling you this in confidence, you understand, only a handful of people know about it, at least right now. Coupla your fellow ministers know; in fact, it was Rev. Ammons and Rev. Stapleton told me I needed to be talkin' to you."

Reverend Clark leaned forward in his chair. "Mr. Simpson, you have me intrigued."

Jack took a deep breath and jumped right in, telling him all about Oddibe. Nice young man, good family, chance to be an outstanding ballplayer. Also, first-ever Negro in the Mountain Empire League. "In fact, as of right now, he'll be the ONLY Negro..."

"Wow. Really? The only Negro, ever?" Reverend Clark was dumbfounded.

"Of course," Jack went on, "we're expecting some, uh, opposition from..."

"Opposition? You'll be getting some venom, some real...real revulsion, Mr. Simpson. And I hate to say this, but some of it will be coming from the grandstands right here."

"I know," Jack sighed. "I'm hoping that, as time goes on and Oddibe shows what a terrific, exciting player he is, that kind-a...behavior, language, will go away." Reverend Clark audibly snickered, which prompted Jack to say "Well, maybe slow down quite a bit?" He smiled, but thinly. "That's my hope, anyway."

"Time will tell, Mr. Simpson. Time will tell. But I'm glad you came here to share this with me. Gives me a chance to get my congregation..."

"And this is exactly why I wanted to talk to you like this, Reverend. See, we hafta...um, we...uh, lemme ask you, how much do you know about Jackie Robinson's first year in Brooklyn, back in '47?"

"I know it was one of the great events in the history of the Negro in America. Was celebrated in houses all over the country, not just in Brooklyn. Several of my congregants put his picture up on one of their walls, right next to Jesus." Simpson laughed, but the minister did not. "I'm serious. To many of my people, Jackie Robinson can do no wrong, he is the Black Moses."

"I understand, Reverend, I do, but listen. Before Jackie played his first game in Brooklyn, there was already great...oh, anticipation, I guess you could say... anticipation in Brooklyn, all over the country, really. And concern, a whole lotta concern as to what might happen. Kinda like what I've got now." Reverend Clark nodded silently while Jack shifted in his chair.

"Mr. Rickey...Branch Rickey, he was the Dodgers' co-owner and general manager and the man responsible for signing Jackie and bringing him to Brooklyn. He was afraid of the bigots, of course, just like we are now. But he was also...worried about...about...another group that could..." Jack was searching for the right way to say what he had come to say, and his discomfort was readily visible to the Reverend.

"Mr. Simpson, we've only know each other for a few minutes, so let me tell you something about myself. If something is on a man's mind, I very much appreciate it if he just comes right out and says it. No need to beat around the bush. Please, sir, please just tell me..."

"Sorry, Reverend, sorry I'm bobbling the ball here. OK, nice and straight. Mr. Rickey was also concerned that Negro groups could also do things to make it difficult for Jackie to succeed. He was afraid they'd, oh, celebrate, have parties and parades and shit…'scuse me, sorry. They'd do all sorts of celebrating, which would get people, white people, all riled up, even more-n what was expected. He was afraid different groups would throw banquets for him left-n-right, get him all fat and outta shape, and he wouldn't be the ballplayer he could be, the star they were expectin' him to be. He was afraid that if these Negro groups went…went overboard like this, that some-a his teammates, his white teammates, would get all jealous and resent him, resent all the attention. He knew…Mr. Rickey knew how hard things were gonna be on the field, but the clubhouse, that needed to be Jackie's sanctuary." Simpson looked around the church. "Kinda like this, you know? The clubhouse needed to be where Jackie could catch his breath. Last thing they needed was for some teammates to be all pis…ticked off because of all the attention Jackie was gettin' from different groups." Jack sighed. "Sometimes I'm not so good at expressin' myself. I shoulda brought my wife with me, she's much better at this-n me. Reverend, do you understand what I'm tryin' to say?"

Reverend Clark nodded his head. "I must admit, Mr. Simpson, I was not expecting…that. You have caught me off-guard, twice!" He chuckled, and the salesman in Jack recognized that one more point could close the deal.

"Now Reverend, look, I'm not saying you have to be quiet about this. People can come out to the ballpark and cheer for Oddibe all they want. And I'm sure he'd appreciate a home-cooked meal every now and then, but not every night, maybe just once during a homestand."

"Now that will not be a problem" Reverend Clark's eyes sparkled. "I will make sure my congregants understand that perfectly."

"Good," said Jack. "But they also…I think it would be important for them to agree that there won't be any parades, or fireworks, or trumpets in the stands. And another thing Mr. Rickey did was, he encouraged the Negro community to print up signs, we could do the same thing here. All it would hafta say is 'Don't spoil Oddibe's chances.' They did that for Jackie in Brooklyn. Put them all over, in stores, barber shops, community centers. We need…we ALL need, to give this young man every opportunity to succeed on his own. With his own talent. Can't be puttin' any more pressure on him."

The clergyman nodded. "I can understand that. But I have a question, Mr. Simpson. This has not gone public yet. When can I start talking to the members of my church? When can I tell them…all these things you've just told me?"

"Soon, Reverend, soon. We'll be goin' to spring training pretty quick, I'm sure his name will start poppin' up in the *Gazette*, maybe even in the *Times* or *News*, if the Kingsport people decide to cover the story and send someone over to our training camp. We're not plannin' any big announcement, that's something we're doin' different from Branch Rickey. He splashed it all over, we're gonna be, um, more low key."

There was silence for a moment or two, and finally the Reverend Clark stood up.

"Mr. Simpson, I thank you very much for coming in to see me today. I'm sure you realize you have my complete support, and will have the backing of the Jericho Chapel

AME Church. And we'll be careful, I promise! I'll take care of getting some of those signs printed up, just as soon as this news goes public, don't you worry about that at all. And you'll be seeing us out at ballgames this spring and summer, you can count on that. Bet you even make quite a few new fans for the Wolves."

This was one of those occasions when a handshake was more powerful than a million words.

There were two Tate sisters, Coletta and Lakieta, and one of them worked at Adams Market, Nashota's source wasn't sure which one. Didn't matter, of course, she was sure either would do, so she drove over to Ryan Road, where she was surprised to find a very full parking lot. In fact, she had to park the car a block away and walk up an inclined street. *Well, this will please my mother, she keeps telling me that exercise is good for the baby.*

The store seemed to be crammed with merchandise, and its narrow aisles didn't help with the traffic flow. Nashota waited her turn on line and then asked the short, somewhat-stout woman at the cash register for Miz Tate. "I'm Coletta Tate," the woman replied. "What can I do for you?"

Nashota identified herself and then, as quickly as she could (there were now a couple of people lined up behind her), spoke about needing a room for Oddibe.

"He's a real fine young man," she concluded. "Quiet, doesn't get into any trouble. He should be able to pay on time because he'll be getting a paycheck from us twice a month, and…"

"No," said Miz Tate, with some finality. "Don't want him."

Nashota was taken aback. "I'm sorry, but you seem so…so definite, may I ask why?"

Coletta Tate had that tired look that seems to inflict so many people who work retail. But her eyes were firm and cold. "He be trouble. Don't matter he a nice boy, come from a good Christian family, all that you said. This boy gonna be trouble and we don't need that at our front door, no way."

"Miz Tate, I assure you…"

"Looka-here, Miz Simpson, I'm sure he ain't a-comin' here to cause no trouble, he jes' wanna play ball, I understand. But trouble…" She paused for effect. "Trouble gonna find him, sure as we breathin'. There be some folk won't like havin' him out there on the ballfield, no indeed, they won't like it one bit, and they be the ones causin' trouble. They find out where he livin'…'scuse me, lemme ring up Miz Muse here." Nashota stepped aside while Coletta Tate smiled and took care of a lady wearing a blue print frock. An attractive woman with a flowery yellow dress allowed a man to get ahead of her when she saw he only had a carton of cigarettes, and when Miz Tate took his money, she looked again at Nashota.

"We got Klan here in this area," she said. "Last thing I want is for them to bring their…their ways to my front door. Our neighbors don't want it, neither, I know that for a fact. We bring this young man into our house, Lord knows what might happen. Sorry, Miz Simpson."

Nashota stood outside the store for a moment, not quite sure what to do next. This had seemed like a great lead, *I was so sure...*

"Ma'am? Ma'am?" The voice belonged to Miss Flowery Yellow Dress, who was leaving Adams Market with a couple of bags. She came over to Nashota.

"Sorry, but I couldn't help hearin' your conversation in the store. Gotta tell ya, Coletta is right to worry. We do have Klan 'round here and they can make trouble." All Nashota could manage was a very weak "Oh."

But now Miss Flowery Yellow Dress smiled. "Klan won't bother me, though, they flat-out leave me alone." She gave a short laugh. "When they come 'round to my house, they ain't wearing no sheets." She then looked right at Nashota. "Ma'am, I got a room at my place over on Light Street, happy to show it to you right now if you like."

The day had suddenly gotten better.

"You parked 'round back?" Nashota shook her head and said "No, about a block away."

"I'm in the lot back there. Blue Chrysler New Yorker. I'll pull out and you follow me." Nashota smiled, nodded, and the two women started to walk towards their respective cars before Miss Flowery Yellow Dress called her again.

"Did you say your name was Simpson? Related to...to that Jack Simpson with the Wolves?"

"Yes, he's my husband. I run the office, handle the business end..."

"Well, don't that beat all." Miss Flowery Yellow Dress smiled broadly, then held out her hand.

"My name is Jasmine, Jasmine Brunét. Nice to meet you."

She had been born and raised in Baton Rouge, Louisiana, where her real-world education began at the age of thirteen. Trying to help her sick mother and baby sister Rose, she stole some food and was chased into a dead-end alley by a policeman. She told him her tale of woe and was surprised when he offered to let her go—"I'll just tell 'em you was way too quick for me and got away." There was a condition, however, as he unzipped his fly while pushing her down to her knees. Lesson #1 helped to stave off the family's hunger pains for at least the next couple of days, and it taught Jazz that money could be made, easy, tax-free money, and she quickly became the sole bread-winner of the family. But while she may have been able to stay on the good side of Johnny Law, she learned the hard way that her skills meant nothing to the Grim Reaper—that heartless bastard claimed both her mother and Rose before Jasmine turned sixteen.

With nothing keeping her any longer in Baton Rouge, she began riding the rails, eventually landing in Pine Bluff, Arkansas in 1927, where she was accepted by Ida Holmes at The Apollo. Her travels had taught her that The Apollo was considered by many to be the finest bordello in the area, perhaps in the entire state, and this was an instance where rumor proved to be fact. Jazz settled in and, over time, became one of Ida's most popular girls. She even found herself a steady beau, Guynn Galimore, the trombone player with Max West's Hot Five, a group of itinerant jazz musicians who booked themselves into juke joints all around the South. Max and his boys came to The Apollo one night and she happened to get paired with Guynn (he pronounced it Gwin, "rhymes with win, 'cause I's a winner!" he would say and give off the biggest smile this side of John Bubbles). She loved his happy personality, which he attributed to playing jazz, eating cornbread whenever he could, and regularly puffing on a strange-smelling cigarette. She tried it when he told her it would make her feel better. "Will it help me sleep?" she asked. "Sometimes...there be nights I see my baby sister and I has trouble sleepin'," she told him. "Don't know for sure," he replied, "but I knows it'll make you feel more relaxed, and that gotta help you with sleep, doncha think?" It wasn't perfect—Rose still made occasional appearances, but they were fewer now, and she did sleep better.

When the depression hit, it affected The Apollo as much as any other business. Gigs for The Hot Five became rare as the economy bottomed out, and Max gave his musicians permission to find work wherever they could. Guynn washed dishes at a country club, shined shoes, would take almost any job at all, but he hated everything except playing the trombone. "That's what I do best, baby," he once told Jasmine. "I's happiest playin' my horn, and bein' with you, 'course."

In October of 1932, Guynn was washing dishes at a speakeasy just a few blocks from The Apollo. His night over, he began walking home when someone grabbed him from behind and demanded money. "I ain't got no money, you dumb shit," he said. "Who do I look like, Duke Ellington? I'm just a dishwasher." Then he tried to turn around and fight off his assailant, and for his efforts was rewarded with a knife in his belly. The other man twisted the knife a time or two, grabbed Guynn's wallet, and vanished into the night. The man's tattered shoes were the last things Guynn ever saw.

Rose was now joined by Guynn. The sleepless nights came back to Jasmine, and she decided she needed to leave Pine Bluff.

She hit the rails again, plying her trade in bigger cities like Birmingham and Atlanta and Memphis. "There be big money in big cities," she said to someone who shared a boxcar with her for a day or two, "but life...hoo boy, life sure is hard there." And expensive. The only work she was able to find was on street corners, not in a nice comfy house like The Apollo, and the pavement was rarely kind. She got beat up so bad in Memphis that she had to go to a hospital for a couple of days, and then she had to blow an orderly so he'd help her sneak out without paying. Birmingham was also dangerous, so many white people she saw looked at her like they'd just as soon kill her as say "good evening."

Atlanta was too damned big but one good thing came out of it. She met a young traveling salesman named Keith who took a real liking to her and suggested she come along with him as he toured northern Georgia. They would sleep in motor courts every night, nothing fancy, just second-rate places but all had real beds with real mattresses. Some were better than others, of course, but they were all huge improvements over life on the street. *Maybe things is lookin' up.*

They went to Chattanooga, his hometown, and he introduced her to his parents, a Cherokee mother and a Negro father. Mom seemed genuinely happy to meet Jazz and was very nice to her, but his father made it very obvious that he thought she was dirt, the kind of Negro that gave the whole race a bad name. One evening she was washing the dishes, as she always did, and he came up behind her, put his hand under her skirt and whispered, "Don't you say a word." She was so surprised she complied at first and let him feel her up, but when she heard him pull down his zipper she turned around and said "no!"

"What you say to me, bitch?" His face was full of anger, a black version of the faces she had seen in Birmingham.

She tried to control her voice. "You heard me, I said no. Me-n your son, we together now, bein' with you just wouldn't be right, be...be weird..."

He slapped her face. "You live in my house and eat my food, you do what I want, understand? Understand?"

"Yessir," she said. Her street-savvy brain went into overdrive. "But your wife, and Keith, they just next door, they'll hear us. We need to wait, maybe after they been sleepin' for a while, we could come out here, or the parlor, or wherever you say, and then..." The professional Jazz took over and she carefully rubbed his chest with one hand and his crotch with the other. "Then we can have a good time, yessiree, I can show you a way good time. OK? That OK with you?"

He grunted and re-zipped his fly. "Meet me in here 'bout one," he said, then walked out.

It was before midnight when Jasmine quietly got out of bed, threw her few belongings in her worn-out old suitcase, gently kissed Keith on the forehead, and slipped out the back door. She found her way to Highway 58 and stuck out her thumb every time a vehicle went by. She figured she'd been walking for a couple of miles when a truck driver finally stopped and opened the door.

"Where ya headed, honey?" he asked, to which she replied with her biggest and sweetest smile, "Where you goin'?" He laughed and said. "Tri-Cities area," to which she said, with great wonderment in her voice, "Why shut my mouth, that just where I wanted to be!" She of course had no idea where the Tri-Cities were, or what three towns they were, but it would be someplace new for her and perhaps she could make a fresh start...again.

She originally chose Johnson City to be her home base, because there was a college there and no matter where you lived, college boys were college boys. Six months after she arrived, however, war broke out in Europe and, while the U.S. remained neutral, some of her clients repeated the same mantra: "Only a matter-a time 'fore we be gettin' involved." That worried Jazz, because it meant that a great many State Teachers College students would be headed off to war.

The police were also problematical, regularly bringing in the girls and keeping them locked up for at least several hours, which essentially meant losing a night of work. It started happening often enough that Jasmine began thinking once again of trying to find a better place to live and work.

Every girl had her regulars, guys who wanted to only be with her. Jazz had two, one of whom was 76 years old and mostly just wanted the company. The other was much younger and simply went by the initials D.L. One evening he approached her with a big smile.

"I have been saving up for a month or more, Jazz, but I've got enough for the whole night."

They got right down to business, and when they were finished Jasmine asked him what he had in mind for the rest of the night. "We gonna do this again? We gonna talk, or sleep, or what? I'm yours for the night, you paid your money, I's only curious. Don't often have just one person for a night, and if-n I do it usually means business be slow."

"As a matter of fact, there is something I wanted to talk about."

What he had in mind was a business proposition. In the town of Edens Ridge, just some 27 miles away, there was this old house that was practically falling down. "It's been condemned, could get it for a song." He was thinking that he'd buy it and renovate it, make it real nice and comfortable, and then "I'll turn it into a…well…you know…a house…um…for you girls…"

"You mean a whorehouse? You want to make a new whorehouse? You crazy, D.L.? Cops shut it down 'fore you can even blink. They on us as much as our clients, know what I mean? This is a tough area for workin' girls, I truthfully don't know how long I gonna stay here with all this heat. This a bad idea, D.L., I gotta say."

"Police won't bother us, Jazz. See, my uncle is the Chief up there, and he'll look after us. Hell, this is his idea, he said he'd do it himself 'cept he wants to keep his name outta it. As long as I pay him a fee, he'll make sure his boys look the other way. It could be a sweet deal."

Jazz looked at him warily. "What you mean, us? Who-all gettin' involved?"

D.L. smiled. "My plan is to have you run it. You live there, you hire the girls, you run the place. We divvy up the money: some goes for everyday expenses, some goes to the girls, of course, some comes back to me, some stays with you. How does that sound?"

"What about this war? Everybody says that, sooner or later, Mista Roosevelt gonna hafta send our boys to Europe. What about that?"

"Not everyone will be going. They might change the rules, of course, but if we went to war right now I'd get to stay home because I have flat feet. Can you imagine that? My feet will keep me from getting shot at!" He laughed, then finished his thought. "So I'll be here and I imagine others will be as well."

Jazz looked at him for a moment. She had become a pretty good judge of character over the years, and he seemed to be serious. "Why you wanna do this, D.L.? Think you gonna get rich, do you?"

"Yeah, sort of. If I claim it as rental property, I'll be able to keep a lot of my share for myself. Seems like a good way to make some money. And I get to keep my day job, too, which I like."

"What you do, D.L.? I really know nothin' 'bout you…"

"I'm a plumber," he said, reaching for a cigarette. "I fix toilets for a living. Which means I'm good with my hands, so I figure I can fix up the house myself, maybe get a coupla buddies to help out…"

"I'm kinda good, too, I know how to use a hammer and a wrench," she said with a smile, a kiss, and then more.

It took nearly a year for all the paperwork to be taken care of and all the work to be done. Jazz spent many an afternoon over there, and with the promise of a nice warm place to stay, she was able to recruit a couple of other girls to help as well. D.L. was there on weekends and a few different people showed up at different times. One fellow, Jake, seemed to be there every time she turned around.

The war did come, of course. They guessed they were only a couple of months away from being ready to move in when the Japanese bombed Pearl Harbor. They lost Jake to the Marine Corps, but the work continued, and Jazz and two other girls, Emma and Charlotte, were able to move in by the first week in June of 1942.

It was obvious to Nashota that Jasmine had done this before.

"We had to do a awful lotta work on this house to just keep it from fallin' down. The foundation was good but some-a the wood was rotten and other pieces were hangin' crooked, that all had to be fixed. And the insides was terrible, just terrible, I wouldn't let a dog stay here overnight. We had different people to help us, though the main ones was me and my business partner and his friend Jake, who's now my man. Some-a the girls helped, too." That led her to explain about "the girls," and how the house was a business as well as a residence. Jazz noticed that Nashota's eyebrows raised just a bit, but she otherwise seemed to be unaffected.

"The outside looks nice, nothing seems to be crooked now," Nashota said. The porch railing had been freshly painted, and holly bushes, still taking their winter naps, ringed the building. On both the east and west side of the building was an area that was obviously earmarked for plantings. "We put in vegetables and a few flowers," said Jazz when she noticed her guest's gaze. "Started growin' food during the war, helped us out a lot. Flowers we mostly grow in pots up on the rail, people like lookin' at 'em when they walk up, even when they just drive by. We'll have more as the weather gets nicer."

They walked onto the porch. "We need to paint every coupla years. We did it after the war was over, in spring of '46, then we did it again in '49, was it? No, it was '50, that's when it was. Maybe we'll do it again next year, maybe we'll wait 'til '54."

Nashota was surprised when they went inside. She was expecting something out of a book or movie, maybe red and gaudy, like Belle Watling's place in *Gone with the Wind*, but this wasn't anything like that at all. The only stereotypical piece of furniture was the piano over in the corner; otherwise there were two small couches and several chairs, all covered tastefully in muted colors. They surrounded two small tables that featured a variety of current magazines, and one book, *Pride and Prejudice*, which surprised Nashota.

"That belong to Emma, she forever readin' somethin' and she always leave it layin' 'round. One time she was readin' some book and she couldn't find it, tore the place apart lookin' for it but weren't nowhere. She got all upset 'cause some fella had given it to her, could barely keep her mind on her work. Anyways, maybe two weeks later this boy come in, he been here before, and what you know, he had it with him and brought it back. He picked it up and started readin' it down here, while he was waitin' for Emma, and then he took it on his way out 'cause he liked what he'd read and wanted to see how it come out. Told Emma he used it in a book report at school, too." Jazz let out a little laugh, and Nashota said "School?" Jazz nodded. "Told you he was a boy. Don't know where he got the money but he paid in full every time." She grabbed the Jane Austen book. "Always tell her not to leave her…stuff layin' out, but she likes to come down here and read when she ain't…workin'."

"Does this mean she's, um, working now?"

A smile slowly engulfed Jasmine's face. "Why yes indeed, all my girls is workin' right now, least they oughta be."

"Really?" asked Nashota. "It's only…" she glanced at her watch. "I mean, it's not even four, and…"

Her host couldn't contain herself, she laughed out loud. "Sometime we do gets early birds, but the girls, right now, they all workin' in the house, you know, cleanin', dustin', that sorta thing. We all have our chores, I get to do the marketin', which reminds me, we better put all these things away, 'specially what has to go in the ice box. Follow me." And toting her sacks, she led her guest into the kitchen, with its green countertops and black-and-white checkered flooring.

When the groceries were all put snuggly in their places, the two women climbed the stairs, and Nashota counted seven doors. At the top of the stairs Jazz nodded towards a room just to their left, said simply "that be my room," and then she turned right, walked past two doors and opened up the third, said "this is the empty room," and walked in.

Like the downstairs, it was rather tasteful, and it was surprisingly spacious. The bedroom area was fully carpeted and featured a nice-sized bed right in the middle of the room with what looked to Nashota like a double mattress. A good-sized dresser, with a mirror, was alongside one wall, while a plushy-looking chair sat on the other, next to a floor lamp. There was no window. Just a couple of feet from the lamp was the entrance into the bathroom, which had faded tile but contained a sink, toilet, bathtub and medicine cabinet, certainly adequate for one person. Nashota nodded absently.

Jasmine put her hand out, indicating that her guest should sit in the chair, while she plopped it on the bed.

"I know you gots questions, lemme see if I can answer some 'fore you even ask 'em," she said. "We had this place ready to live in by June of '42. There was just three of us, me'n Emma and Charlotte, who ain't here no more. War was goin' on so business was slow even though D…" She caught herself and stopped for a second, then said "my partner always thought we'd do fine anyway, but lotsa guys went into service, I don't have to tell you…"

"No, I understand," interrupted Nashota. "Though it was a little different for me. I was living in Weare then, down in North Carolina, north of Asheville?" Jazz just shrugged. "I was running a small restaurant/diner-kind of place, and we had a base right outside town, so there were plenty of guys all the time."

"You was lucky," said Jazz. "We have Tennessee Eastman 'round here, and farmers, and our high school, that's it, not much else. Not so many guys came a-knockin' back then, we needed to do something to pay our bills, so we started rentin' rooms, four of 'em. Really helped us get through the war." She sighed, then continued.

"Dropped that bomb, whole lotta guys came back, and business really took off. We hired two more girls, then a third, but we couldn't hire no one else 'cause one fella was still rentin' a room and we weren't-a no mind to toss him out." She smiled. "Al Gatti, older man, we all liked him, he was real nice. So we kinda got used to havin' a boarder. We found that six girls was really enough, maybe more-n enough, so there always seems to be space for someone to live here 's-long as he don't mind livin' in a whorehouse." She paused again, and looked intently at Nashota. "I don't pull no punches, Miz Simpson. No reason to get all fancy or nothin', this is a whorehouse, no two ways 'bout it."

"How many girls are living here now?" asked Nashota.

"We got five, 'cludin' me. Two white girls, one other cullud girl, and one-a yours," said Jazz with a smile.

"Mine?" asked Nashota.

"Injun. Linda—her name's Linda, and she from some tribe in Mississippi. 'Course," and here Jazz just shrugged, "it don't matter none to me." Nashota didn't say anything, so her hostess went on. "Two rooms is empty right now. One girl, Millie, she left just 'fore Thanksgiving, said she'd saved up 'nuff money and was goin' home, Jackson I think. Gonna go to business school, wants to be a secretary. Her room was the one next door. This one here," and she waved her arm, indicating where they were sitting, "it belonged to a Mr. Cooper, he was here for a year or so, maybe fifteen months. Worked at Eastman and didn't like it so he quit, least that's what he told us, and he left at the end-a January. So we been tryin' to rent both these rooms for a while now."

"Well, the thing is, I can't rent it today," said Nashota. And she proceeded to tell Jasmine about Oddibe, how he'd be the first Negro ballplayer in the Mountain Empire League, and he needed a place to stay and eat but he wouldn't be in town until April, still about six weeks off.

Jazz scratched her head. "I prob'ly oughta talk with my partner, and with Jake, he got a good head on him." She smiled. "Two good heads, if you know what I mean," she said, and then she laughed, and Nashota couldn't help but laugh along. "But I tell ya, I'm thinkin' it be a good thing to have your boy livin' here, which you might think is kinda funny, but lemme tell you why. He workin' at night, just like all-a us 'cept Jake, so he be sleepin' when we-all be sleepin', which means he most likely will get plenty-a rest. And with me-n four other girls around, he'll be momma'd and big sister'd to death. What I'm sayin', Miz Simpson, is that we'll look afta him real good, make sure he eats right, 'course he gotta throw in for vittles like we all do. And if there is any trouble, we got Jake here, Jake is strong as an ox, person gonna think twice 'fore they tangle with him, that for sure. And my girls, they'll all leave him be unless he can pay for it, like everyone else. No one but Jake gets freebies and ain't really free for him, neither. He does work 'round here when we need it and when he can do it, he's the manager out at the lumber yard, he there now," she said, and Nashota could hear the pride in her voice.

"Oddibe has a girlfriend, I know, back in Asheville, where he lives. I don't know if he…" But Jasmine quickly interrupted.

"He a male, ain't he? He be tempted, very least, but hey, that just show he normal and healthy." She laughed again. "Besides, a whole bunch-a our clients are men with wives, so just 'cause this boy got a girl back home…"

She stopped herself, realizing she may be talking herself out of a sale. Quickly she said "Tell you what, Miz Simpson, I'll give you my word as the…the manager of this place that I'll personally make sure he stay on the straight-n-narrow. No messin' 'round for Mr. Oddibe 'cept if his girl comes to visit. Huh," she said, as she suddenly had a new thought. "Wonder what Little Miss Asheville will think about where her boyfriend be livin'? Wonder what his Momma and Daddy will think? Might could be a problem, Miz Simpson?"

Nashota had not considered that. "Let me talk to my husband," she said. "I have to tell you, this is a very lovely house, the room is real nice, I'm sure he'd love living here, but you raise a good point, especially about his parents. His mother is a real firecracker, father is an old ballplayer…"

"Did your husband play with him?" asked Jasmine.

"No," said Nashota, "They weren't letting Negroes play with whites back when Jack played." She looked at Jazz very intently. "How did you know that my husband played ball?"

You gotta big mouth, Jazz, she thought while shifting around on the bed.

"I go out to the ballpark sometimes, mostly for day games," which was true. "I know who he is, know he played some 'fore he come here." All true, she just was leaving out one little fact—that back in Pine Bluff, a young Jasmine Brunét had "popped the cherry" of a very young ballplayer named Jack Simpson.

Nashota stood up. "Well, like I said, let me talk to Jack, see what he thinks, and then I can get back to you."

Jasmine also stood. "Miz Simpson," she said, "What you found at Adams you likely to find everywhere. No one wants no trouble, and they prob'ly nervous 'bout what might happen when young Mr. Oddibe start playin'. I may be wrong but, like I said earlier, I think you might have a hard time rentin' him a room anywhere else in Edens Ridge. Not here, though, we won't have no problem with him livin' with us. And I can tell you that…that…um, without goin' into too much detail, I can say we have a…a…good relationship with the local police, very good. If trouble do come to these doors, it goin' away real fast." She cleared her throat. "Fact, I'll make a promise to you here-n-now. I knows the police chief real well, and I will talk to him myself, soon as you give me the word, glad to do it. Yes, ma'am, we-all be happy to look out for your ballplayer, we take real good care-a him."

"Thank you, Miz Brunét. I'll be sure to tell my husband what you said when I see him later tonight."

The two women walked back downstairs, where one of the girls was sweeping out the parlor. Jasmine opened the front door and escorted Nashota out onto the porch, then extended her hand.

"Thank you for comin', Miz Simpson," she said, "Appreciate you lookin' at the room. And I hope you allow us to help you with this, it'll be our…our civic duty, our way of contributin' to the ball team." They shook hands, Nashota smiled, and Jazz felt pretty sure she had made a sale.

SIX

It was a long trip, longer than any he had ever taken before. Of course, truthfully, Oddibe had rarely been out of North Carolina—a couple of times to South Carolina, once over to Tennessee, that had been it. There had never been money for frivolities like vacations.

But this was no vacation, this was life, his new life, as a professional baseball player.

He had received a letter in the mail from the Edens Ridge Wolves, his new employers, *that has a nice ring to it!* Signed by Jack Simpson, it told him when he was expected to report to their spring training facility in Okaloosa County, Florida, and what he needed to bring with him, and most importantly, it included a bus ticket to Fort Walton Beach. He and RubyAnn had gone over to the library one evening and looked at maps to find these places. Just looking at the names got him excited, but he quickly suppressed it because he heard a quiet sigh come from RubyAnn, and he felt her shoulders tighten a bit. He knew that she was anxious about his leaving, and sad because they wouldn't be seeing each other for at least a couple of months. He realized that, at this moment, he needed to be there for her.

But on the Greyhound bus, it was just him and his thoughts as they made the journey to…what? What would he be facing? Oddibe knew he was a good ballplayer but that was in and around Asheville, what about against these older fellows, these professionals? Would he be able to hit their pitches? Were the fastballs faster, did the curveballs drop further? Could he catch up to their long shots to the outfield? More importantly, would any of his teammates, his white teammates (because they would, indeed, all be white) act friendly, or even civil? His father had reminded him that it had taken a little time for the Dodgers to accept Jackie Robinson, and even then not everyone had come on board. "Some people not gonna like you, Oddibe," his father had said to him a couple of days before he left. "That's OK, you already know that true from working at the Grove Park, right? But it be important that they respect you. Respect you as a player, respect you as a man. You respect them and they should respect you, sooner or later, and the ones that don't, yeah, they don't deserve no respect, no how, no way. You get their respect and they'll be with you, no matter what."

He thought about those words as the bus made its way south. More than 500 miles from start to finish gave him plenty of time to think.

And to read—he had brought lots of reading material. His parents had bought him a brand-new Bible, and his mother had reminded him "All the answers are in there, son. If things ever get dark for you, this will lead you to the light." He had a couple of Mark Twain books with him, he loved Twain, especially *Huckleberry Finn* and *A Connecticut Yankee in King Arthur's Court*. They made him laugh and think all at the same time, so even though he had read them both before, he wanted to have them close to him. And RubyAnn had saved up her money and bought him the newest from A.B. Guthrie, Jr., *The Way West*. She knew he had loved *The Big Sky* and wanted him to have the next volume in the set.

He thought about RubyAnn a lot. She meant so much to him and had for such a long time. He had been respectful of her, agreeing to her request to "wait, please, just a little while longer." He was, actually, content with what they did, how they played with each other. She had let him see her naked, let him touch her all over. Once, when they were the only ones home, she let him rub his penis on her small breasts until he boiled over. They showered together and, when they kept touching each other, they both climaxed a second time—man, was that special!

He shifted in his seat, didn't want anyone to see what his body was doing. He tried not to think about her but that was impossible, especially after last week. They had gone out and parked in their usual secluded place and things were getting hot and heavy in the car when she moaned and said, "Take me, Oddibe, take me now, make me your woman."

That stopped him right then and there. "You are my woman, RubyAnn, there ain't no one else for me, never will be."

She sat up. "I know that, O, I know. I see it in your eyes every time we together." She kissed him. "What I mean is...I think...I...I'm ready, my body..."

"Honey, you don't have to do this 'cause I'm leavin', you be comin' up to see me in Tennessee, and then I'll be back 'fore you know it, we talked 'bout this, no need..."

"This ain't 'bout you leavin', O, this 'bout you and me, this 'bout..." She paused and looked away, trying to find the right words. Finally she looked him in the eyes. "This is because it's time. I'm ready. I want this. I want you."

He took a breath. "I don't have no protection, Roo. I wasn't 'spectin'..."

She kissed him again, a long, wonderful, meaningful kiss. "I trust you, my darling, my wonderful man. I know you'll do the right thing." And with that she removed the rest of her clothing and lay back. He took another breath, undressed, folded his undershirt and put it beneath her, then slowly and carefully penetrated her. She cried out and he stopped, frozen, afraid he had hurt her or done some damage. "No," she said emphatically. "Don't stop, keep going, put it all the way in" and he did, withdrawing when he felt himself getting close.

They cleaned the blood and the gunk as best they could, and her eyes sparkled when she said, "Too bad we can't shower up together like we did before." She told him she was fine, that she didn't hurt, but he noticed she walked a little gingerly when she moved from the back seat to the front. But when they got to the door of her house she gave him another long kiss, a passionate kiss, and said "I love you, Oddibe Daniels. When I come see you in Tennessee, I assume you'll have, um, what-all we'll need to, um, to...to, uh, you know, do this again, yes?"

"Next stop is Montgomery, we are coming to Montgomery, Alabama." The bus driver's words woke him, he had evidently fallen asleep thinking about RubyAnn and their new-found intimacy.

Montgomery meant the trip was about half over, maybe more. The first bus had taken him to Atlanta, where he changed for this one, and now he would be getting on another Greyhound bound for Tallahassee, where he would then have to switch one last time, to the bus marked for Fort Walton Beach. Mrs. Simpson had promised to meet him there.

Sitting in the very back, as his parents instructed him, he patiently waited until everyone else got off the bus, then he grabbed his duffel bag and walked to the door marked "Colored Entrance." There he used the bathroom, bought a package of Nabs, stretched his legs and shoulders, and found his new bus.

He slept a little, read a little. Twain was so funny, he especially loved the sequence in *Connecticut Yankee* when Hank tries to teach those old Brits how to play baseball. Oddibe laughed to himself when Twain wrote that they had to wear their armor while they played and wouldn't even take it off in the bath. But he couldn't restrain himself, laughing out loud at the section describing how umpires were, literally, killed over their decisions, which made umpiring "unpopular." Several people on the bus turned around to wonder why this young man was laughing so hard.

The roads in southern Alabama seemed to be worse than any of the others, it was hard to read as the bus went *bumpety-bumpety-bumpety-bump* for hours on end. He couldn't concentrate on Twain, so he tried Guthrie, and eventually he just stared straight ahead.

What? What was that? He was sure he heard a voice, a familiar voice, how could he hear a familiar voice here? He listened again and this time it was clearer, it was…it was…no, it couldn't be but he kept listening and now he was sure—it was Arch McDonald, the radio voice of the Washington Senators. And was he saying his name?

> *OK, fans, we're back, and Stengel has brought in Ostrowski to try and save this game for young Tom Morgan, who pitched real well for eight innings but tired here in the ninth. Mickey Vernon led off with a double, moved to third on Noren's grounder and then Mele was hit with a pitch and that was it, Casey came and got him and brought in the southpaw Ostrowski to face the rookie, Oddibe Daniels, lefty versus lefty.*
>
> *So there's ducks on the pond for Daniels, who has great speed and will be tough to double up, but that's what Ostrowski wants, two dead birds to end the game and send the fans here at Yankee Stadium home happy.*
>
> *Infield at double-play depth, Coleman maybe a step or two towards first. Daniels gets in the box, waves the bat but that doesn't bother an old vet like Ostrowski. He stares at the youngster, now he checks his runners, and delivers the pitch…STRIKE says Larry Napp, and it was, right down Broadway. Ostrowski doesn't waste much time, he looks at Vernon, tying run at third, looks at Mele, now he fires, JUST OUTSIDE FOR A BALL. Daniels thought about swinging but laid off. Now he steps out, knocks the dirt from his cleats, takes a look at Harris coaching over at third. The fans are yelling for Ostrowski to put him away. Southpaw steps off the rubber, removes his glasses and wipes the sweat, it's a warm one today in the Bronx. OK, back on the hill, he gets his sign from Berra, nods, comes set, delivers…*
>
> *HIGH BOUNDING BALL UP THE MIDDLE, to the right of second. Rizzuto has the best angle, he comes across the bag, jumps and…IT TICKS OFF*

THE END OF HIS GLOVE! *Coleman chases after it in short right-center. Here comes Vernon, that ties up the game, and Mele is heading for third...AND LOOK AT DANIELS! HE MAKES THE BIG TURN AND IS RACING FOR SECOND. Coleman throws to McDougald, who has come over from third to cover, so Daniels will make it...WAIT, HE'S STOPPED JUST SHORT OF THE BAG, DELIBERATELY STOPPED, now they have him in a run-down and he's dancing around like Jackie Robinson, AND NOW HERE COMES MELE, COLLINS THROWS TO BERRA, COLLISION AT THE PLATE, AND HE'S......*

"Tallahassee, last stop on this bus is Tallahassee, we are coming to Tallahassee, Florida." *Oh, man, it must have been a dream, wonder what happened at home plate? Hey, it's a dream, right? I can make it end however I want. Mele scores, Berra starts to argue, Daniels heads for third, Berra throws down but no one is covering the bag and the throw sails into left field. Daniels scores, giving the Senators a 4–2 lead. Harris brings in Sandy Consuegra and he gets the Yankees out 1-2-3 in the ninth, striking out the rookie, Mantle, who is sent up as a pinch-hitter.*

He smiled as he walked through the "Colored Only" door to use the restroom and then find the bus that would take him the 164 miles to Fort Walton Beach.

"Missus, you can't be in here, this here is for culluds only, and you is..."

"I'm not white, sir, if that's what you're saying. If you think I'm white, then sorry, but you're wrong. So if I'm not white, I guess I ought to be in here, right?"

The Negro janitor didn't know what to make of this crazy lady smiling at him. He just shook his head and went back to work, quietly muttering "she pretty but done lost her marbles."

Nashota had been dealing with this all of her adult life, ever since she had first moved to Asheville. While she certainly wasn't what the authorities would classify as "colored," she had never ever identified as a Caucasian, which was something of a problem in a region that seemed to define everything as either black or white. When she and Jack were in the early stages of their relationship, he once called her "exotic" while they were out having dinner. That proved to be unfortunate, because she had just begun to drink her beer but found the term to be so hilarious that she laughed out loud. The brew came spewing out her nose, all over the table, which made her laugh even harder, causing her to pee her pants a little, which made her laugh even more. Eventually she had to excuse herself to go to the ladies' room, where she laughed for a solid three minutes at the whole sequence of events. An embarrassed Jack, meanwhile, did his best to clean the table and not make eye contact with any of the other patrons in the room. Needless to say, that was the last time they ate at that restaurant, though whenever they happened to drive past it she could never refrain from giggling, which always caused Jack to ask her if she needed a beer, and they both would laugh.

She had gone to the bus terminal in Fort Walton Beach to wait for Oddibe, and had instinctively walked into the "Colored" section because, of course, that's where he'd go once he collected his bags. But in truth, this whole "Whites Only" and "Colored Only" business had been bothering her for quite some time. It ignored her and all people like her, not just Cherokee and all other native tribes, but also immigrants from places like China and India. Mostly, though, it bothered her because, in her heart, she knew this just wasn't right. Those words in the Declaration of Independence—"…all men are created equal"—they weren't really true, certainly wasn't being practiced in the USA in 1952. *By now,* she thought, *we should be better than this.* A war had been fought to end slavery, but another system had been developed that denied basic freedoms to those who had been in chains. Eight decades later, another war was fought against nations who wanted to enslave the whole world, and yet, and yet…She sighed, audibly. *Our Negro soldiers came home and were met with the same…indignities as ever. They were placed under the same yolk they had left when they had gone off to liberate Europe and Asia.*

Her thoughts made her tear up as she waited for the bus from Tallahassee to arrive. She sat there quietly, dabbing her eyes, and paid no attention when Negroes would look at her as they walked in or out of the room. The only person who spoke to her was the janitor, which was fine with her. *I need to calm down, I need to be the friendly face that Oddibe expects to see.*

The bus pulled in just a few minutes late and Nashota stood up and positioned herself near the door so that Oddibe could spot her right away, which he did. He smiled and headed straight for her, while she did the same, reaching to take one of his suitcases.

"Oddibe, how are you? I am so glad to see you. How was your trip? Here, let me take that from you, no need for you to carry everything."

"Thank you, Miz Simpson, appreciate it," said Oddibe, allowing her to grab his new piece of luggage; well, it was new to him, anyway. His parents had purchased it for him at a second-hand store, and it contained everything he was not able to get into the old duffel bag his father had insisted he take. "This is what I used to use when I played for the Asheville Royal Giants," Walter Daniels told him. "Was generally able to get everything in there. Me-'n this ol' bag, we traveled some miles together." He paused, and Oddibe could tell that, in his mind, his father was off on another road trip, though only for a moment. "Use it well, son," he said, looking at his eldest boy. "Maybe it'll take you farther than it took me."

As they walked to where she had parked the Meadowbrook, she was conscious that he stayed a couple of steps behind her at all times, and her blood began to boil once more, but she quickly caught herself. *This boy…YOUNG MAN!…is going to have to be dealing with plenty of shit soon enough, no need to start right away.* They walked silently to the car, put his stuff in the trunk and drove off.

After a minute he said, "Nice car."

"It's OK, it gets me where I need to go." He didn't say anything. "Are you tired?" she asked. "Yes'm," he said. "Long way from Asheville, North Carolina."

"Ever been to Florida before?" she wondered.

"No, ma'am," he said. "Never been south-a Greenville, South Carolina before. This all…different…very different for me." He paused, then said "I didn't really expect to see you here, Miz Simpson."

She smiled. "I don't usually come to spring training, but this year…it's…uh…it's different, special." She liked that word, so she said it again. "Special. Because of you. I decided I ought to be here right at the beginning, help you settle in, make sure things are OK for the first few days. Then I'll go back to Tennessee, we still have a lot to get done before Opening Day."

"Yes, ma'am," he said. "Thank you for doing that."

She hesitated, then decided to get right to it. "My brother, one of my brothers, is a major in the Air Force, which is one reason we're training here, Eglin Air Force base is here. He's done a lot for us, the league, the last few years, helping to get some of our facilities. Anyway, I spoke with him after we signed you and asked him about finding a place for you to live while we're here, and he was able to line up a room in someone's house. Very nice young couple, Senior Airman Ellis and his wife and their young daughter, they said they'd be happy to have you, so I'm going to take you over there, Mrs. Ellis is expecting us. I kinda figured you'd want to rest up today and then go out to the field tomorrow, is that OK?"

"Yes'm," he said. "I reckon I could stand to stretch out in a bed. Do I get a bed, or a couch, do you know?"

She smiled. "They have an extra room, so you have a bed waiting for you. Now, I have to tell you, I don't know exactly what they're going to be charging you for rent and all, that'll be between you and Senior Airman Ellis, you understand," and Oddibe just nodded. "Good," said Nashota. She paused for a moment then continued. "I also have a place for you to live once we get back to Edens Ridge. We may need to talk about it, but today is probably not the best day," she said as she saw that his eyes had closed.

"I'm awake, ma'am," Oddibe said, but very softly. "Just restin' my eyes. My momma says that all-a time and we always tease her 'bout it, but now I understand." And they both smiled.

She had reached the beginning of the military housing. "Oddibe," said Nashota, "We're going to do everything in our power to make this a good experience for you. We're going to try to keep the…the…the garbage down to a minimum, best as we can. We'll do…"

He opened his eyes. "Appreciate that, Miz Simpson," he said. "I really do, but don't worry too much 'bout it, always gonna be someone, somewhere. I may have some rough days, but the nice thing 'bout baseball is there's always a new game the next day. Unless it rains," and with that he gave out a little laugh. "Though sometimes we play in the rain, ain't that right?" And of course she had to agree.

It had been more than a bit awkward.

No one had really known what to expect, but the players, for the most part, were polite. They kept their distance, mostly just nodding at him, occasionally flashing a very brief smile before moving on. A few paid no attention or stared right through him and Oddibe knew exactly what that meant, quietly hoping that those fellows did not make the team.

The Mountain Empire League

Of course, technically, they were all trying out. In the majors, even a bad club (like the Cubs or Browns or Senators) could count on having the same dozen or so players year in and year out. This, however, was not the major leagues. This was, in fact, as far from that level as one could get and still be called a professional ballplayer. This was Class D, and an independent league to boot, unaffiliated with any of the majors' 16 teams. No one had a guaranteed spot on the roster, everyone had to prove to the manager that they could play.

Now in actuality, Jack Simpson already knew a few of the men who would be suiting up on Opening Day. Like Peter Sevareid, the big first baseman from North Dakota who could hit the ball a long way and whose sense of humor always kept the clubhouse loose. Terry VanLandingham, commonly called TVL, was a speedy, handsome outfielder from Las Vegas with a generally sunny disposition, which always seemed to go over very well with the ladies. Ken Crockett was a little lefty from eastern Kentucky whose chief claims to fame were his devastating screwball and his insistence that he was a direct descendant of Davy Crockett himself. They had all played on the team last year but had not been picked up by any club in a higher classification, which mystified Jack, who knew they were all better than Class D players. In fact, over the winter, he was sure he had a deal for Crockett with Lafayette in the Class C Evangeline League, but then they began to hesitate, and when Jack tried to bargain, they told him they'd changed their minds, sorry. Damn them! These three, and a couple of others, showed up in Okaloosa County with the quiet knowledge that they'd be heading to Edens Ridge in April.

And Oddibe, of course, would be on the team, that was a given. After all the trouble they had gone through to get his contract approved, then all the talks with sponsors and city leaders and religious leaders and others (like Win Appleton), there was no way this young man was being sent home any time soon. Jack Simpson was very upfront with everyone, a break from normal spring training protocol.

"See that young man shagging flies out in center?" he asked several potential recruits. "His name is Oddibe Daniels and he's my center fielder. If we give you a try-out, you may find yourself sitting next to him in the dugout, or on the bus. If you make the team, you may have to shake his hand if he hits a home run. Think you can do these things?" Some people said sure. "I'm from Jersey," said outfielder Jerry Brodie, though out of his mouth it came out a bit differently. "I seen Jackie play lotsa times, even in Joisy City back in '46, when he was with Montreal. Don't matter much to me." A little lefty from Texas, Tommy Nathan, had a different perspective. "Is he a good outfielder?" When Jack said he was one of the best he had ever seen, Nathan nodded and said "Mista Simpson, I been livin' on a farm in east Texas ever since I was born. Be honest with you, I ain't seen many Nigras in my life, so I don't know much 'bout 'em. But look, I'm a pitcher, and what's important to me is havin' guys behind me who can make the plays. If I give up a shot and he can go git it, that's all I really care 'bout."

But not everyone felt that way. "Shit, are you crazy, man?" "Who you think you are, Branch Rickey?" "We can't be havin' something like that, not in Tennessee." "What you tryin' to do, cause a riot?" Words along those lines were enough for Jack to thank the young man for coming, but he would not be offered a chance to try out. "You don't even wanna see me throw?" asked one freckle-faced kid. "I can throw hard and throw strikes, I'm as good as anyone you got in this-here camp," said one. "I can hit like Ted Williams and run like Joe DiMaggio," said another. But Jack held firm, and often got cussed out for his resolve. "How can you just sit there and take it?" asked Mike Hamblen, the team's coach/trainer/bus driver/clubhouse man. "I think I'd be practicing my left hook on guys like these." Jack gave out a short laugh. "Makes me think that I must be doing something right. Besides, it kind of puts me in Oddibe's shoes, 'cause I know he'll be hearing this, and worse, every day. Every single fucking day."

Unless you seriously suffer from allergies, you probably love the spring, and why not? It is a beautiful time of year, as the grey, cold winter gives way to bountiful colors and warmer weather. Spring means beauty and renewal, flowers and trees and birds, spring means life is good again.

It also means baseball is back.

Wells Boggs loved the spring. As anyone who had ever worked behind the scenes could attest, the regular season becomes a series of days and nights, chores and meetings, attending to business and putting our fires. During all those years he ran ballclubs, Wells would rarely see more than an inning of a game, here and there, before he was needed somewhere. When he was in charge of the Knoxville team, he found that if he ever wanted to see a game, just sit down as a fan and watch a ballgame, he would have to drive over to Nashville or Chattanooga or Morristown when his Smokies were on the road. But it was different in the spring. Even after he became a league president, he found he could sit in the stands, relax and watch the action between the lines, like anyone else. Except, of course, when someone might happen to recognize him. "Aren't you the Mountain Empire League president? Thought so. Listen, mind if I bend your ear for a minute? Somethin' I been thinkin' 'bout, and I wondered...won't take but a minute." They would then spend a good quarter-hour chattering about some trivial matter...*Ah well, comes with the territory, I suppose.*

There were not a lot of relaxing moments in the spring of 1952.

Wells' strongest desire was for every team in the Mountain Empire League to become affiliated with a major league club. It would create great stability for each franchise and, frankly, would be a real personal achievement. In his opinion, the very best minor leagues, like the International or the American Association, were affiliated, and he sought that status for his league. On the Mountain Empire's bottom-rung Class D level, only the Appalachian, PONY and Wisconsin State leagues were fully affiliated. Boggs saw integration of the league as a way to demonstrate to the majors that they were worthy of becoming fully affiliated and, therefore, one of the elite.

This, more than anything else, was what guided Wells. He understood the legalities that had been raised, and he supposed this was the right and moral thing to do. But making his league a full-fledged working partner with the big boys was his ultimate goal, and if integration was the route they had to take, then Herbert George

Wells Boggs would drive that train. And so, despite having personal reservations, he completely threw himself behind Jack Simpson's experiment with Oddibe...*what's that boy's full name again?*

In the meantime, the eight clubs were all unaffiliated and therefore needed to recruit, sign, and pay all their own players. (Affiliated teams, such as Knoxville and many others, didn't have to go through all that rigamarole. The major league club signed all the players and paid them directly from headquarters.) Knowing that each team would be working to fill their roster, Wells had sent his letter (the one that so upset Truck Maxwell), then followed it up with telephone calls. Upon arriving in Okaloosa County (early, it must be noted), he met with each manager and team president individually, and emphasized that their off-season vote had been decisive and reminded them of their responsibilities. He also let them know, in no uncertain terms, that "I intend to keep order in our league. I will come down, swiftly and convincingly, on anyone who tries to cause trouble, no matter who it might be, got that? And listen, if y'all think I don't mean what I say, jus' try me, hear? If you decide to test my mettle, that will be a test you will fail." Everyone looked him in the eye and told him they understood.

Trouble started right away.

Gene Conn spotted Wells eating breakfast in the Gulfview Hotel. "Mind if I join you?" he asked, and Wells, with his mouth full of eggs, just nodded and pointed to an empty chair. The former catcher was one of Wells' favorite people in the league, quiet and polite in mixed company, firm but fair with his players and a good, sharp baseball man. Lionel Ticknor and Bob Rhodes had both stated, on separate occasions, that they expected Gene to manage in the majors someday. He was not the type of person to complain, so whenever he happened to expressed a concern, Wells made sure to pay close attention.

"Wells, I have to tell you I've already lost six players or would-be players. Two guys I had last year—Martin, my second baseman and Hopkins, that tall lefthander with the scraggly moustache, remember him?—they both told me a coupla weeks ago that they'd rather not play against a Negro. And then down here, holding tryouts, I've told everyone right away, just like you asked us to, and four guys walked out, just shook their heads and left. Can you imagine? Chance to maybe play professional ball and..." He shrugged. "It's...bothersome, Wells, it's not good." The league president said nothing until Gene asked him "Did you hear about Lionel? I understand he got into a real shouting match with someone," and Wells quietly said "Yes, I know all about that."

In fact, Wells had been one of the peace-keepers. He had been visiting the Bees' practice field and was casually chatting with John Robertson when they both heard some shouting and saw the players start running towards the dugout. Boggs and Robertson did the same thing and quickly saw the veteran skipper pushing and yelling at a young man that neither of them recognized. Wells thought he heard the phrase "n— lover" but couldn't be completely sure. He was, however, positive he heard Lionel call the kid a cock-sucker and told him to get off his practice field, which is when the boy clenched his fist and raised his arm. Wells instinctively pushed through the audience of ballplayers that had gathered and grabbed the young man from behind in a half-nelson, while John Robertson thrust himself between this kid and his manager and pushed Ticknor out of the way. Didn't stop the shouting, though, and finally Wells spun the young man around and said, "I don't know who you are but I do know you are not welcome here, now grab your gear and git!"

"Who the hell are you, old man?" snarled the boy, whose blonde hair was closely cropped.

"I'm the president of this league, you sonofabitch," said Wells, who rarely swore, "and what I say goes. Now you leave this instant and never come back."

The players, silent observers up to this point, now joined in and started hollering at the young man. When two of the Bees' veterans, catcher Tom Hart and outfielder Dave Walters, began walking towards him, the young man decided that now might, indeed, be a good time to take his leave. Grabbing his small duffel bag, he said "OK, OK, I'm going, I don't need no fucking escort," and he headed for the door. As the yelling continued, he raised his middle finger without breaking stride, which turned up the volume. Suddenly Dave Walters began running towards the departing player, but was blocked by Wells, who shouted "Walters! Stop right there! WALTERS!! Take another step and it'll cost you fifty bucks!!" That had the desired effect.

The clubhouses that Okaloosa County had built for the league a few years back were often described as cozy, which was a polite was to say small and cramped. John Robertson took his manager there and Wells followed after he instructed the players to go back to what they had been doing. When no one moved at first, he said simply "Fungo practice! Infielders, to your positions, outfielders, go out and shag flies." Then he went to find out what had happened.

"What happened," said Lionel, "was that this squirrely bastard said he wanted to try out for the team and I said fine, go find a uni. Then I remembered and said 'Oh, while you're looking, let me tell you about something that's happening in the league this year, something we think is real exciting.' And I told him about Daniels and he just stopped in his tracks, turned around and said to me 'You mean you gonna have a n— on this team?' And I said no, not on the Bees but on another team in the league, the Wolves, and he said 'Well don't that beat all, what's this world a-comin' to when a good old southern league starts allowin' n—s in, country's just goin' to shit.' I interrupted him right there, told him I didn't like that kind of talk, and if that's the way he felt he could leave right now, he wasn't welcome on my team. Well, he starts hollerin' and cussin' and sayin' all sorts-a things, and when he said somethin' about 'lynchin' 'em all,' I just blew up. Sorry John, Wells, I know I shouldn't-a lost my temper like that, I'm supposed to be the adult around these boys, but I couldn't stand listenin' to his shit…"

"That's OK, Lionel, it's OK, really," said Robertson. "I probably would have just hauled off and decked him, at least you didn't do that," to which Lionel replied, "I was sure thinkin' 'bout it," and that made all three of them laugh. After a brief pause, Lionel said, quietly, "Guess I oughta go out to my team," and he took a breath and strode back out onto the field.

Later on Windy Haines came knocking on Wells' hotel room door. "I heared what happened with ol' Lionel today," said the one-time major league catcher in his

Kentucky drawl. "Coulda had sumptin like that in our camp today, too. Different fella, I imagine, but spoutin' the same garbage. Didn't lose my temper, boss, but if-n he had pushed me just a bit further, don't know what I'd-a done. Thought I'd letcha know." He turned to go, stopped, then looked at Wells again. "Keep an eye on Vic, boss, I hear he may not…um…he may be a little more, uh, uh, forgivin' of people and their pin-yuns, if-n you know what I mean. And this new guy, Axford, the player-manager, don't know much 'bout him, but I do know he was in the Dodger system and got released in '46 or '47. Don't know if that means anythin' or not, just…just passin' it on, boss." And with that he left.

Wells was tempted to leave, too. He thought about calling the airline and changing his ticket, going back to Knoxville early, Georgia and the kids would certainly be happy to see him. He sat in his sterile hotel room and stared at the phone for a long time.

Then he went to bed. He was the Mountain Empire League president and couldn't just leave, couldn't run out at this crucial point in league history.

They started hearing it with the very first exhibition game.

Since the entire league was rather isolated there in Okaloosa County, they only had each other to play against, but that was OK. For a lot of players, the veterans, they just needed a little time to get the kinks out, shake off a winter's worth of beer-drinking and carbohydrate-loading and not getting the kind of exercise they really needed. For those not virtually assured of a roster spot, it was important to make an early impression on the manager. If you could show him you could at least hold your own with the other players in the league, that might possibly go a long way in securing a job for yourself.

Larkin Samuel "Trig" Swinney found himself in a unique position. He was a veteran player, but was trying to make a new (to him) team in a new (to him) league. He needed to show manager Karl Hines that he could still wallop the fastball and handle the breaking ball, and that he hadn't lost a step in the outfield. He had spent the winter in Texas, as usual, working on the family farm, but he also took on extra chores so he could work off the calories; that big boy always could eat! When cold weather set in, limiting what they could do outside, he made sure to carve out some time to run, keeping his legs in shape and his body warm. He also made a conscious decision to limit his Lone Star beer intake, though some weeks proved to be more successful than others.

After consulting with his daddy, he decided he would drive to Florida and then (hopefully) to Kentucky, so he also spent some time working on his '49 Chevy 3100, making sure that old half-ton pickup was up to the challenge of a long road trip. New spark plugs, new air filter, new wipers, and two new tires, which he put on the rear. Changed the oil, filled up the coolant, checked the air on the old tires, he was ready to go. The drive proved to be boring, and long, but he made it to Okaloosa County without incident.

He started hitting just as soon as he suited up. Didn't matter what these kids threw him, or where they put it, he was able to get his bat on the ball. And they really were kids—he was the oldest one in the Shirley camp by better than three years. One day in practice a skinny right-hander tried to move him off the plate and threw it high and tight, but Trig just arched his back so the ball wouldn't hit him, and then he smiled as he stepped back into the batter's box. Sure enough the kid tried it again, and this time Swinney was ready—he got his bat up, slid his hand up the barrel so the wood was parallel to the ground, and pushed a bunt down the first-base line. The skinny pitcher raced over to field the ball, putting him right in the baseline, and Trig never hesitated, plowing over the youngster like he was just a bump in the road. The boy went sprawling, the ball kept rolling, and by the time the first baseman was able to glove it, Swinney was dusting himself off at second base.

"What are you doing?" shouted the catcher, who was helping the woozy hurler get to his feet. "Didn't you see him in front of you? You could have killed him!"

"Base path belongs to the runner," said Trig, calmly, from second. "Man gets in the way, he's gotta be prepared for the consequences."

Karl Hines—a former outfielder who had made it as far as Triple-A in his playing days—came out to check on his pitcher as several players gathered around and opined about how maybe Trig was playing dirty. The youngster was still seeing stars, so Hines looked at his bench and nodded at another young man, a redheaded southpaw from Massachusetts. "You, Red, you throw for a while, let's see whatcha got." As the kid sprinted off the bench towards the mound, Hines turned towards those players who had gathered along the first-base line.

"What he did was perfectly legal," he said. "And what he said was correct, the base path does belong to the runner. Can't block him out, this ain't fucking football. An umpire would have called interference on the pitcher and would have awarded the batter/runner first base." He looked up at Trig, standing calmly at second. "Fact that he's at second shows he's a smart baserunner." He looked at his players, veterans and wannabees alike, then spoke loudly so all could hear. "We don't play dirty on the Cardinals but we do play smart. That was a smart play, Swinney." And with that he walked back into the dugout and sat next to the young pitcher who'd just had his bell rung.

(Later on, when their workouts were all done for the day, Hines quietly came over to Trig. "Nothing wrong with what you done, Swinney," he said. "Just try not to kill these young-uns, will you? I ain't sure I got enough capable bodies to take north, and it don't help if some of 'em get hurt on the job." Then he slapped Trig on the knee and ambled back to his little office. A couple of days later the skinny right-hander was sent home to West Virginia.)

The eight teams in the Mountain Empire League played on several fields that had been built by the county, with ample assistance from the Air Force. During the ten months or so that the ballplayers were not in Okaloosa County, the airmen used the fields for both recreation and occasional military maneuvers. The fans who attended these spring training games were similarly a mixture of local folks and military men, and their respective families. The flyboys were from all over the country and represented all walks of American life, while the others were primarily people who had always lived in northwest Florida.

Jack had not made any attempt to hide what he was doing, though he hadn't publicized it, either. His goal was simply to conduct a normal spring training camp, which meant choosing the best players to represent Edens Ridge and getting them ready to play the arduous season. It didn't take long, then, for the word to be spread, quickly making the Wolves the #1 topic of conversation in living rooms, barber shops, and taverns throughout the county.

Wells Boggs was concerned and came to see Jack.

"There's a lotta talk goin' round, Jack, lotta talk, not all of it good. I was thinkin' that maybe you might wanna, um, play closed games, you know, not have any fans…"

"Wells, are you nuts? That's the craziest…we're ballplayers, we're used to playing in front of people, that's all there is to it."

"Maybe at first, Jack, maybe the first 2–3 games, get people…"

"What, more fired up? That'll just make it worse. People will really be chompin' at the bit, wanting to see Oddibe, and my players will be real anxious to be playing in front of fans. No changes, Wells, no coddlin', no…no nothin', we play our full schedule, right? Right?"

Wells nodded, but his heart wasn't really in it.

League tradition held that the first pair of games were always intrastate contests, which simply meant that Edens Ridge would take on Kruse. A coin flip determined who would be the home team for the first game, and Ducks' manager Vic Rutherford correctly called "heads," so the Wolves would come to the plate first. (They would reverse roles the next day.)

Unlike standard minor league facilities, these grandstands had not been built to hold a great many fans, maybe 1,000 people, give or take. Most of the time, they were, perhaps, half full, but on this day the place was jam-packed.

There was a very audible buzz in the crowd as Kruse took the field. The Wolves, meanwhile, all tried to be nonchalant as Oddibe grabbed a couple of bats and swung them as he walked to the on-deck circle. His very appearance onto the field sent a jolt through the crowd, but they didn't react until he was officially announced: "Leading off, in centerfield for Edens Ridge, number six, Oddibe Daniels. Daniels, number six."

A handful of people cheered, including Oddibe's "landlords," Senior Airman Ellis and his wife and daughter. A very small number of Negroes came to the game and they cheered also, but they were quickly drowned out by boos…and worse.

"Lookie here, we got us a n— on the field!"

"Glad you're here, n—, I need me some fresh gator bait."

"Call the zoo, one-a their monkeys done escaped!"

"Hey, rastus, go back where you belong, this here's a white man's game."

Coaching at third base, Jack heard them all and knew that Oddibe could hear them, too. He looked into his Wolves' dugout and saw some of his players shuffling around a bit, looking at their feet, embarrassed for their young teammate. He heard Pete Sevareid shout out "OK, Oddibe, OK, let's go now, let's get 'em," which led several of the other Wolves to join in. *Good for you, Pete.*

For this first game of the spring, Rutherford had started a tall, husky right-hander from Arizona State University, Will Thomasson, whose warmups seemed to Oddibe to be harder than anything he had experienced back in North Carolina. *No going back now, no sir, now get-on in there and show 'em, show 'em what you got.*

Thomasson looked at his catcher, nodded, wound up, pivoted just a bit and threw from a three-quarters arm angle. The ball was fast and straight and Oddibe watched it sail by, heard the umpire holler "STRIKE!" He also heard other sounds, including the slurs coming from the stands, but also words of encouragement coming from his dugout.

"No pitcher out there, no pitcher."

"That's all he's got, Oddibe, you can hit him."

And he clearly heard his manager, Jack Simpson, clapping his hands up the third-base line and saying "Let's go, let's go, be a hitter out there."

The next pitch was another fastball, almost the same spot. Oddibe swung late and just nicked the ball, which dribbled harmlessly in foul territory.

"They play for real in this league, snowball" came from the stands. ("Snowball?" asked reserve catcher Allan Miggs. "Where do they come up with this shit?")

Now Thomasson tried a curve ball, but it bounced in the dirt right in front of home plate. "Ball One," said the ump.

Oddibe knew he'd be seeing another fastball, so he mentally geared up for it and was not disappointed, it came in low and fast on the outside part of the plate. He swung and hit a line drive to the left of second base. The Ducks' shortstop, a veteran named Barry, had been shading Oddibe to pull, so he was closer to the bag than normal; he took a couple of quick steps, then dove and knocked the ball down. He quickly got to his feet, grabbed the ball and fired to first base, where his teammate stretched about as far as he could.

The ball and Oddibe seemed to arrive together. The umpire made his right hand into a fist, swung it like he was throwing a punch, and shouted "OUT! HE'S OUT!!"

Jack thought his speedster had beaten the throw, but he didn't argue, he just waved his arms a bit. *Gotta pick your battles.* Oddibe also thought he was safe but he didn't fuss, he just turned and trotted back into his dugout, where several teammates patted him on the back and offered words of encouragement, including "You'll get him next time." That didn't happen, though, as he popped up and hit a weak grounder to second before Jack brought in a new set of players. He did, however, make a fine running catch in the fifth inning that prevented an extra-base hit, which brought shouts from his bench and silence from the slur-mongers.

After the game, Win Appleton wandered into Jack's office, carrying a couple of beers. "Lift those from the press room?" Jack asked with a grin. "Yeah, right," growled Win. "Grabbed 'em as soon as I finished my pheasant."

The two friends sat there for a couple of minutes, silently sipping their beers. Finally Win said, "Well, it wasn't too bad for him out there."

"No, not at all, as long as you don't count all the n— remarks, and coon and gator bait and…and…there was one in there I'd never heard…"

"Rastus," said Win. "Comes from the Uncle Remus books. Disney made that 'Song of the South' film a coupla years ago based on those stories."

"Hmmm," said Jack, taking another drink.

"In the first inning, looked to me like he was safe. You?"

"Are we on the record?" Jack wanted to know. Win shook his head. "Looked safe to me, but then, I was over by third, not the best angle. Tell you, though, he ain't gonna get the close calls, not for a while, anyway, not 'til he proves himself, as a player, and more. Like Jackie."

Win took a drink. "Should-a been out by ten feet. Ball was hit hard, it didn't roll too far, ordinary runner, he's out by ten feet. That boy can run, Jack."

"Told you, told you that when we had snow on the ground. And don't call him a boy, especially around 'Sho."

"I know, I forgot, sorry." They both concentrated on their beers for a moment, then Win said, "So when can I write him up?"

"Why don't you wait 'til he does something better than oh-fer?"

Win finished his beer, set it down by Jack and stood up. "I can do that, just give me the heads-up, yeah?" Jack nodded and Win ambled out.

MOUNTAIN EMPIRE LG. ENTERS THE 20TH CENTURY
By Win Appleton

Okaloosa County, FL—Last July, the National League trounced the American League in their annual All-Star game by a score of 8–3. Two of the starters for the NL were Jackie Robinson and Roy Campanella, both of the Brooklyn Dodgers. Their teammate, Don Newcombe, pitched the sixth, seventh and eighth innings and did not give up a run. Over in the AL dugout, Cleveland's Larry Doby and Chicago's rookie sensation, Minnie Minoso, each made it into the game. And the Giants went to the World Series last year with Monte Irvin, Hank Thompson and Willie Mays making significant contributions.

All the players mentioned are Negroes, except for Minoso, who is actually Cuban but with such dark skin he was able to play in the Negro National League.

When Jackie Robinson broke the minor-league "color line" in 1946 and the major league barrier the following year, he was looked on as an oddity, an experiment. Now we can see he was just the herald, announcing the readiness of the Negro ballplayer to make his mark on the game.

Which brings us to what is happening this spring in Okaloosa County, Florida.

Our own Jack Simpson, the grizzled former outfielder who leads the Edens Ridge Wolves both on and off the field, is dedicated to finding the very best ballplayers, who will win often enough to challenge for the league championship. He believes he has found a young man, 21 years old, who will do just that. A speedy native of Asheville, North Carolina, Simpson thinks he "has the potential to be the best outfielder we've ever seen on the Ridge, maybe the best ever to play in our league." And if he hits, he might just bring the same kind of excitement on the basepaths that Robinson and Mays offer to National League fans. And oh yes, like them, he is also a Negro, with the intriguing name of Oddibe Daniels.

"It's about time this league started signing the very best talent," Simpson told this reporter. "Senators bought Charlie Dowell so we need a good centerfielder, and this kid is better than good, I think our fans are really gonna like him out there."

But there never has been a Negro player in the Mountain Empire League, what about that, Jack?

"Don't matter to me what color skin he got. My job is to put the best players out there, game in and game out. When I look at how our roster is shaping up, I feel confident that Daniels is just that—one of our very best players." And there was no mistaking the look of resolve in Jack Simpson's eyes.

Certainly Daniels makes the fan want to watch him. His speed is breathtaking, which is most evident when he chases down fly balls in the outfield. So far this spring, he has shown he can catch balls that seem to be over his head just as easily as he can prevent Texas Leaguers from dropping into No Man's Land.

This observer, however, is not yet convinced that Mr. Daniels can handle that all-important leadoff slot. To date he has 17 official at-bats and has collected just four singles, a .235 average, and only two of those hits left the infield. A man batting at the very top of the order needs to get on base more, and that, no doubt, is what this young man must work on for the balance of spring training.

Meanwhile, there is the larger issue. At this juncture, none of the other M.E.L. teams has a Negro in camp, so Oddibe Daniels may very well be the league's lone pioneer this year. Which means that our rookie fly-chaser will be under a microscope, but so will we, the people of Edens Ridge. How we treat him will be carefully looked at by the other seven teams in the league, that's for sure, but it won't end there. We will also be monitored by minor league headquarters in Columbus, Ohio, and by the sixteen major league teams, who are always on the prowl for good places to park their prospects. When the games start for real in just a few weeks, we'll need to welcome him with good old Northeast Tennessee hospitality. Show him that we fans know he's a part of the team, OUR team, as we launch what we hope will be a successful season for the Edens Ridge Wolves.

There were different reactions to Win's *Gazette* piece all over town. On the East side, the Reverend Ish Clark was thrilled and excited, but a little dismayed, all at the same time. He was thrilled that his hometown baseball team was taking such a bold step, and excited that he and his parish had been consulted in advance and could get to play even a small role in this great venture. But after his conversation with Jack Simpson, he had asked around and found that none of his parishioners were willing to house Mr. Daniels. He was disappointed in his congregation, and saddened when he learned what accommodations had been found for the young man.

Downtown, the police chief of Edens Ridge, Newell Gregory, had read the article with interest, knowing that it meant something different to him and his small force. He wondered whether he needed to seek out advice from other communities, but he wasn't sure just where to go. And while he was thinking, he started getting concerned calls from folks who were worried about what might happen in their normally-tranquil little town. He also received angry calls from people who told him, clearly (and often quite loudly) what might just happen "if this Nigra shows up here. Jus' warnin' you, Newell." And a note arrived in the mail, containing a copy of the article and a piece of paper that read *This has to do with what we were talking about. Don't forget what you promised.* The note was unsigned but it didn't have to be, he was very familiar Jasmine Brunét's return address.

On the south side, Orley Pepper threw his newspaper on the floor. "Good goddam!" he exclaimed, using his favorite expression, which he immediately followed with "son of a fucking bitch," also up there on his personal hit parade. "A n— playin' ball right here, right here in Edens Ridge? We'll have to see about that, now won't we?" And with that he grabbed his hat and his car keys and went out the door.

The *Gazette* piece also drew a lot of responses from the Edens Ridge Wolves.

"Oh my, I do declare, your speed just takes my breath away," said pitcher Patrick Head in falsetto. "Frankly, my dear Scarlett, I don't give a flying fuck," said outfielder Jim Altman, which shifted conversation from Win Appleton's article to the film version of "Gone with the Wind." ("Gable wanted to say 'flying fuck,' everybody knows that!").

"Good piece on you," said the studious Anthony Valenza, known to all as Coach because of how he automatically took charge of the infield from his shortstop position. Aside from "hi there" every day, these were Valenza's first words to Oddibe, but they were said without rancor or sarcasm, which the youngster took to be a positive sign.

Not everyone was encouraging. "Says here that a fellow with just four hits and a .235 average is 'one of our very best players,'" said catcher Rob Boxleiter, holding the paper in his hand. "If that's the case, we must just suck." Boxleiter was a crude, snide young man from Staten Island who could hit the ball a long way, just not very often. Jack had tried to sell his contract over the winter but had been unsuccessful. When training camp began, he was hoping that a better backstopping candidate would materialize so he could tell Boxleiter he didn't need him this year, best of luck to you. Allan Miggs, however, was proving to be the only other competent catcher trying to make the team, and his strength was his glove and his grit, making it likely that

Boxleiter would win the starting job again. Thinking about his catching situation made Jack spit. *Damn! Sure wish Box was every bit as good as he thinks he is.*

(Jack only had one comment on the article, by the way. "Grizzled?" he asked his old friend the day after it ran. "I'm only in my thirties, how could I be grizzled?" "Jack," Appleton replied. "I believe you were born grizzled. And now you're balding, as well.")

To Oddibe, however, the Appleton piece was serving as an ice-breaker. "More people are now talking to me," he wrote in his daily letter to his parents, in which he also enclosed the article.

Even for someone who was quiet by nature, it was a lonely existence. Away from the field he had no interaction with his teammates. Mrs. Ellis brought him to the field every day and generally picked him up, though sometimes, if she was running late or practice ended early, Jack would simply drive him back himself.

There were two movie houses in the area he could go to in the evening. The one over at Eglin was technically off-limits to civilians, but Senior Airman Ellis brought him in a couple of times as a guest and no one said anything. The other contained a very specific Negro section, which were the last six rows of the balcony. They had better films than the ones on the base, first-run features. He had gone a handful of times and really liked the Western, "High Noon." He had expected "The Quiet Man" to be a Western, because it starred John Wayne, and was surprised when it wasn't, but it was good and fun, he had enjoyed it. But he always felt very conspicuous there, even in the darkened theatre, so he didn't go all that often.

One time the Simpsons invited him over for dinner and that went well, though everyone seemed to be acting more polite than usual. Mrs. Simpson said something about doing it again, but then she went back to Tennessee to finish preparations for the regular season, and that was that.

He missed his family, even Berenice. He especially missed RubyAnn, and if he thought about her too much he'd have to quietly take care of himself. He looked forward to having them all visit him during the summer, though he wasn't sure how they'd react if they learned the truth about where he'd be living.

Oddibe had actually found that whole thing to be amusing. The Simpsons had brought it up when they had him over for dinner.

"I spoke with several people, Oddibe, about renting you a room, but no one was willing to step up, there seemed to be...um, I hate to say it but I could tell there was some fear, they're not...no one is really sure how the community is going to react..."

"That's OK, Miz Simpson, I know you tried your best."

"But I did find something, I didn't totally strike out!" she said, laughing at her baseball metaphor. "A nice old house, really lovely old house, seems like a decent neighborhood, close to a grocery store, I saw that myself, not too far from the ballpark, and they are eager to have you!"

"They?" Oddibe wondered. "Is it a family, like the Ellis family?"

Nashota gave Jack a withering look when he made a snorting noise.

"No, not exactly, though it is...kind of a family. Several women live there, and they are all anxious for you to move in, it'll be like living with aunts and big sisters, they've promised to look after you real good."

"Huh," said Jack.

Oddibe suspected that something was up, he wasn't dumb. "Skipper, what is it that y'all ain't tellin' me. I'm a big boy, I can take it, whatever it is."

The Simpsons looked at each other but no one spoke until Oddibe, after a moment of silence that seemed more like an hour, simply said "Please!"

Nashota cleared her throat and began. "Well, Oddibe, it's not really a big deal, not to us, certainly, probably not to you, either. It's…it's…don't forget, we weren't having any luck finding anything else…"

"It's a whorehouse!" Jack exploded. "We just gotta spit it out, 'Sho." He looked at Oddibe. "What Nashota said is correct, we were turned down a coupla times, and this place, it just fell into our laps…"

"The room is a good size, I've seen it, been in it," said Nashota. "There are two bathrooms on that floor, second floor, another on the ground level, big kitchen which you can use, and you won't be getting in anyone's way, they…"

"They're working at night because they're working girls!" Jack said. "Prostitutes, hookers, call 'em what you want." He leaned forward in his chair. "Look, Oddibe, we know it ain't ideal, ain't even particularly good. If you don't like it, if it bothers you just one little bit, you say so and we'll go back, talk to more people, see if we can find you…"

"Sounds alright to me, Skipper, Miz Simpson. Don't matter to me what those girls do, everybody gotta make a living, you know? Besides, I kinda like the idea of having aunties keeping an eye on me…"

"What about your family, Oddibe, especially your momma?"

The young man chuckled briefly. "Momma will not be happy, no, no, not at all, so…ha! I just won't tell her. Same with RubyAnn. When anybody come to visit, I'll make sure they don't spend much time over at my place, and if they have to see it, I'll work it out with…with who, who's in charge?"

"Miss Brunét, Jasmine Brunét," said Nashota.

"Jasmine Brunét," repeated Oddibe. "I'm sure we'll get along."

"She's always liked ballplayers," Jack muttered and then, when he realized he had actually said that out loud, he quickly added "I mean, I know she comes out to some of our games. Occasionally. Once in a while." *Oh, boy, am I gonna hear about this later on.*

Shortly after Win's article appeared, the Wolves played the Shirley Cardinals on an absolutely beautiful, sunny Friday afternoon in northwest Florida. It was the kind of day that every Chamber of Commerce around the country likes to say is oh-so-typical of their community.

The Cardinals were having a hard time coming around. Those were actually the exact words of their manager, Karl Hines, as he and Jack made small talk a couple of hours before the game.

"Had to watch a lotta players walk away, Jack, you know why," said Hines, and Jack nodded. "Still tryin' to put all the pieces together, and I tell ya, I ain't for sure that

I got them all here. Some-a these kids…" He paused and surprisingly let out an audible sigh. "Some-a these kids don't belong here. My centerfielder, Swinney, he oughta be in Class B, at least in C, but a few of the others should be selling shoes back home. We're having a hard time comin' 'round, this could be a rough year for us."

Hines started a tall right-hander from Missouri named Jeff Mackey, whose chief problem that spring was throwing strikes, so when the second pitch Oddibe saw sent him sprawling onto his butt, no one thought anything of it. But on a 3–1 pitch, Oddibe practically had to do a backflip to avoid getting drilled in the knees by a low, inside fastball. Jack began yelling to the umpires from his spot in the third-base coaching box, and a couple of the Wolves started shouting as well. "Hey, he's throwing at our player, he's throwing at our player." Oddibe said nothing as he trotted to first, then moved to second when Squirrel Davis hit a high chopper to the right side. He quickly stole third, and scored when Mac McElvain ripped a single to right-center, which was followed by a two-run blast by Sevareid that cleared the scoreboard in left-center.

The next inning the Wolves were threatening again, with Jerry Brodie on second and two out, when Oddibe came to the plate. He wanted to hit the ball through the infield, allowing Brodie to score, but the first pitch from Mackey came straight for his chin. Oddibe fell backwards to get out of the way, and in doing so he left his bat sticking straight up in the air. The ball hit the bat and dribbled slowly towards the mound, where Mackey easily fielded it and threw to first for the final out while Daniels was picking himself up off the ground.

As Mackey and his teammates headed into their dugout, the pitcher said, with a smirk, "That's how we play professional baseball, jigaboo."

Heading out to his post at first base, Pete Sevareid stopped in his tracks, turned and yelled at Mackey. "What did you just say?"

The two men were about the same height, but Pete had at least twenty pounds on the hurler, who simply replied "Weren't talkin' to you, meat," before sitting down in his dugout.

The third inning was quiet, the fourth was not.

Terry VanLandingham led off with a hit and went to third when Boxleiter hit a ground-rule double to left. Brodie's fly ball scored Terry, and Coach Valenza singled to center, plating Box with the Wolves' fifth run of the game.

This brought up Harry Neville, the pitcher, and he laid down a bunt. The Cardinal catcher pounced on it and fired to second, trying to get Valenza, but his throw was high. His shortstop had to leap to grab the ball and keep it from sailing into center, and everyone was safe.

Oddibe took a couple of pitches and this time none of them was out to kill him. He then saw one he liked and singled up the middle, which scored Coach and sent Neville to second.

Karl Hines wearily walked to the mound and removed Mackey from the game. As he headed for the dugout, the battered pitcher started yelling towards Daniels, who was standing on first base.

"Fucking coon, you don't belong here, why don't you go home and pick some cotton? Or come over and shine my shoes, you nappy-head sonofabitch."

The fans on the first base side heard every word and started hollering; some of them telling Mackey to shut up, others cheering him on and adding their own invectives.

Jack Simpson ran over to the base umpire to implore him to take control of the situation before it got out of hand. Someone else was running, too—it was Pete Sevareid, and he ran right to Mackey, blocking him from retreating into his dugout.

"Out of my way, cocksucker," shouted Mackey.

"Not 'til you apologize to my centerfielder," yelled Sevareid.

"Fat chance, lard-ass, now get out of my way," and with that Mackey pushed Pete, which was the only incentive the big first baseman needed. A right to the head, a left to the chin, and the pitcher quickly found himself on the ground. Both benches emptied and the ballpark erupted as little skirmishes suddenly broke out everywhere.

Oddibe wasn't sure what to do—should he join his teammates, or stay where he was? This was all new to him, there never had been any brawls when he played for the InnKeepers. Suddenly he saw someone running towards him and yelling his name. It was Buck Hightower, a big, swarthy righthander from LSU trying to make a comeback from a serious ankle injury suffered in 1950, when he pitched for the White Sox' Class B club in Waterloo, Iowa.

"Skipper says don't you move," said Hightower in that deep voice of his.

"OK, I won't." Buck just stood there. "Yeah, got the message, Buck," Oddibe said. "Listen, if you wanna join in over there…," and he nodded towards the various combatants.

Buck just folded his arms. "I'm here 'til Skip says different," to which Oddibe just said "Oh."

It took the two umpires, with the help of both managers and a couple of players, about eight minutes to get things quieted down. Pete Sevareid, of course, was tossed out of the game, as was reserve infielder Doc Andrews, who had made the mistake of cold-cocking a Cardinal player right in front of one of the umpires. Meanwhile, in the stands, a couple of off-duty MPs took it upon themselves to tell all the fans, clearly and firmly, to settle down or they'd be forcibly ejected, any questions?

The game began again, runners on first and second, one out. Hines had brought in a lefty to face Squirrel Davis, who was quite talented at going with the pitch, and hit a curve the other way. The third baseman did a good job of scooping up the grounder, straightened and threw to second, where his shortstop was waiting.

Stepping on the bag meant that Oddibe was out, and a throw to first would probably get Squirrel for a double play, end of inning. But the shortstop held the ball for an extra second, looking at the sliding Oddibe the whole time. And Oddibe recognized that look, the look of pure hatred, and he knew what was coming.

The shortstop threw the ball to first but threw it low, low enough to possibly hit the incoming runner right between the eyes. Oddibe threw up his hands in self-defense and deflected the ball, prompting the umpire to immediately thrust his right fist in the air and yell "Interference! Runner interfered with the throw, it's a double play, inning over!"

Welcome to Round Two.

Jack came tearing over from the coaches' box, screaming something about "intent"—"that throw was meant to injure my baserunner!" Benches emptied and fans started screaming again and suddenly Mackey came bolting out of the dugout, at full speed, heading right for Oddibe Daniels, who was picking himself up near second base.

Oddibe heard footsteps and saw Mackey charging. He knew he could easily outrun the big pitcher, but that would simply get him a reputation as a coward, so he steeled himself for a fight. But then he heard more running, and saw a big body flash by him, a body wearing Cardinal red. It was their new centerfielder, Trig Swinney.

Trig stood a few feet in front of the bag and directly in the path of the on-rushing pitcher. "What the hell are you doing, Mackey?" shouted Trig. "You're out of the game, you tryin' to get yourself suspended for a month or longer?"

"Don't matter anymore, I ain't makin' this fuckin' team, now get outta my way, cowboy, I'm doin' me some coon huntin' 'fore I go."

"You ain't doin' shit, you dumb prick. Get yourself back to the dugout, or else…"

"Else what? You gonna do somethin' there, Tex? Feel like messin' with me?"

Trig looked Mackey right in the eye. "You already been knocked down once, dipshit. Won't be that hard to do it again."

The pitcher clenched his fists and started to advance when Karl Hines—seriously out of shape and out of breath—came up behind them and shouted "Mackey, stop right now! Mackey, that's an order!!"

Mackey turned, saw it was his manager yelling at him, thought for a second, then spit in Hines' direction and whirled back towards second base. Trig Swinney was right there, and he didn't hesitate, delivering a hard right to the jaw. This staggered the pitcher, but he straightened up, let out his best rebel yell and charged Swinney, who responded with a left-right combination, then a left to the belly and another right to the jaw. Mackey hit the dirt and just lay there.

By this time, all other activity in the ballpark had stopped; it had, in fact, become as quiet as a funeral service. While teammates do fight among themselves on occasion, it is generally not done in public, so the players on both squads were shocked and fascinated by what they had just seen. And the fans were completely dumbfounded, no one had ever witnessed anything quite like this before.

Hines had waved his arm and a few of the Cardinals were now reaching him. "Get him out of here," he commanded, and two of them helped Mackey to his feet and guided him towards the dugout. The umpires came over to Hines and said "Karl, we hate to do this, but we need to toss Swinney out of the game, you understand. And Mackey, too, of course." Hines nodded, looked at Trig and nodded again, and then, as the big Texan picked up his glove and headed off the field, said "Wait for me in the dugout, Trig, will you?" "Sure, skip," was Trig's quiet reply.

Hines then took a few steps towards Oddibe Daniels, still standing, transfixed, at second base. "I'm really sorry this happened, son," said Karl Hines. "I'd like to apologize to you on behalf of the entire Shirley Cardinals organization. You…you don't deserve this." Hines then turned and started walking towards first base, but suddenly saw Jack Simpson and went over to him.

"I apologize to you, too, Jack. That was..." He was searching for the right word. "Disgraceful. Inexcusable. And...and...un-FUCKING-believable! I ain't never seen anything like that, have you?" Jack shook his head, then put his arm around Hines and walked with him towards his players. As they approached the dugout, Hines asked "Shall we call it a day, Jack? I can tell the umpires we're forfeiting, and honestly..."

"Karl, I think that's sending the wrong message. We're here to play baseball, we need to get back to playing baseball. This game ain't over, I don't think you and I should end it."

Several players from both teams muttered their agreement—"he's right," "play ball," "let's get back to it."

Karl and Jack looked at each other, then Hines nodded and looked at his players, while Simpson clapped his hands and said "OK, Wolves, inning's over, we're in the field, let's go, let's go."

Karl Hines looked at his players, who were all quietly standing in the dugout. Then he looked directly at Trig Swinney. "Trig, you're out of the game, but what you did out there was special. If you get fined by the league, the team will pay it." He then looked back to the other players. "What happened out there was disgusting, and it was not reflective of the Shirley Cardinals. We've all discussed this before, but I'll say it again—if anyone has any objection to playing against a Negro, be a man and tell me. Won't be able to play for me but at least you'll be honest, and a man. Understood?" No one said anything, so Hines continued. "All right, everyone, we're up. Let's get some runs back. O'Neill, grab a bat, you'll be hittin' for Swinney."

After the game, the umpires, as they were required to do, filled out reports about the incidents and hand-delivered them to their league president. Wells Boggs read the reports, sighed profusely, and then, as it was necessary for him to do, called both Karl Hines and Jack Simpson and arranged to meet them, separately, to find out just what had happened. He also, as he had promised to do, sent a copy of the reports to Bob Rhodes in Columbus. And upon receiving and reading these reports, Rhodes booked himself on a flight to Florida, because he felt it was the essential thing for him to do.

SEVEN

Spring is a very busy time for the Simpsons, with Jack putting together his team in Florida and Nashota getting the ballpark ready for the new season. This year had been different, but with Oddibe now settled into the Ellis household, Nashota had no real reason to stay in Florida, so she headed back to Edens Ridge. She needed to oversee Nick Felix, Richie Waters and Max Broome, their three-man grounds crew. Concession and souvenir supplies were coming in and they needed to be inventoried. And the office needed to be managed.

Elnora, with a soft spot in her heart for her old employer, had been able to provide a service to the ballclub even after she had departed to start her secretarial business. Knowing they needed a reliable secretary/office manager for the spring and summer months, she recommended Jessica Fisher, the newly-married daughter of one of her old friends. Jessica had grown up in Kruse, and her new hubby was beginning law school at the University of Tennessee in Knoxville. Jessica's mom was thrilled at the thought of having her daughter living "at home" for about six months. "Didn't you say Emory had decided to go to the summer session? Shoot, he'll be busy going to classes and studying all the time. If you come home, you can make a little money, he can drive up here or you can go down there on weekends when the team's out of town. And living with us, you won't have to pay any rent!" Jessica proved to be a wonderful employee, very bright and possessing a positive, sunny disposition. But when the Simpsons got a Christmas card from her, she said she was pregnant and due in July. Coming back to work for the Wolves was no longer practical.

The young woman they had hired to replace Jessica was a strawberry blonde named Louetta. She had just graduated from high school the previous spring and, honestly, was not sure what she wanted to do in this life, aside from getting married and having babies. She was as green as grass, which meant they'd need to teach her almost everything. "I dunno, 'Sho," Jack had said, rubbing his chin. "I know anyone we hire will need to get some instruction, but…"

"But this way we can teach her, right from the start. Show her how we want things done, mold her, you know? She doesn't come in with any pre-conceived notions." Jack just grunted.

"I like her, *tsu-na-da-da-tlu-gi*, and I'm impressed that she wants to learn, seems eager to learn. Besides, she's not a complete rookie, she's worked games for two years and has a pretty good grasp of the food operation, that's a start, at least."

They brought her on board in mid-February. Nashota, though, felt it was still too soon to leave Louetta by herself for very long, so she made sure that she hurried home. She also had the baby to consider, and though she was now in the second trimester, she didn't think she ought to spend too much time away from her doctor, just in case something went wrong.

Win Appleton's *Gazette* piece changed everything. The phone started ringing incessantly, sometimes with congratulations, sometimes with profanities, often with requests for tickets for opening night. Most people bought two or four tickets. The Reverend Ishmael Clark came over and bought 56 tickets for his Jericho Chapel AME Church and said he might eventually need a few more. "We are the largest Negro congregation in this area," he said with pride. "If we don't need more for opening night, we'll certainly be buying for other games this season." Rabbi Halevi came in and bought 21 ("14 adults, 6 children, and me!"), which greatly pleased Reverend Thomas when he dropped by and purchased 24 tickets. "I can't wait to let him know I'm bringing in a larger group! If he waltzes in here and buys more tickets, you be sure and call me, hear?"

The radio stations called, too, and since Jack and all the players were still in Florida, they had to settle for Nashota. All identified her as "the wife of Wolves manager Jack Simpson" before getting around to mentioning she was also the team's business manager; one station, WOPI, ignored her title altogether. But she had good interviews with WJHL and WCYB, and an especially good one with Dave Young from WKPT, who frequently came out to games if he didn't have to pull a second shift.

Dave had conducted the interview in Nashota's office. When they finished, they opened the door into the outer office so he could purchase a couple of books of tickets for he and Priss, and they found Louetta speaking with a tall and very thin young man.

"Oh, Nashota, you're done, good, perhaps you could help this gentleman, he has some questions I can't answer," Louetta said.

"Be happy to; sir, if you could wait for just a moment…"

Dave quickly jumped in. "You go on and help him, I'm sure the young lady here can sell me a couple of books. Just remember to have Jack call me, collect, before they get back to town, so I can have my exclusive." Then he pulled out his wallet, looked at Louetta and said, "I'd like to buy a couple of books, if I may."

Nashota took the slender fellow into her office and asked, "How may I help you, sir?"

"Well, I was tryin' to find out about ticket prices. Group of us is wantin' to come out, prob'ly the second game of the year, that's a Friday, right?" and Nashota nodded. "Easier for us to come on a Friday, most-a us are off on Saturday, you know. Might have a good group, not sure a how many jus' yet, but maybe hunnert, maybe more, maybe less, ain't for sure today, but we wanted to know if we'd get a lower price with so many."

"Are you a church group, or with a school or lodge or…"

"Lodge, ma'am, yes indeed, a lodge, well, kind of a lodge, uh huh. We all got a common interest, you might say, and we get together here and there, now-n-again, as we need to, dependin' on, well, diff-urnt things, diff-urnt reasons. Thought this might be a good time for our next gatherin'."

He was nice and polite and well spoken, and seemed clean, and he certainly was plenty country, nothing unusual about that. But something bothered her, she wasn't sure what it was. Some of those words—*kind of a lodge, good time for our next gathering*—caused a red flag to start waving in her head.

"Well, sir, we...excuse me, I'm sorry but I didn't get your name."

"Pepper, ma'am, Orley Pepper."

"And I'm Nashota Simpson, good to meet you. Mr. Pepper, if you actually do bring a hundred people here one night, we can give you a real good discount. You might even want to think about a deal we have that includes a hot dog or hamburger for everyone, plus a bag of chips and a drink, and the tickets, of course. Everyone would wind up saving quite a bit, but I'd need to know the exact number of people you'd be bringing several days ahead of time."

He looked down at the floor, then looked up at Nashota. "That sounds awfully good, ma'am, but I ain't for sure...not everyone be wantin' to eat, prob'ly...fact, more I think on it, more it seems we be best jus' buyin' tickets, can we do that?"

"Well certainly, we're happy to sell you tickets. Again, if you do have a hundred people, even close to that many, you'll save quite a lot. Did you want to buy them today?"

He was shuffling his feet. "No, ma'am, lemme talk to my people, see if we can figger out how many might be-a comin', then I can get back to you, is that OK?"

She gave him a smile. "Yes, of course, you just call me or drop by any time. Maybe call first to make sure I'm here, this time of year is so busy, I often have to be out..."

"Thank you, ma'am, I'll do that, 'deed I will. Appreciate your time, ma'am, and the information." He offered up a little lopsided grin, nodded, and left.

Nashota thought for a moment, then went back out to their small main office area.

"Louetta, do you know that man?"

"No, ma'am, can't say ever seen him before."

"Did he seem a little...oh, odd, maybe, or a bit...off? Nervous?"

"Think I'd say he was a might squirrely."

"OK, thanks," said Nashota, who turned and went back to her office, where she called the Edens Ridge Police Department and asked for the Chief, Newell Gregory. He was out so she left a message. Then, after a moment's thought, she dialed Jasmine Brunét, and found her in.

Well, at least on the grounds. It was a pleasant day, a bit cool and overcast but otherwise a good day to prepare the yard for planting. She had been out since a little before nine and was planning to stay out until her belly told her it was time for lunch, but that changed when Vicky came out to tell her that "Jack Simpson's wife Nashota is on the phone."

"Mrs. Simpson, this is a surprise. I hope you're not callin' to tell me that our boarder won't be comin' after all."

"Not at all, Miss Brunét, not at all. He'll be here in just a couple of weeks, along with all of our other players. No, I had a visit from someone a few minutes ago, and I wondered if by chance you knew him."

"Mrs. Simpson, you flatter me, but really, I don't know every man in Northeast Tennessee! But who is he, maybe I can help."

"He said his name was Orley Pepper."

Jasmine sat up straight. "Orley Pepper! Let me ask you, was he kinda tall and real rail thin?" And when Nashota said "That sure does describe him," Jasmine exclaimed

"Oh shit yes, I most certainly know Orley Pepper! I know who he is and what he is and bet I know why he was visitin' you."

"I'm guessing," said Nashota, slowly, "that he wasn't here 'cause he's a big baseball fan."

"I'm sure he likes baseball bats, Mrs. Simpson. He's Klan, and I'd be thinkin' he's plannin' somethin', a demonstration, a rally outside the ballpark, maybe…worse. What he say he wanted?"

"Said he was interested in buying tickets, maybe a hundred. Not for Opening Night but for the second game, Friday night."

"Huh, prob'ly figures he'll catch you off guard. Call the police yet?"

"Yes," Nashota replied. "I was told Chief Gregory was out, so I left a message."

"Lemme call him, he'll get back to me right quick, he always does, is that OK with you? Sometimes I stick my nose in where it don't belong, so if you don't want me gettin' involved, just tell me and I can stay outta it, and you won't be rufflin' my feathers none, know what I'm sayin'?"

Nashota smiled, she found Jasmine to be a most interesting woman, very direct. "Feel free to get involved, Miss Brunét. I reckon it can't hurt to have both of us working on the Chief."

Jasmine laughed. "You got that right, honey child. I'll call him soon as we hang up. But listen, you and I, well, we workin' together on this, ain't we? For young Mr. Oddibe? Seems like we…um…look, I think you can call me Jazz, or Jasmine; fact is, I'd like it if you would."

"Fine, thank you…Jazz. And you can call me Nashota."

"OK, Nashota. I'll ring up Newell and then let you know what he tells me. You-n me, we need to stay in touch."

"Agreed. We'll talk later. And Jazz…" Nashota paused, then simply said "Thanks."

"My pleasure, Nashota, my pleasure. We all gets to play our parts."

Newell Gregory looked at the pink message slips on his desk and made a decision. *It's been a busy day and I'm too tired to answer any-a these today, they'll keep 'til tomorrow.* He did wonder what the pretty Cherokee baseball lady wanted, and groaned when he saw that Jazz had called, *ain't never a good sign when she wants to talk.* But he went on home.

The next morning, still in his pajamas, he walked down his driveway to pick up the *Gazette,* and saw a blue Chrysler New Yorker parked right in front of his house. As he got closer the passenger door opened and Jasmine Brunét said "'Morning, Chief. Brought you some coffee."

He did not get in. "Jasmine, what are you doing here so early in the morning? You know I don't like…"

"I know what you like and don't like, Newell," she said with a wicked grin. "I know you don't like me comin' round here. But I also know you didn't call me yesterday…" He opened his mouth to respond but she cut him off. "Uh, uh, uh, I don't wanna hear no excuses. Now get in here and have you some coffee. I promise this won't take long."

He knew that arguing would just prolong the inevitable, so with a sigh he got into the car, and she quickly fired up the V-8 engine and roared off. They only drove a few blocks, to the nearby city park, where she stopped.

"Now here's what we gotta talk about. Orley Pepper been over to the ballpark, askin' 'bout buyin' a bunch-a tickets for the second game of the season, a Friday night. Bet you know as well as me what that means."

He didn't want to give her the satisfaction. "Could be anything, Jazz. Could be he just likes baseball and he and a mess-a friends want to…"

"Don't you be bull-shitting me, Newell Gregory, you know he's Klan and you know we got a Negro player comin' to town and you know that mixes up 'bout as well as gasoline and a match. He up to somethin', no two ways 'bout it."

He sighed again; he found himself doing that a lot around her. "If he wants to buy tickets, I can't very well stop him. Still a free country."

She glared at him so sharply that he had to look away, and while he did she said, in a low voice, "You remember them words 'free country,' Mr. Chief-a-Police, when this young cullud boy comes here to live and play ball. Free country for him, too, you understand what I'm saying to you, Newell?" He nodded. "Good," said Jasmine. "Now look, I know you can't stop him from buyin' tickets, but he mentioned gettin' maybe a hundred. You and I both know the only way this peckerwood knows that many people is if they all be wearin' sheets. He plans on bringin' his Klavern out to the ballpark, maybe even more-n just our local boys." She paused to let that sink in while Gregory let out a groan. "You need to be workin' with Mrs. Simpson," she continued. "She also called you yesterday, and if he does bring a shit-load of them bastards, you need to be ready for 'em."

"Since when are you so against the Klan? I know they bring business your way…"

"And I don't like it one bit, but I do it 'cause business is business, I got mouths to feed, bills to pay. I also don't wanna see my house go up in flames any time soon." She looked away. "I don't let none-a them shits touch me, not that they'd want to anyways." She quickly looked back at the Chief. "This ain't 'bout money, it's someone's life, and a boy at that, just a boy, ain't hardly lived at all. He's comin' here to our town and he be expectin' you and your crew to be protectin' him. Only sayin', Newell, you need to be prepared to do your job."

They looked at each other for a long moment, then she began massaging his crotch. He moaned, then said "No, Jazz, stop, not today, I don't need this today."

She smiled and withdrew her hand. "Fine," she said, "But you do need to call Mrs. Simpson, you will be doin' THAT today, right?" When he nodded, her smile got wider, she started up the New Yorker and hustled him back home. And as he walked up his driveway, she called after him, "Good chattin' with you, Chief."

Oh, that woman…

Born in 1916, Orley Pepper never really knew his father, who enlisted in the Army when America entered the Great War, and lost his life in the summer of 1918 when death rained down on his 52nd Infantry Division during the Aisne-Marne Operation. He had only vague recollections of how hard life had been for his mother, Ozine, as she tried to raise her child and keep the farm going. He did remember, though, seeing the happiness on Mama's face when a man named Frank O'Farrell started helping out with some of the chores before he eventually moved into the house. Things seemed to be going pretty well for a couple of years and young Orley liked Mr. O'Farrell well enough. When he was having trouble with both his reading and his arithmetic, Mama suggested asking Mr. O'Farrell for help; "ain't never been much good with them two, m'self," she said, "but Frank...Mr. O'Farrell, he's a smart man, betcha he can work wichya." The older man also taught the boy how to throw and catch a baseball, how to whittle, how to catch a fish. "You'll never go hungry, Orley," Mr. O'Farrell once said, "long as you're near some water." He wasn't all that good with a gun, but that was OK, Mama was one of the best shots in the area, and she'd made sure her son could handle a pistol and a rifle.

A man named Al Smith changed everything. Smith was the Governor of New York and actively sought the Democratic Party's nomination for President in 1924. Smith was also a Catholic.

Orley really didn't know what that meant. Since he was just eight years old and lived in little old Edens Ridge, Tennessee, he didn't know there were a great many religions in the world. His Mama and everyone he knew went to the Brookdale Baptist Church on Sundays and special days, like Christmas. Everyone, that is, except for Mr. O'Farrell. "His beliefs are a little diff'ernt from our-n," Mama said one time when Orley asked why Mr. O'Farrell never came to church with them. "He's a Catholic and they's...well, they's...uh, they don't...aw shoot, they's just diff'ernt, boy, now quit asking me questions like that and tie your shoes, we gonna be late and you know I hates bein' late to church!"

That evening Orley and Mr. O'Farrell were sitting and whittling when Orley suddenly asked "why don't you ever come to church with us, Mr. O'Farrell?"

O'Farrell snorted. "Where did that come from, boy?"

"Dunno, I was jus' thinkin' 'bout it. Asked Mama this morning but she never did give me no answer. She said you a Catholic, does that mean you don't believe in Jesus?"

"We sure do believe in Jesus, we absolutely believe in Jesus. Believe he was the Son of God, and He died for our sins and came back after three days and then went to heaven and sits right by his Daddy. We believe it's wrong to kill and steal and lie..."

"They teach us all that in our church, too," said Orley. "So why don't you come with us on Sundays?"

Mr. O'Farrell said nothing, he just whittled. Finally he said, "All I know is I ain't welcome in your church." And when Orley began to protest, Mr. O'Farrell quickly cut him off. "It's way bigger than you-n-me, Orley, way bigger. Let's just leave it at that, hmmm?" And he concentrated on his whittling.

But some people couldn't leave it alone. When Orley went to town with his Mama, he often heard talk about this Mr. Smith and how if he was elected the country would be ruined and we'd all have to eat fish on Friday. That was actually OK with Orley, he loved fish and was happy to eat it any day of the week, except for Sundays. Mama almost always made fried chicken and taters and cornbread on Sunday, sure better than the hash they ate the rest of the week. They also said that this-here Mr. Smith, if he got to be President, really wouldn't be President at all, he'd be taking orders from some man named Pope in Rome, wherever that was, must be near this New York they also talked about. Both of 'em were just terrible places, horrible cities where no self-respecting, God-fearing Southern man or woman would ever want to live, wouldn't even want to visit. Least-ways, that was what a coupla them boys said at the feed store and others nodded their heads, so it must be true.

One night Orley heard his Mama talking to Mr. O'Farrell and telling him he needed to leave, get out of town for a while, maybe 'til this election mess is over, lotta bad talk in town.

"Now, now, Ozine, all be jes' talk, these boys get all riled up 'bout one thing or t'other ever-so often, this time it's Smith and the election, they'll all calm down…"

"Not this time, Frank, this time they serious. One ol' boy, Backus Gamadge, you know who he is, doncha? Got that big-ole farm north-a here. You know what group he runs with, Frank, rides with, really, ever'body knows, nobody does nuthin' or says nuthin' 'cause we don't want no trouble. Well, Backus Gamadge, he looked me right in the eye and said 'me-n my friends, we gettin' mighty uneasy with having one-a them-there Papists in our town. If-n your Mr. O'Farrell knows what's good for him, he'll be lookin' for work someplace else, someplace where his kind is welcome. Don't know where that might be, Miz Pepper, but if I was him, I wouldn't be wastin' much time.' Then he said 'day' and just ambled off. Frank, you need to light out, you need to light out tonight, tomorra at the latest!"

Mama had raised her voice and Mr. O'Farrell told her to quiet down and after that Orley couldn't hear anything else they said. When morning came, they all ate breakfast together, as usual, and went about their day as they always did, and at night there was no sign that Mr. O'Farrell was thinking of leaving.

It was pitch black two nights later, no clouds at all, no wind. Everyone had been in bed for a while, at least an hour, and Orley was dreaming that he was fishing and catching them like crazy, having the best fishing day of his life. Suddenly there were horses, lots of them, they were scaring off the fish, *get outta here, you're…*There were men on these horses and there was shouting and now Orley woke up. *This is no dream, they's actually horses right outside my window.* Men were yelling, and they were wearing sheets and odd-looking, triangle-shaped hats on their heads, *who wears somethin' like that?* Three of them had Mr. O'Farrell and were putting him into a wagon, but suddenly there was his Mama with her rifle, and she fired it in the air and all the yelling stopped.

"You let him go right now or my next shot's gonna go right in someone's heart, same with the one after that and the one after that. If you wanna leave here alive, y'all are gonna have to take me out too, Backus Gamadge."

"MAMA!" Orley screamed and instinctively started climbing out his second-story window.

"Stay right where you are, Orley," she said to him. "Don't you move a muscle!" She then looked back at the men assembled by the front door. "Now look what you went and did, you waked my boy. Fine thing for him to see, fine way to spend his summer." A couple of riders shifted a bit in their saddles. Mama pointed her weapon directly at the men in the wagon holding Mr. O'Farrell. "You boys will be first, second and third. Got me? If-n you don't think I'm serious, jus' give me five seconds and then you'll see." More shifting, and the men in the wagon now looked at one of the riders.

"We don't want no trouble, Miz Pepper," he said, and Orley knew his Mama had been right 'cause he recognized the voice of Backus Gamadge. "We got nothin' 'gainst you, or your boy, you're both fine Christians, but I warned you, this man here…"

"Is also a good Christian man, no diff'ernt than you, any-a you, maybe better. Works hard, don't drink, is good with my Orley, treats me right. Can't ask for better. None-a you stepped up after my husband died and offered to help out here, but this man did, served his country and then came here lookin' for work, is all." She paused, thought, then continued, in a soft voice that Orley had never heard before, and actually made him shiver. "This ain't got much to do with religion, do it? Shame on you, Backus, shame on all-a you. Y'all ain't got no right to judge."

There was silence for a few seconds. Everyone else seemed to melt away, even Mr. O'Farrell, except for Mama and Backus Gamadge, who finally broke the silence.

"Make you a deal, Miz Pepper. We'll make sure you get help, all the help you need, 'til you find someone else to work on the farm. You're on your own with the boy," and with that Mama snorted loudly, while Gamadge continued by pointing at Mr. O'Farrell. "He leaves first thing in the mornin' and never comes back. Not ever, understand?" Now he spoke directly to Mr. O'Farrell, still standing in the wagon. "Don't care where you go 's-long as it's nowhere near here. Agreed?"

Mama and Mr. O'Farrell looked at each other for what seemed like an hour. Then he spoke for the first time.

"She and Orley won't be hurt at all?"

"Got nothin' 'gainst them, mister," said Gamadge.

Mr. O'Farrell looked down and Orley thought his voice sounded funny when he quietly said "I'll leave at first light." And Orley wept like a baby while Mr. O'Farrell was helped off the wagon and went inside the house, as the men rode off.

A few days later Orley finally got up the nerve to ask his mother the one question that had been on his mind ever since that night:

"Mama, why didn't we jus' go with Mr. O'Farrell?"

She never looked at him. "Thought about it," she said. "But this land is ours, been livin' here for such a long time. Couldn't just walk away, Orley, I couldn't. Once this lecshun business is over, I 'spect people will calm down, then maybe he'll come back." Almost under her breath she said "Hope so."

They never saw Mr. O'Farrell again.

Gamadge and the Klan did keep their word by sending a couple of fellows around to help Ozine on the farm. The older man, Mr. Torbett, was all right, he went about doing his work without a fuss, but the younger one always had something to say to Orley's mom, trying to act friendly, but she never did trust his smile. "He has mean eyes," she told Orley one day. "Don't you get close to him 'tall, and don't you listen to nothin' he has to say." First chance she had she contacted Backus Gamadge and the next day Mr. Torbett reported for work with a different partner, a guy named Lamar Herman.

Mr. Herman was tall and muscular, with rough hands that said he was not afraid of hard work. He wasn't old but his hair was graying along the sides; when Orley asked him about it one time, he just smiled and said "I done a lot of livin'." He wasn't from Tennessee but he never did say where he grew up, just that he'd "lived all over, one time or t'other." Actually, he didn't like to talk about himself but had no trouble talking about the most important thing in his life.

"Klan will always take care-a you, boy," he would say to Orley. "Klan is my family, my only family. They look after me, they lookin' after you and your Maw, and they always will. That feller who lived here, he was no good, he was a Catholic bastard, a fish-eater, can't have none-a them 'round here." Orley hated hearing something bad said about Mr. O'Farrell, who would maybe come back some day and Mr. Herman sure wouldn't like that and then what would happen? If they could become friends, ah, that would be just the best thing, Orley would love that, but the way Mr. Herman talked, he didn't think that was very likely.

"This Smith, Governor Smith," said Herman as he spit on the ground, "he's a Catholic who wants to be the President of this-here country-a ours, and we can't have that, no siree. Can't have no one who pledges hisself to that Pope in Rome, we can't have no President takin' orders from no one, specially that Whore-a Babylon." He looked at Orley and grinned, something he didn't do all that often. "Don't you tell your Maw I used that kind-a language 'round you, hear? She'd skin me alive." Orley smiled back because he had a mental picture of his mother with a knife, slicing Mr. Herman like he was a rabbit.

"No, can't be havin' no Catholics, can't be havin' no Jews, they killed Jesus, you know, and can't be havin' no n—s, 'cause they's just stupid and useless. That's why we got the Klan, they lookin' out for all us good and decent Americans, just like we lookin' out for you and your Maw, see?"

Orley did see, and the more he talked and worked with Mr. Herman, the clearer he saw it all. When, in early July, Al Smith failed to win the Democratic nomination for President, Orley felt happier than at any time since Mr. O'Farrell had been forced to leave. And from that point on, he was a dedicated supporter of the Ku Klux Klan. Four years later, Smith was back at it and this time actually became the party's official candidate. By that time, Orley Pepper was twelve, old enough to join his fellow Klan members in helping their neighbors understand the dangers of electing a Catholic to the highest office in the land. That help often took on a rather violent form.

Orley may have been happy, but Ozine wasn't, and she had no problem expressing herself to her son.

"That Klan is no good, Orley-boy," she said. "They ain't God-fearin', no matter what they say, they is all about hate, and nothin' good ever comes from hate. Can't you see that? They ain't for anythin', they jus' 'gainst things, 'gainst people, mostly, that ain't no way to be."

"We for America, Mama, we for America and Americans. We don't want no furriners takin' over our country."

"Mr. O'Farrell weren't no furriner, shug, you know that, you know he was a good man, a decent man, treated us good, taught you things, looked on you like you was his own son. You remember that, don't you? Mr. O'Farrell weren't no furriner, but your blessed Klan ran him off, took him outta our lives. What about that, hmmm?"

Orley wasn't sure what to say, so he said nothing.

Ozine sighed. "Nothin' worse than hate. I only loved two men in my life, and hate took 'em both. Your daddy was a good man, Orley, but he hated the Germans, got all agitated jus' thinkin' 'bout 'em. Don't rightly know why, but when we went to war 'gin 'em, he had to join up. 'I have to go fight them Huns, Ozine,' he said to me, and off he went and came back in a box. Then Frank, Mr. O'Farrell, he was..." She paused and looked away and was silent for a moment before she began again and while she wasn't looking at her son, Orley could definitely hear a catch in her voice. "He was such a good man, he made me feel special, no one ever did that, no one ever said things to me like he did, no one ever did..." Now she looked right at him. "No one ever made me feel like he did. But hate took him from me, from us. US! You'd-a be diff'ernt if he was still here." She paused again. "Don't like it one bit, Orley. You my son and I love you, I'll always love you, and if you love your mother you'll quit this Klan. They is bad, chile, bad people, you better-n that, better-n them, I know it. You stick with them and you'll get in trouble, get throwed in jail or worse. I don't wanna come visit you in prison, and I sure as shootin' don't wanna be buryin' my only chile. Quit 'em, Orley, quit 'em while you can."

Orley Pepper couldn't say no to his Mama, not ever, so he laid low for a while, 'til circumstances changed.

Just a few weeks after Ozine implored her son, much of the world fell under the cloud of economic depression. The Peppers kept themselves fed, as they always had, by producing their own food, but they weren't able to sell much of their excess and, when they did, they were only receiving a fraction of what the crops had brought them just a year or two earlier. The day before Thanksgiving of 1931, Orley was awakened by an unfamiliar sound; when he went into the kitchen, he found his mother sitting at the table and crying.

"We gonna hafta sell this place, Orley-boy, can't think-a nothin' else to do. I ain't been able to pay the mortgage for 'most a year, and we owe so much on taxes, it's only a matter-a who gonna come git us first, the sheriff or the bank. I hates to leave this farm, I love it, I really do, but this depression is doin' us in."

"Who you gonna sell to, Mama? Nobody 'round here got much money."

"I'll talk to some people, see if they knows anyone wants a nice farm," she said. "Won't ask much, just enough to pay what I owes, that's all. They be gettin' a deal, tell you what."

"And then? Where we go, to town?" Orley asked. He waited for her response. And waited. She just looked at him with sad eyes 'til the tears came again, and finally she choked out "Don't rightly know. Don't know what we'll do, or where we'll live, or where our food..." She couldn't continue.

"Mr. Gamadge knows a lot of people, I can talk to him..."

"NO!" Ozine shouted. "I don't want nothin' to do with that man. Never you mind, I'll figger somethin' out, I jus' gotta do it quick."

There was no such thing as "quick" during the Depression, and eventually the sheriff came calling. He gave them 72 hours to either pay the back taxes, or pack up and move out.

"Won't be so bad, Mama," said Orley, as they tried to decide what to take with them. "We can find a little place in town, and I'll get me a job, any sorta job, and..."

"Can't do it, son, I can't live here no more, can't show my face in town, ever-body know I been kicked off-a my own farm and ever-body know why, can't live with that, I jus' ...jus' ...can't."

"What you thinkin', Mama?"

"Maybe we could hop the train, lotsa people do it, take it out to Californy, they's jobs there, 'swhat I hear, anyways. Getta fresh start in a new place, make us a new life..."

"Mama," Orley interrupted her. "I, uh, I, Mama." Not being used to contradicting his mother, he spoke slowly, haltingly.

"I don't really wanna leave. I love it here, love these mountains, love seein' the mist hangin' low in the mornin'. Don't think...um, I wouldn't be happy elsewhere, 'specially way out there in Californy." She could see tears in his eyes—she had never known him to be so serious before. "Mama, you go. You go make you a new life, maybe find you a new man, someone who can take care-a you. I'll stay here, 's-where I belong. Maybe, who knows, maybe someday I'll have me enough money I can buy this old place and you can come back and we can..."

"You only 16, boy, you can't be livin' here all by yourself. Where you gonna sleep? How you gonna eat? Boy your age still needs his mama."

"I be fine, Mama, don't you worry none. Like I said, I can find a job, and I'll find a bed somewhere, plenty-a folk be happy to rent me a room, gimme a little grub, I be jus' fine. Prob'ly time I was earnin' my own keep anyways."

He helped her sneak onto the train one evening and rode with her through Kingsport. Eventually, though, he hopped off in Church Hill 'cause he knew if he stayed much longer he'd never leave her, and now was, indeed, the time. Besides, he knew she'd be good, she had her pistol with her, and plenty of bullets, no one would be getting the drop on his Mama!

He hadn't told her he had already spoken with Mr. Gamadge, who was happy to help. He promised him a job in the funeral home he owned, a bed in an empty room (one that didn't have bodies in 'em, he just couldn't be sleepin' with no stiffs!), and use of the kitchen, as well. And of course, he'd be welcomed back to the Klavern. He just told her to write to him care of Imalove Calcote, the postmistress of Edens Ridge, she'd know where to find him and he'd write back with his new address. And once he'd made his fortune, he'd come out to visit and then bring her back with him, no one would dare look down their nose on the richest man in Northeast Tennessee!

Opening Day is also important to the grounds crew, because it's their first opportunity to show people what they've been doing for the past several weeks. The playing field will actually look much better in the month of June, but this is the first time people will be sitting in the stands and looking at their handiwork, and they want everyone to be impressed. Or at least say "Field don't look so bad for this time-a year, do it?"

This would be the fourth year that Nick Felix and Richie Waters were "crewing" together, and the third year since they were joined by Max Broome. Their different personalities made for an interesting work environment, but one thing they had in common was that they were hard workers who took great pride in the appearance and functionality of "their" playing field.

No one disputed that Nick was the head man. A good fifteen years older than Richie, he just seemed to naturally take charge when they both were hired in January of 1949. He was 34 at the time and was actively looking for a new job. A Texas transplant, he had originally moved to Northeast Tennessee shortly after the war because he'd heard that Eastman was hiring. "I was planning to just stay here for a couple of years, make some good money, then go back to Texas," he had told Nashota one time. "I wasn't really planning on living here forever, not with these cold winters. Then I met Belinda and everything else went out the window."

"Meeting the right person can certainly change your life, believe me, I know," Nashota had said with a smile, and Nick had smiled back at her and nodded. She did not know, however, how "right" he and his wife were for each other. Not only had they both moved north for work, they were both also hiding a secret from their conservative, predominantly white neighbors.

Belinda's grandmother was a Negro, which meant that, even though she herself was two generations removed, she was considered, by the standards of the Jim Crow South, to be a Negro as well. No one could tell—Belinda was very fair-skinned, with green eyes and straight hair, much like the 1930s actress Fredi Washington. She had been so determined to get hired at Tennessee Eastman that she had checked the "white" box on her job application, and no one had ever questioned it.

Nick, on the other hand, was of Mexican ancestry. His father had been born in Tampico and had come to the United States—illegally—as a young man, then decided to stay for good after settling in San Antonio and eventually marrying Isabelle. The family name was originally Feliciano, but Nick's father had changed it to Felix "just because it's easier," he once told his son, who simply continued the tradition. Only one person had ever asked him about his family history, and Nick had a ready lie.

"We're Greek," he said with a straight face. "My great-great-grandfather came over here after Greece's War for Independence, which took place in the 1820s. They won their freedom but, afterwards, he was just plumb-tired of war and thought America would be a calmer, safer place. I'm told he was heartbroken in his later years when Texas joined the Confederacy but, well, what can you do?"

People never questioned him, since battling for liberty was far more acceptable than sneaking over the border.

Tennessee Eastman did pay very well, but Nick found the assembly line to be boring, and he was not successful in trying to get on in another department. He would have loved to become one of the people who tended to the grounds, so when he heard about that kind of job being open for the Wolves baseball team, he eagerly applied. Nashota was skeptical.

"Mr. Felix, you seem very qualified, but I have to tell you that we don't pay anywhere near what I assume Eastman pays you. You have a wife and a newborn, I'm not sure you'll be able to manage. And don't forget, you won't be working, or getting paid, from the beginning of October until maybe mid-February or later, depending on the weather. We've found…"

"Mrs. Simpson, I understand all that. Sorry for interrupting, but ma'am, I really want this job, I know I can make this the best playing field in the Mountain Empire League, all I need is the chance. My wife is still at Eastman and we'll make out just fine, don't worry about us. If you give me this opportunity, I guarantee you won't regret it." Which proved to be correct.

Richie Waters, on the other hand, was a local boy, born and raised. He was a troublemaker in high school, suspended twice during his four years there. "I'm on a first-name basis with both Newell Gregory and Jeff Davis Tucker," he laughingly told Nick during their first year together in 1949. But it was Tucker, the principal at Edens Ridge High, who had recommended him to Jack Simpson. Strongly.

"Let me get this straight," Jack had said. "You've got this kid who's a serious fuck-up—oh, sorry, 'scuse my French, Mr. Tucker—but you want me to hire him to work on my playin' field. My playin' field, which is probably a lot like the inside of your school—it needs to be in great shape so's nobody gets hurt. The infield has to be in the best possible condition at all times, and the outfield can't have no chuckholes in it. The foul lines have to be just right, all of foul territory, for that matter. And the mound! The pitching mound has to be perfect, at the right specified height and slope. And you think that a kid who's been tossed outta school twice for disciplinary reasons would be a good fit? Think you could, um elaborate on that, Mr. Tucker?"

"Yes, sir, because I knew you'd ask that question; hell—'scuse MY French, Mr. Simpson…" and they both laughed before Tucker continued. "Hell, if we were on opposite sides of this matter, that's the question I'd be asking. OK, let me tell you about Richie Waters. He's one of five kids living in what is really a two-bedroom house. There's actually a sixth child, his older brother, but Jay is in jail because he robbed a grocery store and pulled a knife on the cop when they cornered him. The Mom and both daughters sleep in one room, while the Dad and Richie and the two younger boys sleep in another. When the old man gets, um, randy, then it's kind of like your "wheel play," everybody moves. The girls go into the boys' room while the boys move into the living room, and I think someone winds up sleeping in the tub. Dad drinks and, as you might expect, has trouble holding onto a job. I've heard a rumor that Richie had to pull Pop off the oldest sister one time, but it's only a rumor, don't know if there's any truth to it." Jack groaned out loud.

"Thing is," J.D. Tucker continued, "through all this, Richie is basically not a bad kid. In a different household, he's probably a B-plus student, a candidate for a small college like Maryville or Lincoln Memorial, maybe, those would both be good choices for him, under different circumstances, of course. But that's just not happening for him right now, maybe not ever."

He took a sip of water. "But he can be a hard worker, I've seen it for myself. He worked with our maintenance people for a month or so and they told me he did a good job and didn't cause any problems. If he likes what he's doing, I think he can be really productive, which is why I thought of your grounds crew. And if he has strong supervision, a positive role model…"

"You think I'm a positive role model?" Jack asked with a laugh. "Do you know how many times I've been tossed from a game, goin' back to Eau Claire, Wisconsin in 1933?"

"You work with young men every day, older than Richie but still young, and there's never any hint of trouble. I'd be proud to have any boy of mine work for you, Jack Simpson."

There was silence for a moment, broken only by Jack drumming his fingers on his pant leg. He finally looked the principal in the eye.

"Mr. Tucker, why don't you send this kid in to see me some time, he and I can talk. Understand, that's the only promise I'm giving you—we'll talk. After that…" Jack shrugged, and Principal Tucker nodded.

In October of 1949, shortly after concluding his first year as a member of the Edens Ridge grounds crew, Richie came in to see Jack.

"Wonder if I could ask you for a favor, Jack? Hate to do it, but…"

"Don't worry 'bout it, Richie," Jack said. "Go right ahead, tell me what's on your mind."

Waters took a deep breath. "I got a chance to rent an apartment over on Conger Street," he said. "Nice place, two bedrooms, both good-sized. My thought is to have my sisters share one room, get 'em away…" He cut himself off and looked down at the floor, then back up at Jack and said, "You know what I mean, right?" Jack quietly nodded.

"I saved up some money from workin' here this summer, and I got a job at the Piggly Wiggly, unloadin' boxes and crates and shit," Richie continued. "I ain't great with numbers but I been figurin' a bit and I can pay the rent and the food, I think, but I need money up front for a deposit, hunnert-n-a-quarter. Nick says he can give me the quarter, and I was wonderin'…" He trailed off again.

All summer long Simpson had been mentally patting himself on the back for deciding to take a chance on this kid; without telling anyone, he had even sent two season tickets to J.D. Tucker with a note that simply said, "thanks for sending Richie our way." Now he pulled out the ballclub's checkbook and asked, "How 'bout I give you two bills, just to make sure you and the girls have enough to eat through the winter. No interest, and you can pay me back next summer."

When he got into his car, Edens Ridge High tough-guy Richie Waters drove around the corner, parked next to the sidewalk, and cried.

In stark contrast to the other two members of the grounds crew, very little was known about Max Broome. He was older than both of his "partners," older than Jack Simpson by probably a good ten years. He did reference the war occasionally so they were pretty sure he had been there, and one time he mentioned "that god-damned Patton," which they assumed placed him in the European Theatre, perhaps at the Bulge. But that was it, he generally steered clear of the subject and clammed up if anyone wanted to talk about it.

Max was as strong as an ox, with large hands and the arms of a wrestler, which he once mentioned he had been in high school, "coupla lifetimes ago." Didn't say where, though, so they had no real idea where he grew up, or in what circumstances. He didn't talk very much at all, actually, though he was always polite and respectful, especially to Nick, whom he seemed to like. He treated Richie like an annoying kid at first, but as the 1950 season wore on and he saw that the youngster was a good worker, he warmed up to him a bit, actually gave him some pointers about the job. The person he talked to the most was Jessica, the pretty brunette who worked in the office. He obviously was a little sweet on her, even if she was married and a couple of decades younger than him.

No one even had any idea where Max lived. He must have been staying close to the ballpark because he didn't drive any sort of vehicle, he always walked in early in the morning, around 6:30 am, and then walked out again when his day was done. If asked where he was living, he generally just said, "Here and there."

"What if I need to reach you?" Nashota had asked him when he first came around looking for work in early 1950.

"Why, you can talk at me when I's here, cause I 'spect I'll be here most-a the time."

"But what about..."

"Don't really see no need for us to be talkin' any other time, do you?"

One day, Jack was sitting in the business office before a game and watched as Max was putting down the foul lines. Nashota looked out the window and said simply, "I think Max has some Indian blood in him."

"Really?" asked Jack. "What makes you say that?"

"Oh, little things," she replied. "Way he moves, very graceful, very controlled. He's pretty quiet, certainly doesn't talk about personal stuff, that's a very Indian quality, in my book, at least. He's got those cheek bones and the ruddy complexion..."

"He is out in the sun an awful lot," Jack interjected. "That certainly accounts for the skin tone, if nothing else."

Nashota shrugged. "Just a feeling I get. I don't know if I'm right or wrong, and I doubt I'll ever know, he certainly won't say. It don't matter, of course, I was just offering up an opinion." She smiled but then it disappeared. "And there's his bouts with alcohol. I know lotsa people drink, but, well..."

Once or twice a year, Max would lose his temper, generally over something totally trivial, which meant he needed to go off on a bender. It was no secret that Max liked his alcohol, and he was doing his very best to control it. But usually in late March, as they neared the opener, Max would disappear for several days, then suddenly return and put in long days and evenings. "When he gets like that," Nick Felix once said, "he works like a machine that's been cleaned, oiled, tuned up and recharged." This would get repeated sometime during the long season, generally in July or early August. His fellow crew members, as well as Jack, had learned to recognize the signs and simply let him go off to do what needed to be done, because they valued his abilities during those long stretches when he was "right."

These different personalities had meshed over time to create perhaps the best grounds crew in the Mountain Empire League—at least, they all thought so. More importantly, they had been working hard for more than a month, and now they had Bill Washington Park ready to go for the 1952 season.

EIGHT

Opening Day! It's a phrase that can make the heart beat just a little more quickly. While spring training is wonderful, it is also something of a tease. After all, most people are, most likely, reading about it in their newspapers, drooling over the warm-weather pictures while still suffering through the late stages of winter. For them, the beginning of the baseball season means the end of cold weather is finally in sight, and the inexorable, day-to-day struggles on the diamond are now to begin anew, sucking us in like great theatre.

Opening Day! Professor Robert Behn fervently believes—and is happy to tell all within earshot—that it ought to be declared a National Holiday. For baseball fans, that is a moot point—it already is.

Situated in northeast Tennessee, just ten miles or so from southwest Virginia, Edens Ridge was a small community of some 17,000 people, most of whom worked for Tennessee Eastman, headquartered in next-door Kingsport, just a dozen miles to the west. Seeking to expand as business improved in the late 1930s, Eastman had purchased two prime tracts of land in "The Ridge" and built a couple of new facilities, one of them managed by Bill Washington. Eastman, Edens Ridge, and Bill Washington all prospered, even after the war ended.

When Bill Washington decided to pursue a Mountain Empire League franchise, the Board of Mayor and Aldermen had agreed it would expand and renovate the former high school field, primarily because they thought Bill was howling at the moon. Being selected as one of the league's founding four surprised everyone not named Bill Washington, and now it was time to pony up. The dilapidated old grandstand needed a thorough overhaul, which would cost tens of thousands of dollars, money that the City simply did not have on hand. Washington was not going to let them off easily, so he extracted a written agreement that outlined a gradual but scheduled modernization of the field.

They replaced the old seats for that first season of 1946, more than tripling seating capacity to 1,768, and they also built new clubhouses and concessions. The lighting was upgraded in 1947, and a souvenir area was added as well. Because the team was drawing so well, it was decided to put in more seats for 1948, bringing capacity to 2,585, but even that proved to be inadequate, so a whole new section was added in time for the 1951 season, allowing it to hold 3,207 fans.

The field was formally re-christened Bill Washington Park on Opening Day of 1950 because of a tragic event. After the 1948 season had ended, Washington had abruptly and unexpectedly resigned as team president, blandly saying he needed to spend more time with his family. "Jack Simpson will succeeded me in the front office while also continuing in his role as field manager of the Wolves," Washington had stated in his press conference. Jack had agreed to this because he was one of the very few people entrusted with the real reason for Bill Washington's resignation, and he also solemnly served as a pallbearer in July when pancreatic cancer took his dear friend at the age of 64.

For that Opening Day of 1952 (actually a misnomer, it was really Opening Night), Nashota's records showed they had sold almost 2,800 tickets. This did not include the 457 season ticketholders, or the numerous economical, undated book tickets, always so popular with people and a great source of pre-season income for the ballclub. In other words, the ballpark was going to be packed. After a couple of late-night telephone conversations with Jack as the team was making its way north, the Wolves had to do something they had never done before:

WOLVES' OPENING NIGHT A SELLOUT
By Win Appleton

Edens Ridge, TN—Nashota Simpson, Business Manager of the Edens Ridge Wolves and wife of the team's President/Field Manager, announced today that Thursday's Opening Night, against the Kruse Ducks, has officially been sold out.

"We have sold so many tickets just for Thursday, and when you add in our season tickets and book tickets, well, we expect an overflow crowd," she said. "So we will not be selling any more seats for the opener. We ask that, if you don't already have a ticket for Thursday, please do not come to the game. Book tickets will, of course, be honored, but if you're planning on using a book ticket that night, we strongly recommend that you come out early; gates will open at 6:00 pm."

Mrs. Simpson also mentioned that there are plenty of tickets available for Friday night's contest against Kruse. Both games are scheduled to begin at 7:30 pm.

This notice also went out to the four local radio stations, who were asked to read it as often as they could.

Not good news for Chief Gregory. As if he didn't have enough on his mind, he now had to handle the traffic and parking problems that a thousand or more vehicles would be providing.

But good news for everyone else. Nashota ordered extra food, soft drink canisters, candy and popcorn. She made sure they had stocked more than enough toilet paper and paper towels, and she lined up more game-day help than they regularly utilized, figuring it couldn't hurt to have extra people on hand.

She also tried to get a leg up on Mother Nature. She sent a note to Reverend Ammons, Reverend Clark, Father Feeney, Rabbi Halevi, Reverend Stapleton and Reverend Thomas, asking them all to pray for good weather. The Rabbi was the only one who responded, just to tease her, or *kibbitz,* as he called it.

"I don't know, Nashota, you're asking a lot, wanting me to use my extraordinary powers for something so trivial as weather. I usually save them for more important things, like war and peace and finding knishes in Northeast Tennessee."

Many of the region's ministers mentioned the Wolves to their congregations, at least in passing. For the Reverend Ishmael Clark, baseball became an integral part of his Sunday sermon.

"It's easy to say that something like evil can't happen here, but it can, friends and neighbors, it can, indeed. *(Yes it can!)* Just because the Klan was able to force a Negro man to drop out of the City Council race in Gaffney, SC, doesn't mean we should say, 'oh, that's South Carolina, they're nothing like us fine Tennessee Negroes.' Fact is, same thing could happen right here, anywhere around this so-called Mountain Empire." *(Amen!)*

"We can stop it, you and me, all of us, all our friends and neighbors, and we are now getting an opportunity! You may not be a baseball fan but y'all know Jackie Robinson, know what he done a few years ago with courage and dignity. *(Yes he did!)* And now we're going to have our own Jackie, a young man who'll be playing for Edens Ridge, the very first Negro to play baseball in the Mountain Empire League. He will be vilified, he will be spat upon, he will be treated as sub-human, lower than dirt, y'all know it's true! *(Yes, yes!)* They may even try to kill him like they did with poor Mr. Moore in Florida, and on Christmas Day, no less, may God have mercy on his soul. *(Amen!)* But we need to support this young man, support him in every way we can. Many of you are coming with me on Thursday to watch him play, and we will be letting him know we're there for him! *(Yes we will!)* Those of you who aren't coming this time, I want you to be praying for good weather and praying that he will do well and PRAYING that no one tries to do him any harm. And I want you to go out to the ballpark this summer and cheer him on, and cheer LOUDLY so he KNOWS his people are with him. *(We'll do it, Reverend, you know we will.)* I want you to invite him to your homes, feed him some good food, 'cause he's probably already missing his mama's cooking. *(Oh, you know he is!)* I DON'T want him to be like that man in South Carolina and drop out because he fears for his life. WE don't want that to happen. *(No we don't!)*. WE CANNOT let that happen *(No we can't!)*. Because this is OUR moment, this is OUR time. *(Yes it is, yes it is!)* Friends and neighbors, let us pray."

If anyone knows that Opening Day/Night is special, it's the ballplayers themselves. From game #2 through the last game of the regular season, each day is much like the other—show up for work, play the game, go home. But that opener is different, and everyone deals with it differently. Some players just loll around, being lazy, saving up all their energy. Others have trouble sitting still and have to be up and moving. For everyone, each minute that passes seems like an eternity.

Oddibe Daniels was like a mousetrap just itching to be sprung. He wished they had decided to move the start time of the game up to ten in the morning—he wanted to get it played and out of the way. He tried reading some Twain but Huck and Jim floating down the Mississippi just made him more restless. He read a few pages of Guthrie, but the story about the wagon train traveling west in the 1840s had the same effect. He headed for the front door.

"Where you think you're goin'?" That was Miz Brunét's voice, for sure.

"Out for a walk, ma'am," he replied. "I'm feelin'…oh, kinda cooped up. Gotta do something."

"Know how to use a broom?" she asked. "We like to keep our house clean, so if y'all needs to get rid of a whole lotta energy, no one would sure object if you ever wanted to pitch in."

He wasn't sure if she was being serious or not, but thought it wasn't a bad idea, so he said "And where would I find me a broom?"

Jasmine hunted down Vicky, told her that Oddibe wanted to help and that she was being placed in charge of him. In doing this, Jasmine was thinking about more than housecleaning. Vicky was the youngest of her girls, and Jazz thought that being given this small responsibility might help her grow and mature. Vicky was surprised but happy to have a new charge, especially this cute ballplayer, and she showed him what areas needed to be swept. He was happy to do it, but later drew the line at dusting, even when Vicky asked him sweetly and gently touched his arm. Dusting was flat-out boring.

By two o'clock he couldn't stand it anymore and told Jasmine he was going to the ballpark. She offered to drive him but he politely refused, saying the walk would do him good.

"You remember which way to go, now? That be the safest, in my opinion," she said, to which he nodded and replied "Yes, ma'am, I do, I be all right." "You remember that safe-passage shortcut, too?" He smiled, she was almost like his mother. "Yes, ma'am, I remember." He was practically out the door when she called his name. "When you get there, you call me here, let me know you's safe and sound, understand?" He smiled and said "Yes, ma'am," turned back towards the door but stopped when she said "And have a good game, hear?" He smiled at her once more, said "Yes, ma'am" again, and left.

He was a little surprised to see that the police had already put up traffic cones on the streets around the ballpark. He was more surprised to find that he wasn't the first person in the clubhouse, even though no one was required to report for more than an hour. The team's jack-of-all trades, Mike Hamblen, was sitting at a table with shoes spread out in front of him, giving them a final shine before batting practice began. Meanwhile, off in a corner, the manager was quietly talking with tonight's "battery," starting pitcher Greg Bombard and catcher Rob Boxleiter. They paid no attention to him when he walked in, but Hamblen did, flashing him a big grin when he said "Hi there, Oddibe. Beautiful day, eh?"

Hamblen was stocky and muscular, typical for a former catcher. He had, in fact, caught the very first pitch thrown in the Wolves' very first game, back in 1946. He had made it as far as Class B, Wenatchee in the Western International League, before being released in June of 1949.

Being home in Bellingham, Washington for half the summer, rather than playing ball, drove him (and, by extension, his family) nuts. Before he and Andrea were married in September, he talked her into waiting until after Thanksgiving to go on their honeymoon. She really wanted to see our nation's capital and he said that would be fine with him, this way they could also go to Baltimore the first week in December, when baseball would be holding its annual winter meetings. Once they arrived, he spoke with a lot of people at the Lord Baltimore Hotel, but no one seemed to have an open roster slot for a 28-year-old who had not made it through a full season since 1947. There was one person, however, willing to offer him a job.

"You can be my emergency catcher," said Jack Simpson. "But I really need someone to be my coach, my second, plus drive the bus and act as trainer and clubbie. You may not get any at-bats, Mike, but you'll be playing a valuable role, several of 'em, in fact. Plus, you know the town and the area, so you'll be able to help Andrea adjust. I think I can help her find a job, and I may also be able to help you find something to tide you over during the winter..." Hamblen had said yes before Jack could finish his sentence, before they even had a chance to discuss money.

He loved working in baseball, loved being at the ballpark, and it showed, as he was almost always positive and upbeat. The players sometimes teased him about it, calling him Pollyanna, but he didn't mind and, in fact, enjoyed the back-and-forth repartee that would quickly send the clubhouse or the bus into hysterics.

To Mike Hamblen, every day was a beautiful day, but none was ever more luminescent than the first game of the season.

That new shower area, built especially for Oddibe, also featured a few nails where he could hang his street clothes when he changed into his uniform. He found it laying out on a small bench that had also made its way into "his" room (thank you, Mike Hamblen). He slowly changed into his new, freshly washed-and-pressed uniform, adorned with the team name on the front and his number—6—on the back. He lingered just a moment while rubbing his hand along the name—Wolves—and then went out on the field to do some stretching and running. It was just a way for him to burn off a lot of his nervous energy, though he was careful not to tire himself out before the first pitch had even been thrown. He cooled off by walking around the outfield track.

He heard another set of feet and looked up to see Jack Simpson endeavoring to catch up to him, so he slowed down.

"Hey, you didn't have to do that, I'd have reached you sooner rather than later," his manager said, smiling. "I'm not THAT old, you know."

Oddibe tried to smile back but was only able to muster something lopsided. "No reason I can't help you out, Skip, you got enough on your mind today."

"Every day, my friend, every fuckin' day, comes with the job." They walked together silently for a moment, then Jack asked, "How's the room? The one here in the park?"

"Fine, skip, just fine. Got all I need, really."

Jack shook his head and grimaced a little. "You know if it was up to me, you'd be..."

"Stop right there, skip," said Oddibe. "No need for you to be sayin' somethin' that might get-cha into trouble. That room is fine, it'll work real well."

"Glad you think so. Me-n Bob Dean and a coupla his railroad buddies put it up before I went down to Florida. City gave us money for the materials, on the QT, of course. They just put it under 'ballpark expenses.'" Then he shrugged, and the only sound to be heard was their feet moving along the outfield grass.

Jack decided to resume the conversation. "Nervous?" Oddibe gave him that lopsided look again, nodded and said "Yes, a little."

"Good," said Jack. "You oughta be. Wouldn't be human, in fact, if you wasn't." He paused to let that sink in, then said "Won't last long, though. Once you get that first at-bat outta the way, you'll be fine. After that first at-bat, it's just another game."

"Is it, Skip, is it really?" Oddibe stopped walking by the bullpen in right field, so Jack stopped, too. "Do we sell out every game? Do we have traffic cones out hours before the game is s'posed to begin? This ain't just any game, this is like a World Series. And it's all cause-a me, all these people, they comin' to see me." He looked down at the grass. "You bet your ass I'm nervous." And they started walking again.

"You're right, there's gonna be a shit-load-a people here, most of them to gawk at you. And guess what—we'll have that at least seven more times, whenever we go into a town for the first time. Startin' on Saturday, in Kruse, so you might as well get used to it." Oddibe didn't say anything, he just kept walking, slowly. "What I figure, though, is those people, all those people, tonight and every night, are going to see exactly why you're here." This time it was Jack who stopped walking. "Do you know why you're here, Oddibe? Do you?" Oddibe wasn't sure what to say. "I told you, and your father and mother, your sister and brother, too, the day you signed our contract, I told you I thought you could play in this league, play professionally. I don't think it any more, I KNOW it, and that's why you're here, because you can play. Not because your skin is black, not because I think I'm some minor league Branch Rickey or Hubert Humphrey. You're here because you can play and help us win ballgames, plain and simple. OK?"

Oddibe smiled, a real smile this time, nodded his head. "OK, Jack." He looked up at the sky, exhaled and gave out a short laugh. "Still nervous, though."

Jack clapped him on the back. "That first at-bat tonight? One of those pitches is gonna put you right on your butt, I guarantee it. Don't be so nervous that you forget to get back up."

Wells Boggs and Bob Rhodes had long known where they would be when the 1952 baseball season began. Wells had called Nashota about three weeks earlier and asked her to reserve a room at the Holston Hotel, the very best one they had, in his name. He would be coming in on Wednesday and would be around "just in case I'm needed," he told her. He planned to stay until Sunday. "I'll take in Kruse's opener, too, so might as well drive back and forth." And oh yes, please be sure that the room—"the very best one they have, did I already mention that?"—had two beds, "because Bob Rhodes will be staying with me. Don't worry 'bout him at all, I'll pick him up at the airport. And if you could, please tell the hotel that we'll be splittin' the bill, or I guess I can mention it when I check in. Who's your contact there?"

People were still straggling in as public address announcer Bill McDermott called for the two teams to line up along the foul lines. It was an Opening Day feature begun by Bill Washington with the Wolves' very first game back in 1946. "They do it at the World Series," Washington had said at the time, "and I think the first day of the regular season is every bit as important."

In the Wolves' previous six seasons, no one could remember the small press box being this crowded, with unfamiliar newspaper and radio reporters from Kingsport, Bristol and Johnson City jockeying for space with the regulars from Kruse and Edens Ridge. The presence of the President of the Mountain Empire League, and a representative from the National Association of Professional Baseball Leagues, made it apparent that this day was, indeed, different from all other days.

The Ducks' pitchers and reserves were announced first, followed by the manager and coach, and finally the starting lineup. Then, just as soon as Bill intoned the name of the starting pitcher—"…and on the mound tonight for Kruse, number 41, George Thomas"—the low buzz of the ballpark ratcheted up a couple of levels in anticipation. "And now, fans" said McDermott, his voice rising slightly. "Please direct your attention to the first-base line and welcome your own, your very own, 1952 Edens Ridge Wolves!" And the crowd, more than 3,000 strong, erupted with typical Opening Day enthusiasm. The players (except for the starters) came out and lined up along the line as they had been instructed.

"First our pitching staff," said McDermott with mounting enthusiasm. "Number 29, Patrick Head…" As each player's name was called, he would take a step forward, smile, doff his cap, and step back to the line. Occasionally someone would wave to the crowd, like the effervescent Buck Hightower. More than occasionally, one player would say something to another, generally off-color, that would elicit laughter from those within earshot.

Bill continued. "Our reserve position players are number 22, catcher Allan Miggs…" The small group of non-starters was announced, and then there was a pause for dramatic effect. Sitting in the press box, Win Appleton leaned forward in his chair and quietly said "Here we go" as Bill McDermott said, with great enthusiasm, "And now the starters for tonight's game!"

In the far grandstands, the ones along both foul lines that were furthest from home plate, the fans stood en masse and screamed and cheered and clapped and made so much noise that all those reporters stopped taking their notes and just stared. The Negro fans, nearly a thousand of them, were making themselves heard, and Oddibe had not yet stepped onto the field.

In the dugout, the players looked at each other; none of them had ever heard this much noise on a ballfield. Finally Jack said, "OK, mullions, this is for you, let's get out there. Valenza, you lead," and the team ran out as the rest of the overflow crowd stood and cheered.

The noise level went up. "Sounds like fucking VJ Day all over again," Rhodes mumbled.

"The manager of the Edens Ridge Wolves is number 1, Jack Simpson." The cheering and clapping continued. Underneath the stands, in the concession and souvenir stands, the game-day workers, especially the veterans, all looked at each other in disbelief—the ballpark was practically shaking, no one had never experienced this before. Standing on a ramp and looking out at the field, Nashota began to cry.

"Our coach is number 5, Mike Hamblen." Later on, the players would tease him: "the crowd sure got quiet when you was announced!"

"Leading off for the Wolves and playing centerfield, number 6, Oddibe Daniels."

There was no booing, but Win, quickly scanning the crowd, could see that some people had quieted down. Others stood on their toes to try and get a better look. But the noise from the far grandstands seemed to soar to new levels. Bill McDermott wisely let it go on for a moment, then tried to give the rest of the lineup but stopped himself and let the outpouring continue.

For his part, Oddibe was rather embarrassed. He had waved his cap and stepped back, like he was supposed to do, but the cheering continued. He looked down at his feet until he heard Squirrel, standing next to him, say "Wave your cap again, man," so he did. Nashota hustled down the ramp and went straight into the ladies' rest room so she could bawl without anyone seeing her. Standing on the field, her husband got a little misty, too.

McDermott gave it another go, and this time he succeeded. "Batting second and playing third base, number 2, Ronnie Davis. Batting third and playing second base, number 8, Ross McElvain. At first base, number 3, Pete Sevareid. In right field, number 20, Terry VanLandingham. Doing the catching tonight and wearing number 27, Rob Boxleiter. Playing left field is number 11, Jerry Brodie. At shortstop is number 17, Anthony Valenza. And pitching for the Wolves and warming up in the bullpen is number 28, Greg Bombard. Ladies and gentlemen, these are YOUR Edens Ridge Wolves!"

The ROTC color guard from the high school now came out from the bullpen in right field and raised the flag. This was followed by Krissy Martino (daughter of Paul Martino, the Miller Beer distributor) singing the National Anthem, which was followed by Bill McDermott's final pre-game pronouncement: "LET'S PLAY BALL!"

The Wolves all ran out to their positions as the crowd collectively took their seats and settled down. In the press box, the reporter from the *Johnson City Press* asked, in all seriousness, "Wow, that was something, is it like this every night?" To which Win quickly replied "Oh yes, it's a regular hootenanny here all the time," causing Bob Rhodes to nearly spit out his beer.

Bombard, the stocky right-hander from Riverside, California, set down the side in order, and now the noise level began to grow once again. Oddibe, who did not have a ball hit his way that half-inning, ran into the dugout and grabbed a couple of bats, one of which was his, and stepped back out onto the field, swinging the bats over his head.

"Look alive out there, O," said Pete Sevareid, and Oddibe turned, looked at him, and nodded.

The far grandstands now rose once more and began cheering as loudly as they could, with the Rev. Clark exhorted them on—"let him know we're here, y'all!" Very few people actually heard Bill McDermott announce the batter, but it wasn't really necessary—everyone in the ballpark knew who was coming to bat.

Oddibe tossed aside the extra bats and strode to home plate. He looked at Jack Simpson, coaching at third, to see if there was any special sign, but his manager was just clapping and yelling the usual encouragement. Oddibe adjusted his cap, which was his indication that he understood, and planted himself in the left-handed hitter's box. The crowd quieted some, enough for him to hear the Ducks' catcher mumble "Our manager wants us to say hello." It was enough of a distraction for Oddibe to let a perfectly good fastball go by; "strike," yelled the umpire, causing the partisan crowd to boo.

Oddibe knocked some dirt off his cleats and looked at the catcher, whose gaze was focused on his pitcher, George Thomas. A veteran minor leaguer, Thomas had, in his career, ascended as high as Class AA, but now was just hanging on. His next pitch was a curveball that was low for a ball. *Bet he comes back with the hard one,* Oddibe thought, and he was right, but it moved in on him and stung his hands when he pulled it foul. Even though it was nothing more than a strike, it was enough to bring cheers from the Negroes sitting in those far grandstands. *What's next? Another curve, or maybe a slowball.*

Wrong on both counts. The fastball sailed up and in, moving closer and closer to his chin until Oddibe had to bail out and hit the dirt, butt first. The Negroes started shouting at the pitcher—"whatcha doin', cracker, tryin' to kill our boy?"—while others yelled at the umpire, a young man named Hank Putnam—"did you see that, Mr. Umpire? Throw him outta this game!" Up in the press box, Bob Rhodes watched to see if anyone might be stirring in either dugout, but all was quiet. He and Wells exchanged quick glances.

Oddibe stood up, looked at Thomas, then got back in the box. The next pitch was a slowball and the youngster got a piece of it and rolled it foul. *What he gonna throw now? Ah, don't guess, just react.* It was a good fastball and he hit it towards left-center field. The centerfielder had been shading him to pull so he had to run to his right, but he was able to reach up and snag the ball before it sailed past him. One out.

Oddibe had just rounded first base when the ball was caught, so he calmly turned and headed back to his dugout. And as he did he heard it again, that groundswell of cheering coming from those far grandstands. *They're excited I made an out? That's fucked up.*

A couple of his teammates said things like "way to hit it" or "nice shot." Pete Sevareid asked him "fastball/curve?" and Oddibe said "slowball, too," and the big first baseman nodded.

Maybe because it was the beginning of a brand-new season. Maybe because of the size and enthusiasm of the crowd. Whatever the reason, both pitchers had everything working for them that April night, and it quickly became apparent that hits and runs would be hard to come by. Coach Valenza got the first knock for the Wolves, a one-out grounder in the third that just snaked by both the third baseman and shortstop. Greg Bombard tried to sacrifice but popped up instead, which brought Oddibe go the plate for his second at-bat. The first pitch was a fastball up and in that backed him up a bit, nothing more. Another fastball was low and inside and he tried to stop his swing when he realized the pitch was probably under the knees. He couldn't and the umpire called it a swinging strike, the right call even if the fans loudly disagreed. Then came a big old slow curve, Oddibe hit just the top of the ball, causing it to roll harmlessly to the first baseman, who stepped on the bag, ending the inning.

Hits by Mac in the fourth and Brodie in the fifth led nowhere. Meanwhile, Bombard ran into a bit of trouble in the top of the sixth as the Ducks put men on first and third with just one out, but he induced a foul pop that Squirrel caught behind the third base coaching box, then got a strikeout on a sweeping curve, ending the threat.

Oddibe led off the sixth inning and had a plan in mind. He took the first two pitches, both fastballs out of the strike zone, then set himself mentally for a breaking pitch, and got it, that tantalizing slowball. Tough to hit, certainly with any authority, but a good pitch to bunt. Oddibe slid his left hand up the bat, moved the wood so it was parallel to the ground, and just pushed at the ball, which began rolling along the third-base line.

It wasn't a perfect bunt, had a little too much spin on it, but it stayed fair. The Ducks' catcher chased it, grabbed it, spun to his right and made a futile, off-balance throw. The first baseman had to hustle a few feet off the bag to prevent the ball from bounding out to the outfield, and Oddibe was on with his first professional hit.

The fans in the furthest reaches of the ballpark erupted with glee. *Did you see our boy run? Man, he's fast!* And now the whole park was abuzz again, waiting, hoping, expecting…

Both Oddibe, standing on first, and Squirrel Davis, standing just outside the batter's box, were looking at their manager, Jack Simpson, who was in the third base coaching box. Relaying signs makes the manager or coach look like he has an uncontrollable itch, but these various arm gyrations are actually his strategic instructions, and it continues a baseball tradition that dates back to the 19th century. Oddibe and Squirrel both touched their caps, indicating they'd received the sign, then Davis got into the right-handed batter's box.

He showed bunt on the first pitch, which was a fastball outside. While a bunt wasn't likely, the quick feint at least put the possibility on the table. George Thomas decided that, first, he ought to pay attention to the Negro dancing around off first base, so he threw over, but Oddibe got back in plenty of time. Thomas peered in to his catcher, but suddenly he moved his left foot off the pitching rubber, whirled and threw to first again. Oddibe got back but it was a closer play, he had to slide in. This made Thomas' decision easier—he'd throw fastballs to Davis, at least until he got him to two strikes.

As Thomas delivered an inside fastball, Oddibe took off for second. Squirrel swung, aiming for right field, a classic hit-and-run (another misnomer, it really ought to be correctly called run-and-hit, since that is the exact sequence of events). By any name it is a thing of beauty when executed properly, but Squirrel just fouled the ball back.

Ducks' manager Vic Rutherford flashed a sign from the bench. Thomas threw another fastball, this one high and outside. Squirrel took it for ball two but the catcher, Bradley, quickly stood up, caught the ball and fired down to first in another attempt to pick off the speedy Daniels. Another close play and, again, base umpire Al Geiger signaled "safe."

"Shit," said Rutherford in the dugout, and then, more to himself, "fucking n—." And then he made a decision—well, acted on impulse is more like it—that would eventually affect the rest of his career: he ran out to argue the call.

"Hey, blue, you can't be intimidated by all the n—s in the stands. He was clearly out, my man nailed him, you need to call it, you gotta be fair, man."

The argument took the young umpire by surprise. He said nothing for a few seconds, then simply stated "The runner was safe."

"Safe? Are you crazy? This coon was out, I could see the white ball hit his black hand plain as day. You need to stand up for your people, for white people, out here. Make the call!"

All over the ballpark, the fans were screaming at Rutherford, even though they couldn't hear the words he was using. Up in the press box, Bob Rhodes said, to no one and to everyone, "What's he doing? He has no argument, Daniels was clearly safe." No one had a good answer, but Wells Boggs made a mental note to talk to his umpires after the game.

"I've made the call, Vic," said Geiger. "His hand hit the bag in plenty-a time, he's safe." Just as he had been taught, he turned away and headed back to his position in an effort to stop this before it got worse.

"That's weak," said Rutherford, "That's horseshit. Anyone with two good peepers could see he was out. You…"

The umpire turned around and calmly cut him off. "Let me remind you that there are some important set of eyes here tonight, like our league president, and the personal representative of the head of the minors. You sure you want to be doing this in front of them?"

Vic Rutherford stared at the young man, then kicked at the dirt a bit and said "Just get 'em right out here, for all the white boys and white fans, hear?" And then he went back to his dugout as the crowd—black and white alike—showered him with jeers.

Oddibe, of course, said nothing through all this, nor did anyone else, for that matter. George Thomas spent his time thinking about the next pitch to Squirrel Davis, and by the time his manager had gone back to the dugout, he had made up his mind. His catcher signaled for a fastball and Thomas shook him off; the catcher tried again and again was rebuffed.

"TIME!" Pitcher and catcher held an impromptu meeting on the mound.

"Curve? Are you nutty?" asked the catcher. "Their guy's gonna be running, curve gives me less chance to throw him out."

"I'm down 2–1 in the count, I need to get a strike. All he's seen so far is fastballs, he needs to see somethin' else." The catcher opened his mouth but Thomas immediately cut him off. "I been fuckin' this game for 13 years, kid, I think I've learned a thing or two 'bout pitchin'. Now get back there and prepare to nail the prick at second."

Oddibe increased his lead, Thomas noticed and threw over. Then again. Then a third time, and the fans began to boo. *Fuck 'em, he's taking a shorter lead, just what I wanted.*

He threw the curve, a good one, lots of spin and a big break. And he got the hoped-for response, as Squirrel swung and missed to even the count.

Oddibe, however, had taken off for second as the crowd roared. The catcher caught the pitch, came out of his crouch and fired the ball. With a right-handed batter up, the second baseman raced over to receive the throw, which was strong though a little to the shortstop side of the bag. It hardly mattered, as Oddibe executed a perfect hook slide and was comfortably on the base two or three seconds before the second baseman applied his futile tag. Umpire Geiger spread his arms out and shouted "safe," and many in the stands celebrated by stomping their feet.

New situation now called for new strategy. The reason that baseball is popular with intelligent people is because a new tactic is often necessary for each pitch, and with a runner in scoring position, both teams had to think differently. Squirrel needed to hit the ball to the right side so Oddibe could get to third, while Thomas needed to prevent it. Best way to do that, he reasoned, was with a high, inside fastball. Davis was expecting that, however, and took just a half swing, more of a chop, and the ball bounced to the right side. The first baseman moved to his right, fielded it and tossed towards the bag, where George Thomas hustled over, caught the ball and stepped on first base for the initial out of the inning. Oddibe, meanwhile, advanced to third.

Vic Rutherford came out to talk to his pitcher, specifically to ask one question.

"This mullion," he said, meaning the next batter, Mac McElvain, "is a lefty hitter, and a good one, generally gets the bat on the ball. On-deck batter, Sevareid, is a righty, good power but slow, good double-play candidate. I'll let you choose who you want to face."

Thomas didn't hesitate. "I hate walking guys." Rutherford nodded, patted him on the rump, said "Go get 'em," and left.

"I'll start him with heat, up, then go with breaking stuff," Thomas told his catcher, who didn't argue. So the first pitch came in about neck high and Mac let it go, and the next pitch was a curve that he swung at and missed badly.

All this time, Oddibe was dancing down the line at third, trying to distract the veteran pitcher, who may not have been disturbed but was certainly aware of what was happening. He stepped off the rubber and looked right at Oddibe, who walked back to third base. He had a real urge to say something to him but thought better of it. *Fuckin' jig, you ain't gonna rattle me.*

He turned his attention back to Mac and decided to throw a slowball. It came in low and outside, and out of the corner of his eye he could see Oddibe coming down the line again. Mac saw it, too, and took a short swing, just trying to hit the ball somewhere. He did, over towards short, where the shortstop backhanded the ball. He took a quick look, saw that he had no chance of getting Oddibe at the plate, then threw to first. It was low and bounced once, forcing the first baseman to stretch out. The ball hit his glove and went up in the air. He jumped and grabbed it, but Mac's foot hit the bag before the first baseman came down with the ball. The umpire yelled "SAFE" and the crowd howled in delight.

Rutherford, in the dugout, and Thomas, on the mound, both cussed, the manager a lot louder than his pitcher, who now turned his attention to Pete Sevareid. Knowing that the cleanup hitter loved the fastball, the catcher called for a curve, and the pitcher agreed. Both, however, were expecting something better.

It spun slowly and did not break very much, just enough to cross the strike zone thigh-high, perfect location for a hitter like Pete, and he jumped all over it. The whole ballpark could hear the CRACK, and they watched the ball soar high and deep, deep,

deep into the night, far over the fence in left-center field. The long two-run homer gave the Wolves a 3–0 lead.

Thomas got VanLandingham and Boxleiter on fly balls to end the inning, and as he walked off the mound, most of the press box crew figured that his night was over. They were wrong. Even though two men were warming in the Ducks' bullpen, he came out for the seventh. "Huh, must be trying to get one more inning out of him," mused Win Appleton. It didn't happen. On a 3–2 pitch, Jerry Brodie sliced an opposite-field double, and Rutherford made a pitching change.

The young right-hander he brought in was not effective. Valenza ripped a single up the middle, scoring Brodie, and then Bombard deftly bunted Coach over to second. With the left-handed Oddibe due up, Rutherford made another move and brought in a lanky southpaw named Hunt.

To Jack Simpson, it seemed like the manager was spending extra time talking to his new pitcher. To Oddibe Daniels, that conversation was as clear to him as if he'd been standing on the mound with them. As Vic Rutherford walked back to his dugout, he stared at the young Negro every step of the way, fixing him with a look of sheer contempt. Oddibe knew what was coming. So did Wells Boggs, who had recognized the same thing from his press box perch.

The first pitch was a fastball over the plate but high, ball one. The next would have nailed him squarely on the chin if Oddibe hadn't hit the ground. He dusted himself off, picked up his bat, and returned to the batter's box. Next pitch was a breaking ball that Oddibe weakly hit foul. *Maybe that was it, just one beanball.* Wishful thinking—the 2–1 pitch was way inside, though lower than the one that had sent him sprawling. Oddibe only had enough time to turn away before the ball hit him right on his butt. The umpire, Hank Putnam, simply held up his hands and then, pointing to first, said "Take your base."

Jack came down the third base line, yelling and gesturing. "They're trying to kill my player! You have to do something!!" As Oddibe trotted down to first, Mike Hamblen came over to check on him, see if he was hurt in any way, but the centerfielder waved him off before he could get very far, saying "I'm fine, Mike, I'm fine." It hurt like hell, of course, but you don't acknowledge it, don't rub it—you don't ever want to give the opposition the satisfaction.

Jack walked slowly back up the line, but now he looked into the Kruse dugout, where he saw Vic Rutherford standing on the top step, hands on hips, wearing a "what you gonna do 'bout it?" look. Jack stopped walking and stared right at Rutherford, then he pointed his finger at him.

"You want to play dirty, Vic? Huh, is that what you want?" He waved his arm towards the crowd, which was now on its feet and shouting. "I've got three thousand people I can bring to this knife fight, what you got?" Rutherford just grinned at him, knowing that, while fans are behind the home team completely, they generally only offer their support from the comfort of their seats. "I also have the league president and an assistant to George Trautman here today, watching this, watching you." Rutherford stopped smiling, he had forgotten they were here. "So play dirty all you want, Vic. We'll be here again tomorrow, but will you?"

The Mountain Empire League

The fans, again, couldn't hear the words, they could just see Jack's mouth going, his arms waving, the angry look in his eyes, and they joined right in, calling Vic Rutherford every name they could think of. Putnam, fully aware that his boss (Wells Boggs) was at the game, ran over to Jack and told him to get back in his coaching box. Jack wanted to ream him out for letting this happen but said nothing, he just glared at the young man in blue and walked back to his spot.

Hunt stayed in the game to pitch to Squirrel, who hit the second pitch into right field, a little looper that dropped in for a hit. Coach rounded third and headed for home, and behind him Oddibe never hesitated, cutting the bag at second and flying into third. The right fielder retrieved the ball and instinctively threw it towards the plate, but it was wild and way off the mark; Valenza scored as the catcher had to chase after the ball. Oddibe had just arrived at third base and, seeing what was happening, immediately raced for home as Hunt correctly came down to cover. The catcher grabbed the rolling baseball, planted his right leg and threw it to his pitcher, who straddled the plate so he could receive the ball and tag the sliding Oddibe.

Later on that night, when he wrote to his parents, Oddibe simply said "Instinct took over." He hit the ground so that he led with his right leg, which hit home plate well ahead of the tag. His left leg, however, was up in the air, and he made sure his cleats hit the pants of the young Mr. Hunt, cutting him.

The lefty yelped and went down. Putnam gave the safe sign as the Ducks bench erupted, with Rutherford and a couple of his players jumping onto the field. Oddibe picked himself up and stared at them, defiantly, with a look that said if you want a fight, come and get it. Jack rushed down the line and stood by Oddibe, telling him "Go back to the dugout, back to the dugout." The Wolves, led by Pete Sevareid, massed themselves by Oddibe. Oh, and through all this, Squirrel kept running and got himself to third base before anyone had the good sense to officially call a time-out.

Wells had jumped out of his seat and walked to the press box door when Jack had started hollering at Rutherford. Now he threw the door open and raced down the stairs as the benches were emptying. When he reached the railing, he tried to get anyone's attention, but his shouts were drowned out by all the noise in the ballpark. So he climbed over the railing and onto the field and put himself right in the middle of everything.

"Everyone go back to your dugouts," he shouted. "Right now, and I mean RIGHT NOW. Go on, get moving or you'll all be paying big fines." The players recognized the league president, since he had spent so much time with them in Florida, and they proceeded back to their respective sides of the field. Wells now looked at his umpires. "You two get ahold of this situation right this minute, or you'll be out of a job just like that," he said, snapping his fingers. "And you two," he concluded, pointing his fingers at Vic and Jack, "There will be nothing more like this the rest of today, understand? Otherwise it will cost each of you a month's salary. AND you will meet me in the business office THE MINUTE this game is over, DO I MAKE MYSELF CLEAR?" Both men nodded and headed back to their respective dugouts with their players.

A new pitcher came in and got Mac on a slow roller that plated Squirrel, then Pete struck out because he wanted so badly to hit a 900-foot home run.

A little out of rhythm due to the long delay, Greg Bombard finally cooled off and was touched for three runs in the eighth before Jack brought in Buck Hightower to bail him out. Which he did, getting the last four outs in the Wolves' 7–3 victory.

The meeting was short and sweet. Jack could tell that Wells was angry, but to his credit the league president kept his composure.

"What I saw out there, gentlemen, was despicable. You want to knock a boy down a time or two, fine, that happens. But your pitcher was head-hunting, Vic, and there's no excuse for that, none whatsoever."

"Wells, when Sal Maglie or Early Wynn does it…"

"Shit, Vic," said Wells, and that's when Jack knew he was pissed, 'cause words like "shit" only come out of his mouth as a last resort. "Your boy ain't no Maglie or Wynn, he's a fucking rookie in Class D. If he weren't throwin' at Daniels, you oughta give him a bus ticket home. That your plan?"

The question caught Rutherford off-guard. "What? Home? No, no, the season's just started, it's just one bad outing…"

"Didn't think so," said Wells. "So I'm finin' him fifty dollars, and I'm finin' you twenty-five dollars. I'd like to fine you more and suspend your ass for a few days, but I can't prove you told him to hit Daniels, so the fine is for not controlling your players. Understood?"

"That sucks, Wells," said Rutherford. "Boy ain't hardly making enough to eat on, and you gonna take fifty from him? Ain't right." He shook his head. "Ain't right, all because of that…that…"

"That what, Vic? What you wanna say, hmmm? Finish your sentence, please."

"You're protectin' Jack's nigra, Wells, and it ain't right. Boy needs to prove he can play professional baseball, this ain't no North Carolina industrial league. He's bein' tested, we all were tested when we played, right Jack?" Simpson kept his mouth shut. "You gonna hold his hand all season, Wells? He's gotta prove hisself…"

"I saw you," said Wells, his voice dropping an octave. "I saw how you looked at him when you brought in your lefty. I seen hate before and I saw it tonight, from you."

"Wells, I grew up in Jacksonville. Can't help how I was brought up, how I feel. And you can't fine me for that."

"Which is why your fine is only twenty-five. But I can make it more if you like. If you want, you can pay both fines outta your own pocket."

Wells waited, but there was silence in the room. He looked at Jack.

"I'm finin' you fifteen dollars for stirring up trouble, Jack. It didn't help nothin' when you started hollerin' at Vic, here, 'long the third base line."

Jack nodded. "I can have Nashota write you a check tonight," he said.

"I want it comin' directly from you, not the team," Wells said emphatically, and Jack simply nodded his head again. "She can take it outta my next check," he said, to which Wells replied "OK." He thought for a few seconds, then continued. "Now, as for tomorrow, and the next day, and every day after that, there will be absolutely no repeat of what happened here tonight. There will be no beanballs, no spikin', no name-callin', nothin' but good, clean baseball. That's what the fans want, that's what Mr. Trautman wants, that's what I want, and that's what we're gonna have!" That last word was said with great emphasis. "Is that understood, gentlemen? If we have to have this conversation again tomorra, or any day this season, you'll regret it, I can assure you of that. Are we clear?" Both managers mumbled an assent, and Wells said "Good. Now go back to your teams and make sure they all understand, too." As they were leaving, Wells thought of one more thing. "Oh, Jack," he said, and Simpson turned around. "Nashota can pay me when she sees me tomorra. Vic, I'll be calling Don tonight to fill him in." And with that they all went their separate ways.

No one had been willing to speak for publication; Win couldn't even get his friend Jack Simpson to talk off the record. Vic Rutherford had tersely answered "No comment" to all questions. Even the umpires were unavailable, meeting with Wells Boggs after the game before quickly heading off to their hotel. The only thing Win had been able to get was Pete Sevareid's remark that "we stand together as a team." When asked—no, prodded, and then begged!—to elaborate, the big first baseman shook his head and walked away, mumbling "I've said too much already."

Win thought that perhaps a new day might bring him new information, so he got to the ballpark a little earlier than usual on Friday. And he found the place crawling with cops.

Well, OK, "crawling" may be an exaggeration. The Edens Ridge Police Department was 29 strong, and on an average night two were assigned to a Wolves game. Casually roaming the stands, they were very visible to the fans, which was generally enough to dissuade any trouble. On Opening Night, knowing that a huge crowd would be on hand, Chief Gregory had sent over five officers, and every one of them had earned their pay. During that wild seventh inning, the officers covered the grandstands, each taking a position in front of the first row of seats and continually scanned his "region." Remaining on high alert throughout the uproar ensured that no fired-up fans got overly enthusiastic and jumped onto the playing field, or started a fight with any of the Kruse people who had made the short drive to cheer on their boys.

But when Win arrived at Bill Washington Park that afternoon, he counted half a dozen constables already positioned outside. Were they expecting Kruse to launch some sort of counter-attack? The first couple of young men he questioned said the same thing, which was no help at all. "The Chief just told me to be here until the ballpark emptied out after the game, that's all I know, sir." Another fellow, however, mentioned that "Sergeant Yates might be able to tell you more, he's inside."

Win Appleton was a year behind Philman Yates in high school, they knew each other just enough to say hello in the hallways. When Yates came back to town after the war, Appleton thought it might be good to interview someone who had been at Pearl Harbor, but Yates wasn't interested in talking. Appleton got his interview by agreeing to a simple sentence: "Petty Officer Yates was one of those wounded during the

Japanese sneak attack of December 7, 1941, and after he recuperated, was reassigned to the Naval base in Norfolk, Virginia." The two-part article on Yates' naval career proved to be a good one, and helped to establish a solid bond between them, which Appleton hoped to capitalize on now.

Inside the ballpark, Win found Yates walking through the empty stands with Jack and Nashota. He trailed them for a bit, making mental notes of what portions of the conversation he could hear. He then sat down, pulled out his notebook, and wrote it all down before it disappeared from his brain.

He heard a sing-song "Whacha doin'?" as two people sat down on either side of him. Nashota was giving him her mega-watt grin from the right, while Philman's grey walrus mustache was frowning at him from the left.

"Nothing, just jotting some notes," he said, closing his book.

"You can't be writing this up, Win," said Yates. "We'd lose our advantage over these people, if we even have one."

Appleton didn't know who "these people' were, he hadn't heard any names mentioned, though of course he had an idea. He wasn't going to tip his hand, however. "Whatever I write won't be published 'til tomorrow morning, so you have nothing to worry about, I won't be ratting you out. What can you tell me, for the record?"

Yates stood up. "For the record? Looks like it'll be a nice night for a ballgame. Now please excuse me, I have more work to do." And with that he shuffled off.

Win looked at Nashota. "I came here early today so I could talk to people about what happened last night. Where did Jack go? I'd love to spend a few minutes…"

"Leave it alone, Win, please," she said. "I can tell you that Jack, and everyone on the team, is upset about what happened, and embarrassed, too, but that was yesterday and this is today, gotta game tonight, and…" She hesitated, then said "That's all. New day, new game." She stood up and started walking back to the office.

He followed her. "You and Jack and Phil were making plans like it was D-Day, what was this all about? Are you telling me this has nothing to do with last night? Come on, Nashota, are you expecting some sort of retaliation from Kruse fans? 'Cause that's kind-a how it looks."

She stopped walking and turned back to him. "You think…oh, that's good, I like it!" She giggled and gave him a kiss on the cheek. "Yes, sir, Mr. Appleton, you got us. I took a call this morning and a big group from Kruse asked about reserving tickets for tonight. Maybe 60, 70, 80 people, he said, just good Ducks fans, but I got suspicious and called Chief Gregory. He sent Sgt. Yates over, and he has determined we need extra police presence for tonight. Hopefully the sight of all those uniforms will make the Kruse folks think twice about acting up. That sure would stop me." Her smile softened. "Walk me to the office?"

She lowered her voice as they made their way along the concourse. "You know exactly what caused everything last night. It really won't help matters, Win, if you splash it all over the papers. Wells is handling it, he fined the pitcher and Vic and even Jack, just to be fair, I guess. And Bob Rhodes is keeping the National Association in the loop." They were almost at the door to the office, but she stopped walking and looked him right in the eye. "We need things to cool down, Win, and an article…I'm afraid what it might do. We have a whole season to go, we've only played one game…" She was actually starting to cry. She looked up at the sky and plaintively said *"U-nequa!"* She looked down at the ground and then back at Win, tissue in hand. "I seem to cry more easily now that I'm pregnant," she said, forcing a smile. "Could you please hold off, just this once? For me?"

He looked away, then looked back at her, thoroughly defeated. "OK, for you. And Jack. And your baby. But this is the only pass you get, understand?" She smiled, a little brighter now, kissed him on the other cheek, and said "Thanks, Win." She started to go into the office but stopped and gave him a much bigger smile. "Do you realize, I've kissed you more today than I've kissed my husband?" She laughed out loud and went inside.

The plan was simple. They were all to meet at the Piggly Wiggly parking lot, fully dressed. Orley would give everyone a ticket, and then they would march the four blocks over to the ballpark. Once inside they would split up, with half the group sitting in general admission along the third base line while the other half sat on the first base side. They would be respectfully quiet until this Daniels boy came up to bat in the bottom of the first, and then they'd start their chanting and hollering.

They had not counted on extra police, and Orley wondered why they were there, and so early, too. He had been tipped off by a friend that the cops were already camped out at the ballpark and there were more than the usual two, damn! He wondered if it was because last night had been such a mess, that must be it, no outsiders knew what they'd been planning, everyone had been really good about keeping tonight's "meeting" quiet. Still, they would now have to contend with extra police, a whole boatload, actually, which complicated matters. And when things got complicated, Orley often got confused.

A total of 36 Citizens gathered in the parking lot, wanting to know what to do, looking at their Exalted Cyclops and waiting for answers.

"Are we still going, Orley?"

"Sure are a bunch-a cops over there, I saw 'em as I was drivin' over."

"We gonna be able to get in dressed like this?"

"I's happy to go in there and scream and shout and shit, but I don't wanna be gettin' 'rested, I gotta family and a job, can't be losin' my job, Orley…"

"Me either, new baby be comin' in June, I can't be gettin' fired 'cause-a no n—…"

"You always gotta baby comin', Roy, ain't you ever heard-a rubbers? Or just goin' to sleep?"

"Quiet, y'all." Orley spoke sharply, he'd had enough of their yammering. Part of his responsibilities as Exalted Cyclops was to lead them, they'd made him the leader and expected him to lead and now he put his foot down. "HUSH UP!" That got their attention.

"I admit things are a bit, um, tougher, little bit tougher than I 'spected, but we got tickets, they hafta let us in. And we got rights, we can go to a damn baseball game if'n we wanna. And lookit, let's not forget why we're here. No n— gonna play in this-here league, for OUR team, not if the Klan has anythin' to say 'bout it." Orley was determined to stay on track and see his plan through.

"Dunno, Orley, I gotta funny feelin' 'bout this, seems they's waitin' on us." Orley recognized the voice of Gray Gamadge, his Kladd, who owned the Kettle Creek flower store and was Backus' son. Orley liked Gray well enough, but he sure didn't have his old man's balls.

He did have a point, but there was no reason they couldn't change on the fly.

"We don't go in as a group," said Orley. "Just two or three or four-a us at a time, few minutes apart, and we walk in from diff'ernt directions, so it don't look like we's all together. And nobody wears their robes, least-ways, not now. Let's take 'em off, stuff 'em in our pants or under our shirts, whatever, then we go to the bathrooms and put 'em back on and go to our seats. I got all our tickets right here, be happy to hand 'em out now. Whaddya think, Citizens?"

There was some muttering, then Nick Mancuso, the barber, said "'Spose we wait just a bit, 'til after they play the Anthem? If we walk in now, still plenty-a time to throw us out, but if we wait, we can at least do what we need to do when that boy come up to bat, know what I mean?"

More murmuring, and now someone asked "Is the Klavern still payin' for the tickets?" "Yes, you cheap bastard, the Klavern is payin'," said Orley, which brought on a small cheer.

Gray Gamadge said "I think Nick's gotta good idea, we wait a bit. And Orley's right, too, let's take off the robes and hoods and not put' em on 'til we get into the ballpark."

Orley jumped on this. "That OK with all you Citizens? That what you wanna do?" Several people said "yeah," there was even one "hell yeah!"

"Anyone wanna back out?" Orley continued. "I don't wancha here if-n you don't wanna be here, if you're 'fraid of a few police." He knew that would get them, no one would admit to being scared, and he was right, everyone stayed put. "Then let's split up," he said. "Small groups, not more-n four, but don't just be four, let's have plenty-a two's. Wander in after the Anthem, a few here, a few there. Kruse team be up first, don't forget, then when they go out and we come up, that Daniels boy gonna be first and that's when we act. Got it? Any questions?"

Everyone seemed clear, so they (literally) disrobed and disbursed. Orley jumped into his pride and joy, his two-tone, 1947 Plymouth Special Deluxe, to change his clothes and maybe park a little closer to the ballpark. A simple plan is really the best.

That Special Deluxe was well-known around town; Orley called it "my snazzy-lookin' vehicle" (which he pronounced "vee-HICK-ul"). Everyone in Edens Ridge, it seemed, knew who owned that Special Deluxe, including the police. On a couple of occasions, Sgt. Philman Yates had found it necessary to stop that shiny car and have a chat with its owner. "Where you goin' in such-a all-fire rush?" Sergeant Yates would ask, and Orley would stutter some sort of answer which never prevented him from getting a ticket. Yates suspected he was late for a Klan meeting, but there was nothing he could do about it. Going to a meeting of any sort wasn't against the law,

The Mountain Empire League

and besides, in these parts, those boys were mostly harmless, full of hot air and not much else.

There had been exceptions, of course. When he was still on the "Chitlin' Circuit" and using his given name of Richard Penniman, Little Richard played in Kingsport and a full-scale riot broke out. His hard-driving piano style was popular with young Negro audiences and was now catching on with some whites as well, which appalled the Klan, who thought this music, and its effect on "our innocent children," was immoral. Just minutes after he began playing and singing, several Klaverns burst into the hall and attacked the stage, which prompted a few patrons to fight back. Completely surprised and overwhelmed, the Kingsport police put out a quick call for help to neighboring law enforcement agencies, including Edens Ridge, and among those that Philman Yates arrested that night was Orley Pepper.

"Oughta be banned, oughta be a law," he said when they hauled him in. "That jungle music, it's dangerous, gets them nigs all fired up, gets 'em dancin' and screamin' and hoppin' 'round. Whoo boy, next thing we know, they be attackin' us and our wimmin. Our wimmin! We can't have that, no sir, can't have them doin' whateverinhell they wanna do. Can't you see that, Sergeant? You arrestin' the wrong people, we just tryin' to protect our way-a life."

"Lots-a people got arrested tonight, Orley, black and white. And protecting, that's what we do. If you let us do our job, you'd be home right now, 'stead of heading for a cell."

"If you was doin' your job, you wouldn't ever let that n— in town to play his music, his so-called music, you'd just…"

"All right, enough out of you, now get in there and keep quiet 'til we take you to see the judge."

Something similar had happened when Little Esther had come to town, not nearly as violent, but the Klan did make its presence felt. They stood at the back of the room, wearing their robes and sheets, and shouted a series of invectives at the young singer, unnerving her and causing her to flee the stage in tears. Needless to say, this upset the people who had paid good money to hear her perform, which led to more hollering and a few punches being thrown before the police could break it up. Orley was part of that fracas, too, so he and Sergeant Yates had developed more than a nodding acquaintance.

Thus, when the veteran policeman stopped along the ballpark's concourse to have a quick smoke as the fans were filing in, he happened to catch sight of that two-tone, 1947 Plymouth Special Deluxe driving by. *Oh shit,* he thought, understanding that their fears were about to be realized. He quickly put out his cigarette and went inside the office so he could issue a radio command to all his officers without being overheard by the fans happily buying their food and beverages. Then he went out on the street to join his men.

Orley and two of his Citizens sauntered up to the gate, reached for their tickets, and found themselves face to face with Sergeant Philman Yates.

"Evening, Orley," he said before nodding to the other two, whom he did not recognize. "Where y'all going?"

Orley gave a short laugh. "Nice to see you, Sergeant. Well, since we's standin' in front-a the ballpark, and we have these-here tickets for tonight's ballgame, I'd say we are a-gonna go see our Wolves beat up on them Kruse Ducks."

"I didn't know you was such a fan, Orley. Tell me, where'd you get those tickets?"

"Why Sarge, I bought 'em myself. Came right down here one day and paid cold hard cash for 'em. Is there anything' wrong with that? Looks like lotsa other people done the same thing," said Orley, waving his hand at fans who were passing through the gate unimpeded. "Don't understand why you should be stoppin' me-n my friends and not no one else."

"Tell you what I don't understand, Orley. I been told you bought way more-n three tickets, you actually bought 37. Where is everyone else?"

Orley had not been expecting this, and he knew he had to answer carefully; the wrong response could kill their plans right then and there.

"Diff'ernt people done give me their money…I think I mentioned to someone that I was a-plannin' to come out tonight, and this guy told that guy who told 'nother, and 'fore I knew it, I was bein' asked to buy 37 tickets. Yessir…" Orley was really getting caught up in his story. "So that's what I did, took everyone's dough and bought 'em their tickets and gave 'em all out. Ain't that right, boys? Imagine some-a them are here already, people just gonna get here when they get here, and sit wherever they can find a space, I reckon. Looks like a nice crowd, eh Sarge?"

Sergeant Yates knew in his gut that Orley was lying, knew the Klan was up to something, knew that trouble was brewing. But he had no proof, just intuition, and he couldn't very well bar Orley from entering since he had legitimately purchased his tickets and hadn't done anything to call for a police action. He just glared at the three men grinning in front of him, and finally he stepped aside.

"Enjoy the game, gentlemen," he said. "But just know that I'll be keeping my eyes on you all night long. If you even think of causing any trouble, I'll have cuffs on you so fast you won't know what hit you. Understand?"

"Yessir, Sergeant Yates," Orley said with a big smile. "Yessir, I'll remember what you said. You gonna watch me in the bathroom, too? 'Cause I gotta tell you, I really need to pee, you wanna be eyeballin' that? If-n you do, well, be my guest, you surely be in for quite the sight!" The three Citizens all laughed as they walked through the gate.

But Orley's mood shifted once inside the ballpark. "Fan out, y'all," he said to his two companions. "Try to find some-a our people, let 'em know the cops are here a-watchin' us. Tell everyone you see to spread the word that we still doin' this, for sure. Just be careful, don't say nothin' to nobody, don't tip your hand. Got me?" The two men nodded and then all three went off to find their compatriots.

Friday nights were generally good ones for the Wolves, for most minor league teams, in fact. It was a good way to celebrate the end of the work week, blow off a little steam and not have to worry if you woke up with a hangover. Plenty of tickets had already been sold, but after the fireworks of Opening Night, the ticket office had been busy right through lunchtime, when the very last seats were purchased. Nashota put their TONIGHT'S GAME HAS BEEN SOLD OUT signs up at the ticket window and the front gate, and asked all the radio stations to pass that information along. Exciting for the team, but a further headache for the police.

Public address announcer Bill McDermott was making his final pre-game announcements as tall, muscular Patrick Head threw his warm-up pitches. A native of Wichita Falls, Texas, he was probably the hardest thrower on the team, and was also in the process of developing a good slider and slow curve. When he had control of all three pitches—hell, when he was able to consistently throw even two of them for strikes!—he was a legitimate big-league prospect. But he liked the nightlife, which had already led him to be released by two organizations, the Red Sox and Indians. In Florida, Jack had spent a good deal of time talking to him, emphasizing that this was most likely his last opportunity to make it to the majors.

"You've got all the ability in the world, Pat," Jack had told him one morning when they met up for brunch. "You could be a real star in the majors, an All-Star. You throw harder than Reynolds or Lemon or Maglie, or Bubba Church, how in hell is Bubba Church a 15-game-winner and you're still in Class D? You're way better than Bubba Church and you know it. But you also know why you're here, why two teams have already given up on you." Head looked away. "You control your future, Pat. Stay outta the bars, stay off the bottle, and I guarantee you'll have a great year and the big guys will come calling again, with their deep pockets. That's all you gotta do, 'cause you've got the stuff." Head had nodded and said, "I know, Skip, I know," and had behaved himself throughout training camp, earning the #2 spot in the rotation. He showed every bit of that potential right at the outset, retiring the Kruse Ducks in order on a weak ground ball to Squirrel Davis, a foul pop caught by Mac McElvain, and a called strike three on a pitch that painted the outside corner.

People now hustled from the concession stands to their seats, heads turned towards the home dugout so they could get a glimpse of HIM. Oddibe Daniels, an Edens Ridge resident for just a couple of days, had very quickly become the most talked-about person in town, to say nothing of Sullivan, Washington and Hawkins counties.

The object of their curiosity grabbed a bat and strode towards home plate, Bill McDermott's smooth voice guiding him along.

"Leading off for the Wolves and playing center field is number six, Oddibe Daniels, number six." There was a buzz throughout the stands, mixed in with raucous cheers from the Negroes in the far bleachers, and…and…what was that?

People started talking to each other excitedly. "Who's yelling?" "Where are they?" "What are they saying?" And as the fans looked around the stands, they quickly saw a sea of white robes and pointy hoods. They came out of the restrooms, marched through the concourse and went down the aisles—two down one aisle, two down the next, two down every aisle between first base and third base. They marched all the way to the screen that separated the fans from the playing field, until everyone in the park—players, fans, officials, media, everyone—could see the Ku Klux Klan.

And hear them as they shouted.

"No n—s in our ballpark!"
"Go home, you baboon, we don't want you here!"
"Time to take our country back from the Commies and the coons!"
"Get out of here, camel lips, this is OUR town!"

Oddibe stopped several yards short of home plate and looked at them. Several players jumped out of the dugout, a couple with bats in hand, but Mike Hamblen, coaching at first, shouted "No, no" at his players as he ran towards them. Jack Simpson, meanwhile, raced down to home from his spot in the third-base coaching box, waving his arms and yelling.

Oddibe looked at the Invisible Empire, not so unseen at this moment, then looked at his dugout, where more of his teammates were already out on the playing field, ready for action. He just smiled, shook his head, then looked at the sheeted group, gave a short laugh and walked towards home plate. He laughed! They all saw it, and it was the equivalent of turning up the heat on a stove—the Klansmen screamed even more, and a few of them started pounding their hands against the screen.

Last night's umpiring crew was working the game, of course, but they had flip-flopped their assignments: Hank Putnam was working the bases while Al Geiger had the indicator to call balls and strikes. This was standard procedure in the minors and had nothing to do with Wells' criticism of how they had handled things the previous night.

Geiger took off his mask and assessed the situation. The noise around the ballpark had ratcheted up several-dozen decibels. The coach at first base was screaming at his players, who were coming out onto the field; the manager was racing down the third-base line, waving and screaming. This was not a situation found in the standard umpiring manual.

Geiger strode up to meet Jack. "What in hell is going on here, Jack?" asked the young umpire. "Is this a ballgame or a political convention? You've got to get control of your fans, we're going to have a riot out here if we're not careful."

"Al, Al, this isn't a riot, this is a few crazy fans. This is no worse than when they disagree with some call you've made. Let me get my players back in the dugout so we can continue…"

"Geiger, you're right, we need to maintain order here." It was Vic Rutherford, joining the discussion without being invited. "I'm afraid for my players. Jack here is the general manager, he needs to get control of his ballpark, or else I'll be forced to pull my players off the field." Vic now looked smugly at Jack as if to say *you asked for this, Jack Simpson*. "And I'm sure the league president would completely agree with me." It was all Jack could do to keep from socking him in the jaw.

Putnam now joined the group, and after a brief discussion they made a decision. "Both teams, back to your dugouts. Jack, you and your people need to restore order in this ballpark, or we'll have to consider forfeiting the game in favor of Kruse. And Vic, we'll have no rabble-rousing out of you or your players, understand?" And with that the two umpires began purposefully moving the athletes off the playing field, leaving Jack standing there, momentarily dazed, wondering what he was supposed to do.

The police, caught totally out of position, were now reaching the aisles, guns drawn, hoping to nip this right then and there. But the Citizens were not about to go quietly, especially since they held a five-to-one advantage. They started throwing punches.

In the press box, Wells Boggs looked on in horror. Throughout the winter he had envisioned all sorts of terrible scenarios, but this had the potential to be worse than any of them. He couldn't just stand there, though, he was the League President, so he raced to the door and headed down the stairs, ignoring Bob Rhodes, who was yelling "what do you think you're doing?"

Near home plate, a Klansman, having knocked a policeman to the ground, was feeling pretty good about himself, but that sensation lasted maybe four seconds, because he happened to be standing right by Vernell Gibson's long-held seat.

The owner of The Specialty Shop stood up. "You sonofabitch, you can't do that in our ballpark. Get the hell out of here right now, or…"

"Or what, old man?" asked the Kluxer. "You gonna do something, hmmm? I'm scared!"

Gibby may have been about to turn 70, but in his mind he was still in high school. "You oughta be," he said. With his left hand he grabbed the hood and jerked it off the man's head and then, before the young Citizen could react, he threw a right cross that would have made Joe Louis proud. "That'll teach you to mess with a season ticketholder," Gibby said as the boy crumpled to the ground.

This galvanized some of the other fans. Ron Bruce, the printer, ran down from where he was sitting, grabbed a Klansman from behind, spun him around and sent him to the ground with a head-butt. He then put his foot on the man's back until a cop came over to make the arrest. Sitting near the first-base dugout, Paul Martino, the big New Jersey native, found a unique way to form a posse. First he cold-cocked one Citizen and then, when the fans in that section cheered, announced he would personally buy a cold Miller for everyone who "helps me drive these miserable mother…oh, 'scuse me, damned bastids outta OUR ballpark." Six or eight people immediately jumped out of their seats, and the Klan quickly learned they were no match for a group of thirsty fans.

Jack, meanwhile, had begun to climb into the stands. *Vic Rutherford, damn him, is right, I'm the General Manager, I have to…* He needed to do something, even if that meant beating a few of these shitheads to a pulp. Just as he was about to jump over the little fence that separated the first row of seats from the playing field, he heard a familiar voice. "Stay where you are, Jack Simpson." It was Wells Boggs.

"Wells, I gotta help out, I…"

"Your responsibility is with your players. Looks to me like a few-a them wanna get in here and mix it up. Can't have that, Jack, can't have that. If they come into the stands they'll be violatin' league rules and I'll hafta fine 'em, maybe even suspend 'em. No matter they doin' the right thing, the moral thing, I gotta go by league rules. You keep your players on the field, hear?" He paused, looked around and actually smiled, just a little bit. "I think…looks to me like this is bein' taken care of, Jack. You got good fans here in Edens Ridge." Jack looked in the stands and was able to see the police, assisted by a few of those fans, dragging the Klansmen up the aisles *(OUCH!!)* and out of the ballpark. He then looked back at Wells. "Yes, sir," he said, and he jumped back on the field and went to his players.

What Jack had not seen was one particular fight. A Klansman was being marched up the stairs by an officer. As they reached the concourse, he suddenly turned and threw a few punches, knocking the startled policeman down. But before the Citizen could rejoin any of his compatriots, he was attacked by two people, one of whom jumped on his back. Eventually the three hit the ground, where the two fans proceeded to pummel him until the recovering officer was able to regain his feet. He pulled them away, handcuff the bloodied Kluxer and carted him outside, ignoring the two people who quickly picked themselves up off the ground.

"Don't you dare tell my husband what I was doing," said Nashota.

"You were doing? It was all me, darlin', all me," said LaDonna Holmes, and the two women laughed before Nashota said "LD, you need to go into the bathroom, your lip is bleeding."

LaDonna just laughed again. "All in a day's work."

The whole fracas had taken about 27 minutes, from the time the Klan first began their hollering until the last Citizen was removed from the ballpark. Nashota herself walked down an aisle by the first-base dugout to tell Jack that it was now all over, but her words didn't register nearly as much as the sight of her scuffed face. "What in hell happened to you?" he bellowed. "Nothing, nothing at all; look, the police have things under control. I just wanted to give you that info, the all-clear, OK?" She needed to continue her lie before her husband caused a scene. "Listen, I have to, um, I, uh, I have to fill out some forms for Sergeant Yates," she said, quickly running up the stairs to the office.

The umpires called the managers together at home plate. "We'll treat this like a rain delay," said Al Geiger. Everyone can take a few minutes to stretch, warm up, get themselves ready, then we begin again, bottom of the first, Wolves' leadoff man coming to bat. Understood? Any questions? Good." He then called over a ball boy. "Tell the PA guy to announce that we'll be getting underway in just a few minutes, got it?" The boy nodded and hustled off, and about ten minutes later, Bill McDermott once again said "Leading off for the Wolves and playing center field, number six, Oddibe Daniels, number six." And this time the whole ballpark cheered.

NINE

Following the Klan Klobbering (credit Win Appleton for that one), the Wolves had gone off on their first road trip of the year. They split their two games in Kruse, then won two-of-three in Mettin before losing two-of-three in Beck.

Jack, however, didn't feel right that whole week. He was still upset about Nashota's participation in the brawl, and it must have been apparent in his voice, as things were definitely frosty between them during their daily phone calls. It also cut down on his sleep, as his brain had trouble shutting down. *Is it possible that the two of us squabblin' can affect the baby's health? If she's feelin' at all like how I've been feelin', we're gettin' off to a pretty shitty start as parents. Jeez, nothin' like ruinin' the kid before he's even born! Or she, no way to know what's actually cookin' in the oven, now is there?*

He was anxious to get home and make things right again, and then—wouldn't you know it!—that last game in Beck went eleven LONG innings, finally ending in a loss. *(Sometimes it seems like these guys are bein' paid by the hour, I just hate these slow-ass games.)* Mike didn't wheel the bus into town 'til close to three, Nashota was sleeping, of course, and when he finally woke up she was long gone. He drank some coffee, ate two pieces of toast, and went to the ballpark early, bypassing the clubhouse for the business office.

She was surprised to see him but smiled, though it wasn't her trademark beam that could illuminate Mammoth Cave. She walked around her desk and gave him a little peck on the cheek, but he was here to deliver a message. He put his arm around her shoulder blades, looked into her eyes, then very firmly drew her to him and gave her a long, hard kiss. Louetta, who was also in the office, stopped what she was doing and stared and then said "Oh" just a second before the same word came out of Nashota's mouth.

Jack looked at the secretary. "Been gone for a week, Louetta, and we got in real late last night, so I'm just saying hello. To my wife."

"Sorry, Jack, sorry, sorry," Louetta stammered. "I, I, I didn't mean anything...I was...it just slipped out, sorry. I'll shut up now," she concluded, and quickly buried her head in her work.

Nashota and Jack went out into the concourse. "That was certainly a nice hello," she said. "We haven't kissed like that in, um, quite a while, I guess."

"And that's my fault, I've been a butt," said Jack, and when his wife began to protest, he cut her off. "I may have been right to be upset, but it should have been over that night. Or a day later. I'm sorry I let it drag on for so long, that just wasn't right, 'Sho. I'm real sorry."

She felt like crying, but she just smiled. "And I shouldn't have been mixing it up in the stands, pregnant or not. I'm the team's Business Manager and I should have been trying to keep the peace, not make things worse. You were right to be angry at me, and I need to think more like an expectant mother."

Now it was Jack's turn to smile. "Don't beat yourself up, hon, you were just bein'…well, you. But yeah, you need to be thinkin' 'bout our baby, we want him or her to be born completely healthy, not with a lump on the forehead 'cause Mama got into a fight. Even if the bastard did deserve it."

They just looked at each other for a moment, until Nashota put her hands in Jack's. "No extra innings tonight, OK? Maybe we can even have a quick game so you can be home kinda early?" Then she laughed. "If you want, I could go out onto the field and, you know, strictly by accident, of course, turn on a sprinkler or two so that the infield is just too wet to play on…"

They both laughed. "Tempting as that may be," said Jack, "I'd rather play Weare tonight than have to play two tomorrow." He kissed her again, not so hard this time. "But I like the way you think, *asiule ehu*. See you later." He gave her one more kiss then headed to the clubhouse.

You know you're going bad when a walk is the highlight of your night. That was Oddibe's thinking when he declined Jack's offer of a ride home after the game. "Walk will do me good, skip, but thanks," he said, and Jack just nodded, reminded him to "stay alert," and let him be.

A decent crowd for a Tuesday, nearly 1,200, had seen a good game, with the Mustangs and Wolves trading the lead back and forth. Going into the bottom of the eighth, Weare held a 5–4 lead but Rob Boxleiter opened the frame with a single up the middle. Jack sent Quizenberry in to run for the lumbering catcher, then Brodie sacrificed him over to second. When Coach Valenza settled himself into the batter's box, a loud whistle came from the visitor's dugout, and everyone could see Gene Conn standing on the top step, holding up four fingers. Pitcher and catcher both nodded, and after four pitches were thrown wide of the plate, Coach trotted down to first on the intentional walk.

Ken Crockett, the Wolves' third pitcher of the night, was due up but Jack called him back and told Jim Altman to pinch-hit, which caused Gene Conn to bring in a lefthander. Jack had anticipated this but wasn't concerned because, though he swung from the left side, Altman had so far been successful against southpaws, and tonight was no exception—he hit a grounder up the middle. The Mustangs' second baseman made a hell of a play, ranging far to his right to get his glove on the ball and then shovel it to his shortstop, forcing Valenza. The shortstop wisely held the ball while keeping an eye on Quiz, who had rounded the third-base bag but now retreated safely. This put runners on the corners, two out, and the entire ballpark leaned forward, knowing that THIS was THE big moment in the game. And Oddibe was due up.

He hadn't hit the ball out of the infield all night, and now here he was, with the game on the line. He looked back to the dugout, expecting to see Miggs swinging a bat. It made perfect sense: Boxleiter was out of the game so Al would have to come in to catch, he was a right-handed hitter, this was the perfect time for him to pinch-hit. Jack did give it a fleeting thought, as did quite a few fans, who were shouting out this suggestion to their manager, just in case he had suddenly forgotten how this-here game ought to be played. He quickly rejected it. Being right-handed was certainly an advantage Miggs had over Daniels, but Jack's gut told him to leave his young Negro in the game. *Showing confidence in him might help him break outta this slump.* So Jack just clapped his hands in the third-base coaching box, hollered "let's go, Oddibe, let's go, pick him up," and Miggs just continued strapping on his catching gear.

The fans didn't much like it, and there was some loud booing as Bill McDermott intoned "the centerfielder, number six, Oddibe Daniels, number six" over the PA. Most of the catcalls were aimed at his declining production, but there were a couple of "Get that n— out of there, Jack" cries once his name was announced.

Wait for a good one was the only thing running through Oddibe's mind as he settled into the batter's box. The first pitch swept away from him and dipped low for a ball, then the next one was a fastball that rode in and he had to back away to avoid being hit. "BOO!!" screamed the crowd, led by the Negro fans out in right field, even though the pitch had not been all that close to his chin. Now he was ahead in the count, 2–0, and he looked down at Jack, who was clapping and chattering, but in the midst of his gyrations, the Wolves' manager also put his fists together, and Daniels touched his cap. *Wait for a good one and hit it hard.*

The pitch came in, fast but with a little break away from him, about thigh high, and Oddibe swung and connected. Hit hard, the ball was pulled on a line to right field, curving towards the right field corner, maybe for extra bases, and sinking, sinking, far away from the nearest Mustang outfielder. Finally, with every eye in the ballpark following its flight and every throat yelling "AH," it hit the ground…foul, just foul, foul by inches. Foul ball, strike one.

Oddibe had been halfway to first base when he heard the crowd groan and looked up to see the base umpire holding his hands up in the air, the universal symbol for a foul ball. He also saw Mike Hamblen, coaching at first, kick at the dirt in disgust, the way DiMaggio had done when Gionfriddo robbed him of extra bases in the 1947 World Series.

He was dejected when he got back to home plate. *First solid hit I've had in weeks and it hooks foul, damn!* He heard the umpire call time and then say "son, your manager wants to see you," and he looked up to see Jack walking towards him. Oddibe sprinted up the line to meet him halfway. "Sorry, skip," he started to say, but Jack cut him off.

"Oddibe, you hit that pretty good, nice solid stroke. Good job. Now forget that it went foul, shake it off, and do it again, you can do it."

The next pitch fooled him completely, coming in fat on the inside part of the plate but then suddenly dropping, dipping underneath his bat as he pitifully missed it. The crowd let out a collective groan. Now with two strikes he really had to be careful, so he choked up a bit on the bat just to make contact.

The 2–2 pitch moved the same way as the very first one, and he watched as it bounced in the dirt for ball three. He stepped out of the batter's box and looked at Jack, who flashed a sign meant primarily for Jim Altman at first: *head for second when the pitcher makes his delivery.* Standard baseball strategy with a full count, everyone knew it, including the pitcher, who threw over to first a couple of times to try and keep Altman just a bit closer to the bag. But finally he delivered, that fat inside pitch again. Oddibe held himself back, made sure he did not commit too early, like he had a couple of moments before. The ball dropped down again, he pulled the bat back and was relieved to hear the umpire holler "BALL FOUR, TAKE YOUR BASE."

Gene Conn and several of his players yelled at the ump from their dugout. "Broke his wrists, blue," meaning they thought Oddibe had offered at the pitch, but the arbiter just looked over to them and shook his head. The pitcher picked up the resin bag, fondled it for a second or two and then threw it on the ground in disgust. There were still two out, but now the bases were loaded.

That changed in a hurry. Squirrel Davis hit the second pitch up the middle for a solid hit, scoring both Quiz and Altman and sending Oddibe flying into third. Mac hit a hard shot that bounced off the third baseman's chest. He picked it up as quickly as he could and then, since he was facing home plate, threw it there to try and nail Oddibe. Daniels' speed served him perfectly, however, as he slid in well before the catcher could grab the ball and apply the tag. That run made the score 7–5 in favor of the Wolves, and with Larry West throwing a scoreless ninth, that's the way it ended.

Which is why Oddibe decided to walk home. He was happy that the team had won but upset that his only contribution had been to coax a base-on-balls. Sure it was as good as a hit, and had been part of their winning, three-run rally. Sure his speed had taken him to third and then home with the insurance run. But he still wasn't hitting, so maybe the walk home would help him clear his head, figure things out.

The house on Light Street was not quite two miles from the ballpark. Oddibe had walked it before, generally in about thirty-five minutes, a quiet stroll through a couple of residential sections in the eastern part of Edens Ridge.

The ballpark had, at one time, been a part of the high school, constructed in this neighborhood because it was, after the Great War, approximately the center of the small town. But things changed, primarily because of the economic growth of Tennessee Eastman. Government contracts had helped them come out of the Depression a little earlier than many other businesses, and when the U.S. had entered the Second World War, the company began manufacturing the explosive RDX for the military, and business really boomed (pun intended). With a greater influx of families, Edens Ridge took the pro-active step of building a brand-new high school in a different part of town, one that was now perceived to be (more or less) the new population center. The old school was converted into apartments, leaving the ballpark idle until Bill Washington secured his Mountain States League franchise and renovations became a necessity.

So while the park was still in a residential neighborhood, it was now on the edge of town, rather than smack dab in the middle. When Oddibe walked eastward for just two blocks, the landscape changed from a cluster of homes (and those apartments) to sparsely-populated streets that featured a few industrial concerns, a few empty buildings, and quite a few vacant lots.

That part of town was playing a role in the Edens Ridge mayoral race, one that featured two big baseball fans, season ticket holders, and members of the booster club, the "Wolves Pack." The incumbent was motor lodge owner Dick Curtis, who had been so hateful to Nashota when he learned that the team had signed a Negro ballplayer. His opponent was Bob Dean, a long-time railroad man and the current head of the local chapter of the Transport Workers Union. He was also the man who had helped Jack Simpson build Oddibe's "dressing room," and his wife, Dorothy, helped out all over the ballpark, whenever an extra set of hands was needed. Curtis and Dean loathed each other, had for years, and a couple of their arguments at booster club meetings had already become legendary, repeated frequently around town and even at Mountain Empire League gatherings. In launching his campaign, Dean had accused Curtis of favoring business interests over those of ordinary citizens, and he vowed to "clean up the east side." "It's a blight on our fair city," he said about the area where Oddibe was now walking, promising to "turn it into a place where people want to live and work." Between the baseball team and the juicy election, the people of Edens Ridge found themselves living in a daily drama the equal of "Search for Tomorrow," "Guiding Light" or "Hawkins Falls."

Leaving the ballpark, Oddibe walked down Rockwell Boulevard until he reached an alley. This was Miss Brunét's shortcut, and he headed down the alley, which emptied out onto Polk Avenue. Oddibe then made a left at Polk, which eventually intersected with Light Street. A right turn, two short blocks, and he'd be in his bed.

Polk Avenue was one of those areas of "blight" frequently mentioned by Bob Dean. A nice wide street, it had once contained several thriving businesses, but the good fortune that had touched most of Edens Ridge seemed to pass over Polk. The best thing one could say about it at this time was that it was quiet and afforded a young man the opportunity to think while he walked.

What am I doin' wrong? I hit one ball hard tonight, just one, and it went foul, what is wrong? Am I startin' my swing too early? Am I grippin' the bat too tight? Do I need glasses? I don't think I need glasses, I see as good as I ever did. Am I missin' RubyAnn too much? I know I miss her a whole bunch, but I ain't thinkin' 'bout her when I get to the park every day. Jack says not to worry, just hang in there, everybody goes through a slump but this never happened to me in Asheville, I was always able to hit, always the man, but not here. 'Course not, you fool, what a stupid thing, this ain't Asheville, this ain't no industrial league, this is professional baseball, guys play here who have a chance to make the big leagues. Maybe that's it, maybe I just ain't all that good, maybe I don't have what it takes to be a professional. Maybe I oughta just call Dad, have him come get me, take me home. I can probably get a job back at the Grove Park, or maybe somewhere else, make some money and marry Ru...what was that?

He stopped walking and concentrated. Had he heard something on the quiet street, something other than his own footsteps? He stood still for a moment and just listened. He had pretty good hearing, honed by his years of playing the outfield and listening for a teammate calling him off the ball. "I got it!" was a phrase he heard less and less, and hollered out more and more, as he took control of the outfield, which is something a premier centerfielder needs to do. *In Asheville,* he thought, *in Asheville, man, you were the BEST out there, but not here, not in this league, here you're just a kid trying to play a man's game.* He caught himself and went back to concentrating on whether or not he had actually heard anything. He let a few seconds pass before he decided it must have been the wind; there did seem to be a breeze blowing up. *Shit, better get a move on, wanna be home 'fore it starts in to rainin'.*

He continued down Polk. *Dad will be mad, he'll kill me...no he won't, he'll be disappointed and that's worse. He has such high hopes for me that maybe I'll make it, play with Jackie and Campy, or against Jackie and Campy and those guys, wouldn't that be great? Wonder if they ever had trouble hittin' the ball? Must have, everyone goes through a dry spell every so often, Pete ain't hittin' much now and says he's gonna set fire to his bats if things don't...*

He heard it again, he was sure of it. *Wind don't make no noise like that, like somethin' hard hittin' 'gainst somethin' hard. Maybe a shoe against the pavement, or a bat against...*

Now he heard his father's voice, loud and clear. Before he took the bus down to Florida for spring training, his Dad had told him several times, "Be careful at all times, AT ALL TIMES. There gonna be people out to get you, maybe even on your own team. Look out for yourself 'cause no one else will." *Now*, he thought, *now might very well be one of those times.*

He was sure he could out-run whoever it was, even if there were two of them. If there were more, though, that could be a problem. And if he/they knew where he lived, they'd know where he was going and how he planned to get there. So he began walking again, a little more slowly than normal, so he could be thinking, planning, while he was making his way home.

Polk runs right into Light, they might be waitin' at that intersection. But it sounded like the noise came from behind him, *so if they're gonna attack, it will be on Polk 'cause there's just no traffic on Polk this time-a night.* He remembered that Miss Brunét had told him about another shortcut, a "safe passage," she had called it, and he had told her he remembered it, *now would be a good time, punk, to bring it up front. If I can remember Jack's signs, I oughta remember what she taught me. If I want to live, I'd better remember.*

There was a green house across the street, abandoned, used by winos and other low-lifes, but the color triggered his brain. Acting as cool as possible, he casually crossed the street to the green house, took a step or two forward as if he was going to continue on Polk, then suddenly wheeled around and ran down the alley next to the house. And now he knew for certain that he hadn't just been hearing the increasing wind.

"He's runnin'!"

"After him, he's gettin' away."

"Get him, get the n—!"

He heard the squeak of a screen door and increased his speed, kicking into the next gear like he was trying to score from first on a double. Someone definitely said "shit" behind him, and he could now tell that he wasn't the only person running down that alley. *Somewhere down here, one of these lots has a wooden fence...*and then he saw it, just a few yards ahead, and he geared himself up, *like chasin' down a long fly and havin' to leap...*He veered just a bit to the right, mentally gauged what he needed to do, then took two quick steps to the left and hurdled the fence, landing just a bit awkwardly but maintaining his footing. Whoever was his nearest pursuer did not fare as well, he could hear a body go *splat* as he tried to vault the fence, followed by a string of curses. Now in open field, Oddibe really turned on the jets, sprinting as if he was trying to prevent a little pop fly from dropping safely in short center. And he could hear more footsteps and voices.

"There he goes, get him!"

"He's heading over to Light, dammit, stop him!"

The next street was, indeed, Light, and he hit it at full speed. Miss Brunét's house was just two blocks away.

Oddibe could now tell that he was leading a small parade—with all their shouting, they were making almost as much noise as a brass band. Which proved to be a good thing.

The house was now clearly in view. He could see the flowers, the porch...*wait, was that someone comin' out onto the porch? Two someones? Looks like, could be, yes, that's Jake and Miss Brunét, and she's holdin' somethin', isn't she? What is it?*

Jake came running down the stairs. "Come on, Oddibe, come on. Get in here, man, run, run hard, come on!" *Does he think I'm out for a midnight stroll?* Jake was waving his left hand, and in his right hand he was holding something silver. Meanwhile, he could now clearly see Miss Brunét on the porch carrying a shotgun.

Oddibe reached the house, raced past Jake and bounded up the stairs. Jake's right hand swiftly came forward, revealing a handgun, which he pointed directly down Light Street. At the same time, Jasmine took several steps forward so she was at the edge of the porch. Raising the shotgun to eye level, she fired once into the air. The parade came to a screeching halt.

"All right, y'all, that's far enough. Anyone takes one more step and they'll either get cut down by my Crosman or Jake's Luger. You got a preference? Don't matter to me which one-a us kills any-a you."

No one moved, no one probably even took a breath. In the distance they could all hear the wail of a police car.

Jasmine continued. "My suggestion is, y'all just turn around and walk away, right now, and never come anywhere near my place again, hear?"

She looked at everyone, standing stock still yards away, and then fixed her gaze on one man.

"Orley Pepper, you listenin'? You know me, I ain't spoutin' off no bullshit here. I got no problem blastin' away, Orley. Me-n-Jake can get a whole bunch-a you 'fore the police show up, and I'll bet they agree I's just protectin' my property, know what I'm sayin'?"

Orley looked down at his shoes, then he kicked at a rock and said "shit, boys, let's get outta here 'fore Johnny Law arrives." There was a lot of grumbling but the group quickly disbursed, so that when Sergeant Yates got out of his car, he found only Jasmine and Jake sitting on the porch, waiting for him.

"I get here extra early this morning and you STILL beat me in, DAMN, Jasmine!" Chief Newell Gregory sighed and shook his head. "Come on into my office, Jazz.

Want some coffee? We always have a pot on. How'd you even know I'd be coming in early today?"

"Yates told me last night he'd be callin' you right away, let you know what-all happened," she said. "I know you gen'rally get here 'round 8 and figured you might wanna get a jump on things, 'stead of your usual runnin' this police department like it's some la-de-da bank. And yes, I'll take a cup-a Joe, thank you kindly."

He shook his head again, walked out to where Regina always had hot coffee waiting, poured two cups, threw a lump of sugar into one and brought them back into the office and sat down. He took a sip from the sugar-free cup, sighed, then said "Could you please close the door, Miss Brunét?" He took another sip while she did that, then put his cup down, looked her right in the eye, and said "That was downright nasty and uncalled for."

"You bet your ass it was, chasin' that poor boy for blocks, armed with sticks and bats, I saw 'em, Newell, saw 'em with my own eyes…"

"That's not what I'm referring to, Jazz, and you know it. We have a good police force in this town. I'm proud of my men, I think we offer a high level of protection, maybe the best in the whole area. We're certainly better than Johnson City or Rogersville, and they're both way bigger than we are and can afford to hire more officers…"

She cut him off. "Chief Gregory, a young man livin' in this town, this town that you and your men protect better-n anywhere else 'round here, 'cordin' to you, was chased last night by men holdin' weapons. They weren't wantin' to talk to him 'bout the ballgame that just ended, Chief. They weren't gonna offer advice as to how he could do better when he's battin'. They weren't tryin' to invite him to come out with them for a late-night beer and a sandwich. Now, I guess you could say they were kinda inquirin' 'bout his health, since they had every intention…" and here she raised her voice considerably…"OF CHANGIN' IT RIGHT THEN AND THERE. I'd be a-willin' to wager everythin' I own that not-a one-a them got theirselves a medical degree." She paused, took a breath, then continued. "I agree with you, we got ourselves a good police department. But last night not a-one-a them was anywhere to be seen 'til someone heard me fire my gun, I suppose, and called it in and Sergeant Yates came a-runnin'. Now how good is that, hmmm? How good would it have looked…" and now she stood up as she raised her voice again…"IF THIS YOUNG MAN HAD BEEN BEATEN TO A BLOODY PULP ON THE STREETS OF EDENS RIDGE?" She sat down and he noticed she was quivering a little, and when she spoke again her voice was cracking.

"He just a boy, Newell, did you know that? Only 21 years old. You see him out at the ballpark and you think he's older, he acts older, maybe, but he only 21. Don't deserve to be beaten like…like…I dunno what, but he don't deserve it. What else they gonna do? Break open his skull? String him up like they done to so many-a my people over the years? That what you want here, Newell? Wanna be talkin' to all the papers, not just the *Gazette* but the *Sentinel*, and the *Banner*, maybe more. And all the radio stations 'cross the whole state, tellin' 'em why you can't protect a BOY, a 21-year-old boy, who's just here to work, try and become somethin'…" By this time she was sobbing, so much so she couldn't go on.

He offered her his handkerchief, which she gladly accepted. "You know I don't want that, Jazz. But are you talkin' 'bout protecting him all the time, 24 hours? I dunno if we can do that, I dunno if he would even want somethin' like that, do you? Make him feel kinda like a prisoner, honestly, I know that's how I'd feel."

"Don't need no round-the-clock protection, like some Mafia boss. Just a ride home, Newell. You always got at least one cop at the ballgame, sometimes two, you just have one wait for him to come out and drive him to my place. Take five minutes, well, plus the wait time."

"We don't pay those officers who work the ballpark, Jazz, did you know that? Since they're officially off-duty, they get paid by the ballclub, and they might feel they deserve extra for having to wait around an extra hour or so…"

"You leave that to me, Chief," said Jasmine. "I'll talk to Nashota, we friends, she and I, we work it out 'tween us. You arrange it from your end, I'll do it from mine. Yes? Can we get this done today? Today?" She offered his handkerchief back but he waved it off. "What, don't want my black germs in your pocket?" she asked with a wan smile.

He just shrugged. "Today, huh? OK, I'm sure I can make the arrangement. In fact, tell you what I'll do, I'll call Nashota myself and work out all the details, then give the orders to all my officers. How's that? Is that fast enough for you, Miss Brunét? Same-day service, you can't hardly do better-n that." He gave her his hand and she appreciatively took it as she rose from her chair. They started to walk to the door when she stopped and grabbed her coffee. "Not bad java, Chief, I'll tell 'Gina on my way out."

"I am sure she'll appreciate the compliment," he said as he opened the door. "We'll get it done, Jasmine. We know how to protect our own, and we are the best."

She did tell Regina that she enjoyed the coffee. She also asked if she could borrow a telephone book and, perhaps, use a phone for just a couple of minutes? "Got another stop to make," she muttered, really more to herself.

Jack was so angry he could not sit down, he kept roaming about the office, hitting his right fist into his left hand. Nashota attempted to calm him—"try and relax" she had said a couple of times—to no avail, he just wordlessly glared at her.

Jack had been in the shower when the phone had rung. Nashota, preparing to leave for the ballpark, first wondered who could possibly be calling before eight in the morning, and then another thought took hold as she walked to the telephone: *this can't possibly be good.* And when Jasmine identified herself, she instinctively said "What's happened to Oddibe?"

"He's OK," said Jazz, "he ain't hurt, but I wanted you to know…"

"Jasmine, what happened? Just tell me."

"Let me come over to your house, or meet you at the ballpark, better to talk 'bout this in person, I think. But he's OK, don't you worry none."

They hustled over to the park and Jazz told them everything she knew about the attempted attack, including the fact that she recognized Orley Pepper for certain. She told them about her conversation with Chief Gregory, and how he was going to make sure that Oddibe had a ride home every night. She also said she would personally drive him to the ballpark every afternoon, "generally a real slow time for us, you know," which the Simpsons both ignored. She thought she was being as soothing and as reassuring as she could possibly be, and Nashota seemed to be all right, but her husband just wouldn't sit still.

"Jack, I been up much-a the night, and I gotta tell ya, watching you pace 'round this room is makin' me even more tired," said Jasmine, and her voice really did reflect her weariness. "Our boy O is OK, I told you ten times already, we gettin' this taken care of…"

He finally stopped, grabbed a chair, turned it so that its back was facing the two women, then he sat, leaning over, with his hands clutching the top.

"He's not OK. I haven't seen him or spoken to him yet, but I know he's not OK. How would you be if a group of men were planning on bashing your body or head with clubs, bats, pipes, sticks, whatever the FUCK they were carrying? If it was me and I was just 21 and away from home for the first time and already the most targeted player in every city in the league, including the one I play in, I think…" He stopped and seemed to be gazing over the heads of both women, and Nashota recognized that look, knew he was having a thought, knew some important decision was about to be made. And she was right—Jack stood up, looked at his wife and said "We need to go to him, right now, 'Sho. We need to talk to him immediately." Now he looked at Jazz. "Is that all right? Can we go to your place?"

"'Course, Jack, of course you can. Wanna all ride in my New Yorker? Plenty-a room."

"Jack, I'll need to tell Louetta that I'll be out for a bit, she'll be here in just a minute…"

"I'll ride with Jazz, you follow quick as you can," he said, and instantly was out the door.

The two women looked at each other. "Not every day you see a black woman drivin' a white man 'round town," said Jazz, and her little smile got bigger when Nashota burst out laughing. Then, quite unexpectedly, Nashota gave Jasmine a hug, and suddenly the tears came, and it took no time before they were both sobbing and trying to console one another. Finally Jazz pulled back, grabbed a tissue from her purse, and said "Gotta go, bet he's all anxious, doncha think?" And Nashota, using her own tissue, nodded and said, "I'll be there directly."

They sat in total silence for most of the short drive, the only noise coming from the Chrysler's V-8 engine, and its tires rolling through Edens Ridge. When she turned onto Light Street, Jack suddenly said "I've never thanked you for taking him in. I know Nashota has but I haven't, and I'm sorry about that, I should have…"

"No need, Jack, no need. I know your wife speaks for both-a you…"

"She does, but I should have said something. Or sent you a note, or called. It just…well, it feels a little, um, awkward, even now. Know what I mean?"

She gave him a brief glance, and smiled when she saw him looking at her. "Coupla lifetimes ago, Jack Simpson. You was just a boy then, and you know, I wasn't all that much older-n you. 'Sides, ain't like we was datin' or nothin', you was just a customer. Nice guy, cute guy, sweet guy, but just one-a the boys who came a-callin'. A customer."

There was more silence until they pulled up at the house. When she cut off the engine, Jack said "I really don't like being called 'sweet,' drop that one, will ya?" A quick smile, then he got out of the Chrysler.

They found Oddibe sitting in the parlor, staring at the floor, and Gail was with him, speaking softly and stroking his hand. She stood up when her boss came in, and the two women went over to a corner of the room to talk while Jack sat down next to Oddibe.

"You look like you could use some sleep," Jack said.

Oddibe just nodded, so Jack continued. "Night off will probably be a good thing, O. I'll play Altman in left and move Brodie over to center. Squirrel can lead off with Altman behind him, or I could maybe move Terry up top, I've always liked his great power-and-speed combo…"

"Do I hafta come to the park tonight, Skip? Don't know if I really feel much up to it."

Jack rubbed his chin. "Tradition says you oughta be there unless you're in a hospital or something. Injured players always suit up, unless they get special permission, same if a guy's gotta sore throat or laryngitis or some such bullshit. It's one-a them unwritten rules, I guess."

Oddibe looked up for the first time. "Maybe you could give me one-a them special permissions? I'm just not real sure I can be out there tonight, tomorrow, maybe forever." He looked right at Jack for the first time. "Thinkin' 'bout callin' my Dad later today, after he gets home from work. Maybe tell him this here 'speriment ain't really workin' out, maybe he could drive up here and get me, bring me home. Just don't know if I'm cut out for playin' ball, least not professionally. Too bad there ain't a Class E, you could send me down there, maybe I would do better, but there ain't none, I know, this is it, lowest rung on the minor league ladder." He let out a very audible sigh. "I ain't doin' shit and I got people that hate me, people I don't even know, and now people wantin' to kill me or, least, hurt me, rough me up. They would-a, Skip, I swear, they would-a if I hadn't been able to out-run 'em all. Tell ya, comin' down Light Street, I think I was runnin' 'bout as fast as I ever run, I could-a beat Jesse Owens, or Harrison Dillard, or Arthur Wint, any-a them Olympic guys. Thing is," he finally took a breath, then went on, "thing is, those guys, Owens and them, they was runnin' for medals and history, but me, I was runnin' for my life. And that ain't right, Skip, that ain't right. I just wanna play ball, what they want from me?" And now he leaned into Jack's shoulder and the tears came freely. He wasn't the only one: Gail let out a sob, covered her mouth, and ran from the room. Jasmine got all misty-eyed again and also walked out, though she had an excuse, she had to answer the knock on the door which was, as she expected, Nashota.

Over the next hundred minutes, a lot of words were exchanged and a lot of tears were shed. The residents of the house steered clear of the parlor while Jack explained how the on-duty cop would drive Oddibe home every night, and when the young man seemed embarrassed by Jasmine's offer to take him to the ballpark each afternoon,

Jack volunteered to personally come over and get him, if he preferred. "Truthfully, I like the walk," Oddibe said, but he agreed to let his manager pick him up every afternoon around three o'clock; Jack always liked to get to work plenty early and start planning for that night's game. Jack also made him another promise: "I know you're in a slump right now and it seems like you'll never get out of it. You will, I know you will, I've told you that before and I'll keep on tellin' you. Meantime, I've got me an idea, I wanna talk to someone and this could take a few days to put together, but let me work on it, OK?" And here Nashota jumped in. "Please don't go callin' your Dad, you don't want to worry him, or your Mom, get them upset, let's see what we can do here first, Oddibe, that's…let's do things the grown-up way, all of us. My Jack, I know him, and I know that right now he wants nothing more than to find that Orley Pepper and beat the living shit out of him, and all of those guys he had with him, right Jack?" Husband looked at wife in amazement but then he silently nodded. "That's what he'd like to do, but that's not what he's gonna do, cause that's not…it's not very adult. And we…we all want…we all NEED to act like adults, to be adults. I gotta tell you, Oddibe, going back home, that's the easy way out, probably the most painless, but it's not adult, it's just running away. And when you do that…"

"Those bastards win," Jack said emphatically. "You leave and they'll know they drove you off, and they'll gloat about it for years and years. That what you want? Don't even think about baseball for a minute, just think about you, and them. You said it, O, ain't right, definitely not right, you just wanna play ball…" He coughed and shook his head. "Know what? This…this thing…it's getting to be bigger-n baseball, bigger-n all-a us. I'm sorry 'bout that, I didn't really expect it to be quite like this…" He stopped, rubbed his face a little and shook his shoulders, like he was coming in out of a light drizzle. Then he looked back at Oddibe.

"But it is, and who do you want to win this one, you or them? Nashota and I, we want you, we're with you a hundred percent, a thousand percent, and we're doin' everythin' we can to make sure you come out on top. This is probably the biggest contest you'll ever be a part of, son, bigger than the World Series, even, but you gotta stay here and play."

There was silence for what seemed like an eternity as Oddibe once again was studying the floor. Finally he said "In our house, we like ol' Harry Truman. He's pretty scrappy, ain't he? I like how he says 'if you can't stand the heat, get outta the kitchen.'" He stood up and looked at Mr. and Mrs. Simpson. "Always did like hot weather, I play my best in hot weather." He attempted a smile. "I'm gonna go take a nap now, if y'all don't mind. And I'll see you at three, Skip."

Jack was able to smile for the first time. "But you're on the bench tonight, you can sit next to me. Win Appleton asks, I'll just tell him you need a night off. And O, look, if you wanna tell the guys what happened last night, or not tell them, that's up to you. I…we won't say anythin' to anyone."

Oddibe nodded. "Maybe on the next road trip. No tellin' what Pete might do." Then he smiled, nodded, said "Miz Simpson," and went up to his room.

In a town the size of Edens Ridge, however, it's hard to keep this kind of news quiet for long. The grounds crew were the first to know, because of Max. Max seemed to live in the shadows and often had information about things before others, which he would share quietly, in dribs and drabs. But when his work-mates would ask him, "How do you know this, Max? Where did you get this information?" he would just shake his head, give them his crooked little smile and say, "I jes' know, is all."

He knew because the chase had begun on Polk Street, his street, the dilapidated neighborhood where, most nights, he slept. He had heard the voices, seen the runners, and had followed them discreetly, until they retreated in defeat. No one had seen him, but he had seen everything.

"Orley Pepper," he said to Nick and Richie. "Ain't he the Klan guy what was involved when we had that fight in the stands few weeks back?"

"Yeah, that's him. He's a little peckerwood," said Nick, with disdain. "Guys like that..." He stopped and spit out a wad of tobacco juice. "He's just an ignorant shit, I ain't got no respect for a person like him."

"He ain't that bad," said Richie. "I've talked to him before, he's OK, a little odd, maybe, but ain't we all, right?" He was expecting some sort of affirmation, but his two co-workers were just looking at him.

"Well it ain't like I agree with everythin' he says and does," said Richie in protest. "Ain't never talked about the Klan with him, or anythin' like that." Now that was a lie. Orley had tried recruiting Richie into his Klavern, but so far had not been successful. So far. Not because Richie wasn't sympathetic, he just wasn't all that worked up about race the way Orley Pepper was. Besides, Richie had spent his life talking his way out of tight spots, and had gotten to be pretty good at it. As a member of the Klan, however, he recognized there may well be times when being glib would have to take a back seat to being physical. He might have come across as a tough guy in high school, but violence had never really been a part of Richie's makeup.

"He's a little piss-ant," said Max, to which Richie replied, "He's ...oh...he's kinda funny, actually, funny-ha-ha, you know, he says things to make you laugh." Once again there was silence. "He is pretty fanatical 'bout race, I admit that."

Max stood up. "Don't like people like that. I seen fanatics 'fore, they strange, weird, rather kill theirselves..." He caught himself and stopped in mid-sentence before he said more than he should. He just shook his head. "Little piss-ant gonna go too far one-a these days. Make the wrong person mad, that'll be the end-a him." It was his turn to spit. "Ah, 'nuff-a that shit, let's get back to work, fellers."

The Buchanan Bees followed the Weare Mustangs into town. It didn't matter how good or bad or in-between either team was that year, the two always seemed to play especially hard against one another. That was because of the close personal relationship between the two managers, which was well known throughout the league, as well as in many baseball circles. Both relished matching wits and trying to come away with bragging rights, even if it was just for one night. But this time, Jack had a special reason for welcoming Lionel Ticknor to The Ridge.

LaDonna knew to keep a table in reserve when the Bees were in town, since Jack and Lionel invariably met at The Back Porch for lunch. (Lionel returned the favor, making sure that a table was waiting for them at The Kopper Kettle, a local eatery owned by his girlfriend, Jeannie Grayson.) Lionel was now in the habit of getting there early so he and LaDonna could indulge in a favorite pastime—exchanging good-natured barbs and insults, as well as the occasional off-color joke. So it was no surprise that, on this Friday, Jack found Lionel seated in the back, kibitzing with LaDonna.

"Coffee, black, coming up, Jack," she said.

"And LD, you can bring me your chicken salad special, on rye, light on the mayo, please."

"Sure thing. Want your coffee first?" Off she went when he nodded.

"Lionel, I got a problem that maybe you can help me with."

Ticknor smiled. "And hello to you, too, old friend. Why, I'm just fine, thanks for asking. And how's that beautiful wife of yours? She and baby doing well?

Jack offered up a weak, sheepish smile. "Sorry, Li, that was rude-a me. We're fine, 'Sho's great, growin' every day. Last visit to the doc went well, we're excited. Thanks for askin'. How are you doing? How are things going with Jeannie? You two ever going to get married?"

Ticknor almost choked as he drank his coffee. "Bite your tongue, you bastard. I ain't never gonna make that mistake again, told you that before, didn't I? 'Sides, me-n Jeannie got a good thing goin' for us just as it is, no pressures, no expectations, just… well, you know, we're there for each other. Though I gotta tell you, since you asked, she did mention somethin' lately about me maybe movin' in with her, least durin' the season…"

"Ha!" said Jack, slapping the table. "You old rascal! Love it, that's just great, you gonna do it?"

"Quit makin' so much noise, you little prick, ain't you learned anythin' from your wife? As for movin' in with Jeannie, I ain't had time to think much about it, got me a team to manage and, in case you ain't noticed, I ain't doin' such a good job of it so far, we're three under."

"Ah, you'll get 'em straightened out, I know you. Just wait 'til next week, will ya?"

LaDonna brought the coffee, including a refresher for Lionel, and asked "know what you want, Goose?" And Lionel did—"chopped steak, medium well, peas and carrots and taters, no dessert, then I'll take a tuna on white to go."

"You oughta try the chicken salad, it's pretty damned good," said Jack. "You always get tuna for your pre-game meal, be a little daring for a change, eh?"

"I was daring a coupla nights ago and it cost us the game," Lionel said with a grunt. "We're in Kruse, it's the top of the ninth, score tied, we get a man on, Paulson, our third baseman, good hitter but can't run a lick. So I replace him with Leigh, fastest guy I got, and then I flash the hit-and-run for Taylor. Pitcher throws, Leigh takes off, Taylor swings, hits the ball to the right side, just like he's s'posed to—right into the glove of their first baseman. Big galoot steps on the bag, double play, our threat is over, just like that. Shit! Then, in the bottom of the ninth, they get their leadoff man on, next guy bunts, our catcher picks it up and heaves it into center, gives 'em runners at the corners. I bring the infield and outfield in but it don't matter, their catcher hits a long fly to center, runner easily scores, that's the game. Man, was I pissed!"

"Why?" asked Jack. "You played it right, even your batter did what he was s'posed to do, he hit it the other way. Just tough luck. You know as well as I that somewhere during the season, you'll steal one like that." He looked at his old friend. "Somethin' else bothering you, Li?" Jack never called him "Goose," like LaDonna did, which was short for Mongoose, it was always Li.

"Nah, it's just that these kids..." He trailed off for a moment, thinking, then returned. "They're nice kids for the most part, good kids, but as a group, they're not real bright, they make dumb mistakes. Gonna be a lot of work with this cluster of fucks." He chuckled. "I probably shouldn't be tellin' you this, you'll use it against us somehow." He lifted up his coffee cup, clinked it against Jack's, and said "Cheers!" They drank, then Lionel said "You mentioned a problem when you came blowin' in here, what's up?"

"Yeah, that. It's my centerfielder, Oddibe Daniels. He's provin' to be more of a project than I anticipated. Got off to a good start, but he's been in a slump for nearly two weeks now, and it's really draggin' him down. I think part of the problem is his, um, circumstances. I mean, he...you know, he...um...he hears shit all over, even here at home, some. We had a, a, near calamity the other night, some guys chased him home and they wasn't after autographs. Gotta be a load on him, must feel like he's wearin' cement." Jack leaned forward. "You worked for Veeck up in Cleveland, do you know any-a his Negro stars? I was thinking if, maybe, a guy like Satchel Paige could talk to him, just talk to him, calm him down, somethin', it might help. I'm doin' everythin' I can to keep his spirits up but I think, um, it would, um, I think it would be more effective comin' from someone who wasn't white."

LaDonna came with their food and said she'd be right back with more coffee.

"Satch is in St. Louis, playin' with the Browns, you know that. Be real tough to get ahold-a him, but I'll try for you, I will. Prob'ly be able to get to him by goin' right through Veeck. I've introduced you before, haven't I? Thought so. Great guy, best baseball mind there is, better than Rickey, if you ask me."

Jack reached into his pocket and pulled out a couple of pieces of paper. "I brought these, just in case you said 'yes,'" he declared. "One is our pocket schedule, so you could tell Satch where we are. The other has a list of our hotels and their phone numbers, and I've also written my home number down there as well. Tell him he can call me at any time. Any time. Thanks, Li."

"Don't mention it," said Ticknor. "Now you do somethin' for me, OK? You're startin' Neville tonight, right? Tell your pitcher to just lay 'em in for my guys, we need to have a night of just BP, OK?" He grinned, and Jack said "sure thing, sure thing. Maybe I'll just put everybody in positions they never played before, have a lefty out there at short, things like that. Work for you?" They both had silly smiles on their faces, and Lionel said "would you, old buddy? That'd be just great, 'preciate it." Jack just shook his head as he took another bite out of his chicken salad (excellent!), and said "you old fuck."

A little later, standing outside The Back Porch, Lionel said, with a toothpick in his mouth, "'Case you hadn't guessed, I'm seriously considerin' Jeannie's proposal."

Even though it was just for one game, Jack felt that giving Oddibe the night off would be beneficial, and soon enough the young outfielder agreed. Sitting on the bench had given him a chance to see the game from a different perspective, even to question his manager as to why he made certain moves in certain situations. It didn't help, though, that the Bees throttled the Wolves by a 12–2 score, and the next night Oddibe was back in there. Got a hit, too, and scored twice as Edens Ridge rebounded with a 5–4 victory, and Oddibe thought that perhaps his seemingly-endless slump was at an end. But in the rubber match of the three-game series, he struck out twice and popped up twice, including in the bottom of the tenth, when the Wolves had the bases loaded and any sort of a hit would have successfully ended the scoreless tie. No dice, and Buchanan eventually won with a run in the twelfth.

So now the Wolves were off to North Carolina, starting with three games in Weare. Jack always enjoyed going there, since it allowed him to see Tehya and Chris and Gwenelda, who seemed to be growing up so quickly. "That's what happens," said Tehya. "First they're *usdigas*, so tiny and helpless, then before you know it they've developed their own personalities and are driving you crazy!" She laughed. "Gwennie's pretty good, but give her time, she'll be displaying the Cozens side of her before we know it. *U-ne-qua*, help me!"

On their second day in town, following a come-from-behind 6–4 win that was accomplished despite Rob Boxleiter hitting into a triple play, the phone rang in Jack's room. He had just finished showering and was stark naked, *maybe it'll be Nashota, we could have some long-distance fun.*

It wasn't. It was, in fact, an unfamiliar male voice.

"This Jack Simpson?"

"Yes sir, it is, who is this?"

"Satchel Paige. Talked to my old buddy Lionel Ticknor yesterday…no, day before, sorry, and he was tellin' me 'bout this young man you got playin' for you down there, North Carolina is it?"

"No sir, we're from Northeast Tennessee. Lionel's team is in Carolina, same league, in fact we happen to be in…"

"Don't matter, young man, don't matter 'tall. Fact is, you got a young Negro ballplayer who needs some help, is that right?"

"Yes sir, he's just twenty-one, first time in Organized Ball, and strugglin' some."

"Position player?"

"Yes, sir, he's my center fielder, fast as hell, great glove, but havin' trouble gettin' on base…"

"They harassin' him? Yellin', screamin', all that bullshit?"

Jack paused, then quietly said "yes, sir, he's seen…we've all seen, a fair amount of that this spring. I've tried…"

"Nothin' you can do 'bout it, Mr. Simpson, you ain't gonna stop it, not just you alone. But I'm sure that's part-a his problem, I'd be willin' to bet 'most anythin' on that." He paused, but Jack didn't comment; he wasn't sure what to say. So Paige continued.

"Look-a-here, Mr. Simpson, I'd love to help you, but I really can't, I'm pitchin' here in St. Loo, I'm sure that bastard Hornsby wouldn't let me take a few days off, even Mr. Veeck would prob'ly say no and he treats me real good. And I'm a pitcher, your young man needs to talk to a position player. Someone…you know, someone who can talk better 'bout hittin' than me, though I reckon—ha!—after all these years of missin' bats I qualify as somethin' of-a expert on hittin'. But listen, I know a feller might could help you, old teammate-a mine when I played with the Crawfords, "Bug" Gillen. He lives in South Carolina, I reckon if you pay his bus fare and give him a place to sleep and maybe a coupla meals a day, he'd be glad to help out for a while. Now, he played mostly infield, second base behind me, but you just need help with his battin', right? Bug do a real good job for you there, he was an ornery cuss 'bout gettin' on base and makin' his way home, know what I mean?"

"Yes sir, I sure do. Thank you so much, Mr. Paige, I really appreciate your takin' the time…"

"No big deal, son. Ol' Goose tells me this kid-a yours is pretty damned good, maybe a big-leaguer someday. Lord knows, we needs to develop more good, talented Negro ballplayers for the majors. Maybe we can get him here in St. Loo, we could certainly use all the help we could get, startin' with that manager-a ours, Hornsby. Won a World Series back in '26, been livin' on that glory ever since. 'Course, it helped that he was in his prime as a player and could put hisself in the middle of the lineup… Aw shit, listen to me ramble and gripe at you, nothin' you can do 'bout the Browns, you got your own worries. Anyways, I'm happy to help a young Negro ballplayer, wish I could do more, but I'll get a-hold of Bug and I know he be callin' you."

"We check out day after tomorrow, Mr. Paige, heading for Buchanan, that's our next stop. Do you have that list…?"

"Got it right here, young man, got it right here, everythin's copacetic."

When he hung up the phone, Jack sat down on the bed. He was rather overwhelmed and wasn't sure what he ought to do next. He then realized he was still naked, so he got dressed. The clock in the room told him he still had a couple of hours before Gene Conn would be coming over for lunch, so he called Nashota.

"Honey, you'll never guess who I just talked to. I gotta tell you, this is the most excitin' thing that's happened to us in quite a while. Good excitin', not like some-a the crap we've had to deal with lately. This is big, well, it could be…yeah, yeah, I know, I'm babblin', sorry, lemme start at the beginnin'…"

For Floyd Gillen, Lexington County, South Carolina was a fine place to grow up, because he got to play about as much baseball as he wanted. His world was his family, his friends, school and baseball, that was it. He never gave a second thought to the fact that just about all of his classmates were Negroes, this was simply the norm at that place and that time. He paid no attention to the crazy war taking place in Europe, he was more interested in learning about baseball from his Pops and playing baseball with his friends.

His parents saw that Floyd was good with numbers and quickly insisted that he be diligent at school and get good grades, with his immediate reward being that they would then allow him to play baseball. Learning wasn't easy in the ramshackle building the county called a school, replete with old desks and even older textbooks. Many times he was tempted to quit, just light out like his older brother had done, off to who-knows-where? "No, we never hear from him, but if I knows Bert, he prob'ly somewhere fun and exotic." Floyd never tired of talking about the life he imagined his brother to be living. "Bet he's in a big city like Noo York, 'cause he loves his baseball, jus' like me. Did you know that, during the season, major league baseball is played every day up there? Every day! They have three teams, so at least one-a-them is always playin' at home, April through September. Think-a that, a city so big that three teams can be playin' and doin' well all at the same time!"

Sometimes he day-dreamed about wearing a uniform like that, just like fellow Palmetto Staters Joe Jackson or Del Pratt, playing in huge stadiums in front of thousands and thousands of people. But he wouldn't even get close if he didn't do well in school. "Finished all your work for the day, boy? Lemme see. All right, then go on wichya, but y'all be back by dark." While his parents insisted he bring home good grades, they were also proud of the talent he was developing on the field. So in the classroom he worked hard despite the inferior building and obsolete primers, and on the diamond he worked hard to make himself into the best player he could possibly be.

He liked that "scientific baseball," manufacturing runs by using your head and your legs and your skills, not just bashing the ball over the fence. He proved to be a fast runner, fast enough to steal or take the extra base, fast enough to scoot either left or right and get to ground balls that otherwise would have snaked through the infield for base hits. Because his throwing arm was only average, he found himself playing second base rather than shortstop, but that was fine because he was playing. His speed gave him his nickname. One day, after stealing both second and third, the father of one of his friends yelled out "that boy sure is fast, he remind me of a water bug." Just like that he was "Bug," and it was a name he would wear proudly for life.

By the time he was a senior in high school, there were scouts following him, and when he graduated in 1925 he signed a contract to play for the Winston-Salem Pond Giants, a team in the Negro minor leagues. Thus began a journey that eventually took him to the Negro National League and a career playing with such great stars as Josh Gibson, Judy Johnson, Cool Papa Bell, "Double Duty" Ted Radcliffe, playing-manager Oscar Charleston, and Satchel Paige.

As a baseball man, Jack Simpson knew a little about Negro League baseball, he certainly knew the names of Paige and Gibson and Bell. He had frankly never heard of Mr. Gillen, but if the great Satchel Paige was recommending him, Jack was eager to determine if he could, perhaps, help young Oddibe Daniels. Gillen called him while the Wolves were playing in Buchanan.

"Me and the missus, we run a restaurant in Charleston, a fine place on Meeting and Hasell, you know Charleston at all? You never been? Man, you gotta come down here some time, this is one of the great cities in the South, in all of America, if-n you ask me. 'Course I'm prejudiced, we've lived here for years, Maudene grew up here, though we met in Pittsburgh…well, hell, you don't care 'bout my life or where I met my missus, let's get down to business. Our restaurant is doin' good so I can afford to leave it for a few days. Maudene can take care-a things just fine, and we got plenty-a help, there's lotsa work here in Charleston. This is such a great place to work and live, did I mention that already? Sorry. Ain't perfect, 'course, no place is, I guess, but Charleston do come close, I believe. Now, we do get us a hurricane ever now-n-then. And the humidity, whoo boy! But see, I'm from South Carolina so I grew up with all that…that…stickiness, you know, it just second-nature to me, I don't think much 'bout it, but people who visit, they fuss and fret…"

Jack cleared his throat. "Mr. Gillen, not to be rude, but we have a game tonight and…"

"Oh sure, son, sure, sorry, I like to talk and can get onto this-n-that, you just feel free to stop me any-old time. OK, like I says, I can leave here and come see you. We only got one car and Maudene's gonna need it, so I'll hafta take the bus up to you, which means I'll buy the ticket and you can reimburse me. And then I'd need a place to stay…"

"Of course, Mr. Gillen, and I was hoping you'd honor us by staying with us, my wife and I. We have an extra room so you wouldn't be putting us out none, and this way we'd be able to feed you at least a coupla meals a day. And we'll pay for your evening meal, there are good places around here, especially one…"

"That sounds fine, Jack, just fine. And listen, call me Bug, everybody does, even my wife. Mr. Gillen was my dad and he ain't with us no longer, so it's Bug, y'hear? And I'd be happy to stay with you and your wife, the honor be all mine"

"Thank you, sir…Bug."

"OK, let's talk 'bout expense money. Meals and a bed is all well and good, but even as a favor for my good friend Satch, a man gotta look after hisself, know what I mean? What you say to thirty dollars a day?"

Jack winced a bit. He and Nashota had been expecting to pay a per diem, but had hoped to get by for less, more like, say, $12.50. Bug wasn't biting.

"Jack, like I said, I got a business to run, if I come up there, it's as a courtesy to you and to Satch. I know you're in minor league ball and you don't make a lot, I know all 'bout that. But look, I think I can help you with your young man, I seen it before and I 'spect I can do somethin' with him. You don't manage your ballclub for free, do you? You eat a meal in my restaurant, you know you gotta pay. Same thing here—I oughta get paid for my services. But I 'preciate your circumstances, I do, how 'bout $25?"

This was like negotiating contracts with ballplayers in the winter, except then the team always held the upper hand; not now. "Boy, Bug, that's still a little rich for our blood. I think I can swing $20, though, can we do it for twenty?"

There was silence on the other end of the phone as Bug thought it over. Then he said "tell you what, Jack. You make it $22 and I'll get me on a bus in time for your next home stand, OK?"

Nashota will probably kill me, she wanted to stay under twenty, but… "it's a deal, Bug, you have my word." *I sure hope this works, otherwise, may God have mercy on my soul. And you, too, U-ne-qua.*

TEN

Things happen every season that only the Baseball Gods can explain. For one night, an otherwise-mediocre pitcher is completely unhittable. On another night, a pitcher most certainly bound for the Hall of Fame is drubbed by the league's worst team, sending him to the showers in the third inning. A light-hitting infielder whacks a home run in a crucial World Series game, driving his team to an improbable championship. The best-fielding outfielder in the game misplays a routine single into a triple, ending a nail-biting, extra-inning contest. A sure home-run ball suddenly loses altitude, hits the wall, and the ensuing relay cuts down the potential winning run at home plate. Only the Baseball Gods can explain, and they never speak for publication.

Making a swing through the southeastern states that make up part of his territory, Bob Rhodes passed along some information to Jack Simpson.

"Friend of mine gave me a tip, told me about a catcher he saw playing in an Ohio semi-pro league, down around Athens, maybe about 75–80 miles from our office in Columbus. Big farm boy named Monroe Hicks. Big NEGRO farm boy. Went to see him play one evening, and he's a good hitter. Well, a decent hitter, big power but he swings-and-misses a lot. But his defense, man, it's spectacular! Blocks balls in the dirt like Campy or old Bill Dickey, got a gun for an arm, real take-charge guy behind home plate." He stopped, waited for a reply, got none so he continued. "If you want, I can put you in touch…"

"I got two catchers, Bob, and a full roster, I can't use him, sorry. I'm sure there's another team somewhere on your route…"

"Sure, sure," said Rhodes. "There's several I could talk to about him, several that might sign him. Yeah, I'll talk to them, I just thought he might be good for you, good for Oddibe, too, have a fellow…um…another…well, you know. But I understand, Jack, I do, no need to give it a second thought."

And he didn't, until the Baseball Gods decided to get involved. On the first night of a road trip to North Carolina, Edens Ridge and Weare went 16 long, grueling innings before the Mustangs pushed over a run to win, 8–7. Jack wanted to give everyone a night off but, with the league-mandated 19-man roster, including seven pitchers, he could only rest four players at a time. Sitting Rob Boxleiter was a no-brainer since he had caught the entire game; he noticeably winced just climbing onto the bus to go to the ballpark. Miggs went behind the plate and, as usual, was solid with the glove but an easy out in the batter's box. And damned if this game didn't go extras as well! So in the tenth Jack rolled the dice and, with two out and no one on, he sent Box in to hit for Miggs. The big kid from Staten Island timed a curve perfectly and blasted it far over the wall in left-center, then went in and caught the bottom of the inning as the Wolves evened the series with their 6–5 win. In the finale, Jack sat the other four players, which included Pete Sevareid, which was problematic because not only was he the team's most productive hitter, he was also the only real first baseman on the roster. But Jack knew that Box had played a handful of games there in the past, so he wrote his name in at first base and batted him in the cleanup spot. All Box did was have the game of his life: two home runs and two doubles, six runs batted in, and no problems in the field. Even Miggs had a big night, at least for him, with a single and double, and the team bus was rocking on the winding road to Buchanan after their 10–2 triumph.

The ensuing three-game sweep of the Bees could have easily been called The Rob Boxleiter Show. Game One: another homer, plus a double and two singles, driving home four in an 8–3 win. Game Two: two singles and (most importantly) the game-winning run RBI with a sacrifice fly in a 5–4 victory. Game Three: an early two-run homer, followed by a bases-clearing double late as the Wolves came from behind to win again, 7–6.

Unbeknownst to Jack, a scout from the Boston Braves had been in Buchanan. The Braves were horrible—they would lose 89 games in 1952 and finish next-to-last in the National League, ahead of only the Pittsburgh Pirates, one of the worst clubs in major league history. The Braves' starting catcher was Walker Cooper, an eight-time All-Star who was now 37 years old and in serious need of a night off here and there. They had someone they could bring up from their Triple-A affiliate in Milwaukee, which would create the usual ripple effect of players moving up all along the chain, but ultimately, one of their clubs would be short a catcher. Boxleiter's hot streak suddenly made him a very desirable commodity, which allowed Nashota to suggest asking for top dollar.

"Six thousand bucks? 'Sho, no team in their right mind will pay $6,000 for Rob Boxleiter."

"They might, they're desperate. And if they balk, it gives us a nice place to begin negotiations."

Boston did cringe at the high price but, needing to act quickly, they kept the bargaining to a minimum, and the two teams settled on $4,400, a figure that made the Braves comfortable and the Wolves ecstatic. But now Jack needed another catcher, and where do you find one who's any good this time of year? He could probably ask Bob Rhodes to get him a list of players released from National Association teams…wait. *Bob Rhodes, Bob Rhodes, didn't he say something a week or two ago about some kid he saw, or heard about, or…dunno, something, ain't for-sure, but wasn't that kid a catcher?*

Nashota was happy to do the legwork. A call to Columbus provided more information than she wanted, because Sara sure liked to talk. Before getting what she needed, Nashota heard about the weather in Ohio, an update on Sara's newest grandchild, even a health report on Mr. Trautman, who's "been fightin' a cold for several days but he won't stay home!" Mixed in *(wa-do, U-ne-qua)*, ultimately, was Bob's whereabouts; actually, his complete itinerary for the next two weeks. Today he was in Cordele, Georgia, but a call to the hotel proved to be fruitless. Yes, they had a reservation for him; no, he had not checked in yet; yes, he'd be happy to take a message. Nashota then called the ballpark and, sure enough, he was there, had just arrived moments ago, in fact.

Nashota explained the situation to Rhodes, concluding with "You mentioned to Jack a young Negro catcher…"

"Monroe Hicks!" Bob yelled it so loudly that Louetta could hear him even though she was in the next room. "His phone number is in my bag, and I haven't unpacked yet, obviously. Let me look for it and I'll call you right back."

It took him about forty minutes before he got back to her, but he had a good excuse. "I thought it might be best if I called him first; after all, I had seen him play, and had spoken with him, briefly. So I called his house, spoke to his grandma, she told me he was out in the field, they got a farm there in Morgan County, but she said she'd go get him. Didn't take long, he called me here and I gave him the heads-up that you'd be reaching out to him right away. Anyways, here's his number, gotta pencil?"

Though she wasn't even thirty yet, Nashota always felt so old when she talked to these ballplayers, especially the real young ones, because they "ma'am-ed" her so much.

"Mr. Hicks, my name is Nashota Simpson, I'm the Business Manager for the Edens Ridge Wolves in the Mountain Empire League, I believe you just spoke to my friend Bob Rhodes from the National Association."

"Yes, ma'am, I did, yes, ma'am."

"Maybe he told you, we need a catcher, our starter just got purchased by the Braves organization, and Mr. Rhodes spoke real highly of you. Think you'd be interested in giving pro ball a try?"

"Oh yes, ma'am, nothing would please me more, been my dream since I was in short pants."

"Now you know we're Class D, that's the bottom rung of the minors, and we make no promises, give you no guarantees, our manager decides when you play…"

"Yes, ma'am, I understand, I gotta prove myself, I understand, ma'am."

"And you know we're in Tennessee, specifically Northeast Tennessee, and the other teams in our league are in Virginia and Kentucky and North Carolina. I have to be honest with you, Mr. Hicks, there is only one other Negro player in this league, though he is on our team. He's had his problems with fans and other players, not the ones on our team, but, um, he has had a few difficulties, Mr. Hicks, you need to know that right up front. And if that bothers you, or you think it might bother you or be a problem, just say so and we won't…"

"Ma'am, please, with all due respect, won't be nothin' I ain't faced here in southeast Ohio. They ain't gonna say things I never heard, know what I mean? I can take care of myself, ma'am."

Nashota paused for a moment, then said "Well all right, Mr. Hicks. If you give me your address, I'll send you a standard contract, plus a bus ticket. Will take a few days, of course…"

"'Scuse me, ma'am, don't mean to interrupt, but you said you need a catcher, I imagine that means real quick, am I right?" Nashota said "yes," not sure where he was going with this. "If I gotta wait for that contract and bus ticket, that means you won't have a catcher…"

"Oh, we have one, Allan Miggs, he's been our backup and now he moves up…"

"But do you have someone behind him, ma'am?"

The Mountain Empire League

She was starting to hate the word "ma'am." "No, Mr. Hicks, that's why we need you…"

"Yes, ma'am, I understand. Guess what I'm tryin' to say is I can get on a bus tomorrow, day after at the latest, be to you that night, prob'ly, maybe even in time to suit up. I can buy the bus ticket here and you can pay me back when I get to town, and I can sign that contract then, too. This way we both don't hafta wait all that time, mail can be awful slow comin' out here."

As Jack said later, "gotta love that kind of enthusiasm!"

Shirley, Kentucky was a town that was showing its age. Coal was its primary business, and baseball and basketball were its residents' primary diversions from the mine. Unless there was a snowstorm or a cave-in, the high school gym was generally filled during the winter when the Terriers were playing. When the weather warmed up, the Cardinals' little ballpark was invariably packed on Friday and Saturday nights, and management could count on at least 1,000 of its 2,270 seats occupied on other nights (except Sundays), unless it was raining or there was a problem at the mine. The ballpark, however, was sub-standard, even after the City spent some money upgrading it. Terriers Field was a good high school yard but a poor professional facility. It had short fences and poor lighting and a rocky infield and a small clubhouse and (mostly) bench seats for the fans, though that last point didn't concern the players at all. Tommy Nathan, the Wolves' southpaw who hailed from south Texas, described it as "puttin' lipstick on a pig. No matter what you do with her, she's still a pig." Bob Rhodes had recommended to Mr. Trautman that he lean on team owner B.J. Lewis to improve the facility, starting with the lights and the infield. The NAPBL President had talked to Wells Boggs about it, and Wells, in turn, had tried to impress on B.J. the importance of making these necessary changes. Lewis, however, always pointed to the Cardinals' great attendance figures as proof that the fans didn't care. "In fact," he said on more than one occasion, "they think our park is charmin' and quaint and wouldn't have it no other way." He knew that Wells, fearing a lawsuit, wouldn't try to yank the team away from him, and he truthfully doubted they could find another town that would support the franchise so well. Boggs, however, was thinking of the Big Picture, which meant major league affiliations for all eight clubs, and he had been told confidentially that no big-league team was about to send their players to his lipsticked pig.

But now B.J. had hit on a new idea, and he was just itching to try it out on Wells. He had almost called him up, long-distance, as soon as he thought of it but decided to wait, knowing that the league president was "coincidentally" coming to town for this series with the Wolves.

Wells Boggs' visit to Shirley really was a coincidence, he had decided almost three weeks earlier to make a swing through Kentucky and Virginia. One of the requirements of being a league president is the necessity of getting out of the office to visit your teams periodically during the playing season. This is a good news/bad news situation. It's good to get out there, sit in the stands, mingle with the fans and hear what they think, what they like and dislike about the operation of their team. It's always good to be watching some baseball. There are even times when it's good to get away from the family for a few days. But the league president also hears everyone's gripes, from his team operators' complaints about the umpires to all the fans' concerns. And the fans are not shy about venting. "Cold hot dogs and warm beer? I'm really not the person to talk to about that, sir." "The umpires? Yes, they do work for me, why don't you tell me what happened?" Those arbiters, by the way, also generally had a laundry list of problems to discuss, like lukewarm water in their shower stalls, or not getting baseballs on time before a game so they could be rubbed up. Wells generally found that, after just three or four days of this, he began looking forward to getting back home, even listening to his teenagers.

Planning to leave first thing the next morning, he was making a priority list for his secretary when she buzzed and told him that Bob Rhodes was on the line.

"Wells, this is a heads-up. You probably know Jack Simpson needs a catcher, I gave him a tip on a kid and it looks like he's gonna sign him. His name is Monroe Hicks and I wanted you to know that he's colored."

"Oh," said Wells. "I see."

"Kid's from Ohio, been playin' semi-pro for a coupla years and really, REALLY needs someone to take a chance on him, so…"

Sometimes Wells just couldn't help himself, and the Southern in him would come pouring out.

"Does he hafta sign a cullud boy? Ain't there no other catchers out there?" Then he realized what he said and quickly retreated. "I'm sorry, Bob, I didn't mean it like that, it's just…"

"No, I understand. Look, Wells, this will be good. It gives Daniels some company on the team, especially on the road. And it makes you and the league look good in the eyes of the majors, and you know what that could mean. Just keep thinking of the long term."

"I will, Bob, I will. You know the league comes first with me." But after they had hung up, Wells mumbled to himself "the short term, though, could be a bitch."

He deliberately left Knoxville early so he could get to Shirley early; no sense putting off the inevitable. And he went straight to B.J. Lewis' Chevy dealership.

"Why Wells, what a pleasant surprise, I didn't 'spect to see you 'til tonight. Don't tell me you finally decided to get smart and trade in that old Studebaker-a yours?"

"My Champion DeLuxe still got a lotta life in her. No, B.J., I wanted to tell you about this new player Edens Ridge just signed…"

Lewis cut him off. "Already heard 'bout it. Fact is, I got a call from my constable, tellin' me he got this young coon down in the jail, they just waitin' for Jack and his team to arrive."

Wells literally leaped out of his chair. "Jail! Jail! What did he do, why is he in jail?"

"Relax, sit yourself back down. Boy ain't in no trouble, he just went to the hotel by mistake." Lewis chuckled. "Ol' Raymond got scared, I guess, and called Porter, who decided he could wait there in the jailhouse just as easy as anywhere else." Wells eased himself into his chair as B.J. went on.

"Another nigra in our league, Wells, another nigra, and he's gonna be playin' tonight in my ballpark. This is hard for me to imagine, how 'bout you? Now they got two-a them! Wells, this ain't right, this ain't what we voted on, Jack was only bringin' in one, now all-a sudden he's the new Homestead Grays!"

"Oh B.J., having two cullud players don't hardly make them the Homestead Grays. He needed a catcher after they sold Boxleiter to the Braves and this boy was available. Prob'ly cheap, too, you oughta 'preciate that."

"You mean there ain't no other catchers he could sign? In the whole You-Nited States, he can't find him one white catcher? Hell, sittin' here with you, I can think of two—Aaron Robinson and Bob Scheffing. Bet either one-a them would love another crack at the big leagues."

"B.J., please be serious. Robinson ain't available, he's playin' in the PCL, Portland, is it? And Scheffing, I don't know where he is right now, he may be scouting, but he's gotta be forty, or close to it. This kid is young, the kind we have in our league..."

"Man, you just don't get it. You holed up in a office in Knoxville, you ain't out here, in the trenches, 'cept ever-so-often, you don't hear things, what people sayin' in your town. Bad enough we had to take one-a them, now we got another? Where does it end? Ain't good, Wells, I tell ya, it just ain't good. People gonna be mighty upset."

"Why? It's only a three-game series, then they leave..."

"But they'll be back later this summer. How many-a those people he gonna have then, huh? Three? Four? All nineteen?"

Wells sighed. "I can't reject a contract just 'cause the boy's got black skin. 'Sides, you know Trautman and Rhodes would have my hide if I tried to do anything like that. I think..."

Lewis was now getting animated. "That's the problem, Wells, you ain't thinkin'. You ain't thinkin' 'bout what might happen. Maybe here, maybe in Mettin, maybe even in Edens Ridge. Somebody gonna do somethin', somebody gonna stand up for our way-a life and do somethin'."

There was a very pregnant pause, then he went on.

"And maybe, maybe, it be me." Lewis leaned back in his chair. "How 'bout you and me talk turkey, league business, right now? That all right with you?"

Wells wasn't sure where this was going. "What...what do you have in mind?"

Both men moved forward so they were only a foot or so apart, elbows propped against the desk. "You been after me for, what, two years, three, to make some changes to Terriers Field, right? You know I don't think we need to do nothin', I think this ballpark is jus' fine the way it is, but here's what I propose. This off-season we'll get us brand-new lights, best lights money can buy, just as good as they got in Atlanta or Nashville or Chatt'nooga. Look-it, I know Joe Engel, I'll call him tomorra and have him tell me where I can get lights as good as his and we'll get 'em installed, maybe even 'fore this season is over. Then, come fall, we'll strip the infield, have the whole thing re-done, make it the very best in the league. Tell you what, I'll even start lookin' into expandin' our clubhouses, both-a them, maybe have that done in the winter, too, or maybe the winter after. Whaddya say to that, Wells?"

"I say that'll be great, these things should-a been done 'fore now. So why do I think you're expecting something from me in return?"

Lewis laughed. "No wonder you're the league president, you one smart cookie. All you gotta do is reject this new contract, tell this new porch monkey he can't play in this league, in OUR league, you can make somethin' up, I'm sure. You do that and I'll be on the phone to Joe Engel in the mornin'."

Wells just sighed. "B.J., you know I can't do that. No reason this fella can't sign a contract with Edens Ridge. I do what you ask, I'd be standing on quicksand. George Trautman would have me up in Columbus 'fore I could take a breath, then he'd prob'ly send Bob Rhodes here to run this league. I like my job and have no desire to get shit-canned just 'cause you don't want your pitchers facing a second Negro player. And he's just a backup catcher, for cryin' out loud! I ain't about to get fired over a backup catcher!"

Lewis picked up some papers that were on his desk and slowly shuffled them in his hands. "Wells, we can talk 'bout this some more tonight at the game, if-n you like. Fact, I'll let you think on this the whole time you're here in Shirley. But if you stick with what you just said, I'm tellin' ya, somebody gonna do somethin', and it won't be pleasant, I can guarantee it. Don't say I didn't warn ya, Wells." He looked at those papers in his hands. "Now I hope you don't mind, but I gotta lotta work to do. I'll see you tonight, we can talk."

Once the league president had left his office, B.J. Lewis sat and thought for a moment, then grabbed his league directory, found the page he was looking for, and made a long-distance call.

"Hey there, sugar, this is B.J. Lewis in Shirley, Kentucky, with the Cardinals' baseball team, you know? How are you? Well, that's good, glad to hear it. Listen, hun, does your boss happen to be in? Ah, well, you expectin' him later today, maybe? Oh, around game time? Well, that'll be good, think you could ask him to call me at my ballpark? We got a game, too, but I really need to talk to him, sooner rather than later, so if he could call me tonight…Thanks so much, darlin', I appreciate it, I'm gonna write myself a note to bring you a big box-a chocolates next time I come over to Mettin."

Keener and Trula Rodgers lived in a neat and tidy bungalow that had a fresh coat of gray paint on the outside and colorful, welcoming roses leading up to the front door. Mrs. Rodgers was there to greet them, and immediately offered them some sweet tea and biscuits, which none of the men saw fit to refuse. As far as having a place for Monroe to sleep, however, that was not such a simple matter.

"We only have the one child, Mr. Simpson, never could have 'nother. With KJ in the Army, fightin' over there in Korea, we got a empty bed for now, that's why we can rent it to Oddibe." She looked at Monroe and smiled. "Sure hope you don't take 'fence, Mr. Hicks, but you're a big-un. Dunno if that-there bed will put up the two-a you."

The sweet way she said it made Jack Simpson laugh out loud. Monroe jumped right in.

"No 'fence, ma'am, none at all. I can sleep on that couch you got in the livin' room, if you-n your husband don't object. Fact is, I don't need nothin' fancy, I can just lay on the floor…"

They went back to the living room and looked at the couch. "I know I'll sleep like a baby," Monroe said, but he was, no doubt, being overly polite—it was small and narrow and a bit threadbare. Oddibe piped up.

"You won't fit there, hoss. I'm smaller than you, I'll sleep on the couch."

"Man, you were here first, I don't want you givin' up your space, I can sleep right here…"

"Ain't MY space, just where I sleep when we're in Shirley. Tell you what, next time we're in town, we'll switch, I'll take the bed, you take the couch."

"We could do it now. You sleep in the bed one night, I'll sleep in it the next, and the third…"

Simpson quickly interrupted. "Here's what we oughtta do," he said with a smile. "When we was drivin' over here, I noticed an Army-Navy store. Let's go in there and buy a sleeping bag, and the two of you can alternate between the couch and the bed and the bag. Then we can take the bag with us in case we need it in other towns. How's that sound?"

Everyone agreed it was a good plan. Jack and Mrs. Rodgers easily came to terms on how much the team would pay her for the extra lodger—"we'll just double what we normally pay, OK?"—and then he left, reminding his two ballplayers that the bus would be back later that day, around 4:45 pm, to take them to the ballpark. That afternoon, as they were leaving the house, Mrs. Rodgers cheerily said "Have a good game, boys." They both smiled, but as they climbed onto the bus, Oddibe said softly "Better to wish us a quiet game." Monroe would quickly learn what that meant.

On this night the two squads proved to be evenly matched; when one team scored, the other quickly tied it up. When the Wolves pushed over a run in the eighth inning to take a 4–3 lead, Jack brought Ken Crockett in to pitch. The little lefty from eastern Kentucky had been the team's most reliable relief pitcher, taking charge in the eighth or ninth inning and closing things out. On this night, however, he couldn't control his curve, which allowed the Cardinals to sit on his fastball. Before Jack could get Larry West into the game, WHAM! WHAM!! WHAM!!! Three runs had scored and the Wolves were down, 6–4, heading into the ninth, and set to face Lee DeYoung.

Just a few days away from the halfway point of the season, DeYoung was easily the league's most valuable player. A star at Crawford High School in San Diego who once struck out Ted Williams three times in a game, he signed a professional contract with Detroit and moved up the minor league ladder. Like so many ballplayers, however, he exchanged his baseball uniform for military fatigues after Japan bombed Pearl Harbor. Seeing combat in Europe, DeYoung fought in Sicily and France and the Battle of the Bulge, and then came home, anxious to resume his baseball career. But he did not return alone. He would wake up at night, sure he was under fire. Loud noises made him jump. Trying to calm his nerves he began to drink, and when that seemed to provide relief, he happily increased his alcoholic intake. Released three times in four years, he decided to quit baseball after the 1949 season, a has-been at the age of 31.

He went back to San Diego and tried driving a cab, then worked construction. Neither made him happy or curbed his drinking. And then one day in January of 1951, he got a call from a former teammate, Karl Hines. The outfielder was now a manager in some town he had never heard of, Shirley, Kentucky.

"Karl, I appreciate you thinking of me, but I can't pitch no more, I'm through. I'm a drunk and I know it. I'd love to get off the sauce but every time I try…" His voice trailed off.

"Don't want you to pitch, Lee," said Karl. "I need a coach, and a guy who can drive the bus and maybe patch up a scraped knee. You been around long enough…"

"Damn, Karl, it makes me feel good that you want me, but it also makes me feel like shit 'cause I know I can't do it and I'd sure hate to let you down. I don't…"

"Lee, I know all about booze. I been battling it forever, since you and I were teammates. Maybe I held my liquor a little better-n you, or hid it better, I don't know. I do know it kept me outta the bigs, I'm sure-a that. But listen, I been sober for seven years now, and I can help you. I need a coach and you need a friend, I think we could help each other out here."

So DeYoung headed east. He found that he liked tutoring the young players and, with Hines' help, he worked hard at laying off the booze. And then in July, the Cardinals lost two pitchers to injuries, right after they had sold their best hurler to the Giants. DeYoung went to his skipper.

"Karl, activate me, I can eat innings for you."

"Lee, you haven't thrown in anger for over a year, are you…"

"We need bodies, man, and I'm here, activate me, at least until you get some young studs."

DeYoung started two games and did OK, nothing great, but he kept his team in both games. By then Hines was able to find a couple of hurlers who had been released by big-league clubs earlier in the year, but he decided to play a hunch. He did not take his old teammate off the active roster, instead he shifted the big lefty to the bullpen, and it was like the sun had suddenly broken through the clouds. Needing just two primary pitches for an inning or two (three at the most), DeYoung saw that Class D hitters had no idea how to handle either his "sweeper" (his name for a slider) or his screwball. Over the final few weeks of the season, Lee DeYoung was virtually unhittable. Given "the best contract of my life" by B.J. Lewis, Lee DeYoung picked up in 1952 right where he had left off the previous season, mowing down Mountain Empire League hitters with relative ease. And now he was brought in to finish off Edens Ridge.

Oddibe, set to lead off the ninth, came in from the outfield and immediately headed for the bat rack, where he found Jack waiting for him.

"Skip, ain't you s'posed to be out in the third base coaching box?" he asked with a sly smile.

"He's gonna stay outside on you with that sweeper-a his. Don't try to pull it, best thing to do is simply go with the pitch."

"I was thinkin' 'bout a bunt…"

"They'll be lookin' for it," said Jack, as he started for third base. "Go with the pitch."

Oddibe saw that both the first and third basemen were creeping in, so he made a last-minute decision to reinforce their mindset. He feigned a bunt, but because he didn't actually offer at the pitch, it was called a ball. Jack shook his head before continuing his normal routine of clapping and shouting encouragement—"attaboy, good eye out there, good eye, make him work now, here we go, here we go."

DeYoung combatted the perceived threat of a bunt by throwing his fastball up and in. Daniels leaned back so he didn't get hit in the jaw, but the ball nicked his bat and rolled foul for strike one, bad break.

"That's OK, that's OK, you can do it, make sure you get a good one." Jack said that one a lot.

And the next pitch was a good one. It was one of those sweepers, but it didn't break quite as much as DeYoung wanted. Oddibe stepped directly into it and just met the ball; he didn't try to kill it, just hit it hard ("squarely" in baseball's unique parlance). The ball went on a low line towards third base and quickly shot past the bag into the outfield and rolled all the way to the wall as the left fielder chased it and Oddibe quickly turned on the jets and steamed around the bases, easily making it into third without having to slide.

The Shirley crowd was beside itself. "Goddam!" "Fuckin' n—!" "Kill that coon, just shoot him right there at third." "Whatsa matter with you, DeYoung, givin' up a hit to that jigaboo!"

Monroe Hicks sat in the visitor's dugout, dumbfounded, his mouth agape. His new teammates snuck sideways glances at him and could see the look of absolute incredulity on his face. He had experienced some discrimination in Morgan County, certainly been called names, but he had never heard so much venom in such a quick and concentrated form before.

Squirrel Davis did what he did best—he hit a multi-hopping ("squirrely") ground ball up the middle, just beyond the shortstop's last-ditch dive, and into center for a clean single. Oddibe trotted home, cutting the Cardinals' lead to 6–5. Mac McElvain did the same, and suddenly the Wolves had runners on the corners, and DeYoung still had not registered an out.

The big lefty was cussing at himself behind the mound when he heard footsteps, and saw his young catcher trotting his way. *Damn, I ain't got time for this shit.*

"What do you want? Get back behind the plate, meat, and just catch what I throw you," snarled DeYoung to the stunned young catcher. When the young man hesitated, the pitcher took a couple of steps towards him and shouted "Go on, get back there. Goddammit!!"

A fly ball would have tied the game, but Pete Sevareid, over-anxious, struck out swinging for the inning's first out. DeYoung never had trouble with Terry VanLandingham, who always appeared over-matched, and today was no exception as the Edens Ridge outfielder weakly fouled to the catcher. Two out, and now Jerry Brodie was the Wolves' final hope.

Jack got the umpire's attention and called time. He trotted over to his dugout, where all eyes were on him. He scanned his players quickly, then looked right at his newest player. "Hicks, grab a bat, you're hitting for Brodie." Jack passed along this change to the home plate umpire, then went back to the coaching box.

Monroe Hicks sat there for a second, looked at his new teammates, then jumped up and found a bat. Oddibe went with him.

"Ignore them, man, the fans, all-a them. Just concentrate on the pitcher, on the game, that's what I do." Hicks just nodded and went to home plate for his first professional at-bat.

Like a verbal landslide, the hatred descended on him from the stands. He had heard all the words before, of course, many times, but never by so many people all at once. Never had he felt so much animosity directed right at him.

"Jig." "Coon." "Alligator bait."

"Go back to Africa, you monkey."

"Kill him, Lee. Hit him in the head, right 'tween his buggy eyes."

It was like…really, he couldn't compare it to anything he had ever experienced before, so he just walked up to home plate and set himself in the batter's box.

Having observed DeYoung's pitching style, Monroe was expecting a screwball and got one—and he missed it by a foot as the pitch darted underneath his swing for strike one. A stretch by the lefty, a check of the runners, another screwball, and this time Monroe got a piece of it, hitting the ball foul over towards the first-base dugout.

Now he was down two strikes, one more would end the game. He moved his left foot out of the box, looked at the pitcher, glanced at Jack, stepped back in, trying not to pay any attention to the blistering attacks coming from all over the ballpark.

"Got you now, n—."

"Strike him out, Lee. Send him back under that rock he came from."

DeYoung decided the rookie might be ripe to be fooled, so he shook off his catcher's signal for a screwball and said yes to a fastball. Thrown up and in, he was hoping that Hicks would chase it and either pop it up or miss it altogether and he and his Cardinals could go into the clubhouse and pop open the PBR. The ball went right where he wanted it to go, but Hicks spoiled the strategy by fouling the ball back. *Shit*, thought the veteran southpaw. *This burrhead may be raw but he ain't dumb. Fouled off the last two pitches, guess I actually gotta think out here.* DeYoung shook off the sign for the screwball, then the fastball, which brought his catcher hustling out to the mound.

"You again? OK, meat, here's what we gonna do. First a sweeper, give him somethin' else to think about. Then another fastball and hopefully that'll be it. Got it? Good." And DeYoung turned his back and picked up the resin bag, abruptly ending the conversation. *Asshole.*

The sweeper was low, in the dirt, and the catcher had to impersonate a hockey goalie to block it and keep the runner on third from scampering home. But for DeYoung, that was simply a set-up pitch. He expected that the rookie would now be looking for a screwball, making the fastball a surprise. *He'll miss it and this damned game will finally be over.*

Monroe did not miss it. He did not pop it up. He hit it on a high arc out to left-center field, and deep. Both the left fielder and the center fielder went back, towards the wall, back, back, and then watched as the ball struck the fence. It hit the ground and bounced once, twice, and was finally picked up by the left fielder, who immediately whirled and threw it towards the infield.

Squirrel trotted home with the tying run, grabbed Monroe's bat and tossed it out of the way, then got down so he could signal McElvain, who was flying around the bases.

And all eyes were on the race, the ultimate in baseball drama. The throw came in from the outfield and was grabbed by the shortstop, who whirled and fired home. Squirrel was on the ground, a few feet away from home plate, pounding the dirt with the universal signal of SLIDE, SLIDE. And finally, the runner and the ball and the catcher all converged at home plate, seemingly at the same time. The players and fans all held their breath, waiting for the umpire, who looked carefully before spreading his arms apart and hollering "SAFE! SAFE!" This quickly turned the fans' wrath away from Monroe Hicks and onto the man in blue, although one leather-lunged fan had a word for the man on the mound:

"DeYoung, you dipshit, how could you let that big n— hit the ball?!"

Monroe was left stranded at second, so the game moved into the bottom of the ninth. Jim Altman went into left field to replace Jerry Brodie, and Larry West went back onto the mound, though Buck Hightower began warming up in case West faltered. Having re-taken the lead, Jack now really wanted this win, and West, a handsome, amiable right-hander from Pittsburgh, was up to the task, retiring the Cardinals in order for a 7–6 Wolves' victory.

The next morning, B.J. skipped the pleasantries as soon as Wells walked into his office. "You can't blame me for all that noise comin' outta the stands, fans gotta right to cheer and boo…"

"There weren't any booin' goin' on, B.J. Booin' don't bother me, but the stuff they was hollerin' was downright offensive. If it was offensive to me, an old Southern white boy, 'magine what those cullud kids felt like, hearin' that shit. And good mornin' to you, too, got any coffee?"

"Margaret, could you bring us some coffee in here?" Lewis yelled to his outer office. Hardly a moment later his secretary appeared, toting a tray that contained a small pot, mugs, sugar and creamer, set it down on B.J.'s rather large desk and scurried out without saying a word, closing the door behind her.

"I can't regulate the fans, I can't tell 'em when to boo or when to cheer or what to yell or anythin' like that, Wells, you know it, you ran clubs…"

"We agreed, when we met in the winter, do you remember that? We all agreed that we would try to make it as easy as possible for this young man to come into our league and play and not get harassed, not get the shit scared outta him every night…"

"I hear," B.J. interrupted, "that it's just as bad for him in his own park, with his own fans. Not the nig…culluds, of course, but the rest…"

Boggs quickly jumped in. "You don't need to concern yourself with the fans in Edens Ridge, just your cranks here in Shirley, that's all we talkin' 'bout here today. I'm well aware of what's gone on in Edens Ridge, and I also know that Jack and Nashota are workin' real hard to make things better. I'm confident they're very much on the right track, are you? Sure didn't look or sound like it last night."

"What you want me to do, Wells, hmmm? Our fans are…" He searched for the right word. "Passionate. Our fans are passionate 'bout their Cardinals, and they express it, they express themselves. Can't put a muzzle on 'em, now can I? Wouldn't even wanna do that. Might be a fun promotion, though, Muzzle Night, maybe I could get a pet store…"

"B.J., there's a real difference between bein' passionate and bein' mean, bein' vile. I was sittin' in the stands last night and your fans…" He looked down and shook his head. "Your fans was just evil." He looked up again. "It's gotta stop, B.J. Big-league people hear horseshit like that comin' from the stands, with nobody sayin' or doin' nothin' to stop it, they gonna pass us by. We'll never hook up with the majors and without them, we won't be able to make it. In time…"

"What you talkin' 'bout, Wells, we all doin' fine, you said so yourself at the Winter Meetings, all our teams are makin' money, some a little more-n others but still, we all…"

"The day is comin', B.J. Somethin' is happenin' in the minors, and it ain't good, not for us, anyways. There were 59 leagues operatin' just three years ago, last year there were 51, and now there's 43. Sixteen leagues gone, poof, just like that, in three years. And more are in trouble. Florida State League lost Gainesville and St. Augustine, they both folded up just a few days ago, you heard that, didn't you?" Lewis nodded, and Boggs continued. "I hear there's trouble in the Mississippi-Ohio Valley and the Alabama-Florida. These leagues…"

"It's that damn TV!" yelled Lewis. "They put major league games on free TV, fans are gonna stay home, why should they pay me fifty-cent when they can sit at home and drink beer and see the best players in the whole world? This TV shit is the problem."

"Won't argue with you there, but B.J., it's also these Negro players. More-a them are gettin' signed by the majors, and if a town or a league won't take 'em or accept 'em, then the bigs are gonna send their players elsewhere and those leagues are gonna go bye-bye. And that could be us, B.J., that could be us 'fore long." He paused, and Lewis thought that he suddenly looked very tired. "We're all in this together. 'Way I see it, if we wanna make it, we gotta all be rowin' in the same direction, know what I mean?"

B.J. thought for a moment, then leaned forward in his chair.

"I can, prob'ly, maybe, talk to a guy or two here in town, spread the word, try to keep a lid on. Can't guarantee nothin', y-understand, but I can, maybe, do that." He smiled. "Fact, as I think on't, I can do even better-n that. Remember what we talked 'bout yesterday? My offer still stands. Fact, I promise I'll start workin' right away to calm things down in the stands, you just find a way to get rid-a this Hicks fella. We'll accept Daniels, we voted on him-n all, but we'll get the fans straightened out if you get Hicks outta the league. Then I'll start fixin' up Terriers Field this fall, and you won't let no more culluds into our league. Simple, eh?"

There was silence in the room. B.J. tried again. "Whaddya say, Wells, we gotta deal? And we don't have to say nothin' to nobody, can just be 'tween the two of us. Shake?" He extended his right arm.

Wells Boggs just looked at him, then shook his head and stood up. "You haven't heard a word I said. You're not seeing the big picture here. This is 'bout a whole lot more than a coupla cullud boys playin' baseball. This is about us—you, me, Jack, Truck, all-a us in this league—makin' a livin', survivin'. Why can't you see that? It's right there in front-a us, big as life. It is life, our lives." He shook his head again. "Damn you, B.J. I ain't makin' no deals. And you keep your fans in check, startin' tonight."

The fans, however, were no different that night; if anything, they were more vicious as the Wolves pounded out a 10–5 win. With every hit by Daniels and Hicks, with every run they scored or drove in, the tirades grew worse. Wells didn't even stay for the ninth inning. He could only hope that Blackmer would be better.

Like Shirley, Blackmer was a typical Kentucky town, built on coal, supported by coal, owned by coal. Unlike Shirley, however, just 44 miles away, Blackmer displayed a little more tolerance. A significant reason may have been Charles Underwood.

The owner of the Blackbirds was the principal banker and possibly the wealthiest man in town (the owners of the mines certainly didn't live anywhere near where their money was made). Yet despite the income disparity and the fact that he was always impeccably dressed in his bespoke suit, Underwood was well-liked and, more importantly, well-respected by everyone. It was, no doubt, because he had always made it a practice to be respectful of everyone else, no matter who they were or where they lived or how they dressed. It was how he had been brought up, and he lived by the Southern credo: "don't get above your raisin'." Quiet and dignified, he had always put the interests of Blackmer ahead of everything else, and his fellow citizens recognized and appreciated that.

Underwood had been responsible for convincing Wells Boggs and the owners of existing Mountain Empire League clubs that Blackmer could support a professional franchise and then, once it had been granted, in getting Blackbird Park built. He had picked the brains of some long-time minor league operators on how to run a ballclub, like Dick King and John Henry Moss. The latter, from the little town of Kings Mountain, NC, told him to never, ever, think like a banker, and that simple sentence may have been the most helpful of all. Life was hard in a coal town like Blackmer, so Underwood and his small staff worked very hard to make sure that whoever came through the gate had themselves a good time. From Day One, the team had consistently drawn well and made money despite their small population base.

Underwood was always easy to find in the ballpark, as his hand-tailored suits were in stark contrast to the overalls and jeans and hand-me-downs worn by nearly everyone else. And when the red-hot Wolves came to town, that suit could be seen everywhere. A good-sized crowd was expected, larger than normal for a weekday, causing congestion at the ticket window. Underwood jumped right in, stationing himself alongside the line with a roll of tickets, shouting "No waiting here! I'm selling general admission seats, step right up, no need to wait in line! Exact change is appreciated." Once he had cleared up that bottleneck, he stood by the ticket-takers and greeted each fan as they came through the gate. Of course, he did have an ulterior motive. Every so often, he would spy someone he knew and would smile and greet him by name. He would then put his arm around the new arrival and, walking him into the concourse of Blackbird Park, speak quietly to the man—it was always a man—before giving him a pat on the back. Each individual who received this personal touch was someone that Underwood knew to be a potential troublemaker, and he was being singled out for his own special and private message. "Now John/Clyde/Marcus/Whit, there ain't gonna be any trouble here tonight, is there? This has the makings of being a real good game, and I'd hate for you to miss any of it. You agree with me, don't you? Good, now go on, cheer hard for our boys, and have fun."

He stood at attention when the anthem was being played, hand over his heart, and then he remained standing, eyes darting about, inspecting each section of the park. When PA announcer Will Dingus intoned "Leading off for the Edens Ridge Wolves is their centerfielder, wearing number six, Oddibe Daniels. Daniels, number six," Charles Underwood held his breath as he looked about and listened. And what he heard was…not much. A muted response, certainly not what the Wolves had been hearing everywhere else, including in their own ballpark. Just a handful of catcalls but no epithets, no denigrations of Daniels or his family or his heritage. Pretty much the same thing heard by all visiting players on all visiting teams. Charles Underwood exhaled deeply, and began to casually stroll through the grandstand, down the first-base line.

Blackmer was starting a left-hander and his first pitch was a called strike, then Daniels swung on the next and dribbled it foul. Oddibe stepped out of the batter's box, tapped his bat against his cleats, and as he stepped back in, a voice from the stands rang out clearly and with great gusto:

"OK Jonesy, now kill him, hit that fuckin' n— right in the head!"

Oddibe glanced up but quickly went back to concentrating on the pitcher. Charles Underwood, however, immediately sprang into action. He quickly changed direction and moved towards the general sound of that voice, and as he approached a section near the third-base bag, several fans stood and pointed. "There, Mr. Underwood, the fellow there with the green shirt, that's the one, that's the man who shouted just now." Underwood walked down the stairs until he was standing just a few feet away from the fellow, whom he did not recognize.

Standing in his usual position in the third-base coaching box, Jack Simpson had a unique bird's-eye view of the proceedings.

"Sir? Do you think I could speak with you for just a moment? Only a moment, sir, I promise."

"Got nothin' to say to you, Mr. Fancy-Pants. 'Sides, I ain't done nothin', I'm just a-sittin' here, watchin' this-here game."

Several fans chimed in with "Don't listen to him, Mr. Underwood, he's the one, he's the guy what yelled."

"I didn't yell nothin', you bastards, and if-n I did, it's a free country, I can say what I want. I fought at Guadalcanal, was with MacArthur in the Pacific, I…"

"Sir, I assume you're new to Blackbird Park, I'd just like to speak with you about how we treat people here. Please, this will only take a moment, then you can go back to watching the game."

"Fuck you, you rich-ass sonofabitch. I paid my money, I served my country, I…"

He continued his stream-of-conscious rant while a few fans started yelling back at him: "Shut up, man, we're tryin' to watch the game"; "Hey, I was at Omaha Beach, don't got nothin' to do with this ballgame"; "Yeah, really? I was there, too, what outfit was you with?"; "Jiminy crickets, y'all are missin' the game, didja see that?" Oddibe had reached first by beating out a slow ground ball, then had attempted to steal second. The catcher, trying to throw him out, had instead heaved the ball into right-center field, allowing the Wolves leadoff man to pick himself up and trot easily into third. Meanwhile, Charles Underwood had signaled to one of his security people, who now forcibly removed the Guadalcanal vet, loudly proclaiming his rights as "a free white man in these-here United States, no n— gonna get me 'rested, there'll be hell to pay for this, you'll see, I got friends, 'portant friends, they won't stand for this, no n—..." That's when the security guard slapped the back of his head and the fans on the third-base side, and the left-field bleachers, too, cheered. This was actually quite bizarre, because that was just when Squirrel Davis punched a single up the middle. Oddibe scored, and for those elsewhere in the ballpark (including the dugouts), it sounded for all the world as if the Blackmer fans were applauding their team giving up a first-inning run.

Damn, thought Jack to himself. *Just when you think you've seen everything in this game.* Then he had a totally different thought: *You're a damned good man, Charles Underwood.* Similar thoughts were going through Wells Boggs' brain, as he watched from the press box. *Why can't B.J. Lewis, and Truck Maxwell, be more like Charles Underwood?* He quietly shook his head while, out on the field, Jack Simpson softly admonished himself—"Shit, better get my head back in the game."

When one door closes, another one opens. Or something like that. It was a lesson Trig Swinney learned in the Mountain Empire League in the summer of 1952.

At the beginning of the season, Trig had pounded the ball as if his life had depended on it, and as far as his baseball career was concerned, it did. Playing in Shirley was giving him a fresh start and, hopefully, a chance to move up to a higher level, Class B or C. Best way he knew to prove himself was to hit the snot out of the ball, so that's what he concentrated on doing and that's exactly what he had done. In the season's first three weeks, he batted .361, with ten doubles, a couple of triples and four home runs; he even stole three bases. His 17 runs scored led the league and his 13 runs batted in were just one behind the leader. He was on fire.

And then, just like that, the blaze was extinguished. Perhaps he was thinking too much about a rumor circulating around the ballpark that a scout from the Gulf Coast League had been spotted in the stands. *He's gotta be here lookin' at me, right? That would be just perfect, a Class B league based primarily in Texas!* Perhaps pitchers learned that his weakness was a fastball up and in. *Lay off, lay off, DAMN!* It always looked so...tempting, and he always popped it up. Perhaps it was just the Law of Baseball Averages, which only fleetingly allows a career .284 hitter to sniff the rarified air of the .360s for very long. Whatever was the case, Trig came thudding down to earth, so that by the end of May he was hitting just .268, and was now playing only against left-handed pitching.

When Trig got to the ballpark on June 10, Karl Hines was waiting for him. "Let's go into my office," the manager said. Swinney knew instinctively it wasn't to tell him his contract had been sold to a team in the Gulf Coast League. He'd been released in both Wenatchee and Lamesa, he could recognize all the telltale signs.

"Trig," said Hines, "You're a great guy, a great teammate, a positive and solid influence on these younger players. I wish I had more fellas like you. If I did, though, I'd want 'em to be hittin' a little better than .182 in their last 77 ABs."

"Skip, it's just a slump, I know it, I don't have to tell you…"

"You may be right, son, you may be right. But we got a tough league this year, real tough. Only team that looks like they got no chance at the post-season is Kruse, everyone else has got a shot, which means there's seven teams battling for four playoff berths. And my owner…" He made a face and shifted in his chair. "…has told me that we may not turn a profit unless we get ourselves a home playoff game or two. And if we don't make money he may not 'find it in his heart' to bring me back next year. Find it in his heart, my ass. 'Tween you-n me, Trig, this B.J. Lewis is one-a the biggest pricks I ever run across in baseball, and I been fuckin' this game for a long time, this is my thirtieth year, did you know that? I been around, so believe me when I say this guy is a real shit. Dunno if I wanna be back here next season, but right now I'm under contract and my job is to do the best I can for the Shirley Cardinals, win as many games as possible, and try to make the post-season. And Trig, I'm sorry, but right now I don't think you can help us do that."

Both men exhaled, almost simultaneously. Karl Hines then broke the awkward silence.

"But we're not gonna release you just yet. There may be somethin' developin', a deal may be in the works, so just sit tight, don't say nothin' to nobody, and I'll keep you informed, let you know when I know, OK?"

"OK, yeah, sure, Skip, sure, but listen, what kinda deal are we talkin' here? Does somebody want me? Where is it? I was hopin' that maybe the Gulf Coast…"

"I don't know much, Trig, really, but I do know that it's right here in the Mountain Empire, not the Gulf Coast. Shit, you go up to the Gulf Coast, you take me with you, hear? I got to play in Class B in 1928 and '29, Terre Haute in the Three-Eye, good league, tough league." He smiled. "Good memories, real good memories. That's where I met my wife, in Terre Haute. Her folks ran a general store…ah, you don't care 'bout this old shit. Look, all I know is one-a the teams in this league got their eye on you. Dunno which one so don't ask me that, I honestly don't know. For now, you're still a Card and I'll still play you against lefties and bring you in as a pinch-hitter and for late-inning defense, and soon's I hear somethin', I'll tell you. We gotta deal?" Trig nodded. "Good," said Hines. "Now go on, get yourself ready for the game tonight. Oh, and Trig, right now, no one else on the team knows 'bout this so we'll just, uh, you-n-me, we'll just keep it 'tween us, yeah?"

Trig smiled—both externally and internally—nodded again, and went onto the field.

The other team was the Kruse Ducks. Just a couple of days before he would be heading up to see games in Kentucky, Wells Boggs had received a call from Don Harrell, who said "I need some advice, Wells."

"Really? I'm flattered, Don. What kind of advice do you need?"

"I want to get rid of Vic Rutherford. I think he's a horseshit manager, which is one reason why we're in last place. More to the point, he's a lousy evaluator of talent, he brought in most of these guys and you see what they can do, which is not all that much. *Can't disagree with that,* thought Wells. But the biggest reason is that he's a shit…"

"Don, whoa, I'm not sure I've ever heard you use that word, and now you've used it twice in a matter of seconds."

"Sorry, Wells, you're right, I don't usually talk like that, but he really…ugh, he just makes me wanna spit! He's negative and hateful and foul-mouthed and…and…and just a bad person. I hate being around him, and I'd say that even if we were in first place by twenty games. Biggest mistake I ever made was hiring him, I kick myself every day for doing that, every single day."

"So, Don, just fire him," said Boggs.

"And that's where I need your…advice, maybe your help, Wells. The guy I want is not on our team. He's in our league, but…"

"All right, Don, hold it right there. You know the rules, you can't tamper with another manager, you'll have to…"

"He's not a manager, Wells, he's a player. I don't even know if he'd be interested, that's why I'm coming to you. How do I go about this? Do I just try and trade for him and then hope he'll take the job? Can I approach him in advance, or maybe have someone else act as my agent? What can I do here?" By this point, Boggs thought that Don Harrell sounded almost desperate.

"Who's the guy you have in mind?"

"Trig Swinney," said Harrell.

"The Texas boy playin' for Karl Hines in Shirley? Big kid, can hit the ball hard…"

"But he hasn't been hitting it all that often these days. Karl and B.J. might be willing to make a deal, Wells, and if they did I'd like to grab him and make him my playing-manager, if he was interested. That's what I don't know."

Boggs leaned back in his chair. "Don, I'm curious, why him? Why are you all focused on this Swinney fella?"

"He's a natural-born leader, Wells," said Harrell. "I saw that right away, in spring training. The way he carried himself, the way the other players responded to him. I heard about how he decked one-a his own teammates, that pitcher who was after Daniels. That impressed me, especially from a guy with no guarantees, simply tryin' to make the team. And they've been here in town twice so far and both times he just…I dunno, he just looks and acts like a leader, the captain. He's been around a few years, played in C-Ball, ain't never gonna make it as a player, too many holes in his swing. But I think maybe he could be a good manager and now, now might be a good time for him to give it a try."

Harrell paused to take a breath, he didn't usually string that many words together all at once.

"Are you askin' me to talk to him, feel him out, see if he might could be interested in takin' over the Ducks?" asked Wells.

"Could you? Could you do that? That would be OK, right, since you're league president-n-all?

There was a long pause, so much so that Harrell asked "Wells? You still there, Wells? Hello?" He then heard a very perceptible sigh, followed by the league president's voice.

"I'm going up to Shirley and Blackmer day after tomorrow. I s'pose I could casually ask Swinney if he's ever thought about being a manager. I won't mention you at all, I'll simply…it can just be two guys talkin'. How's that?"

On June 21, 1952, the Shirley Cardinals put out a small press release, announcing the release of outfielder Trig Swinney and the signing of Errol Hungerford, a local boy from nearby Pineville. The next day, the Kruse Ducks put out their own press release. Manager Vic Rutherford had been "relieved of his duties," and former Shirley Cardinals outfielder Trig Swinney had been signed to be the team's playing manager for the balance of the season. Team president Don Harrell was quoted as saying "We think he has the makings of an excellent manager, another Stanky, and are eager to be the ones to give him his first assignment. He will, of course, continue his playing career, joining Garner Axford of Beck as a Mountain Empire League playing-manager."

Not quoted was Vic Rutherford, who gave Win Appleton an earful, most of which was unprintable, about that bastard Don Harrell and the "mother-goddam-fucking way he's running his ballclub. No wonder they're at the bottom of the league, but big-fucking-deal. This whole league is bush, bein' taken over by n—s and n—-lovers, hellwithem, to hell with all-a them!" He said he was going back to Florida, find honest work with honest white men. Appleton chose not to run this "rebuttal."

Four days later, Swinney put an outfielder, Thomson, on the disabled list, and released two Ducks, both of whom were backups with batting averages under .200. They were replaced by an infielder named J.W. Wingate, a one-time teammate of the new manager, as well as his cousin, an outfielder named Floyd "Lightning" Haskell. Both of the new players were Negroes, and both contracts were approved by the league office.

Those two signings, however, coupled with Monroe Hicks joining the Edens Ridge club, served to reignite Orley Pepper.

He and his crew had all been hit with disorderly conduct charges after the ruckus at the ballpark, which was better than the rioting charge that could have been leveled against them. They all then decided to lay low, though it didn't prevent Orley from having "strong suspicions" he was being watched.

Damn, how'm I gonna do what I need to do? He mulled it over, then hatched a plan.

For three dollars, he got his buddy Roy to help. One day after work, Roy strolled over to Nick Mancuso's barber shop for a haircut. About ten minutes later, Orley did the same. Inside the shop, they exchanged clothes, which was a bit of an inconvenience for Roy since he was about four inches taller than Orley and at least thirty pounds heavier. No matter, he pulled his fedora down near his eyes, ducked his head, and walked out the door, so that if anyone was tailing Orley they would now follow him instead. A few minutes later, Nick and Orley quietly left the shop, got into Nick's 1949 Nash Airflyte, and headed up the road for Mettin, Virginia.

Truck Maxwell was not happy to see Orley Pepper. They had met before, here and there, primarily at Klan rallies. The owner of the biggest independent trucking company in all of Virginia (which was how Maxwell liked to introduce himself) found the little guy from Edens Ridge to be just a bit too, oh, maybe squirrely would, indeed, be the best word. How'd he ever become Exalted Cyclops, anyway?

And then, he showed up at Maxwell Motors, uninvited, with a bat-shit-crazy plan, complete with hijacking and kidnapping and murder. It was bizarre, to say the least, and more violent than even Truck was willing to contemplate, something right out of a Mickey Spillane novel. The last thing he needed was to get mixed up in a bizarre plot that had no chance of doing anything other than bring down Maxwell Motors. He was not about to see his life's work disintegrate because of this strange little man. He was also not about to break the promise he had made to someone years ago. He told Orley, and Nick, to leave his office while their legs still worked.

"I thought you was on our side," whined Orley. "I thought you wanted to get rid of this n— as much as me, as us," and here he pointed at Nick and then himself. "Thought you were this big Virginia Ku Kluxer, ain't 'fraid-a nothin', that's what I 'member you sayin' one time. What a bag of hot air! You ain't no better than our blowhard politicians. What a…a…what a turd you are, Maxwell. C'mon, Nick, let's get outta here, this place stinks-a turd real bad, it's startin' to get all in my nose and mouth, make my eyes water." They headed for the door, but Maxwell's voice stopped them.

"Pepper!" he shouted. "C'mere." Orley didn't want to move, afraid of what Maxwell, who was way bigger than him, might have in mind. Truck seemed to read his thoughts. "I ain't gonna hurt you. Here," he said, grabbing a piece of paper and holding it out. "Write down your name and phone number on this. I'll give it to…to someone, someone who can maybe help. I 'spect he'll be calling you real soon." Hesitantly, Orley put the requested information on that piece of paper. All three of them then just looked at each other for an awkward moment until Maxwell finally said "Next time you boys are up this way, make sure the Foxes are in town, I'll give y'all box seats. Free, on the house, OK? But look-it, right now I have a whole lotta work to do 'fore I can leave here for the night, so please shut the door behind you."

"Wonder who he's gonna talk to," said Nick as they were driving back to Edens Ridge. "Hope it ain't the cops."

"He ain't gonna call the cops. He ain't gonna call nobody," said Orley with more than a trace of disgust. "He's just a blowhard, all he is. Waste-a time our comin' up here. Least we was able to find us a good chicken joint, this stuff is pretty tasty, eh?"

A few nights later, Orley Pepper's telephone rang. The conversation was extremely short.

"You Pepper? Truck Maxwell told me to call you, said you might have a job."

"Oh, we got a job, all right," said Orley. "We got n—s playin' baseball on our local team and we need to get rid-a them. However you wanna do it is fine by us."

The man on the other end of the line was quiet for a moment, then said "Baseball players? You want me to kill baseball players? That's a first, who wants to kill a baseball player? Well, there was that chick in Chicago coupla years ago, shot a guy, what was his name? Miksis? Waitkus? Bobkis? Something like that. But she was nuts. You nuts, Pepper?"

Orley was taken aback. "No, no, I ain't nuts, not at all. Weren't you listenin'? These ain't any ole players, these is N—S. We can't be havin' n—s playin' our American game, don't you see? We tried to run one outta town but…didn't work. Now they's 'nother one here, plus a coupla new ones on 'nother team. I…we just wanna get rid-a them, for good, once and fer-all."

There was a sigh on the other end of the line, then the man said "This will be a high-profile job, the kind that gets in the newspaper. That costs more, twenty grand."

"Twenty thousand dollars? Are you serious, twenty thousand dollars? Who's got that kind-a money? Now who's nuts?"

The man actually chuckled. "Were you expectin' to have this done for free? Maybe for, what, a few oil changes? This is business, Pepper. Man's gotta eat, you know?"

"Hey, listen, pal, I knew we'd have to pay, I just figured, well, you know, we're Klan…"

"Nobody gets a break, I don't care who you are. I don't play politics or anythin' like that. I'm in it for the money, nothin' more. No deals, no discounts. The price is twenty gees. I'll call you a week from today, and if you have it or can get it, we can do business. Otherwise, I'd suggest just enjoy watchin' the ballgames, that's what I do when I ain't workin'." He hung up, figuring that nothing would come of this.

Orley found a pencil, jotted down some names on a piece of paper, then grabbed his hat and hit the streets of Edens Ridge.

ELEVEN

Since it was almost a straight shot from Asheville, the Daniels family decided to drive to Weare to see their eldest son play professionally for the first time. On the one hand, Oddibe was happy about that, since it meant he could continue to avoid the inevitable confrontation about his Edens Ridge living arrangement. But on the other hand…

"Ain't no gettin' 'round it, O," Jack said when his young outfielder told him about his parents' upcoming visit. "You're gonna be nervous just knowin' they're in the stands. Happens every time and it happens to everyone, no exceptions, I can guarantee that." Jack pulled into the small parking lot of Bill Washington Park, turned off the car, and looked at Oddibe. "You need to try and block 'em out, just forget they're up there, and lemme tell ya, I know from experience that's easier said than done. I remember the first time my folks came to see me play, it was 1937, I was already in my fifth year in the minors."

"Really? It took 'em that long?" asked Oddibe.

"Yeah," said Jack. "Dad runs the newspaper in our little town and thinks the world will stop if he ain't there to give people the news, so he hardly ever takes any time off. My Mom always bugged him but he didn't wanna leave, plus I was in Wisconsin and Arkansas and Missouri, nowhere near Pennsylvania. When I got to Norfolk, though, Mom finally put her foot down, so they came to see me." He laughed at the memory. "Was nervous as shit and struck out my first AB, against Harry 'The Cat' Brecheen! He's slowin' down now but man! He was good back then, awfully tough and really rough on left-handed hitters. I might-a struck out anyway, but knowin' my folks were up there, watchin', just made it worse. Shit, didn't even foul the ball off, just swung like a Little Leaguer. Remember it like it was yesterday." He looked down, shook his head, then looked back at Oddibe. "Next time up, though, I pulled one through the hole on the right side for a hit. Then in the eighth," and Jack shifted his body so he could fully describe the moment, and Oddibe was surprised to see excitement in his manager's eyes. "Game's on the line, two on, two out, and I rip a triple that puts us ahead to stay, and sent The Cat to the showers. One-a my all-time favorite memories." He smiled, and Oddibe could tell that his manager was 22 years old again, playing ball in Norfolk, and the world was his, everything was still possible.

The moment passed, the young outfielder was gone and the Edens Ridge manager was back. "It ain't easy, O, but you just hafta play the game, play it like it's just another ballgame because, you know, in the end, that's all it is. Just figure you're gonna screw up at least once while they're watchin' you and hopefully it won't cost us a win. I'm sure that don't help none but really, there ain't nothin' more I can say. Just play the game." He clapped the young man on his shoulder and said "Just play the game. Which is what we gotta do today, let's go in and get ourselves ready, yeah?"

First thing that needed to be done was to find them a place to stay for a couple of nights. That was hardly an easy task, it's not like there were hotels that catered to Negroes in the small town of Weare, North Carolina. Thankfully, Nashota had connections.

"Can't put up all four-a them," said her sister, Tehya, "but I do have room for two. Maybe mother and daughter would stay with us? I could always use an extra hand or two with Gwennie." That was a start, and now Nashota reached out to her old boss, Brian Stevens.

"Nashota, so good to hear from you, it's been a while, how are you? When are you due?"

"I'm fine, Brian, doing well, feeling well, considering I'm lugging around what feels like a medicine ball. My legs ache, I can't sleep comfortably, and I have to pee all the time, but other than that…"

Stevens laughed. "You can't fool me, we've been friends for a long time—you're loving it, right? 'Fess up."

"Well," said Nashota, "I do wish I could sleep more but yeah, being pregnant is pretty special, I can't deny it. Don't know if I'll want to go through it again, but…"

"You will," said Stevens. "I know you, you will."

"You're probably right," said Nashota. She decided this was a good time to get down to business, so she explained about Oddibe's family. "Tehya said she'd be happy to take in two people and suggested Mrs. Daniels and her daughter. Frankly, she's being a bit selfish, thinking they might be able to lend a hand with the baby, but that still leaves Mr. Daniels and their other son, Willie I think. Would you know of a place they could stay for a coupla nights?" She was hoping he'd take the bait, and he did.

"I've got plenty of room in my house, still just me after all these years. As long as they don't mind that I won't be around much. I can get 'em an extra key so they can come and go as they like. Won't be no charge, I'm happy to do it. Course, it'd be nice if they ate at the B&N, at least one meal a day, but I can't force 'em, even if we still have the best food in town. Maybe not quite as good as when you were cooking, but we keep using a lot of your recipes, so we think we're still the best. I hear rumors about a fried chicken place from Kentucky looking at maybe coming in here, but I can't see it, we're so small and people really like making their own fried chicken at home. Anyway, you tell Mr. Daniels that I'll be happy to host him and his son."

"You won't get in any trouble?" Nashota asked.

"Nah, no one will care. Klan isn't very strong in these parts, they're mostly down east, closer to Wilmington, long way from us. We mainly got the bootleggers and they only care about staying away from the Feds."

Lilly Daniels was not crazy about the idea of the family splitting up, even briefly, but Walter was philosophical. "We can drive back and forth ever' night and sleep at home, if you like, but you know I don't see all that well in the dark and you just hate drivin' at night. Ain't no cullud hotels up there, what else we gonna do? We could change our plans, go up to Edens Ridge, Oddibe said he thought there was a place in Kingsport we could stay, but he weren't for sure. Look, Lil, we don't have a lotta options here. We both wanna see our boy play, I think this is the best offer we gonna get."

US Highways 19 and 23 run together as they head north out of Asheville. It was a pretty stretch of road, and smooth, something that could be not said for US Highway 19-W in Yancey County. The state of the road drew several comments from his passengers, primarily Berenice, who was trying to read Agatha Christie's *Crooked House* but was having a hard time concentrating with all the bumps in the road. "DAD," she cried with exasperation after one-too-many jolts. "I can't read my book!" "Ain't doin' it on purpose, sweetheart," said Walter. "Can't make the road any better-n what it is. Won't be too long and we'll be in Weare."

A sign welcomed them to town, and Lilly read the directions Nashota had sent: "Go to the third stop sign, that's Main Street, make a right, go two blocks and make another right, that's Ward. The B&N is on that street, so just find a place to park and go on in!" When they did, a man and a woman were sitting at a table, and they immediately stood up. "You must be the Daniels family," said the man, extending his hand. "I'm Brian Stevens, this is my restaurant, and this…"

"You have to be Miz Simpson's sister, you look a awful lot like her," said Lilly, with a smile.

"But I'm the good-looking one! Shorter, older, but much more attractive. I'm Tehya," she said with a laugh, shaking Lilly's hand. "We are so happy to have you here in our little town."

As introductions were being made, Brian asked "Is anyone hungry or thirsty? Can I get anything for anyone?" Berenice was not shy. "Could I use your restroom? I really gotta…go."

"Sure thing," said Brian, and he pointed. "There's one all the way in the back." Berenice walked in the direction of his finger, but slowed down as she saw both a men's and women's restroom close by. "No, not there, in the back, you have to…well, you know." Berenice frowned but kept walking, and Brian looked at the elder Daniels with some embarrassment. "Sorry about that, but you know how it is…"

"Don't need to think anythin' of it, suh," said Walter. "We used to it."

The Mustangs followed common minor league practice—batting practice began at five o'clock, with the home team getting a full hour and the visitors just half that. Walter really wanted to see BP, but gates didn't open until 6:30 pm. Jack, however, had spoken to Jules Gray, who said it would be OK as long as the Daniels' sat in the colored section, and then went back outside and bought their tickets. "We asked for comps," said Jack, and Gray quickly retorted "There's how many-a them, four? You know the rules, Jack, can't have more-n two per person." *Oh for cryin' out loud.* "Fine," Simpson snorted. "Jules, please put Walter and Lilly Daniels down as comps of Oddibe Daniels, and Berenice and Willie Daniels down as comps under my name. That work for you?" Gray considered saying something about there being no need to be snotty, but he could tell that the Wolves' manager was in no mood for a debate, so he simply nodded.

The Daniels family ignored the disdainful look of the man at the gate, who let them in when he saw their names on his pass list, though he made it a point to say "you know you have to sit out in the colored section, in right field." "We do, yes suh, thank you," said Walter, guiding his wife and children up the ramp to their right. "Dad, you were sure a whole lot nicer to him than he was to us," said Berenice, to which Walter replied "We here to watch our Oddibe play, not get into no fights." This gave Lilly an opportunity to also chip in. "Berenice, you remember what it says in Matthew? 'But I say to you, love your enemies and pray for those who persecute you.' We get to our seats, we can say a prayer for that man." If a teachable moment suddenly presents itself, always take it.

Oddibe didn't see them at first, but as soon as he stepped into the batting cage he heard them, cheering and calling his name. *Oh Lord.* He pulled a ball foul, then hit a little dribbler towards short. *OH LORD.* His teammates sensed his discomfort—they'd all been there before, had similar experiences with family members, so they did what you'd expect.

"Yoo hoo, Oddibe, over here, Oddibe, over here."

"Hey there, short, dark, and ugly, new in town?"

Jack was throwing BP and he quickly stopped. Though he was smiling, he looked at his bench and shook his head, a clear message to his players to back off. But before he could toss another pitch, he heard "Is that all you got?" and he saw his young outfielder looking at his fellow Wolves and laughing along with them. "Damn, O," Jack mumbled to himself, then aloud he said "OK, Oddibe, get back in there and hit this sumbitch, willya?"

Walter was too far away to hear exactly what was being said, but he could hear what sounded like falsetto tones. *Huh? What?* When he saw his son laugh, it brought him back to his own playing days and the unique camaraderie of teammates. *He a part of this team,* he thought with a sudden sense of pride, and he surprisingly started to tear up. He quickly choked it back, *real man don't cry, certainly not over some silly BP banter.* Hurriedly, he clapped his hands and shouted "All right, Oddibe, you can do it, Oddibe, let's see you hit that ball," and young Willie, sitting right next to his father, did and said the exact same thing.

A short while later, they saw someone walking towards them and quickly recognized it to be Nashota Simpson. There were hugs all around, and when Lilly said "I so wanna thank you, Miz Simpson, for takin' such good care-a my boy," Nashota quickly replied "I haven't done very much, he's proving that he can take care of himself." The women chattered throughout BP ("I'm feeling pretty good, I haven't thrown up in quite some time"), while Walter and Willie kept their eyes glued to the field. Infield practice was next, which is really a misnomer, because the outfielders chase their share of fly balls, too. The Mustangs went first and only left ten or twelve minutes for their opponents, yet another long-standing minor league tradition. By this time, a very small handful of Negro fans had come to the park early. When Oddibe trotted out to center field, those fans, plus Nashota, all joined the Daniels family in standing and applauding. Now for the very first time he acknowledged them, smiling and waving, then he quickly looked back when he heard the sound of a bat hitting a ball. It was a routine fly and he ran effortlessly to his right and caught it with ease, then grinned when he heard them scream like he had made the greatest catch since Gionfriddo.

The public-address announcer gave the lineups and there were some boos when he said Oddibe's name, but there were a few cheers, too, all from the colored section, of course. A local Girl Scout troop sang the National Anthem, the Mustangs threw the ball around the infield, and Oddibe grabbed a bat out of the rack. Just as he did that, he heard Jack Simpson's voice behind him. "Regular game, all it is. Don't try to do too much, just play your game," and then he was off, running up the line to the third base coaching box.

He walked towards home plate as his name was being announced over the scratchy PA system. More boos, of course, that was to be expected. And there were catcalls, shouts of "coon" and "n—" and one particularly loud-mouthed fan who hollered "go back to Africa, you jungle bunny." But there were also a few cheers, from right field to be sure but he also thought he heard a smattering of applause coming from near third base. *Nah, must be an echo or somethin'.*

He had thought about trying to bunt his way on, but Gene Conn, knowing that Oddibe loved to utilize his speed, had both his first and third basemen playing in, and they both charged towards the plate as Daniels took a mediocre fastball for a called strike. The next pitch was a curve that didn't bend and wound up above his shoulders, ball one. Oddibe stepped out of the batter's box and banged his bat against his cleats. *Both pitches kinda slow, he must be a junkballer,* he thought. *Good to know.*

The third pitch was outside and dipped just a little bit, but it still came in around mid-thigh. Oddibe timed it just right and hit a slashing line drive up the middle, to the left of the second base bag. The shortstop took a couple of steps to his left and then dove in the air, but his glove was nowhere near the ball, which bounded into center for a base hit.

Out in right field, the four members of the Daniels family stood and cheered like they did when the Nazis had surrendered. Willie began jumping up and down and then did his own impromptu dance, which drew laughter from the other fans in their section.

Everybody in the ballpark expected Oddibe—the top base-stealer in the league—to light out for second just as soon as he could. Jack Simpson, however, had a different thought, and with their hand-signals he passed that along to his batter, Squirrel Davis, as well as to Daniels. Nothing happened for a few minutes, however, as the pitcher threw over to first several times, trying to keep Oddibe from getting much of a lead.

"BOO! C'mon, Ace, throw the ball to the plate, you gotta man standin' up there," yelled Walter, who was anxious to see his boy try and steal.

"BOO! BOO!!" mimicked Willie.

Eventually Squirrel saw a pitch, he didn't swing and Oddibe didn't move. "Ball one, low," said the umpire. Davis stepped out, looked over to Jack, saw that the sign remained the same, touched the brim of his cap to indicate he understood, stepped back into the batter's box. Oddibe also touched his cap, took his lead, hustled back to first when the pitcher threw over again. And again. Now there were even Mustang fans booing their own pitcher, including Mr. Leatherlung, who hollered "Geez, throw the fuckin' ball, willya?"

He did, and this one was to Squirrel's liking. But he didn't swing, he bunted, towards the first baseman, who had been anchored to the bag to be on the receiving end of his pitcher's endless toss-overs. He had absolutely no chance to get to the ball, so it fell to the catcher. The backstop moved as quickly as he could and, when he got to the ball, he saw that Squirrel was at least halfway up the line. Still time to get him. He paid no attention to Oddibe, *no fuckin' way I can get that speedy booner.*

The catcher grabbed the ball, planted his left leg and threw it wild, off the first baseman's glove and into foul territory, allowing Squirrel to dash for second. Oddibe, meanwhile, having rounded second base, saw Jack jumping up and down by third base, furiously windmilling his arm, so without hesitating he raced to third.

Weare's second baseman had been following up the play, as he was supposed to do, so when the ball got away he chased it down, grabbed it in foul territory, spun around and threw it back to the infield. Jack, meanwhile, decided to play it safe, which would put runners on second and third with no one out and the heart of the batting order coming up in just the first inning. *Good way to start the day*, he thought, so he danced down the line a bit and put up both of his hands, the universal stop sign. Oddibe, however, had a different idea. When he got to third base, he slowed down for a second, looked over his shoulder, decided he could out-run the baseball, and sprinted for home plate, his manager's "NO!!" barely audible over the noise coming from the stands.

The first baseman grabbed his teammate's throw and heard someone yell "cut four." This meant he needed to throw the ball to home plate, so he wheeled and fired for all he was worth. His catcher had run back to his post and was waiting to make the play. Oddibe came roaring down the line. The umpire made sure he was in the best position to make the correct call. And the fans…the fans were just besides themselves.

Ball and runner arrived at home plate simultaneously. The backstop reached for the ball, then spun to his left to apply the tag. That action allowed Oddibe to execute a perfect hook slide, curving his right leg while keeping his left away from the catcher's outstretched glove. Leg hit the plate before glove hit the other leg. "SAFE!" bellowed the young umpire. Two batters in and Edens Ridge had quickly taken a 1-0 lead.

Oddibe calmly brushed off his uniform pants and trotted back into the dugout, where his fellow Wolves were on their feet, eager to greet their speedy lead-off man. Up in the press box, the official scorer said to no one in particular, "hit for Davis, error on the catcher's throw, runners both move up on their own." In the covered grandstands, the crowd was almost apoplectic. "You're blind, blue/he was out/he got tagged before he hit the plate/what a busher" they screamed at the umpire. "What's wrong with you/field the damn ball, willya?" was aimed at their infield. "Damned n—/we gonna kill you, boy" had just one target.

Out in right field, however, there was nothing but joy, especially around the Daniels family. People they had just met were congratulating them, clapping them on the back, grinning from ear to ear. These were Weare residents and Weare fans, but Weare didn't have any Negro players and this young man, one of their own, had just done something exciting, spectacular. "Just like Jackie," said one, and for Walter Daniels, that was all he had to hear. His eyes grew misty again, and he looked at his wife. She was blinking real hard, and that moment became, for them, just like a photograph, frozen for all time.

Edens Ridge was having very little trouble timing the junkballer's serves. Two more runners crossed the plate by the time Gene Conn signaled for someone to start warming up in the bullpen. He then trotted out to the mound amidst a chorus of catcalls from his own fans ("Noise wake you up there, Gene?") to try and calm his pitcher down and at least get him through this inning. Another run would score, however, before the onslaught ended. "Four runs, five hits, one error, no one left on" intoned the PA announcer, somberly, while the home crowd cheered derisively.

Given a four-run lead, Harry Neville followed the book for such a situation—don't be cute, just throw strikes. He gave up a two-out single but that was it and Edens Ridge came up again. Gene Conn decided to let his soft-tosser continue, pitchers can sometimes turn themselves around after a bad inning, and it looked like a good decision when Coach Valenza bounced out and Neville struck out, which brought Oddibe to the plate.

This time the ballpark was relatively quiet, except for the cheers coming from right field, until the loud-mouth fan yelled "Stick it in that n—'s ear!" A couple of fans laughed but most remained quiet. On the Wolves' bench, a couple of the players shifted in their seats before beginning their own chatter. "OK, O, you can do it, get a hit, now, get a hit." "Good hitter, good hitter." "Take a good rip, O, good rip, good rip." "He's just throwin' junk out there, piece-a cake, you can hit him."

The Mustangs' infield was not looking for a bunt this time, certainly not with two outs and a four-run lead. They got that right, Oddibe wasn't thinking bunt at all.

The first pitch to Daniels was outside for a ball, but the next one was one of those medium-speed fastballs, a little inside, just above the knees. Oddibe swung and the ball lifted on a high arc out to right field. The outfielder ran back towards the fence and the foul line, and the fans watched it all, mouths open. *Will this ball stay fair or go foul? Can our guy catch up to it for the third out?* No, he could not. The ball bounced just inside the line, fair ball, signaled right away by the home plate umpire, who was doing his job and hustling up the first base line. The ball then took a high bounce, hit the wall, then the gravel, where it must have hit a rock because it suddenly bounded away from the right fielder and started rolling towards center. The Mustang player reacted as quickly as he could and chased it down, picked it up and fired it to his second baseman, who had raced into the outfield to receive the throw.

Oddibe, meanwhile, just kept running, and this time, when he got to third base, Jack Simpson was dancing down the line, whirling his arm and yelling "GO, GO." And Oddibe did just that, sliding into home well ahead of the relay throw, safe, with the team's fifth run and his first—his very first!—professional home run, an inside-the-park job.

The right field stands erupted. Walter threw his hands in the air and screamed with joy, while Lilly and Nashota—who had defiantly stayed in the "colored" section ("I'm not white and I'm not black, so I feel I can sit wherever I like, and tonight that's with y'all. If you'll let me, of course," she had said after the National Anthem had been played)—jumped up and down, hugged each other and cried. Willie went back to doing his crazy dance, and even Berenice, who wasn't completely sure what was happening, grinned and applauded. The fans around them were equally as enthusiastic, yelling and cheering, making so much noise they all missed Squirrel Davis' routine grounder to third that ended the inning.

Next time up, Edens Ridge found itself facing a new Mustang hurler, Chandler, who shut them down. Meanwhile, Weare began chipping away, and after five they only trailed by three, 5–2. In the sixth inning, the Wolves put runners on first and third with just one out. Terry VanLandingham worked the count full, then tried to out-guess Chandler and was totally fooled by a slow one. TVL started to swing, realized his mistake, tried to hold up but was unsuccessful and futilely came up empty for strike three. He slammed his bat on the ground and heard it crack, which angered him even more since each player was responsible for buying his own bats. *Shit!* Even with the discount they got from Louisville Slugger, that was still $6.50 out of his pocket. *Sonofabitch!* Jerry Brodie, however, singled to center, scoring the sixth run, before Coach, mired in a slump, ended the inning by bouncing back to the mound. Conn brought a new pitcher in for the eighth, a lefty, and Edens Ridge roughed him up for a pair, giving them an 8–2 lead. Insurmountable? Never say never in baseball. A couple of hits and a long fly ball that Oddibe ran down near the fence brought in a Mustang run. Jack began thinking of warming up a new pitcher, but before he could act, the next batter stroked a grounder between first and second for another single.

At least, it should have been a single. The ball bounded into right field towards VanLandingham, who ought to have been charging the ball so he could scoop it up and be in position to throw out the runner trying to advance from first to third. But TVL wasn't thinking about the ground ball heading his way, or the baserunner who had decided to try and make it to third base. He was still focusing on that last, miserable at-bat of his. He didn't react until the ball was almost upon him, when he hurriedly put down his glove to try and grab it. Too late—the ball kept rolling and the Las Vegas native quickly gave chase, but not before the runner on first had scored and the batter had easily made it into second, where he dutifully heeded Gene Conn's stop sign.

Jack jumped out of the dugout and ran to right field. "Terry, are you alright? Did you hurt your leg, pull a muscle or somethin'?" VanLandingham saw that his manager was genuinely concerned, which made him feel even worse. He looked down at his cleats. "No, skip, I'm fine, I just…screwed up. My mind wandered off…" Spoken aloud, it sounded horrendous. "I'm so sorry, Jack," he said, looking his manager right in the eye. "It's my fault, won't happen again."

The two men looked at each other. Simpson pursed his lips, nodded, turned to walk back towards the infield, and then stopped. Looking back at his outfielder, he tersely said, "Come on, follow me." Jack Simpson then trotted towards the mound, with his right fielder just behind him.

When they got to the hill, the entire Wolves infield had gathered. Their manager looked at all of them, then said to VanLandingham "Tell Harry what you just told me." TVL was silent. "Go on, tell him, tell him what you said out there. You need to be apologizin' to your pitcher, not to me." Terry stammered about how sorry he was, he made a mistake, it will never be repeated. All the other players were shocked, and Harry Neville finally just mumbled "hey, man, that's OK." He was about to say something else when Jack cut him off.

"No, it's not OK." Simpson was furious, and everyone could clearly see it. "That was a bone-headed play and it cost us a run, cost YOU a run, made your ERA go up. It's very definitely NOT OK!" He then looked at VanLandingham. "Take a seat in the dugout, you're through for today. Go on!" he barked when TVL hesitated. Then he hollered over to Mike Hamblen, who was standing on the top step. "Mike, send Altman out to play right." Finally, he looked at his catcher. "Miggsy, is Harry losin' it? Do we need to get someone hot real quick?" Miggs hated being put in the middle like this but he knew it was part of the job of a catcher. "Stuff is flattenin' out a bit, skip," he said, then he looked at his pitcher and shrugged.

"OK," said Jack. First he yelled back to Hamblen "Buck, right now!" Then he looked at his pitcher. "Harry, pitch carefully to this next guy, stall a bit, throw extra pitches, walk him if you must, we're gettin' Buck up now and I'll bring him in soon as he's ready, OK?" Neville nodded, he really was feeling kind of tired. The infielders went back to their positions, pitcher and catcher had a brief conversation ("make like somethin's in your eye, that always works"), while Simpson trotted back to the quiet dugout and sat next to VanLandingham.

"I want you to lead the cheerin'," said the manager to the outfielder. "We'll talk after the game, got that?" TVL nodded silently.

The umpire didn't buy the dirt-in-the-eye con when they trotted it out after just a couple of pitches, he quickly went out to the mound and said "OK, guys, enough of this shit." Harry ran the count full and then made sure ball four bounced in front of the plate. But Buck wasn't quite ready, so Harry faced one more batter, and his third pitch got too much of the plate and was hit right back up the middle for a hit. A run scored, and suddenly Weare trailed by just three, 8–5.

With two men on base and momentum definitely swinging the Mustangs' way, Simpson now summoned Buck Hightower, and the big righty was equal to the task. He struck out the first man he faced, ended the inning with a routine ground ball, and then breezed through the ninth, anticlimactically ending a game that no one would soon forget.

Willie was getting sleepy and Berenice was getting bored. The Daniels family was waiting outside the ballpark so they could congratulate their son on his big game, but the Edens Ridge Wolves were sure taking their sweet time coming out of the clubhouse.

And then, when the players finally did appear, they looked more like the losing team—no one was laughing or joking, no one seemed happy at all. Oddibe did, however, smile when he saw them, and he went over to where they were waiting.

Willie gave him a big hug. "Oddibe, you were great! You hit a home run, you ran so fast, you were the best player out there!!" That elicited a few chuckles. Berenice was more reserved, she simply hugged him and said "you were real good tonight, big brother." Lilly, of course, gave her son a big kiss on the cheek. He was embarrassed and said "Ma!" but she said "I don't care how old you are, or who-all is watchin', if I wanna kiss my boy I'm gonna do it!" Walter stood there beaming, then grabbed him and gave him a huge bear hug. Nothing was said for a moment, it was not necessary. But finally Walter asked about the team's delay in coming outside.

"Um, skip had...there were a coupla things...I gotta go, Dad, the bus is waitin' and..."

"We can take you where you need to go," Walter said, but Oddibe demurred. "We travel as a team, Dad, even if it's just up the road. Look, how's this, let's all meet at the B&N for breakfast in the mornin' and I'll tell you everythin', OK? OK?" Then he gave everyone, one by one, a quick kiss on the cheek, and he hustled to the door of the bus before turning around. "Eight o'clock, OK? Well, maybe closer to 8:30!" He grinned, waved, and got on the bus, last man on, as Mike shut the door and pulled the big coach out of the parking lot.

The players had not known what to expect when the Mustangs made the last out. They knew Jack wasn't happy, but they also knew that Oddibe's family was visiting, maybe the skipper would wait until tomorrow to talk with TVL. He could do it privately, in his hotel room, that would be best, that's surely what he'll do...

"Daniels. VanLandingham. In my office NOW!" Guess not.

There were two main reasons why a town was in Class D. The most important one had to do with size—being the lowest rung on the minor-league ladder, Class D municipalities were expected to be small, and the eight towns that made up the Mountain Empire League were just that. And it would stand to reason that a small community would have a small ballpark, which was also true. None of the yards in the MEL would ever be confused with, say, Yankee Stadium, or even smaller, cozier big-league facilities like Fenway Park or Ebbets Field. This meant that the locker rooms were small and the manager's office wasn't a whole lot larger than the toilet. That's why the Wolves figured Jack would wait until morning to dress down TVL, he could do it privately so he could scream to his heart's delight and no one else would hear. Calling him in right now meant that Jack was beyond pissed, whatever level that might be, and that wasn't good. Why Oddibe was getting called in, too, though, was a mystery, at least for a few minutes.

"Terry, what you did out there was a disgrace. The worst part is, you're a veteran, you've been in this game for a few years already, you should know better. I KNOW you know better, but you still screwed up. I don't get worked up 'bout an error, everyone makes errors, it happens, it's part of the game. But this was no error, you could have fielded that ball but your goddam mind was elsewhere. What the hell was going on out there?"

"Skip, I'm sorry, I messed up, I know it. I was...shit, it sucks to even say it, I was thinkin' 'bout my last at-bat, how bad I looked, how I let the team down, men on base and all..."

"Geez Louise, Terry, you can't bring your at-bats out on the field, that's just...shit, that's just basic baseball, you know it, everybody learns that in grade school. That's a horseshit reason, just horseshit." Jack stopped for a moment and did not—could not—look at either of his players who were standing there, he just fumed. Then he stared intently at VanLandingham. "What do you think I ought to do, Terry? How should you be punished?"

The outfielder was shocked, as was the rest of the team, listening in that small clubhouse. They hardly had a choice, after all, this was like a radio that could only pick up one station.

"I dunno, skip," Terry stammered. "Maybe, uh, maybe a fine…"

"Damn straight," Jack said quickly. "When we get home you'll give me twenty-five bucks, and for right now you're on the bench 'til I cool off. Brodie's playing right, HEAR THAT BRODIE?" Boy, no pretext at all! Very quietly, Brodie said "yes, sir."

"As for you," Jack said, looking at Oddibe. "I know you hit an inside-the-parker tonight and that's great, but first inning, FIRST FUCKIN' INNING, you ran through my stop sign." Daniels opened his mouth to say something but didn't get the chance. "No back talk! I know you scored, that's because you're the fastest man in the league. But it ain't your job to make that kind-a decision, that's why I'm out there. You're 'sposed to hit and field and run and follow 'structions, got that? If I tell you to stop runnin', you stop runnin'. Understand?"

Oddibe just nodded, and Jack continued. "I'd sit you down, too, if your folks weren't here. What I am going to do is fine you ten dollars and put you on notice that, when we get back to the Ridge, you'll be on the bench for at least one game, maybe more." He paused again, looking at both of his players, then he asked "Have I made myself clear?" They both shook their heads, but that wasn't enough for Sergeant Simpson the Younger. "I can't hear you," he yelled, and both Daniels and VanLandingham shouted back "YES, SIR!!"

"All right," said Jack, opening up the door to the tiny (and hardly soundproof) office. "Let's all get on the bus, Mike's waitin' for us.

Lilly was aghast. "He can't do that," she said, putting down her B&N breakfast special of eggs and bacon and biscuits. "You scored a run, why would he fine you for scorin' a run?"

"Mom," said Oddibe, but she wasn't finished.

"I don't think that's fair, and it's most certainly not right. The object of the game is to score runs, to score more-n the other team, and here you are…"

"Mom." Oddibe tried again, and now his father attempted to break in.

"Lilly, you need to…"

"Walter, don't interrupt me, please, I haven't finished what…"

"Lilly, you need to stop talkin' now." The rest of the family just looked at Walter, they were not used to hearing him speak sharply, certainly not to his wife. "Jack Simpson is the manager of the ball team, he got every right to chew out our son, and anyone else who play for him. And he has every right to fine him for breakin' the rules." Walter looked directly at Oddibe. "Manager throws up the stop sign, boy, you stop. He tells you what to do, and you do it, understand? I'm surprised at you." There was silence at the table. "If I was you, I'd apologize to Jack when you go in today. Tell him you're sorry and you won't ignore any-a his signs again. That's what I'd do. Hell, I'd also tell him that he can sit me down if he wants, don't matter who's in the stands, but I'll leave that up to you." He looked at Berenice and Willie. "When y'all get older, you'll be workin' somewhere, and you'll have a boss. The boss tells you to do somethin', you do it; he tells you not to do somethin', you don't. And if you ever gets to be boss, you'll expect people to follow your 'structions. Jack Simpson is Oddibe's boss, he told him to stop runnin' and Oddibe ignored him. Yes, he scored a run and it was excitin', 'specially for us, but what if he had been throwed out? Point is, his boss gave him an order and Oddibe paid him no mind. Gettin' fined is right and proper." He looked again at his oldest son, who simply said "Yes, sir, you're right. I made a mistake. I'll apologize." Walter just nodded, then put some eggs in his mouth. "Man makes a real fine breakfast," he said, "real fine."

There was a dress shop around the corner, on Main Street, that both Lilly and Berenice had noticed when they drove in, and now the ladies announced that they were going to check it out. Lilly gave Walter that defiant look he had seen before; she was angry at him for lecturing her, even if he did know more about the game than she would ever know. Walter didn't argue at all, no sense using up all that energy, he and his sons simply walked slowly behind them.

"Mom's pissed," said Oddibe.

"Ain't the first time, won't be the last," replied his father, and they both chuckled. Walter decided that this might be a good time to bring something up.

"You got two hits last night, that was good, you hit the ball hard both times. Then they tied you up rest-a the night. You tryin' too hard? Maybe squeezin' the bat a little too much?"

Oddibe sighed. "Been like this ever since I had that good first week. I can't get into a rhythm. I'll get a hit and then nothin' for a day or two, then I get a hit but that's all. Leadoff man needs to get on more-n I do, Dad, I dunno what's wrong, and I don't really know what to do. Had some extra BP with Jack and he's made a suggestion or two, Mike too, and I try 'em but nothin' seems to work. Maybe…I dunno, maybe I'm just not cut out for this, for professional ball, maybe I'm just a good industrial league player."

"Don't say that, son, that ain't true…"

"You're just sayin' that 'cause you're my Dad, but I ain't hittin' all that much, ain't helpin' the team at the plate like I oughta. These pitchers up here are tough, they throw all kinds-a stuff, pitches I never seen before. And the fans…" He stopped, he didn't want to bring that up, it just slipped out. He quickly backtracked. "I been thinkin' 'bout…Dunno, maybe I oughta just come on home, go back to work at the Inn or someplace else, sock away a little money so RubyAnn and me can get married, just play some ball on weekends."

His words hung in the air for several seconds, then Walter stopped walking, forcing his sons to halt as well.

"Is that what you want? What you really want? 'Cause if it is, we don't need to be wastin' time, walkin' 'round this town. We can go get your stuff and drive you back to Asheville. 'Course, I guess you got most-a your clothes-n-things up in Edens Ridge, but we could do that, drive up and get everythin' and then head on back home. If that's what you want, boy, let's go find Mr. Jack Simpson and you can tell him you're done, through, you quittin' here-n-now. Thanks for the opportunity, suh, but I just can't cut it in this-here league, I'm gonna go back to Asheville and, what, what you gonna do? Bus tables at the Grove Park Inn? Think that's gonna provide for you-n RubyAnn and however many kids the two-a you make? That what you want?"

"Dad," said Oddibe weakly while carefully examining his shoes.

"Don't you 'Dad' me," Walter snapped. "You wanna quit, then quit. These smart pitchers too much for you? Quit. These cracker fans gettin' the better-a you? Quit. Teammates don't give a shit 'bout you? Quit. Miss gettin' it reg'lar from RubyAnn? Quit." Oddibe looked up at that remark and his father knew he had touched a nerve and went for the kill.

"We go on home, don't matter to me, you know, we can take you home. But you gotta promise me that when we get there, you'll tell everyone that you quit, and why. Can't say you got released, 'cause you didn't. Can't say you got hurt, 'cause you didn't. Gotta tell people 'yeah, I quit, I couldn't handle it, all-a it, decided to come back here, it's safer. I can live a nice, simple, safe life here, go 'bout my business, never stand out, never make no waves. Learned me a good lesson—things get a little tough, just quit. Winnin' and losin' don't matter. Don't matter that they win and I lose, better for me to just quit.'"

He was seething, that was the only word that accurately described it. The son had never seen his father like this.

"That's what I want you to tell people," Walter continued. "Hell, maybe we can take out a full-page ad in *The Asheville Citizen* or *The Carolina Times*. What you think?"

They just stood there on the street and stared at each other. Young Willie looked first at one, then the other, and then back again. He was the only one who saw his mother and sister come out of one store and disappear inside another one, just three doors down. *When was someone gonna say somethin'?*

"Jack, uh, Jack mentioned somethin'...Oddibe spoke haltingly. "Said somethin"bout bringin' in a fella, an old-timer from the Negro leagues, says he's got some ideas, some methods, that might could help me at the plate. Bug Gillen's the name, know him?"

Walter kept looking right in his son's eyes. "I 'member him. Don't know him, never played 'gainst him, but I 'member him. Played some with Satch." His tone was softer, the storm had passed. "Got lotsa experience, bet he could teach you plenty. You just hafta wanna learn."

Oddibe nodded. There was silence for a few seconds, finally broken by Lilly's voice.

"Walter, come over here. I need you to tell me what you think of this hat."

They had agreed to wait outside, of course, which would make it easier to identify them—a balding white man and a young Negro boy, standing together. And it worked perfectly when several Negro men got off the bus from Asheville, but one walked right over to them, thrust out his right hand and said "You must be Jack Simpson and Oddibe Daniels. I'm Bug Gillen." They shook hands all around, but Bug could tell that Oddibe was a little less than enthusiastic. Before he could say anything, however, Jack spoke up.

"We have a game tonight, Bug, you probably remember that. I thought I'd take you over to my house, our house, me and the wife, and then I didn't know if you maybe wanted to stay there tonight, rest up after your long trip, get started tomorrow..."

Bug quickly cut him off. "It was a long trip, that's for sure, but I slept plenty on the bus, 'specially the one outta Charleston. Truth is, I can sleep 'most anywhere, always been good 'bout that, was real helpful when I played 'cause we spent lotsa time in buses and cars, ain't that a fact. 'Sides, you ain't payin' me to sleep, so I just as soon be out at the ballpark, watchin' the game. Even after all these years, a ballgame gets me revved up, makes me feel young again. Best feelin' there is!"

They made the relatively short drive from the bus depot in downtown Kingsport to the Simpson house in Edens Ridge, and Jack and Oddibe both found it amusing that, just moments after the car started moving, Bug Gillen nodded off. He awoke, though, when Jack cut off the engine in front of a cute little house. "Nothin' wrong with a good little cat-nap," he said with a yawn. Inside, Jack gave him a quick tour and everyone took turns using the bathroom before heading off to the ballpark. Oddibe went to the clubhouse while Jack wanted to take Bug to the office to meet Nashota, but the old infielder first took in the panoramic view of the field. He stood there for a moment and smiled. "Ain't nothin' like a ballpark, nothin' at all, 'cept maybe a beautiful woman," he said with a chuckle. "We got a team in Charleston, the Rebels, awful name but nice yard, College Park, maybe a little bigger-n this. Don't get too much of a chance to go out since the restaurant is busy so many nights, but we closed on Mondays so sometimes I'll go catch a game." He looked right at Jack. "You know that pitcher Harry Byrd, doin' so well with Connie Mack's team?" Jack nodded. "Saw him pitch 'gainst us jus' last year, he was with Savannah, Athletics' farm club. Gave up seven or eight hits, always seemed to be pitchin' from the stretch, but jus' when you think he's on the ropes, he gets a strikeout, inning over. Went eight and they beat us, 5–2, I think. Won 18 for a team finished 'bout ten under, so no surprise he's winnin' for Mack." Bug smiled. "Bein' in a ballpark sure do get a fella's brain goin' hunnert miles-a hour, yeah man!"

The office door opened and Nashota came out. "I thought I heard voices," she said with a smile. "Is this Mr. Gillen?" She extended her hand.

Bug took off his hat. "Yes, ma'am, Bug Gillen, so pleased to make your 'quaintance," and instead of shaking her hand he kissed it, causing Nashota to giggle.

"Bug, this is my wife, Nashota. She's the team's business manager, but really she runs this place. There's probably no baseball in Edens Ridge if she's not here."

"Brains and beauty and baseball, you can't beat that with a stick," said Bug. "Mrs. Simpson, I wanna thank you for lettin' me stay in your house, we stopped there for a few minutes and it is a lovely place, lovely place." Bug dropped his eyes just a bit and exclaimed "Well Lordy Lord, look-a here, we gonna have us a little Simpson 'fore too long, how wonderful!" He gave Jack a friendly jab in the arm. "You never said nothin', skipper, 'bout havin' no child, that's jus' t'rrific." And then back to Nashota: "When you due, ma'am?"

"Sometime in September is what they tell us."

"Oh, that's wonderful, wonderful. This your first? Me-n Maudene, we had four, one passed, unfortunately, but the other three are fine and healthy, maybe too healthy, they all likes to eat three meals a day!" He laughed, then turned serious. "Look, I didn't know you was 'spectin', ma'am. If my bein' in your house is gonna be a problem, jus' tell me, I can stay in a hotel or boardin' house. Maybe where Oddibe stayin', help me get a little closer to him, that boy sure is awful quiet..."

"Trust me, Bug, you don't want to stay at his place. Well, actually, to be honest, your wife wouldn't like for you to be stayin' there, OK? It's, uh, it's..."

"A house-a ill repute? Ha, seen guys live in places like that 'fore, kinda common when I played, actually. And you're right, Maudene would not be pleased, and she'd know, I wouldn't hafta say nothin', she'd know, don't know how but she would." They all laughed. "Well, look," Bug continued. "If I ever get in your way, either-a you, jus' tell me to move my ass...pardon my French, ma'am."

Nashota laughed out loud. "Bug, I live with a baseball man, so I'm sure I don't have to tell you that 'ass' is one of the kinder words heard 'round our house." And they all laughed again.

Mike Hamblen got there first, unlocking the gate and then the clubhouse before changing into his uniform. He then went down the right field line, where the Wolves kept a shed filled with field equipment, including the small tractor that Nashota had been able to purchase from Donnie Lake at what he described as a "major league discount for a minor league team." Mike quickly fired up the tractor and drove it further up the line, stopping when he had gone as far as necessary. There he hooked up the batting cage to the tractor and drove down to the home plate area, and was getting ready to set up the cage when he heard a car door shut, then a second, then a third, and voices.

"Wait for me, Mike, I can help you."

"I can get it, skip, no problem."

"Dammit, Mike, no need to be stubborn, let me help out." Still in his street clothes, Jack Simpson helped maneuver the cumbersome batting cage into place, then disappeared into the clubhouse. Mike was about to follow him when Win Appleton arrived.

"Geez, Mike, you'd think it would be a bit warmer for nine o'clock. Got any coffee?"

"Sorry, Win, I been dealing with the batting cage. But Jack and Oddibe are here, in the clubhouse, and I thought I saw them carrying some bags, bet it's coffee and pastries. Hope so, anyways, I could use a slug myself." Win and Mike headed inside.

"Look who it is, our shaggers!" Bug was annoyingly cheerful for this early in the morning. Last night's game went the normal nine, but both teams seemed to be playing in slow motion. By the time the Wolves pushed over a run in the bottom of the ninth, it was 10:40 pm, which meant that no one got to sleep until after midnight, and now here they were, back out just hours later. All the other Wolves, and the Cardinals, for that matter, were probably still snuggled up in their beds, or somebody's bed, but not this little group. They were putting on their jocks and sanitary hose and preparing for...say, what were they doing out there?

Bug insisted on a uniform, and he proved to be an easy fit because, despite being 45 years old, he was still pretty trim. "Put on a few pounds since I played my last game six years ago, but not all that much, not really. Gotta tell you, Maudene is one fine cook, it'd be easy for me to balloon up. You seen Frisch when he was managin' the Cubs last year? He can't play no second base any more, could maybe be the infield tarp, though!" They all laughed, and he continued. "Now, the Bug, he could still get to plenty-a ground balls. Course, I can't promise I could play nine…" That brought more laughter, even from Oddibe.

Finding a jersey and pants for Win Appleton, however, proved to be a little more difficult until Jack remembered something that was stored away. "Last year…no, wasn't either, was the year before. We had that big Dutch kid, right-hander, escaped the Nazis early on and came over here, he and his sisters lived in Wisconsin, I believe, what was his name?" Jack and Mike and Win put their heads together and finally remembered—Thomas Janssen. "Yeah," said Mike, "we haven't had anyone quite that big since he left, bet Win could fit into his uni." It actually proved to be a bit snug but it worked. "Hope I can play better than him, he was a real rag-arm," said Win. "Where is he now?" Jack just shrugged. "Nice kid, tried hard, but not much of a pitcher. I hated to release him 'cause I liked him and he lost his folks-n all, but we needed someone who could get outs." There was silence for a moment, then Jack said "Speaking of out, let's get out on the field, shall we? Do what we're here to do."

Mike and Win grabbed gloves and walked until they were about ten or twelve yards beyond the infield, with Mike in short right-center and Win more towards left-center. Jack stood on the mound with a bucket of baseballs, while Oddibe settled in to where the batter's box would be if they had taken the time to chalk it in. Bug chose to position himself right behind the batting cage. The exercise was simple: Jack would throw, Oddibe would swing, and Mike and Win would retrieve, assuming that Oddibe made contact.

At first he did, regularly, but then Jack began to spin the ball, throwing curves and sliders and an occasional slow ball, and that's when Oddibe began having more difficulty. Bug, meanwhile, didn't say anything; he was so quiet, in fact, that at one point Oddibe turned around to make sure he was still there. "Pay no attention to me, young man, you just concentrate on the baseball."

After about twenty minutes Bug yelled out "Time! Let's take a break." From his vantage point he could see that Appleton was huffing and puffing, perfectly understandable since he wasn't an athlete. But he also needed to ask a question.

"Son," he said to Oddibe, "what you see when you standin' there in the box?"

"What do I see? Well, the pitcher, the infielders, you know, the usual."

"Uh huh. What about the ball?"

"Well sure, I see the ball, that's just…" Oddibe was a little annoyed. He really didn't want to be here, didn't know how this old-timer could help him, and now he was asking stupid questions. "Just natural to see the ball, right?"

"When do you see it? How soon you see it?" Bug asked, and Jack knew immediately where he was going with this. *Damn, why didn't I think of that? What a horse-shit manager I am!*

"How soon? I dunno, prob'ly, oh, maybe, uh, I, uh, tell you the truth, Mr. Gillen, I don't know, never really thought about that before."

"Son, what you…"

Oddibe cut him off. "Mr. Gillen, no disrespect, but could I ask you not to call me 'son'? I'd rather you use my name, if you don't mind. Again, no disrespect…"

Bug smiled. "Understand, young man, understand. But look, Oddibe, what you need to be doin', what I think you need to be doin', is watchin' the baseball and nothin' but the baseball. Forget them infielders, forget the pitcher, just concentrate on the ball, and try to see it the instant, the very second, it leaves his hand. Soon as he throws, you be on it. Not when it passes the mound, or is halfway to you, but just when he lets it go, understand?" Oddibe nodded. "All right now," Bug said, to everyone, "let's do this again."

They worked for another twenty minutes or so, took another break, then picked it up again. By this time the usual game-day activity was taking place at the ballpark and provided a bit of an audience. The clean-up crew, for instance, which had begun working minutes before Jack started throwing, decided to take a quick break to watch Oddibe swing the bat. The usual vendors were making their deliveries, bringing hamburger and hot dog buns, beer, candy and the like, and they would all pause to observe the proceedings for a few moments. Not really sure what this was about, though, and having other stops to make on their routes, they soon headed off. Even Nashota came out to watch, leaning against the railing nearest to the office. Jack saw her standing there and smiled.

"'Sho, what time is it?"

She looked at her watch. "Almost ten-thirty. How long do you want to be out here?"

Jack looked at Bug. "That's a question for you, I think. How long do you want us out here?"

If it was up to him, Bug would have stayed there for another hour or two, maybe more, he was just loving this. Of course, he wasn't hitting or pitching or running, either, and he could tell that the newspaperman, Appleton, was pretty worn out. "'Nother few minutes, let's say, ten more swings and we call it, that all right with you, Oddibe?" The young man nodded (Win Appleton quietly grunted to himself), and Jack threw again and again, ten more times, and Oddibe connected some more, ten more times. After the tenth swing, Bug hollered out, "OK, that's it for today." And to his pupil he said, "you done good, Oddibe, you done good."

Mike drove the batting cage just a few yards away. "We'll be using it again later," he said to Jack. "Seems silly to haul it way out to its normal home, then haul it back, then haul it one last time. It'll be all right where it is and besides, saves us money on gas, right?" Win got some water in the clubhouse, downed it quickly and poured himself some more. He washed his upper body and put on fresh deodorant before changing back to his street clothes and ambling up the stairs. He correctly figured that making innocent small talk with Nashota would help him completely catch his breath before he headed off to the paper.

Oddibe got into the back seat of Jack's car, as he had on the way over, but this time, Bug Gillen climbed in next to him. "Drive on, Rochester," he said merrily, and the two older men laughed, while even Oddibe managed a smile.

After a few quiet moments, Bug leaned forward a bit. "Jack, who that guy, left-hand hitter, tall and skinny, won a battin' title a few years ago playin' for two teams…"

That was an easy one for Jack. "Harry Walker," he said quickly. "Outfielder. Season was only a coupla weeks old and the Cards sent him to Philly for…for…yeah, it was Ron Northey, 'nother outfielder. Gave 'em lots more power, guess they thought they needed it to beat the Dodgers but it didn't work. I think that might-a been Jackie's first year…"

"It was," said Oddibe, quietly.

"He still playin'?" asked Bug.

"Might be back in Triple-A," said Jack. "Played there last year, I know that, and I ain't seen his name in any box scores this year. Gettin' kinda old to play every day, he must be my age, or close to it. Why do you ask?"

Bug looked at Oddibe. "How big your bat? How many ounces?"

"Been usin' a 34 but I was thinkin' 'bout switchin' to a 33, maybe that will…"

"No, no, no, you don't wanna go lighter, make it just that much easier for pitchers to throw the ball by you. No, the kinda hitter you are, or oughta be, you need to go heavier. Harry Walker swung a 38 and he led the league in hittin' that one year, '47."

"Lotsa guys have won battin' titles, Bug," said Jack, with his eyes on the road. "Musial's won a bunch, same with Teddy Ballgame, Reiser, Jackie won coupla years ago, why pick on Walker?"

"Cause that's the kind-a hitter Oddibe should be. His approach, Walker's approach, is perfect for Oddibe. Use a heavier bat, 36 or 38 ounces, maybe choke up a bit, hit down on the ball or go with the pitch." He looked right at Oddibe. "You run real good, young man, you 'bout as fast as anyone I ever seen, 'cept for Cool Papa. Ain't no one ever as fast as Cool Papa, now that a nat'ral fact. But you can run, really run, and you gotta use that, take 'vantage-a that. Everyone knows you can't steal first base, but you…you can use that speed-a yours to get on base. That's what we need to work on. 'Cause look, once you get on, you causin' trouble, the other team gotta worry 'bout you and 'fore you know it, they're makin' mistakes, you're comin' on home, and puttin' up a run for your side. See what I'm sayin'?" He tapped on Oddibe's leg. "Use your speed, that speed God gave you, right from the start, right in the batter's box. The other teams, they know they gotta worry 'bout you if you get on base so they workin' hard to get you out, and what you doin'? You jus' helpin' them 'long by tryin' to pull everythin'. We get you to hit DOWN on the ball, you gonna get on base more often, I guaranTEE it!" He practically shouted those last two words.

There was silence, especially from Oddibe, who wasn't sure what to say. Finally Jack, rather quietly, said "I think you may be on to something there, Bug."

"I know I am, boys, I jus' know it." Once again he looked directly at Oddibe. "Whaddya say, Oddibe? You game to give it a try? We can go out there and work on this for a few days, see if you can get the hang of it. I can stay as long as you like, as long as Jack and Miss Nashota can put up with me."

"You're no trouble at all, Bug," said Jack, which was all the old Negro Leaguer needed to hear.

"How 'bout it, Oddibe?" implored Bug.

Neither man was really aware that Jack had stopped the car, they just looked at each other. Finally Oddibe said "Bug, we gonna need shaggers, like today?"

A bit perplexed, Bug said "Yes, sir, 'spose we will need a couple."

"I don't know if it's a good idea to ask Mr. Appleton to help out again, thought he might have a heart attack out there!" The laughter was so intense that the three men were startled when someone knocked on the car door.

"What got y'all howlin' like hyenas?" Jasmine always paid attention whenever a vehicle stopped in front of her house. Recognizing it as Jack's, she was about to go back to reading her book on the front porch when she heard cackling coming from inside the Meadowbrook. "What in tarnation is goin' on in there?" she said aloud as she ambled over. She hoped Oddibe was one of those laughing; she had barely seen him smile over the past couple of weeks.

"Nothing," said Jack. "Oddibe said something we thought was pretty funny."

"Oddibe said somethin', did he? Well Lord have mercy, that's good to hear."

"Anyway, here you are, O. See you a little later," said Jack. But before the youngster could open the car door, he felt Bug's hand on his arm.

"Like to see the place, if I could. Mind if I come in for a bit? Jack, we gotta hurry off?"

Jack got serious real quick. "No, but, um, Bug, we uh, this, uh, this is…"

"Yeah, yeah, we already talked 'bout it, I know what this is, Jack. Think I was born yesterday? I been in places like this before. When we was barnstormin', there was a coupla times we stayed in a house like this. Don't worry, I won't be long, I just wanna have a look around. Come on, Oddibe, show me your room. Come on, Jack."

Jack had become visibly uncomfortable. "No, that's OK, Bug, you go, I'll just wait here…"

"Nonsense, come on in. Sittin' here in the car makes you stand out, 'specially if the police happen to come by. Come on in, I'm sure this nice lady here won't bite, least, not unless you pay her some money." That got Bug laughing again, and even Oddibe began to giggle when Jasmine laughed louder than any of them.

They all went inside, with Oddibe and Bug going upstairs, and Jack finding a chair downstairs. He didn't sit for long, however, and soon he was pacing, which distracted Jasmine. She was having a hard enough time getting into this book—*Black Boy*, by a man named Richard Wright, recommended by Emma—and Jack wasn't making things any easier. "Jack Simpson, why don't you and me set ourselves out on the porch? Otherwise you'll wear a hole in my carpet, and I'm tryin' to get least 'nother year outta it."

They sat in silence for a few moments before Jasmine finally said "Ain't you got nothin' to say today, Jack Simpson?"

He looked at her. "How are you, Jazz?"

She gave him a big smile. "I'm just fine, skipper, how 'bout you?"

He grunted. "OK. We're tryin' to get Oddibe straightened out. His hittin', I mean. He's gotten all depressed because…"

"I know," said Jazz. "We talk, him-n-me. I told him to just relax, make believe he's back in Asheville, guess that ain't so easy to do."

Jack paused and let that sink in. Then he said "The guy with him played Negro League ball and was recommended to us by Satchel Paige, that's praise from the best, you know? Name-a…"

"Bug. Oddibe told me that, too, but I remember the name. Now I 'member the face and…ha!" She let out a little laugh. "Other things as well." And she laughed again.

"No! Really? Him too?" She nodded. "Is there any man in America you haven't… um…?"

"Ain't never met Mr. Eisenhower, or Mr. Truman, neither. Don't much like politicians, tellya the truth, they generally all older and flabby, nothin' very excitin'. You baseball folk, you mostly all strong and athaletic and I always did like that type, still do." She looked at Jack and smiled. "Back in Pine Bluff, this travelin' cullud team came through one year, late, think it was October, and a bunch-a them fellas came to The Apollo and I got to be with someone named Bug. Been a long time, 'course, and I guess there could be more-n one ballplayer with the same nickname, but now I see him…"

Jack had to smile as he shook his head. "I'm surprised you didn't jump up-n-down when I mentioned Satchel Paige."

"What about Satch?" It was Bug. "Great guy, smart guy. You ever meet him, Jack?"

"No, we just spoke on the phone that one time, like I told you."

Bug was looking at Jasmine. "How 'bout you, ma'am? Ever meet Satch?"

She stood up. "Now where would I get to meet a man like that? I know who he is, don't get me wrong, but I'm just a small-town whore and he's a big-league ballplayer, and a legend 'mongst us cullud folk." She looked at Jack, smiled and gave him an ever-so-slight nod, then back to Bug. "If you gen'lmen will 'scuse me, I got some things to do 'round here." And she disappeared into the interior of the house.

Bug's eyes followed her as she sashayed past him. Kept looking, in fact, even after she vanished from view. Jack felt free to insert the needle, baseball man to baseball man. "Now what would Maudene say?"

Bug turned back to face his host, and gave him a broad smile. "She say it all-a time: 'you can look 'slong as you don't touch.' And she tells me she 'spects I'll always look." He made his voice higher, imitating his wife. "'Day come you don't look at a pretty girl, I'll know it's time to throw dirt on you.' Ain't it the truth, ha! But I gotta tell you, Jack, somethin' 'bout that gal looks awful familiar. I was just wonderin'…"

"You ain't never been in these parts before, have you, Bug?" The old Negro Leaguer shook his head. "Then I reckon you ain't never met her, she's strictly a local girl. Oddibe OK?"

"Yeah, he fine. Was a little embarrassed to show me he lived in a whorehouse, but I told him, ain't nothin' to be 'shamed of, lotta guys 'fore you done the same. 'Sides, it's a bed and prob'ly pretty comfortable. He said yeah, and the girls are all nice and leave him alone and I said that's all he can ask for."

As they drove back to Jack's house, Bug reminisced.

"I can't lie, I been in several cathouses in my life, not lately, 'course, but when I was younger, long 'fore Maudene. Had a teammate in Nashville name-a Blackbottom Wesley. Big lanky right-hander, almost threw sidearm. Loaded up ever once-in-a-while. Anyways, he liked to live in whorehouses, any place he played he found a nice one and lived there. Said they always treated him great, and sooner-r-later he'd get one-a them gals to feed him and fuck him. He played in a lotta places, more-n me, I'd say, and it always seemed to work for him, so I told Oddibe not to worry 'bout it, enjoy it if he can. Says he's loyal to his girl back home, though. Maybe he just needs to get laid, whaddya think, Jack?"

"Actually, I've had that thought myself, more-n once."

"Might be time for her to visit, eh?" And the two men looked at each other and smiled.

TWELVE

Before the season had begun, Nashota had given the Wolves' complete schedule to Jasmine, and had pointed out the nights when the team would be coming off the road at some "ungodly hour." That was Nashota's phrase, to which Jazz just chuckled and said "Honeychild, that just normal business hours for us." So shortly after 2 am, Mike parked the bus in front of the house on Light Street and closed his eyes for a short snooze as Jack escorted Oddibe and Monroe up the steps, where Jasmine and Jake were both waiting. Jack felt it was his responsibility to introduce Monroe to them, and to thank them for making sure his new player had a place to sleep.

"Happy to help, Mr. Simpson," said Jazz, being playful with Jack by being so formal. "I got the room, least for this boy, but don't know if I can put up any more, though, just lettin' you know." Then she turned her attention to her new charge. "Mr. Monroe Hicks, been readin' 'bout you in the paper, we real glad to have you. Me-n Jake here'll take good care-a you, you can be sure-a that. Lemme show you your room, OK?"

"Yes, ma'am," said Monroe. "I'm lookin' forward to sleepin' in a bed, I can tell you that. After two nights in a barn, I think that wherever you put me will seem like the White House!"

"Hey, the barn ain't so bad," said Oddibe, as they wearily went inside the house. "I slept there, too, you know, was OK. Didn't hurt your hittin' none."

Jack said his good-nights, then he and Mike took the bus back to the ballpark.

The next night, Tommy Nathan was practically unhittable early on—13 of the first 14 Cardinals who came to the plate went back to the bench grumbling. "Goddammit, that little shit don't throw harder than my kid sister." "He ain't got nothin', we oughta be hittin' the piss outta him." Karl Hines finally got tired of the grousing and snapped "Quitcherbitchin' and just hit the damn ball." And with two out in the fifth they started doing just that, stringing together four hits and, along with an untimely error by Coach Valenza that would have ended the inning, Shirley suddenly had a 4–2 lead. And when the first two Cards reached in the sixth, Jack hustled out and returned with Nathan in tow and Buck Hightower now on the mound. His job was to staunch the bleeding, which is exactly what he did, and then some. A foul pop ended the sixth without any more runs scoring, and then, in the bottom of the inning, Miggs led off with a single. Valenza, trying to make up for his error, put down a bunt, ran his ass off, and not only beat it out but advanced to second when the throw went wild. Jack thought about replacing Buck with a pinch-hitter but, with runners on second and third, he figured that would just result in an intentional walk, whereas they'd be inclined to deal with the pitcher. "Go get 'em, Buck" Jack yelled from the coaches' box, and the big righty just grinned and nodded, looked at a pitch low and inside, then blasted the second one high and deep to left-center. The Cardinal outfielders just watched it sail over the fence as Wolves' fans stood and screamed and yelled and stomped their feet. In fact, they made so much noise that even Win Appleton, sitting in the press box, said to no one in particular, "Damn, that's about as loud as this old ballpark has ever been." Of course, Jack now had to let Hightower throw the seventh and, with his adrenaline obviously working overtime, Buck got three quick outs, needing just eight pitches. Edens Ridge scratched out another run and Buck got three more outs, then Larry West was brought in to finish up the ninth and nail down the 6–4 win for the home squad.

The clubhouse was loud and boisterous, as if they'd won the World Series, rather than just some regular-season, Class D ballgame. And absolutely no one was more boisterous than Buck, who stood on a table and held court.

"I am the LORD," he shouted. "Did you hear those fans? They loved me and were makin' that noise, that joyful noise! 'Make a joyful noise to the Lord, all the earth.' I heard 'em, yes I did, yes I did, and I know what they was doin', who they were cheerin', that be me. Ha ha, we did it tonight, didn't we? We sure got 'em tonight, didn't we? Ha ha ha."

Eventually he decided to take his shower, and on his way in, he stopped by where Oddibe and Monroe were sitting.

"How 'bout we three go out tonight and celebrate?"

Oddibe laughed. "Really? Sounds great, man. And where you suggest we go that will be happy to serve two black guys and a white guy? Even if the white guy did hit a home run tonight."

Buck crinkled up his nose. "You're right, sorry. Tell you what, I'll buy us some beers and we can go over to your place, bet your landlady won't mind," he said with a grin.

They sat in Monroe's room and drank. As soon as he had finished his beer, Hicks waved his hand and declared "I'm startin' tomorrow, so I've reached my limit. Can't be comin' to the yard hung over."

"Hung over this quick? What's wrong with you?" Buck asked. "Lemme tell you, hoss, you need to be able to drink if you wanna play in the pros. You a big boy, strong, you oughta be able to handle your alcohol."

Monroe just smiled. "I do OK, but like I said, I'm startin' tomorrow and can't afford to screw up, I'm tryin' to make an impression," to which Buck raised his bottle and said, "We ALL tryin' to make an impression, partner." He passed them both a second round and they all nodded and clinked their bottles, but Oddibe and Monroe both sipped their refills while Buck swigged his down. When he saw them looking at him he laughed. "I threw three and a third tonight, I won't be brought in unless we go extras." He laughed again. "So you guys make sure we take 'em in nine, OK? Deal?" They laughed and clinked again.

It didn't take long before the talk turned to the other residents of the house. "Anybody gettin' any?" asked Buck. Monroe shifted a bit in his chair and said, "I just got to town, man," while Oddibe said "I gotta girlfriend back home." Buck laughed and looked at Daniels. "Well, she ain't here now is she?"

"They're all nice girls," Oddibe said as Buck snorted and Monroe chuckled. "Really. Yeah, I know what they do for a livin', I know what's goin' on here, but I see 'em some durin' the day, talk to 'em, I even…" He stopped and Buck pounced. "Even what? Even fucked 'em all coupla times, that it? Quit holdin' out on us, boy, talk!"

The room quickly became silent and cold as Oddibe stood up. "Ain't no boy," he said icily. "I may not be as old as you but I ain't no boy, and neither is Monroe. You white folk, it always gets down to that, we just boys, never men…"

"Hey, hey, hey, whoa, slow down, wait a minute," said Buck. "I didn't mean nothin' by it, certainly not what you think. I could never be like that, not me, not ever. I…" And then he stopped and got real quiet, not the norm for him, not at all. And he stared, looking past them, at nothing they could see, but for Hightower there was… something.

Oddibe and Monroe looked at each other, then at Buck. No one said anything until Hicks asked, "You was sayin', Buck?"

More quiet. Oddibe finally stood up and said "we gotta game tomorrow, better get me some sleep." He began walking towards the door but Buck stopped him.

"Wait a minute, just a minute. Well, maybe two or five, OK?"

Oddibe went back to where he had been sitting as Buck grabbed another beer, took a big swig, and said "this stays here, right? Don't leave this room, not tonight, not ever. Right?" The other two just nodded.

"OK," said Buck as he took another drink. "OK. Y'all know I'm from Louisiana." He pronounced it LOOZ-EE-ANNA. "Ever been there?" His two young teammates shook their heads. "Great place. Beautiful. This here, Tennessee, is beautiful, too, but Looz-ee-anna, we got it all. Plenty of fishin', I sure love to fish, and boatin', love bein' out on the water. We got the best food, everybody knows that, and those old plantations, and Mardi Gras…"

"And swamps," said Monroe with a smile. "I hear you got lotsa swamps, full-a alligators."

"You hear right," said Buck. "Just another thing that makes it great, and special." He took another drink. "And people, we got different people, all sortsa people, different kinds, different races. Kinda like America in miniature, you know? Find it all in Looz-ee-anna. Y'all need to come down and visit some time, you can stay with me and my family, glad to have you." Another drink, then he looked at the floor and said nothing for a moment while Daniels and Hicks just waited. Finally he looked up at them.

"Our politics is crazy," he said. "And some people, some people high up, still make a big deal outta race, gets 'em elected. Lotta folks don't, though, and that's because lotta us Looz-ee-annans got all kind-a blood in 'em, you know. State was settled by Indians and Canadians and Spanish and Africans and Europeans and prob'ly a few others, too. Ha!" He laughed and took a quick drink. "Men and women got together, didn't matter what they looked like, what color their skin was, what language they spoke. He thought she was a dolly, she thought he was a flutter-bum, she invites him in and next thing you know they're raisin' a child." He smiled, then lowered his voice. "My grandpappy," he smiled at the thought of him, then continued. "He quite the fella. My grandpappy, he's every bit as dark as y'all. Married an Indian girl, Coushatta tribe, I can even speak a little Coushatta. My mother identifies as Indian but she married a white man, just like our Nashota. I been raised white and Indian, but I also been taught some by my Paw-Paw. Taught me 'bout slavery long 'fore I got to school, taught me 'bout race riots in N'awlins and Colfax back after the Civil War, taught me to be proud…but careful. So I don't tell folks 'bout him, just 'bout my white side and Indian side. But I got as much black in me as white. No one here knows, no one but you."

The two younger players looked at each other again, dumfounded, not sure what to say.

"I figured," Buck continued, "I figured right away you needed a friend, O, and I didn't know how many others would step up, that's kinda why I did. The guys have mostly come around, Box was a prick but he gone now, pretty funny we brought Monroe in to replace him, eh? Anyhow, way I look at it, the Edens Ridge Wolves now have three Negroes on the team, but we're the only ones what know that and you hafta promise to never say nothin', understand? Can't say nothin' 'round here, can't say nothin' in any places we play." He took a quick swig. "Can't say nothin' to nobody, not even Jack and Nashota, they don't know and I'm askin' you to please keep it to yourselves, OK?" A brief pause. "OK? We drink to that?"

They clinked their bottles in brotherhood and that seemed like a good time to call it a night, so Oddibe and Buck departed. The outfielder walked down the hall to his room, while the big pitcher, swaying some, unsteadily made his way down the stairs, where he saw one of the girls sitting all alone, reading Look magazine. It was Linda, who was waiting to see if there were any stragglers that night. She quickly sized up the situation and smiled. "Need a place to sleep, bull? I ain't sure you can make it home tonight, and I know that Jack Simpson would be awfully mad at us if somethin' happened to you and he found out we let you leave here. Won't charge you hardly anythin' just to sleep, and if we do more-n sleep, well…" She smiled coyly. "…we can work somethin' out."

Buck looked at her. She was awfully pretty, especially when she smiled. And he saw something familiar, a look he'd seen before.

"I'm Coushatta. I may be wrong, but are you Choctaw?" Which got him an even bigger smile and, in the morning, a deep discount.

She looked so pretty when she got off the bus in her little red-and-white sun dress. She looked around, saw him and her face lit up as she ran over and kissed him, hard, not caring that they were in public and people would talk. They hadn't seen each other for nearly four months and she wasn't looking at anyone else, didn't see anyone else, just him.

She looked positively stunning when, as soon as he took her home to Light Street, she quickly undressed. No surprise that his release was all-too-quick, but being young means needing just a short rest before being up and at it again, and this second time was taken much more slowly, and was much more satisfying for both of them. And as they lay there in each other's arms, physically and emotionally satisfied and blissfully in love, it was, he thought, the time to tell her.

She didn't look so pretty any more.

"This is what? You are livin' in WHAT? Oddibe Daniels, how could you? You're…you…you been raised better-n that, you're a Christian, a good Christian, your parents…Oddibe, do your parents know? Your mother? She can't know, if she did you'd be dead by now, she'd-a come up here and killed you herself. Oh Oddibe…"

"Calm down, honey, please calm down," he said, trying to smooth things over while mentally kicking himself for bringing the matter up. "It's just a place for me to sleep, nothin' more. Jack and Nashota, they looked all over and couldn't find no place in town, Miz Jasmine was the only one who said sure, I gotta room. And look, she been great to me, make sure I'm fed, do her best to keep me safe, her-n Jake, everybody, really, treat me so good, like family…"

"How much like family, hmmm? These…these…girls, runnin' 'round here half-naked or totally naked, for all I know, they actin' like your wife, that what you mean?"

"No, no, you got it wrong. I'm like a brother, their baby brother, that's all. 'Sides, I don't actually see the girls all that much, I leave for the ballpark 'fore they come downstairs, mostly, and when I get back I come straight here, I'm tired and just wanna sleep. By myself! That's it, Rube, this is just a place for me to sleep and eat, all it is. Whatever else is goin' on don't have nothin' to do with me." He decided, on the spot, not to mention that night he was chased home and Jasmine and Jake were pointing their guns at his pursuers, or about how he frequently helps the girls with the vacuuming and general clean-up.

"Well, I don't know, I don't know if I can stay here, sleep here, knowin' what's goin' on in the other rooms. It just ain't right, O, it ain't how we been brought up."

He wanted to say that they hadn't been brought up to have sex before they got married but that hadn't stopped them just now. Twice. Didn't do anythin' different than what Emma and Vicky and Linda and Gail are doin', only difference is that Emma and Vicky and Linda and Gail get paid for their efforts. He wanted to say something like that, but he didn't.

She fussed some more. When she said "maybe I oughta just go on home," he reminded her that she had only now arrived, they've been waiting so long to see each other, and besides, how would she explain her speedy return to her parents? When she countered with "well, maybe I might could stay with the Simpsons," he countered with the fact that Nashota was pregnant and didn't need to be dealing with anyone else right now, especially someone who wasn't family. Family, she said, had he told his family? He just shook his head.

Jack came to get them a little early, as had been agreed upon in advance, and he thought that they were rather uncomfortably quiet on the short drive to the ballpark. Once they arrived, Oddibe took RubyAnn to the office to introduce her to Nashota, and then he excused himself. "I gotta do my stretches," he said, and quickly left.

When Oddibe had talked about RubyAnn, he never failed to mention her bright, bubbly personality, which made Nashota eager to meet her. But the girl sitting in her office did not match the description. When the older woman would ask her a question—"How was your bus trip?" or "I'll bet you were excited to see Oddibe after all this time, eh?"—she got simple, one-word answers: "Fine" and "Yes." She tried a different approach.

"I've got a couple of things I need to do around the ballpark to get ready for tonight's game. Wanna come with me? We can keep talking, and…"

"No, thank you, ma'am," said RubyAnn. "If it's all the same to you, I'd just as soon sit here 'til the ballgame begins. I brought a book with me."

Something was up. Nashota took a chair, pulled it so it was right in front of the young girl, then she sat down and looked her in the eye. "OK, RubyAnn, I know we've only known each other for a few minutes, but I'm pretty sure that something's bothering you. Let's talk about it, maybe I can help. I'm older than you and…"

"And you shoulda known better!" Nashota was taken aback by RubyAnn's sudden sharp tone. "You're right, you're older, you're married, you're gonna be a mom, yet you put him…there, and you let him stay there. How could you, you and your husband, you're supposed to be lookin' out for him, he's got all this…this stuff goin' on, with people yellin' and throwin' things and he's just tryin' to play ball…" She began to cry but that didn't stop her, she was on a roll. "And then he gotta come home at night to…to that…that place, no wonder he's havin' trouble, no wonder he ain't hittin', how could you, Miz Simpson, how could you?"

Guess the cat was out of the bag. "Ruby," she said, but was quickly interrupted. "It's RubyAnn, Miz Simpson, if you please." Nashota smiled. "Sorry, RubyAnn, I apologize, my fault. Anyway, there really are things that I have to take care of before ballgames, and I would love to have a little help. Why don't you come with me, and we can talk while we're working?" She smiled again, and this time she saw a bit of a crack in the ice. "OK," said RubyAnn, and the two women left the office.

Behind the workplace there was a small storage area, and they stopped there first. Nashota unlocked it and pulled out two speakers. "These are new," she said, handing one to Ruby. "We don't want them exposed to the elements, and we don't want them stolen, which has happened before, can you believe that? So we put them up before every game and take them down before we leave at night and lock them up. Come."

They walked along the concourse. Out on the field, several players, including Oddibe, were doing some light running and stretching. Mike Hamblen was driving the tractor out to the bullpen area, where he would get the batting cage, hook it up to the tractor and bring it back to the infield, setting it in place for batting practice. All else was quiet. Nashota and RubyAnn walked to an area behind home plate, then went up to the top row of the grandstand. "Wait here a moment," Nashota said, unlocking the press box door and disappearing inside. RubyAnn could hear her walking inside, then she heard what sounded like a window being unlatched and opened, and then more footsteps. Nashota now popped out of the press box, picked up the speaker she had previously set down, and carried it over to the first-base edge of the long press box window. There she climbed on the bench seat and carefully fit the speaker into the waiting empty cradle, fastened it as tightly as she could, then threaded the wire through a small opening in the window she had unfastened. "Now we'll do the other one," she said, and they walked over to the third-base edge of the window. "I'll take that," she said, relieving RubyAnn of her speaker. Nashota fastened this one just as she had done a moment before, then said "We're almost done with this task."

They went inside the press box. A long desk stretched most of the length of the room, and on that desk was a metal apparatus that had switches and knobs, as well as a microphone. Nashota took the dangling wires that had been threaded through the window and connected them to the back of that machine, then she flipped a couple of switches, picked up the mike and said "testing, testing." Her voice could now be heard all over the ballpark.

Nashota offered the mike to RubyAnn. "Wanna say something? You could say hi to Oddibe." The girl just shook her head. Nashota shrugged her shoulders, turned off the mike, took a seat and said "OK, let's talk." RubyAnn could see it was not a request, so she, too, sat down.

Nashota looked down at the floor, which she had swept up yesterday, then looked at RubyAnn. "Do I remember," she asked, "that you have just graduated from high school?" A slight smile from the young girl. "Yes, ma'am. Stephens-Lee High School, one of the best in all of North Carolina." Nashota nodded. "I agree. I lived in Asheville for a few years. Didn't go to school there, I was finished with school when I moved to town, but I remember it being praised for its academics and its athletics. And you live with your parents, right? Never lived on your own?"

"No, ma'am," said RubyAnn.

"Um-hmm," said Nashota. "I'm sure your parents are wonderful people, good people, I can tell because I see the kind of young woman they have raised, now ready to go out into the world. I'm sure, because you've received this good education, you've read about things, read about how things are in these United States, but maybe you haven't seen them in person. This…"

RubyAnn cut her off. "I've seen prejudice, Miz Nashota, I've seen hatred. I've had people yell at me and say horrible things to me. And Oddibe, he's told me some-a the things that have happened to him this year, things people say…"

"Did he tell you that he got chased by a group of people who wanted to bash his head in?" RubyAnn's eyes grew wide and her mouth dropped open. "He'd be mad at me for talking 'bout it, but I'm telling you this for a reason. These…these *a-s-gi-nas*—devils!—chased him for several blocks until he got home, to the house that you think is so evil, and there he was protected by Miss Brunét and her boyfriend, Jake. They used guns, RubyAnn, they pointed guns at those fiends and made them back off. Now tell me, if he lived in some apartment building, you think anyone would have come out to shield him? You know the answer to that as well as I do, because you're a smart young woman who's been taught well at the Stephens-Lee High School." She paused for a moment, but RubyAnn said nothing, so she continued.

"You've never had to worry about putting a roof over your head, I'll bet, and that's good, that's wonderful, that's the way it oughta be for people. When our players come up here after spring training, the first thing they have to do is find a place to live, that makes sense, right?" RubyAnn silently nodded. "And we help them, we have a list of places they can go and get an apartment or a room in someone's house. But we've never had a Negro before, never been one in this league before, I know you know that.

So when I went out in January and February and talked to people and told them that Oddibe was coming, this nice, decent, well-mannered, proper young man, know how many people told me they'd be happy to rent him a room? Take a guess, RubyAnn, how many people do you think were anxious to have him for the season?"

She stopped talking, waiting for an answer, and after a few seconds the young woman realized that she was supposed to respond. "Just one?" she asked softly.

"That's right, just one. All our good Christian folks were afraid, 'don't want no trouble' they'd say to me. Other folks said worse, like, 'we won't have no n— living here, why are you bringin' him in anyway?'" This last part wasn't true, not exactly, and Nashota knew it, but only because she had never approached any white people about renting to Oddibe. What was the use? They wouldn't dream of doing something like that, wouldn't dream of rocking the boat. If she had asked, however, that's precisely what they would have said, she had every confidence.

"Yes, Miss Brunét runs a whorehouse, no one denies that," Nashota continued. "But I can tell you for a fact that she takes good care of Oddibe, not in a sexual way but as a big sister or…or an aunt, that's prob'ly a better description. She has put her neck on the line for him more than once, and now she has taken in our new player, Monroe Hicks, who I haven't even met yet!" She chuckled, then she turned serious again. "Don't matter where you sleep, RubyAnn, what matters is what you do when you're awake. Oddibe is living a good life, trying to make it in baseball. He's getting help from some fine people, and Jasmine Brunét is one-a them." She stood up. "You got nothing to be ashamed of, and nothing to be afraid of, at Light Street. I hope you understand. Now we've got some more chores to do before we open the gates at 6:30, and time's a-wastin' 'cause I been runnin' my mouth. Come on." And with that they left the press box and headed back to the office, with Nashota explaining "we have to give the umpires twelve brand-new baseballs, and then we have to check…"

The gloomy, wet weather in Southwest Virginia was something of a metaphor for the country as a whole. The war in Europe, now in its third year, seemed to be making eyes at the United States in October of 1941. The German navy had torpedoed an American destroyer, the Kearny, just a few days earlier, killing 11 and wounding twice that number. This came on the heels of President Roosevelt asking Congress for permission to arm our merchant ships. "Hell, we ain't even at war and we's losin' boys to them Nazis. We gotta do somethin'," one fellow said.

War talk uncharacteristically dominated the Klan meeting that evening. Many were pleased that the Wehrmacht was whipping the Red Army, beating them everywhere and pushing them deep into Russia. That bastard Stalin and his Commie friends had already fled Moscow, it was surely only a matter of time before Hitler would triumphantly enter the city, just like he did in Paris a year ago. "Then they can concentrate on that fat fuck Churchill and the Brits, and then, THEN, Roosevelt will have to back down…" Somebody yelled "You mean 'Rosenfeld,' don't you?" which always got a few laughs, but the man went on. "Whatever. Point is, I think it's only a matter-a time 'fore the Nazis are over here, in charge, and then we can link up with them and take care-a our problems once and for all. Our n——s and mackerel snappers and kikes, they'll learn, they'll get what's a-comin' to 'em!" Cheers all around, a better day was just around the corner, courtesy of the Third Reich.

Plenty of speechifyin' and good fellowship at the meeting, as always, which meant plenty of beer was on hand. So much so that, by the end of the evening, Truck Maxwell did not feel confident in his ability to drive home. "Let's go Beau," he said to his 19-year-old son. "You can drive the half-ton tonight."

"Geez, Dad, you know I don't like that truck, never will un'erstand whyinhell you bought it to begin with."

"Looks great, it's snazzy, I like it."

That wasn't enough for Beau. "Yeah, but the hood is too high and rounded, makes it tough to see, and they moved those headlamps up, that was a mistake..."

"Shut up, boy, and drive. 'Sides, I need me a smoke," said Truck as he lit up a fresh Pall Mall.

It appeared that the rain hadn't stopped the whole time they were in the meeting. Beau drove carefully, his sight diminished by the weather and the high, rounded hood, even though his father kept urging him to go faster between puffs. "This baby can do a lot better-n 20!"

"I wanna get us home in one piece," Beau said, the exasperation apparent in his voice. His father was always sniping at him, critical of everything, and he was tired of it. He had actually been thinking about getting away, as far away as possible. He expected it was only a matter of time before the U.S. got into this war, no matter what those citizens said. Roosevelt ain't gonna let Hitler just come marchin' in here without a fight. Beau wasn't a Democrat but he sure wasn't a Nazi, either, and the way he saw it, a winner-take-all fight between the U.S. and Germany was inevitable. I need to get in on that, and soon. Joining the military seemed like the answer for him, he just needed to decide which branch had the most appeal, and right now the navy...

"Holy shit!" Beau yelled as something darted in front of him on the road. He swerved to avoid it, and the truck began to slip and slide on the wet ground. He could feel them hit something, must have been a big rock or a tree stump, and now the Plymouth was airborne. It spun in the air and hit the ground hard, with a loud CRASH, then rolled down an embankment several times and finally stopped completely upside down, near a tree, somewhere in Wise County. Beau Maxwell could hear his father yelling something, maybe calling for help, he couldn't tell for certain. His head hurt and his left hip and leg really hurt, and now the world seemed to be swirling again and getting darker, he didn't think it could get much darker, but it did. Suddenly the sun was shining and he was lying on the ground, grass all around, cool breeze blowing, and he felt...calm, all calm and serene. This was great, this was beautiful, he could easily stay here forever, didn't know where he was but no matter, this was so peaceful...

A bright light shone on him, not the sun, something different, and his eyes were fuzzy but he thought he could see people hovering around him. He was no longer lying on the grass, though he was still lying down, felt soft, might be a bed, and the people around him were wearing white, who were they? Doctors? Angels? They were busy talking to one another, and then one put something over his mouth and told him to take deep breaths, and he felt light-headed and now he felt like he was on a merry-go-round going faster and faster and…

The Brooks family was home that Monday night, where else would they be? October is a very important month for farmers, who are busy harvesting their crops. Come evening, then, they would be exhausted and would relax by listening to the radio before turning in. All too often, Lathan found himself saying "4:30 a.m. has a habit of comin' 'round real quick-like."

They were listening to the "Lux Radio Theatre" when they heard a noise off in the distance. At first they believed it was part of the program, a comedy starring Abbott and Costello. But young Garland, the 17-year-old, thought he heard someone shouting, so he got up, put his ear against the window for a moment, then said "Dad, I think someone's in trouble out there."

"No, son, it's on the radio, sit yourself back down."

Garland was insistent. "Dad, please, come over here and listen a minute. Please listen."

Lathan was tired and comfortable and enjoying Bud and Lou but he slowly got up and walked over to the window, listened, then said, with a sense of urgency, "Grab your jacket, Garland."

Outside they ran in the direction of the voice, a man weakly calling for help. Must have been a mile they ran, maybe a little less, but they soon found a Plymouth pickup truck off the road, upside down, with a man lying on the ground a few feet away. The man was bleeding and badly bruised, but when they approached him his first words were "My boy. My boy is still in there. Help him, please help him."

Lathan and Garland looked inside and they could see the boy—a young man, really—on the driver's side, apparently passed out. Hopefully just passed out and not passed on. They tried opening the doors but they were stuck.

"If we break the window, I think I could crawl in there, Dad," said Garland, and his father responded by kicking at the window with the heel of his boot until it shattered. "Careful, son," he said as the teenager slowly wedged himself inside the cab.

The first thing Garland Brooks did was to feel the young man's neck, something he remembered from a Health Ed class he had taken at school. "Got a pulse, he's still alive!" Then he rolled the inert body towards him and attempted to pull the boy back towards the broken window. No luck, he was just dead weight. "I can't hardly move him, Dad."

"Kick at the door with your heels, maybe you can get it un-stuck," said Lathan. Garland tried but it wouldn't budge, maybe he wasn't strong enough, or maybe he couldn't get the right leverage. "OK, try the window, do like I did on this side," instructed his father. This took a couple of minutes but eventually the window gave way. "Good boy," said Lathan, running around to the driver's side. "Now roll him back this way…that's good, you got him…now see if you can get under him and push him up so's I can grab him and pull him out. That's it, that's good, little more, little more, OK, I got him. Grab his feet, Gar, that'll help me lots. Good, good, a little higher, that's good, OK, here we go," he said as he pulled the body out of the truck. The inert young man grunted several times as he was being pushed and pulled, and then again as he was put onto the wet ground, but that was his only verbal response as his eyes remained closed.

"OK, Garland, you run-on home, you're way faster-n me, and bring the truck 'round. Grab some blankets, too, many as you can find, have your Mama help you. Throw them blankets on the truck bed, we'll use 'em to cushion the ride for these fellas. Hurry up, now, no dawdlin'!"

The closest hospital was in Norton, and Lathan made a quick decision that the ride over there, on this rainy night and in his old 1933 International, might further damage these two injured men. So they drove them over to Doc Bolling, who did a cursory examination and then called the hospital to request an ambulance, and he made sure they'd put a rush on it by saying "I got two white boys here that's hurt real bad." "Don't know how long they'd take if they thought I was callin' 'bout cullud folk," said the doctor to Lathan and Garland when he hung up the phone. "They don't hurry themselves for us."

The medics were accompanied by Sheriff Hart. A short, pudgy man who liked his cigars, the sight of him walking up to your front door was hardly ever welcomed in Negro households. This evening, however, he simply wanted details of the accident, and Lathan, Garland and Doc Bolling all told him as much as they knew. The sheriff wrote everything down, nodding now and again, before asking a few questions.

"Anybody see anythin' or hear anythin'?" No. "Didja see anyone else out there on the road?" No. "Did Truck or Beau say anything 'tall?"

"Who are Truck and Beau?" asked Lathan.

A smile slowly spread across Sheriff Hart's face. "Those fellas who got hurt, who you helped, they're Truck Maxwell and his son, Beau, di'nt you know that? Di'nt you rec-a-nize them?"

The three black men looked at each other before Lathan spoke. "No, suh, they was both pretty banged up. And it was dark, and rainin'. 'Sides, we, uh, we ain't exactly, um, you know, we…"

"I get it," said the sheriff. "Y'all don't go fishin' together." He chuckled, then looked at Bolling. "Good-a you to treat 'em, Doc."

"That's my job, Sheriff. I took an oath. Man needs medical help, my job is to take care-a him, no matter his color."

"Yeah," said the sheriff. "OK, guess I got what-all I need, boys. Thanks for your help," and with that he left.

Several days later, with evening approaching, an unfamiliar car drove up to Lathan Brooks' house. A man got out with some difficulty, walked around to the front of the vehicle, sat on the bumper and called out "Brooks. Lathan Brooks. This is Truck Maxwell, come on out here."

Having just come into the house a few moments earlier from the farm, Lathan was annoyed at having to delay his evening meal for this cracker. *What could he want, anyway? Well, quicker I find out, quicker I gets to eat.* Brooks ambled out onto the front porch, but not before telling everyone to stay inside.

"What can I do for you, Mista Maxwell?"

"You already did it, and I wanted to thank you-n-your boy for helpin' us the other night. We may not have made it without you and Doc Bolling, and I wanted to thank you, in person. I just came from the Doc, he told me where to find you." The two men looked at each other for a moment, then Maxwell said, "Thank you."

"My pleasure, Mista Maxwell. Happy to help." There was another moment of silence, and then Lathan asked, "How's your boy?"

"Still in the hospital. He was banged up pretty good. Prob'ly be there a few more days, but they say he'll recover, be OK. Prob'ly walk with a limp from now on, won't be able to play no ball, coupla teams were lookin' at him but now..." He looked at the ground and shook his head.

"Least he alive," said Lathan.

"Yes," said Truck, "Least he alive." He looked up at Brooks. "He oughta be good, in time, be good 'cept for that left leg." He looked down again and shuffled his feet. "Thank you, Lathan Brooks, and your boy, what's his name?"

"Garland."

"Garland. Thanks to him, too, you'll tell him?" Lathan nodded, and with a grunt and some effort Truck slowly stood up but didn't leave and the silence was deafening. Lathan was about to ask if Mr. Maxwell needed something else when Truck spoke again.

"You and your family...well, look, nothin' will ever happen to you, know what I mean? You took care-a us, we'll take care-a you. For life. Know what I'm sayin', Brooks?"

Brooks nodded, and Maxwell continued. "This just stays 'tween us, hear?" Lathan nodded again, and with that Truck carefully got back into his car, nodded at the farmer, and drove off.

OnaRuth had just fed her baby when she heard the sound of wheels coming up their gravel road. She looked at the clock in the kitchen, which told her it was a little after five. *Now who comin' here at this time-a day?*

She went outside and saw an unfamiliar car, a shiny Cadillac with those fancy whitewall tires. She admired the look of the Series 61—*damn, sure wish we could have us one-a those*—before becoming apprehensive—*don't know nobody who drive somethin' like that, this can't be good.*

A big beefy white man with salt-and-pepper hair and a graying mustache got out, walked to the front of the car, and eyed OnaRuth. He took the cigar from his mouth and said "Evenin'." OnaRuth just nodded, slightly. "Lookin' for Lathan Brooks, think I could talk to him?"

"He ain't here right now," she said warily. "Ain't come in from the field yet. I reckon..." and here she glanced up at the sky, "reckon that on a nice day like this, he work 'slong as he can, maybe 'nother coupla hours. Sir." Maybe if she was polite he'd go away.

The man shook his head. "Think you might could find him? Got some important information I need to share with him, sooner rather later. He really needs to know this. Ma'am."

"Gotta baby in here, plus 'nother, three years old, sir. All due respect, but I really don't wanna wander 'round our land, carryin' these young'uns with me. You could tell me…"

"No!" The man spit it out quickly and emphatically. "I really need to talk to him, young lady, and talk to him today."

"Well, you welcome to come inside and wait, or sit here on the porch, I could fix you…"

He pursed his lips. "All the same to you, I'll wait right here."

She had seen that look before, many times in fact, from practically all the white people in and around town. She had tried to get Garland to move, out of Mettin, out of Wise County, maybe somewhere closer to Richmond or Norfolk or maybe even up in the Shenandoah Valley, but he didn't want to leave his father. "He's getting' older, needs my help more." He also wasn't sure they'd be treated any better elsewhere in Virginia. "Prob'ly gotta go someplace in Pennsylvania, maybe even further north, and right now just ain't the right time." *Never gonna be a good time.* "Suit yourself," she said to the white man, and went inside. Her conscience bothered her a little, though, so a few moments later she reappeared, holding a glass.

"Thought you might like some iced tea. Nice-n sweet, made it myself. Lathan likes it real well."

He just looked at her, then said "Thanks. You can set it down on the porch."

What a snake, she thought.

Lathan or Garland oughta put her in her place, he thought.

He relit his cigar and leaned against his car; after she had been inside for a few minutes, he ambled over and picked up the tea and took a sip, then another. *Not bad for a pickaninny.*

He had been waiting and smoking for perhaps twenty minutes when Lathan suddenly appeared. As luck would have it, Garland had forgotten one of his tools and his father (who was feeling a little tired but would never admit it!) volunteered to go get it for him. As he approached the house, Lathan saw the Cadillac and knew exactly who was standing there.

"Evenin', Mr. Maxwell."

"Lathan."

"Won't you come in? Be happy…"

"This won't take long, Lathan." Truck thought he saw a curtain move. "Let's take a little walk, shall we?" And the two men moved away from the house.

They moved slowly, showing the effects of time. Age is an expert at making bones creak and joints ache and body parts wear down, and it was proudly showing off its handiwork with both Lathan Brooks and Truck Maxwell on this 1952 summer afternoon. They picked their way along the gravel, being especially careful so they would not fall and break something. Perhaps this is why nothing at all was said for several minutes, until they had moved about fifty yards or so away from the house. Truck then stopped, pulled out his lighter, asked "Mind if I smoke?" and relit his cigar when Lathan shook his head.

"Crops doin' good this year?" Brooks was taken aback by this question, so he simply said "Seem that way, 'least right now. Could use more rain, 'course, but that's normal for summer. I guess they be OK."

"Good. That's good," said Maxwell, taking another puff, which seemed to trigger something. "I'm sorry, Lathan, can I offer you a cigar? I got plenty, be happy to…"

"No thanks, Mista Maxwell, I don't smoke no more. Never did go for cigars but I use-ta smoke cigarettes. Gave 'em up during the Depression, had to cut out several things to save money and I never went back. Thanks all the same." *This is strange.*

Maxwell nodded, took another puff, said nothing. They just stood there, out on the gravel road, half a football field from the house.

Lathan Brooks' stomach growled. "Look, Mista Maxwell, I don't wanna be rude, but I been workin' all day and me-n Garland, we got a little more we'd like to do 'fore the day wears out on us, know what I mean? Is there somethin' I might could do for you?"

Maxwell's eyes got narrow and he fixed Lathan with a cold stare as he inhaled and exhaled the smoke one more time. Then he spoke.

"Want you to listen, and listen good. Don't ask no questions, hear? Just listen." Lathan nodded.

"Good. Now you know what…who I run with, what I am in these parts. Little while back they asked me…some fellas were upset 'bout this cullud boy playin' ball in our Mountain Empire League, plenty-a folks were upset, but they didn't say much, just grumbled some. But now Jack Simpson has signed him another ni…Negro boy, and that really got 'em riled up. I'm mad, too, and me-n others talked to Boggs, our league president. He's all right but he got…we don't see some things the same way, not hardly." He gave out a short laugh and took another puff.

"So these fellas were mad and they came to me and asked if I knew anybody who, um, who was, uh, who had been in the war and was known for his, uh, his abilities with guns. I told 'em I did and I…I prob'ly shouldn't-a done that but I did and now…" He paused, looked away, shook his head, inhaled and exhaled more smoke. "I got a reputation 'round here, people know me so I gotta do certain things…" The two men looked at each other. "Don't know what might happen, prob'ly nothin', man don't work for free, you know. But I thought I'd tell you 'cause I know that boy, that Daniels boy, he stays with you when his team's in town, and I made you a promise and wouldn't want nothin' to happen to you or your family. I can…"

"What about him? Daniels I mean, what about somethin' happenin' to Daniels?"

Truck Maxwell looked at Lathan Brooks quizzically. "Not sure I follow…"

"Daniels…he di'nt save your son's life, so it's all right if he dies?" Brooks looked at the ground. "I'm sorry, suh, pardon me, I was just 'sposed to listen."

"Look, Lathan, I didn't have to come to you. Could-a kept my mouth shut, just gone 'bout my business. I didn't. I was thinkin' and decided…I figgered you must know people you could talk to, tell 'em what you know, maybe no one has to get hurt. Jack Simpson is kinda a pain in the ass, and his wife's real mouthy but very pretty, easy to look at when we have league meetings, you know?" He gave out a short laugh. "And that Daniels kid, I don't know the other boy they brought in, we ain't played 'em yet since he signed on, but Daniels is a good little ballplayer. Can really go get 'em in the outfield and is fun to watch on the bases. He just needs experience, time to learn…" Maxwell shuffled his feet. "Hate for him not to get that 'cause I…I…I…shit. Just lemme tell you what-all I know and I'll be on my way."

Lathan had a fitful night, and in the morning he got Garland to drive him up to see his sister in Beck. She swore up and down quite a few times, but finally she said "You wuz right to come to me with this, Lathan, I'll make sure this information gets where it needs to go." And just as soon as her brother and nephew left, she got on the phone to Jeriome Hoffman.

The Beck Bears' owner was surprised to hear from Marzella Brooks. He found her to be an interesting woman, fascinating, actually, so full of life for someone her age. Their relationship had become…different, maybe even a bit bizarre, but had never included a phone call before. Back in February, he had been told she might be able to house Oddibe Daniels when Edens Ridge was in town, so he had gone out to see her. She had, in turn, taken him to visit her brother, Lathan, down the road in Mettin. He drove her back to her house, and when she asked if he wanted some coffee, he suspected she meant more than a cuppa-joe. He began making regular trips over to see her, and almost every time she suggested some new position, even though she always said, "This gonna make my arthur-eye-tis hurt like a sonofabitch, but it be worth it!" Divorced for more than three years, Hoffman was happy to be getting laid again.

But he also felt guilty. This woman was 74 years old, 17 years his senior! And she was a Negro. It's not like white men didn't bed black women in Virginia (or anywhere else in the South, for that matter), but he had never done it before and had, in fact, always looked down on anyone who had. He was not a racist, no sir, no one could say that about Jeriome Hoffman. He had hired a great many Negroes over the years to work at his beer distributorship and had never had a problem with any of them. Well, except for that one man, Herk, Herk something-or-other, who had been making noises about bringing a union in, they had to get rid of him, he was most obviously a Red. Otherwise, all the others were good people, real credits to their race, because they understood how things worked and what was expected of them and where they stood in the company hierarchy. They were very good at following instructions and speaking respectfully. In return, they were treated with respect and paid well and even received a couple of extra benefits, including overtime pay and a small pension if they retired after thirty years on the job. Don't need no union 'round here!

He wasn't prejudiced, he wasn't like Truck Maxwell or B.J. Lewis, those two were most likely Klan. Still, it felt weird to be…having…relations with a Negro woman, even though they were both unmarried and very consenting adults. He always made sure to go over there at night and leave after just a couple of hours. He told no one what he was doing, no one at all. He almost felt like a criminal, and yet, he couldn't stop himself from visiting Marzella. And she was always very happy to see him.

But she never called, so when she did he was concerned, especially after she said she had to see him. "A matter of extreme urgency" were her exact words, and it would be better to discuss it in her house, not over the phone. Except for one irrational, bizarre thought, he had no idea what on earth it could be, so of course, just as soon as she opened the door he went straight to crazy—"You're not pregnant, are you?" She had to sit down, she got to laughing so hard. Once she regained her composure, she said, "Well, don't someone have a real high 'pinion-a hisself?" That made him laugh.

She then told him what was so urgent, and gave him the piece of paper her brother had given to her, the one that contained the information dictated to him by Truck Maxwell. "There's prob'ly lotsa folks who need to know 'bout this," she said. "Not really," he said., and when she looked at him in surprise, he continued. "Only our league president. And Jack Simpson and all the other team presidents. Every police chief in every town in the league. Everyone, like you and your brother, who are offering Daniels a place to sleep. And…well, most likely there's other people I haven't thought of right off the bat. That's all."

He thanked her profusely and left. There was no thought this day of getting naked.

At least twice every summer, someone came to the ballpark during the day and wanted to look around. Generally it was a party of two or three or four, though once in a while it was just a single guy. Always a guy, never any girls, with the exception of one time, Nashota remembered, two or three seasons ago, when a young couple was spending part of their honeymoon going to ballgames in Virginia and Tennessee.

And it was always the same—he or they would get out of their car and quickly walk into the ballpark and immediately look at the field, without stepping into the office first. If there were more than one person, they would talk excitedly:

"Field seems to be in great shape, doesn't it?"

"Look over there, a small rise leading up to the outfield wall in right, that must be fun!"

"Especially for visiting outfielders!!"

"'Bout average size, I'd say, holds maybe 4,000, you think, give or take?"

Sooner or later Nashota would see these fellows and wander over to them. They could be from anywhere, of course, but were generally from along the east coast, though occasionally from elsewhere. She had greeted several from Arkansas, as well as the Mississippi-Alabama area, and maybe once a year someone would hail from the Midwest. She'd offer to give them a brief tour, if they'd like, and of course they would, their faces always lighting up like Times Square. If the players hadn't arrived at the park yet, she'd take them into the clubhouse and they would practically wet themselves, they'd be so excited. Eventually she would sell them tickets for that night's game, give them directions to the Holston Hotel, and recommend breakfast at The Back Porch. And that night she always made it a point to check in with them in the early innings to make sure they were enjoying themselves. "Everything going good?

Glad to hear it. If you need anything, y'all know where I am, in that office up there, just come in and see me, be happy to help." And she would always remind them to tell their friends back in New Jersey/Maryland/Indiana/wherever to come to little ol' Edens Ridge sometime and see the Wolves play.

Today's visitor was alone. Wearing a white tee-shirt and a pair of blue jeans, he stood there, hands on hips, looking at the field. He was not short but not tall, either, and well-built, muscular, obviously someone who frequently lifted weights. He had a bushy brown mustache that was raised in a small smile and broadened when she slowly made her way towards him.

"Ma'am, hope it's all right that I'm lookin' 'round a bit, and whoa! You all right there, ma'am? You look very…um, you are…"

"Pregnant, the word is pregnant, you can say it and I won't get offended. Yes, I'm fine, the warm weather just bothers me some these days, but in a coupla months…" She patted her belly and smiled.

"Well, don't mean to put you out none, ma'am. I'm just passin' through, slowly makin' my way back home to 'Bama, Citronelle, little town north of Mobile, ever hear'd-a it? Thought not, most people ain't." He looked back over to the playing field. "I love baseball, love seein' cute ballparks like this, we got League Park in Mobile, 'course, it's OK though I don't like Mobile much. If I feel like drivin' for three hours or so, Anniston's got Memorial Field, more fun an'…" He stopped, shook his head and the mustache tilted upwards. "Listen to me, prattlin' on, sorry 'bout that, I get like this 'round pretty women, sorry."

She smiled. "Thank you for the compliments, to the ballpark and to me. Now I have to tell you, you're welcome to look at the place, in fact I'd be happy to show you around, if you'd like. Our team, though, is out of town, will be for a few days yet, so I can't invite you to stay for a game."

He shrugged his shoulders. "Shoot, just my luck. Well, really shouldn't stay anyway, love to but I got people to see. Gotta be in Knoxville and then Dayton tomorrow, then Fort Payne, then…oh, there I go again, sorry. But I'd be happy to walk 'round with you for a bit, if-n you're up to it, hate to put any strain on you."

She waved her hand. "Walkin' does me and the baby a whole lotta good, according to my doctor. We just have to take it a little slow."

She gave him the standard tour and he was attentive, but he didn't act all ga-ga like so many others, and he seemed to look up a lot, paying special attention to the upper reaches of the park. It took some forty-five minutes to wander around the yard—"we'd been done in half an hour if I didn't have all this extra weight," she said with a grimace—and before he left she handed him a pocket schedule. "If you find yourself this way again, come on back and see us," to which he replied "I sure will. Thank you, ma'am, thank you very much, really 'preciate it."

He wasn't being completely truthful. He did take US 11-W down into Knoxville, but he kept going, through town, south and west, until he came to Lenoir City. A mile or so out of town, he turned onto Hurley Road, which began as dirt but quickly degenerated to simply gravel, and old gravel at that. There was no sign of life for at least two hundred yards before a ramshackle old house appeared off to the right.

Experience had taught him to blow his horn as he approached, which brought the owner to the porch, shotgun in hand. He cut the engine, slowly opened the door and yelled "Buford. Buford. Cap'n, it's me!"

Once inside, Buford Hurley proudly poured a couple of drinks. "Special stash," he said. "Made it myself, 'course, and this may be the best batch yet, if-n I do say so. Whatcha think?"

His guest practically choked. "How can you drink this stuff? Oughta pour it in my car, bet I wouldn't need none-a that dinosaur gas for a month." Didn't stop him from taking another, smaller, swallow, then he shook his head. "We had better stuff in the Philippines, Cap'n, and that practically tore a hole in my gut. I 'member you even said somethin' 'bout using it to make explosives. Doncha got any beer?"

Hurley gave him a disapproving look, then slowly got up and went to the icebox. "This is way better-n what we had out there. You gettin' soft, don't 'ppreciate good likker when it goes down your throat," he said, pulling out a bottle of Miller and setting it down on the table. "Body demands good alcohol, ya know, this shit'll kill ya."

They sat quiet for a moment, each ingesting their respective beverages, before the visitor wiped his mustache and spoke again.

"Ballpark won't work. Roof's too far off and there ain't a good 'scape route. Concourse is way too open, too many people could see me or get in the way, plus they got netting, sturdy stuff, could deflect a bullet's path. Have to be perfect shots and as good as I am, ain't real sure I could get off more-n one under these conditions. I…"

"You ain't givin' up, are ya?" asked Hurley. "I never know'd ya to be a quitter 'fore, Steve, that ain't like…"

"Who said anythin' 'bout quittin'? I'm just tellin' ya what I found. Thought I'd report in, Cap'n, letcha know why the basic plan won't work. Figgered I could stay the night here, then head on back, reconnoiter a bit. I got a few days, team is outta town 'til Friday. Lady there gave me a schedule for the rest-a the summer, so if I can't get it done this time, I know when else they'll be 'round. They play into September, you know, be plenty-a chances."

"Sooner we makes our statement, though, the better. Hear there's coupla more-a them on 'nother team, and some boys be getting' anxious."

Steve took another swig from his High Life. "Nothin' to worry 'bout, Cap'n. You hired me to do a job, you'll getcher money's worth. Like always. I ain't never letcha down." He wiped his mustache again. "Got anythin' to eat 'round here?"

THIRTEEN

While serving as business manager of the Montreal Royals in the early 1930s, the innovative Frank Shaughnessy created the post-season playoff format. Aimed at making late summer games more meaningful for both players and fans, it called for the team with the best won-lost record to play the fourth-place team, while the second and third-place teams also squared off. The winners of those two series would then face each other for the league championship. After the Mountain Empire League expanded into Virginia and Kentucky, they adopted those Shaughnessy Playoffs, and enjoyed exciting races as teams battled into September for a post-season spot.

But 1950 and 1951 were nothing compared to 1952, as every team in the league, except for Kruse, had a legitimate shot at getting into the playoffs. The Buchanan Bees had gotten off to a great start and jumped ahead early before slowly coming back to the pack, which was waiting to pounce. The Shirley Cardinals and Weare Mustangs were virtually tied for second, just two games out, the Beck Bears were only a half-game behind those two, while Edens Ridge, Mettin and Blackmer were all within another 2½ games of being in that top four. With seven weeks still to go, everyone was primed for a spectacular race that might not be decided until the last pitch of the regular season.

This upcoming long homestand, then, was critical for Edens Ridge. Weare would be coming in for three, followed by Buchanan for four (making up an early-season rainout), and would end with a home-and-home four-game series with Kruse. Playing two of the league's best, Weare and Buchanan, would be difficult even in the best of circumstances, but now—of all times, now!—the team had run into a major roadblock.

The trip to Kentucky had started off so well. The Wolves took two of three from Shirley, and almost made it a three-game sweep. The Cardinals were able to win the final game of the series when a little ninth-inning pop fly, hit by veteran slugger Mel (The Hammer) Hamilton, eluded four Edens Ridge fielders and drove home the tying and winning runs. Still, can't complain about winning a series on someone else's field, so the Wolves motored over to Blackmer for their four-game set. The Blackbirds were strong on Friday night, blasting three home runs in an 8–3 rout, but the Wolves bounced back on Saturday behind Greg Bombard's four-hit shutout, knotting the series. And when Pat Head flirted with a perfect game for $6^2/_3$ before giving up a hit in the opener of Sunday's doubleheader, the 4–1 win seemed to give momentum to Edens Ridge.

And then it shattered in an instant.

With the Wolves holding a slim 3–2 lead in the nightcap, Coach led off in the seventh. He watched two pitches go wide, then he got the inside fastball he was expecting, and hit the ball hard, just what he wanted to do. It did not, however, go through the infield or between a couple of outfielders; no, it went straight down and smashed his left ankle. Valenza immediately screamed in pain and dropped to the ground as if he'd been shot.

Jack and Mike helped their injured athlete limp off the field. Bill Quizenberry was sent up to pinch-hit for Coach (he struck out), and then went out to play shortstop in the bottom of the inning. The team seemed to lose heart, especially when Quiz made a critical error in the eighth, which keyed a three-run inning and led to a 6–4 Blackbird victory. Meanwhile, the multi-talented Hamblen quickly iced Coach's ankle and then took him to the emergency room at the local regional hospital.

Splitting a doubleheader and a four-game series on the road was generally acceptable, especially when it came against a tough playoff contender. But having to leave one of their own behind, even temporarily, made for a very somber bus ride home. Jack tried to be as upbeat as possible.

"Fellas, this is a blow, no doubt, but we're tough, we're a good team, we can get through it. Besides, everyone suffers through injuries, look at Buchanan, they lost Demeter earlier in the year and they're still in first. We don't know yet 'bout Coach, we oughta hear somethin' tomorrow or the next day, he might only be out for a little while. But we'll be fine, I have faith in you, all-a you."

The truth, of course, was different—this was devastating. Pete Sevareid got a lot of headlines because he hit homers and drove in runners, and Oddibe was, well, Oddibe. But everyone associated with the Wolves, even the kids selling popcorn in the grandstands, knew that Anthony Valenza, better known as Coach, was the most indispensable man on the team. He was a good solid shortstop who seemed to know the hitters and was therefore able to position himself so he got to more ground balls than any other infielder in the league. He complemented that talent with a strong right arm that frequently helped him get tough outs on balls hit into the hole. Quiz and Doc Andrews were the backup infielders, but neither, frankly, had the arm to be considered as a long-term option at the critical shortstop position. Now everyone was, silently, afraid that Coach would be out for quite a while, and with those games against Weare and Buchanan coming up, gloom was riding the team bus back to Tennessee.

Born in Elmwood Park, part of the Greater Chicago metropolitan area, Coach had received his nickname while still in high school. "Valenza just naturally takes charge of the infield, kind of like an on-field coach," were the first words ever written about him, in a local paper, while he was still a freshman. After graduating in 1943, he enlisted in the Army and was assigned to Major General Beightler's 37th Infantry Division, seeing action at Bougainville, Luzon and Manila. He came home unscathed and hoped to get started in baseball, but the glut of returning veterans made it nearly impossible for an untested player to get signed by a major league team. Valenza wrote to independent teams all over the country, and a fellow "goombah," Joe Valenti, signed him for his Hammond team in the Class D Evangeline League. After having a fine year for the Berries, Valenti sold his contract to the Boston Braves, and Valenza bounced around the Braves' ladder for several seasons before getting released in June of 1951.

He thought about quitting but that just wasn't in his make-up. He once again wrote to independents, and heard from someone named Jack Simpson. "Come to western Florida for spring training and we'll give you a look-see," Simpson had written. "I make no promises, you understand, other than I'll be fair in my judgment and choose the best players I see in training camp to come back to Tennessee with us. Oh, and you'll need to pay your own way to Florida." The best spring of his life secured him the job as Edens Ridge's shortstop. Yeah, he was back at the very bottom again, Class D, playing for an unaffiliated club at age 27. He could hear the clock ticking, loudly, but that was OK, it spurred him on. Besides, he was doing what he loved the most, playing baseball, so he still might have a shot of making it to the bigs.

And now this.

The next day, the report from Kentucky was about as bad as it could be: broken ankle. "It will take several days for the swelling to go down. Once it does, patient will need to be fitted for a cast, which he will wear for a period of four-to-six weeks, followed by approximately six weeks of physical therapy. Exact determinations should be made by local physician." The hospital signed him over to Doc Nelson, who authorized Mike to drive back up to Blackmer (in his own car, not the team bus) to pick up Coach and bring him back to Edens Ridge. And when Doc examined him, he simply confirmed the hospital's report—Coach's season was definitely over.

The three games with Weare proved to be a disaster. Doc Andrews started at short and made an error the first night that led to the go-ahead run as the Mustangs defeated the Wolves, 7–5. He kicked another one the following night but, more importantly, was unable to get to a couple of grounders that Coach likely would have reached, including one that slipped under his outstretched glove in the twelfth inning. The runner on first moved to third and scored moments later on a fly ball, ultimately giving Weare a 4–3 win. Quiz was back at short the next night and made no errors but he did bounce two throws, proving once and for all that he did not have the arm for shortstop. At the plate the Wolves were pathetic, managing just an eighth-inning double by Jerry Brodie, in a 3–0 whitewashing.

The clubhouse was particularly quiet after that game, which marked the first time the team had been swept all season. Before long, Allan Miggs and Squirrel Davis poked their heads into Jack's office. "Could we talk to you for a moment, skip?"

Jack and Mike had been sitting there, very quietly discussing where they might find a competent shortstop at this late date, but they waved their players in.

"We been talkin', me-n Squirrel," said Miggs, "and we was thinkin'…"

"Nothin' against Quiz, or Doc, neither, you understand, they're both good guys," said Davis, to which Miggs quickly added "Great guys, they're great guys, we got great guys on this team."

"Yeah, sure, they're great guys, I agree, but not shortstops, not startin' shortstops. What's your point?" said Jack, a little sharply.

The two ballplayers looked at each other. "Skip, I've played some third base before. I ain't no George Kell or Willie Jones, y'understand, but I can play the bag," said Miggs.

"And I've played short before. I ain't as good as Coach, that's for sure, but I can make the plays and make the throws, you know that," added Davis. "Again, I ain't… we ain't talkin' against Quiz or Doc, skip, but the team…we just thought…"

"If you're maybe tryin' to come up with somethin' different," said Miggs, "try to shake up the team a bit so we get off the schneid, you know, maybe this would…"

Simpson gave them a long, serious look. "Why don't you both meet me out here tomorrow mornin', ten o'clock, for a little infield, hmmm? That be OK?" Jack's eyes seemed to be a little brighter as he spoke, as Miggs and Davis nodded vigorously. "Good. Mike," said Jack, turning to his coach. "See if Pete can come out, too, play a little first for these guys. And I'll want you to come as well." Mike jumped up and smiled. "Sure thing, skip," he said as he went into the clubhouse to find Sevareid. A few seconds of awkward silence was broken by Jack. "Thanks, fellas. I really appreciate this." Miggs and Davis smiled, nodded, and left their manager alone.

It was pretty quiet in the car a short while later as Jack drove Oddibe and Monroe back to Light Street, but eventually the silence was broken by Daniels. "Skip, I hope I ain't outta line, but I want to tell you that I've played short before. Been a while, 2–3 years maybe, and not at this level, 'course, but I have played and I ain't bad. Better in center, that's my natural position…"

"Shit," said Hicks with a grin. Oddibe ignored him.

"All I'm sayin', skip, is I can move over there if you'd like. TVL can play center, he plays a good center, not as good as me…"

"SHIIIIIIT," Monroe said, much louder this time and drawing the word out, which actually made Jack laugh. Oddibe continued to ignore him.

"Brodie, Altman and TVL is a good outfield, I think. They can all go get 'em, got good arms…hell, I don't need to tell you. I'm just…just makin' the offer, is all."

Jack Simpson said nothing for a few seconds; it sure was quiet in the dark car. Then he spoke.

"I'll swing over here tomorrow mornin', 'bout 9:30, take you over to the park, run you through some infield drills, OK? I already got Squirrel and Miggs comin' out, so we'll see, we'll see what y'all got, see if somethin' different will help. Think you can be ready at 9:30, O?"

"That means no foolin' 'round for you tonight, my man," said Hicks with a broad grin.

Oddibe punched him in the shoulder. "Shut up, candy-ass." Then he looked at his manager. "I'll be waitin' for you on the porch, skip."

The jarring sound of the telephone woke Orley Pepper, who fumbled for the receiver.

"This Pepper?"

"Who inhell is callin' at this ungodly hour?"

"The answer to your prayers. You awake yet? I need you to have a clear head."

"Wha…who is this? What prayers? What kind of bullsh…"

"Call you back in five minutes, Pepper. Go pee, splash some cold water on your face, have some coffee or Mountain Dew. I need you to be alert. WE need you to be alert…Citizen." Click.

That last word got Orley's attention, and he followed instructions. *How did he know I had Dew in the icebox?* A few swallows did the trick, though, and he was ready for the next call.

"I'm told you have the money and you're the man I need to work with. I plan on comin' to town soon, very soon, and there's a few things I'm gonna need. Got a pencil?"

Orley searched for one that had enough lead to be usable, found it, then said "OK, ready."

"Good. First off, I'll need a map of the town, a map of Kingsport, too, and Kruse, if you can get it. No, tell you what, make that an order, I want those maps. I'll also need you to show me places where I can sleep, no hotels, just quiet, secluded areas, away from main drags, understand me? When I come to town we'll meet somewhere and then we'll drive around and you can show 'em to me. I'll need to look things over, scope everythin' out, 'cludin' different ways to get outta town, good ones, maybe ones that don't get used much…"

"Yes, sir, but we're a small town, ain't a whole lotta ways in and out and…"

"FIND 'em!" The voice on the other end of the line was sharp and emphatic. "That's your major assignment, Pepper, that and those maps. This is your town, I was told you're the man to know, the man who can help…help me the most, so find 'em. Be creative. You wouldn't want me to go back and tell people that you failed, would you? Would you?"

"No sir, not at all, sir, no sir. Don't worry, I'll get you what you need, you can trust me, I'm your guy. Sir."

"Good. We're countin' on you, Pepper. I'll be back in touch in a few days, then we can make more direct plans. Where's a good place for us to meet? Tell ya, it'd be nice if there was cold beer on tap."

"Warren's Watering Well is the best place in Edens Ridge for that. The only place, actually. It's on Fifth and…"

"Save it, you can give me directions next time I call. Oh, and one other thing, Pepper. I wouldn't mind me some female companionship when I get to town, you know? Got any whorehouses there in that burg-a yours?"

Orley smiled. "Oh yes, sir, we sure do. I think you'll like it real well, and not just cause-a the girls, neither. There's a coupla boys livin' there, right in the house, and I'll bet you can guess their names and…"

"Hush up, Pepper. That's all we need to say to each other right now. You'll be hearin' from me, make sure you get me those maps and have everythin' else worked out in your head." Click.

McDermott Brothers Flooring and Carpets generally stayed open until 6 pm, as a convenience for working folks. On game days, though, Wes McDermott knew that his brother would be out the door no later than 4 pm, maybe even a few minutes before that, because he loved getting to the ballpark early. As the public address announcer for the Edens Ridge Wolves, he really only had one major responsibility before the game began—write down the starting lineups for the two teams. (If anyone had a new player on the roster, he also wanted to make sure he could correctly pronounce their name. Bill prided himself on his professionalism, as well as his diction.) But he liked being at the ballpark and hanging around with ballplayers; "beats selling carpet for a living," he had said more than once.

Besides, this series with Buchanan had now become crucial for "The Ridge." Having lost all three games to Weare, the Wolves had slipped to sixth place, four games out of a playoff spot and a mere half-game ahead of Blackmer. If they were going to try to climb back into the post-season picture, they were going to have to do it right now, against the league's best team, and with a gaping hole at short. All this should make for some interesting conversation in the clubhouse and out by the batting cage, and if there was one thing Bill loved it was talking baseball with baseball guys.

He was expecting a quiet clubhouse, but instead it was lively and full of chatter. Quiz and Doc, who had both been trying (unsuccessfully, in Bill's opinion) to fill Coach Valenza's shortstopping shoes, were being interviewed, in tandem, by Win Appleton. Bill saw some of the other players drifting over that way to say something to the two infielders, and his internal warning system started flashing. *Something's up,* he thought. *Have they been released, or traded? No, not likely, they're both in their uniforms. What's going on?*

He decided to question Mac McElvain, who was lacing up his cleats. He began walking over to his locker, but his journey was interrupted by the voice of Jack Simpson.

"All right, mullions, let's get out there. We got plenty-a work to do, boys, plenty-a work, so c'mon, get to it"

Bill checked his watch and was surprised, this was a good twenty minutes before they normally went onto the field for batting practice. He expected to hear a chorus of complaints from the athletes, but instead there were several remarks of "OK" and "let's go," and a couple of enthusiastic shouts of "yeah!" To a man, the players ran around him and out onto the field as if they were high school kids about to play for the state championship. Quizenberry and Andrews were the last ones out the door, and Bill tried to engage them, either of them, briefly, but Quiz just said, "Can't talk, Bill, gotta get out onto the field."

The manager, meanwhile, handed Bill that night's lineup, then followed his athletes. McDermott glanced at it briefly, looked around and saw Win Appleton still in the locker room, jotting in his ever-present notepad. He walked over to the writer, who glanced up and gave him a quick smile.

"Damndest thing," said Win. "But I guess you gotta give Jack credit, he's tryin', and the guys are still tryin', they haven't gotten down, not too much, anyway. And Quiz and Doc, they're OK, they're puttin' the best face on it. They've both had a chance to step up, take over at short, and they've both fucked it up, can't blame anyone but themselves."

"What are you talking about, Win?" asked Bill. "Who's at short tonight? We got a new player?"

Appleton chuckled. "That tonight's lineup there in your hand?" Bill nodded. "You might wanna look at it before you flip on your mike."

Bill unfolded the hand-written sheet, studied at it carefully, and let out with a "Huh!"

1)	Daniels	6
2)	Davis	5
3)	McElvain	4
4)	Sevareid	3
5)	VanLandingham	8
6)	Hicks	2
7)	Brodie	7
8)	Head	1
9)	Altman	9

"Oddibe is…wait, is this right? This can't be right. Oddibe playing short, the pitcher is batting eighth and Altman is batting ninth? Who made this lineup? Who wrote this?"

"Who handed it to you?" asked Appleton with a smirk, and when McDermott said "Jack," the reporter just grinned, said "Uh huh," and walked out.

Unbeknownst to Bill McDermott, Jack Simpson had called Win Appleton around one o'clock to tell him what he had decided to do. He called Lionel Ticknor at the Holston Hotel and told him there'd be a slight change in the batting and fielding practice schedules. He grabbed Quiz and Doc as soon as each of them had arrived at the ballpark and explained it to them.

"This is just an experiment, fellas, I want to see what kind-a options I've got. Tomorrow I'm gonna play Miggsy at third and Squirrel at short and see how that goes. Meanwhile I'd like you both to keep workin' on your glovework and throws, especially from the hole, OK? You are both valuable members of this team and will stay that way, understood? Any questions?"

There were none. Next step, then, was to speak privately with Jim Altman.

"You're startin' tonight, battin' ninth. I want you to understand—this DOES NOT mean I think Pat Head is a better hitter-n you. Just the opposite, actually. I like the idea of havin' you and Oddibe hittin' back-to-back…"

"I could bat second, skip, I've done it before," said Altman.

"Sure, you could, and I thought about it. But Squirrel is great in the two-hole, you know that, we've seen it all season, and I decided it would be best to leave him there. And like I said, if you're ninth, then after the first inning it's you and O and I can just see the two of you creatin' chaos out there, hit-and-run, things like that. Whaddya say, Alt-Man?"

The outfielder scowled. He was still uncomfortable having Negroes on the team, and now his manager wanted him to join the speedy coon (as opposed to the husky coon) as part of some new team strategy. *Won't ever work, whoever heard of someone other than the pitcher battin' ninth? But he is the boss, and I want to play so I guess I gotta go along.* "Yeah, I see your point. Yeah, skip, this could be fun. Different, at least."

Batting practice for the Wolves normally began at 4:45 pm, but today they got started at 4:30 pm. The Bees went out there at 5:30 pm, then at 6:20 pm Edens Ridge came back out for extended fielding practice, specifically to give Oddibe a few more pre-game reps at short.

It was a pretty typical Thursday night, with (eventually) 641 in the stands, but there was a collective gasp when McDermott read the lineup over the PA. The fans were agog. *Oddibe at short and the pitcher batting eighth? Has Jack flipped his lid?*

Crazy like a fox was more accurate. Daniels didn't make any errors, though he was not able to get the ball out of his glove when he had to go into the hole in the second inning, Appleton generously ruling it an infield single. Later in the game, however, he flashed behind the bag at second and flagged down a ball that seemed to be heading into center field, easily making the throw to Pete for the out. He and Mac also smoothly turned two double plays to help Pat Head stay in the game until the seventh. And he and Altman did execute one hit-and-run which keyed a three-run third, giving the Wolves a lead they never relinquished in their 6–4 victory.

Jack hated to break up a winning combination but he had made a commitment, so the next night, with 1,380 on hand, Squirrel Davis moved over to short and Allan Miggs played third, while Oddibe went back to center, VanLandingham slid back over to right and Altman sat. The results were the same, primarily because Tommy Nathan pitched his best game of the year, giving up only three hits, one of which was a two-run homer, the only major blemish in his 5–2 win.

Great crowd the next night. Weeks ago, Nashota had set up a promotion with area Cub Scouts and Boy Scouts. Kids in uniform got in for a quarter, and with no threat of rain on a Saturday, and two straight wins over the first-place team, they came pouring in. Unfortunately, the "Altman lineup" wasn't up to the task, and despite a ninth-inning rally, 2,726 went home disappointed with a 6–5 loss.

Back to the "Miggs lineup" on Sunday. Smaller crowd, of course, because it was Sunday, but 1,117 was OK, and Greg Bombard was on, getting the Bees to flail at his curve as if he was Sal Maglie. Miggs was the game's other hero, with Win Appleton writing "he was plus-two for the day." In the second he singled home Brodie, then in the sixth the Bees' pitcher left a fastball up and Miggs got all of it, driving it over the left-field fence, scoring Hicks ahead of him. Those more than made up for his error in the top of the inning, which led to a Buchanan run. Bombard was able to nurse his cushion into the eighth, when Larry West came in and got the last four outs in the 4–2 win, putting the Wolves just four games out of first, even though they sat in fifth place.

Jack felt he needed to see more, though, so he continued to alternate the two lineups. A series in Weare produced three more tough games, though, so by the time the team bus pulled into Buchanan, he was ready to make a commitment...almost. First he needed to have breakfast with Mike Hamblen.

"We been movin' guys around for better-n a week now, Mike, I'd like to hear your thoughts."

Mike took a bite out of his sausage biscuit. "You're the manager, Jack, the final call is yours. I'll support you, whatever you decide."

"I know that, dumb-ass," growled Jack. "You don't hafta give me a lesson in How to Be a Minor League Manager. I think I know what I wanna do, but I'm askin' for your opinion. Should we keep alternatin' lineups, or just stick to one, and if we pick one, which is the best?" Mike was mute, like he suddenly did not understand the English language. "I really would like your thoughts here, Mike. Look, I know that someday you want to be a manager and you may have to make a decision like this. What would you do if this was your ballclub?"

Hamblen put down his fork. "OK, since you want to know. Oddibe's a good shortstop, better-n Quiz and Doc. But he's a great centerfielder. A GREAT centerfielder. In a coupla years, he'll be as good as DiMaggio ever was, and I mean Dom, he was the better fielder, in my opinion. TVL can sub for him well enough, but we lose a little somethin' out there by movin' O to short. Squirrel does OK at short, he's better at third but he can make the plays, and we keep his bat in the lineup. Miggsy's been swingin' good lately and we sure need all the hits we can get. That's what I'd do, skip, since you asked."

Jack nodded. "Exactly what I been thinkin'," he said. "But we'd need to get a new backup catcher, can I activate you?"

"Me? I'm a little old for this league. Shit, I'm a little old for most leagues, 'cept for the American, eh? If I was on the Tigers, their average age would drop. And just think, if I was on the Browns and caught Satch, we'd prob'ly set some sorta record for the oldest battery ever!"

"It would only be for emergency purposes. If I need to take Hicks out for a pinch-runner, say, I can move Miggsy back-a the plate and put Quiz or Doc in at third."

"No, you can't. Jack, neither-a those guys can play third, even for an inning, they don't have the arms. Truthfully, since we're layin' 'em out here, I think they're both horseshit players. Good guys but horseshit players, and we're tryin' to win games. I think we oughta get rid-a them, at least one, bring in someone who can make the throws, you know? Be good if he can hit a little, too, but we really need someone who can throw. Hey, maybe Buck knows how to play third, you can put him in there in a pinch." He laughed.

"One crisis at a time, Mike," said Jack with a smile. "We move Squirrel to short and Miggs to third full-time, O plays center every day, we activate you temporarily while we look for a new backup catcher, that sound right?" Hamblen nodded. Jack took a bite of his pancake, then said "And I'll see about findin' a better infielder for the left side. Not the top priority, understand, but I'll make some calls."

Jack had Nashota file the activation form on Hamblen, then later on, at the ballpark, he called Miggs and Davis into his office and told them what he had decided. That went well, as expected; different story with Jim Altman.

"Back to the bench? Why? I been doin' good out there, skip, doncha think? I..."

"It's not you, Jim, it's shortstop, we need a shortstop, you know that, and I like Squirrel out there better-n Oddibe. And if Squirrel plays short then I need Miggs at third, and O goes back to center, TVL goes back to right, and..."

"And I get fucked," yelled Altman. "I deserve better-n this, Jack. I can play this fuckin' game, almost made Double-A three years ago, Beaumont, and now I can barely get ABs in a backwater, piece-a-shit, n—-lovin' indy D-league. It sucks! It sucks, skip, you suck, this whole fuckin' world sucks!" He slammed the door as he stormed out.

The "Miggs" lineup produced five runs that night against the Bees, often enough for a win but not when the pitchers get roughed up for 11. The Wolves rebounded the next night, however, with a crisp 4–2 triumph. In the morning, Jim Altman was waiting for Jack in the hotel lobby.

"Pretty early for you, ain't it, Alt-Man? asked Jack, with a sense of uneasiness.

"I wanted to talk, skip, and thought this might be the best time to catch you."

They both ordered some breakfast and then Altman confirmed his manager's fears. "I think I can play, Jack, and I'm not gettin' the chance here. When we get back to Edens Ridge, I think I'll just pack up my shit and go on home. We got a team there in Hannibal, the Stags, I might be able to catch on with them for the last few weeks, then decide what I wanna do next year, and the year after…" He smiled thinly. "And the year after that."

"You could do that just as well here, Jim. You don't know if they'll have a spot for you in Hannibal, least here you're gettin' a paycheck, guaranteed 'til the end of the season, and we still got a shot at the playoffs. You get home, the Stags are full-up, now you ain't playin' AND there ain't no money comin' in. Why don't you just stick 'round here, could be fun down the stretch." Altman didn't seem to be moved, however, so Simpson played another hand. "Tell ya what, and this is just 'tween you-n me, but I'll guarantee you more starts in left. Brodie, I think he might be wearin' down a bit and could use more time off. How 'bout I tell you right here, man to man, that you'll be in the startin' lineup two…no, three games a week, every week, and if you get in a good groove, you'll stay there. That seems fair, don't it? Whaddya say, Alt-Man, let's see if we can chase down a playoff spot together?"

Altman stood up, took two dollars out of his wallet and handed it to his manager. "For breakfast," he said, then he glanced down at the table before looking Jack right in the eyes. "I think I just wanna go home, skip. Sorry."

"Win probably thought this was amusing," yelled Jack. "Well, I'm not fuckin' amused!" He threw the newspaper down on the kitchen table and stomped outside.

Nashota slowly walked over and picked up the *Gazette*. Jack often grumbled about something Win had written, but he rarely got angry, or marched off like that. And he never cussed this early in the morning, especially these last few months during Nashota's pregnancy. She had even asked him about it. "'Sho, I know this'll prob'ly sound crazy, but what if our baby can already hear us, and understand us? I mean, we don't know, right? If he can hear us, well shit, instead of the usual wailin' when he's born, he might just come out the chute swearin' like a ballplayer! And if he's a she…oh, brother!"

She had gotten a big kick out of that. Win Appleton's article, however, was different. Nashota started reading and quickly decided to complete the article sitting down.

HELP WANTED:
CATCHER, OUTFIELDER, MAYBE AN INFIELDER, TOO
By Win Appleton

Edens Ridge, TN—As the weather gets hotter and the days and nights get longer, it's not unusual for all sorts of aches and pains to finally begin catching up with a baseball team. In the case of our hometown Edens Ridge Wolves, however, it is manager Jack Simpson who seems to be the one who most needs a good rubdown, maybe even a few days in Warm Springs, Georgia.

That's because what he needs the most is a new catcher—again!—plus a new outfielder and, maybe, a new face for the infield. All in July, when we have already zoomed past the halfway point in the baseball season. Most teams are pretty well satisfied with their rosters by now, and any unemployed ballplayers are out of work for a reason, with that reason being they're not all that good.

Let's break it down. When starting shortstop (and Most Indispensable Player) Anthony "Coach" Valenza was lost for the season with a broken ankle, a new shortstop had to be found. After trying several different combinations, Simpson has apparently decided on moving third baseman Ronnie "Squirrel" Davis over to short and installing catcher Allan Miggs at the hot corner. That's why a catcher is needed, because as strong as Monroe Hicks seems to be (try shaking hands with him sometime, you'll quickly understand!), he is also very inexperienced, and at the very least will need a day off every now and then. And if you put Miggs back behind the plate... wait, I'm getting ahead of myself.

Then there's the need for an outfielder. The NEW need for an outfielder. Unable to dislodge the starting trio of Jerry Brodie, Oddibe Daniels and Terry VanLandingham, Jim Altman packed up his bags and went home to Missouri, suddenly making another outfielder a necessity.

OK, the Wolves need a catcher and an outfielder, but why an infielder? Bill Quizenberry and Richard "Doc" Andrews are still on the roster and are capable backups, right? Well, that depends on your definition of "capable." Both are adept at second base, but Jack Simpson's recent experimentation proved to him—and anyone with two reasonably-functioning eyes—that neither had the range nor arm strength to play shortstop. And if that position was challenging, it doesn't take a baseball genius to realize that third base would be simply impractical. Which means if you move Miggs behind the plate, even for an inning, you're left with two options at third, bad and just-as-bad. Hence, from the perspective of this writer, there is a dire need for a new infielder, one that can play the left side without making everyone hold their breath when a ground ball is hit their way.

But where do you find even one decent ballplayer at this time of year, let alone three? That's a question that would likely stump even the knowledgeable "Information Please" panel. Simpson seems to have his work cut out for him.

Nashota started to stand up, had difficulty, sat back down and called out to her husband, who was still outside. "Jack, give me a hand, please," she said. He hustled back in and grasped her extended arm, giving her the lift she needed. "Whose idea was it to have children?" she asked, "and why does it have to be so damned uncomfortable?" He was not familiar with the next few words she angrily tossed out, but he suspected that, if he ever uttered their English equivalent to an umpire, it would get him banished to the clubhouse for the rest of the night.

Jack waited for the brief explosion to end, then he said "Sorry I cussed like that, 'Sho, but that column just…man, I never get that mad at Win, but you read it, right? He not only talks about our personnel problems, he's positively mean to both Quiz and Doc. He's right, neither one-a them can play short or third, but he shouldn't say that in the paper, not like that. They never did nothin' to him, far as I know. He and I'll be havin' words later today, you can count on that."

Calmer now, she looked at him and smiled. "Don't be too hard on Win, he's just trying to help, and he's probably almost as frustrated as you are. Besides, it might prove to be the kick in the butt that Doc and Quiz need."

"You're always the optimist," he said, as she grunted while slowly walking to the sink for a glass of water. "Well, most of the time, when you're not…you know…like this."

"You mean pregnant? You can say the word, Jack, it's a condition, not an insult."

Retreat! Retreat! "Point is, no matter what Win writes, no matter how hard they try, Doc and Quiz have to play with the cards they've been dealt. Neither were given strong throwin' arms, that's all there is to it. I'm gonna need to find someone who can back us up on the left side." He smiled. "Maybe one-a those words you spouted out a moment ago would be appropriate for me right now, wanna give me a lesson?"

That made her laugh. "Last time I taught you a few Cherokee cuss words, you got run anyway. You might as well just stick with English, *tsu-na-da-da-tlu-gi*."

Information began coming in quietly to police departments, large and small, throughout the Southeast. *Be on the lookout for a white male, medium height, muscular, close-cropped hair, last known to sport a full mustache. Extremely proficient with all kinds of weapons, especially guns. Has used a variety of names including Alan Michaels, Michael Allen, Steven Darby, Richard Howe, Harley Puckett, Mark Mundy, Carl Swain, Charlie Davis, and no doubt many more.* **Is extremely dangerous.**

They had known Wells Boggs was coming, he had called Nashota a few days earlier to say he'd be making one of his regular in-season visits when Beck and Mettin came to town. He didn't say anything, though, about his guest.

"I swear, darlin', I didn't know he was comin', he literally walked into the hotel 'bout two minutes after I did," said Boggs. He and Nashota were looking at Bob

Rhodes, who was using the office phone to call Marge in Columbus to see if he had any messages. "Don't know what he's doin' here, honest I don't, maybe it's just a friendly visit, like mine." He smiled when she looked skeptical. "'Course, as it turns out, you may be needin' some extra help today, eh? Got some special mornin' promotion?"

Nashota sighed. She truthfully had no idea what was going on. All she knew was that about a half-hour after she got to the park, young men started showing up and knocking on the office door. A couple were wearing softball uniforms, but most were just in jeans, and all were carrying cleats and gloves.

"I read the article in this morning's paper, ma'am, and I wanted to try out..." "Read what Win Appleton done wrote and thought I'd offer up my services..." "I'm a damn...'scuse me, ma'am...darn good outfielder, and..." "Got a gun for an arm, everybody says so, man's gotta be faster-n Pee Wee or that Cuban mother...er, Minoso, to steal off-a me..." "Been playin' third all-a my life, was born to play third, ma'am, if you just give me a chance..."

She had called Jack, who was surprisingly calm, more than she was, actually, which was unusual. "Have 'em sit in the stands, tell 'em it might be a while, maybe an hour, 'fore we can get people there, but we'll at least talk to 'em all. But whatinhell is Bob Rhodes doin' here?" Funny, that was what got a rise out of him. "Maybe you can find out" was the last thing he said as he hung up.

"I'm just making my usual rounds, is all," Bob said. "Spent a few days in North Carolina, checking in on the Coastal Plain League. Ever heard of Roanoke Rapids? Little town, maybe 8,000 or so, right near the Virginia border...don't matter. They got this kid, Ted Abernathy, tall and husky and I stayed an extra day just so I could see him pitch. And man, Nashota, can he throw! Side-armer, you know what that is, right? Thought so. Anyway, this is his first season as a pro, and those Coastal Plain hitters can't touch him. Team's only so-so, hangin' 'round .500, mainly cause-a Abernathy. He could win twenty in his first year, first God-damn year! Only 19..." Bob always could ramble on if he was talking baseball.

Mike Hamblen showed up a short while later and Jack followed right behind, accompanied by both Oddibe and Monroe; Pete Sevareid and Buck Hightower appeared moments later. The Wolves contingent then assembled in the grandstand, standing in the walkway to face all the would-be ballplayers. Rhodes, Boggs and even Nashota decided to sit down and eavesdrop.

"Boys," said Jack. "I'm Jack Simpson, I'm the manager and general manager of the Edens Ridge baseball team. I'm sure you know we are professionals, members of the Class D Mountain Empire League. Our league president, Mr. Wells Boggs, just happens to be visitin' us today, he's sittin' right over there, wearin' that very red sport coat." Jack waved his hand in Wells' general direction, then grinned. "Wells, it's gonna get plenty warm here today, you might wanna ditch that jacket." There were a couple of low snickers, Wells just smiled and nodded.

"I appreciate your comin' out here today. I hafta admit, I'm surprised, I wasn't expectin' any kind-a reaction to Win Appleton's piece..." Jack stole a quick glance at Nashota, who rolled her eyes. "...but at the very least this shows you can all read..."

(That brought some chuckles) "…and that you are all willin' to take some initiative. In case you don't know that word, it's a good thing, boys, a good thing."

He looked around him for a second or two, then continued. "Now these fellas standin' here are all members of the Wolves, they're all my players except for this mullion standin' next to me, he's my coach and bussie and trainer and all sorts-a other things. Mike Hamblen. They was all good enough to agree to come out here and help us work y'all out, see if anyone can maybe play in this-here league. Now lemme ask you, anyone-a you a catcher?" Two people, including a tall man who was the only Negro in the group, raised their hands. "Good, we're gonna start with you first. This big drink-a-water is Buck Hightower, one-a my best guys outta the bullpen, real reliable, throws a good heater and slider and slow ball, too. I wanna see each one-a you catch his stuff. We'll start with that, OK? Rest-a you, limber up a bit, like you would 'fore a game, then you shortstops and second basemen, go man the infield, let these catchers feel like there's a real game goin' on in front-a them. All right, let's go!"

They all went out on the field. Mike caught Buck's warm-up throws, then yielded his spot to one of the two catching applicants, the white one, who got into his crouch as Mike stood behind him, like an umpire. Buck began throwing fastballs, then followed with breaking pitches, some of which he deliberately threw wide and in the dirt. After maybe five or six minutes, Jack nodded at Oddibe, who trotted over to first base.

"This is Oddibe Daniels," said Jack to the young backstop, who was now standing. "He may be the fastest player in our league, he's certainly the best base stealer. We're gonna test your arm, son." Then he looked at the fellows hanging around the infield. "I want different people to cover the bag," he shouted. "First one, then another and another. Got it? Don't matter to me who goes first."

The young man proved to have a good arm, as did the Negro catcher when he got behind the plate. Neither, however, was able to nab Oddibe attempting to steal either second or third base. Mike then donned the catching gear—often dubbed "the tools of ignorance"—and both young men were given an opportunity to swing the bat. It was here that the Negro separated himself, hitting several line drives to left and left-center, balls that most likely would be hits unless a superior outfielder was able to run them down. The ball really "jumped" off his bat, unlike the other fellow.

"Let's take five," yelled Jack. He then went over to both men, spoke to them quietly and shook their hands. In the stands, Nashota saw her husband point to her, then nod in the direction of the Negro. She watched both of the catching aspirants climb back into the stands, but the white man just kept walking and left the ballpark, while the black man came up to her.

"Mr. Simpson says the pretty lady will give me an official contract. Those were his words, ma'am." He smiled.

Bob Rhodes walked over to him. "I've seen you before, haven't I? Didn't you play in Canada a few years back?"

"Yes sir, I did. Our St. Jean Braves team won the Provincial League championship in '49. How'd you remember that?"

Bob laughed. "Part of my job is to remember talented players. And do I remember you have an…er, unusual first name?"

Now it was the young man's turn to laugh. "Yes sir, I surely do. Yam Yarnell, at your service."

"Yam, that really is unusual. May I ask, how did you get the name of Yam?" Nashota inquired.

"Yam, Yam," mused Bob. "There was a player named Yam something…Yam… Yaryan, that's it, played a little for the White Sox, I think, long time ago. Think I saw him play somewhere…"

"Yes sir, that's him, Yam Yaryan. Played in Birmingham a lotta years, that's where I was born."

"I played in Birmingham," said Rhodes. "Part of '17 and '19. That would have been long before Yam got there."

"My daddy, he's a great baseball fan, he might-a seen you play! But ol' Yam was his favorite player, don't know why, 'zactly. Maybe 'cause he could hit like a sonofa…'scuse me, ma'am, I just mean to say that ol' Yam was quite the hitter, power and a high average, so my daddy insisted on that name for me. Funny thing is that Yam was just a nickname for Mr. Yaryan, I learned that his real name was Clarence, but me, mine's Yam, and I'm pretty proud-a it. Gets your tenshun, don't it?" And they all chuckled.

"Well Yam, let's you-n I go into the office, and we'll get you to sign a contract. I also have some information that I'm required to give all players, a list of league rules, then we'll go find you a uniform. Come with me, and please forgive me for moving slow, as you can see…" She patted her very pregnant self as the two of them walked off.

"'Member this winter, Bob?" It was the soft drawl of Wells Boggs, who had been silently observing all this time. "Not really that long ago, but…" He smiled wistfully. "We talked 'bout all the things we needed to do to prepare for Oddibe Daniels. Was a big deal, and still is, 'course, but now…" he said, waving his arm in the direction of the Wolves' office. "Edens Ridge is signin' their third Negro player, and Kruse got two. Buchanan even thinkin-a addin' one, backup infielder named…shoot, what's his name? Can't remember right now." He looked directly at Rhodes. "Point is, we never had none 'fore and now, in less-n a year, we've added five Negro players, maybe six. Hope you remember that this winter, Bob Rhodes, when I work on gettin' us some big-league 'filiations." Then he turned back to the field, where the tryouts were continuing.

Monroe was hitting grounders to several young men who were all stationed between second and third. Each player was asked to simply field the ball and throw it over to first, where Pete was stationed. Oddibe, meanwhile, was hitting fungoes to the two outfielders who had come out. Jack and Mike were standing in foul territory, just a few yards beyond first base, giving them a good vantage point to watch and evaluate all the aspiring Wolves. Buck, meanwhile, was lounging in the dugout, enjoying the break. Finally Jack hollered out "OK, come on in," which brought Buck off the bench. As the group of hopefuls jogged in, he ambled over to his manager and coach on his way to the mound.

"See that skinny little kid over there, one with the sandy hair? Just crossed over the mound…yeah, him. Way I see it, if he can hit, even a little, he's our guy. Moves real smooth out there and he's got a good arm. Not great, not like Coach, but good. Can see him getting' a little playin' time at short. Just my opinion," he shrugged, and walked out to the mound.

Batting practice was relatively short. Each player got about a dozen swings, and then Jack called a halt. It was late July, after all, and the sun was already starting to make things hot and he did not want to tire his regulars before the game against Beck that night. He sent all the job applicants back to the grandstand. "Just wait for us there, we'll join you in a few minutes," and he led his players into the clubhouse so they could all offer their viewpoints.

Sitting there in the stands, no one spoke. It was eerie, almost as if they were at a funeral, or taking an exam. It even affected Bob and Wells, who kept their whispered conversation to a minimum. When Nashota returned and slowly made her way down the stairs, the noise of her shoes almost sounded like a gong.

"What's going on?" she asked, in a normal voice.

"We're waiting for Jack to come back," whispered Bob, to which Wells added (also in *sotto voce*), "They're waitin' to see if any-a them got chosen. Like the cullud feller earlier."

"I figured that," said Nashota, now speaking very quietly. "But why are we whispering?"

Rhodes shrugged. Boggs began—"Well, you see...," then abandoned his thought when Jack, Mike and the players reappeared on the walkway, facing the seated aspirants. The manager cleared his throat.

"I want to thank all-a you for comin' out. When that article appeared this morning, I gotta tell ya, it was a surprise to me, I didn't ask Win to write it, I didn't know he was writin' it, and I was kinda upset when I read it. But now I'm happy it was there, because I got to see some...some nice players. You all did real well out there today, and I wish I could offer jobs to all-a you. But I can't."

There was some uncomfortable shifting of butts.

Jack looked at the sandy-haired boy whom Buck had identified. "You, what's your name?"

The young man pointed to himself and asked "Me?" Jack nodded, said "Yes, you," and the boy responded "Danny, sir, Danny Chase."

"You looked good in the infield, Danny Chase, ever play any outfield?"

Young Mr. Chase had started to smile, but his mouth quickly turned down. "Just a bit, sir, but honestly, not all that much, maybe just a coupla innings here or there. Infield's really my..."

"Stop," said Jack. "I got eyes, I know what I saw." He turned to Oddibe and they spoke quietly for a brief moment, then he turned back to his assembly. "You, wearing the Dobyns-Bennett shirt, what's your name?"

The young man jumped up. "I'm Raburn Reece, sir" he drawled.

"You still in school, Raburn Reece? Same question for you, Chase."

Both shook their heads but Wells Boggs immediately spoke. "Gonna need proof-a age, boys." There was no response. "I'm the league president, 'member? We require everyone to be at least 18 years old and outta school. Don't matter if you got a diploma, you just gotta be outta school."

Both boys fumbled for their driver's licenses and showed them to Wells. "I just graduated," said Chase, while Reece said, "I got out last year."

"Either-a you workin'?" Jack asked. Chase shook his head while Reece said "Was workin' at Eastman for a while but I quit that in the spring, it was really boring. My uncle owns a construction business and I'm workin' with him 'til I figure out what I really wanna do."

Jack nodded. "Can I assume that you're both free to play with the Wolves for the next few weeks? You both have to understand, you'll be backups only, bench players, nothin' more. You'll have limited playin' time, and it's just for the balance of this season, that's all I'm concerned about right now. Got that, mullions?" Reece smiled and nodded, but Chase was simply beside himself. "Yes, sir, yes, sir, I understand, sir. I'm so grateful for this opportunity, sir, I've always wanted to play baseball, you won't be sorry, sir…"

"Enough!" Jack's sharp tone immediately quieted the boy. "No need to call me 'sir,' I ain't your dad. I'm Jack, or skipper, or skip, that's it." He took a breath, then continued. "You two go into the office, and my wife…" He nodded in Nashota's direction, as she eased herself up. "…will get you all fixed up. The rest of you, again, 'preciate your comin' out, sorry I…"

Mike stepped forward and whispered in the manager's ear. Jack nodded and continued.

"My coach here, Mike Hamblen, has a good suggestion. Why don't y'all go into the office and write down your names, addresses, phone numbers if you got one, and what position or positions you play. Then you can go. 'Sho, you can have Chase and Reece start fillin' out their paperwork while you collect contact info on these boys."

As everyone stood and started heading for the office, Wells walked over to Simpson.

"Jack, I think you may be forgettin' somethin' here." The manager looked quizzically at his league president. "How many on your roster right now? Right now, as we speak?"

"Well, Altman's gone, and Coach is gone, of course, 'least til next spring and maybe forever, though I been thinkin'…"

"Numbers, Jack, numbers. League rules say you can't have more-n 19 on your roster at any time. How many you got now?"

"17, Wells, and these two new boys…"

"No, you got 18. Did you forget, you activated Mike, here, coupla days ago? You got 18 right now, and just today you had Nashota sign that big ni…big catcher, one that Bob saw play in Canada, 'member? I assume he signed a contract when he went into the office. He's number 19, Jack, and these two boys would make 21 and you'd be over the line. I'd hafta fine the ballclub for breaking the rules, and two people would be declared ineligible for the rest-a the season. 'Course, I assume that this Canada boy's replacin' Mike and we can get him off-a the active roster real quick-like, but you'd still be one over."

Simpson was looking at him rather blankly. "My numbers are good, Jack, trust me here, this is a big part-a my job, after all. Way I see it, you got a decision or two to make here, son. You wanna sign all these fellas, that's fine, but I figure you first need to deactivate Mike and then cut someone else. Understand what I'm sayin'?"

The Mountain Empire League

"Shit!" was Jack's response, and he bolted for the office, taking two steps at a time and yelling "Chase! Nashota! Wait! Wait!" Jack Simpson probably hadn't run that quickly since the Netherlands, maybe even Normandy.

Out of breath, he explained the situation, making sure to add "It's just a temporary glitch. We still want you," he said to Chase, who had been reading the contract. "We just have to do somethin' today to make room for you so we ain't breakin' league rules. Just come back tomorrow afternoon, say around 3 pm, bring your gear, come into the office here, sign the contract and then I'll take you into the clubhouse myself. OK?"

Chase was a little disappointed. In his head he was already a member of the team, taking part in infield drills, getting into the batting cage, bantering with the guys, his teammates, being a BALLPLAYER. Yeah, sure, he could wait 'til tomorrow, what's one more day, but in the back of his mind there was a little voice whispering *What if they can't clear up this glitch? What if this is as close as you ever come? You were practically there, you were holding the contract in your hand, and then...WOOSH, they pull it away, right outta your hands. Could that be it, could that be the end of your dream?*

And it had been his dream, ever since his father had taken him to see the new Kingsport Cherokees in 1938. He fell in love with the game, learned how to hold a bat, how to slide, how to make a proper throw. When Little League Baseball came to Northeast Tennessee, seven-year-old Danny Chase started playing on an actual team, and he soaked up everything his coaches taught him. At Lynn View High School, he took over the starting shortstop position as a sophomore and held it for his final three years on campus. He and Raburn Reece had a nodding acquaintance, since Lynn View and Dobyns-Bennett were long-standing rival Kingsport high schools. Taller and older by a year, Reece swung from both sides of the plate and could hit most pitches with real authority. He wasn't a great outfielder but he caught everything he could reach. Since high school, however, he had gone to several try-outs and there always seemed to be someone who was just a little better, a little faster, a little more, oh, hungry, and that guy, that was the guy who got the contract. This time, however, would be different. Now, in late July of 1952, Raburn Reece finally signed a contract to play professional baseball, with the Edens Ridge Wolves. And Danny Chase was told he'd be signed tomorrow. *Just wait 'til tomorrow, they said, sure hope they're tellin' me the truth.* He wasn't sure he'd be able to sleep and, as it turned out, sleep proved to be difficult for many in the Mountain Empire that night.

For Jack, perhaps the toughest part of being a manager came when he had to cut a player, and as Wells had so correctly pointed out (later confirmed by Nashota), someone had to go. Mike had no problem with being deactivated; he was, in fact, relieved that they had not needed him to go into a ballgame. But one of the infielders had to be released, and that was painful. Jack and Mike spent the better part of an hour discussing the pros and cons of Bill Quizenberry and Richard Andrews. "Neither one's ever gonna be a star, or even solidify someone's infield," said Jack. Nor did one have a distinct advantage over the other, offensively or defensively. (A Shakespearean scholar might have compared them to a minor league version of Rosencrantz and Guildenstern.) In the end, it was an off-field activity that tipped the scales. Andrews was known to everyone as Doc, had been for years, because he was studying to be a dentist, and was really only playing ball so he could help pay his tuition at Michigan. That, ultimately gave him the final edge. Jack told Quiz when he got to the ballpark, and frankly the New Jersey native took it better than his manager.

"I figured you was gonna hafta make a move, skip, and I thought it might be me. I 'preciate your tellin' me straight off like this. Ya needs me to clear out right away, or what?"

"No, Quiz, new guy won't start 'til tomorrow. Stick around, I'll even get you in the game tonight, if you'd like."

"Sure, skip, I can do that," Quiz said. "Maybe you can give me an AB? Might be my last, don't know if I'll try to play anywheres next year. Ain't gettin' no younger, and no better, I guess. My girl back in Passaic, her dad builds houses, says he could always use a strong back…"

So with the score tied in the seventh and Miggs on first, Jack sent Quiz in to bat for a tiring Tommy Nathan, and damned if he didn't lay down the prettiest bunt, moving the runner over to second. The Wolves didn't score, though, and the manager played a hunch. "Quiz, go out there and play second." McElvain was pissed, he hardly ever came out of a game, and he sat down next to Jack.

"I never complain, skip, but why'd you…"

"I'll tell you after the game, Mac."

"But skip, I'm…"

"Later!"

The teams were still even in the bottom of the eighth. After Sevareid flied out, VanLandingham lashed a double to left-center, and Garner Axford, the Bears' manager, decided to walk Hicks to set up the double play possibility. Jack countered by sending in one of his new players, Raburn Reece, to run for Monroe, and it paid off. Brodie hit a ground ball to second and Reece, showing both speed and moxie, came in hard to upend the shortstop, preventing the double play and keeping the inning alive. Miggs worked a walk to load the bases, bringing up Quizenberry. Everyone, even Quiz, expected Jack to send in the other new player, Yarnell, to pinch hit, but Simpson simply clapped his hands and shouted "All right now, let's pick him up, pick him up." Sitting in the press box, Win Appleton said, to no one in particular, "What the fuck?" A moment later he shouted out those same words as Quizenberry, after watching a pitch bounce in the dirt, lined the next one over second and into center for a hit that brought in both TVL and Brodie. Larry West got three quick outs in the ninth, sealing the 6–4 Edens Ridge win. Afterwards, Jack hated to bring down the jubilant clubhouse, but his players needed to know that one more roster move needed to be made, and everyone eventually said goodbye to Quiz. Jack Simpson had never felt so shitty after a win, and it took him almost two hours to fall asleep that night.

Over at the Holston Hotel, sleep was the culmination of a life-altering event.

In the fall of 1950, Lemuel Moon had explained to his family that he was strapped for ready cash. "We ain't broke, in fact, things have been looking up these last coupla months. I think this old hotel is finally primed to turn a profit. But I don't have a lot of money for Christmas presents this year, so I'm going to be a bit creative."

And for his oldest daughter, Phoebe, that meant giving her something she had been talking about for months—a place of her own. Almost.

"You've really learned a lot about managing a hotel, Phebes," he said. "I've been able to turn more and more over to you, by this time next year, I'll bet you'll pretty much be running the place. Makes sense, then, I think, for you to have your own apartment right in the hotel. How's that sound? Kitchen, bath, bedroom…"

"Living room, too?" asked an eager Phoebe, but her excitement was quickly dashed as he shook his head and said "No need to get crazy, now."

Even without a living room, Phoebe loved her little apartment, loved having a space to just kick back and decompress every night, loved having a daily commute that consisted of nothing more than an elevator ride.

And then she had met Rabbi Yitzhak Dov Halevi.

They were such an unlikely couple. She was very outgoing, he was more introspective. She had, for the most part, grown up in Northeast Tennessee, while he was from Louisville, a much larger area. She had wanted to go to college, but her father thought she would learn more about the hotel business directly from him. Dov, meanwhile—she had taken to calling him Dov, which he liked—had received his bachelor's degree from Western Kentucky before spending five years studying to be a rabbi.

And, of course, he was a rabbi, no getting around that! He was not just Jewish, but a rabbi, the only rabbi around for miles. She wasn't particularly religious and didn't come from a religious family. Her parents, though, had always encouraged her to explore, and she had come to believe in a benevolent God, the Ten Commandments and "love thy neighbor," though so far had not, in Northeast Tennessee parlance, found a "church home." She felt that these beliefs, and her open-mindedness, would play in her favor as her relationship with Rabbi Halevi deepened, but there was some problem, an invisible barrier, that she did not quite understand. Wasn't she eagerly learning more about Judaism from him? Didn't she frequently attend services on Friday nights? (Not on Saturday mornings, though. Saturdays were generally busy at the hotel, she needed to be at work, and he said he understood. *Oh, could that be the problem?*)

He would get especially quiet, as if his brain had flown off somewhere and left his body behind, even when they were kissing and petting. She could feel it and would ask "Where are you, Dov? Where have you gone?" One night he finally answered.

"How would it look, Phebes, if the rabbi married outside the faith? We aren't a large congregation, you know that, you've seen, but still…"

"I'm ready to convert, Dov, I've told you several times. We can start the process whenever you'd like…" But he hesitated, and the barrier remained.

Then there was sex—they had not gone "all the way" yet. They were both virgins and were naturally nervous. There had been a couple of times when she thought *this is it, we're going to do it,* but then he had backed off. And one time she had been the one to say no. They were in his car, and she had always vowed she would not be one of "those girls" who lost her virginity in someone's back seat. When he started moving forward she stopped him, and after she got home she cried and cried, then came to a firm decision. It was most definitely time to take advantage of that nice apartment her father had fashioned for her. She found the irony quite amusing.

Yitzhak Dov had a weakness for food, so she insisted on cooking for him, a meatless meal of rainbow trout with rice and vegetables. Afterwards they adjourned to the couch and then to the bed. She let him touch her, caress her, and she gladly took off her blouse and her bra and tingled all over when her breasts were in his mouth.

"Oh Dov," she panted, "I ache for you."

"I do, too," he said, in a very husky voice. "Can we...can we get naked?"

They both undressed and began to explore each other's bodies, and then he positioned himself over her. She spread her legs and...nothing. Worse than nothing, actually, because they both wanted this, wanted this so much, but it wouldn't go in. She was so tight, and whenever he pushed she would give out a little cry which stopped him. "I don't want to hurt you," he said far too many times, until they finally gave up. That's when the tears began, first hers, then his, making her apartment look like it was hosting a wake. He left feeling ashamed, inadequate and frustrated (to say nothing of horny), while she cried herself to sleep, believing she had lost him forever.

But she couldn't let it end like this, she had no desire for it to end at all. *(What was that poem they forced us to read in high school? Ends with the line "not with a bang...? That kept running through her mind.)* She needed advice, she needed to talk to someone, but who? She could hardly go to her mother ("you want to do WHAT?"), there must be someone...

"This has to be really important," said Nashota with a smile, "for you to come to me, and bring sandwiches as well!"

"Well," said Phoebe, "I don't know if I'd call it important, but...um...I guess... yeah, it's important, at least to me, and to Dov."

"Dov, is it? I like that, it sounds nice, endearing."

They were sitting in the stands. At this time of day, there was very little activity at the ballpark, so they had the place to themselves. They sat in the shade and, while munching on their sandwiches, Phoebe unburdened herself, becoming emotional when describing their failure to consummate their love. Wiping her eyes with a napkin *(thank goodness I asked for extras!)*, she finally mumbled "I'm sorry, Nashota, I had promised myself I wouldn't..."

"No, no, no need to apologize, it's important to let it out." Nashota put her hand on Phoebe's knee in sympathy. "And I have to say, I'm very flattered that you came to me, Phoebe. I can see why you wouldn't, oh, bring this up with your mother."

"She would be horrified, shocked! She'd probably try to send me off to a convent or something!" They both giggled, then Phoebe asked "Have you ever heard of something like this before? Did you have any...problems...the first time..."

"No, not at all. Of course, I was younger than you and a little more, oh, you might say, adventurous. I was 19 and living on my own in Asheville and trying to, uh, experience as much of life as I could." This made them both smile.

"I'm 25, guess I'm slow," said Phoebe. "I've always been taught 'good girls don't do it 'til they're married,' 'boys won't buy the cow if the milk is free,' crap like that. And I guess I just took it as gospel, 'til now, 'til I met someone I want." She started tearing up. "And I do want him, Nashota, I love him so much, it…it just feels…right, we feel right together, and I want to be with him, I want to do this, my body aches and I was excited and thrilled and then…" The waterworks started again.

Phoebe ran out of napkins, but Nashota handed her a tissue from her purse, then spoke.

"I didn't have this…happen to me, like I said, but I've heard of it, I know it does happen with some people. You just need to relax, and I know," she said, as Phoebe gave her a sharp look, "I know, easier said than done, but really, that should be all it takes." Nashota thought for a moment before continuing. "Have a glass of wine, maybe two…"

"Maybe three?" asked Phoebe with a little smile.

"Well, you don't want to get blitzed, you won't know what happened, you won't even know when it happens, that's no fun!" Nashota said with a short laugh. "And it is fun, Phoebe, it's great fun, especially with someone you love. I think, maybe, no more than two glasses of wine, that should get you relaxed. Maybe a hot bath…ha! Here's an idea: why don't you both take a hot bath, together, both have a glass of wine in the tub…oooh, sounds kinda sexy, doncha think? I think I've made myself tingle, though it might just be this baby moving around or something…" They both chuckled again.

Two nights later, as both Danny Chase and Jack Simpson were having trouble falling asleep, Phoebe Moon and Rabbi Yitzhak Dov Halevi slept like logs. After first having had some California sherry in the bathtub (one glass for each, though she had had one before he arrived), and after first kissing and petting, they suddenly coupled right there in the tub. This had not been suggested by Nashota or planned by Phoebe, it just happened spontaneously. The wine and warm water and the mood struck all at once, even proved to be practical as the water washed away the little bit of blood that came from her and the sperm that came from him. And they dried each other and nuzzled against each other in the bed, satiated, at least until the middle of the night, when a normal trip to the bathroom led to more loving, with no wine or warm water necessary. It took a very persistent alarm clock to wake them up.

Weeknights were generally slow on Light Street, a regular or two, hardly ever any college kids or strangers, perfect nights to get in a lot of reading. If Emma was caught up in a good book she could easily ignore the other girls' conversations and chew up page after page, and now she found herself immersed. *Three Blind Mice and Other Stories* was a series of mysteries by Agatha Christie, and not only was it wonderful, but it had been marked down because it was already a couple of years old.

She had just begun a new story, in which Miss Marple *(what a great name, so British!)* is looking into thefts from the Skinner household, when the door opened and a man walked in. Muscular, broad-shouldered, wearing a brown shirt and jeans, he was carrying a (very obvious) bottle in a sack, and was greeted, as per usual, by Jasmine. They spoke for a minute or so, then walked into the parlor, where all the girls smiled as they rose to greet him.

He was of medium height but, because he was muscular and well-built, seemed to be larger than he really was. He had a bushy brown mustache and grey eyes that, Emma felt, were already penetrating her. Most men made their choice strictly on what they liked—tall, short, white, black—but this one appeared to be looking more deeply, examining their inner workings, as if he were a human X-ray machine. If he'd actually had that ability, he would have seen four girls with very different personalities but a common goal—make enough money to leave "The Life" far behind. Well, maybe not Vicky, she seemed to like the work and, most definitely, the money. Her parents, living in nearby Wise County, Virginia, were poor farmers who thought their daughter worked in a fancy Kingsport restaurant, which is what she'd told them to explain the money she sent home every month. Lately, though, she'd been thinking that the time might be right to move back up that way, closer but not too close, you understand. Maybe somewhere in eastern Kentucky, some coal county where the miners needed a place to unwind and forget about their jobs and what was happening to their lungs. She could be like Jasmine, own her own house, and be closer to maw and paw, who seemed to be aging very quickly.

He would have learned about Gail's Hollywood dreams. The Springfield, Ohio native saw herself gracing the silver screen. "I'm prettier than Dorothy Dandridge or Lena Horne," she would say and then, when the other girls just hooted, she'd back off a little bit. "Well, I'm as pretty, at least…right? Right?" She was forever playing with hair, hers especially but, more frequently now, one girl or another would ask her to "do something with this damned mop," and Gail would happily spring into action. The result would always be very flattering, making the recipient more alluring, which would bring her more business. "Forget about Hollywood, Gail," Jasmine said one time. "You oughta open a beauty parlor, I think you'd do real good, you got the touch." She had nodded and thought…*well, maybe, why not go to California and do my cuttin' and stylin' in Tinseltown?* She might be able to convince Monroe to move out there, he'd even said to her "They got two teams, you know, Pacific Coast League, 'cludin' one right in Hollywood. Lotta stars come out to games, I hear." That excited her. "Sounds ideal, for both-a us," she had said to him, but then all he did was grunt. *Well,* she thought, *he didn't say no, we can talk 'bout it again, some other time.*

Like Buck, the new customer might have recognized Linda as a Choctaw Indian. If not, he certainly would have noted the quality of her clothing and jewelry. The Mississippi native, while proud of her Indian heritage, felt constricted by life on the reservation, so she and a cousin had packed up and hitched their way east once they turned 18. But they could only find menial jobs in Montgomery and Atlanta. Linda really wanted to sell either jewelry or clothing to well-to-do white women, but no one was interested in hiring a "squaw" for their upscale shops. While working in a diner in Savannah (her cousin stayed in Atlanta, having met "the man-a my dreams"), she got to talking to a traveling salesman. It was a slow night and he had a pleasant smile and before she knew it she was pouring out her tale of woe. He listened patiently, sympathetically. "This is your lucky day, sweet pea." There was money to be made in the hills of Northeast Tennessee, he said. "Seen it for myself, and I'm fixin' to move up there to start making some. How 'bout you come with me?" All she had to do was make sure he climaxed every night, hardly a chore. When they got there, she quickly learned that money could, indeed, be made…if you were white. It was about the whitest area she had ever seen, but it was pretty, and much less hectic, and her experience with the salesman had taught her there was more than one way to earn a dollar. In Johnson City she met a lady named Jasmine Brunét, who was looking to staff a new place in the smaller community of Edens Ridge. "I'll tell you what I tell everyone else, Miz Brunét. I want my own place, a store, selling ladies finery. I plan on catering to high-end clientele, fancy white women with plenty-a money to spend." "Fine," said Jasmine. "I gots no problem with that. And I can practically guarantee—you work with me for a while, you'll be sellin' your fancy duds 'fore you know it. You'll give me a discount, right?" Last time she had looked at her bank statement, Linda knew that day was almost here.

It is likely, however, that his "X-ray vision" would have failed when it came to Emma. She may have desired to "read everything on every shelf in the library," but she herself was anything but an open book. Would he have seen that her father was in prison for beating Maddox Jones—a family friend!—to death? "Raped me is what he done. I was a whole 12 years old," she told Linda one night. "Weren't askin' for it, weren't expectin' it, sure didn't know a blessed thing." Very quietly, she began to cry while Linda held her tenderly. "Maddox and my Daddy, they was best friends. We was all neighbors in Greene County, he lived just down the road, he and Daddy went fishin' together, shot pool." She paused, took a deep breath. "One night no one was home, they was all out somewhere, and come's a knock on the door, it's Maddox, says he lookin' for Daddy. Came in, got him a Coke outta the ice box, took a drink, gave me some. Then alla-sudden, he moved in and kissed me. No one had ever kissed me on the lips 'fore, I was surprised, I just said 'Maddox!' He grinned. 'Like that?' he asked, then he didn't wait for me to answer, he kissed me again. I didn't have no boobs but he started feelin' me, and 'fore I knew it my panties were off, and he had me on the floor and he was inside me, it hurt and I cried…" They were both sobbing at this point, so loudly that Jasmine knocked on the door and opened it, but when she saw them holding each other and crying, she simply closed it and left. Emma composed herself so she could finish her story. "Don't know how long I lay on the floor, they tell me I prob'ly passed out. Next thing I remember is my parents findin' me, and my Daddy askin' 'who did this?' and I told him, I wouldn't lie to my Daddy. Momma took me to the hospital in Greeneville. When I said I wanted to see my Daddy, they told me he was locked up, he had killed Maddox, just pummeled him 'til he was dead. That was 1941, just a few weeks 'fore Pearl Harbor, and he been locked up ever since." Linda, speaking ever-so softly, said "Maybe it's time to forget, Em. Been more-n ten years, now might be time to let it go and…" "Can't ever forget it, Lin, not ever. And not sure I wanna forget. 'Specially his eyes when he came at me. That was evil, or somethin' real close, the kind-a evil that…that…" She searched for the right analogy, and found it. "Evil we saw chasin' Oddibe down the street. There's a…a look, Lin, a certain look, I don't wanna ever forget it, I wanna be able to reck-nize it right away."

And one night it walked in the door, wearing a brown shirt and jeans, carrying a bottle in a sack.

Something about him made her shiver, figuratively, and she hoped he would choose one of the other girls. He seemed to be leaning towards Linda and she'd be perfect, athletic and sexy, a guy built like that would no doubt enjoy her. But no, he veered off like a hurricane changing course, looked right at Emma and said, "That one, the short brunette." *Damn!*

Jasmine felt the same way; after all these years, she most certainly recognized trouble when she saw it. She had even done something about it a few years before. Back when Sergeant Yates was sweet on Millie, one of her original girls, he expressed concern about what he called "unsavory elements" coming to the house and, perhaps, "harmin' my sweet girl."

"We get unsavory elements alla time, Sergeant," laughed Jasmine. "Prob'ly makes up half our business, maybe more."

"Still, doesn't mean you shouldn't have a little protection," he said, and when she started to tell him that both she and Jake had several weapons on hand, he quickly interrupted. "That's not what I mean. Maybe 'warning' is a better word. I can set it up for you, Miz Jasmine, prob'ly only take a few days...."

It was a simple buzzer system, and he put one in every room. If a girl was having trouble with a client, or thought that something bad was about to happen to her, she was to push the button, conveniently located under the bed. It would ring in Jasmine and Jake's room, on a board that they had hanging on a wall. Each room was denoted by a light, and when the buzzer sounded, the correct bulb would light up, which meant a girl needed help. It was even in Oddibe's room, of course, and Jazz hadn't mentioned it at first, but after a while she thought, *yeah, he oughta know 'bout this, too.*

So when the newcomer chose Emma, Jazz whispered to her "Don't forget 'bout your buzzer."

He proved to be rough. He liked slapping her butt, hard, making it all red, and he liked to pull her hair, hard, from behind. He never asked her to turn around or get into a different position, those muscular arms just picked her up and tossed her about.

There wasn't much talking. "I paid for all night," he said when she took him upstairs. She always tried to make a little small talk at first, she found that helped people to relax, but after he told her his name was Steve he ignored her questions while undressing. He simply gave her a steely look and said "Just shut up and get naked, bitch. I didn't pay for no conversation."

In truth, none of this was totally foreign to Emma. She'd had her share of rough customers before, and plenty of men weren't interested in talking. But the hanky was a new one for her.

It took him a little while to climax, but when he did he came in torrents, which made her happy because she figured he'd shot his wad and might just sleep for the rest of the night. After a few moments he wandered into the bathroom, came out and sat on the side of the bed; she took the opportunity to go in there as well and clean up. When she came back into the room, she saw him sitting there with a handkerchief over his nose and mouth, breathing deeply.

"Are you all right, Steve? Do you need anything?" In the back of everyone's mind was always the fear that someone's heart wasn't really up to this kind of physical activity, though that worry was always more prevalent with some of the older men who occasionally wandered in. Widowers mostly, some divorced fellows, though it was not unusual to see old boys who were married and had been for years, ain't that right, Congressman? "My wife ain't int'rested no more, but I can still get it up, just takes me a little longer, so bear with me, sweet thing…" Emma would always smile and say "That's all right, honey, you just take your time." But she wouldn't have expected a young, physically-fit person like Steve to have any health problems.

He didn't. "I'm fine," he growled at her. "Never you mind 'bout this, you just get back on that bed, we only now gettin' started."

And he sure wasn't lying. After taking a few deep breaths, he literally pounced on her like some big cat on the savannah, and they went at it again, as if it was their first time, only now he added biting to his repertoire, which she did not like. "That hurts, Steve," she said one time, and now he grinned. "Like it? Was hopin' you might."

"No, not really, teeth are OK but a little lighter, please…OW!" He paid no attention, and now she thought about pushing the buzzer. Before she could reach it, however, he moved her onto her side, a bad position for her, but at least the biting stopped. And afterwards, he actually lay down and closed his eyes. *Good, maybe now I can get some sleep,* she thought, and it took her no time at all to doze off.

At some point she heard a noise and she looked over to him. He was sitting up, but he seemed to be asleep and talking. More like mumbling really. *Must be dreaming.* She couldn't really make out what he was saying until she heard "Oddibe Daniels," followed shortly by "blow him away, and that other n—, too." After that, Emma found sleep to be impossible. Oh well, at least she was awake, and prepared, when he took her once more, sometime before the sun rose.

He left in the morning and, despite being rather groggy, she wasted no time telling Jazz what she had heard, and the two of them quickly hightailed it over to Newell Gregory's office. The Chief questioned Emma thoroughly, asking her twice whether she was sure she hadn't dreamt that part about Oddibe and shooting.

"Chief," said Emma, as serious as she could be. "I know what I heard. I wasn't dreaming, why would I even dream of such a thing?'

Gregory sent the women over to the Kingsport police department, where there was a sketch artist on staff. Emma worked with him to develop the best possible rendition of Steve, after which they were thanked and allowed to head on home. On the way back, Jasmine told Emma she could have the night off, a piece of news Emma missed at first because she had already fallen asleep in the car.

FOURTEEN

It didn't matter to Danny Chase that it was lightly drizzling when he reported to the ballpark, or that the forecast said there was a 60 percent chance of showers that night, and at least 40 percent for the remainder of the week. Told to report to the office between 3:00 and 3:30 pm so he could sign his contract and get issued a uniform, Danny arrived around 2:30 pm, focused simply on the fact he was going to become a professional baseball player.

"I'm sorry I'm so early, Miz Simpson" he told the pregnant woman in the office. "I just wanted to be sure I got here in plenty of time. I know I've got things to do first and then I'm gonna meet the other players and I figured Mr. Simpson might wanna talk to me and…and…"

Nashota couldn't help herself—she laughed out loud.

"I know, I'm excited, this is my first time as a ballplayer, I mean, a professional ballplayer, I haven't slept all that much since they told me I might make the team, and…"

"Slow down, son, slow down. No need to apologize and, honestly, I'm happy to see someone who's so eager to be here. I'm Nashota, by the way, I manage the front office and in my spare time I'm also Mrs. Simpson."

They both laughed and then she gave him the contract, which he signed immediately. No one ever reads all the legalese but most fellows at least look at the line that lists their salary. Young Mr. Chase simply grabbed the pen and signed. Louetta then escorted him to the clubhouse *(he's really cute!)*, where he proudly put on a jersey with the number 19 on it and waited until his manager arrived a short while later, with two of his new teammates, the Negroes Oddibe Daniels and Monroe Hicks. He had never shaken the hand of a Negro before but that became another first for Danny Chase that day as Oddibe immediately extended his hand; Monroe just nodded.

He practically bounded into the manager's office when he was called. "Hope you don't mind that I change into my uni while we talk," said Jack.

"No, sir, Mr. Simpson, not at all, no, not at all."

"Good, 'cause I was gonna do it anyway." Jack smiled. "Lighten up, kid. I know this is your first job and you're just 'bout to pee your pants bein' here, but…"

"I have worked before, I worked at Donny Lake's landscaping business for three summers and even some after school when he needed me, and I also…"

"This is a real job, young man, not somethin' you do 'til classes begin again. You're gonna go up there with a bat in your hand and some man who is a lot older than you is gonna throw a baseball travelin' 'bout 85, 90 miles an hour, and it'll have real movement. Even more likely, you're gonna be at second tryin' to turn two and some man is gonna come at you with his spikes aimed at your nuts. We ain't plantin' flowers out here, Danny. And call me Jack, everyone does, the only one who calls me Mr. Simpson is my wife and that's when she's hoppin' mad at me."

Danny smiled, a little weakly. "Yes, sir, Mr. ..., er, Jack."

"Better," said Jack, at this point clad only in his underwear. "Now listen, I wanna make sure you understand your role on this team. We've had an infield crisis recently, our regular shortstop…"

"Valenza, yes, sir, um, Jack, I know, Valenza got hurt, he's done for the year, and you've been movin' guys around…" The manager just looked at him. "I come to games all-a time, Jack. I live here, you know, in Kingsport, that is, and I come to games here and at J. Fred Johnson, mostly. Sometimes I even go over to Johnson City and Bristol, maybe once or twice a year. Anyway, I know what's been goin' on here."

"Good," said Jack, buttoning his jersey. "So you know the score. I got Miggsy over at third now and Squirrel at short, which means two guys are out of position, but it's the best I can do at this stage of the year. I want you backin' up Squirrel, there might be times, late in the game, when I pull Miggs and move Squirrel back over to third and put you in at short, understand? And I also got you penciled in to back up Mac at second, though that won't happen much, maybe not at all. Got all that?"

"Yes, sir, yes…Jack. Sorry, I'll get the hang of it."

Simpson had to smile, he wasn't used to having such a greenhorn on his team. "All right, then, any questions? When we go on the road this weekend, you'll room with Reece. What I suggest now is that you go back to the clubhouse, introduce yourself to all the guys and keep it short, just tell 'em your name and that you're an infielder and, uh, listen, Danny." He sat down and looked his new player right in the eye. "We had to release a fellow, Quizenberry, to make room for you. Quiz was a popular guy 'round here. A good guy, but just a fair player. You got a better arm, that's why I've hired you, I need a good arm at short and Quiz didn't have it. But some-a the guys may, um, they may not be too crazy to be losing Quiz, understand? So if you introduce yourself and they don't wrap their arms 'round you, don't worry 'bout it. First time you nail a guy from the hole with that gun-a yours, they'll be fine. Understand?"

Danny just nodded and Jack grabbed his uniform pants. "OK, go on out there. And be sure to talk to Mike Hamblen, you know who he is, he'll tell you how it'll be when we go to Kruse day after tomorrow, and then up to Virginia a coupla days later." They both stood up, and as the newcomer headed for the door, his manager said, "Glad to have you here, Danny."

"What a piss-shitty day." With the likely exception of Danny Chase, Jack's expression perfectly summed up everyone's feelings that night.

It rained on and off all day. Rain a little, stop. Rain a little, stop. Sun would come out, start to dry things off, then the clouds would move in and drop a little more moisture, and stop. It never really poured, it would just rain enough to be annoying, and then stop. By 6:30 pm, when some fans began to trickle in, Nick, Richie and Max were already a tired grounds crew, tired and more than a bit frustrated. They added more sand to the area around shortstop, the traditional low spot in the infield, as well as in front of the first-base dugout. The umpires were also slogging around the outfield and shaking their heads, but Bill McDermott had cheery music playing over the PA so hopefully…and then it began to drizzle again.

"God damn it to hell!" shouted Jack, looking up at the sky to make sure The Almighty knew exactly how he felt.

It didn't last long, however, and shortly after 7:00 pm Nick and Richie and Max ran out with more sand. This time they were joined by a couple of fans who jumped out of the stands. One was Bob Dean, the Eastman engineer and mayoral candidate who was one of the team's most fervent fans, a member of the Booster Club (wife Dorothy was the president), and a nightly presence at the ballpark. Bob and Dorothy always made themselves available to help out here and there, and this was hardly the first time Bob had hopped the fence to work on a damp field. The other set of hands, however, came from an unexpected source—Jehosie Jackson, the small auto repair shop guy. He didn't come to all that many games, he was often too tired after a long day of crawling under people's cars. But he happened to be there on this rainy, drizzly night and, on the spur of the moment, he left his seat, ran over to Nick and asked "Anything I can do?"

There were probably fewer than 200 people in the stands, which was understandable—bad weather almost always keeps people away. With such a small crowd on hand, one voice could sound especially loud, and as soon as Jackson had asked his question, someone on the first-base side boomed out "Get that n— off the field!" And for a few seconds, everything stopped.

Jehosie Jackson looked at Nick Felix. "Sorry, man, I didn't realize…" and he turned around.

"Where you going?" asked Felix. "I thought you wanted to help."

Jackson turned back to the group. "Don't wanna cause no trouble. Sure don't want anyone here gettin' hurt…"

"No one's gonna get hurt, not unless they come outta the stands, I'll tell you that," said Bob Dean, and he handed Jackson his rake. "Here, take this, I'll grab another. We'll smooth out the first-base line, OK?" "You sure 'bout this?" asked Jackson. "Fuck yeah!" said Nick Felix, who clapped his hands, looked at the grandstands and yelled loudly, "Let's go, let's get to work, we gotta ballgame to play tonight."

As Bob grabbed a new rake, he thought he heard the phrase "n— lover." He walked so that he was as close to the stands as he could be without sitting in the first row.

"Anybody got a problem, come on down here and say it to my face. Tell you what, I'll even let you take the first punch. Be your last, though." He paused for a few seconds. "Anybody? Anybody at all?"

There was silence from the grandstand. Bob Dean was not tall, but his years of working in the railroad yard had sculpted his body. His moon face was almost always set in a smile, he was generally very friendly and very funny, quick with a joke and quicker to laugh. He liked almost everyone, which meant he was your friend for life and would do anything for you. But if you got on his bad side, then you'd better have the strength and stamina of Rocky Marciano, because otherwise you were going to get seriously hurt. And that night at the ballpark, apparently, no one was ready to go fifteen rounds with Bob Dean.

Some 25 minutes after the scheduled 7:15 pm start time, lineup cards were exchanged, the Wolves took the field, and home plate umpire Al Geiger shouted out "Play Ball!"

The drizzle began again in the top of the second inning. Nashota could hear it pitter-pattering on the park's metal roof, and her first thought was *Oh God, what's Jack gonna do?*, so she left the office and toddled out into the concourse to see for herself. Play was continuing, though she did see Al Geiger glance up at the sky after about every third pitch. Once the managers exchanged lineup cards, the game was in the hands of the umpires. They were the only ones who could call a halt to play and order the tarp brought out, and she knew that thought was in Geiger's mind. She also glanced over to the dugout and saw Jack standing there, arms crossed, frowning deeply. Just then, the Wolves' batboy, Kevin, ran over and thrust a folded piece of paper at her.

"The skipper asked me to give this to you," he said, a bit out of breath. "And he told me he wanted an answer right away!"

You really ought to lose a little weight, Nashota thought, *you're way too young to be out of shape.* She kept her opinion to herself, however, opened up the paper and laughed out loud:

Got any credit with U-ne-qua? Or maybe you can perform some Cherokee magic and make this damned rain stop for the next two hours? Hmmmm?

Well, at least he hasn't lost his sense of humor…yet.

"Kevin," she said, still grinning. "Please tell our manager that it will take a lot more than a little drizzle to get me and my…no, OUR…*u-s-di-ga* to cash any heavenly chips we may have. Got that?"

She had to repeat the word *u-s-di-ga*, slowly, and then, when young Kevin still looked confused, she said "It's the Cherokee word for baby, just say baby, OK?" The youngster nodded and left, and Nashota wondered what message Jack would actually receive.

Playing baseball in the rain is a difficult thing. The ball is wet, so pitchers have trouble controlling it. The field is wet, slowing down ground balls and turning the basepaths into mud pits. Raindrops, even only a drizzle, can interfere with a batter's sight of the ball. And no one—players, managers, coaches, umpires, even fans—really wants to be out there. Just think how you feel when you've left your umbrella or rain hat in the car and need to run through the parking lot because a storm has developed while you've been stocking up on your beer.

No surprise that it was a sloppy game. It was hard for anyone to set their feet and make decent throws, either from the infield or outfield, and running the bases felt more like running in a swimming pool. Everyone had to slow down and be careful at all times, the complete opposite of what they had been taught ever since their fathers or grandfathers had first put a ball and bat in their hands. Jack Simpson and Trig Swinney were keeping up a running commentary from their respective dugouts:

"Sure is slippery out there, Al." "Someone could get hurt out there, blue, let's get these fellers off the field." "Gotta good ground crew here, Al, let 'em do their job, once this rain stops, eh?"

For whatever reason, the umpires let play continue.

In the bottom of the fourth, Edens Ridge struck for three runs, taking the lead when a low pitch slithered away from the Kruse catcher. Trig came out to argue that the field had become unplayable and his vehemence was rewarded by Al Geiger: "You don't like it out here today, Trig? Why don't you go enjoy the warm, dry clubhouse—YOU'RE OUTTA THE GAME!"

Now holding a 4–2 lead, Jack grabbed his pitcher, Harry Neville, just before he headed out to the mound and gave him a simple instruction: "Get three quick outs."

In every game, the fifth inning plays a pivotal role. It is the halfway point of the contest, and with its completion, the game is now official, just as if a full nine innings had been played. This is especially important to the home team involved in a rain game. If the home team holds the lead after the visitors have completed their at-bats in the fifth, it could rain for days as far as they're concerned, this game is official and they've won. Which is just where Edens Ridge now found themselves, hence Jack's instructions to Neville—three more outs would constitute an official game.

Of course, all this did was put extra pressure on the stocky right-hander, who gave up a hit and a walk, prompting Jack to come out to the mound at a trot.

"Harry, what the fuck is wrong with you? We got the lead, don't cough it back up."

"I'm tryin', skip. I'm havin' a hard time..."

"Look, no excuses. If you can't do the job I'll get someone else in here. Want the 'W'? Just throw the fuckin' ball over the fuckin' plate. Got that?" Without waiting for a reply, Jack trotted back to the safety of his dugout, where he signaled for Buck Hightower to start warming up, and make it snappy! Neville, however, got the message. He got two ground ball outs, though the second produced a run, bringing the Ducks to within one, 4–3. Then he really bore down on J.W. Wingate and got the Kruse shortstop to fly out to Oddibe, ending the inning. The game was now official, let the heavens do their worst!

And they did, in a manner of speaking.

VanLandingham led off the bottom of the fifth, took a ball, low, then swung at the next pitch and hit it hard but foul. It soared over the dugout, constantly rising, until it hit one of the light towers. Not just any light tower, though, it hit the one that was roughly parallel to the infield cutout on the first base side. The one that contained the transformer.

The likelihood of hitting that transformer were astronomical. After all, they'd played more than 300 games in Bill Washington Park since the Wolves had first taken the field back in 1946. At least a dozen foul balls flew in that general direction every single night, and the transformer had never been hit before. Not once. The next day, Win Appleton would make a couple of calls over to the mathematics department at East Tennessee State College, where he eventually located a professor who, after asking a few questions, did some figuring and determined that the odds were around 5,000–1. One has a better chance of being struck by lightning.

But on this night, this drizzly, "piss-shitty" night, a foul ball off the bat of Terry VanLandingham hit the transformer and plunged the ballpark into sudden darkness.

The small crowd of 280 hearty souls let out a loud collective yell, much more forceful than one would expect from 280 throats. Then everyone seemed to turn to their neighbor to ask "Well, hell, what happens now?" before turning their heads instinctively towards the office, where Nashota sat, as stunned as the rest of them. The difference, though, was that she was the Business Manager and she was expected to do something, and right now!

The telephone still worked, thank goodness, so she grabbed it and dialed the Operator.

"Mabel? Hi, it's Nashota Simpson over at the Wolves ballpark. We…oh, I'm fine, thank you, the baby is good, I think, kicking up a storm, thanks for asking. Say listen, we have a problem here, all our lights just went out, do you think…yes, that's why I called you, do you think you could put me through to Russ?"

Of course she could, and in just a minute or so she was speaking with a regional vice president for Kingsport Utilities, Inc., who was also, coincidentally, a season ticket holder and member of the Booster Club. Hearing the anxiety in her voice, Russ Francis was succinct: "I'll get a crew right over, Nashota, don't you worry." Then he chuckled. "Might be a good opportunity to sell some hotdogs while they're still hot!"

Good idea, she thought, as she ambled over to the press box. *Why didn't I think of that?*

She explained things to Bill McDermott, who grinned when she asked "How can we tell people what's happening?" "Leave that to me, Nashota," he said, opening the press box window. Leaning out as far as he could go without tumbling into the stands, he used his loudest and most authoritative voice.

"Ladies and gentlemen, Kingsport Utilities has been called and tells us that a work crew will be here quickly. Sorry we can't play any music for you, but hot dogs are now on sale, two for a quarter, get them while they're still warm! Same with popcorn, now just ten cents."

Quite a few people laughed, but a few others got up to see if ol' Bill was pulling their leg or not. Hey, can't hardly beat two for a quarter, right?

Jack Simpson actually smiled and very simply said, "My wife's a fuckin' genius." Not too many people heard him, however, partially because he spoke more to himself, but mainly because another, louder voice was now making itself heard. It was one not yet very familiar to the Wolves, since it was new and, up 'til this point, had not been used all that much.

"Gentlemen," came a deep rumble from the bench, "I think we oughta give these fans a little phantom infield while we're all waitin', whaddya think?" It was the new catcher, Yam Yarnell.

Standing almost six-foot-three-inches in his bare feet, Yarnell was one of the taller players on the team, behind Buck (of course!), and Pete, and tonight's starter, Harry Neville. He had broad shoulders and muscular arms that were adorned with tattoos above both elbows—a Celtic cross on his left arm, and a heart on his right containing the initials OY + PY, homage to his parents, Opal and Peter. No one had asked him yet about either one. In fact, not too many of the players had spoken much to him. He was quiet and kept to himself, mostly, though he was polite when he did speak and smiled readily. He had been energetic at warming up pitchers, taking batting practice, and doing whatever Jack or Mike had asked him to do before a ballgame. He had also been a strong voice on the bench, cheering on his new teammates when they put men on base, and constantly encouraging the pitchers. He was friendly with everyone, and knew what to do out on a baseball diamond and inside a locker room.

He was also rather secretive. He told everyone he was originally from Birmingham and had been playing ball for a while, though no one knew just how long "a while" was. He had grown up at Rickwood Field, watching the Barons play in the Southern Association and the Black Barons play in the Negro National League; he preferred the latter because he didn't have to sit so far away from the action.

Pearl Harbor got him all fired up, and the day after he graduated from A.H. Parker High School, he joined the Navy and was lucky enough to be assigned to the USS Mason, a destroyer escort that was the first ship in the Navy to feature a predominantly-Negro crew. They made six trips across the Atlantic and stopped in places like the Azores and Northern Ireland and Algeria and England. When the war ended, he came home and spent a season with the Black Barons and then, in the wake of Jackie Robinson, began playing in the previously-all-white minor leagues. Seasons in Stroudsburg, Pennsylvania and St. Jean, Quebec, Canada (where Bob Rhodes saw him play) led him to Las Vegas, Nevada, which proved to be a fun place to live and work. It was also where he met Opal, a hat-check girl at the Sands, where he also found work during the off-season. She was pretty and smart and sassy, and shared her first name with his Mama. But when she found out that her father was ill, she headed east to some little burg he had never heard of, not even with all his travels. This was how he came to be living in Weber City, Virginia, just a small handful of miles from Northeast Tennessee towns like Kingsport and Edens Ridge. He didn't play anywhere in 1951, since he was too busy helping Opal's parents with their farm, but he did find the time to marry Opal. Yam looked around for a place to play in 1952, but the only opportunity that came along was way out in Yuma, Arizona and paid a mere $175 a month. That wasn't nearly enough to make it worth his while to be away from Opal and her family, their family. But then he read Win Appleton's "help wanted" article in the Gazette.

"Way I figure, Opal, this is at least worth a try, you know? I mean, it's just a short drive, and it'll only be for a few weeks, and it'll put some extra money in our pockets 'fore harvest time."

"Plus you be playin' ball, right?" Opal asked with a knowing smile.

She knew him so well. This would give him the opportunity to be doing what he loved the most and, you know, can't never tell what might could develop, right?

Now, on this "piss-shitty" night, the bass voice of Yam Yarnell could easily be heard all over the ballpark in almost every inning. But this was the first time he had addressed his teammates directly.

Larry West was the first to respond. "Need some source of light. You gotta car?"

"I do," said Yam. "Ford Meteor, bought it when I played in Canada coupla years ago."

"We'd need more-n one car, though," said Miggs.

"What about our bus?" asked Terry VanLandingham, enthusiastically.

"I'm sorry," said Oddibe. "I'm...I'm not quite following this. What in hell is phantom infield?"

"Yeah, that's a new one on me, too," said Danny Chase, to which Pete good-naturedly replied, "Everything is new to you, meat," which got a laugh in the dugout.

"Phantom infield, you boys never heard of phantom infield? Man, you as green as grass," said Yam. "Well, look, it's simple, we take infield practice, just like we did 'fore the game began, but we don't use a ball. This way we can get to make all sorts-a fancy catches and trick plays, kinda stuff you dream 'bout when you was a kid, or when you sittin' on the bench!" Here he laughed, and then continued. "No one gets hurt, 'cause there ain't no ball, see? And the fans eat it up, they just love it. Keeps 'em occupied, least for a while. That's phantom infield."

The new players just nodded, then Mac quietly said, "Bus would work best, Skip." All eyes now turned to Jack.

"Gas is up to 24 cents," he said. "We ain't exactly drownin' in dough here, I mean, look at tonight's crowd, if you can even call it a crowd. Bet Jasmine gets this many some Saturday nights." There was some snickering at that, but no one said anything.

Jack looked out at the field, then into the stands. He could see movement, people coming back with hot dogs in tow, others just strolling down the steps, back to their seats, probably returning from the bathrooms.

"We got no idea how long this might take," he mused. "Could be quite a while. Could be they can't fix this 'til morning. Least it's an official game, eh?" He looked at Mike, who just shrugged and said, "Your call, skip."

"Yeah, yeah," sighed Jack. He continued to stare out at the drizzly ballfield, then he suddenly raised his voice.

"What the hell, this night's been crazy already, let's just top it off. Fire up the Maxwell, Mike," and the bench erupted in cheers as Hamblen ran into the clubhouse to get his keys. Jack then turned to the young batboy and said, "Kevin, would you please run upstairs and tell Bill the PA guy to yell out that we'll be havin' phantom infield out here in just a few minutes? You might want to tell my wife, as well, if you can find her." Then he addressed his players. "OK, first off, if you're gonna go out there, you gotta change into tennis shoes. NO CLEATS, that'll rip up the tarp. No leather shoes either, too easy for you to fall and get hurt. You wanna just wear your hose, go ahead, but remember they'll get real wet. Then, everybody gets a turn, understood? Pitchers, too, if you wanna go out there, though I'd rather you didn't. And work in shifts. But no one does anythin' stupid, hear me? If anyone gets hurt fuckin' around out there, I swear I'll make you pay for the doctor's bills outta your own pocket. Everybody understand?" A little mumbling, not enough to please the manager. "Rain made you deaf? I asked if EVERYBODY UNDERSTOOD!" and this time he was met with a loud chorus "Yes, sir, Mr. Simpson!" Aye, aye, Cap'n," things like that.

Bill McDermott was enthusiastic when he opened the press box window again. "Stick around, folks, we're going to have a real treat for you—our players will be giving us a demonstration of an old baseball classic, the phantom infield! Be just a few moments."

By this time, maybe a quarter or so of the fans had already headed for home when they saw the tarp being laid down. Those who remained, however, gave a little cheer, which grew louder when they saw the team bus being driven down the warning track, and then maneuvered so that it faced the infield with its engine off but its lights on. The players let out a collective whoop, and the starting infield ran out to their positions.

The next day's edition of the *Gazette* contained two small pieces by Win Appleton. The game story was standard—how teams scored, who got key hits—and was short, reflecting the brevity of the game itself. But the sidebar, complete with a picture by staff photographer Gordy Shaw, was all about the players' extra-curricular show. (Ironically, Shaw had been packing up to go back to the paper when he heard the announcement about the hot dogs. *Hmmm, two for a quarter fits very nicely into my budget,* he thought. This was the only reason he had stuck around, but he quickly recognized the opportunity and took numerous photos. The one chosen to run in the *Gazette* would eventually earn him a statewide award.)

WOLVES WIN PLAYS 2ND FIDDLE TO "PHANTOM INFIELD"
By Win Appleton

Edens Ridge, TN—Most baseball games are entertaining, especially if your team wins. Last night, the Edens Ridge Wolves defeated the Kruse Ducks by a score of 4–3, for a couple hundred folks at Bill Washington Park, that wasn't what made the night pleasurable; no, "memorable" would actually be a much more accurate word. Because what they got was an extravagance fans rarely get to see, a display of something known as "Phantom Infield."

Leading off the bottom of the fifth inning, right fielder Terry VanLandingham hit the second pitch foul. Turned out to be not just any foul ball, this one hit a transformer, knocking out all power in the ballpark. All of it. Of course, Kingsport Utilities was called and they worked for a good forty minutes or more before they passed along the information that they would have to resume their efforts in the morning, when they could operate under natural light. And presumably, without the distraction of a steady rain. This effectively ended the game, giving the Wolves the win in the minimum amount of time needed to count in the Mountain Empire League standings (4½ innings), but not before the players put on a little sideshow to take people's minds off the darkness and drizzle.

Using only the lights from the team bus, driven onto the field for just this special occasion, the team's starting infield of Pete Sevareid, Mac McElvain, Squirrel Davis and Allan Miggs took their usual positions and pretended to be fielding ground balls, just like they do before the start of every inning. They were pretending because they weren't using a ball, and you hopefully understand why they weren't throwing a baseball in the dark.

But it was a performance worthy of Keaton or Chaplin. Miggs, the "reformed" catcher, made a couple of diving "stops" that would have made Billy Cox or George Kell proud, had they been done for real. Davis ranged into the hole from his shortstop position, then did a pirouette as he leaped in the air and "threw" to first, presumably nipping the mythic runner by a step.

The Mountain Empire League

A few moments later, a new group came out, this one featuring two catchers. Monroe Hicks stationed himself at first base (where he has actually appeared on occasion since joining the club), and newcomer Yam Yarnell, all six-foot-three inches of him, staked out third base. With regular center fielder Oddibe Daniels scampering about at shortstop, (newcomer and local kid Danny Chase was over at second), it meant that the Wolves were displaying—if only for fun—an infield that was three-fourths Negro.

The fans seemed to be having almost as good a time watching this bit of vaudeville as the players had in performing their excellent pantomime. It was hard to tell, in fact, if the booing from the grandstands was because the real game was called off, or because that meant the end to the "phantom infield." Whichever was the case, this observer cannot remember any occasion when fans expressed disappointment over leaving a wet ballpark. Thanks, Wolves!

Among those who were dissatisfied was a muscular, well-built man with grey eyes and a bushy brown mustache.

Gail was acting kind of strange. After splitting the two games in Kruse, Monroe thought that maybe they could have a little play-time, since the team would be leaving the next day for Beck and Mettin. She wasn't interested, said she'd had a tough night. *Huh, she seems to have had a few of those lately but that's OK, prob'ly normal in her line-a work.* Same with him, he'd just fanned twice and hit into a double-play and was startin' to feel a little tired. *Shit, been catchin' every game since Miggs moved to third but I ain't gonna ask for a night off, no sir. That Yam looks like he can PLAY and next thing you know, I'll be Wally Pipped and no one wants that, no sir, not ever.* He just smiled and said, "All right, darlin', I'm pretty tired myself, make sure you say 'bye 'fore we leave in the mornin'," and she promised she would.

None of the girls were downstairs while he and Oddibe were eating their breakfast, but there was nothing unusual about that, the girls often slept late. They did hear someone knock on the door and some muffled voices, but didn't give it a second thought, a few guys preferred mornings.

They cleaned up their dishes and were starting for the stairs when Jasmine stopped them.

"When you boys leavin?"

"We're goin' upstairs now to pack," said Oddibe. "Jack will prob'ly be around to get us in an hour or so."

"Less," said Monroe. "Won't even be an hour."

"Well, look, 'fore you do that, can we talk 'bout somethin'? Won't take long, I promise, just a few minutes."

They went into the parlor and all the girls were sitting there, waiting for them. And if that wasn't surprise enough, Sergeant Philman Yates was with them! He stood up, smiled and spoke.

"Morning. Sorry 'bout the game last night, but you'll get 'em tonight, we know you can beat those Bears, you've got a good record 'gainst 'em this season."

Well, that was awkward. No one else spoke for several seconds, so Sgt. Yates tried again.

"Have a seat, boys…men, fellas," he said quickly. "We got somethin' we need to discuss, and thought this was as good-a time as any."

Monroe and Oddibe looked at each other, then at Jasmine, who just nodded. Gail patted the space next to her and Monroe walked over there, while Jazz took Oddibe's hand and sat with him on the unoccupied couch. Sgt. Yates remained standing, and now Oddibe noticed that Jake was there, too, standing off to the side of the room, his arms crossed.

Yates cleared his throat. "We wanted to let you know…we have heard about, been looking into…well, see, there may be somethin', but maybe not…"

"Oh, for heaven's sake, Phil, I'll do it, you never was no good at talkin.'" Jazz was nothing if not blunt. She made sure she looked at both ballplayers, in turn, as she spoke.

"Emma had a customer t'other night and he was…he was bad, weren't he, Emma?" asked Jasmine, and the younger woman just nodded solemnly.

Jazz continued. "His money ain't welcome here no more, tell you what. I don't let nobody mistreat my girls, but that ain't why you're here. This piece-a-shit talked in his sleep and mentioned you, Oddibe, said your name out loud and said somethin'…" She stopped and was suddenly hesitant.

"Not so easy, is it?" asked Sgt. Yates, with a small smile. He looked at the two Wolves, who were both obviously just as confused as when they had walked into the room. "He threatened you, both-a you. Mentioned you by name, Daniels, not you, Hicks, just called you 'that other n—,' but said he was gonna…gonna take care-a both-a you. And we believe him, we believe he's here in town, somewhere, and he's gonna try to harm you."

The room grew quiet, then Monroe spoke.

"Had threats before, plenty-a them. We get called shit alla time, don't really pay 'tenshun to it. What's so special 'bout this cracker?" And he actually chuckled.

"We heard…we got some information 'bout a week or so ago," said Yates. "Very good source, really good. We have a general description, don't know his real name, he uses a lot of aliases. But, we got the word out all over, Jack and Nashota know, all the other teams know, too, plus police and sheriffs 'round the league, keep an eye out for this bastard, he's probably armed and definitely dangerous." Yates took a breath, then looked at Emma. "This young lady here, she came in the other day, with Jazz, told us 'bout this creep she'd been with, told us what he said. Her description-a him fit the general one we had, we think it's the same guy we been warned 'bout in our tip. We think you two are in some danger here."

The parlor went silent again. Gail squeezed Monroe's hand. No one knew just what to say. After a moment Jake walked towards Monroe and, without a word, handed him a pistol. "You know how to use one-a these?" asked Yates.

"More used to a huntin' rifle," said the catcher. "Don't have one-a them in your pocket, do ya, Jake?" That brought some smiles around the room.

"Sorry, Monroe," said Jake with a grin. "Just another one-a these," and he produced another handgun, which he took over to Oddibe.

Daniels looked at it, then at Jake, then at Yates, and finally at Jasmine. "I never…I never even touched a gun before. We don't go huntin' in Asheville and just…never had no use for a gun."

"Your dad must have one," Jazz said, quietly.

"Maybe when he was younger. Grew up in the country, in Georgia, bet he shot a gun back then. If he got one now, I ain't never seen it or heard 'bout it. And I never touched one and really…" He hesitated, not sure if he should continue his thought. But they were all looking at him, so he took the plunge. "I thank you, Miss Jasmine, and you, Jake, and you too, Sergeant Yates, I thank y'all, truly. But if it's all-a same to you, I'd rather not start now."

"For your own protection, boy," Yates said sharply and unapologetically. "We don't have the manpower to have someone with you 24 hours a day. We think it's a good idea for you, both-a you, to be carrying this at all times. Except when you're on the field, of course. I don't think the league would give you permission, even under the circumstances."

"I wouldn't want you to be squattin' behind the plate and accidentally shoot somethin' important," Gail said, looking at Monroe with a sly grin, which made the other girls laugh, and even Sergeant Yates could not help but smile.

"Monroe got experience with a gun, I don't," said Oddibe. "Sorry, I just ain't comfortable…"

"Take the gun, Oddibe. It's for your own good," said Jasmine, and the girls all chimed in with similar words of encouragement.

"I'll take it," said Monroe. "He's right, if he don't know nothin' 'bout this, he'd prob'ly just hurt himself. Can't have him shootin' off a toe, we need that speed-a his these last few weeks." He opened the chamber of the gun he'd been handed and saw it had six bullets. "Same with this one," said Jake, handing him the gun that Oddibe had rejected. "And if you need more…" He now produced a box of bullets and handed that to Monroe as well.

"Thanks," said Hicks. "I'll give this to Yam, I'm sure he's held one before." He chuckled. "I think ol' Yam has done all sorts-a things in his life that we know nothin' about, and prob'ly never will!"

"You may not wanna know, either," said Jazz with a smile. She stood up. "But look—don't you be thinkin'-a this when you're out on the field, now. You boys just play ball, we wanna see you in the playoffs! Just be careful, extra careful, gettin' on and off the bus, or if you're wanderin' around Beck and Mettin. Hear?"

"Miss Jasmine," said Oddibe. "No Negro in his right mind ever gonna be found just wanderin' around Beck and Mettin."

In Beck, Marzella Brooks was only too glad to put up another ballplayer. "Y'all tell that boss-a your'n that he oughta field a whole team-a Negroes, 'cause I'd find places for 'em to sleep and make me a shit-pile-a money!"

She assigned them their rooms, giving Yam the largest one "'Cause you one tall, well-built specimen, you gonna need more space." A few minutes later there was a knock on Oddibe's door and his two teammates walked in. Yam was holding one of the handguns Jake had given out before they left town.

"True what he tellin' me? You had guys tryin' to kill you, least-ways beat you, right in Edens Ridge? And you don't know how to use a gun, never even touched one? What Moses here says, all that true?"

"It's Monroe," said Hicks.

"Done had a coupla scrapes this season, that's a fact. Don't know if them crackers who chased me woulda killed me, but they wasn't lookin' for no autograph, that's for sure. And yeah, I ain't never touched no gun."

Yarnell whistled before he spoke again. "Well, shit, if that don't beat all. Don't think I know any culluds that don't know their way 'round a handgun, do you, Morton? Even my Opal, she as sweet a dolly as they is, but I can leave her alone, like now, and know she can take care-a herself, and her folks, with her .38."

"It's MONROE," said Hicks, loudly, with a trace of annoyance in his voice.

Yam just laughed. "I know, just givin' you shit, buck." Then he looked back at Oddibe. "I can show you how to use this-here gat, won't take but 2–3 minutes. I don't need it, I got my own, but you…"

"Don't want it, don't wanna learn," said Daniels, with emphasis. Then he took a breath. "Sorry, don't mean to be rude, Yam. But no, thank you but no, I do not want the gun, don't wanna learn how to use it. Appreciate your offer, but no."

Yam sat down on the bed. "Why not? You lookin' to get killed? Doncha think you oughta be protectin' yourself?"

"For RubyAnn, man," said Monroe. "For nothin' else, you oughta learn how to use one, for RubyAnn." The husky catcher then looked at the tall catcher. "That his girl, RubyAnn. She live down in Asheville." Yam just nodded, then looked back at Oddibe.

"I think," said Oddibe, then he stopped and they could see he actually was thinking, trying to frame his answer. After a moment, he continued.

"I think RubyAnn would be upset if she knew I had a gun. Even if she thought I was in danger, I don't think she'd want me to be carryin'. Same with my Mom, and my Dad, too. We don't have one in our house, never had, far as I know. That's just…it ain't how we are."

Hicks and Yarnell waited for more of an explanation, and when nothing more was forthcoming, they both reacted.

"Man, I don't get it," said Monroe. "You think she want you to get shot down? Bet she'd rather have you alive than dead."

"Sure she would, but she wouldn't want me to be someone I ain't, and I ain't no gun man. And look, if someone really wants me dead, he gonna make that happen. Don't matter how many guns I'd have, in my hands, in my pockets, all over, if he wants me dead, I'll be dead. Look at Gandhi, famous man like that, argued against violence, lived his whole life 'gainst violence, and what happens? Shot and killed, out in the open. Nothin' he could do 'bout it."

The two backstops knew it was pretty hard to argue against Gandhi. They all simply looked at each other, and finally Yam stood up.

"What time we go over to the ballpark? And how do we get there?"

In her first year working in the "front office," 19-year-old Louetta Henry was certainly learning a lot. Stands to reason, since she was the youngest full-time member of the Wolves' staff. She was also the first face one saw when they walked into the office, making every day a new adventure, of sorts, as she came in contact with different people and unique and interesting situations. To help her remember things, she had also taken to writing down different procedures and tasks on index cards, and even, occasionally, people's names, titles, and significance to the ballclub.

One thing she had learned very early on was a minor league saying: *the best thing about road trips is home stands, the best thing about home stands is road trips.* She had heard Nashota say it back in April, when the team bus rumbled off to Kentucky for the first time, and she thought *that's kind of odd,* so she asked just what it meant.

"When the team is at home, we're just busy-busy…hell, you saw what it was like, it's practically non-stop. So we're happy to see the boys leave because now we'll have a little peace and quiet, and time to breathe! We can work normal days, normal hours, and catch up on all the things we had to put aside in order to just get ready for the gates to open each night."

"But we miss 'em when they're gone, and we especially miss that nightly income, so by the time the next home stand starts, we're ready for it, and all the craziness that comes with it!"

The two women had established something of a routine, more or less. Nashota liked getting to the ballpark early during home stands, opening the office no later than 8 am, and she gave Louetta permission to come in an hour later, which the youngster often interpreted to mean closer to 9:15 am. *That's OK,* she rationalized to herself, because around six o'clock she transitioned back to her old job in the concession stand, and stayed until around the eighth inning. Of course, Nashota was generally also the last person out the door, and even then she didn't go home right away. A stop at the bank to drop off the night's receipts came before she could finally—FINALLY!—head to her own house and her own bed. It was not unusual for Nashota, and that baby growing inside her, to have put in a good 15 hours that day.

During road trips, like this one, Louetta was the designated early-bird, which she took to mean about 8:30 am; there was no game that night, what's the rush? During road trips they could work at a leisurely pace and go home for the day around 5 o'clock or so. It was nice.

Once in a while, Louetta would arrive at the ballpark and find Nashota already at work. "The team's out of town, remember?" she would ask, and Nashota always said "I know, but I've got a few things I want to do today, might as well get an early start." "Well, make sure you go home early, I can lock up," Louetta would earnestly respond, and her boss would tell her that she would, but it never happened. "You go on, I'll be right behind you" was the typical rejoinder from Nashota when it was pointed out that it was already past five o'clock. Louetta didn't need a hand-engraved invitation, she would gather her things and say good-night, which was usually met with a friendly smile and a wave. No telling how late that woman stayed.

It was not a surprise, then, when the teenager saw Nashota's car in the parking lot that morning. It was unusual, though, not to see her in the office. *She's probably in the bathroom, she is pregnant, after all, and she does pee a lot.* Louetta poured herself some coffee and got busy typing up invoices for businesses that had asked to pay their bills on a monthly basis. These were the team's larger accounts, primarily for fence signs, or packages that included some combination of signs, program ads and tickets. Many businesses were more likely to spend more if they could make monthly payments, and one of Louetta's index cards was a reminder to SEND OUT INVOICES DURING THE FIRST ROAD TRIP OF THE MONTH.

She typed up her second invoice and still no Nashota, so Louetta knocked on the bathroom door.

"Nashota? You in there?"

No answer, so she slowly opened the door and saw…nothing. *Oh well.* She returned to her typewriter, rolled in another piece of paper, but then stopped herself. *This isn't like her.* Louetta decided to take a few moments and see if she could find her boss.

She walked to the grandstands and saw Nick, Richie and Max working on the field, like they did every morning, but no one else. She walked down the stone steps, all the way to the fence, and called out to Nick, who trotted over, still holding his rake.

"'Morning, Nick. Have you seen Nashota?"

"Sorry, Lou, I haven't seen her at all so far today. She's not in the office?"

"No. Her car's in the lot so she must be somewhere, I just thought she might be out here. Well, I'll find her." And with that she walked back up the steps and then down the ramp to the breezeway. Three pair of eyes followed her progress until Nick grinned and said, "OK, mullions, let's get back to work."

Louetta, meanwhile, walked back towards the office. Unlikely that Nashota was in one of the bathrooms along the breezeway, maybe she was in the concession stand? *She has no reason to go in there, or in the souvenir stand, Rowena always made sure it was all neat and tidy every night. Maybe she's…*

Louetta stopped. *Did I hear something?* She stood still, but heard nothing. Maybe the wind. She began walking again and this time she was sure, she definitely heard something. "Nashota? Nashota? Is that you? It's me, Louetta, where are you? Talk to me, Nashota."

Now she heard a…a noise, like a thump, and then a moan, but where was she? "Do that again, Nashota, one more time." *THUMP!* Coming from her left, in…in… the souvenir stand! Louetta grabbed her keys, fumbled a bit for the right one, then opened the door.

Nashota was on the floor, with her back slightly elevated against one of the boxes of Topps cards. Her skirt was down around her ankles and there was a little bit of blood on her panties. When she saw Louetta she reached out her hand. "Help me up, Lou, please." Her voice was barely above a whisper.

"Nashota!" Louetta wasn't sure if she had ever screamed so loudly in her life! "What happened? Did someone…was there someone…were you…?"

"There's no one here," said Nashota with some difficulty as she used Louetta's hand, and the box of cards, to get back to her feet. "It was me, I started feeling pains, felt like…OOOOOOH!" Her face became distorted and she doubled over. Louetta grabbed her and steadied her so she wouldn't fall again. Nashota took a series of quick breaths, then slowly rose.

"Pains like that. It may be contractions but I dunno, I've never had them before, and it's too early, baby's not due for more-n a month and first babies are often late…" She took a deep breath, then another. "I'm OK, but I think we ought to go into the office."

The women slowly walked out of the souvenir stand and over to their two-room space. Louetta generally occupied the outer office, but Nashota immediately sat in the guest chair and said "Lou, bring your chair over here, please." As soon as it arrived, she put both legs up on it and, with a heavy sigh, whispered "I probably need to see a doctor."

Louetta immediately shifted into another gear. "Sit right there, don't move," she said, and then she dashed off into Nashota's office, found Doc Nelson's phone number and dialed.

"This is Louetta Henry, I work with Nashota Simpson in the Wolves' office, and she's having pains…yes, she says it may be contractions…yes, I saw a little blood, not a lot…no, well, let me check." She put down the phone and ran back to what was normally her space to ask, "Did your water break?" She then dashed back to the phone to report "No." A moment later she was back on the run. "How often are the pains coming?" And back to the phone. "She's not sure, maybe every 3–4 minutes." Another question—"Has the frequency changed any, or is it holding steady at every 3–4 minutes?" The answer to that was "steady."

Louetta spent the next minute or so listening to the voice on the other end of the line before she asked, "Not to the emergency room?" A pause, then "OK, we'll be there just as soon as we can." She hung up and went back to Nashota. "Doc Nelson's nurse says to bring you in to her, not to emergency. I would have thought…"

"You were talking to Nurse Wendy, I'll bet. She's real good, I have faith in her, she knows what she's doing, she and Doc both." Nashota put her legs down but struggled to get out of the chair.

"We need to man the office, Nashota. Let me call Dorothy, she'll come over." Nashota, slowly taking deep breaths, simply nodded.

Within twenty minutes they could hear a police siren getting louder and louder until it stopped in their parking lot and Dorothy Dean, President of the Booster Club, burst through the door.

"I called Newell and he had Officer Montgomery bring me over. We went through red lights!" she said with a laugh. Then she went over to Nashota. "Come on, honey, he's waitin' for us outside." But as Nashota began to rise, she had another pain and sat down again.

"Give me a minute, Dorothy, these pains seem to pass. And listen, I hope you don't mind, but I'd like Louetta to take me over to Doc Nelson. Why don't you stay here and mind the place, answer the phone, that kind-a thing, 'til we get back?"

"Nashota, I'm happy to drive you, we got this wonderful police escort…"

"And I appreciate you gettin' that, love, I surely do. Here, help me up, will you? But I think I'd feel more, oh, at ease, if I knew you was here runnin' things while we're gone. You've worked in here before and…"

"I've also had babies before, 'Sho, I think…"

"Please, Dorothy," said Nashota, and there was something about the look on her face that told Dorothy Dean to back off.

"Sure thing, shug, just leave this place to me. Let me help you out, at least." And the three of them slowly walked into the parking lot, where Officer Montgomery immediately took over, gently placing Nashota in Louetta Henry's car, as he was instructed.

"Want me to try and find Jack?" Dorothy's question was met by an emphatic shaking of the head as the young policeman turned on his siren and the two cars roared off.

Louetta waited outside as Nurse Wendy immediately put Nashota into an exam room. She came out a short while later, smiled and said, "She's fine, no cause for alarm," just as Doc Nelson went in. "Be right back," said Wendy, and less than ten minutes later, she poked her head out and said, "You can come in now, Louetta."

"She has something called prodromal labor, it's very common, nothing to worry about," said Doc Nelson. "It's kind of a false labor, happens a lot. There's no need to fret and I've told her that, but she needs to go home and rest. And when I say rest, I mean full rest, in the bed, do nothing for at least today." He was looking directly at Nashota when he said that, then he turned back to Louetta. "Can you make sure she gets home OK?" Louetta, trying to process what she was being told, was silent until Doc Nelson said "Ma'am?" It served as a slap in the face.

"Yes, sir, yes, doctor, I'll take care of her, don't you worry none. Does she need any medicine, or does she have to take anything?"

Doc Nelson actually smiled. "She's not sick, young lady, she's pregnant. But a hot bath or shower would be good, and rest, bed-rest, like I said, and if she could sleep, that would be even better. You got that?" Louetta nodded and emphatically said "Yes, sir." He started for the door but stopped when she asked, "Dr. Nelson, do you know what caused this?"

"No, we don't know why this happens. Like I said, it's pretty common, though. And it won't affect her baby, or her pregnancy, or her delivery." He held the door open for her. "I will check on her, at home, tomorrow morning. She knows all this, I've already told her everything."

There was no police escort this time. "Too bad," said Nashota. "Made me feel like Bess Truman or Queen Elizabeth, someone like that." Then she asked Louetta to take her to the ballpark. "I need to get my car," she said, but Louetta immediately protested.

"The doctor said you was to rest, I don't think driving home is what he had in mind."

"I don't live all that far away, and I need my car," but now Louetta was determined.

"I'll take you to the ballpark, Nashota, and Dorothy can then drive you home, I 'spect you'd be a little more comfy having her help you with your bath, am I right?" Nashota nodded. "Good, then it's settled. We'll worry 'bout getting you back into your car tomorrow, or another day, OK? Right now, we're just gonna follow the doctor's orders."

Jack didn't learn about all this until the team got to Mettin. Since it was a short drive between the two Virginia towns, they motored over after the last game in Beck so they could get a good night's sleep before playing the three-game set against the Foxes and their very rowdy, unfriendly fans. And Jack needed to get some sleep after that damned series in Beck. Edens Ridge had won the opener, 5–4, on Pete Sevareid's ninth inning sacrifice fly. The next two games, however, really stuck in his craw. "I lost these last two games, Mike," he mumbled to Hamblen on the bus. "Not the players, me. Fucked up both nights." His coach/trainer/bus driver quietly disagreed, but Jack just shook his head. "First I yanked Harry too quickly, he prob'ly could-a gotten a coupla more outs. Surely couldn't-a done worse than the bullpen," he said, remembering the four runs that quickly crossed the plate, putting the game out of reach. Then the next night, Greg Bombard kept the Bears off-balance for nine innings, but his counterpart, Ed Ottinger, was equally as good. Jack had decided to let Bombard pitch the tenth, but he loaded the bases before Simpson could replace him with Ken Crockett. It looked like the Wolves had lucked out when Crockett induced a ground ball, but the Wolves failed to turn the double play and got on the bus with a tough, 2–1 loss in their throats. "Can't blame anyone but myself," Jack kept saying as they headed to Mettin.

When they got to town, they dropped their three Negro players off at the Brooks farm, then headed to the hotel. As the players were checking in, the front-desk clerk handed Jack a note. He stuck it in his pocket until everyone had their keys and bags and were trudging up to their rooms, then read it as he was heading for his room. He stopped, read it again, then raced back to the clerk.

"Did you take this message?"

"Yes, sir, I did. I assume that was your wife? She wanted me to tell you not to worry at all, she's just fine, and to BE SURE and not call her tonight! The doc said she needs her rest, so she'll be sleeping by the time you read this note. And she said...well, you can read it all right there, I wrote down everything she said."

"And how'm I s'posed to sleep, not knowin' how she is, did she tell you that?" This young man had suddenly become no more than a dumb old umpire in Jack's eyes.

The neatly-dressed clerk calmly straightened his tie. "Your wife warned me you might get a little, um, testy, sir. She told me to press upon you that she is FINE and she'll tell you everythin' in the mornin' after you both have had plenty-a sleep." He gave out a little laugh. "She told me I had her permission to tuck you in, might could help you sleep, but I said I was sure that would not be necessary." And he smiled.

Jack gave him the evil eye—this kid was definitely no better than an ump!—said "Hmmmmff," and walked off.

Despite her assurances, it took Jack a little while to grudgingly admit that worrying wasn't helping things any, and only then did he fall asleep. It was almost nine when he woke up, and it was only minutes later that he placed his call.

Nashota was feeling much better and told him so. "I stayed home all day yesterday, Dorothy was in and out, and Louetta was able to handle things at the yard, only called me one time. That girl has really grown up right before our eyes, Jack, we did good hiring her. Tell you what, she was quite the lifesaver when I needed her most, kept her a level head, suggested calling Dorothy, we need to give her a raise!" She hoped he would laugh, or grunt, or something, but he just stayed on point.

"So whatinhell is this pro…pro-dribble…pro-double labor? Does everybody get it? Is it serious? Does it affect the baby at all?"

"It's prodromal labor, dear," she said, trying to sound soothing. "It's a…a false labor and yes, a lotta women get it. Doc Nelson and Nurse Wendy both said it was not at all unusual, they told me to rest, take a hot bath, which I did and BOY, it felt great! Little thing like that made me feel so much better, hard to believe. In fact, I been thinking that I might could go over to the ballpark for a while, there's a few things…"

"I don't know if that's such a good idea, 'Sho," said Jack. "Team won't be home for a coupla days yet, there's prob'ly no need…"

"You know as well as I that there is still plenty to do when you're on the road. But I certainly don't hafta stay out there all day, *asiule ehu*. Maybe…um, maybe I can go over after we finish this chat? Then I promise you, Jack, I swear to *U-ne-qua,* that I will come home early, maybe three or four o'clock, and do the same tomorrow. Maybe after that I get back to a regular schedule, depending on how I feel, what do you say, hmmm?"

He knew his wife, he knew she had already made up her mind that this is what she was going to do. But he couldn't give up without at least a mild protest.

"I dunno, hon, you yourself told me the Doc and the nurse both said you oughta rest, and you'll certainly rest better at home than out at the yard. Why don't you stay home one more day, then go in tomorrow, after we talk on the phone?"

"But there are things…Jack, look, as great a job as Louetta's been doing, there are just some things she can't do, doesn't know how to do. Suppose I stay here 'til, say, noon or so, and then only work 'til around four, could you live with that?"

My goodness, she's actually not being pig-headed about this! Wonder if this pro…what was it? Prodromal thing, maybe it scared her a little. Don't know if I've ever seen Nashota scared. "Yeah, I guess," he said. "And I'll call you tomorrow, maybe around this time or a little before, and if you're feelin' OK, you can try a longer day, like, say, 5–6 hours. How's that sound?"

It felt good to get a win on the home front, because after losing those two tough games in Beck, Jack was afraid a playoff spot was slipping away from him and his Edens Ridge Wolves.

FIFTEEEN

With less than a month to go in the season, three clubs were practically assured of post-season slots—Weare, who had now climbed into first place; Buchanan; and hard-charging Shirley. It was the fourth and final berth that was very much up for grabs, with Beck, Blackmer, Edens Ridge and Mettin all separated by just three-and-a-half games. This three-game series, then, was crucial to both the Wolves and the Foxes.

It was Pat Head's turn to pitch, and he was excellent. He gave up a leadoff double in the second inning when the ball was jarred loose from Oddibe's glove after he crashed into the fence in left-center. This not only pleased the Mettin fans, but gave them free reign to heap even more derision upon their favorite target.

"Couldn't catch a cold out there, n—!"

"You'd-a held onto it if it were some fried chicken, now wouldn't you?"

On previous trips up to Virginia, Jack had spoken to the umpires about doing something about the verbal abuse coming out of the grandstands, but they were not inclined to get involved. "The fans paid their money, they have a right to say what they want, Jack, you know that. Same thing applies when your fans get on players down in Edens Ridge. We know to get involved if it becomes physical, but aside from that…" A shrug of the shoulders was the umpires' best response, so he knew better than to say anything, and watched as the Foxes pushed across a run. And that was the only scoring through eight tense innings, as Head matched serves with Mettin's grizzled Jasper Gillis, who claimed to be 39 but, like Jack Benny, was probably older. Gillis had pitched for Hazleton when Jack played for Binghamton in 1938, and Jack had a strong memory that Eastern League managers and players had constantly accused him back then of throwing a spitball. Ever since Burleigh Grimes had retired after the 1934 season, the spitter had been outlawed, but Gillis was still (likely) throwing it, and effectively, too, as witnessed by the Wolves' inability to get any kind of a hit against the old pro.

With Pat Head scheduled to lead off the ninth, Jack called on Raburn Reece to pinch-hit. The first pitch was outside, but the next one dropped a foot as Reece swung through it. He stepped out of the batter's box, looked over to Jack, and then laughed! "That's some fuckin' pitch," he said to Mettin's catcher as he stepped back in. "Can't wait for him to throw it again," to which the catcher quickly responded, "You won't hafta wait long, meat."

The next pitch, though, was a fastball, up and in, which put Reece on his butt as the Foxes' players and their faithful howled, and Gillis glared at this raw rookie who had dared to laugh at his bread-and-butter pitch. Reece said nothing, he just stepped back in without even brushing himself off. When the count went full at 3–2, Reece knew he'd be seeing that piece-a-shit pitch, and geared up. It came in, the rookie started to swing and then it dropped; he pulled his bat back and the umpire, Joe Gallagher, sang out "Ball Four, take your base."

The Mettin players, and all their partisan supporters, began heaping serious abuse on young Mr. Gallagher! A lot of remarks were directed at someone who wasn't even present—his mother—while others questioned his eyesight, his intelligence, his abilities, and even (in one case) the length of his penis. He simply called time, took out his whisk broom, dusted off home plate, then frowned at the fans as he returned to his position behind the plate and motioned for the game to continue. While this was going on, Jack has asked for "time" and had trotted down the third-base line so he could speak with Oddibe, who met him halfway. This increased both the intensity and the decibel level of the fans' venom, which forced the manager to put his arm around his young outfielder and speak right into his ear so he could be heard.

"First pitch will be a spitter," said Jack. "I want you to bunt it, maybe between the mound and third, if you can. But if you foul it or miss it, don't worry, see if you can then slap the next pitch to left, they won't be expectin' that, OK?" Oddibe nodded and smiled when his skipper slapped his butt as the two headed back to their respective posts.

This display caused the fans to go nuts. With alarming speed, the ballpark became a raging cauldron of vile, with screaming coming from virtually every section. And now a couple of fans seated near home plate began shaking the protective netting, as if they hoped to pull it apart and race onto the field, or at least yank it right out of its moorings. Having lived through this kind of furor several times during the season, as far back as spring training, Jack Simpson recognized the potential danger and ran down the line again, this time going straight for Gallagher.

"You have to get control of this before it gets out of hand. My players won't be safe if these fans come out on the field. You have to do somethin' NOW."

As base umpire Mark Aubrey joined them, Jack repeated his plea. Aubrey, the crew chief, immediately directed Jack and Oddibe, and even Raburn Reece, to go back into the dugout "until we get this straightened out." (Later, Jack would admit that he was actually surprised when they acted so quickly.) Gallagher, meanwhile, ran over to the Foxes dugout, where Beau Maxwell came out to meet him.

"These fans need to calm down. I won't restart the game until they do, and if it lasts very long, I'll call it off right here and Edens Ridge will win in a forfeit, 9–0. Understand me, Beau?"

The Mettin manager needed to scream so he'd be heard. "You can't do that!"

"I can and I will unless you get control of your fans!"

Beau looked around and saw that his father had come down to the first row of the grandstand, right next to their dugout. He ran over to him.

"Umps are threatenin' to forfeit unless the fans calm down, Dad. You need to get on the mike and shut them up."

"They can't do that!" said Truck, to which Beau quickly replied, "Yes they can, and we both know it." He took a breath, then spoke quietly into his father's ear.

"Look, Dad, these umps have been real lenient with us, I know it, bet you do, too. But they can't have a riot break out, and these fans…our fans, we can't have our fans cost us a game, not now, not when we're fightin' for a playoff spot. Dad, if we forfeit this game, our season is over and I'll tell you, we'll have a real hard time tryin' to get guys to play here next year or any year after that. This is our season, right here, so if you wanna have a chance at any post-season dough, you gotta do somethin' now, and I mean right now."

Truck Maxwell was not used to this kind of talk from his son, but he nodded and moved as quickly as he could up the stairs, disappearing into the press box.

"Ladies and gentlemen, this is Truck Maxwell. Y'all know me and know how I feel 'bout…things. But I also want to win or lose a ballgame fair and square, and these umpires seems to be afraid that y'all are gonna cause a riot or somethin'. Now, I know that ain't gonna happen and you know that ain't gonna happen, but we gotta prove it to 'em or else they gonna forfeit this game to Edens Ridge."

The booing increased in intensity.

"Friends, friends," said Truck, raising his voice. "Looky-here, y'all can boo, that's fine, but you gotta at least sit down so they don't think you're comin' out there with pick axes or what-not. We only gotta get three outs, let's get this-here game started again so's our boys can wrap up this win. Tell you what, y'all do that for our team and we'll keep the beer stand open and give out a free brew to anyone who wants one. That a deal?"

The boos changed to cheers and everyone sat down. The umpires gave Jack, Oddibe, and Reece the OK, and the game began anew.

Mettin's third baseman crept in, expecting a bunt. As Jack had predicted, Gillis threw his illegal pitch and Oddibe tried to bunt but could do nothing more than foul it off to the left. This emboldened the third baseman to move in a little closer, and this time the veteran pitcher decided to throw a fastball up and in, hoping to induce Daniels to pop the ball up for an out. Instead, the young Negro hit the ball "inside out," a baseball term that describes hitting the ball the other way (in this case, to left field), even though the pitch was thrown inside. It flew over the head of the drawn-in third baseman and into the outfield for the Wolves' first hit of the night. Raburn Reece briefly thought about trying to make it to third, but his manager threw up the stop sign and he went back to second base, standing on the bag as if he were some ancient explorer claiming this land in the name of his sovereign.

Truck Maxwell had signed Jasper Gillis in early May, when it had become apparent that the Foxes needed more pitching and he had learned that the spitballer, something of a minor league legend, was looking for work. However, the age difference between the veteran and his manager had made this an uneasy marriage, at best. The two, in fact, had grown to dislike each other, and the clubhouse was now divided between "Pro Jasper" and "Pro Beau" players. The young manager was convinced that this chasm was the reason his team wasn't closer to guaranteeing itself a playoff berth.

About three weeks earlier, Beau had argued with his father, vehemently trying to convince Truck to release Gillis and two other players as a means of reestablishing his authority and reuniting the team. "We can win this thing, Dad," he had said. "If we just get rid of Gillis and a couple of his toadies…"

"Gillis is a helluva pitcher," Truck had said that night at the house. "He can pitch us to a pennant, that's why I signed him."

"You signed him because he's been playing forever and you think he's hot shit. He thinks he's hot shit, too, but…"

"Already won 13 games for us, ain't he?" asked Truck. "Only been here three months and he's second in the league in wins. We'd be fightin' Kruse for last place without him."

"We'd be fightin' Buchanan for first without him, in my opinion. He's divided the clubhouse, you seen it yourself. That ain't no way to win a pennant, we all oughta be Mettin Foxes, nothin' else. If we release him, plus Malcolm and Isaacs, that immediately clears the air, brings the whole team together. I guarantee, Dad, I absolutely guaran-fuckin'-tee, that we'll get ourselves in playoff position in no time at all. I know my team, I know they can do it, as soon as we get rid of that jagoff Gillis."

But Truck wouldn't hear of it. Jasper Gillis was a name, and a winner, and people came out to see him pitch, more people than on other nights, and more people meant more money, and more money always made Truck Maxwell happy. So when his son had gone to bed that night, after having lost his argument, he had made himself a vow. *I love this game and I love managin', and next year I'll be managin' somewhere else. Somewhere, anywhere, but not in Mettin.*

Now, in the ninth inning of this important game against Edens Ridge, Beau Maxwell had signaled for some bullpen action, and he slowly ambled his way to the mound, expecting the worst. He got it.

"Don't need no pep talk, child," Gillis growled. "My arm's fine, I ain't tired, and I got plenty-a stuff left to get these chicken-shit hitters. Get your ass back in the dugout so I can do my job."

Beau looked his pitcher right in the eye. "I got Forbes gettin' hot in the pen. One more hit and I'll be back out here to get you," he said before turning to walk back to the dugout.

"Yeah, you and what army?" sneered Gillis.

The younger Maxwell stopped, turned around, and glared at his pitcher. This wasn't the first time that the hostility between the two had been on public display, and he was tired of it.

"You'll leave the game when I tell you to leave. If you give me any shit, you'll earn a police escort right to the fuckin' bus depot. Understand?" The two glared at each other, then Gillis spit on the ground as Beau headed back to the dugout.

A bunt by Squirrel Davis moved up both runners and brought Mac McElvain to the plate, with Pete Sevareid in the on-deck circle. Gillis actually glanced at the dugout but Beau gave him no sign, as if to say "you think you invented this game, you make the decision." With first base open, one could opt to walk McElvain, which would load the bases but set up the possibility of a double play, or maybe a force at home plate. It would also bring up the Wolves' most potent bat—Sevareid—in the ultimate run-producing scenario, one in which he thrived. To walk or not to walk, that was the question. The manager usually made that call, but in this case, Beau Maxwell (who favored issuing the walk) was deferring to his experienced veteran.

Gillis decided to be careful with the good-hitting Edens Ridge second baseman. First pitch was inside for a ball and the next one bounced in the dirt. The righty felt he could tempt Mac with an outside pitch but McElvain, thinking along with righty, stepped into the ball, meeting it squarely and hitting it on a line over second base, a clean single. Reece scored easily and Daniels, running hard from the outset, flew around third and slid in, comfortably ahead of the throw to the plate. Beau Maxwell walked out to the mound and silently took the ball from his hurler, who also said nothing as he trudged into the dugout on the short end of a 2–1 score, which is exactly how the game ended.

As promised, Jack called Nashota in the morning and she sounded good and felt good, even better than yesterday, she said. She had gone over to the ballpark, worked for less than four hours, and went home when she began to feel a bit fatigued. And she got plenty of sleep, too—"I was in bed reading, around, oh, maybe 9:15, but I couldn't keep my eyes open, so I just closed the book and turned in."

Jack told her a bit about their game, skipping over that little fear-of-a-fan-riot thing. She seemed impressed.

"Wow, winning the game after not being able to get a hit for eight innings, that's terrific!"

"Yeah, it was a good win for us," he said.

Her plan was to go to work once they hung up and stay 'til maybe four o'clock, but "if I feel tired like I did yesterday, I'll just come on home. I need to save my strength for when the next homestand starts in a coupla days."

"Listen, about that, do you think you could give me Dorothy's phone number? I want to see if she can spell you during the day once we get home." She started to protest but he cut her right off. "Look, 'Sho, I'm not the type of husband who dictates to his wife, you know that, but there won't be any discussion on this one. Ain't nothin' more important to me than your health and the health of our baby, and I'll do whatever I need to do to make sure you don't over-exert yourself. I've thought about just bannin' you from the park and payin' for off-duty cops to keep you at home…" He'd hoped she would laugh at his joke, but she didn't…"but I think it would be better if we paid Dorothy to split the job with you until the baby is born or the season ends, whichever comes first. Now may I please have her phone number, my love?"

Dorothy, of course, was only too willing to help, which Jack had fully expected. He even knew she wouldn't want to get paid, but he insisted on it, so they agreed she would get the current minimum wage of 75 cents an hour. "I'll even bring in a cot that we have at home and put it somewhere so she can lay down for an hour or so whenever she wants," said Dorothy, which Jack found to be amusing.

"You may have to force her like you would a toddler," he said, which made them both chuckle.

"I remember those days. Lord, there were times that Burt would pitch a fit when I tried to get him to take his nap. Ha, guess I'll just tell her the same thing I used to say to Burt—sooner you lie down, sooner you can get back up. Where do you think we could put that cot?"

Jack thought for a few seconds and then said "The visitor's dressing room, it's darker in there, she might actually be able to sleep. Have one-a the groundskeepers move it for you, tell 'em I said to do it. There's a closet in that room, when Weare comes to town, they can fold it up and put it in there."

With those calls out of the way, he began to shave when the phone rang. *Wonder if it's Nashota, or maybe Dorothy forgot to ask me somethin'...*

Wrong with both guesses—it was Beau Maxwell, wanting to take him to breakfast. "My treat," said the young manager, a proposition that Jack could hardly refuse. He wondered, though, what this was all about, and why Beau said to wait for him in front of the hotel and not in the lobby. Guess he'd find out in half an hour.

Standing on the street, Jack heard a noise and looked to his left. He could see a red car moving swiftly, going much faster, actually, than it should have on Mettin's Main Street. *Sure hope...damn, it is him* he thought as a Crosley Model CD Convertible screeched to the sidewalk and Beau Maxwell said, "Hop in!" The thought *he'll be careful, now that he has a passenger* quickly gave way to "SLOW DOWN THERE, BEAU!" shouted out a couple of times.

When they crossed the railroad tracks, Jack began to wonder where they were going, prompting that very question. "Grits. Best eatin' in town, maybe the whole county, for that matter. We'll be there in 'bout five minutes or so," to which Simpson mentally added *If we live that long.*

There was nothing fancy at all about Grits. It was an old brown building that sat by itself off to the side of the road, and the inside was equally nondescript. But the smell of food was unmistakable, especially bacon being fried in the clearly-visible kitchen. Jack also saw a couple of waiters bringing out huge stacks of pancakes, plus big, fluffy biscuits with gravy, eggs, sausage—his mouth was watering already. And despite the early hour, the place was jumping! No one seeming to care about the drab and unassuming decor, they were all too busy eating.

Jack also noticed one other thing—he and Beau were the only white people in the place. *Beau Maxwell likes to eat at a Negro diner?*

No sooner had that thought popped up in his head than a large black woman came over and gave them a big smile.

"Beau, good to see you, been a few days, y'all musta been outta town, am I right?"

Beau smiled. "We were. Just got back a coupla days ago, this is the first chance I've had to come see you."

"Well OK," the woman said. "Guess I forgive you. Glad you here now." She looked at Jack. "And who this fine man what's losin' his hair?"

"Jack Simpson, ma'am, I manage the Edens Ridge team, we're in town..."

"Oooh, yes, I know you, seen you 'fore, at the ballpark, course, you a good manager, you always seem to give our boys fits." She had a hearty laugh. "Glad you finally found your way out here." She then took a quick look around. "Beau, all I got is a little table, kinda in back, may be a bit small for ya, I dunno. If you want somethin' else, it'll be a few minutes, not too long, I 'spect. I can bring you some coffee while you wait..."

"That little table is just fine, Oree. Sittin' in the back, actually, be good today. OK with you, Jack?" And hearing no objections, the woman led them to a small table where they did, in fact, have to wedge themselves in. She waited for them to be seated, then she quickly wiped it off and said, "Be back with that coffee directly."

"That's Oriole, like the bird, or the IL team in Baltimore," said Beau. "Don't know if that's her real name, but that's what everyone calls her. She owns the place. I brought you here 'cause the food's great, plus it's outta the way, not likely anyone will see or hear us."

Jack smiled. "Does your daddy know you come out to a…a…a..?"

"Who do you think brought me here in the first place?" replied Beau, and then, more quietly, "Don't read nothin' into it, hear?"

Oriole brought a tray with silverware, napkins, coffee cups and a pot of coffee, plus a couple of menus. As soon as she poured, Beau said "I know what I want, Oree—full breakfast, and make sure the bacon is extra crisp, last time…"

"That man done gone, had several people complain 'bout the bacon." She looked at Jack. "Need a moment, sir?"

"What's the full breakfast, ma'am?" he wondered.

"Name's Oriole, sir. Two pancakes, two eggs, any way you like 'em, sausage, bacon, grits or hash browns, coffee. 'Nuff food to last you the whole day, unless your name is Beau Maxwell." She let out that big laugh, and Jack joined in.

"I don't think I could do justice to all that, ma'am… Oriole. Maybe I could get two eggs, over easy, with a biscuit, no gravy but butter, hash browns and some-a that crispy bacon?"

"Sure thing, Mr. Simpson. Be out in a jiffy." And she made her way into the kitchen.

Beau took a sip of coffee. "Oh, that's good. And hot. Gets the ol' engine goin', you know?" He took another sip, then leaned back in his chair. "Bet you're wonderin' why I invited you out this mornin', eh?"

Jack nodded. "The question did cross my mind."

Beau laughed. "OK, let's get right into it, Jack. My team…it's a good team, pretty much, I like these fellas, don't get me wrong, but I don't think we're gonna be able to make the playoffs, 'specially after last night. Last night…," and here he whistled. "Your boys really took it to us, get off the floor after bein' no-hit for eight innings, that's a good team, Jack, that's a good bunch-a guys. Y'all deserve to be in the post-season but Beck and Blackmer, they're both still ahead-a you and the clock's tickin'."

"I know all this, Beau. Where you headed here?" Jack hated beating around the bush.

"Right. Look, I think I can help you, and help me, too. I'm sure it ain't no secret that me and Jasper Gillis don't get along at all. Man's a good pitcher but…"

"He oughta be," Jack interrupted. "Been pitchin' forever, I even batted against him in the Eastern League. Think that's where it was, definitely before the war. He oughta be chewin' up Class D hitters."

"And he is, you saw that last night. I prob'ly shoulda yanked him when I had the chance but I didn't, I fucked up, cost us a game. Maybe cost us more-n that, I think we may be done. After you guys scored, we had no life, you saw us, a quick one-two-three, we're out. No life, no fight. Your team is still scrappin', even with Beck and Blackmer ahead-a you, I like that, I admire that, actually. I'd like to see you grab that number-four spot, Jack, so here's what I'm thinkin'. We could help each other out here, one simple deal, could give you the push you need, gets rid of my biggest headache and gets me started on plannin' for 1953." Even though Beau was hoping to be elsewhere next season, you never knew in this business, he might wind up spending yet another year as the Foxes' manager, so it didn't hurt to be thinking ahead.

"A deal, eh? You want me to take Gillis off your hands." Now that the coffee had cooled off a bit, he was finally able to taste it and Beau was right, it was pretty damned good.

"I gotta tell you, Beau, I'm not sure he'd be any less of a pain-in-the-ass with me than he's been for you. Think I got a hit offa him, he's prob'ly still steamed." They both laughed. But Jack had some interest, and why not, he'd be adding a veteran who'd already won 13 games. "Whatcha want in return?"

Buck leaned forward and lowered his voice, although no one around them was paying attention to anything except the plate in front of them.

"I'd need a pitcher, of course, and I was thinkin' Neville, I'm sure you wouldn't part with any other starter, not this close to the end. And maybe that new kid you got, Reece, I saw him takin' BP, and he drew that key walk last night. Looks like he can play, might be the kinda guy I could build on next year. Hmmm?"

Jack had to laugh. "Two for one? Where'm I gonna get an outfielder at this late stage, eh? Not a chance, Beau, sorry." But the younger Maxwell was ready for that.

"I understand, Jack, sure, I'd feel the same way if it was you makin' this proposal. I got a guy named Malcolm, Carl Malcolm, you seen him before. Good player, can hit and field..."

"He's a piece of..." Jack looked around, then decided to be discreet in a public place. "Piece of crap, and you know it. Don't want him on my team, not even for these last few weeks, sorry."

"OK, fine, you're entitled to your own opinion. Don't take Malcolm, how 'bout Isaacs, Charlie Isaacs, good little..."

"Infielder, but I don't need an infielder. I got Danny Chase and Doc Andrews behind my starters, so, tell you the truth, Beau..."

The truth would have to wait a moment, because Oriole brought their plates to them. They fell quiet while she laid everything out on the table.

"That sure looks good, ma'am...Oriole, sorry," said Jack. "That biscuit...wow, I can't wait to taste it, I have a real weakness for biscuits."

Oriole smiled. "Go 'head, have a bite, tell me whatcha think." Jack was only too happy to comply, and the biscuit did not disappoint.

"Ooh, doctor, that is purely delicious. Miss Oriole, one bite and you've already made my day!"

She laughed and gave him a little curtsy. "Thank you kindly, Mr. Simpson, thank you. We aim to please. Now you boys enjoy."

Maxwell was already diving into his mountain of food. "You gonna be able to eat all that?" Jack asked. Beau nodded, swallowed, then said, "Never had to ask for a doggy bag yet. But Jack, you was sayin', 'bout the deal..."

The Mountain Empire League

"Yeah, the deal." First he needed some eggs and hash browns. That accomplished, he looked at his young colleague.

"I like my team, Beau. Gillis might be able to help us, but he might also prove to be more of a distraction. I know how he is, thinks his turds don't stink, and that ain't gonna change no matter what uniform he's wearin'. I know you're in a pickle here, and I'd like to help you out, but we don't have all that much time left in the season, and then you never have to see the SOB again."

There was silence for a moment as they both ate their breakfasts.

"Jack, come on, maybe…"

"Beau, thanks for bringin' me here, I really love this food, I'll hafta remember it for next year. Gotta say no to a deal, though. Think I'll fight this battle with the platoon I got. Sorry."

There wasn't much talking for the rest of the meal, nor on the drive back to the hotel. When the convertible reached its destination, Jack put out his hand.

"Thanks for the meal, and the conversation, Beau. No hard feelings?"

Maxwell grabbed the extended hand. "Course not. Your team, your decision." They shook and Jack said "See you tonight" as he got out of the car.

The younger man nodded and drove off. When he was out of earshot, though, he quietly said "Shit" to no one in particular.

When the team returned home, Win Appleton wrote a fair assessment of their playoff chances, and concluded with

> So now Gene Conn brings his boys into town this weekend, starting tonight, and all the Weare Mustangs have done since we saw them last was to vault over Buchanan and into first place. They will be followed by the Bees, and Lionel Ticknor's squad will be eyeing a return to the top spot and the coveted home field advantage throughout the playoffs. This has the makings of a do-or-die homestand for the Wolves. Game time tonight is 7:15 pm, and the gates will be opening at 6:00 pm, a bit earlier than usual, in anticipation of a big crowd. If you want to find a seat, we suggest getting to the ballpark early these next few nights.

The fans were listening, and began congregating in front of the ticket booth just after 5:30 pm. Nashota authorized ticket manager Patty Cantwell to open her window a few moments later, after first announcing that, after buying their tickets, fans would then be asked to form a new line in front of the main entrance. She drafted the ever-reliable Dorothy Dean to serve as a second ticket seller, and then Nashota herself went outside and stood near the box office, a roll of tickets in her hand. "If you've got the exact amount," she shouted, "I can help you right here." She also opened the gate. Getting people into the ballpark was her primary concern; they can't buy any food or souvenirs until they're safely inside. In less than an hour all 3,207 seats were filled, but there were still people reaching for their wallets as they approached the windows, so

Nashota made a snap decision. Once again going outside, she announced that no more seats remained but that she would sell a limited number of standing-room tickets. Ever mindful of the fire laws, she had Dorothy count out 200 tickets and give them to Patty, with the firm instruction that "once you've sold these, put up a SOLD-OUT sign and close the windows." She also passed that information on to Jimmy at the front gate.

And the fans got to see a ballgame that was, probably, the most entertaining one of the year. Even reading Win Appleton's write-up the next day was great fun.

> "Because the Edens Ridge Wolves were on the road in early July, area fans were not able to have a traditional holiday celebration at Bill Washington Park. But the team made up for it on Friday, with a huge assist from the Weare Mustangs, as the two teams shot off fireworks all night long. And we're not talking bottle rockets or Roman candles, but base hit after base hit after base hit, leading to runners scampering around the bases like jackrabbits, and runs being scored in unprecedented numbers. And when the smoke finally cleared, the hometown heroes looked at the scoreboard, took a deep breath, and collapsed in their locker room with a chaotic 16–14 win in their collective pockets."

It was the Mountain Empire League's highest-scoring game of the year, despite both teams starting their best pitchers. Greg Bombard went first, getting knocked out of the game after giving up seven runs in the third inning, while his Mustang counterpart, Ted Young, departed shortly thereafter during a four-run fourth that tied the game at eight apiece. Both skippers were then required to utilize their bullpens, which led to this Win Appleton zinger: "Jack Simpson was ready to pull out the remaining hairs in his head, but he quickly discovered he doesn't have any."

There was also a sideline note that was not reported in the newspaper, primarily because it was only noticed by the players. Trailing 14–11 in the eighth inning, the Wolves loaded the bases with one out, causing Gene Conn to bring in yet another hurler.

"Now pitching for Weare, number 51, Eulisio Campana, number 51," Bill McDermott announced over the PA.

After two warm-up throws, Yam Yarnell jumped off the bench, leaned on the top step of the dugout and stared intently, then turned around and faced his teammates.

"Eulisio Campana my ass! He ain't no Mexican, or whatever he sayin' he is. That there is Eulis Belle, I'd know him anywhere, we played together in Vegas coupla years ago."

The players laughed, while Yam turned back to the field and waved his arms, catching the attention of his manager standing in the third-base coaching box. Simpson quickly called time and ran down to his dugout and conferred with Yarnell.

"You sure that's him, Yam? Well I'll be damned!"

"Lemme swing the bat, skip, I know just how he throws, I caught that bastard for a whole season out there in the fuckin' desert."

The next batter was Oddibe and Jack wasn't inclined to pull his sparkplug and best defensive player on a hunch, so he just said, "I'll letcha know," and returned to his spot near third.

Daniels, no doubt trying too hard, fouled out to the catcher, which meant that Squirrel was due, but now his manager called time once again, whistled, and pointed to Yam. A disappointed Davis went back into the dugout, replaced by the tall newcomer.

"Now batting for Edens Ridge, number 35, Yam Yarnell, number 35."

The pitcher stared as Yam strode to the plate, and then flashed a wide grin. Yarnell looked at him, nodded, then swung the bat a couple of times and ended up by pointing his lumber directly at the man on the mound, sending his fellow Wolves into howls of laughter. Gene Conn, meanwhile, paced nervously in his dugout.

The first pitch was high and tight, rocking Yarnell back on his heels. The fans screamed, but Yam just smiled. The next pitch was low and away, and now the big man from Birmingham stepped out of the batter's box, knocked some dirt off his spikes, then stepped back in. He knew what was coming, fastball low around the knees, and he hit it solidly over the shortstop's head into left-center field, scoring two runs. Mac skied to center to end the inning, but the Wolves now trailed by just a run.

After Danny Chase made a nice play at short to end the top of the ninth, Pete Sevareid led off for the Wolves and hit a hard grounder that went past the diving third baseman for a single. Jack thought about asking VanLandingham to bunt but then decided *no, this game has been crazy right from the get-go, let's play it straight and see what happens,* and TVL responded with a single up the middle.

This brought up Monroe Hicks, who had not been asked to bunt since, well, he actually couldn't recall ever having been asked to bunt. And though it was traditional and safe baseball strategy, no one in the ballpark was expecting him to bunt.

Campana/Belle's first pitch was called a strike, though the Wolves all thought it was outside, as did the fans, who were not averse to sharing their collective wisdom with the umpire. The next pitch was fouled back, and now Monroe was down, 0–2. The third pitch, though, was up and in, and the broad-shouldered catcher shifted his feet just a bit and swung mightily. As soon as his bat hit the ball, there was no doubt that it was gone, the only question was whether or not it would stay fair. The Wolves, and their fans, needn't have worried. The long three-run homer ended the game, a 16–14 Edens Ridge victory, after three hours and 38 minutes. "Monroe Hicks kicked a game-winning field goal just as time was about to expire," wrote Win Appleton.

After such a long and emotionally-draining ballgame, Jack and Nashota were both tired and moving a little slowly the next morning, so they were especially startled when the phone rang. It was Louetta.

"Nashota, do you know when you're gonna be in? Only reason I ask is there's a man here, name-a Fred Hofmann, he's with…who'd you say you was with?…the St. Louis Browns, and he wants to talk to you-n Jack about Monroe. Whatcha want me to tell him?"

"Oh shit! Louetta, please be nice to him, and tell him we'll be there in half an hour, OK? And please make sure we have plenty-a coffee!"

Talk about a wake-up call.

They sat in the grandstand with their cups of Maxwell House. Fred Hofmann was a husky, friendly man, probably in his mid-fifties, with a red "drinker's nose." He smiled easily and didn't mind dropping names.

"I played for the Yankees in the 1920s, didja know that? I was just a backup catcher, never got in more-n 72 games with 'em, but I roomed with the Babe for a little while, as much as anyone roomed with him. Ping Bodie would say he roomed with Ruth's trunk, 'cause the Babe was never in the room, even to sleep, know what I mean? 'Scuse me, miss," he said to Nashota, who just laughed and said "No need to apologize, Mr. Hofmann. I know how things are, you ain't sayin' nothin' I don't already know."

"Not everyone is like that, miss. Now, your husband…I'm sure your husband here is the very salt-a the earth…," which got Nashota to laughing so loudly that Louetta could hear her in the office.

Confused by her laughter but definitely not wanting to pursue it, Hofmann simply continued.

"The Babe was just like that. Dumbest thing he ever did was get married, and he did that twice! Guy like that oughta just played 'round, least while he was in the bigs. He liked the ladies, and they liked him, 'specially liked his money, he sure could spend."

He took a breath, had a little coffee, and continued.

"He liked to live fast and hard, which I'm sure you know. All those stories you've heard 'bout him, they all true, all-a them. Do you know the one where he supposedly died in a car crash? I was there for that, I was with him! He had just bought a new car, was a Ford, maybe, not sure. Anyways, the Yankees gave him permission to drive to Philly for our series there, and he asked me if I wanted to go with him. Sure thing! But it wasn't just the two-a us, his wife Helen was there, too, and one-a our coaches, Charley O'Leary, and another guy, Frank Gleich, ever hear-a him? No, not many people did, outfielder, only played a few games in the bigs. So the Babe is drivin' to Philly and he'd had a pop or two, we all did, even Helen, and he's drivin' fast, which he liked to do, and we came up on this one curve and the car skidded and flipped over. That'll sober you up real quick, lemme tell you. No one got hurt, though, none-a us, and we finished the drive into Philly. Someone musta talked, though, 'cause one paper had a big headline that the Babe was dead! Prob'ly just wishful thinkin' from that Philly writer, his team stunk, lost over a hundred games, while we almost won the pennant. Anyway, the Babe…"

"Don't listen to a word that bootnosed backstop says!"

Another tall, burly man stood briefly at the top of the steps and then began his descent towards them. Hofmann frowned and shook his head. "Oh, heaven help us, it's Howie Haak."

He was nattily dressed in his sport coat and tie, and he was carrying a notebook and plain cup. Nashota thought it strange that a man would be walking around with coffee, but when he sat down in the row behind them and spit tobacco juice into that cup, she realized it wasn't being used for drinking. Made her feel a bit queasy, though it might have been the baby moving, these days it was hard to tell. He nodded to her, displaying a bit of a tattoo when he shook Jack's hand.

"Mr. and Mrs. Simpson, I am, indeed, Howie Haak, and I represent the Pittsburgh Pirates organization. And I would like to talk to you about a couple of your ballplayers, if I could. Without any interference from this sorry excuse…"

"I was here first, Howie," said Hofmann. "Can't help it if I can get outta bed earlier-n you."

Haak waved a very bent and crooked finger in Hofmann's direction. "You prob'ly ain't even been to bed yet, Bootnose. Judgin' by the look-a you…"

Hofmann stood up and clenched his fist, but Jack quickly got between them. "Gentlemen, gentlemen, there's no need to cause a ruckus right here in the stands. Mr. Haak, how 'bout you-n I go into the office up there while my wife and Mr. Hofmann stay right here. As you can see, Mrs. S is very pregnant and movin' around can often be difficult for her."

Actually, Nashota had been contemplating standing up, maybe walking a bit. Sitting on those wooden benches hurt her butt, and since her back ached most of the time as it was, she had been thinking about seeking some sort of relief.

"Jack, if you don't mind, I think it might be better if I went into the office. I'll be happy for either Mr. Hofmann or Mr. Haak to accompany me, and we can talk in there."

"Let me, ma'am," said Fred Hofmann, offering his hand as support as she slowly rose, then his entire arm as they made their way up the steps and into the office.

"She looks like she's due any day," said Haak, to which Jack replied "Close, 2–3 weeks or so."

"This your first?" Haak asked, and when Jack nodded, he said "I always tell brand-new parents that the first one is generally late, but this guy may be here 'fore you know it, she looks like she could pop at any time."

This kind of talk always made Jack begin to sweat, so he quickly changed the subject. "You mentioned a coupla our players, wanna talk about 'em now?"

"Sure thing," said Haak. "That's what I'm here for." He opened up his notebook, took a quick glance, and then fixed his attention on Jack.

"We're interested in your two Negro players, Hicks and Daniels. That Hicks sure hit the ball a long way last night. I've seen him before, he can handle the bat. Not sure about him behind the plate, but when a man can hit the ball that hard, we can teach him the finer points of catchin' and, if that don't work, we can always find a place for him to play. I was impressed with how quickly he reacted to that inside pitch, supposed to be a waste pitch and he crushed it. As for Daniels, you know we been lookin' at him for a few weeks now and think he has possibilities. You can't teach speed and he's got that in spades."

Jack frowned at Haak's choice of words, and the old scout immediately picked up on it.

"Oh, OK, sorry, 'scuse me, didn't mean nothin' by it, just an expression. What I mean is, he can go get 'em out there, he can steal bases, go from first to third without breakin' a sweat. He's just gotta prove he can hit and we think we can work with him on that."

Jack kept quiet, so Haak continued.

"I'm a physical-ability man, Simpson," he said. "What I mean by that is I look at what a feller can do right now and then estimate what he might do later, with the proper trainin'. We can help both-a these Negroes-a-yours make somethin'-a themselves, and by that I mean major league players. That's why I'm here; hell, that's why Fred's here." He waved that crooked finger towards the office. "Fred's not a bad guy, tell you the truth, he drinks too much but a lotta guys do in this business, I don't have to tell you. But look," and here he leaned in and lowered his voice, even though there was no one else around. "You've prob'ly heard the rumors 'bout the Browns and I can tell you I'm absolutely positive somethin's gonna happen 'fore too long. Baseball can't continue like this, it's just a black hole there in St. Louis, they draw six or seven thousand in Sportsman's Park most nights, teams barely make expenses when they go in there. Philly and Boston, they got problems, too. New York and Chicago, they may be the only places that can support more-n one team any more. But St. Louis also has Veeck, and most-a the other owners hate him, especially Topping and O'Malley and Yawkey. Wrigley thinks he's amusin' but would never stand up for him, not by himself. The owners want him out, they want out of St. Loo, and there are plenty-a towns just beggin' for a major league team. Baltimore, KC, Houston, Milwaukee, and the whole west coast, though I don't see the owners lettin' someone go out there, not by himself, you know? That's a long trip to play just one three-game series, even a five-game series. But the Browns are goin' someplace, soon, and without Veeck."

He spit in his cup. "You're wantin' to look after your boys, I'm sure, plus make a few bucks. If you sell 'em to the Browns, who knows where they might wind up? Houston, Baltimore, those are southern cities and I ain't certain what kind-a reception they'll get, know what I mean? Don't even know who the owner'll be, or the GM, might be people that don't want 'em. But we got Branch Rickey, you know he signed Jackie and Newk and Campy and those fellers when he was with the Dodgers. Now look, I know we suck in Pittsburgh this year, we already lost 93 games and we still got a whole month to go. That's why we need young blood."

He looked inside his notebook once again. "I am prepared to offer you $5,000 for both boys, Hicks and Daniels. I'm happy to shake on it now and let 'em finish out the season here. I know you're tryin' to make the playoffs and you'll be needin' both-a them, that's not a problem for us. Once your season ends, whenever that is, I'll come back, we'll fill out the paperwork, and I'll give you a check for five grand. I've heard you give your players a cut, that right?"

Jack nodded. "They get fifteen percent, as long as the sale price is over $300. This would be way over, they'd each be gettin'…"

"$375," said Haak, who laughed when he saw the look on Jack's face. "I was always good at math. Each player gets $375, you get $2,125, times two, that'll buy you a lotta baseballs next year, Simpson."

Meanwhile, inside the office, Fred Hofmann was making his pitch to Nashota.

"Look, there's no doubt we are…I mean my team, the Browns, when I say 'we.' We have a great organization and the best owner in the business in Bill Veeck. Have you ever met Bill? No? We oughta fix that, if you come to the Winter Meetings this December in Phoenix, we'll make sure it happens."

"My husband has said lots of nice things about Mr. Veeck over the years. I think his information has come mostly from Lionel Ticknor."

"Yeah, Lionel worked for us a coupla years, and now he's down here in this league, right? Good guy, good baseball man. Anyway, Bill is just tremendous, we all love workin' for him. But that doesn't mean we hafta wear rose-colored glasses. We all know he's havin' money problems. Team doesn't draw too well and we haven't contended since the war ended. Doesn't mean we can't keep lookin' for talent, though, that's the best way to turn things around. We got a coupla good young players right now. Ned Garver won twenty last year, though he won't do it this season, and Roy Sievers was Rookie of the Year in '49 but mostly been hurt this year and last. Scraps, Clint Courtney, is having a good solid rookie season, same with Bob Nieman. We got the start of somethin', I think, we just need more good young talent, and you've got some here. Tell you what, if it was up to me, I'd make you an offer for a bunch-a your boys, Hicks and Daniels for sure, plus the kid throwin' tonight, Head, maybe even the first baseman, Sevareid, though we already got Sievers. Ain't up to me, though, least-wise when it comes to money. I got just so much, $3,300, that's it. If you'll take that for both-a your colored boys, Hicks and Daniels, then we can sign today. But my guess is that ain't nearly enough for both-a them, and I'm bettin' that ol' Howie out there…," and he jerked his head towards the grandstand, where Haak and Jack were still in conversation, "…he'll have more money in his pocket. Rickey likes to spend, especially on coloreds, even though his Pirates, they're worse than us on the field and don't draw a whole lot better. Ah, what can you do?"

He finished his coffee and stood up.

"Daniels would be my first choice, ma'am, then Hicks, then Head. We got $3,300, Miz Simpson, I can guarantee the money can be here on Monday, Tuesday the latest. You prob'ly want to keep all your boys while you're chasin' a pennant, that's understandable. Your word is good with me, so if you tell me you're willing to sell me one-a them boys, I can wait 'til your season is over and then come back." He smiled. "You'll have had that baby by then, I'd wanna see him. Or her, I just love babies. Then we can get the paperwork done, dot all the I's and cross the T's, I'm sure you know what I mean. You have to talk it over with your husband, I know, I know, that's fine, talk it over and lemme know tonight, one way or t'other. I'm comin' to the game tonight but I'll be leavin' in the morning and drivin' over to Morristown, they're hosting Middlesboro this weekend. The Middlesboro team sucks…'scuse me, ma'am, don't know why I keep talkin' like that in front-a you, I know better. Their team is really bad, they're 'bout twenty games under .500, but they got this righty named Codinachs, from Cuba or Mexico or…I dunno. But he's got an ERA well under 3 even though his team's horse… terrible, so I thought I'd give him a look, maybe he could help us in two-three-four years. I'll check in with you tonight." And with that he nodded, left the office and found his car in the parking lot.

Louetta poked her head in. "Need anything?"

"Just some water, and I can get that, I need to walk a bit."

"He sure could talk, couldn't he?" asked Louetta with a smile.

"Yes, ma'am," replied Nashota, returning the grin while moving, slowly, towards the office door, drinking glass in hand. "I'm not used to a man yakkin' so much. They say us women gab a lot, but Mr. Hofmann was as bad as any woman I've ever met. Puts Dorothy Dean to shame!" They both laughed as Jack and Howie Haak were coming up the steps.

"'Sho, lemme get that for you," said Jack, breaking into a trot towards her.

"I'm fine, Jack, I can get my own water."

"Miz Simpson, you take care now. See you both tonight." Haak and his notebook and his spit cup wandered over to the parking lot.

Jack watched him go, then turned to his wife. "He's made us an offer. We need to talk about it."

"Hofmann made an offer, too. He said he'll be back tonight, sounds like Haak will be back, too. Wanna talk now?"

"Yes," said Jack, "but not here. Don't know who might wander by, or what phone call will come in that has to be dealt with. Let's run home, won't take long, and while we're there you can at least put your feet up, maybe prop up your back with a pillow…"

"SOLD! Getting to put my feet up for a little while would feel real good right now." To Nashota, it almost sounded like a vacation. "I'll tell Louetta," but Jack was already walking towards the office door.

"You go to the car," he said, "I'll join you in a moment. And maybe, um, maybe we need to talk about your work schedule for these last several weeks, hmmm?"

Pat Head was no dummy, he'd been around the block a few times. Around the world as well. He got to see action in the Pacific, came home and participated in the first two NCAA baseball tournaments with the University of Illinois, and then signed a professional contract with the Detroit Tigers. Got as far as Class B with Davenport, Iowa before being released. When he received an unsolicited invitation from Jack Simpson to attend a spring training tryout, he jumped at it, guessing this might be his last chance at a baseball career. And now, as the 1952 season was winding down, he was making the most of it, having already won 11 games and attracting the attention of several big-league scouts. Yeah, Pat Head was no dummy, he could recognize those guys, not too many regular fans come to a game carrying a clipboard.

And he knew what would be expected of him this night even before Jack Simpson took him aside almost as soon as he had put on his familiar uniform #29.

"We had a tough game last night, Pat," his manager said, stating the obvious. "Even if we did win, that was a tough one, we had to use all three relievers, which means…"

"You need me to go nine," said Head. "I know, I started thinkin' that way while the crazy game was still goin' on."

"Maybe just eight, Pat. Crockett only threw seven pitches in the top-a the ninth, so I'll bet he could go a full inning today if we need him…"

"Well, hopefully, we won't need him. Expectin' scouts in the stands again?" Simpson nodded. "Thought so. Nothing personal, Jack, I've really enjoyed playin' here this year, you and Nashota have treated me big-league ever since we met in the spring. But I'm hopin' to get one more shot to prove I can pitch at a higher level, I'm sure you understand."

"Course I do. That's part-a my job, try and get all-a you ready for a higher level. I don't expect to see you anywhere near here in 1953, Pat. But we still got games to play now, and tonight…"

"Yeah, yeah, tonight, I know. Don't worry 'bout it, skip."

And for seven innings, Jack didn't worry at all as Head mowed down the Weare Mustangs. Another standing-room-only crowd, many of whom had undoubtedly decided to come to the game after reading about Friday night's pinball-ish action, were treated instead to a pitcher's duel featuring Head and Gene Conn's crafty lefthander, Dallas Mauk. The southpaw had once been a top prospect in the Cincinnati Reds' system and had been a contender for a roster spot in 1949. Unfortunately, he hurt his arm during a spring start in Tampa, and had been trying to work his way back ever since. He had been a hard thrower before his injury, but now was getting hitters out with a variety of off-speed pitches, and on this night he and Pat Head matched zeroes for six innings.

Mauk's defense let him down in the seventh, however. Mac led off by surprising the Mustangs with a bunt and beating the throw to first. Pete then hit a routine grounder, an easy double-play ball. But the Weare shortstop, perhaps too sure of himself, looked on in horror as the ball went right under his glove for an error. VanLandingham sacrificed both runners over and Conn ordered Monroe to be walked intentionally, loading the bases but setting up several defensive possibilities, including a double-play or a force play at home plate. With Brodie, a lefty swinger, due up, Jack called on Reece to pinch-hit and the local boy hit a ground ball into the hole. The third baseman tried to cut it off but the ball nicked his glove and rolled away. By the time the shortstop had run it down, Mac had scored, the bases were still loaded, and Miggs then brought in another with a long fly to center. Jack thought about going for a bigger inning and lifting Head for a pinch-hitter, but decided that, having yielded just one hit up to this point, the former Fighting Illini deserved a crack at a complete-game victory.

Simpson started to doubt himself when Head gave up a long home run to the second batter of the inning, and he immediately signaled that he wanted Ken Crockett to start warming up. Head got the second out but then walked the next batter, sending Jack to the mound at a trot.

"Whaddya think, Hicks?" he said, addressing his catcher first.

"Fastball may have lost a tick, skip," said Monroe, doing what a catcher needs to do in this situation—be honest with his manager. "They've gotta send up a pinch-hitter for the pitcher here, prob'ly a lefthanded bat, then they got the top-a the order comin' up. If it was me, I'd let him throw to one more batter, at least."

The whole infield was on the mound. Simpson turned to Miggs, the catcher-turned-third-baseman. "Miggsy? If you was catchin'…?"

"I'd say the same thing, boss," said Miggs, without hesitation. "Pat can get us one more out, we trust him."

The umpire was on his way to the mound to move things along; Jack could see him out of the corner of his eye. He quickly turned to Head.

"Hear that, Pat? Your mates have faith in you, so go get 'em!" And with that he clapped his hands and jogged back to his dugout, tossing a polite little smile at the umpire.

Conn did send up a lefty swinger and Head did do his job, getting him to sky to Oddibe, who drifted back and to his right to easily make the catch for the final out in the eighth.

As expected, Jack brought Crockett in to start the ninth. It was a familiar role for the good-looking Kentuckian who, as far back as the last week of spring training, had been tabbed by Jack to come out of the bullpen in the eighth or ninth inning, shut down the opposition, and secure the victory. The role was becoming more important in baseball, with even the Ageless One himself, Satchel Paige, finding success as the "short man."

Some days you're the windshield, while other days you're the bug.

Crockett got the first out, an easy grounder to Miggs, but the next batter split the gap in right-center field and hustled into second base. He didn't stay there long, coming around to score on a sharp single up the middle, which tied the game. Another single put runners on the corners.

Jack felt helpless. He only had three relief pitchers and two of them, Hightower and West, had thrown a lot of pitches in the circus that had passed for a ballgame yesterday. Either would have gladly come into this situation and given his all, he knew that, but he also felt that they both needed the day off. He briefly thought about asking Harry Neville to try and get the necessary outs, but that would make Harry unavailable for his scheduled start on Monday, forcing the other starters to throw on just two days' rest. All of these possibilities ran through his brain over a span of about eight seconds. He processed them all and made his decision—he did nothing.

The next batter hit a fly ball to left. Reece, who had stayed in after pinch-hitting for Brodie, backed up, then moved forward so he could catch the ball and, with his forward momentum, throw to the plate. The runner on third stayed on the bag until the ball was caught (called "tagging up"), and then sprinted towards home. Reece's throw was strong and on the mark, Monroe grabbed the ball and slapped the tag on the sliding runner. The umpire took an extra couple of seconds before spreading his arms out and hollering "SAFE, SAFE."

Hicks threw down his mask and began protesting. Jack came sprinting out of the dugout and pushed his catcher out of the way, because the last thing he wanted was to have that big bat tossed from the game. (Monroe would also not have been crazy about being fined the standard $25 for an ejection). Instead, Jack got run, the fans had a field day venting their collective spleens on the umpire, and Mike Hamblen got to be in charge as Edens Ridge was quickly dispatched in the bottom of the ninth, a heartbreaking 3–2 loss.

After the game, Jack was still steaming, but he managed to find a tiny bit of humor. As Win Appleton was leaving his office, Simpson said, "You know, Win, I think this was the first time all season we've had a bit of a brouhaha out there, with fans screamin' and hollerin', and it had nothing to do with race. Guess we're making progress." Appleton chose not to use that quote.

He did, however, emphasize that the final game of this series would be critical to the Wolves' playoff hopes, and the fans came out in droves, almost packing the place, making it easily the largest Sunday crowd of the year.

Now, even though games began at five o'clock, long after church services had ended, many people in the South were uncomfortable going to a baseball game on the Lord's Day. The Little Rock team, for instance, frustrated that they frequently did not earn even their basic expenses on Sundays, routinely canceled those games when they received the preliminary league schedule, making them up as part of a Friday, Saturday or Monday doubleheader. Mountain Empire League teams were free to follow Little Rock's example, but no one had chosen to do so. They had all seemed to decide that it was easier just to play the game as scheduled and live with the smaller crowd. In the case of the Wolves, that meant an average attendance of about 650 on Sundays, as opposed to over 1,200 on other nights.

But on this Sunday they drew 2,918, for a three-game total of better than 9,300, the best-attended series in Edens Ridge history. In terms of dollars and cents, it was a huge success. In terms of wins and losses, it was devastating.

It was Tommy Nathan's turn to pitch and he was eager for the assignment. "I've been carefully watching their hitters the last two nights, skip," he said to Jack, "and I think I know what I need to do out there." Unfortunately, there proved to be a big difference between "knowing" and "doing." After giving up just one run in four good innings, the roof caved in on the lefty in the fifth, with the Mustangs tallying three more times before Buck came in to stanch the bleeding. The triage, however, proved to be just temporary, as he gave up one in the sixth and another in the seventh. Jack, desperate to stay within striking distance (Weare held a 6–2 lead at this point), decided to yank him in favor of Larry West. There were two on and two out, and the manager had just one instruction for his right-hander from Pittsburgh: "Get the goddam third out."

"Out" was where the ball went, as West's second pitch disappeared far beyond the fence in left field and onto the street.

To their credit, the Wolves did not roll over. They scored two in the eighth and, after a solo Mustang homer in the ninth, they plated two more and had two runners on when Hicks, swinging as hard as he could, drove the ball to deep right-center. The fans stood and shouted as they followed the flight of the ball, then let out a collective groan when the centerfielder put his back against the fence and made the catch for a final 10–6 Weare triumph. The Mustangs headed over to Kruse with a little momentum and a four-game lead over Buchanan. The Wolves, on the other hand, now found themselves back down in sixth place, just a game behind Blackmer but three full games behind Beck in the battle for the final playoff spot. And, perhaps worse, there were only twelve games left in the season, which Jack mentioned several times in his post-game growl with Win Appleton. Jack was the one doing the growling, all Win did was say "tough loss."

"Tough? Nah, this one wasn't tough, this was just a plain, old-fashioned butt-whippin'. Tough was yesterday, losin' in the ninth, that was a goddam killer. We win that and today might've been different, but even if it wasn't, we'd still be closer, and prob'ly feelin' better 'bout our chances. But now? Three behind Beck with just twelve to play, that's a killer, a motherfuckin' killer. Gonna be close to impossible…WAIT, DON'T PRINT THAT, WIN! This just 'tween us, totally off the record."

"Jack, please, there's some good stuff here, your fans are gonna wanna hear your thinkin'. Not the MF part, 'course, but…"

"All off the record, meat, this is just two old friends jawin', with one blowin' off steam."

Win put his notepad away as Jack groused some more.

"We got us a good club here, but Beck ain't gonna collapse these last two weeks, that Axford's proved to be a good baseball man, he's had 'em playing good, steady ball all year long. Likely they'll win seven games, which means we'd have to win ten-a our last twelve, and I don't see it. Nathan and Neville are so inconsistent…" He shook his head. "My fault, I chose to go with three catchers, includin' Miggs, rather than add a pitcher. Could-a had…" He quickly stopped himself as he saw Appleton suddenly eyeing him curiously. "I mean, I could-a gone after a pitcher when Coach got hurt, could-a signed Danny and Reece and then a pitcher, 'stead of Yam. I didn't, so if we don't make the playoffs, it's my fault, hunnert-percent." He nodded at the newsman. "You can print that if you want. Fact, be sure you do, I want people to know why we don't make the post-season."

Appleton smiled. "I'll wait a few days, see what happens, OK?"

Jack laughed for probably the first time all day, a short little snort-y laugh. "Whatever you wanna do. Tell you what, there's one good thing 'bout these last two days," he said, as he stood up and began to undress. "Pretty sure I'll get to be home to see my baby born. Now I gotta shower, so go on and file your story. Give Tal a hug from me, hear?"

Sunday nights were also generally pretty slow for Jasmine and her girls. A couple of times she and Jake had discussed closing on Sundays, but just about then they'd have a busy day or night and realize they needed to be available for their customers. Rather than have everyone just sitting around, they came up with a system that worked pretty well—two girls would be downstairs (along with Jasmine), while the other two girls relaxed in their rooms, doing their laundry or whatever they liked. Those two girls, however, were "on call," so if things got unexpectedly busy, they could be downstairs on a moment's notice.

Gail and Emma were always paired up and this Sunday found them "off" and eagerly taking turns with their washing and ironing, with Emma squeezing in a little reading (too little to suit her!). She had found a used copy of Cornell Woolrich's 1948 novel, *I Married a Dead Man*, was intrigued by the unique title, and now she was completely engrossed.

Downstairs was quiet until one of their semi-regulars, a little old man, wandered in and smiled broadly when Jasmine greeted him by name.

"Haven't seen you for a while, Albert, have you been traveling?"

"No, been in the hospital," he said. "I fell down and hurt my head," and here he took off his hat, proudly displaying a big bandage on his bald dome as if it was a war wound. "Guess you could say I took a little trip," he cackled.

"Goodness," exclaimed Jasmine. "Are you all right? Do you really think you oughta be here? We wouldn't want you to start bleedin' or nothin', be bad for business, as well as your health!" They both laughed.

"I'm fine. Had a nice little rest there in the hospital, they took good care-a me, though I couldn't get no whiskey, not even a beer, they really oughta change those stupid rules they got. Cute nurses, though, one let me grab her ass a few times." More laughs.

"How'd you fall, Albert?" asked Vicky as she stood up. She had been with him several times and knew just what he liked to do.

"Oh good, you're here, I was hopin' you'd be workin' tonight, Vic." He walked towards her. "I'd been at the Waterin' Well and had one too many, I guess. Was walkin' home and I tripped over my feet, cracked my skull. Doc said it was pretty ugly, but they patched me up real good. Tell ya, I don't even know howinhell I got to the hospital, don't remember nothin' after I hit the ground, but I'm good now and in real need of some tender lovin' care, Miss Vicky." He winked at her, then said "Pssst" and jerked his head, indicating he had something he needed to whisper. Since she was several inches taller—and Vicky wasn't tall by any means!—she leaned down with a smile and put her ear to his mouth. "I got me some gin in my back pocket, we can have us a real good time," he said with a wink, as if he was telling her some deep dark secret. She just smiled, nodded, and gave him a little kiss on the cheek as they went upstairs.

"He's so adorable, though anyone with two eyes can see his bottle," chuckled Linda.

"Been comin' here for years, ever since his wife died," replied Jasmine. "I'm told he used to be pretty well respected 'round here, owned the liquor store, if you can believe that. Got too old to work and then when his wife died, he took it hard. Don't know if he has any family, he don't talk 'bout anyone."

"Well, I know he and Vicky get along real well. He'll sleep good tonight."

"Might wind up sleepin' here, it's happened before," said Jasmine, and the two women laughed just as the front door opened again. The laughter stopped quickly, as Steve stood there in his jeans and skin-tight brown tee shirt, his bushy moustache turned up in a smile.

"Hello ladies," he said. "Miss me?" He took a quick look around and then frowned. "Where's Emma? She already…occupied?"

Jasmine stood and gave him a very thin smile. "Think she's in the back. Lemme go check on her. Have a seat, won't take but a minute," she said as she walked away.

He looked at Linda. "Didn't know you had rooms down here."

"Oh yes," she replied, thinking quickly. "We have several. It's a good-sized house, actually. The kitchen's down here, of course…"

"But workin' rooms? Guess I just figgered everythin' happened upstairs."

Linda was silent, she didn't know what to say.

"Well, if Emma's busy, I'm sure you and I can get friendly, right? What's your name, pretty lady? You sure got beautiful eyes and hair, you an Injun?"

"Yes," she said quietly. "Choctaw, east-central Mississippi. Where you from?" The small talk was just a way to stall for time. She hoped that Steve couldn't see she was nervous, but he could. In his line of work, Steve had developed a heightened sense of when danger might be lurking nearby, and now that internal bell began ringing. He started moving towards Linda.

"Alabama," he said slowly. "Might have me some Injun blood, lotsa us do down there. Don't matter none to me." He was inching closer. "Why don't you-n me go upstairs? I'm happy to pay for all night, and for…extras." He smiled. "You ain't told me your name yet, I'm…"

"Steve, hold it right there!" Jasmine had reappeared, this time with Jake, and both had pistols trained right at him.

With one quick movement, Steve grabbed Linda by the throat with his left hand, drew a 25-caliber, Belgium-made FN "Baby Browning," and jammed it against Linda's temple.

"Y'all got a funny way-a makin' a body feel to home," he said as that bushy moustache turned up in a smile. "Now it'd be a shame if this pretty squaw had her brains splattered all over your carpet, doncha think?" There was silence, so Steve continued.

"Don't know what y'all got 'gainst me, I was a good boy last time I was here, paid my bill, with interest, didn't hurt Emma more-n anyone else, I'm guessin'. Was very willin' to spend more money here tonight, but I ain't dumb, I can tell when I'm not wanted." He and Linda gradually began moving to their right. "Now here's what's gonna happen. Me and this pretty Injun—you never did tell me your name, darlin'—we'll be leavin' now, and you two will just watch us walk out the door, understand? Oh, and I'll take those cap pistols you're holdin'. Just put 'em on the floor, real slow, and…no, wait, tell ya what, open up the chamber and take all the bullets out. You first, big boy. Get 'em out, all six of 'em, now bend down and put 'em on the floor. I SAID ALL SIX! That's good, I see you know how to follow 'structions. OK, now you, nig…"

Jasmine fired, striking a picture hanging on the wall. Steve flinched then coolly shot, hitting Jasmine in her right shoulder, causing her to scream in pain and reflexively drop her gun. Steve then looked at Jake, shot him in the leg, and laughed, this was fun! His juices were really flowing now, and he impulsively kissed Linda, long and hard, then dragged her over to Jasmine, who was bent over in pain. He pushed Linda onto Jasmine, sending them both to the floor, grabbed the gun that Jasmine had dropped, and ran out the door, where he could hear a siren off in the distance. Calculating quickly, he jumped into his car, rolled down the windows, stomped on the gas pedal and headed towards Kruse, laughing with unadulterated joy.

SIXTEEN

Newell Gregory was nursing a small cold with his tried-and-true homemade remedy: Earl Grey tea, spiced with a finger (or so) of Jack Daniels. The concoction often made him drowsy, which was good because it seemed to work best while he slept. So even though he was enjoying *The Caine Mutiny (that Herman Wouk can sure turn out a crackling good tale!),* his eyes kept closing, and he had read one passage so many times, he had it memorized. Time to hit the sack…and then the telephone rang, which startled him. *It's just after nine o'clock on a Sunday night, this can't be good news.*

It wasn't. Sergeant Bethel, working the desk, was following protocol.

"Sorry to bother you at home, Chief, but I just took a call from Jasmine Brunét, who said that a fellow named Steve just showed up at her place…"

He was now wide awake, and he gave directions to Bethel, especially making sure that all his officers knew that "this person is likely armed and must be considered very dangerous. But we want him taken alive if we can."

"Copy that, Chief. Over and out."

Mrs. Gregory had put down her sewing when the phone rang, and now looked at her husband with an "oh no, not again" expression and just one question: "Dangerous?"

"Don't you worry, my dear," said the Chief. "I plan on staying in the background until we have him in cuffs. But don't wait up for me."

At the hospital, the Chief was not surprised that Jasmine was being a less-than-perfect patient, loudly barking orders to the nurses as if they were her girls. Jake, on the other hand, was quietly grimacing in pain as the Holston staff was prepping to remove that bullet from his leg. The Chief decided it might be safer to approach him first.

"What happened, Jake?"

"Excuse me," said a nurse, "but who are you? We are about to take this man to an OR, you can't be interfering…"

He quickly flashed his badge. "Newell Gregory, ma'am, Edens Ridge Chief of Police. I just need a coupla minutes with Mr. Church here, he's got information on tonight's shooting."

She gave the Chief a look of disapproval. "I'll be back for you in about three minutes, Mr. Church," said the nurse as she walked off.

"It was definitely Steve?" he asked.

"Oh, yes, no question 'bout it," replied Jake. "Jazz recognized him right away, soon as he walked in. I was in the 'trouble room,' as always, and she came in and called y'all right away, then she got her gun outta the drawer and I grabbed mine and we went back out to the parlor. I thought we could hold him 'til the heat arrived, but…"

"That sonofabitch," shouted Jasmine. "Got the drop on us. He was talkin' to Linda and he just grabbed her and put a gun to her head. I took a shot but missed, then he shot me-n Jake...Nurse! NURSE!! Where them damn nurses? My whole arm feels like it gonna come off and you ain't treatin' me, is it 'cause I'm black? Someone need to come over here..."

"Jasmine! Calm down! Hollerin' like a banshee ain't gonna make 'em work on you any faster, prob'ly make it worse, if you wanna know the truth." Jake had experience stepping between Jazz and someone who had drawn her wrath, and Chief Gregory was impressed that Jake could do this while in pain.

"Jake, baby, it hurts, that bullet musta hit somethin'..."

"Yeah it did," said Jake. "And I know it hurts. I hurt, too, but they can only move so fast, Jazz, they'll get to workin' on you real soon, prob'ly when you start bein' a little nicer to 'em, hmmm?" Jasmine fell silent, and Jake turned his attention back to Chief Gregory.

"Jazz missed, missed him completely, then Steve got her right in the shoulder. Plugged me in the leg, pushed Linda down and took off, I heard him peel out onto the street."

"See which way he went?" asked the Chief, but Jake just shook his head and winced as another wave of pain came over him. "Jasmine, did you see..."

"Didn't see nothin', Newell, sorry. He pushed Linda on me and we both hit the floor. I just heard him run outta the house, and a minute later I heard a car drive off, I assume it was Steve. I could hear sirens, bet he did, too." For the first time, her face relaxed. "That's all I know, Newell, sure wish I could tell you more."

The nurse now reappeared, along with one of her colleagues. "We're ready for you, for both of you. Chief, I'm sorry, but we need to move these two upstairs." She nodded to the other nurse, who went to Jasmine's gurney and began pushing it towards the elevator, with Jake right behind.

"You get him, Chief," yelled Jasmine, as they got onto the elevator. "You track him down and put his ass in jail, 'cause I wanna be able to visit him and spit in his damn face!"

The Holston Valley Community Hospital didn't have too many patients like Jasmine Brunét.

The twin shootings, of course, were reported by all the local newspapers and radio stations. Needless to say, everyone was taking it seriously, although the girls on Light Street, plus Oddibe and Monroe—indeed, everyone who knew Jasmine—found it amusing that she was described as "a local business owner." And people would laugh hysterically when she would say "What's so funny 'bout that? This is a business and I am the owner!"

The injury to Jasmine's shoulder was mild, she was treated and released. Jake, on the other hand, remained at Holston Valley for another couple of days, as the damage to his leg proved to be serious and required surgery. Chief Gregory decided to put a "plant" in the house, in case Steve came back for revenge, or to complete the job, so the house stayed open. "Publicity gonna be good," said Jazz. "More people, new people,

The Mountain Empire League

will start comin' 'round." There was definitely more traffic, but cars would simply come up the street and slow down as they went by the house. Occasionally a car would stop, a couple of people would jump out, photos would be taken, and then they'd get back into their vehicles and drive off. "Hmmmmmf" became Jasmine's favorite expression. Meanwhile, Steve did not return, and the officer was reassigned when Jake got back from his hospital stay.

The shooting was a major topic in the Wolves' clubhouse, as well. The two players living in the house had been at the ballpark at the time, of course, losing their second straight game to Weare, so they missed all the excitement. That didn't stop their teammates from keeping up a steady commentary, led by Yam.

The big catcher was strutting around the clubhouse, wearing nothing more than his jock and sanitary hose, and carrying a water pistol.

"That feller is one lucky SOB, lemme tell you. If it was me, I mean, if I'd been there in that house, I'd have taken him out in a second, know what I'm sayin'? Always carryin', always ready for a battle."

Quite a few of his teammates laughed as he jumped up on a table and started waving the water pistol around.

"He would-a had no chance. POP, POP, I'd nail that mother, nail him good! POP, POP..."

"You'd what?" Hearing the laughter, Jack Simpson had come out of his office to find out what was so funny.

Yam stopped his performance, the pistol raised high over his head.

"Nothin', skip, nothin', I was just..."

"Being stupid, far as I can tell. Talkin' 'bout killin' a man, that's just plain stupid. Have you ever killed someone before? Ever even pointed a gun at someone? Ever held someone's very life in your hands? Ever seen that fear in his eyes, the fear that his life could end in a matter of seconds? Ever have that experience in the Navy, Yarnell? Hmmm?"

The entire clubhouse, including Yam, was silent. Jack continued.

"Didn't think so. If you had, if it had happened to you even one time, you'd remember it, remember every single second, until your dyin' day, maybe longer, who knows? And you wouldn't talk about it so...so...so easily, so jokingly. Probably wouldn't talk about it all."

For a few seconds, Sergeant Jack Simpson was back in Europe. His players couldn't see what he saw, which was just as well, but they could sense that their manager was reliving some wartime incident... and then it passed. Jack started to walk to his office, then he turned back and looked at his players again.

"And I can tell you," he said, quietly this time. "When a man is pointin' a gun at you, it's a whole lot different world than just struttin' 'round and talkin' shit. Man has a gun in his hand, it takes everythin' you got to keep from shittin' your pants. If you'd ever had that experience, you'd know." He paused and seemed about to say something else, then he just shook his head. "Get dressed. All-a you. We got a game tonight."

Harry Neville had one of his better outings, going into the eighth inning with a 3–1 lead, but the Ducks came up with two runs to tie the score. Oddibe then led off the bottom of the eighth with a base hit to right. Immediately thinking "double," he ran hard as soon as he left the batter's box and pulled into second well ahead of the throw from the outfield. The Ducks were expecting Squirrel to try and hit the ball to the right side, so Jack gave him the bunt sign, and the shortstop executed it perfectly. When the first pitch to Mac was high and outside, Simpson gave a new sign, then he coughed loudly to get Oddibe's attention, and flashed the sign to him. The young outfielder just stared at his manager, who stared back. Daniels, realizing he had understood the sign correctly, touched the brim of his cap to indicate his comprehension.

The right-handed pitcher took his stretch, glanced at the runner, then delivered the pitch—and Oddibe began sprinting down the line. Mac meanwhile, simply bunted the ball. It didn't go far, just a few feet, but it forced the catcher to chase it down, leaving home plate unprotected and allowing the fleet Daniels to score on the suicide squeeze. After Sevareid flied out to end the inning, Ken Crockett came in and set Kruse down in order, securing Edens Ridge's 4–3 victory.

Having lost the previous two games, the mood in the clubhouse was joyous, and even Kevin, the batboy, was grinning when he handed Jack a note. "From Mrs. Simpson," he said. The manager read it and nodded, then hollered out "Sevareid!" Pete ran over to him. "The Missus reminds us that we are scheduled to go over to Gillerman Middle School tomorrow afternoon. Meet me over here at, oh, maybe one o'clock and we can drive there together." Pete smiled and nodded.

"Daniels. Hicks," the manager now sang out, and those two players came over.

"You fellas may not know this, but school is back in session here, started last week, right after Labor Day. And Nashota has already scheduled me-n Pete for an event at a school, so she'll be the one coming over to Light Street to pick you up, OK?"

"Regular time?" asked Monroe.

"Yeah," said Jack, and then, as they started walking away, he added "Nice wheels out there, O," which made Daniels thank his manager with a huge grin.

"Girl, you look like you're gonna give birth any minute now! Don't know if any-a us-n can help if you decide to pop right here-and-now on this porch!"

Jasmine and Nashota both laughed.

"They tell me I still have maybe ten days to go, so I guess I won't mess up your doorway," said Nashota, still grinning. "I'm just here to pick up Oddibe and Monroe, Jack is over at..."

"I know, the boys done told me this mornin'. You set yourself down, I'll get those mullions for you, won't be but a minute." Nashota smiled, finding it both amusing and interesting that Jasmine had picked up at least one word heard frequently in minor league clubhouses. Jazz, meanwhile, turned her head and looked inside, but before she could call out to the ballplayers, they were bounding down the stairs. "Guess they heard us talkin'," said Jazz, and as the two young men walked past her, she told them to "Have a good game," and shut the door.

"Nice day," said Nashota, as the three walked down the steps and over to her car. "Forecast is for sunny and warm, then cooling off tonight, as usual. A perfect day for a ballgame." The two young men nodded in agreement as they approached the vehicle.

CRACK!!

The sound split the quiet of Light Street and froze the three people. But only for a second.

"Get down!" shouted Monroe Hicks. "Get down, that's a gunshot…"

Another CRACK rang out and glass shattered. Monroe grabbed Nashota and put his body in front of hers as there was yet another CRACK. The big catcher screamed and stumbled and they both tumbled to the ground, but he remained on top of her. Oddibe took cover behind the car while Hicks, grimacing in pain, pulled out the pistol Jake had given him, turned and fired in the general direction of where he thought the gunman might be stationed.

CRACK!! This bullet didn't hit any flesh or bone, only some pavement, throwing up debris. But Nashota suddenly began yelling.

"Oh God, oh my God, the baby, the baby is…oh, oh, oh, it hurts, we gotta go, we gotta…"

Now there was a new noise, the squealing of tires, and suddenly a solitary car came around the corner and came screeching to a stop behind Nashota's parked vehicle.

Steve got out, holding a rifle, and saw a husky Negro male, bleeding, laying on top of an olive-skinned woman, moaning. He began walking towards them…

He never knew what hit him. Oddibe, hiding behind the car, raced right at Steve and hit him in the gut, as if he was tackling someone in a football game. They both went down and the rifle went flying. Steve, trained in combat, recovered quickly, grabbed Oddibe, raised him up and punched him in the jaw, sending the young outfielder sprawling. Steve then headed for the gun but Oddibe, despite his pain, had the presence of mind to stick out a foot, causing Steve to fall.

"Son of a bitch!" he shouted. "You gonna be first, boy!"

He scrambled to his feet and retrieved his weapon, cocked it and aimed it at Oddibe. *Ever seen that fear in his eyes, the fear that his life could end in a matter of seconds?*

"Hey!!"

Steve turned and faced the house and now saw a man on the porch, holding a rifle. *Ain't that the same feller I shot the other day?* Steve quickly lifted his weapon, and Light Street reverberated with a single BAM!!!

Many of the players were already at the ballpark, so Louetta knew she couldn't just run into the clubhouse, which is what her instincts told her to do. She held back and pounded on the door.

"Jack, Jack Simpson, come out here, please. Jack, it's me, Louetta, open up Jack, PLEASE…"

The door opened but it wasn't Jack, it was Mike Hamblen. "Whatinhell…" His annoyance disappeared when he saw Louetta crying. "What's the matter, Lou? What's happened?"

She could now barely speak but she was able to croak out "I need to speak to Jack, it's urgent, Nashota…" and she began crying again. Mike said "Wait here" and ran inside.

And within minutes a quiet, peaceful, late-summer day—"a perfect day for a ballgame"—became a whirlwind of activity:

- Jack, ashen, let the doorway support his weight as he absorbed what Louetta was saying. Doing his best to remain calm and rational, he then gave instructions to her and to Mike, making sure they both understood what they immediately needed to do.

- Simpson then quickly put his street clothes back on and quickly raced out the door. Only after he left did Mike assemble the players and give them the few details he knew.

- Louetta made the two telephone calls that Jack had said were essential. She was relatively calm when she spoke to Wells Boggs, doing everything she could to be as cool and professional as possible, even when he began screaming "Oh God, Oh God" on his end. But she lost control when she spoke with Dorothy Dean and really wasn't sure she had been completely and perfectly clear. She hadn't been, but Dorothy had been able to discern that there had been a shooting, and Jack was hoping she could come and help Louetta. Well, of course she could! Dorothy immediately called her husband at work and told him he had to get home RIGHT NOW and take her to the ballpark. Once they arrived, Louetta was more coherent and gave the Deans the few details she had. "You go to the hospital and call us just as soon as you know something, anything," Dorothy told Bob. "Louetta and I will make sure this place is ready for a ballgame."

- Wells, meanwhile, called minor league president George Trautman, who was silent for so long that Boggs had to ask, "Are you still there, Mr. Trautman?" "Yes, yes, sorry, Boggs, I'm just…I don't know, shocked, stunned, horrified, none of those words seem to be sufficient." He collected himself, shook his head, and cleared his throat. "Boggs, I need to be in Edens Ridge, WE need to be in Edens Ridge. How long will the team be at home?" Learning that tonight would be the final home game of the year, Trautman didn't hesitate. "Boggs, I will fly to Asheville. Marge will get back to you soon with the details so you can pick me up at the airport, then we'll drive to Weare together. I'll see if I can find Bob Rhodes, too, but for sure you and I will go to Weare."

Bill McDermott was the first to get the news when he stopped into the office, which he always did when he got to the ballpark. Dorothy would have preferred telling Win Appleton first, but it was Bill who poked his head in and he was on the need-to-know list, as well as on Jack's explicitly-worded admonishment.

Win was coming up the ramp as Bill slowly closed the office door, and the veteran reporter quickly perceived that something was amiss.

"Bill, what's wrong? You're as white as a ghost, what…"

"Let's go up to the press box, Win. Shouldn't be anyone else around at this time of the day, this way I can tell you what I know, which ain't much, but we're s'posed to keep it on the QT."

Appleton slumped into a chair when he heard the words "assassination attempt," and he began to shake when Bill told him that Nashota was one of those rushed to the hospital. When Bill had finished—"that's all we know right now"—Win stood up and said quietly, "I can't stay here, I have to go to the hospital," and he headed towards the press box door.

"Win, you can't, Jack doesn't want anyone there, he specifically told Dorothy… well, Louetta, actually, but she told Dorothy, who told me…Win, stop, STOP!"

Appleton was already halfway out the door, but he turned around. "Bill, my very close friend is in the hospital, anything could be…I can't just…just sit here and…and watch a baseball game all night. I have to…"

"You have a job to do, Win. You're a professional and you have a job to do. Besides, Jack is there with her, and with Hicks and Daniels, too, don't forget, and that's his job." Bill stood up and began pacing around the press box. "He left specific instructions with Louetta that we're not supposed to tell anyone until he gives us the OK, which means, I guess, he's gonna call us at some point, likely as soon as he knows somethin'. Look, Win, I'm with you, I wanna run over there to the hospital, and I wanna tell all the fans, but we gotta respect what Jack wants. She's his wife, man, that's his baby she's carryin', we just have to…" And now Bill McDermott began to sob.

"Yeah, yeah," said Win, closing the door and walking back into the press box. He put his hand on Bill's shoulder as the veteran public address announcer wiped his eyes, blew his nose, and shook his head to indicate he was composed. Win offered him a lopsided smile. "You would have to play the 'professional' card." He sat himself in his usual spot and said "Shit."

News like this traveled at the speed of sound, and soon the grandstand was abuzz:

"Did you hear what happened?" "Oddibe AND Monroe, are you sure?" "But she's pregnant, she's due this month, what about the baby?" "Blown away? Right on the street? Good grief, what's happening in our town?"

The very announcement of the night's altered lineup, by an unusually-subdued Bill McDermott, seemed to be a verification of the rampant rumors. Mike Hamblen's presence in the third base coaching box simply confirmed the horror.

In the fourth inning, the sound of a police siren could be heard heading towards the ballpark from several blocks away, and the fans in Bill Washington Park began to buzz. What was going on? Does this have anything to do with…? Those sitting in the top row could see a car pull up to the players' right field entrance, where Louetta Henry was waiting. When a young Negro man jumped out and practically flew through the door that Louetta held open, the word quickly spread—"Oddibe's here!"

Kruse broke the scoreless tie in the top of the fifth inning, and just as the two teams were changing sides, Oddibe dashed from the clubhouse onto the bench. The

746 fans in attendance heard the collective shout that came from the Wolves' bench, and could see the team jubilantly surrounding their young centerfielder. Those closest to the field could also hear the home plate umpire, who found it necessary to walk over to the dugout.

"Hey, Hamblen. We got a game goin' here, wanna get yourself out there at third, and oh yeah, you might wanna bring a batter with you." The game must go on.

"Put me in, Mike, I'm ready," said Oddibe. "I'm fine, really, I'm OK, I wasn't hurt at all. I just had to give my statement to everyone down at the police station, otherwise I would-a been here earlier. Honest, Mike, I can play, I wanna play. I NEED to play!"

Hamblen shook his head. "Not now. Maybe later. Prob'ly later, when the time is right. Meanwhile, O, why don't you just lead the cheers, yeah?"

Kruse nursed that 1–0 lead into the ninth, when they plated another. The time was now right. As he left the dugout for his spot in the third-base coaching box, Mike flexed his aching shoulders, then turned, looked directly at Oddibe, and said, "OK, O, get something started."

As always, the bleachers erupted in cheers when Oddibe's name was announced. But tonight...tonight was very different. Tonight the applause seemed to cascade from the far reaches of Bill Washington Park, down both lines and into the main grandstands, meeting right behind home. The fans stood and cheered, cheered so loudly that the umpire called time and dusted off the plate and then, as he straightened up, looked right at Oddibe.

"Tip your cap, kid," he said. "You don't get to hear somethin' like this too often."

Daniels stepped out of the batter's box and put his hand on the brim of his cap, which seemed to make the noise level go up. Now, for probably the first time all day, Oddibe smiled and took his hat off and waved it at the fans—his fans, finally, his fans. After at least two minutes, the Ducks' catcher looked at the umpire and implored him. "Blue!"

The ump smiled and nodded and spoke to Oddibe again.

"OK, kid, get in there, we gotta game to play, you know?"

With all eyes having been concentrated on home plate, no one had noticed a man enter the ballpark, go into the office, then bound up the stairs and go into the press box, where he was greeted by shouts from Win Appleton and Bill McDermott. The fans were focusing their attention on Oddibe, who responded with a single to center, the Wolves' first hit since the sixth inning.

Even though they trailed by two, everybody in the ballpark knew that Oddibe would be running. The Kruse pitcher threw over to first base once, twice, three straight times, trying to keep the youngster close. The fourth time was not a charm, as he threw the ball well wide of the bag. His first baseman did not really make the extra effort needed to get it, he just waved his glove as it skipped past him, bounced a couple of times in foul territory, then kicked off the wall and rolled into short right field. Daniels took off immediately and never hesitated, picking up a full head of steam as he rounded second and slid safely into third, ahead of the throw from the Ducks' second baseman, who had pursued the ball.

The Wolves' bench exploded in cries of "Olé," a time-honored baseball jeer aimed at a fielder who doesn't go all-out to field a ball, waving his glove as if he was a matador in a bullring. The Ducks' pitcher, Hartsock, was annoyed at both himself and his first baseman and stomped around on the mound. From out in left field, manager Trig Swinney could see what was happening, but before he could call time and try to settle his hurler down, the right-hander was already into his stretch. The pitch to Jerry Brodie caught too much of the plate, and the Wolves outfielder promptly lined it into center for a hit, easily scoring Daniels.

The fans erupted again, giving Oddibe a standing ovation. "I don't get it," he said, as he returned to the dugout. "All I did was score a run."

"Everybody's heard somethin' about what happened today," said Terry VanLandingham. "They're cheerin' you for that, showing you their support."

"This town…we ain't a town full-a evil," said Danny Chase. "They want you to know that."

"Took 'em long enough," muttered Daniels. "Took 'em the whole goddam season."

His remarks, and the tone in which they were uttered, surprised his teammates, who were used to their center fielder being mild, almost bland with his comments. "Yeah, well, they're with you now, meat," said Yam Yarnell. "You need to thank 'em, right this minute. Go on, get out there!" And he pushed Oddibe up the stairs, enough so that he stumbled a bit until he was now standing in front of the dugout. Somewhat awkwardly, the youngster removed his cap and waved it at the fans, causing them to cheer and holler even louder than before. The umpire called time, walked to the front of home plate and dusted it off, then walked behind it and, before affixing his mask, gave Oddibe a stare that clearly said, "that's enough, young man!" Daniels sat down in the dugout, the cheering subsided, and the game continued.

Warmup action had just begun in the Kruse bullpen when Squirrel successfully bunted Brodie over to second, and now Trig called time and jogged in from the outfield to discuss the situation with his players. Speculation was rampant in the stands, as well as in the press box.

"Walk Mac?" asked Bill McDermott.

"Nah," said Win. "That brings Sevareid up with both the tying and winning runs on base."

"But he's slow, and a grounder is an almost certain double play," retorted Bill.

They both turned around and looked at the man pacing up and down. He stopped wandering about long enough to give his opinion.

"Could walk 'em both, set up a force at home, or a DP," said Jack Simpson. "But I think," and here he scratched his balding head. "I think if it was me, I'd pitch to Mac. Carefully."

On the 2–1 pitch, the Wolves second baseman popped the ball into the air. The shortstop and second baseman both ran out, the centerfielder ran in, but the ball fell untouched for a hit. The alert shortstop grabbed it quickly and fired it towards home, where the pitcher cut it off. Runners now on first and third, one out, with leading RBI man Pete Sevareid, walking to the plate. Trig again came to the mound, this time bringing a new pitcher with him. "Hudson," said Jack. "Sinkerballer, keeps the ball down, good call by Trig."

With the tying run on third, Sevareid was consciously trying to lift the ball in the air. He did it, too, twice, and the ball landed in the stands both times—foul. Now down in the count, he had to shorten his swing a bit to protect himself from striking out, and he hit a weak ground ball. The Kruse shortstop moved to his right, fielded the ball, and threw to second for the force on Mac. The second baseman then made the pivot and threw on to first.

Pete Sevareid was not noted for his speed, far from it. But he knew that a double play meant game over, Wolves lose, and if there was any game they had to win, HAD TO WIN, it would be this one, today. So Pete Sevareid ran as hard as he could, probably as hard and as fast as he ever had in his life, hoping to win his race with the ball.

"Safe, safe!" shouted the umpire. "Aaaaaaaa," screamed Pete, sprawling face first just a yard or so beyond first base. The Edens Ridge fans shrieked wildly, realizing their team had just tied the game. And then they fell silent, watching as their big first baseman remained on the ground, writhing in pain.

Mike Hamblen sprinted across the diamond, and several players leaped off the bench to help tend to their prone first baseman. With a cry of "Oh, shit!" Jack left the press box, fled down the stairs and ran onto the field, assisting the distressed Sevareid up. As they made their way to the clubhouse, it became obvious to everyone that he was unable to put any pressure whatsoever on his right leg.

For a moment nothing happened, but as the base umpire headed towards the Wolves' dugout, Jack Simpson reappeared. The two spoke before Jack jogged over to the third base coaching box, while the umpire, looking up at the press box, pointed to both first and third base.

"Your attention, please," said Bill McDermott in his most official-sounding voice. "Now running for Sevareid is number 19, Danny Chase. And now taking over the reins of the team is the manager, Jack Simpson"

Up in the press box, Win Appleton howled with delight. "Wearing street clothes! Haven't seen that since Connie Mack hung 'em up a coupla years ago!"

Hoping for a quick end to the game, Jack tried a hit-and-run, with Chase taking off for second and VanLandingham swinging. Danny would easily have swiped the bag, but TVL's long fly was run down in right-center for the third out, sending the 2–2 game into extra innings.

"Your attention, please." Bill McDermott had briefly become the busiest man in the ballpark. "Please note the following changes for Edens Ridge. Now playing first base is number 35, Yam Yarnell. Now playing shortstop and batting fourth is number 19, Danny Chase. Moving over to third base is number 2, Squirrel Davis. Now catching is number 22, Allan Miggs. Now playing center field and batting ninth is number 6, Oddibe Daniels. Moving over to right field is number 20, Terry VanLandingham. And now pitching for the Wolves and batting eighth is number 34, Ken Crockett." Anyone trying to keep up had themselves one seriously messy scorecard.

Crockett gave up a hit but no runs, and the game went into the bottom of the tenth, and Yam almost ended it with one big swing. His long drive just missed going over the wall in left center, and he had to settle for a stand-up double. Now, with only Doc Andrews left on the bench, Jack had to scrap any thought of sending in a pinch-runner for Yam. A whole host of strategies ran through his head as Allan Miggs stepped up to the plate, and he called time and trotted down the line to give very simple instructions to the Californian. "You need to hit the ball on the ground to the right side. Got it?" Miggs nodded, and a moment later, he complied with a bouncer to the second baseman. His out moved Yam to third.

Because of all the lineup changes, the pitcher was now batting in the eight-hole. Ken Crockett was a typical pitcher when it came to swinging a bat, which meant that he sucked. Jack would have preferred leaving him in so he could keep pitching, but that would have been tantamount to conceding an out, and he knew he still had one option open to him. So he first got the attention of his bullpen and signaled that he wanted Buck Hightower to warm up (putting his hand over his head, indicating Buck's height), then he pointed to Doc Andrews and yelled "You're up."

Out in left field, Trig Swinney was thinking along with Jack, and as soon as Andrews was announced, he came running in to the infield, shouting for a time-out and motioning for his entire interior defense to join him on the mound. After a brief conference, the catcher went back behind the plate, then stepped away to just beyond the left-hand batters' box, and caught four consecutive "wide ones" from Hartsock. "Take your base," said the umpire, and Doc trotted down to first on the intentional walk. A perfect defensive strategy, of course, setting the stage for a possible double play, which would end the inning and maintain the tie. But Oddibe Daniels was now coming to the plate in the reconfigured Wolves lineup, and Trig was not confident that the speedy outfielder could be doubled up. As soon as his name was announced, the Kruse catcher once again stood up, walked beyond the right-hand batters' box, and caught four more easy tosses, sending Oddibe to first and Doc to second, with Yam still on third and just one out.

"Force at any base," said Appleton, to which McDermott replied, "Boy, this game sure has had everything!" And to seemingly emphasize that point, Jerry Brodie promptly lifted a high fly ball to right field, which elicited an "Oh, boy!" from Appleton and, no doubt, similar expressions in the grandstand. It was a routine fly, with the outfielder having to drop back just a couple of steps to catch it for out number two. But that wasn't what was drawing everyone's interest. No, they were focused on Yam Yarnell, who had one foot resting on the third base bag, and who took off as soon as the ball was caught. Meanwhile, the Ducks outfielder planted his left foot and threw the ball as hard as he could towards home plate.

Everyone in the ballpark knew that the Birmingham native brought a lot to the diamond, but speed wasn't one of them. A faster runner might have slid across the plate just ahead of the throw, but in this case, the ball reached the catcher about one second before Yam did. His experience told him he had just one course of action—rather than slide, he lowered his shoulder and barreled into the Kruse catcher, knocking him backwards as the ball bounced away freely. Maintaining his wits, Yarnell then made sure to scramble back and touch home plate with his hand and then look up at the umpire, who spread his hands apart and hollered "SAFE! SAFE!" Final score: Edens Ridge 3, Kruse 2, in ten innings.

Not so fast. "Look at Swinney! Look at Swinney!" hollered McDermott. The Ducks' playing manager was racing in from left field, waving his arms and screaming. He quickly gathered his infield together and directed them back to their positions. His catcher went back behind the plate, his pitcher stood on the mound and then stepped off the pitching rubber and tossed the ball to the third baseman, who stepped on the bag.

"Oh, for heaven's sake," said Win. "He's arguing that Yarnell left the bag too soon."

The base umpire very calmly spread his hands apart, which meant "no, he didn't," and tried to walk off the field, but found his way blocked by Swinney, who was vociferously pressing his case. The home plate umpire immediately joined the fray.

"Let's go, into the clubhouse, everyone, let's go," said Jack. "Harder for them to reverse their decision if we're already out of sight." And while the Wolves headed for the dugout and down the tunnel, Jack jumped into the stands and raced up the stairs towards the press box, waving his arms just as Swinney had been doing a moment before. Appleton and McDermott both saw him coming, and Bill immediately grabbed the microphone.

"Ladies and gentlemen, if I could have your attention, please. Jack Simpson is heading this way and I believe he would like to speak with you about the events from this afternoon. Please, if we could quiet down, I'm sure we all would appreciate an update from our manager."

Some people were making their way towards the exit, while others were still warily watching the on-field debate between Swinney and the umpires. All eyes and ears, however, were immediately directed to the press box, where they could see Jack opening the door. Those players who had not yet made it into the tunnel now shouted at their teammates, "Come out here, come back out, Jack's gonna talk about what happened." They all rushed back, including Oddibe, who knew some of what had transpired but not all of it. Even Trig gave up arguing his case so he could learn just what had caused the Wolves to field a starting lineup that was without two of its stars.

A panting Jack Simpson took the microphone. "Ladies and gentlemen, thank you for your courtesy, I promise I'll be brief. I have to, I'm out-a-breath, as I'm sure you can hear. I don't think I've run so much in one day since I was at Normandy." He took a moment to collect himself, then smiled for, very likely, the first time in hours.

"Some of you may have heard that there was a shooting today over on Light Street, just a few blocks from here, and it involved some of…some of our people. That is true. And you may have heard a rumor that someone died, that is also true."

"Two of our players were the targets, Oddibe Daniels and Monroe Hicks. You obviously know that Oddibe is fine 'cause you saw him out here for the last coupla innings, helping us to win this game. I can tell you that Monroe was shot but he'll be OK. He got shot in, uh, lemme see, how can I say this politely? He was shot in his rear end, and while that might sound funny…"—a few people in the grandstands had begun chuckling—"it is painful. The bullet had to be removed, and he's resting comfortably at Holston Valley. The doctors told me he'll be as good as new in a few weeks, but he is definitely out for the rest of this season."

"The person who died was the potential assassin, a fellow named Steve. And that's what he was, friends, an assassin! He has been stalkin' us for a while, local police have actually been keepin' an eye out for him, and they are sure he was the person responsible for another shooting on Light Street a few days ago. He would have killed Monroe and Oddibe and…and my wife…" Jack stopped for a moment; the very thought of what might have happened flooded over him. He took a couple of deep breaths and went on.

"Monroe and Oddibe are heroes. Monroe shielded Nashota and our baby, took a bullet for them, and we will be forever grateful. Oddibe slowed down this assassin, tackled him and tripped him and took a punch in the jaw for his effort. But he did what needed to be done, he bought enough time for someone, a fellow named Jake, some of you may know him…Jake was able to get his rifle and shoot Steve. Killed him dead, one shot, right between the eyes. The police have spoken to everyone who was there, including Oddibe and Monroe. They've told me they are satisfied that Jake was actin' in the public's interest, and he will not be charged."

He took one more deep breath. "As for Nashota, she's fine…" The ballpark let out a cheer and a collective sigh of relief. "The trauma of the shooting caused her to go into labor a bit early, but she was rushed to the hospital and the doctors did a fabulous job and delivered a healthy BOY, five pounds and eight ounces. They're both good, Nashota is exhausted, as you might expect, least she was when I left the hospital, under her orders, I might add…" That brought laughs from the fans, especially those that knew her even a little. Even Louetta and Dorothy were able to laugh through their tears.

"I'll be headin' on back there just as soon as I finish up here. Which, I guess…"

"Does the baby have a name?" asked Win.

"Oh, good point," said Jack. "Win Appleton wants to know if we've given the baby a name yet, and the answer is YES. Three names, actually—Degugotanv Oddibe Monroe. Degugotanv is a Cherokee word for 'determined,' because that's what he was, he and Nashota both, determined to be born, determined to live, so that's his first name. Oddibe and Monroe, I don't have to explain that. And we're going to call him Dom, made up of the first letter from all three of his names. D-O-M, Dom Simpson—maybe he'll be a major leaguer someday!" He smiled again, then said "OK, I guess this time I'm really finished. Thank you all."

When he got to the hospital, Jack found Nashota awake and holding her baby, their baby. Despite having slept for a couple of hours, she looked utterly exhausted, but he didn't think he had ever seen her so happy. She assured him she was good, just tired, very tired, and she would go back to sleep soon, but she wanted to hold her son for a while.

"And how is he?" the new father asked, and now her eyes sparkled as if they had become the finest of jewels.

"He is a gift to us from *U-ne-qua.*"

Nothing had been ordinary about this season, not a blessed thing, even now, in its waning days. Night before last, when Gene Conn had returned to the hotel in Blackmer after needing twelve innings to defeat the Blackbirds, 9–8 *(such a sloppy game!)*, he had found a telegram from his general manager, Jules Gray: CALL ME IN THE MORNING. *Shit, this can't be good.*

"Gene, did you hear about what happened in Edens Ridge? No, I didn't think so. Let me tell you, it's one helluva mess, just a helluva mess." Jules Gray proceeded to tell Conn all he knew about the shooting, making sure to add "…but the only one who died was the assassin, or potential assassin, whatever. Their big boon…um, catcher, Hicks, was wounded, he's probably out for the rest of the season, Daniels is fine, even got into the game in the late innings and helped 'em win…"

Conn's managerial mind, trained to think several innings ahead, quickly understood why he needed to know what had occurred in Edens Ridge. "So what do you think we can expect, Jules, with the Wolves coming into Weare tomorrow night?"

"I know that George Trautman is coming down here, he and Wells, and maybe Bob Rhodes, too, not sure, but Trautman and Wells are confirmed. They'll wanna talk to Jack, and Daniels, and who knows who else? Gene, the president of all the minor leagues will be in Weare, North Carolina, can you believe that? Never happened before. I'm making sure the ballpark is spotless, and I talked to Bart Johnson and reserved his best room for Trautman, plus one for Wells, guess if Rhodes shows up, he can bunk with Wells. But look, there's gonna be lotsa newspaper guys here, too. Bart told me he's practically full, and the reservations are coming from all over—Atlanta, DC, Baltimore, Pittsburgh, Chattanooga. Newspapers have gotten wind of what happened, Negro papers, and they're gonna try talkin' to anyone they can, includin' you. Thought you might want a heads-up on what's waitin' for you when you get back here."

"Great. Just what we need as we're tryin' to wrap up the pennant."

So instead of sleeping late after the long bus ride home, or having a leisurely shower and big meal, Gene Conn was, instead, standing in his grandstand and fielding questions from the *Washington Afro-American* and the *Atlanta Daily World* and the *Pittsburgh Courier* and the *Chattanooga News Chronicle,* and of course his hometown *Weare Watchman.* Not that he could tell them much.

"No, like I said a moment ago, we weren't playing Edens Ridge, we were in Blackmer the last three days…that's spelled B-L-A-C-K-M-E-R. No, it's in Kentucky, southeastern Kentucky. Edens Ridge was playing against Kruse when this-all happened…certainly, that's K-R-U-S-E, just a few miles from Edens Ridge, they commute back and forth. No, I don't know when they'll be arrivin' here, sometime after lunch would be my guess. Yes, that's about normal for them…"

He saw some familiar faces walking down the steps and grabbed the opportunity to escape from Media Hell.

"Please allow me to bring in one of our owners who is also my General Manager, Mr. Jules Gray, and he can introduce you to the gentlemen with him."

Gray gave him a weak smile. "Thanks, Gene," and then he turned to face the reporters. "We are always pleased to welcome our Mountain Empire League President, Mr. Wells Boggs, to Weare, but today we are especially honored because he has brought with him the President of all the minor leagues, Mr. George Trautman. I'm sure y'all have some questions for these two distinguished leaders, so if you would simply raise your hands and identify yourselves…"

Poor Jules, he has no idea what he's getting into, thought Gene. But he was quick to take advantage of no longer being on the spot and fled to his office, where he hoped he could catch up on at least a little of that lost sleep.

⚾ ⚾ ⚾

When the Edens Ridge Wolves arrived at the Weare-y Traveler Hotel shortly after two that afternoon, they were greeted by a gaggle of reporters, their League President, and a large, hulking man in a grey suit who stood there and scowled. After helping to unload the bus and then parking it, Mike Hamblen walked into the lobby and went directly over to Wells Boggs.

"Mr. Boggs, I'm happy to see you. Your office had called us and let us know you'd be here. I have some papers for you," he said, fishing them out of his equipment bag.

"That's not so important right now, Hamblen, where is…"

"This one," said Mike, waving one official-looking document. "This one puts Monroe Hicks on the disabled list, what a way to end your season, eh, bullet in the butt. That's your copy, here's my copy, Nashota would kill me if I didn't bring back what she needed. And this one activates me, again, thank goodness it's only for a few days, with any luck it won't be necessary to put me in a ballgame. Here's your copy…"

"Mike!" Wells' tone was sharp, like a teacher demanding silence in the classroom. "This is…yes, thank you for these forms, I appreciate your being so thorough. But where is Jack? We want to speak with him. Oh, by the way, this is George Trautman, the President of…"

"Mr. Trautman, so good to meet you, sir. I'm Mike Hamblen, I'm a coach and bus driver and now a backup catcher for the Edens Ridge Wolves." Mike eagerly shook the hand of the obviously uncomfortable minor league leader. Having gotten the formalities out of the way, Mike got down to business.

"Jack's not here, he's still up at the Ridge. His wife, Nashota, she was there at the scene, you know that, right? And that she was pregnant, close to her due date…'course you do. Well, they had to rush her to the hospital, along with Monroe and Oddibe and of course the motherfu…'scuse me, the rat with the gun. He was dead, 'course, but they had to confirm it. So Nashota, she gave birth, little boy! They both seem to be good and healthy and all, but Jack says he needs to be with his wife and son right now. He plans on coming down, he's just not sure when. He's s'posed to call me here pretty soon, I'll know more, but right now I'm the acting manager 'til further notice. We couldn't find any official forms for that, Mr. Boggs, are there…"

"What about Daniels?" asked Trautman. "Is he here?"

Mike and Wells looked at each other, then Boggs, in a soft voice one often uses when speaking to a child or a very senior citizen, said, "Mr. Trautman, you have to remember, we are in the South, not Ohio. No hotel would allow a Negro to stay under its roof. Jack and Nashota spent a lot of time this off-season lining up…um…alternate arrangements for Oddibe. So he is here, in town, but not, um, HERE, right here at this hotel. That's…uh…that's kinda the way it is."

Mr. Trautman cleared his throat. "I knew that. Of course. But Daniels is here, I mean, with the team, right? He didn't stay in Edens Ridge, did he?"

"No, sir," said Mike. "I dropped him off first. In Weare he stays with Mr. and Mrs. Beatty, nice people, they got a farm just outside-a town. They have five children and two of them are now grown and outta the house, so Oddibe bunks in one of the empty rooms, Yam in the other."

Trautman nodded. "Think they'd mind if two old white men showed up on their doorstep?" For the first time that day—perhaps in many days!—he actually smiled.

At the Beatty house, Oddibe methodically repeated the chain of events for Trautman and Boggs. "And you're not hurt, boy…son…Mr. Daniels?" Trautman was obviously feeling awkward and scrambling to hide it.

"No, sir," said Oddibe. "My jaw…he hit me in my jaw and it hurt for quite a while, but that's it. Oh, I scraped my right elbow when I hit the ground, nothin' serious at all. They checked me at the hospital, nurse put some-a that red stuff on it…"

"Mercurochrome," said Wells. "Had to use it on all my children at one time or another."

"That's it," said Oddibe. "Was all I needed, they said. Feelin' fine now, ready to play."

There was a brief, uncomfortable pause before Trautman spoke.

"Mr. Daniels, on behalf of everyone associated with the National Association of Professional Baseball Leagues, I would like to apologize to you for what has happened. It is my sincere hope that you are able to put this all behind you. As sad as it is, it's over now, and you need…I think it is important that you finish the season, rest up, and come back to play somewhere next season. The way to defeat this kind of…of mindless hate is to be like Jackie Robinson, ignore it, and just play all the harder. Beat them on the playing field, in the Game of Baseball, and you will beat them in the Game of Life as well." *(He sounds like he's running for office,* thought Wells.)

But then George Trautman did something unusual—he offered his hand to the young man and smiled. A little lopsided, but a smile nonetheless. Daniels took the outstretched hand.

All this time, Mike and Yam were sitting out on the front porch with Mrs. Beatty, who had served them sweet tea and given Yam permission to smoke his Chesterfields.

"That sh…stuff will kill you," said Mike.

"Oh, and I s'pose your dip is made from lettuce 'n carrots?" The two men laughed as Oddibe and the two presidents came out of the house.

"Ready?" asked Mike, and Oddibe nodded, with a look that said *I can't wait for this to be over.*

And as they all walked to the bus, Mrs. Beatty, with faultless innocence, offered up a picture-perfect antidote to the obvious tension. "You know," she said, "I don't think I ever had this many white men in my house all at the same time 'fore." It took Hamblen several minutes before he could compose himself enough to drive.

"I know it's normal for a first-time father to worry, and after what happened yesterday I don't blame you, believe me." Jack Simpson and Doc Nelson were walking down one of Holston Valley Community Hospital's many corridors. "But please trust me, Jack, I've been doing this forever. Dom is terrific, just as healthy as he can be in his first 24 hours. And Nashota, she's good, too, no pain beyond what's normal after giving birth, all her vitals check out. She didn't sleep that well but her brain probably couldn't shut down after such a traumatic day."

"Great! So how long before I can bring them home?"

Doc Nelson absentmindedly rubbed his chin. "With Nashota, probably two or three days. That's kind of the norm anyway, but considering the circumstances, I'd really like to be especially cautious. With Dom, we have to monitor his weight and make sure he's eating and pooping normally, so it might be two or three days after that."

They had reached an intersection, and Nelson stopped walking. "But lemme ask you something, Jack—what about your team?"

Simpson shook his head. "We've only got six games left, Doc, and no playoffs for us. Mike can handle things, it'll be good experience for him, since he wants to be a manager, crazy bastard! Anyway, I ain't goin' anywhere 'til I can bring my wife and son home."

"I'm not telling you what to do, old friend, you know your job, and your players, way better than I ever will. But I can tell you there's really nothing you can do here, other than visit Nashota and Dom and walk around aimlessly. Now I have to head this way," he said, jerking his head to the left, "while the other people I suspect you're planning on seeing are that-a-way," indicating the opposite direction. "We'll catch up later," he said with a nod, and scurried off.

Pete and Monroe were Jack's other Holston Valley "patients." Pete was first, and he gave Jack a smile—really more of a grimace, which was the best he could do under the circumstances, and asked "When is BP?" He was happy to hear about the birth of Dom, and that mother and baby seemed to be doing well, but otherwise Jack found him to be a little down.

"Jack, I know my career may be over. I'll be 26 in November, who's gonna want someone my age comin' off a serious injury, eh? I know I'm all doped up right now, skip, but…"

"I gotta tell you, some teams have expressed interest in you. You may be right, this injury might scare 'em off, but I'll try to make the best deal I can for you, I'm sure you know that. But look, if nothin' happens, you always have a place here, Pete. I know how to reach you in North Dakota and if I can't get you signed up with a big-league organization, you can just re-up with us. Think you'll remember that?"

Sevareid nodded just as the door opened and three men came in with a gurney.

"Mr. Sevareid, I'm Dr. Kelvin, I'll be assisting on your surgery. We're going to be taking you into the OR, but first I'll be hooking you up…" He now seemed to notice Jack for the first time. "I'm sorry, sir, you'll have to leave now."

Simpson stood up. "You'll do great in there, Pete. They're just throwin' half-speed fastballs, belt high. See you tomorrow, big guy."

Next up was Monroe who was laying on his stomach.

"Hurts if I'm on my back, skip. I can lay on my left side for a while, but mostly they want me on my big belly. I'd rather be catchin' a whole staff of knuckleballers than doin' this." As Jack grabbed a chair, Hicks looked up at his manager. "Skip, whatinhell-r you doin' here? Ain't we got a series to play in Weare?"

"Yeah. I didn't go, least not yet. Gotta make sure my wife's OK, plus you-n Pete." Jack repeated the progress report on Nashota, then told him about the baby. "And I know you'll find this of interest. We've given him three names—first name is Degugotanv, which is Cherokee for 'determined'. We figure that this little booger was definitely determined to be born." Jack coughed, then continued. "His other two names are Oddibe and Monroe, 'cause-a what you two did for him and his mom. We're gonna call him Dom, from all three names, D-O-M, get it?" He gave out a short, quiet laugh.

With a little bit of effort, punctuated by a grunt, Hicks rolled over onto his left side. "Really? You named him after me, at least part-a his name? Wow, skip, that's a…a large charge! No one's ever named nothin' after me before, that's…that's…man, that's…I…" He stopped, looked down, and just shook his head.

The two men were quiet for a moment, then Jack leaned forward.

"Look, Monroe, I know you ain't really thinkin' 'bout next season, but I wanted to talk a bit about it now. In a day or two they'll be releasing you from here, and I 'spect you'll get your gear and head back to Ohio, right?" The big catcher nodded. "I've had some teams ask about you, and in a week or so I plan on following up with them. If I can make a good deal for you I will. Good organization, good solid organization, where you'll have a chance to get major league instruction. You got the talent, Monroe, you got the drive, the personality, the make-up. I can see you catchin' in the majors in 3–4 years, and I ain't just blowin' smoke here, you and Oddibe, you're both big-league players, I'll stake my professional reputation on it."

He paused but Hicks didn't say anything, so Jack continued.

"I just wanted you to know what I'm plannin' on doin'. If I can make a good deal, I will, and soon as that happens, I'll call you. But if by chance I can't get a good price for you, I'd love to have you come back here and play a full season with us. Hell, you get 400 at-bats in this league and we'll have 16 teams linin' up to make offers. Eh, maybe only 15, old man Yawkey don't seem all that anxious to bring Negro players to Boston." They both grinned. "I wanted to tell you this 'fore you left. Eventually I'll be goin' to NC, prob'ly Buchanan, and I'm sure you'll be gone by the time we get back."

Monroe moved back to his stomach. "That really does feel better," he said with a sigh. Then he looked at his manager.

"I 'preciate all you done for me this season, skip. I trust you, I know you'll work to make a good deal for all-a us." He shook his head. "Big-league club, that would be…wow, that would be somethin'. But I gotta tell ya, me-n Gail, we talkin' 'bout maybe goin' out to California." He laughed. "She got this crazy idea 'bout bein' a hairdresser for the stars, and I figure, why not? Why not let her give it a try? Everyone oughta have a dream, right? That's hers."

He paused, framing his thoughts, then continued. "Skip, if you can sell me to a big-league club, you do it. I'll be grateful forever, and I'll be all happy and excited to go to spring trainin' and then to whatever minor league team they send me. Wherever it is, can't be no tougher-n here, right? I mean, I caught a bullet in my butt, can't imagine it'll be worse nowhere else!" They both laughed, though Monroe's ended with a wince. "But if we're out in California," he said, finishing his thought, "and you don't sell me somewhere…" He paused, thinking, then continued. "Nothing personal, skip, but I dunno if I'd wanna come back here to play, leavin' Gail out there all by her lonesome, 'specially if she's tryin' to establish herself cuttin' and stylin' hair, know what I mean? If a major league team is my boss, sure, that's one thing, but if I'm my own boss, if I get to make my own deal, I'm prob'ly gonna see if I can catch on with one-a those teams out west. Understand what I'm sayin', skip?"

Jack nodded. "We'll just have to see what happens this off-season, OK? Listen, if you do go to California, let me know where you are and how to get in touch with you. I really think one-a these teams I been talkin' to might make me a good offer, and I'll need to know where you are so I can call you with the news. Plus send you your cut!" He stood up. "I'll prob'ly pop in later today, and maybe tomorrow, too."

Nashota was awake and feeding the baby, and the way she looked at him when he walked into her room made him happy just to be alive.

He kissed them both before asking how she was feeling. "Good, good. Tired but good. And this *sky-u-sdi*, well…" She trailed off, suddenly misty-eyed.

They sat quietly, the only movement coming from little Dom as he took his nourishment. Jack finally broke the silence.

"Doc Nelson says you're doin' good, you'll be here a coupla more days, they keep all new moms around for a little while. Baby'll be here…um…a little longer, they wanna be careful…"

"We need to call Tehya. And you need to be with your team. You have a job, Jack, a responsibility to the team…"

"I NEED to be here with my wife and child," Jack said, plainly but firmly. "No one gonna blame me for stayin' here with you." He grinned. "No one would DARE!" He shifted in his chair. "Once I leave you I'll go home and call Tehya. If she can come up here, then I'll wait 'til she arrives, then rejoin the team, prob'ly in Buchanan for the last three games. If not, then I won't be goin' nowhere. *Golisdi?*"

She certainly did understand. She understood that determined look in his eye, the way he set his jaw. She had seen it before, not often but when it was there, she knew he would not be deterred. "*Golisdi,*" she said.

Of course Tehya would be there. "Why did you wait so long to call me?" she asked, but didn't wait for a response. "OK, lemme contact Chris and get ahold of my folks, too. I'll call you in a bit, don't go nowhere, OK?" That was more an order than a question.

Down in Weare, Mike Hamblen addressed his Edens Ridge Wolves—plus George Trautman and Wells Boggs—once they had all boarded the bus.

"All right, settle down, settle down. We have a coupla things to talk about 'fore I take you over to the yard. I heard from Jack a little while ago. He says Nashota and the baby are both doing well. She'll prob'ly get released soon, day or two, baby will stay a little longer. Nashota's sister, who lives here in Weare, will be goin' up to The Ridge, so Jack will join us in Buchanan." He paused, then gave his team a wicked smile.

"Which means, you lucky mullions, that I got the conn for at least the next three days." The bus seemed to give out a collective groan. Mike grinned at Boggs and Trautman, who frowned.

Mike continued. "Coupla more things. Pete, he's havin' surgery today, Jack says he'll let me know tonight, or in the morning, how that went. Monroe is OK, they removed the bullet…"

"Prob'ly had trouble findin' it in all that blubber." Yam's deep voice was always recognizable, and his comment drew the hoped-for laugh; even Wells Boggs and George Trautman smiled.

"Very funny," said Mike, trying unsuccessfully not to grin. "Anyway, Monroe is alright, they just have him restin' up for a day or two, then he's goin' home. We won't get to say goodbye, that's too bad." He paused, looking reflectively at the floor of the bus. "And we also had to activate me—again!—for this last week because we're short one guy…"

"That means we're short two guys!" said a voice from the back, which elicited some muffled laughter. Mike was nonplussed.

"I agree. My biggest hope is that I don't have to get into a game. But look—the lineup that we ended with yesterday is the one I'll use while we're here—Yam's at first; Danny Chase, you'll be playing short and Squirrel, you go back to third. Miggsy, that means you're catching. Brodie, you're my back-up at first, 'case I need to move guys around, use a pinch-runner…"

"Mike, I've played first before," said Raburn Reece. "Be happy to go in there if you need me."

"Thanks, Reece," Mike replied. "I may take you up on that. OK, one last thing. We already seen a shit-load-a reporters when we got to town, they'll all be at the yard…"

George Trautman stood up. "Mike, let me say a few words here, if I may." Mike nodded and eagerly backed off.

"Gentlemen," he said, with a firm look. "These reporters are no different from the ones you've seen and spoken to all season long. Different faces, but they are here to do their jobs. Please just answer their questions and by tomorrow or the next day, they'll be gone, chasing down some other story. I would ask you to simply be polite and answer their questions."

"I'd prefer to tell 'em to go fuck themselves," said Yam, which brought some laughter and a couple of cheers, but ended very quickly with a stern look from Trautman.

"You will do no such thing, not if you want to continue your careers with the National Association of Professional Baseball Leagues. You will be polite and respectful. Is that understood, gentlemen?" There was a lot of nodding, plus some muffled "Uh-huh" and "yessir."

Mr. Trautman nodded at Mike and sat down. "OK," said Hamblen. "I think that's it. We got a game to play, let's head on over to the yard," and with that he sat down behind the wheel and turned the key.

A story of this magnitude was, naturally, picked up by the Associated Press and United Press, and distributed around the country. And because of its local connection, both the *Asheville Citizen* and *Asheville Times* ran it on the front page—not in the sports section, but of the whole newspaper!

Running late, Walter Daniels did not have the time to even glance at the newspaper before dashing off to work. He therefore had no idea why several people at Stephens-Lee High School went out of their way to speak with him that morning.

"Glad everything turned out OK, Walter."

"You must be so proud of your son, Walter."

"That was quite the scare, Walter, glad everyone's fine."

Even the principal, Mr. Christopher, who rarely spoke with him, sought him out. "Walter, we are all so proud of Oddibe, and you, too. If you feel you need to take some time off, go right ahead, you have my permission. In fact, if you'd like, I will be happy to pass that information on to Mr. Hebert myself. Walter, if you need anything...," and he patted him on the shoulder.

Walter headed straight for the school's library, where they always had three or four copies of that day's *Times*. He grabbed a copy, and just the headlines caused him to let out an audible gasp.

ATTEMPT TO KILL BALLPLAYERS IS FOILED
LOCAL STAR UNHURT IN MURDER ATTEMPT

"Oh my God," Walter said to himself, as he quickly read the article. But he suddenly had a new thought, which came out much louder—"LILLY!" He sprinted out of the library, quickly found Mr. Hebert and told him he had to go home for a bit, he'd be back as soon as he could, and dashed out even before he had officially received his supervisor's blessing.

He found Lilly crying at the kitchen table.

"My boy," she said as soon as she saw him. "OUR boy, OUR Oddibe. He coulda been killed. We could be goin' up there to get his body and bring him home for burial. Walter...," and she began sobbing, loudly, yet again.

His tears also flowed as he cradled his wife. After several minutes he kissed her, hugged her tightly, and finally spoke.

"But he's OK, Lil, he's jus' fine, not even a scratch. He lucked out, we all lucked out, which means that God was watchin' over all-a us."

"Praise God! Praise Jesus!" said Lilly.

"Maybe we oughta call him. I think we gotta list-a the places he's stayin' at, we should..."

"We should go up there, go right up to Weare and bring him home. Nobody gonna shoot at him here in Asheville, Walter, nobody here want him dead. DEAD!" She put her head on the table and cried some more.

"Season's 'bout over, Lil," said Walter. "He be home soon, maybe in a week, ain't really..."

"Walter!" Lilly's eyes were barely visible but her voice was sharp. "I ain't givin' those…those…animals one more chance at takin' my boy from me. I'm the mom, I'm s'posed to protect him. We need to get up there and…"

"Lilly," said Walter, who surprised himself by being so calm. "We agreed, you-n I, back when he signed that contract with Mr. and Miz Simpson, we agreed that we'd leave him alone, let him do this on his own. 'Sink or swim' we said, and we been doin' that, ever since he got on that bus to Florida. Now he only got a few more games to play, we can't go back on our word, we gotta let him live through this on his own. But I think we should call him and make sure he's all right, maybe remind him that we're right here if he thinks he might need us. What you say, Lil, wanna talk to our young man?"

No one knew Walter like Lilliana Lewis Daniels, and looking at him, listening to him, she knew this was an important moment for all of them. She could tell, by the very tone of his voice, that her husband was determined.

"Think maybe we could go see him play this weekend? They still be in Weare?"

Walter smiled and shook his head. "No, they finish up in Buchanan, Friday, Saturday and Sunday. Little longer trip, but we could go, if y'all want, and if he wants us there, you know?"

She nodded, and he nodded back.

It's only a matter-a time, thought Orley Pepper. *Won't be long 'fore the police come a-callin', 'fore they tie me to this guy, this prick, this failed assassin. Hell, they're prob'ly watchin' me already.* And he peaked out his window for at least the fifth time in the past hour.

It didn't take long for him to pack a bag, he didn't have a lot of worldly possessions, and his valise wasn't all that big anyway. He had been thinking about it for a couple of days and had decided where he ought to go, where he'd be the safest—Albany, Georgia, where he had some cousins. He also had an aunt in Spartanburg, South Carolina and he was closer to her, but he felt that Albany, much further south, would ultimately be a better choice. (Besides, he recalled that one of those cousins was pretty cute and used to be kinda sweet on him!) He also found out there was a bus that originated in Bristol in the evening, heading for Orlando, Florida. Made a lot of stops along the way, including Kingsport, and he could stay on it right through to Albany. So he left the Special Deluxe right where it was and headed for Kingsport on foot. People knew his vehicle and identified him with it, and if he tried to drive it to Albany, someone would notice, someone would notify the Highway Patrol or the local police. Even if he just took it to the bus station, they might could be able to track him down, so he simply muttered "Bye, old girl" as he walked past her in the driveway. *Such a great, great car.*

He walked two blocks north, then crossed Polk Street, heading towards Kingsport. He had given himself more than an hour to get to the bus station, plenty-a time, at his usual brisk pace.

It was dark on Polk, streetlights were out, nothing new, they'd been out for ages. *Wonder if Edens Ridge will ever spend the money to fix these lights, or replace 'em? That would be better, get new ones, prob'ly cheaper in the long run and I'll bet they last longer...* "HEY!"

That last was said out loud as he felt two strong hands grab him from behind. One hand immediately covered his mouth, while the other, and the arm it was attached to, wrapped around his neck and pulled him into an alley. Orley tried to fight, tried to bite the hand that held him, but his captor was taller and stronger, and his big arms and rough hands held fast.

"Goin' somewhere, Pepper?" The voice was just a whisper. "Some reason why you're skippin' town at this time? And not even takin' that fancy ol' car-a yours? Must be a real good reason why you decided not to drive, wonder what that might be?"

Orley was now forced down, seated on the ground, his back resting against this powerful man. He kicked his legs but that just made the man grip him more tightly and painfully.

"Bet that hurts now, don't it? You want the pain to go away, you'll quit thrashin' about, hear?" Orley immediately calmed down.

"That's good, that's bein' a smart feller. Maybe you ain't as dumb as you look. But you sure are a troublemaker, Pepper. Well, we've had 'bout as much as we can stand. Ain't no question you had somethin' to do with the attempt on Oddibe and Monroe and Miz Simpson, and you can't be gettin' away with that, no siree. Not no little piss-ant like you. Those two players, they's good people, and I never run into a finer person than Miz Simpson, not here, not overseas, not nowhere. No call to try and kill any-a them. That other feller, he got what he deserved, and now it's your turn."

Orley Pepper tried to scream but the hand pushed his head back further, further. Suddenly, one hand was on each side of his head, and the man whispered "Say hello to the Devil" just before he gave the neck a quick, hard twist to the right.

The two men remained frozen for a moment, and then Pepper was allowed to fully slump to the ground. The man checked for a pulse and, finding none, stood up, gave the body a sharp kick, and quietly disappeared into the shadows, where he was most comfortable.

Nick and Richie were annoyed that Max went missing when he did, they could really use his help in doing their final clean-up of the ballpark for the winter. And they were surprised, too—he usually has two binges during the year and he'd reached his quota already. It really wasn't like him to pull a drunk at the end of the season. "That guy," Nick said to Bob Dean, who stopped by the ballpark after his shift had ended, just to see if anyone needed any help with anything. "He sure is a strange one. Hard worker when he's here, but..." He shrugged his shoulders. "Oh well, least I don't have to go fish him outta some bar so we can be ready for the next homestand. I'll just wait 'til March 'fore I hafta look for him again, I'm sure I'll find him somewhere."

SEVENTEEN

Tehya blew in like a hurricane. "Chris wanted to give the old jalopy a thorough look-see before I drove over the mountain," she said as she gave her sister a kiss. "Then he decided one tire looked bad so he ran out and bought two and had to put them on. And I needed to bring Gwennie, Chris wouldn't be able to manage her on his own. Now, where's that new *u-s-di-ga?*" After rolling her eyes *(I really think my baby now owns this hospital!)*, Nashota explained that they were keeping a close eye on Dom and would, in fact, be doing so for a couple more days. "Wish I could be bringing him home with me today, but..."

"How can you go home without your baby?" Tehya wanted to know. "I'm sure he's perfectly fine. If they're gonna discharge you, he oughta be goin' with you, that's what I think. Fact, why don't you keep an eye on Gwennie and I'll go find your doctor and tell him..."

"You will tell him nothing other than 'thank you,'" said Nashota, authoritatively. "I've gotten the very best care, right from the start. Look, Tay, I'm happy you're here, and glad you and Gwennie will be lookin' after me for a few days, but there's no need to rock the boat, understand? Understand?"

Tehya may have been older but Nashota had always been the Big Sister. "Whatever," she said glumly. "But look, I gotta ask you..."

She was unable to go any further because at that point there was a knock on the door and a small group of men quietly and carefully filed in. "Good Lord!" exclaimed Tehya. "What did you do, 'Sho? Are they coming to give you last rites or something?"

Nashota rolled her eyes yet again. "Tehya, allow me to introduce you to my friend, Rabbi Yitzhak Dov Halevi, and other members of the area's religious community—Reverend Ish Clark, Reverend Maurice Stapleton, and Reverend Robert Thomas. Gentlemen, this is my sister, Tehya. I am so pleased to see all of you, have you come to meet my new baby?"

The four clerics all mumbled their hellos to Tehya before the Rabbi responded.

"We are all dying to meet him, 'Sho, and we also came to see how you were doing. We are all so...so..."

"Mortified," said Reverend Thomas. "I think that's the right word, YD—mortified." And the others nodded in agreement.

Nashota smiled. "Gentlemen, I thank you so much for your concern. I am doing very well, and I've been told I should be released today. Hopefully soon, before I have to eat another hospital lunch." That got the laugh she was hoping for. "Little Dom is going to have to stay for another day or two or three," she continued. "They are being real cautious with him, which you can certainly understand. But my doctor and all the nurses tell me every day he is fine, healthy, showing no ill effects from being born a bit early, so we feel pretty confident that he'll be coming home very soon." She smiled. "Any other questions?"

"You're so bad," Tehya mumbled under her breath.

"Yes, ma'am," said Reverend Clark. "We do have something…there is something we want to ask you, if you don't mind." Nashota simply nodded, so he continued.

"We been talking, all-a-us here as well as Father Feeney and a few others…"

"Feeney has a conflict this morning, otherwise he'd be here," said Reverend Thomas.

Reverend Clark scowled, he did not like being interrupted. After a brief pause to make sure no one else had anything to say, he continued.

"We feel that we…um, the religious community of this area, this part of the Mountain Empire, needs to say something 'bout what happened. We represent different faiths but we all believe in the Bible, and in one God…"

"The Bible says 'love thy neighbor as thyself'," Reverend Stapleton stated.

"The sixth commandment says 'Thou shalt not commit murder,' and that man tried to murder you, and your players, and your baby, too." The Rabbi was starting to get emotional.

"We feel, Mrs. Simpson, that…we, um, feel very strongly…" Reverend Thomas made sure to emphasize those two words when he repeated them. "Very strongly, that we, as a few of the religious leaders of this community, need to say something, need to speak out, need to…to…"

"Condemn!" Ish Clark was practically in the pulpit. "We must publicly condemn, in no uncertain terms, the act that was perpetrated, and the underlying hatred that nearly allowed it to happen. We have a duty and a responsibility to our parishioners, of course, but also to all the people in this area, and in this state, to speak out against an attitude that allows a man like this to…to ply his trade! Yet they ignore lynchings and beatings and…and degradations suffered by Negroes in this country, a country that just recently fought a war so that people in Europe and Asia could be free…"

"What we are proposing here, 'Sho," said Rabbi Halevi, trying to get to the point before a full-blown sermon broke out, "is, um, we'd like to hold an interfaith rally and have it at the ballpark within the next few days, if we could. We would rent it from you, or the City, I guess, but we wouldn't charge any admission, it would be free for everyone…"

"We would like to stand up for our community," Reverend Stapleton said. "We would like to tell the world that what happened the other day, over on Light Street, was not representative of Edens Ridge, or Northeast Tennessee as a whole. We want to condemn—that is exactly the right word, Reverend Clark—we want to condemn what happened and the thinking that went into it. And we felt that we needed to ask your permission, Mrs. Simpson, to go ahead."

Nashota, taken aback, was silent for a moment, not really quite sure what to say. She looked at her sister, who quietly said "Well, I'll be." Nashota looked back at the group and noticed Jack and Doc Nelson were now standing in the doorway.

"First, let me thank you all for thinking of this, for deciding to do it. I think it is very noble, very thoughtful, very worthy, and…and…and very necessary. We absolutely need for all of you to stand up against hatred and violence. Too much of that in the world, way too much. Maybe our little community can lead the way, eh, Jack?"

They all made sure to shake the new father's hand, except for Tehya, who gave him a big hug and a little kiss on the cheek. "Sorry I don't have cigars," he said, and they all laughed, as he made his way over to his wife and took her hand.

Nashota continued her thought. "As far as renting the park, it is actually our decision."

"That's right," said Jack. "Our contract with the City says we have total control of the ballpark from March 1 through September 30. Since we won't be hosting any playoff games this year, you won't have to dance around our schedule at all. As long as you make this happen by the 30th, you have our permission, right 'Sho?" His wife smiled and nodded. "I doubt any players will be there," she said, "but we'll be there, and baby Dom, too."

"Think we can get the Mayor?" asked Rabbi Halevi, which made both Jack and Nashota smile. They remembered the racist comments Dick Curtis had made to Nashota months ago, but they also expected that he had been smarting over the negative publicity coming Edens Ridge's way these past few days. In this election year, he would likely jump at the opportunity to repair the town's image. "He does owe us one, don't you think?" Jack asked his wife, who chuckled. Then he turned to the clergymen in the crowded room. "Tell you what, why don't we all go over and pay him a visit tomorrow morning? I'm sure he'll be happy to welcome us in!" Nashota laughed out loud, then sheepishly said "Sorry."

"I'm sure I can guarantee a few of my colleagues in the medical profession," said Doc Nelson. "Maybe even get a few of my fellow Rotary Club brothers to come, as well. Oh, by the way, I am Doctor Bill Nelson, Nashota's family physician, and I must ask you all to please leave right now. I am here to examine my patient, make sure she's ready to be discharged."

"Come on, let's go out in the hallway," Jack said to the group. "We can make our plans for invading City Hall!"

"Go, Jack," Nashota had said. "The season is coming to an end, you need to be with your players one last time. We'll be just fine here, and besides, you'll be back in four days."

"But..."

"What, don't you trust me?" asked Tehya. "I think I can take care of my sister, Jack Simpson, and I surely know how to change a diaper once we bring that little *usdi* home. Now go on, get your *tigwali* down to Buchanan."

But as he turned to go, Nashota's voice brought him back.

"And please, tell all our players that I...I thank them from the bottom of my heart. And tell them I love them all." Her voice cracked and the tears came freely. She tried to say something else but could not.

Jack hugged his wife and kissed her. "I'll tell them," he said quietly.

He leisurely drove himself down to Buchanan, checked into the hotel, and eventually climbed aboard the bus amidst a chorus of cheers. (And one laughing comment, from Yam, of course: "Well, look what the cat dragged in," which brought on more laughs, especially from Jack.) Once they reached the ballpark, he was happy to see the whole Daniels family in Buchanan, and not all that surprised. What really startled him, however, was Oddibe asking to speak to him right after the game.

"Jack, Jack, you gotta help me. My Mama's gonna kill me if she…there must be some way…I hate to keep askin' for your help, Jack, you done so much for me, I can never repay you, but now…I dunno, this whole season…"

The young outfielder had been expecting his parents to call him and ask if he was all right. He was sure, however, they would demand that he pack his bags and catch the first bus back to Asheville. But nothing had happened while the team was in Weare, so finding a message waiting for him at Mrs. Cornett's in Buchanan was unforeseen—they were coming up for the last two games, and wanted to take him to lunch. He immediately began preparing his arguments for staying with the team:

- There's only two games remaining in the season,
- "You've always told me to finish what I start,"
- The team would be very short-handed if he left, with no spare outfielders at all,
- He couldn't to do this to Jack Simpson, who had treated him so well right from the get-go.

And then he didn't need to use any of them! The whole family was very concerned, of course, but no one ever brought up bringing him home early. Perhaps emboldened by their show of faith, Oddibe decided to mention something as they walked over to the family vehicle.

"Mom, Dad, there's somethin' I'd like to do, if you don't mind. Last night, after the game, Jack brought up a…a…an event that's gonna be happenin' in Edens Ridge, he's not exactly sure when, but…it's…they're gonna hold an interfaith rally, the different churches are gettin' together, out at the ballpark, and…I dunno, talk about what happened, speak out against it. Since I was one of the targets, the main one, I guess, I thought…maybe…I was thinkin' that it might be a good idea if I was there. Which means I'd have to stay up in the Ridge 'til this thing happened, don't know when it'll be, this month for sure but I don't have an exact day. I'd come home just as soon as it was over, I'd just take the bus home. I hope you don't mind, but I think…"

"Course you stay, you have to," said Walter, and if Oddibe was surprised by how quickly his father had agreed to this, he was absolutely staggered when his mother said, "Know what? I think I'd like to be there, too. I can stay up there for a few days, maybe help Miz Simpson with her new baby, then we can both take the bus home after the rally. What do you think, Oddibe, you mind havin' your ol' mother 'round?"

"Um, no, Mom, no, but where…um, where would you sleep while you was in Edens Ridge?"

"Why, I'll bet they'll have room in that boardin' house you been livin' in all season long, won't they? Monroe be leavin', maybe he already went home, I can stay in his room for a few days, pay the lady for the bed, maybe even help her with breakfast, all the meals…"

Oddibe opened his mouth but nothing came out, which his father found amusing. "Whatsa matter, boy, cat gotcher tongue? Don't you want your Mama stayin' with you?"

"Uh...uh..." Oddibe had suddenly lost the ability to speak. The very thought of his mother even setting foot in Miz Brunét's place made his mouth go dry, and he began to sweat as if he had dashed, full-speed, around the bases—twice. He could picture her seeing the parlor and the girls, in various stages of dress, lounging there every evening; it conjured a mental image of her going toe-to-toe with Jasmine in a match worthy of Tony Zale and Rocky Graziano. He also knew that the only loser of that fight would be him.

"Sure, sure, that would be, um, great, Dad, terrific. I can talk to her when we get back up there Monday morning." *Right after I hop a freight train for the West Coast, or maybe Mexico, yeah, might be safer for me in another country.*

They dropped him off at the ballpark and cheerily said they'd see him later. The Wolves lost again, with Daniels striking out, hitting into a double play, and letting a ground ball go under his glove. The bus had no sooner left the ballpark than Oddibe was whispering in his manager's ear: "Jack, Jack, you gotta help me..."

They both got off the bus at the Cornett house; Mike said he'd come back for his manager in a half-hour or so. On the porch, Oddibe related the conversation he had had with his parents, and when he was finished, a few tears dribbled out of his eyes.

Jack paused, then asked "That it? That the whole nut?" Oddibe nodded.

A smile started to creep over Jack's face, which soon grew to a chuckle, a very audible giggle, and finally a guffaw. Not precisely the response Oddibe had been expecting.

"Jack," he said, with exasperation very much in his voice. "I don't see why that's funny. I've come to you for help on a serious matter, a...a matter-a life and death, really..." This made Jack laugh that much more, but Oddibe barely broke stride. "Yes, MY life and death, don't you see, and you...all you can do is laugh? Laugh at me right to my face? Jack, that's..."

"I'm sorry, O, I am, really, believe me. I know you don't see it, not right now, anyway, but this really is funny." And he laughed again, then seeing the despair on his center fielder's face, he forced himself to cough a time or two, which ended his laughing jag.

"You've been called all sorts-a names this season, some-a the most evil, disgustin' things I've ever heard. You've been chased by a small mob, you've been shot at. You've been decked, uh, I dunno how many times, and plunked more than any man in this league, by far. They've tried to spike you and beat you. They won't let you eat with your teammates on the road, or sleep in the same hotels, but the one thing that bothers you, the one thing that scares you outta your mind, is havin' your mother find out where you been livin' this season." He began to laugh again. "Sorry, O, but that there is funny!"

Daniels still failed to see the humor, so he stood up to go inside, but Jack stopped him.

"OK, OK. I'll talk to 'em tomorrow, if you don't object. I think I can get 'em to change their plans. May I do that?"

Oddibe's eyes brightened—he finally had something that made him smile.

The Daniels' family were among the first admitted into the ballpark, which Jack had expected. Even though the Bees were taking batting practice, he had been sitting on the top step of the visitors' dugout, keeping his eyes peeled. As soon as he spied them, he walked down the right field line to the Negro seating area in the bleachers. The family greeted him at the railing.

After exchanging pleasantries, Jack got down to the point.

"Mr. Daniels, Mrs. Daniels, Oddibe told me you're thinkin' of comin' up to Edens Ridge for this rally the churches are plannin'..."

"Lilly is," said Walter.

"Ah. Good, I think that's good, I think you oughta be there, all-a you if you can. But I hafta tell you that they're just startin' to work on this, and those guys, they're all ministers, and you know what that means! They'll talk and talk and debate and haggle and speechify. If I had a guess, I 'spect it might take 'em a week, two, 'fore they get things set. Miz Daniels, I'm afraid you'd get bored, just sittin' around all day long, waitin' for this thing to come together..."

"I thought I might help the lady what owns the house, you know, help her clean or cook or..."

"Believe me, Miz Daniels, I've known Jasmine Brunét a long time, an awful long time, and she really don't need any help. She got..." He needed to word this just right. "She got that house under control."

Mrs. Daniels had no immediate reply, so he continued. "Now, who might need some help is my wife, this bein' our first baby-n all. But her sister Tehya's come up from Weare, and brought her little girl, Gwennie, with her, which means that right now, I got no room for you. But tell you what, by the time they get this rally organized and scheduled, I'll bet Tehya will be gone and we'll have a bed for you and, no doubt, a real need for someone with your experience to be givin' us pointers."

Mrs. Daniels smiled at this, so Jack rounded third and headed for home. "I know how to reach you. We'll be back in town day-after-tomorrow, and I'll check in with those fellas, see where they stand with the rally. Soon as they've set a day and time, I'll call you, right away, I promise! Then you can make plans to come on up. You know, as I think of it, I'll bet they'll be real excited to have you, prob'ly even want you to say a few words to the crowd..."

"Oh, I dunno, Mr. Simpson, I ain't much for public speakin'," Mrs. Daniels said, giggling a bit, which made Berenice stare and think *I can't remember Mama ever giggling before!*

"Long as you're there, Miz Daniels, I'm sure they'll be absolutely delighted. Now look-it, you have my word, I'll talk to them once I get back home, then I can call you. Sound good?"

That was a good prep, Jack thought, *for the selling season, which will be startin' up again in just a coupla weeks. No rest for the weary.*

In Buchanan's visiting locker room after the season's final game, Jack spoke to his players.

"All right, you guys. I just wanted to tell you to go home and get some shut-eye. I'm driving home myself, you know that, but I plan to be at the yard right after lunch, maybe 1:30 pm. You can drop by then to clean out your lockers before headin' out." He shuffled his feet a bit. "Listen, hope you understand, but I ain't had time to work on your final paychecks yet. I promise, though, I'll do it over the next coupla days and will send them out registered mail."

He was surprised when several players asked if they could see Nashota and the baby. Not knowing what his wife would say, he devised a noncommittal answer on the fly.

"I'll have to see if she's up for visitors," he told everyone who asked.

"No, I don't think I want ballplayers trooping through my house at all hours," she said. "But what would you think about my…um, OUR…sitting in the clubhouse for an hour or two? I'd like to say goodbye to those boys, they've all been so nice to me this year. This has been…" She paused and blinked a time or two. "…a special year, such a special year. This is a very special group." Now her voice cracked. "A lot of them…I'll probably never see again."

The afternoon, then, was filled with handshakes and hugs and more than a few kisses on the cheek. A lot of lingering, too, which is not what you would expect from a team that finished in a tie for fifth. No one seemed to be in a hurry to hit the road, which surprised Jack at first, until Jake brought Oddibe to the ballpark. As soon as he walked through the door, his teammates gravitated towards him. Everyone wanted to shake his hand, a couple insisted on a hug, but nearly everyone said something, like "Been a pleasure playin' with you, man," or "I sure learned a lot from you this year, my friend—thank you."

Not everyone, however, was maudlin.

"If you come to bat against me next year, mullion, you better expect to hit the deck on the first pitch!" said Buck Hightower, with a laugh. "Maybe the second pitch, too."

"That's all right," replied Oddibe, who was holding baby Dom at the time. "If you can actually throw the ball over the fuckin' plate, expect me to line it right back at that fat head-a yours."

Knowing that the players would be in the clubhouse for part of the afternoon, Win Appleton had stopped by, hoping to get a few last quotes. When he saw Nashota and Dom, he quickly called his editor and had him rush over a photographer, and a picture of mother and son, sitting in the Wolves' locker room, ran on the front page of the paper the next day.

Jack could see that Nashota was starting to wear down around 3:20 pm, but it took him nearly a half-hour to shoo everyone except Oddibe out the door.

On the ride back to Light Street, the young outfielder started to say something.

"Jack, I, um, I…"

His manager cut him off as he parked in front of Jasmine's place.

"No need to get mushy there, meat. Don't forget, I'll be seein' you real soon, when you come back up here for that rally. Plenty-a time for girly stuff then."

"Jack!" exclaimed Nashota. "That's not a nice thing to say."

"This game ain't about bein' nice, 'Sho. Nice guys finish last, 'member? This game is about winnin' and losin', and this man…" He was surprised that he needed a moment to gather himself. "This man here is a winner."

He and Oddibe looked at each other briefly, then shook hands. "Have a safe trip home to Asheville," Jack said.

"And call us when you get there, just so we know you made it OK, y'hear?" Oddibe recognized that as more of an order from Nashota than a question, so he smiled and replied "Yes, ma'am." Then, after a brief moment, he said "See y'all soon," and strode up the walkway.

After the long and eventful season, the final 1952 standings looked like this:

TEAM	W	L	PCT.	GB
Weare Mustangs	73	53	.579	—
Buchanan Bees	70	56	.556	3
Shirley Cardinals	67	59	.532	6
Beck Bears	65	61	.516	8
Blackmer Blackbirds	63	63	.500	10
Edens Ridge Wolves	63	63	.500	10
Mettin Foxes	56	70	.444	17
Kruse Ducks	47	79	.373	26

The Shaughnessy Playoffs, then, pitted Beck against Weare, while Shirley faced off against Buchanan. Hosting the first game, the Bears fell behind by six before roaring back to tie it in the ninth with a perfectly-executed suicide squeeze bunt. They almost won it in the 12th inning, loading the bases with just one out, but they stranded their runners and the Mustangs won with a run in the 14th. After the long bus ride to North Carolina, two tired teams played a lackluster game, but Weare completed the two-game sweep with a 3–1 triumph.

Shirley won their playoff opener at home, but they played poor defense when the scene shifted to Buchanan, resulting in a 7–3 Bees win, and a winner-take-all third game. Both teams were ready and produced a back-and-forth contest. The Bees moved ahead with a run in the bottom of the eighth, then held off a Cardinal rally to advance to the final round.

All season long, Weare and Buchanan had been the two best teams in the Mountain Empire League, so it was fitting that they should meet to determine the championship. The Mustangs drew first blood with a 5–2 win on a cool evening, then came from behind the next night, ultimately winning in the tenth and taking a commanding lead in the best-of-five series. Moving to Buchanan, the Bees rebounded with an 8–5 win, but their attempt to send the series back to Weare for a deciding fifth game fell short. The Mustangs scored three times in the second inning and cruised from there. Buchanan only managed four hits and watched Weare celebrate on their field after their 6–1 victory, bringing the 1952 season to a close.

Albert liked being with Vicky. He could tell her about his life, everything he had ever done, and she would listen with respect, maybe even ask questions. He had told her about fighting in the Great War with Pershing, and how he thought Patton was "a piece-a shit." He told her about his aches and pains, and how "gettin' older sucks, Vic." He felt he was doing his part to educate this younger generation. As well as get his rocks off.

So on this Thursday night in September, Albert decided to toddle over to Light Street and pay Miss Vicky a visit. But when he got there, he was shocked to find the door locked. Locked! They're never closed, well, except for Thanksgiving and Christmas, and this wasn't either of those days, he was sure of that. *Nah, ain't cold enough, plus the election hasn't taken place yet, Stevenson and Eisenhower are still goin' 'round the country, pimpin' for votes.* Why would Miss Jasmine close the place up?

He now noticed a piece of paper taped to the front door, so he got up real close—his eyes were failing him too, dammit!—and read what someone had printed:

CLOSED FOR THE NIGHT, GONE TO THE INTERFAITH RALLY AT BILL WASHINGTON PARK. AND YOU SHOULD, TOO!

Well, don't that beat all, thought Albert. He stood there in front of the door for a moment, contemplating his options. *Hell, I don't want to spend a night listenin' to preachifyin'. Guess I'll go have me a belt or two down at the Waterin' Well and come back here tomorrow.*

It had taken quite a bit of haggling. *What day of the week?* They had finally decided on a Thursday because it didn't interfere with anyone's services, or high school football, or anything else for that matter. *What time shall we start?* That one had taken some time.

"It's a weekday night. People have to work the next day, kids need to go to school. This gives us two hours, maybe a little more, plenty of time for a good rally and for everyone to get home at a reasonable hour," Reverend Stapleton had said.

Reverend Thomas seemed shocked. "Two hours or more? You don't think people will get bored and start leaving? I was thinking more like an hour-and-a-half."

This had caused Rabbi Halevi to chuckle. "Bob, think about it—bunch-a preachers standing before a live audience, wouldn't surprise me if we don't push three hours."

They finally compromised with a 7 pm start time, and a promise for everyone to do their best to keep their rhetoric to a minimum.

Jack Simpson had originally decided to open just one concession stand and only sell Coke, but he kept having this funny gut feeling, so he called a few of his most reliable workers. When the gates opened for this Interfaith Night, people found three stands stocked with popcorn, peanuts and even a little candy, along with the Coke.

"Thought you hated selling candy," Bob Dean had said to him as they were setting up.

"I don't hate it. There just ain't no real money in it for us, not like popcorn and soda. But folks like their sweets, and Bob, 'tween you-n-me..." And here he lowered his voice to just above a whisper. "Night like this, people may find that candy will go real good with all the speeches." And they both chuckled.

Jack Simpson's gut wasn't wrong.

A small line started to develop just outside the front gate shortly after six so Jack let them in, then hurriedly found a few leftover packages of frozen hot dogs and threw them in a couple of pots of hot water. This was designed as a peaceful rally, and the last thing he wanted was for hungry people to get angry.

Bill Washington Park held 3,207 but the people kept coming in until the Fire Marshal, who generally only showed up for Opening Night but made himself conspicuous for this occasion, told Jack it was time to turn people away. "Gotta be at least 400 folks just standin', maybe closer to 500, and that's too dangerous for this old yard," he told Jack. That brought plenty of grumbling from those who couldn't get in, but some decided to hang around in the parking lot and listen, as best they could, to the "preachifying."

Mike had not gone back to Bellingham after the Wolves' season ended, he had decided he wanted to stay for the rally. Since he was in town, Jack hired him to build a stage that was placed over the pitcher's mound, stretching almost from third base to first base. "Quiz and Doc Andrews could maybe—maybe!—make that throw," Mike joked. He also set up several chairs along the first base line for photographers. There would be no admission charge for the rally, but donations would be welcomed, even encouraged, with the money being donated, in turn, to the ballclub in lieu of rent. Jack earmarked some of the money for the lights, and to give to the few people he had recruited to work in the concession stands, with the bulk going to Mike for building and tearing down the stage and, finally, getting the infield in shape before it settled down for its long winter's nap.

A few minutes after 7 o'clock, a small procession came out of the Wolves' dugout and mounted the stage. They were led by the quintet who had primarily been responsible for this event—Reverend Clark, Father Feeney, Rabbi Halevi, Reverend Stapleton and Reverend Thomas, and were followed by Jack and Nashota, Bob Rhodes, Mayor Curtis, Oddibe and Lilliana Daniels. They all took seats on the stage except for Jack, who tested the microphone and then spoke.

"All right, ladies and gentlemen, we are ready to begin." He waited a moment for the packed house to calm down *(damn, I sure wish I had more hot dogs to sell!)*, then he said "If I could, let me please direct your attention to the outfield, where Cub Scout troop number 212, led by Scoutmaster Royal Privette, will be raising the colors, followed by our National Anthem." With this cue, Royal led his scouts out to the flagpole in right-center, where they meticulously raised the American flag. Up in the press box, Bill McDermott put on his worn-out recording of the Star Spangled Banner. *It really is quite scratchy, guess I'll have to shop around for a new one this winter.* The crowd, perhaps reflexively, cheered at the end of the record, and a few people even shouted "Play Ball," which made Jack smile wistfully. "Sorry," he said. "No game today, not 'til next April. What we have tonight, though, is more important than any baseball game. Now, at this time, I would like to turn the microphone over to Dick Curtis, the honorable Mayor of the City of Edens Ridge."

Hizzoner had been invited as a courtesy, and because of the animosity that had developed between him and the Simpsons back in the spring, no one had really expected him to attend. But he was politically astute and, with this bitter election campaign going on, he had determined he might be able to pick up a few necessary votes by participating. He thankfully kept his remarks brief.

"The good people of Edens Ridge are here tonight, and I know for a fact that many more had to be turned away, which just proves how many good people we have here in our town. That man, that person, if you want to call him that, who tried to kill our baseball players and my friend, Nashota Simpson, that man was not a part of our community and does not represent any of us who are here. We are celebrating life, we are celebrating people, all people. We are here to reject hate, the kind of hate that intended to commit murder. I am happy to be here, happy to have been invited, and happy to be one of you. Thank you, and God bless!"

As he rose to go back to the microphone, Jack saw Nashota roll her eyes, and he had a good idea what she was thinking. *Now he's such a humanitarian, but back in the spring he was singing a different tune, degrading Negroes, even calling me a squaw. Now listen to him talk, he's such a…a politician. Asshole! Same thing, I guess.*

"Thank you, Mayor Curtis. We're happy you are here, too. Now please allow me to introduce someone that most of you probably do not know, Mr. Bob Rhodes. He is a field representative for minor league baseball, which means he travels the southeast throughout the spring and summer, visiting all the clubs in the region and offering them the benefit of his many years of experience. Nashota and I have been very grateful for his advice over the years but especially this season, and he is here representing Mr. George Trautman, the president of all the minor leagues. Bob?"

Rhodes hated speaking in public but Trautman had insisted he attend as his proxy (as well as a substitute for Wells Boggs, who had to cancel at the last minute when his youngest child came down with the measles). "Besides," said Trautman with a sly smile, "I know you want to see that new baby, right? This lets you make the trip and get reimbursed for it."

Standing in front of the microphone, Bob cleared his throat. "Ladies and gentlemen, I am always happy to be in Edens Ridge. Unlike some other towns I visit, many other towns, as I think of it, my job here is generally pretty simple. Nashota always has the front office, the business side, running like a fine-tuned Swiss watch, so she hardly needs any help from me. And Jack has learned, over the years, to simply stay out of her way." As he had expected, that elicited quite a few laughs. He then continued.

"I am here as a representative of the president of the minor leagues, and I am also standing in for Wells Boggs—the Mountain Empire League president, you all know him—neither of whom could make it tonight. They both want me to emphasize that all of the minor leagues, 45 in all, including one in Mexico, condemn the violence that took place here recently. Senseless violence, aimed at two of our ballplayers. And we want to call it out for what it is—purely illogical, unadulterated hatred for people whose skin is black. Mr. Trautman and Mr. Boggs have asked me to tell you, on their behalf, that they fervently believe there is no place for something like this in these United States. They both plan to work…to continue to work, very hard, 365 days a year, to prevent it from ever happening again in one of their cities and towns. The only dangers a ballplayer ought to have to confront are inside fastballs, or a runner's spiked shoes, or a hard outfield wall. Nothing more. The fact that Oddibe and Monroe, and Nashota, had to stare down the barrel of a gun is appalling. The fact that all of you are here tonight, as a show of unity, is heart-warming. Thank you all for coming out and showing the world what Edens Ridge really is made of."

He and Jack shook hands as they headed in different directions, then the Wolves' manager grasped the microphone again.

"Thanks, Bob, we appreciate your being here, it means a lot to us. Now let me turn things over to the Reverend Ishmael Clark, pastor at the Jericho Chapel AME Church. Reverend Clark."

There was a smattering of cheers. "Ladies and gentlemen, brothers and sisters, I would like to welcome you all to this very special event for Northeast Tennessee, an interfaith rally to support peace and love and brotherhood. We are here tonight because of what happened in this town, just a few short blocks from here. We are here to say to everyone, to the WORLD"—he emphasized that last word by stretching his arms out in front of him and then separating them, as if he was touching everyone in the ballpark—"that this is not really indicative of who we are. I'm sure you all know that there were newspapermen here for a few days, lots of newspapermen from around the country, and they painted a pretty harsh picture of Edens Ridge and all of Northeast Tennessee. Well friends, I don't know if any of those newsmen are here tonight, but we need to show them, and the United States of America, that our community is not at all how they painted us."

The crowd cheered. Up in the press box, several members of the out-of-town press were, indeed, on hand and writing down everything that was said. They were joined by Win Appleton, who had begged his editor for this assignment, and was covering it as "the unusual ending to a most unusual, but historic, baseball season." The *Gazette's* religion editor, Carla Brewer, was also doing a write-up.

"Let me hear you say amen!" Reverend Clark was really warmed up now, as was the crowd, which seemed to Win to be as much black as it was white. The Negroes, however, probably out of force of habit, sat out in the far bleachers along both foul lines, cheek to jowl, and their shouts of "Amen!" reverberated throughout Bill Washington Park.

One by one, the ministers took the microphone and spoke, each echoing a common theme:

- Reverend Stapleton quoted Saint John the Apostle : *"Dear friends, let us love one another, for love comes from God. Everyone who loves has been born of God and knows God. Whoever does not love does not know God, because God is love.'"*

- "It is written in Romans, *'Love must be sincere,'"* said Reverend Thomas. *"Hate what is evil; cling to what is good. Be devoted to one another in brotherly love. Honor one another above yourselves.'"* He then looked directly at Oddibe. "Mr. Daniels, I am truly sorry for what happened to you, and to Mr. Hicks, but please know that I, and my fellow parishioners at The Good Shepherd Episcopal Church, love you for who you are."

- "As a Rabbi, I am much more familiar with the Old Testament than the New," said Rabbi Halevi. "In the Book of Proverbs, we find teachings that are, I think, appropriate, not just for today but for every day: *'Hatred stirs up strife, but love covers all offenses.' 'A friend loves at all times, and a brother is born for a time of adversity.'* What happened to Oddibe and Monroe and Nashota made them all our brothers, and sister, and the fact that you are all here today wholeheartedly affirms that. Also from Proverbs: *'Let not steadfast love and faithfulness forsake you; bind them around your neck; write them on the tablet of your heart.'* And Zechariah tell us *'This is what the Lord Almighty said …show mercy and compassion to one another.'* Love never ends, my friends. Let us all, each of us, vow that it starts right here, tonight, and will never end."

- "Peter commanded us to *'love each other deeply,'"* said Father Feeney. "And John taught us that *'whoever loves his brother lives in the light.'* When we live in the light, when we love our neighbors, when we pay no attention to their skin tone or what church…sorry, correction, house of worship…they attend, then we are following God's law, God's commandments. All of us here must commit to following God's law, and to make sure that we do everything in our power to bring our family and friends with us. I pray that we can all do this."

"This country, this United States of America, was built on one major truth—all men are created equal." It had been decided that Reverend Clark would close the "ministerial" portion of the program. "Just a few years ago, Jackie Robinson showed that Negroes could play on the same field with whites, they were their equal on the baseball diamond." The bleachers exploded in cheers. "And this spring and summer, we have seen Oddibe Daniels and Monroe Hicks and Yam Yarnell prove the same thing here, right here in Edens Ridge!" More cheers, louder cheers, from throughout the park. "We should be celebrating them, celebrating their accomplishments, but instead we are apologizing, apologizing for some evil, hateful man who tried to play God in the most wicked and sinful way possible. Praise be to God, the true God, who prevented him from fulfilling his malevolent desire!" And now the ballpark shook with cries of "Amen!"

Jack returned to the microphone. "Ladies and gentlemen, there is one more person who needs to speak, and if you spent any time at all in our ballpark, here, this season, you're very familiar with him. Although…" and here he grinned. "You may not recognize him all dressed up and not wearing our number six. Mr. Oddibe Daniels."

The ballpark erupted in cheers, which quickly turned into a standing ovation. Remembering what that umpire had told him not long ago, he just stood there and let it wash over him. He waved a couple of times, then finally adjusted the microphone and, clutching the notes he had written on index cards, began to speak.

"First off, I want to thank you for that wonderful reception. That's not the kinda thing I'm used to hearin' when my name gets announced." There was some laughter, especially from the bleachers. "Next, I need to introduce you to my Mom, Lilliana Daniels, sitting right over there..." He didn't need to point her out, but he did. "She and I came up from Asheville, where we live, so we could be here tonight. We thought that, if y'all were gonna take the time outta your busy days to come here and express your feelings 'bout what happened a coupla weeks ago, then we needed to be here." There were more cheers, though this time no one stood. "My Dad stayed home in Asheville, he's got a job, and 'sides, someone had to look after Berenice, my sister, and Willie, my brother. 'Specially Willie, 'cause he's just a little sh..." Oddibe caught himself—he may be in the ballpark, but these were not his teammates. "Oops, sorry, I almost said a word I shouldn't be sayin' in front-a nice folks like y'all. Plus all these men-a the cloth!" The crowd laughed, and even Lilly smirked. "Willie's just a little kid. I also got an older sister, Annie, she's married and just moved to Norfolk 'bout a month ago, Isaiah's in the Navy and plans to stay in even though he got wounded in Korea. Now you know all-a us."

He shuffled his index cards. "I also need to thank Mr. and Miz Simpson for all they did for me this season. They saw me play last year in Asheville, in a little semi-pro industrial league, and signed me to a professional contract. Playin' here was a whole lot better than workin' at the Grove Park Inn, I can tell you. And it paid better, though not a whole lot, if you wanna know the truth." He looked back at Jack and grinned when he said that, and the ballpark howled. "I got to meet some wonderful people here, especially my teammates. In fact, two of 'em are here tonight, sittin' in the stands somewhere, Danny Chase and Raburn Reece. Everyone else has gone home, 'course, but they both live 'round here so they were kind enough to come out tonight." That elicited a little respectful applause.

Oddibe shuffled his note cards again. "I really need to say this. I know a lotta you prob'ly won't wanna hear it, but Miz Jasmine Brunét was great to me all year, she was like a...a big aunt, somethin' like that. She looked after me from the day I met her. And Jake, her boyfriend, or maybe he's her husband, I dunno...well, look, I can tell you for a fact, I wouldn't be standin' here right now if it wasn't for Jake. The two-a them are special people, real special people, and if I were y'all..." He stopped and thought for a moment, should he complete his thought? A voice inside him said *"Hell, yes!"* Well, all right, then. "Don't mean to be preachy, but Miz Brunét and Jake are just real fine people, and I hope you don't mind my repeatin' an old sayin'—you can't tell a book by its cover." No applause here, or laughs, just the sound of a few people doing a little shifting in their chairs.

"I really...my Mom and I really do appreciate everyone comin' out to pray for us and support us. I wanna thank the people of Edens Ridge, most-a the people, anyway. I gotta tell you, there were some people who weren't so, um, friendly, or welcomin'. I got called a lotta names in every ballpark in the league and I expected that, but it even happened here, in Bill Washington Park. Less and less as the season went on, but it did happen, never really ended 'til the very last homestand. I had people spit at me, I had people cuss me, say lots worse than I almost said a minute or two ago. And I got chased one night, after a game here, by men who was carryin' sticks and bats and I dunno what else. Good thing I'm fast, my speed saved my life that night 'cause I out-ran 'em all and made it home. Jake and Miz Brunét were waitin', had their own weapons ready, as those boys got close to the house. Only happened that once but, um, it did happen. Right here, just a few blocks away. Now, I'm sure none-a you were involved in that, bet lotsa you didn't even know this had happened. That's good, that tells me you're the good guys. But you need to know that not all your neighbors are as good as you. Some-a the preachers tonight talked about lovin' thy neighbor and of course they're right, it's in the Bible so I know it's true, but I think…" He hesitated once again, then plowed on. "I think you also need to know your neighbor. And if he or she is not such a good person, maybe they're in the Klan or doin' somethin' illegal, somethin' they ain't s'posed to be doin', you might wanna tell the police or someone. One of the ministers tonight said *"Be devoted to one another in brotherly love."* Way I see it, if you try to help them be a good person, then you are, I think, doing God's work, and that's the best we can do."

There was cheering from the bleachers, but also a smattering of applause from other sections. Oddibe looked at his notes, then looked up at the big crowd, which now became very quiet.

"All we want, all us Negroes…we're just people, and what we want, what we ask you for, is to be treated like any other person, with respect.. And so many-a you did that, did just that, and I'll never forget it. Thank you, Edens Ridge. I learned a lot here, and I'll never forget you." And then he turned and headed back to his chair, but before he could sit, he was met by Jack and Nashota and his mother, who were all crying. Jack shook his hand, the women gave him big hugs, and Lilly added a huge kiss on the cheek, which embarrassed him no end. While this was going on, the Negro section erupted once more, rising and cheering almost as one. The rest of the ballpark was mixed—some people stood and cheered vociferously, some just stood and clapped, and others remained seated and clapped courteously.

"Ladies and gentlemen, if I could, I would like to ask you all to rise." *Jack is getting to be quite the professional Master of Ceremonies,* thought Nashota. "Our ministers, led this time by Rabbi Halevi, would like to close with a special prayer."

Everyone rose as the clergymen came forward. The stood in a line and held hands as the Rabbi intoned: "Let all who dwell on earth simply acknowledge the truth of truths: that we have not come into this world for the sake of quarreling and war, nor for the sake of hatred, jealousy, anger, or bloodshed; rather, we have come into this world only to know You—may You be blessed eternally!"

"Therefore, have mercy on us, and fulfill among us what is written in your Scripture: 'I shall give peace upon the earth, and you shall lie down with none to make you afraid. I shall abolish from the earth the predatory beast. The sword shall never come upon your land. Justice shall roll down like the water, and righteousness like a mighty stream. For the earth shall be filled with the knowledge of The Omnipresent, as the waters fill the seas.'"

Well over 3,000 voices said "Amen" in unison, and as Jack said "Thank you all very much for being here, good night and drive home safely," they slowly filed out.

EIGHTEEN

The Tidewater Tides had spent six weeks battling the Toledo Mud Hens and Pawtucket Red Sox for an International League playoff spot, but their hopes evaporated in the last week of August 1984, and the ballplayers began making plans for the off-season. Many would be going home, while some would be playing winter ball somewhere. But there were also the Chosen Few, a tiny number, who would get the call to join the big club for the final month of the major league season. Power-hitting infielder Kevin Mitchell and hard-throwing right-hander Calvin Schiraldi went first, flying up to New York just as the Mets were playing their second consecutive doubleheader against the Western Division-leading San Diego Padres. Then, on the bus ride back to Norfolk from Richmond, manager Bob Schaefer gave the good word to two more players—speedy outfielder Herm Winningham, and a quick, slick-fielding infielder, Joshua Daniels.

"They want you at Shea on Thursday," said Schaefer. "They'll be sendin' us all your instructions, plus a hotel voucher for a coupla nights. You gotta find your own places to live for the rest-a the month, it comes outta your pocket, which ain't cheap in New York. But don't worry, you'll be gettin' a big-league salary, which means you'll take home more money ridin' the Mets' bench than you did all year bustin' your humps for me here." He smiled as he concluded. "Enjoy the experience, you mullions, you both deserve it."

The next morning, Josh Daniels called his parents.

"I had to...I need to tell you the news, the big news, the best possible news—I got the call! I'm goin' to the majors, Dad, to New York, this week! Be there on Thursday."

"Oh my God!" And then...silence. A long silence, followed by a little noise *(what is that?)* before a very, very quiet "Oh son." And more silence, on both ends of the line, broken finally by a woman's voice.

"Oddibe? Oddibe, who's on the phone, who's calling us so early in the morning?" A son can recognize his mother's voice anywhere, and it was now getting louder. "Oddibe, who is it? Oddibe! Are you..."

"Josh, um, um, lemme call you back in just a few minutes, OK? Don't you go nowhere, don't call anyone else just yet, hear? We'll get right back to you." He quickly hung up and said to his wife, "RubyAnn, our son, our son, our only son, has been called up to the major leagues. The major leagues! I really need a Kleenex."

RubyAnn, organized and professional as she was every day with her greeting cards and knickknacks store in Brevard, North Carolina, made a plan of action. "You go down the street and tell your folks, O, and I'll call Gladys. You know, I think she's workin' today, ain't she on days this week at the hospital? May have to wait 'til later with her. And..."

Oddibe interrupted. "I'll need to call Willie first, he might have a spare room, and, well, you know, easier for me to do that here at home."

His wife nodded. "OK. Meanwhile, I'll call 'Sho and Jack, and they can call the Rabbi and Phoebe, and Mike, bet he can get ahold-a him, and, and…"

"He might also call Jasmine and Jake. I think they may still be in touch," said Oddibe. "And I'll ask my folks to call Annie and Berenice. I'm sure they'll do that." He paused for a few seconds. "What about your Mom?"

RubyAnn frowned. "I was plannin' on goin' over there later anyway, I'll just tell her then. If today's a day she recognizes me, then I'm sure she'll be excited. If not…" They looked at each other a bit awkwardly, and then she shrugged.

"What's goin' on? Who was callin' us so early in the God…gosh-darn morning?" Wearing her robe and bunny-rabbit slippers, Coretta went straight for the coffee pot. Morning was not her favorite time of day, but when her parents told her the news about her big brother, she squealed with delight and initiated a full-body, three-person hug.

As an employee of the St. Louis Browns (and then the Baltimore Orioles, when the Browns moved after the 1953 season), Oddibe Daniels enjoyed some minor league success, but never came closer to the majors than Class B. After Gladys was born, he made the difficult decision to retire, but stayed in the game by moving into coaching, first at the high school level, and then at Brevard College. When he signed his second contract at Brevard, he realized this job was his for as long as he wanted it or, at least, as long as he kept putting a competitive team out on Gil Coan Field. That's when he began, in earnest, working on his parents to make the short move south.

"Dad, that nerve damage in your eye, from the old bus accident, is really affectin' your eyesight, you've said it yourself. Ain't nothin' can be done to fix it, doncha think it might be time to retire? Then you-n Mom can move down here, be close to us. 'Sides, when this new baby is born, Roo gonna need all the help she can get. Don't tell her I said that, though." Father and son had both laughed, but it got Walter to thinking. *Boy got a point, goin' up and down the stairs in our house is more and more difficult every day.* He thought Lilly would resist leaving Asheville after all these years and was surprised when she jumped at the suggestion to move. "Ain't that far away, right? When Annie or Niecy and their families come to visit, we can pick 'em up at the airport and it be less than an hour's drive. And I bet Oddibe-n RubyAnn can help us find a nice house that only got one level." Which is exactly what happened, with the added bonus that the small but attractive bungalow they found put them just five blocks apart.

Oddibe could hear the vacuum running when he got to the door. "Hi, son," said Walter, when he saw his oldest boy walk in. "We just cleanin' up a bit, thought this might be a good day for it, right? It is Labor Day, after all!" And he laughed at his joke, which he had probably used dozens of times over the years.

"Good one, Dad," said Oddibe. "Listen, I got some news, some really good news…oh, hi Mom, 'mornin'." Since she had begun using a cane a few months ago, one always knew when Lilly was approaching.

"Mornin', O. You here pretty early, what kinda news you got? Do I need to sit down?"

"Well, maybe. But it is good news, so don't worry. It also comes with a question—think you might be up for a long weekend in New York City?"

Lilly was only too happy to call her daughters. Annie let out a whoop, and then a shout, and finally an "OMIGOD" when she got the news. Berenice let out a little scream, then she cried, and then she tried to speak. "I just wish...," she said, but the sobs overtook her.

"What, baby?"

It took a moment for her to compose herself enough to say "I wish it had been O, too, Mama. Even for one game."

Lilly wasn't expecting that, and she also choked up. Finally she said, very quietly, "He tried his best, Niecy, you know he did. But you know, bet he thinks this is just as good, maybe better."

Neither of Walter and Lilliana Daniels' girls, however, would be able to get away on such short notice. A resident playwright at the Guthrie Theater in Minneapolis, Berenice had a new play scheduled to open in less than a month. "If it wasn't for the play, I'd fly in, you know I would. Phil can look after the kids for a long weekend, but this is my show and I really..." In Annie's case, it was simply the money. She didn't have to say it, they all knew that, as much as Isaiah loved the Navy, a Master CPO's salary doesn't allow for a lot of unbudgeted items. Even with all four kids out of the house and Annie working a few hours a week at the Piggly Wiggly, it would take them a while to pay off a last-minute trip from Norfolk to New York.

It was understood that Oddibe would call Willie. The brothers were still close, unlike the father and his youngest son. Despite being one of the few dancers able to work steadily in theaters both on and off Broadway, Walter continued to have a problem with Willie's choice of a career, as well as his lifestyle. When Lilly would call, she and her "baby boy" could talk for an hour before she handed the phone over to her husband. Walter, on the other hand, would be on the line for just a few minutes before he'd say, "Well, son, sure nice hearin' your voice, but I gots things to do 'round here." *Bet Dad will have mixed feelings if Josh bunks with Willie this month,* thought Oddibe. *But hmmm, this might prove to be a good thing in more ways than one.*

Had they been giving out trophies for that sort of thing, the award for the loudest scream would probably have gone to Nashota Simpson. RubyAnn had to hold the phone at arm's length for several minutes or risk losing the hearing in her right ear, at least temporarily.

"Sho, you better calm down, I'm afraid you might undo all that construction they're doing on the road linking our two states," she said with a laugh, referring to the work being done on the Linn Cove Viaduct.

Perhaps it was the circumstances of Dom's birth. Perhaps it was the hard friendships they had made, especially in 1952. Perhaps they just liked the beautiful region. For whatever reason(s), the Simpsons had never left Edens Ridge, and the two families remained close all these years, undaunted by the separation of some 100 miles. Jack had remained in charge of the Wolves through 1955, then decided to try and climb the baseball ladder, managing at Fayetteville in 1956, and Danville in 1957 and 1958. Both franchises wound up folding, putting him out of baseball for the first time in more than a decade.

Nashota, meanwhile, got to enjoy being a stay-at-home mom for a year, but when Louetta proved to be unequal to the task of running the Wolves' business affairs, she was persuaded to return following the 1953 season. And the strongest argument was made by Louetta herself.

"Please come back," she cried one morning when she stopped by the Simpson residence. "I loved being the team secretary, I was good at it, least I think I was, but this! This is just too much for me, I can't do it and I don't like doing it. But you, you're so good at it, I'll bet you could even do it from here, right from home. Please!!"

Jack couldn't disagree. He was not particularly happy with how business affairs were being managed, and had been wondering what to do about it. "You and Louetta made a good team," he said after the Wolves returned from their road trip and his wife told him about the meltdown in their living room. "Maybe we can hire a junior assistant that you can train, and maybe that would free you up a little so you wouldn't have to spend so much time at the yard…"

"And what about Dom?" Nashota's eyes flashed and her tone was sharp and direct. "He's not even a year old, what do you suggest I do with him during the day?" Their answer was a small expansion of the office at Bill Washington Park, an added room that served as little Dom's home-away-from-home when his mother returned to her duties as business manager in October of 1953. It was a post she would hold until a tearful Wells Boggs told his four remaining franchises that, once the final pitch of 1957 had been thrown, the Mountain Empire League would cease to exist.

Almost immediately, the Johnson City team offered her a job to be their Business Manager, a position she held for two years. Dom was in school by then, and in 1958 Dorothy Dean gladly picked him up at 3 pm and kept him at her house until one of the Simpsons came for him. In 1959, however, that task fell on Jack, who took a part-time job at the Adams grocery store so he could take his son to school in the morning and pick him up in the afternoon. But not being in baseball drove him nuts; "I'm goin' stir-crazy here, 'Sho," he told her one night.

The City of Kingsport, bereft of a franchise over the previous two seasons, returned to the Appalachian League in 1960 and hired Nashota away from Johnson City to run their business operations. When she saw how eager they were for her services, she used her leverage to "strongly request" that they find something for Jack, telling them "he's just not happy unless he's working with a ballclub." Several conversations with the parent club, the Pittsburgh Pirates, finally led to a job as the team's batting and outfield coach, as well as the bus driver. "Pretty ironic," Jack said one evening when the Simpsons and Appletons were together. "All my years as a player, as a coach, as a manager, and it was my willingness to drive the fu…'scuse me, the darned bus that ultimately sealed the deal. And it's just for one year. They are making no promises after this season. Ain't that a kicker!"

It was, indeed, just for a year, but only because the Pirates hired him to be an area scout, a post he held for five years. Then, when the Milwaukee Braves were preparing to move to Atlanta after the 1965 season, they hired him to be one of their Southeastern scouts, and after nearly two decades, he was just as enthusiastic about the job as ever.

"How long is Jack gonna keep on scouting, 'Sho?" asked RubyAnn. "He's gotta... I mean, no disrespect, but he must be..."

"He turned 69 earlier this year. I've asked him the same question, Roo, but he still loves it, still gets a thrill when he sees a prospect. Sometimes, he starts talkin' 'bout some kid and I swear, for a few minutes he looks and sounds twenty years younger. But back in the spring he promised me he wanted to work 'til he was 70, then hang 'em up, so maybe at the end of next year? We'll see, we'll see if he follows through. If he does, we may think about sellin' The Specialty Shop. You know that as long as we own it, I'm gonna be tempted to go in!"

"How long have you owned that place?" asked RubyAnn.

"Let's see, Gibby had his stroke in '62 and died a few months later. His family took it over but they really didn't show any enthusiasm for it. Meanwhile, when Kingsport lost their team after the '63 season, I worked for a while at the Piggly Wiggly..."

"Oh, you hated that!" exclaimed RubyAnn. "I remember you bitching and moaning about it any time we spoke."

"Yeah, I did hate it, I can't lie. Then Mrs. Gibson came in one day, just needed a few things, and we talked for a coupla minutes. Few nights later she calls me at home and says she has a 'business proposition.' Jack was on the road but I knew he'd be back home 'fore the month was out, so we decided to wait 'til then. Anyway, she offered me a job runnin' The Specialty Shop, with the thought that maybe we'd buy them out in a year or two."

"Jack was a little hesitant, wasn't he?"

"You bet, he wasn't sure we could afford it, and neither was I. That's why we made sure she understood that I really wanted the job, but we might not be able to buy the place. But the longer I worked there, the more I wanted to own it. We started puttin' money aside and by 1967 it was ours. So this is our 18th year." She sighed. "Long time, Roo. May be a real good time to think 'bout sellin'. Meanwhile, we'll call Mike, and the Halevis."

Phoebe Moon began studying Judaism late in 1952. Trying to fit the theology, rituals, history, culture, customs, and practices—to say nothing of learning rudimentary Hebrew!—around her work schedule made it a slow process. But she and Yitzhak Dov were married in August of 1954, at Temple Israel in Columbus, Georgia (where his parents had moved), with Rabbi Horn performing the ceremony. Her new in-laws had been skeptical at first, but time, to say nothing of the arrival of four grandchildren, had eventually brought them around. "My mother spends more time talking to you than to me during our weekly phone calls," he once remarked, which made her smile.

They had stayed in Tennessee until 1960. Shmuel (better known as Samuel, or Sam) was three and Adinah was one and they felt they needed more money, so Yitzhak Dov accepted a job at Congregation Eitz Chaim in Elyria, Ohio, a city in the Greater Cleveland metro area. The increased salary, however, really did not bring anyone increased happiness. After Shoshana was born in 1964, they moved east to be in charge of the Hillel House at the University of Delaware. "It's less money," Phoebe had told Nashota when she called to tell her the latest. "But we both have a feeling about this, a really good feeling." And they were right. The job, and living in a college town, proved to be a much better fit for the Halevis, who were rounded out by Elijah's birth in 1967. By 1974, Phoebe was ready to go back to work and found a job at the Hotel Anjelika, working her way up from Hospitality Manager to her current post as General Manager. Which made her the ideal person to set up the party:

- She knew a good place in Queens, the Siden House Hotel, not all that far from Shea Stadium, that caters to a lot of Jewish customers with their Glatt Kosher menu. She negotiated directly with the manager and, by giving him the maximum number of rooms they might need (it's always easier to cancel than to try to add at the last minute), she came away with an excellent rate.
- She then called the Siden House restaurant. Once again, she spoke directly with the manager and arranged for a Thursday night dinner, which included a cash bar, in their private dining room.
- When that was completed, she called Greg Waters, their travel agent, and instructed him to book two round-trip tickets to New York on Amtrak.
- Only then did she finally call her husband over at the Hillel House.

Nashota also called Mike Hamblen who, like Jack and Oddibe, had remained involved in baseball. He was hired to manage the Valdosta, Georgia franchise for the 1953 season, then two years later he moved to Lubbock, Texas to manage the team in the Class B West Texas-New Mexico League. The Hubbers, unfortunately, folded after the 1956 season, but he had made quite a few good contacts in Lubbock, including a lovely young lady named Drusilla Johnson. He moved down to manage the Corpus Christi team in 1957, but that job was short-lived as the whole league folded in the fall. Minor league baseball was in serious free-fall, as the post-war proliferation of air-conditioning and television combined to keep the casual fan comfortably at home instead of sweating at the local ballpark. Having experienced it first-hand two years in a row, Mike Hamblen didn't need a building to fall on his head. He returned to Lubbock, married Dru and went to work for a landscaping business for a couple of years, until Texas Tech hired him to be an assistant baseball coach in 1960. Six years later, he became head coach. "I'm still enjoyin' myself," he told several people that night at the Siden House. "As long as the kids keep grumblin' about how hard I work 'em, I figure I'm still doin' my job. That, and winnin' games, of course," to which fellow coach Oddibe Daniels agreed, saying "You know that's right."

The gathering at The Siden House was now in full swing. Most had stayed in touch since 1952, through phone calls, greeting cards, celebrations of birthdays and anniversaries and births. Over the years, there had only been a handful of visits, as people moved around and were busy working and raising their families. But the indelible friendships forged by that 1952 Mountain Empire League season remained strong.

A variety of conversations were taking place around the room:

- "I know I've told you this before, Roo," said Phoebe. "Shoshana was just so happy to be able to get advice from your Gladys about medical schools. I think they still talk now and then, though Shoshie says that Duke is really hard, she barely has time to call us…"
- "Man named Tom Butler signed me to a contract in 1923," Walter reminisced. "Went up to Asheville to play for the Asheville Royal Giants. That's where it all started, if you think 'bout it, right Lilly? I played, Oddibe played, and now…"

- "Got my business degree from N.C. State in May," said Coretta, the youngest member of the Daniels family. "But I really think I'd like to be a minister. So right now I'm back in Brevard, living with Mom and Dad, working with Mom in the card store, trying to save enough money for seminary school. Maybe my big-league brother will be able to lend his sister some money…"
- "They gave me number 59, by the way," said Josh, to which Walter quickly responded "Judy Johnson." "Who was she?" asked the Rabbi. "Not a 'she,' rabbi," Walter answered. "Only the greatest third baseman who ever lived, in my opinion. Made it into the Hall of Fame a few years ago, 'bout time, too. Ever see him play, Jack?" Simpson shook his head. "Most of the games we went to were minor league or semi-pro. Once a year, maybe, Dad might spring for a game in Pittsburgh and Philly. Sure wish I'd seen guys like Johnson and Buck Leonard and Oscar Charleston and Cool Papa. My loss. But I did talk to Satchel Paige on the phone once, did I ever…"

It was at that point that the door opened and three more people entered—an elderly couple and a much younger man who, upon seeing everyone, broke into a huge grin and said, "Look who I found wandering around the hallway!"

They moved slowly because they were both in their late seventies, and time has a way of naturally slowing the body down. They moved slowly because of various injuries suffered over the years; he still limped a bit, for instance, from that old gunshot wound.

But they were moving slowly especially because they weren't sure they belonged there. It was something they had debated even after they strapped themselves in and the airplane left Tampa on its nonstop flight for New York. Once they retrieved their luggage at LaGuardia, they took a taxi to The Siden House, and at one point she whispered to him, "Imagine that, my first airplane ride, my first taxicab ride, all in New York City!"

The hotel's lobby was small but tastefully furnished, with no bright, jarring colors to be seen, not a single drop of red. They checked in, had their bags delivered to their room ("Do we have to tip him?" "Yes, I think we do."), and then, after splashing water on their faces, they made their way to the mezzanine level. ("What's a mezzanine?" "Beats the piss outta me!")

They got off the elevator and looked around, not sure where to go. As they hesitated, the door to another elevator opened and they spied a familiar face.

"Miz Jasmine, Mr. Jake, it is so good of you to have come all this way."

"Lordy lord-lord, Dom Simpson, can that really be you? For heaven's sake, stop huggin' me a second and lemme look at you! Why, you just get better-lookin' alla time."

He offered her his arm and she gladly took it, letting him guide her (and Jake) into a private room, where their entrance set off an explosion of shouts and emotions. It began as soon as Nashota and Jack approached, with the two women sobbing on each other's shoulders. Even Oddibe got a bit misty-eyed, but eventually, after waiting for what she felt was a respectful several minutes, RubyAnn broke up the weepfest.

"Miz Jasmine, Mr. Jake, I'd like to introduce you to my son, Joshua Daniels. He's the reason we're all here in New York, after all!"

Josh held out his hand. "I am so pleased to meet you both. My Dad has told us how you saved his life several times during his first season in the minors. It's a great honor for me, ma'am, sir. Guess, ha, guess if it wasn't for you, I wouldn't be here today."

Jasmine looked him over, up and down, then smiled and said "here, young'un," and, by-passing his outstretched hand, wrapped him up in a big bear hug. Jake, a little more subdued, simply shook his hand while continuing the conversation he had begun with Jack, Oddibe and the rest of the men.

But now someone else joined the group, and the room suddenly became quiet as Lilly looked directly at Jake.

"I know who you are," she said. "I know what you done for my boy all those years ago. Never had a chance to thank you for savin' his life, but I'd like to do that now." Balancing herself on her cane, she held out her hand.

"Miz Daniels, I didn't do much-a nothin'," said Jake. "I was just gettin' revenge, that bast...'scuse me, that...that person had shot me, gave me this permanent limp, and now I had the chance..."

"You saved my son, my Oddibe. We all wouldn't be here right now if you hadn't-a shot him. I ain't a violent person, I generally don't approve of violence, I ain't never even held no gun, but you did what needed to be done to save a life and help create more, and I need to thank you."

Jake nodded and grasped her hand in his.

There was one more piece of unfinished business for Lilly, and two elderly black women eyed each other warily.

"I know who you are too," she said. "Can't say that I approve of what you do..."

"I'm retired, Miz Daniels. Jake and I been livin' in Florida for 'bout seven years now. All I do is feed birds and stray critters, do a little knittin'..."

"I'm talkin' 'bout back then, back when Oddibe played with Edens Ridge and lived in your...house. After the season ended, after he came home, he told me what... he told me everythin'. Least..." And here she looked at Oddibe and gave him a little smile. "He told me all he wanted me to know. But I know what you done, I know how you looked after him, and Monroe, too, I know how you cared for those boys like they was your own." She stopped and looked at the floor; this part was the hardest. "And I want to thank you, all these years later. I want to thank you for makin' sure my boy came back to me." She held out one hand while wiping her damp face with the other.

Jasmine Brunét was not a person who shook hands, she liked to hug. But she also was not stupid, and she immediately recognized that this was not a hugging occasion. With a different person, perhaps, but not with Lilliana Daniels. She grasped the outstretched hand.

"Was my pleasure, Miz Daniels. Was all my pleasure."

The oxygen returned to the room.

"All right, all right, if I could have your attention, please. Please!!" Oddibe picked up his glass and tapped it lightly with his fork, which made him feel just a bit like a judge in court, especially when it had its desired effect.

"I would like to thank y'all for comin'. I know that, except for my brother Willie, it was an effort for everyone to be here, especially since we threw this together in just a few days. And right here, let me publicly thank Willie for helpin' to make this happen, and to Phoebe Halevi as well—the two of them are really the ones responsible for gettin' us the hotel rooms and this wonderful space and arrangin' for the meal. I think we need to give them both a big, big hand."

Everyone applauded, and Mike yelled "here, here," then held his glass aloft, which triggered others to do the same and take a drink.

Oddibe stood and waited for the room to get quiet again before he continued.

"My father played ball, semi-pro ball, 'til he got hurt in an accident a long time ago, more-n fifty years now, ain't it, Dad?" Walter nodded. "Then I played ball, in the minors, for nine years, got as high as Class B, very briefly, but that's it." He paused and looked around the room.

"Jack, Mike, you both played in the minors, then coached and managed, and Jack's been scoutin' players for about forever, how long's it been, Jack?"

"This is my 24th year. Gonna do one more, then give it up. Addin' my time as a player and coach and manager, that'll make forty-eight years in professional baseball."

"Here, here," said Mike again, though this time not everyone joined him in a drink. Dru gave him "the look," the one recognized by every husband on earth, the one that told him he'd better quiet down.

"Lotta years we been involved in this game between us, lotta years, but none-a us ever got close to the majors. Not once. But now, now, my son, my son Josh..." He looked down at his feet as his emotions began to rise. "Josh is in the major leagues. He ain't played a game yet and you know, he may not get into one right away, we all gotta remember that. His Mets are in a pennant race and his new manager, Davey Johnson, gotta be more concerned 'bout winnin' games than seein' someone make his big-league debut, but that's OK. He's on the roster, so y'all be sure and buy a program tomorrow, the roster insert will have his name on it." He looked around the room. "And everyone here, every one-a you, played a part in makin' this happen. Goin' back to 1952, actually, 1951, that's when I signed my first contract, in the kitchen of our little house in Asheville." Walter and Lilly nodded, as did Nashota, whose tears began again.

"I talked too much already, but I just wanted to say 'thank you' to y'all for everythin' you did and continue to do, just by bein' here. And I also want to say to my son, my Josh, OUR Josh..." And here he grasped RubyAnn's hand. "How proud we are of you, how very proud."

Hugs. Tears. Smiles. The emotion in the room was overwhelming.

Josh, however, did not want to give a speech. "It means so much to me that y'all are here, it really does," he said. "And I'm sure you know that. Which is all I really want to say," he remarked as he sat down.

"Jack, I got a question for you." It was Walter's distinctive voice.

"Fire away, old friend."

"Yeah, 'old' is sure the right word," said Walter, which drew an immediate retort from his wife. "Watch who you callin' old," she said sharply. "Even if we have been married since the beginnin' of time, I sure don't feel old. Not tonight, anyways." The room erupted in laughter, but once it subsided, Walter pressed on.

"Jack, since we been doin' a lotta catchin' up here tonight, can you tell us 'bout some-a the people who ain't here?"

Jack slowly stood up as he contemplated his answer.

"That's a good question, Walter. Lemme see…well, of course, there are some people who have, um, passed on. 'Sho and I have gone to more-n our share of baseball funerals over the years—Bob Rhodes, Wells Boggs, Win Appleton, Lionel Ticknor, all-a them are gone now. All-a them…" Here he coughed and shook his head. "All such good people, and good friends. Win got stomach cancer, died way too young. That one hurt…" He had to stop again, this time to wipe his eyes. Nashota began to cry as her husband continued.

"Bob died in a car crash in South Carolina, and I'll tell you, the wonder was that it hadn't happened sooner, he was legally blind but was still workin' and still drivin'! Crazy bas…crazy fool."

"Wells died of a broken heart," Nashota said quietly.

"Yes, he never did get over not being able to line up affiliates for the Mountain Empire League, and then of course he finally had to shut it down. He never…never really recovered."

"Gene," said Nashota, her voice barely above a whisper.

"Oh Gene, Gene Conn, you prob'ly remember him, managed Weare, they won the title that year, '52. Tragic death, pancreatic cancer, there's no treatment, no cure, he was only forty-something…"

"Forty-three," said Nashota, unable to hold back the tears.

Jack needed another moment before he could continue. "Bob and Dorothy Dean, they're gone, too, both-a them. Edens Ridge is, um, it's, uh, uh…" He paused for a second, then gave a thin, weak smile. "I can tell you the town is not quite the same without them."

"What about some-a the players?" Jake wanted to know.

"I really only kept up with a few, tell you the truth. Course, y'all know about Buck, Buck Hightower. He went out to California, played in the Cal League, and met some girl who worked for Paramount Studios. They got married and pretty soon he started showin' up in movies and on TV. Usually plays the leading actor's best friend, or an Indian for some reason…" This made Oddibe smile. "But he's had steady work for close to thirty years, so good for him."

"Monroe also went out to California," said Mike.

"That's right. He married a girl…Jasmine, I believe you know a little 'bout this, right?"

Jazz had to laugh. "One-a my girls, and look, y'all know what I'm talkin' 'bout, right, we all adults here. Gail worked for me and she and Monroe took a likin' to one another. Well, after he got better from his gunshot wound, he came back to Edens Ridge and they went out west. She had told me that's what they planned to do, so it ain't like they run off in the middle of the night! He played out there for a while, didn't he, Jack?"

"Yes, he signed with the Hollywood Stars, played there a coupla years, then he quit and helped Gail start her own hair salon, and after a few years they were able to open up more. He manages the money side-a things and she trains the stylists, bet they're millionaires by now."

"Anyone else?"

"Danny Chase, he came to us late in the season, skinny little infielder, local kid, remember? Played for us again in '53 but then decided to go to college. Walters State, two-year school, then Middle Tennessee. Didn't play pro ball, he got into coaching like Oddibe and Mike, but he likes workin' with the high school kids so he's over in Kruse, 'member Kruse? Been the head baseball coach at Kruse High for, I dunno, maybe eighteen or twenty years. Won the state title two or three times, they love him over there. Married our old secretary, Louetta, they got three kids, or is it four, 'Sho?"

"Three."

"Only other one I know about is Pete Sevareid. He got hurt right at the end of the season, tore his hammy, you may recall. Came back to us the next year, played for, maybe, six weeks, then walked into my office one day and said he needed to quit, he just didn't have it any more, and he was right. I was keepin' him 'cause I liked the guy, really great in the clubhouse, and I was hopin' his leg would come 'round, but..." He shrugged, then finished up. "Went back to North Dakota, got his degree, became a teacher in middle school. I think he's coached some Little League, but otherwise he left his baseball days behind him. Married a nice girl, they got two or three kids..."

"Two," said Nashota, and when everyone laughed, she said, "Just call me the Rona Barrett of Northeast Tennessee," which got an even bigger laugh.

"What about that big catcher, 'nother cullud boy you had..." For Walter, some old habits, and words, were hard to break.

"Yam, Yam Yarnell." Jack and Oddibe both began to giggle.

"You gonna let us in on the joke?" asked the rabbi.

"O, you tell it." And all eyes turned to Oddibe.

"Well, it's not really funny, it's actually quite sad," said Oddibe. "He died, bunch-a years ago, maybe 1960? Killed in a car crash..."

"Under mysterious circumstances," said Jack, trying not to laugh.

"Yeah, that's what they said at the time. We found out, though, what happened. He had gone down to Mexico and was playin' ball there and doin' real well, hittin' good, poppin' a few homers and playin' with...with a real flair, which was just his style, he was just bein' Yam. He became real popular with the fans, which included, I understand, quite a few female fans, one of whom was the wife of the town's mayor." A few chuckles could be heard.

"Well, as I hear it, the mayor decided to come home for lunch one day and found his wife with Yam and immediately grabbed a gun. Ol' Yam went runnin' outta the house, jumped in his car and took off, and the mayor jumped in his car and went after him, and somewhere Yam lost control and crashed into a tree and was killed instantly. Didn't stop the mayor from puttin' a bullet in his head, just for good measure, when he got to the scene. Sure sorry Yam's gone, he was a good guy, a fun guy, and a good player. Does make for a funny story, though."

Walter then stood up. "Ladies and gentlemen, I'd like to propose a toast. To all-a them who was so important to my boy Oddibe back there in 1952. Rabbi, I know you Jewish people have a word that could be used here, maybe you…"

"Certainly," said Rabbi Halevi. He rose, held his glass up to eye level, and the rest of the room followed. "L'Chaim." He and Phoebe were, of course, the only ones who said it correctly. "It means 'to life,'" he said, and that phrase resonated with them all. "To life."

Friday night, and more than 46,000 people poured into Shea Stadium, and why not? For the first time in more than a decade, the Mets were involved in a pennant race in the month of September. Though they trailed the Cubs by seven games with only 23 left to play, they realized this was undoubtedly their best chance to make up ground. If they could win all three games, they would only trail the Cubs by four. For the Mets, then, this was a crucial series, and so they started their spectacular rookie righthander, Dwight Gooden.

But for a very small group sitting behind home plate in Shea's loge section, what was most important was a young man wearing number 59. Unseen and unknown by virtually everyone in Shea that night, he was the absolute center of their attention. They cheered him when he came out for batting practice, even if he did just get a couple of swings. They cheered him when he fielded a few balls during infield practice. They even cheered him when he ran back into the dugout shortly before the playing of "The Star-Spangled Banner."

The Mets picked up a run in the bottom of the first but the lead did not last long. Gooden, who would finish with the second-best earned run average in the league that year, didn't have his good stuff on this night and allowed the Cubs to tie the score in the second inning and go ahead in the third. The Mets evened things in the fourth, but Chicago sent Gooden to an early shower with a three-run fifth that gave them a 5–2 lead. The Mets, however, did not give up, and when Darryl Strawberry hit a long home run into the bullpen in the sixth, first-year Cub manager Jim Frey went to his bullpen.

"Ever been to a big-league game before, Walter?" Jake wanted to know.

"Yeah, me-n Oddibe been drivin' down to Atlanta the last few years to watch the Braves play. We go in June, after school lets out and 'fore his summer baseball camp begins. Jack gets us tickets. Go down on Friday and see a game that night, stay for the Saturday game, and come home. I like that a lot, we have ourselves a good time. No wives, just us boys," he said with a wide grin.

"Lord knows what kind-a trouble they get themselves into," Lilly said. "They only tell me 'it was fun' or 'we had a blast,' somethin' like that. Don't know what-all they do, 'side from goin' to the game. IF they even go!" She let out a big laugh, and everyone joined in.

"I ain't never been," said Jasmine, quietly. "Saw plenty-a games in Edens Ridge over the years, went to Kruse now-n-then and Kingsport, too. But never the majors."

"When we first moved to Florida, there was a team in Dunedin, just a few miles away from where we live in Clearwater, and we'd go to a few games," said Jake. "But then they left. Went over to St. Pete a coupla times since then, but not very often. We may be getting' a team in Clearwater soon, that'd be nice."

"We got a team in Nashville, they draw real well, place is always packed," said Dom.

In the seventh inning, George Foster hit a ball off the foul pole in left that tied the score and sent the fans into a frenzy.

"It sure do get loud here!" exclaimed Lilly.

"That's 'cause they're finally winning," said Willie. "I take the subway over once in a while, and I can tell you that I've been here when the crowd wasn't any larger, or louder, than the people that come see us perform at Lincoln Center. It's way different this year." This made Oddibe laugh. "Looks like you maybe did learn somethin', little brother, from my playin' days." Willie smiled and nodded, Walter just said "Hmph."

In the top of the ninth, the Mets' second baseman, Wally Backman, let a routine grounder bounce off his glove. "Josh would-a made that play, easy!" RubyAnn yelled so loudly that several fans around them turned to look at her, so she then had to explain that she was the mother of a new Met. "He's wearing number 59, he's there in the dugout. Look, if you lean forward you can barely see him." A few fans flashed that "Oh, she's just the mother of some rookie" smile. The Cubs, however, were not able to cash in on the miscue, and the score remained tied in the bottom of the ninth.

Ray Knight, recently acquired by New York, was sent to the plate to bat for shortstop Jose Oquendo, and he promptly singled into left field. No sooner had he reached first base than he jogged back to the dugout.

"Now running for Ray Knight is number 59, Joshua Daniels, number 59."

The loge section erupted in screams, tears, high-fives and even a little dancing.

"Sorry, sorry, we didn't mean to be so loud, it's just…just…that's…that's my boy, this is his major league debut…" Oddibe felt he had to explain to his neighbors while he tried to get his group to calm down.

"Sure, mac, sure, we get it. Tell you what, if he scores the winnin' run, we'll all join you in screamin' and dancin', OK? But right now you need to sit down so's we can see!"

Frey made another pitching change, bringing in veteran George Frazier, prompting Johnson to counter with a pinch-hitter, Herm Winningham, who took a pitch outside, then set up to bunt on the next pitch but fouled it off.

"Jeez, crucial spot in a crucial game and Davey sends up a kid, whatsamatta wid him?" grumbled someone sitting next to the Hamblens, who said nothing in return.

Winningham squared again and this time he bunted the ball slowly down the first-base line. Josh was running on contact and hit full speed after just a couple of strides. Chicago's catcher, Jody Davis, screamed "I got it, I got it" so that his first baseman, Leon "Bull" Durham, would stop charging in for the ball and get back to the bag for the throw. The Cubs were willing to allow Josh to reach second base in exchange for an out.

But the throw never got to Durham. It hit Winningham in the shoulder and ricocheted over the bag, rolling towards the fans sitting in foul territory, near where the grounds crew kept the rolled-up tarp. The ball was very much in play.

Josh saw his third-base coach wind-milling his arm, the universal sign for "RUN AS FAST AS YOU CAN, MULLION!" He really needed no encouragement and blazed into third and then, without hesitation, headed for home.

Ryne Sandberg, the Cub second baseman, chased the ball down, heard his teammates yelling "CUT FOUR," and fired the ball towards Jody Davis, who had retreated back to home plate.

It all happened so quickly. The baseball, and Josh Daniels, both seemed to arrive at the same time. Davis grabbed it and reached over to tag the runner, but the newest Met, number 59, bent his body away from the tag while making sure his left leg touched home plate as he was sliding.

The umpire spread out his arms and hollered "Safe! Safe!"

Bedlam reigned at Shea Stadium. Fans all around the ballpark screamed and hollered as the final score went up on the board: Mets 6, Cubs 5. In the loge, everyone joined the Daniels party in jumping and dancing. Several people pounded Oddibe on the back, while others shook the hands of everyone, male or female, who was there that night for Josh.

It took a good five minutes, maybe even more, for people to begin calming down. At that point, Jack Simpson looked at Oddibe, then at Walter, and finally at his wife and said, simply, "Good play."

Glossary of Cherokee Words

There are several Cherokee words used in this book. They are listed below, with their English meanings.

Adadoda	Father
A-do-nv-do-di	Heart
A-ga-la-yv-wi	Foolish person
A-gi-ya	Woman
A-ma	Water
Aneyatahi	Heathen
A-sga-ya	Man
A-s-gi-na	Devil
Asiule ehu	Lover
A-tsa-s-gi-li	Witch
E-du-tsi	Uncle
Galvladi	Heaven
Ga-na-ga-ti	Doctor
Golisdi	Understand
Gu-a-sa-ta	Trash
Gvgeyui	Love
Gvgeyuhi	I love you
Gvlieliga udohiyu	You are very welcome
L-gi-do	Sister
Nigolagvna	Stupid
Nu-da	Crazy
S-te-si	Daughter
Sky-u-sdi	Little man
Ti	Buttocks
Tsi-s-qua	Bird
Tsu-na-da-da-tlu-gi	Sweetheart
Tsv-s-gi-na	Satan
U-dv-sa-nv-hi	Old man
U-na-s-ti-s-gi	Crazy
U-ne-gi-lv-di	Ugly
U-ne-qua	Great Spirit
Unitsi	Mother
U-s-di-ga	Baby
U-s-qua-ni-go-di	Wonderful
U-ya-hia	Husband
Yu-ne-gas	White men
Wa-do	Thank you
Wa'-toli	Penis
Wi-tsv-ke-wa-gwo	Just forget about it

Marshall Adesman

About The Author

Born and raised in Brooklyn, New York, Marshall Adesman will always have one leg in the North. But having spent more than half his life below the Mason-Dixon line, the other leg is most definitely planted in the South. He spent a dozen years in minor league baseball, working as an assistant general manager, general manager and business manager for teams located in St. Petersburg, Florida; Amarillo, Texas; Waterloo, Iowa; Utica, New York; Pulaski, Virginia; and three cities in the State of North Carolina—Durham, Greensboro and Raleigh. Many of the incidents found in *The Mountain Empire League* are based on things he experienced, either directly or indirectly, during his time in the game, and many of the characters found in the book are based on people he knew and worked with in those towns. He is also the co-author of an historical book, *The 25 Greatest Baseball Teams of the 20th Century Ranked,* contributed to two other nonfiction works, and served as an associate editor on the two-volume history, *Baseball's Business: The Winter Meetings.* After 21 years at Duke University, he and his wife retired to the beautiful mountains of Northeast Tennessee in 2009.

photo by Billie Wheeler

Marshall Adesman

www.ingramcontent.com/pod-product-compliance
Lightning Source LLC
LaVergne TN
LVHW061539070526
838199LV00077B/6836